'From Daleks and dingy tower blocks to nuclear threats, this addictively readable book charts dizzying change … To readers addicted to David Kynaston's mighty chronicle of Britain's history since 1945, this collage, sometimes moving, often comic, always fascinating, will seem reassuringly familiar … His tireless research turns up plenty of gems' Dominic Sandbrook, *Sunday Times*

'With a beady but compassionate eye, Kynaston ranges over public records and private diaries, political speeches and TV interviews, in conjuring this fresco of the panoramic and the intimate … Much of it chimes weirdly with our present moment … It is characteristic of Kynaston to present such opposing views and somehow to harmonise them' Anthony Quinn, *Observer*

'Readable and richly detailed … For all its documentary richness, the book reminds us – indeed warns us – how so much can change so quickly' Simon Heffer, *Telegraph*, Best History Books of 2023

'The real strength of the book, and the series, is Kynaston's focus on the voices from below. Drawing on a daunting array of diaries, letters and cultural ephemera ranging from the most pop to the highest brow, the book frames history through the ordinary person's experience' Charlotte Lydia Riley, *BBC History Magazine*, 2023 Books of the Year

'As in the earlier volumes of this vivid history of postwar Britain, Kynaston's primary aim is to document "a ceaseless pageant as, in all its daily variousness, it moves through time". This he achieves with a breathtaking array of treasures: diaries, provincial newspapers, political speeches, films and novels are woven together to provide a kaleidoscope of contrasting perspectives, defying any attempt to create a neat story of progress or nationhood … This is a richly evocative, thought-provoking and, above all, compassionate study of those who lived through the much-mythologised 1960s. We can only hope that when historians write about our own times, they will extend the same generosity of spirit' Selina Todd, *TLS*

'The latest instalment of the social historian David Kynaston's epic chronicle of postwar Britain begins with the Cuban Missile Crisis in October 1962 and ends with the death of Churchill in January 1965 ... *A Northern Wind* holds up a mirror to today' *New Statesman*, Best Books of 2023

'Entertaining, meticulously researched ... A captivating read' Charlotte Heathcote, *Daily Mail*, Favourite Reads of 2023

'The latest volume in a magisterial series on post-war Britain reveals a nation poised for change ... Moves continuously and skilfully between moments of high politics and the daily rumble of normal people's lives' Charlotte Lydia Riley, *Financial Times*

'Here is an intricate tapestry that conveys the essence of the time ... *A Northern Wind* is not a superficial exercise in heritage history, an attempt to dress up the past ... It analyses complexities, teases out nuances and gauges the currents of continuity and change, many of which still flow today' Piers Brendon, *Literary Review*

'A collage of fragments interlaced with penetrating analysis, this book is always humane, often hilarious, devoid of dogma and never condescending' Alan Johnson, *New Statesman*

'Let us be grateful for the collage of little pictures that Kynaston gives us, surely the most hyperreal of historical accounts of this period we will ever have. And let us hope for more volumes soon' *History Today*

DAVID KYNASTON is a professional historian and author. He has written a four-volume history of the City of London as well as a history of the Bank of England. His continuing history of post-war Britain, 'Tales of a New Jerusalem', has so far comprised *Austerity Britain, Family Britain, Modernity Britain* and *On the Cusp*. His three most recent other books have been *Arlott, Swanton and the Soul of English Cricket* (with Stephen Fay); *Engines of Privilege: Britain's Private School Problem* (with Francis Green); and *Shots in the Dark: A Diary of Saturday Dreams and Strange Times*.

TALES OF A NEW JERUSALEM

AUSTERITY BRITAIN
A World to Build, 1945–48
Smoke in the Valley, 1948–51

FAMILY BRITAIN
The Certainties of Place, 1951–54
A Thicker Cut, 1954–57

MODERNITY BRITAIN
Opening the Box, 1957–59
A Shake of the Dice, 1959–62

On the Cusp: Days of '62

A NORTHERN WIND

BRITAIN, 1962–65

David Kynaston

BLOOMSBURY PUBLISHING

LONDON · OXFORD · NEW YORK · NEW DELHI · SYDNEY

BLOOMSBURY PUBLISHING
Bloomsbury Publishing Plc
50 Bedford Square, London, WC1B 3DP, UK
29 Earlsfort Terrace, Dublin 2, Ireland

BLOOMSBURY, BLOOMSBURY PUBLISHING and the Diana logo are
trademarks of Bloomsbury Publishing Plc

First published in Great Britain 2023
This edition published 2024

A catalogue record for this book is available from the British Library

ISBN: HB: 978-1-5266-5757-2; TPB: 978-1-5266-5758-9; PB: 978-1-5266-5756-5;
EBOOK: 978-1-5266-5755-8; EPDF: 978-1-5266-5753-4

2 4 6 8 10 9 7 5 3 1

Typeset by Newgen KnowledgeWorks Pvt. Ltd., Chennai, India
Printed and bound in Great Britain by CPI Group (UK) Ltd, Croydon CR0 4YY

To find out more about our authors and books visit www.bloomsbury.com
and sign up for our newsletters.

This book is dedicated to the memory of Ian Jack (1945–2022), a wonderful writer who had 'post-war Britain' in his bones

Contents

Preface

Any moment in history is Janus-faced: simultaneously looking backwards and forwards. A world where the war was still fresh in the national memory, but where the end to post-war austerity meant that shopping was becoming a leisure activity; a world where homosexual relationships were still illegal, but where a new individualism in taste and identity was starting to emerge; a world where married women still mainly stayed at home and where divorce was still almost unthinkable, but where pop music was disrupting traditional cultural hierarchies and where there was a new impatience with what was now mockingly known as 'the Establishment' – one way and another, the Britain of the early to mid-1960s was undeniably Janus-faced. But looking backwards more, or forwards more? Perhaps backwards, despite the siren call of modernity from politicians, town planners, architects and others. Richard Hoggart, in his justly celebrated *The Uses of Literacy*, had referred in 1957 to how 'old habits persist'; it is a haunting phrase that must give any historian pause for thought.

This book begins five years later, in 1962, the year that lay exactly halfway between two of the most resonant dates in Britain's twentieth-century story. The first was 1945, when Clement Attlee's Labour Party won a landslide election victory, enabling the creation of a seemingly permanent settlement in which all parties signed up to the desirability of a strong welfare state and flourishing public realm, in which the market was the people's servant not their master, and in which the direction of travel was towards a more equal society. At this halfway point, even as Britain was losing an empire and slipping behind its main economic rivals, the foundations of that settlement still seemed secure, as Labour prepared to return to power (for the first time since 1951) in order to build on them. The other resonant date was, of course, 1979, when Margaret Thatcher came to power determined to overturn the collectivist assumptions behind that settlement – and, to a significant extent, succeeded. We continue in the 2020s to live largely in her world.

Tales of a New Jerusalem, a social history of post-war Britain, is about how and why '1945' became '1979': not quite a predestined story, indeed a story involving considerable happenstance, yet one where major, plate-shifting historical forces were at work, mainly in the direction of greater individualism. *Tales* also seeks to show – through as wide a range as possible of contemporary sources, including diaries and letters of the obscure as well as the famous, local papers as well as national, tabloids as well as broadsheets, *Coronation Street* and *The Archers* as well as *Panorama* and party political broadcasts – what Britain looked like, sounded like and felt like during these three decades or more, not least as a monocultural society gave way contentiously but unstoppably to a multicultural one. A partial and incomplete evocation, inevitably, but worth the attempt.

A Northern Wind, starting in autumn 1962 (the day after the Beatles released their first single) and ending in early 1965 (two icons – Winston Churchill and footballer Stanley Matthews – departing the scene), is in effect the eighth book in my sequence of *Tales*. The previous seven are *A World to Build* and *Smoke in the Valley* (gathered together in *Austerity Britain*); *The Certainties of Place* and *A Thicker Cut* (gathered in *Family Britain*); *Opening the Box* and *A Shake of the Dice* (gathered in *Modernity Britain*); and a snapshot of four months on the verge of the semi-mythical 'Sixties', *On the Cusp*. All the books include wide-ranging thematic chapters. But for the most part, my approach has been narrative-driven: the retelling of a ceaseless pageant as, in all its daily variousness, it moves through time.

PART ONE

I

All So Worrying

'Oh such golden weather now, exactly right for the Harvest decorating, in the morning at Church, which we did, with many others,' gratefully recorded Madge Martin, married to an Oxford clergyman, on 6 October 1962. No such cheerfulness this Saturday from the elderly Georgiana Tench, holed up in a convalescent home, probably in south-west London. 'Mostly dry, with *some* sunny periods but *some* very dark & dreary ones. I have not felt very well, & found things very dreary – so much alone.' Loneliness, too, for middle-aged Jennie Hill, living with her tyrannical mother in a village near Winchester, but for the most part managing through the daily round to overcome bouts of depression. Today, just three short sentences: 'Usual Sat work done. Busy day. Good Dixon T.V. programme.' A trio of female diarists, then, none of them with exciting prospects or an obvious claim to posterity's attention; but, like my grandparents living in small-town Shropshire, the 'Sixties' belonged to them as much as to anyone else.

Penelope Gilliatt in the next day's *Observer* wrote appreciatively of how Sean Connery in the newly opened *Dr. No* had played James Bond as a gentle send-up – 'full of submerged self-parody', whereas in the Fleming books 'he is snobbish, brutal and sneering, and his rapacious little character is full of the new upper-class thuggishness' – but Philip Larkin's unreconstructed eyes were more on the *Sunday Express*. 'Jolly good anti-CM stuff,' he told Monica Jones, against a background of Britain's continuing negotiations to join the European Economic Community, aka the Common Market. That afternoon, at 4.10, the comfortably built, middle-aged Mrs Mills, the ultimate pub-style pianist, made an early TV appearance (Granada and ATV only) on *Sing Along*; 40 minutes later, on BBC TV, some 29 per cent of five-to-seven-year-olds tuned in happily to *The Sooty Show*; and that evening, *The Black and White Minstrel Show* returned to the screen after its summer break. A 'Reaction Index' (RI) from viewers of 88 was even higher than the average (84) for the previous series, while percentages of viewers enjoying particular aspects 'very much' were headed by The George Mitchell Minstrels (89 per cent), The Mitchell Maids (82) and The Television Toppers (81), with Leslie Crowther trailing on 69, the same for George Chisholm and his Jazzers. Enjoyed likewise, if in a different key, was the harvest festival at Askerswell in Dorset. 'A fine autumn evening, with a moon to light the way, enticed everybody to service,' noted the Rev. Oliver Willmott in his next parish notes about 'the biggest gathering of the clans for many years', including 'several old boys and girls' of the village. 'After service, people seemed reluctant to leave. They stood renewing old acquaintance, or walked about bestowing well-deserved praise on the decorations. We observed that loyal old son of the church, Mr Norman Adams, drawing the attention of fellow gardeners to his shapely bunch of carrots in the chancel.'[1]

On Monday the 8th, a continuation of *Coronation Street*'s harrowing kidnapped-baby storyline was watched in almost 8.9 million homes (biggest audience yet, almost two years after the serial's start, for Ena Sharples et al.); that evening in Southsea, Tony Hancock started a three-week tour of provincial theatres and was found 'dreadfully diminished' by Kenneth Tynan, least sentimental of critics; next day at a girls' grammar school in Crediton, sixth-former Veronica Lee had 'to see Nutting-bag about universities' and was 'persuaded against L.S.E. [London School of Economics] on the grounds that she hasn't known anyone else go there'; and in Chingford, serious angst for a middle-aged housewife, Judy Haines:

> I talk too much.
>   Forgot to use my lipstick for Choir. John [her husband] didn't see it mattered; and to make up my mind to cancel Choir and go home for it or go in. I felt flat. Went in because I couldn't face going home to silence. Glad I went. The usual silence from John on way home.
>   Didn't want supper. Went to bed. Couldn't sleep. What to do about it? I can't take a job until I find someone to do my present 'Cook-general' one. I can talk less. Then I can't be snubbed.

Compact, BBC's twice-weekly soap, earned that evening a less than glittering RI of 61, some viewers dissatisfied about too much emphasis on romance ('What are they running? A magazine or a Marriage Bureau?'); Larkin in Hull went to see *Dr. No* ('pretty poor film', with Connery 'a cross between an out of work Irish actor and an assistant lecturer in physics'); the Victoria Theatre in Stoke, converted from a defunct cinema in a working-class area and intended as the first permanent theatre in the round, had its opening night; on Wednesday, *Coronation Street*'s baby Christopher was found (a key role in the drama played by Arthur Lowe as Leonard Swindley); at Highbury, after parity over two legs in the European Cup Winners' Cup, little Bangor City at last succumbed (1–2) to mighty Napoli; and also in north London, the local government official Anthony Heap reflected on the tides of change:

> Strange how so many of the things I like and have been buying for years have suddenly gone off the market lately.
>
> First Boots ceased to make and sell Palm Oil Shampoo which I've used regularly for the last fifteen years or so.
>
> Then Littlewoods in Chapel Market surprisingly closed down their provisions department, so I can no longer buy the tinned apple puddings I always got there and have never seen anywhere else.
>
> Next the manufacture of Barons – the brand of long, mild, white filter tipped cigarettes I've smoked these last four years – came to an end.
>
> And now Woolworths have ceased to sell plastic collars in the 'cut-away' style I prefer.

In short: 'What next, I wonder.'[2]

Next for slum housing, the recently appointed housing minister Sir Keith Joseph told the Tory conference at Llandudno that day, was a doubling or even trebling of the rate of clearance 'in the next few years'. The slum-clearance programme, he reminded delegates, had begun in 1956; current rate of clearance was 60,000–70,000 houses a year; more than half a million slum houses were still standing, with one-third of them concentrated in Liverpool, Manchester and Birmingham; and in order to achieve 'the biggest slum clearance drive ever', he pinned his hopes on what he called 'housing from the factory', in other words industrialised (or system) building not reliant on inevitably slower, smaller-unit traditional building crafts. Loud applause greeted these well-intentioned aspirations, with few delegates mindful of the earlier contribution to the debate from one delegate, Mr J. Addey of Huddersfield West. The most pressing problem, he insisted, were the four million households without bathrooms; 'our cry should not be slum clearance, but central heating and hot water for Coronation Street'; and far from all the houses in need of repair were slums. Or as he put it expressively, 'Go to some of the older houses in Lancashire and Yorkshire and call them slums if you dare.' There was also, he might have added, the generational divide; and indeed, when Joseph soon afterwards embarked on a tour of slum areas to see for himself, he 'discovered', noted one report, 'that elderly people liked their slums but that the young didn't, even though they had covered them in the veneer of an affluent society'. For the moment, though, the irresistible force was with indiscriminate, year-zero, carpet-bombing clearance.

On the evening of Thursday the 11th, Madge Martin – in London for a few days – went to the Columbia 'to see the strange, interesting, but rather nasty film "Lolita"'; next day, John Osborne fired off in *Tribune* a diatribe against the 'monumental swindle' of the Common Market ('a desolate affair of obsessive shopping and guzzling'); 'SCHOOLMASTER SAYS RACE HATRED IS FESTERING AMONG HIS BOYS' was the headline in the *South London Press* ('I think there should be more white people on the railways who understand you, than coloured people' being a typical opening sentence in essays at a New Cross secondary school on the recent railway strike); Sylvia Plath wrote the searing 'Daddy'; the incorrigibly upbeat transport minister Ernest Marples claimed on radio that Britain was making 'the greatest blitz on road-building in this country since Julius Caesar'; and Martin and her husband went to Her Majesty's to try *Lock Up Your Daughters*, 'an XVIIIth Century Musical "Romp", which everyone except us seems to have adored'; while Saturday saw Barbara Pym in suburban Queen's Park in north-west London getting ready for the winter ('this morning I cleaned and filled one of the paraffin stoves and the coal shed is full and waiting'), Harold Macmillan laying down the law on Europe (the PM telling his party conference that going in 'must involve some pooling of national freedom of action'), and third time lucky for the Martins, with *The Sound of Music* at the Palace proving 'a thoroughly enjoyable evening', as 'a huge rapturous audience' gave the show (not yet a film) 'additional warmth of atmosphere'. Judy Haines noted in passing on the Sunday that she now had a 'Teasmade'; next day Sussex University began for real on its own site at Falmer (with strikingly modern but expensive buildings by Sir Basil Spence, prompting one member of the University Grants Committee to sigh in later years, 'if only we could have looked after the Spences, the pounds would have taken care of themselves'); and Macmillan on Tuesday was in Scotland, inspecting the new, under-construction Forth Bridge. 'Five town centre projects' announced the *Architects' Journal* on Wednesday the 17th about what lay ahead for poor old Horsham, Wallingford, Lytham St Annes, Coalville and Sutton Coldfield, publication coinciding with the opening that day by the Duke of Wellington of the underpass under Hyde Park Corner ('the tunnel is lovely, but it's chock-a-block at both ends' the instant verdict of a taxi driver); and early that evening, on Granada's *People and Places* (broadcast only in the north and north-west), the Beatles made their first television appearance, singing 'Some Other Guy' and, of course, the recently released 'Love Me Do'.[3]

Macmillan on his Scottish trip also took in the British Motor Corporation's plant at Bathgate in West Lothian. 'This is an entirely new effort & (together with Rootes' factory [at Linwood]) will open a new chapter in Scottish industrial life,' he reflected with satisfaction about what would become the biggest engineering shop under one roof in Europe. 'I was much impressed by the management. The shop-stewards were friendly – or, at least, courteous.' Fewer civilities on display at the notoriously harsh working environment of Ford's at Dagenham, where this Wednesday a popular senior shop steward in the assembly plant, Bill Francis, was instantly dismissed for calling an unauthorised meeting during working hours – even though the meeting had actually been during the dinner break. Protest stoppages at once ensued, and by the end of the day assembly operations had stopped completely, prelude to a nine-day unofficial strike involving over 7,000 men. Reactions to this turn of events included Macmillan privately regretting 'the irresponsible attitude of the shop stewards' and the 'increasing powerlessness' of union leaders; *The Times* arguing that 'the 40,000 people who make up the Ford community are sadly in need of psychiatric study'; and the *Daily Mirror* criticising management clumsiness for undermining 'the efforts of responsible union leaders to curb reckless troublemakers in their own ranks', but reserving both barrels for 'the hamfisted unofficial strikers whose wrecking tactics sparked off this new crisis at Ford's'. As it happened, the evening before the Francis dismissal that lit the fuse, the Home Service had broadcast a documentary by the sociologist Peter Willmott about the people living on the huge working-class housing estate (known as Becontree) created in Dagenham between the wars. 'On their home-ground, discussing neighbours and work and gardens, people can become articulate and understandable in a way that makes you realise what an insult so many plays and novels are to human beings,' commented one radio critic, the writer Paul Ferris. 'The extraordinary thing is that the kind of speech you hear on any London bus any day of the week is still rare enough in radio to give it, as in this programme, importance.'

The main cultural event the following weekend was *A Suitable Case for Treatment*, a television play by David Mercer, with the central part, Morgan, taken by Ian Hendry. 'This story of the bizarre attempts of a non-conformist writer to prevent his wife from divorcing him struck a large number of viewers', noted BBC audience research, as 'utter rubbish. Nearly half the sample, in fact, roundly condemned it as ridiculous, pointless, or quite unsuitable for peak-hour Sunday viewing.' 'It was', the report quoted one viewer, 'completely beyond me. Personally, I look more for something which takes me out of myself rather than something that taxes my brain to its limits and is still incomprehensible.' Or in the words of a retired grocer, 'I presume the title of this play refers to the author!' Not surprisingly, its RI was a meagre 42 (compared to an average of 64 for BBC television plays during the first half of the year), and almost the sole recipient of praise was Hendry: 'To spout all that tripe and still give a good performance was nothing short of genius.' Was this just middle England's lack of imagination allied to a streak of philistinism, about a harrowing play drawing on Mercer's own experience of psychiatric treatment following a nervous breakdown? Perhaps not necessarily, given that the *Guardian*'s Mary Crozier found it 'very boring' and 'pretentious', the *Glasgow Herald*'s Robert Kemp 'a bit of a shapeless mess' albeit 'often quite funny', while the *Observer*'s

Maurice Richardson thought Morgan 'more like a showbiz goon on the job than a personal crisis case', as he 'shaved the hammer and sickle on a poodle, made Milligan-type noises, carted a stuffed gorilla about'. Was Morgan a neurotic? Or a psychotic? 'Some uncertainty,' reckoned Crozier, 'because the words were bandied about so much.'[4]

Next evening, Monday the 22nd, the sociologist Brian Jackson was in interviewing mode at the Huddersfield home – 'small through terrace house, which they are buying, paying money as rent; working-class district; shared toilet outside, no bath; rented TV, car' – of David (26-year-old window cleaner) and his seemingly nameless wife (22-year-old haberdasher, working short time). Surrounded by reproduction furniture (including 'a thing like a Jacobean dresser with plates stacked on display at the top') and contemporary, climbing-leaf wallpaper, the husband spoke of brass bands ('I wouldn't go and listen to one – they strike me as pretty old-fashioned'); of bowls ('perhaps when I get really old, you know about 50 or 60, and I can't throw me time in, in any other way, I might take it up a bit more'); of the semi-pointlessness of elocution lessons ('it's all right, but it's not how you say things, it's what you say, I mean you could pro-nounce everything properly, but you wouldn't know what to say'); and of being Huddersfield-born ('I think I've warm feelings about it, I'm not ashamed of the place anyway'). But she was the more expan-sive, including about the notion of them having separate friends, the prospect of having children, the north/south divide, and Blackpool as their habitual holiday destination:

No, I wouldn't let him go off like that. I don't think it's right. I let him go off for a drink by himself sometimes, you know when he's not leaving me. Real times, when it's the proper time for a man to go, Saturday dinner time and Sunday dinner time. I wouldn't want to go in myself then, it's not a woman's time …

Oh yes, we'd like them to go to Grammar School. And if they don't pass, I'd like them to go to a little Private School. Because at a Private School they'd learn how to talk properly, and that would be nicer for them …

Whenever I've been down South, I've always felt inferior somehow. I've always felt that everybody down there knew a lot more than we did. They're always much more up to date aren't they?

Don't you think so? They seem to have a more modern outlook, and everything down there, it's so much cleaner. They have all these Industries, but everything's clean. You come back to Huddersfield after you've been down South, I was down in Kent, it's all fields and farms. And then you come back up to Huddersfield and it looks black. But I shouldn't like to live down South, I don't think ...

Well, yes, we'd like to go abroad, but it's the expense in't it. And then I think abroad, it's not all it's cracked up to be is it. You get people that go to Majorca and it's just like holiday camp, when they get there. It's not much different at all. I think it's over-rated.

What about politics? 'I'm worried,' she responded, 'because I don't know anything about it':

Are you [i.e. Jackson himself] one of these, that goes and sits down in Trafalgar Square, who are they? I worry about stuff like that. And these people who wear a badge, I don't know what they're all about. I think people ought to worry about it. I talk to them at work about it, but they just tell me to forget about it, and they pull my leg. We had some forms round about Civil Defence, I can't get it out of my mind. If there's something on the news sometimes, and they say that Mr Khrushchev was annoyed, I go into the kitchen and start singing and try and get away from it. And I say, 'Oh dear, don't get him annoyed, try and keep him in a good mood.' Then there's all the weather isn't there? People say that it's caused by the bomb. But you can't get to know anything about it ...

A few hours later, at midnight UK time, President John F. Kennedy broadcast the news that the presence in Cuba of Soviet missile sites had been unmistakeably detected. 'The purposes of these bases,' he added, 'can be none other than to provide a nuclear strike capability against the Western Hemisphere.' Kennedy's address was covered on British radio. 'I was in the black abyss of sleep,' recorded Peter Willmott's wife Phyllis in her next diary entry, 'whilst Petie listened, in bed beside me, and then stayed awake until 2 wondering when the rocket would drop.'[5]

As Tuesday 23 October unfolded, not everyone supported Kennedy's declared intention (backed by the British government) to blockade Soviet ships carrying offensive weapons to Cuba. 'A completely unscientific summary of the day's eavesdropping,' estimated a London-based journalist, 'might be that most people feel emotionally on the side of the President but are unconvinced by his facts and that the "don't knows" are a large proportion.' Among diarists, the East Riding smallholder Dennis Dee made a rare acknowledgement of the world outside ('Big news, America's blockade of Cuba, could be serious'), Frances Partridge of the Bloomsbury group listened horror-struck to the latest radio bulletins before declaring that 'the world may be blown to bits any day – perhaps tomorrow', and Pat Scott, living in Barking, had an unhappy thirty-seventh: 'These things start on my birthday – like the Warsaw uprising – & spoil my day. And then to spoil it even more, Ted [her husband] took his [driving] test for the second time & failed.' That evening, both television channels put on specials – *Flashpoint Cuba* on BBC, *Crisis Over Cuba* on ITV – with critics awarding the honours to Auntie, albeit one noting Richard Dimbleby's 'irritating compulsion to sum up a witness who had just expressed himself with utter clarity and conciseness'. Even so, another critic admired his panic-subduing 'delicacy of touch' at the end of the programme, as he urged all parents to act normally and send their children to school in the morning. 'One misguided breath of emphasis and he could have had a million people streaming out into the streets,' reflected Maurice Wiggin. 'Without actually admitting that anyone might be in need of one, he adroitly administered a sedative at exactly that point in an anxious evening when it was calculated to do most good. And he did it without any manipulation of the facts.' Madge Martin needed more than a verbal sedative. At the end of 'such a keyed-up day', attending a family funeral and then 'hearing on the radio such dangerous and disturbing news of threats of war', she was sufficiently 'scared to death' that she took a sleeping tablet and 'so "put myself out"'.[6]

Only one story vied this week with the Cuban missile crisis for the nation's attention. 'All she could think about was money. That's Bloom for you, the bastard. She was a marvellous wife until she met Bloom.' Read out in a Brighton court on Monday, the words belonged to Harvey Holford, 34-year-old owner of a trendy local nightspot, the Blue Gardenia Club, and now accused of the murder the previous month of his 21-year-old wife, Christine. Bloom was John

Bloom, flamboyant and self-made 30-year-old director of the rapidly expanding washing-machine manufacturers Rolls Razor, whose chairman was a Tory MP, Richard Reader Harris. 'Every bloody day, every stinking day, she kept mentioning Bloom,' continued Holford's statement. 'We had a ruck at Hove Town Hall [where they'd gone dancing]. It was that bastard Bloom and money again. I just couldn't stand any more. So I got my revolver from the top cupboard in the kitchen and shot her.' A statement was also read out from Christine's friend Valerie Hatcher, who related Christine telling her 'that Bloom had promised to instal her in a villa at Monte Carlo and a flat in Mayfair, provided he lived with her, and he promised to give her £20,000 a year'. On Tuesday, giving evidence, Hatcher described the evening at Reader Harris's villa at Cap Ferrat when she had seen Bloom and Christine go hand in hand up to the double bedroom, leaving the obliging parliamentarian to sleep downstairs on a couch. The hearing ended on Wednesday, with Holford sent for trial to Sussex Assizes at Lewes, but not before he had made a tearful statement from the dock, insisting that he had told his wife she was 'in danger of becoming a prostitute and a whore if she went back to John Bloom'.[7]

That evening, the 24th, some 500 demonstrators were outside the US Embassy in Grosvenor Square, clashing with police as they chanted 'Hands off Cuba' and 'Viva Fidel, Kennedy to hell'. 'I suggest you go home,' a cassocked priest said at one point to the crowd after he came out of a house in North Audley Street, adding, 'I want some peace, too.' Earlier in the day, 40 sixth-formers at Midhurst Grammar School not only went on strike in protest against Kennedy's action, but some also took a bus to Petersfield to try to persuade their peers at the progressive-minded private school Bedales to join them. Fertile territory perhaps, to judge by one 14-year-old diarist. 'There could be a nuclear war! Everyone here is taking it VERY seriously, especially Mr Gillingham and all the CND crowd. At Bedales that's virtually everybody!' noted Gyles Brandreth. 'I say that it is because we have nuclear weapons that we are safe, but no one is listening to me! All over school, people are working out where to hide in the event that the Bomb gets dropped – in cupboards, under the oak dining-room tables, etc.' Another teenage diarist, Veronica Lee, was less sanguine:

Oh it is all so worrying ... I don't want to die, not yet when I'm just beginning to have more fun, in a depressing way. Every time I hear a lawn-mower or a plane I think the H-bomb is coming. Irony. Today is United Nations Day. In the lunch hour we made lines of pennies for Oxfam, but no-one will need it ... It's unfair that I and everyone else should have to die, when we have done nothing. Yet Russia can't be allowed to get away with it.

Twice as old, and soon to be published but for the moment still teaching English as a foreign language, John Fowles offered a take on the crisis only marginally less fearful:

It is extraordinary, the little effect this is having on people. They do nothing but joke about it. Endless jokes, in class, in the common-room. 'There's one thing – we've eaten our last English breakfast,' said one of the Greeks. I explained how this part of Hampstead was tilted to receive the maximum blast – huge laughter. And the staff-room full of sick humour. I suggested a notice to be put up: 'Owing to the end of the world today, there will be no classes tomorrow'. Very funny. But for a moment this morning my Proficiency class went out of control: all shouting at the same time, a glimpse of the hysterical anxiety that underlies everything these hours. I had it walking along Fitzjohn's this afternoon – the feeling that at any moment the huge heat-blast would come, all the houses fall. I don't know why, it was the thought of the leaves being blown off the trees that seemed worst ...

Mercifully enough, Cuba was seemingly on no one's minds that after-noon in Leeds when 41 girls from Stainbeck County Secondary Girls' School took their baskets of fruit and sweets to Springvale, the local home for blind women:

On our arrival we were taken into the dining room where all the ladies were having tea. Many of them did not know what was happening but, on being told, remembered how much they had enjoyed our visits in past years.

We handed round the baskets and then one lady asked us to sing. We sang two harvest hymns and some of the ladies sang them with us. The oldest lady there was ninety-five and totally blind. Although she could not see the basket that was given to her, she felt the grapes on the top and began eating them at once.

'We realised how fortunate we are to be young and able to see,' added Betty Longbottom in her report for the school magazine, 'and we came away feeling that we ought to try to do more for those who are less fortunate than we are.'[8]

Next day, at nearby Roundhay High School, the middle school debating society held a so-called 'raft' debate. 'The personalities represented were D. H. Lawrence, Cliff Richard, President Kennedy, Dr Barnardo and a typical teenage schoolgirl. Of these, Dr Barnardo and the schoolgirl were allowed to stay on the raft.' John Gross in that day's *Listener* acclaimed Michael Frayn as the one satirist in the new age of satire who carried a real sting ('when Christopher Smoothe, O. M., and Sir Rollo Swaveley affectionately mull over their bound volumes of *Private Eye* or wander down memory lane with old LPs of Lenny Bruce, they will still turn purple and snarl if anyone mentions the name of Frayn'); the latest episode of *Dr Finlay's Casebook* got an RI of 78 ('a good sensible plot, very good dialogue, everything in character and, last not least, always true to life'); and Judy Haines in Chingford continued to admonish herself: 'Did too much messing about at Keep Fit. Must do better next week.' Thousands of miles away, the US continued its blockade and, backed by new incriminating aerial photographs, insisted that Soviet missile bases were still being built. 'I am indignant though not surprised at the cool reception Mr Kennedy's actions over Cuba have received in the English Press,' declared a cross *Daily Telegraph* reader from London W2. 'Too long has the West turned the other cheek, compromised and lost ... Do we now have to be reminded of Russia's totalitarian goal? Communism demands world domination; let us not lose sight of this fact.' Macmillan made a statement to the Commons, adamant that if Kennedy had neglected the threat 'it would not have been in the interest of a continuance of peace and freedom in the free world', for which he received an immediate rebuke ('made me bristle') from Bertrand (Lord) Russell – in his fastness near Penrhyndeudraeth in Merionethshire, but in seemingly constant contact with both Kennedy and Khrushchev as he sought a peaceful solution. Protests meanwhile continued apace, including 30

Liverpool housewives and their families surrounding the American consulate in the Cunard Building and demanding a halt to the blockade, while the Oxford Union carried a motion condemning the American action as 'an interference to legitimate trade and dangerous to world peace'. A last sober, unadorned word for the day went to the artist (as well as diarist and telephone-exchange operator) William Halle, living in Wandsworth: 'Dreadful news. America and Russia in the thick of a most dangerous crisis which could so easily become a *war*. One thinks of a world destroyed.'[9]

On Friday the 26th, an even stronger sense of the eve of destruction, as a massive build-up of troops in Florida put the rumour mill into overdrive that the US was considering not just bombing the missile sites, but outright invasion of Cuba. Kennedy himself found time to reply to Russell, regretting the philosopher's anti-American stance and remarking that when a burglar broke in, one did not usually condemn the man who caught him. Little comfort to the 250 'screaming, hysterical girls' from Mynyddbach Comprehensive School in Swansea, who at about 11 a.m. 'swarmed out of their classes in protest, so they say, against the Cuban crisis'. 'Amid screams and flaying arms,' continued the local evening paper's reporter, 'their leader told me: "Why shouldn't we strike? Other schools have done the same. We don't want war."' At least one neighbour was unimpressed. 'Their conduct has been deplorable and their language foul. I have never seen anything like it before. I'm sure most of them don't know what it's all about. Strong action is bound to be taken against them.' By this point, a future novelist and a prematurely ageing poet saw the situation very differently. 'I marched around Liverpool in a 200-strong procession, chanting stop this madness,' Beryl Bainbridge soon afterwards informed a friend; whereas when Frances Partridge encountered W. H. Auden, he insisted that Kennedy was perfectly in the right and, asked by her whether he should not in that case have gone to the UN, replied, 'Oh no, there was no time'. Among the diarists, Halle was 'a bag of nerves', Lee asking 'why should the old make H-bombs and use them when the young haven't lived?', and Henry St John, a minor civil servant living on his own in Acton, alert as ever to domestic detail: 'The landlady, who has remained silent on the Cuban crisis and the Chinese invasion of India, commented this evening, after a day of heavy rain and wind, on the "muck" I had brought in, in the shape of leaves and mud, and claimed that although she had been out, she had not brought any in.'[10]

Yet, just possibly, there might be a future. In north London this Friday, the *Finchley Press* profiled the local MP ('she likes to cook, and is all for a bit of adventure, sweets with savoury, and so on', whereas 'Mr Thatcher is a bit wary'); in south London, the Lord Mayor opened the Old Kent Road's new Avondale Square housing estate, complete with three 20-storey blocks of flats; in King's Lynn, the atmosphere at a public meeting at the Corn Exchange to discuss the town's Central Area Development Plan (majoring on multi-storey car parks) was one of 'wariness interspersed with hope, fear, anxiety and congratulations'; and in South Wales the Queen opened the huge new steelworks at Llanwern, near Newport, including a continuous hot strip mill longer than any in Europe. Also new was the England football manager. Announced the day before, the appointment of Alf Ramsey from Ipswich Town was greeted enthusiastically by the *Daily Express*'s Mike Langley, who ended his encomium ('a man with a brain like a combination of camera and computer ... a man able to persuade a camel that it is really a Derby winner') with the prophesy that if England were to win the World Cup in 1966, which they were due to host, then the words would be heard, 'Arise, Lord Alf of Wembley'. Altogether less razzamatazz for the arrival in the charts at no. 27 of 'Love Me Do', but still earning a small feature ('Liverpool's Beatles wrote their own hit') in the *New Musical Express*. 'Why are they called "The Beatles"? The boys laughingly put off this question by saying: "The name came to us in a vision!"'[11]

First thing next morning, the working-class Glaswegian bandleader Tommy Watt was getting very quietly married to his heavily pregnant girlfriend Romany in the registry office opposite Norbiton station in Surrey – timing occasioned by an imminent court appeal (in which he hoped to appear as respectable as possible) after the previous month he had been sentenced to six months' imprisonment for unauthorised possession of Indian hemp. This Saturday was Sylvia Plath's thirtieth birthday; and still in her Devon home, though no longer with Ted Hughes there, she wrote two new poems, 'Poppies in October' and 'Ariel', the latter (notes her fullest biographer, Heather Clark) 'partly about the competing "drives" of creativity and maternity'. For the future historian Juliet Gardiner – nineteen, recently married, living in a bedsit in West Hampstead – it was the regular Saturday afternoon visit to the launderette in West End Lane. 'I sat huddled in my navy duffle coat, watching my underwear going round and round in the dryer, and peering at aerial photographs in my newspaper of hard-to-decipher Soviet ships steaming towards the US military blockade around Cuba,' she recalled. 'I sat rigid with fear, wondering what on earth was the point of having clean knickers, pillowcases and tea towels, since the world seemed about to end in a nuclear holocaust.' Simultaneously, the Committee of 100 (which under the auspices of Bertrand Russell had two years earlier broken away from the less civil-disobedience-minded CND) was holding in central London large-scale demonstrations 'for survival', with 'Hands off Cuba' the invariable chant and many arrests made, especially when demonstrators made a rush from Trafalgar Square into Whitehall. The press paid particular attention to the organisation's field secretary, Pat Arrowsmith, and her colleague Wendy Butlin, rumoured to have been on holiday together in the previous few days. Instead, they asserted in a joint statement, when a nuclear war seemed almost inevitable 'we decided to go as swiftly as possible to a place where we might conceivably survive – the West coast of Ireland'. That evening, reportedly driven out of the country by the prospect of crippling death duties and about to head to the South of France, the owner of *The Times*, Lord Astor of Hever ('kindly, shy, reticent', according to 'Atticus' in the *Sunday Times*) bade farewell to the Kent village. 'After a buffet supper in the primary school, a bound volume of the local people's signatures was presented to him. There was also a silver salver from his tenant farmers, and a silver pencil from the school for his wife, Lady Violet Astor.' Primitive rather than feudal emotions a few hours later, as 20-year-old Christine Keeler and her current lover, Johnny Edgecombe from Antigua, confronted a jealous past lover, Aloysius 'Lucky' Gordon from Jamaica, outside the Flamingo jazz club in Soho. In the ensuing fight, Gordon's face was slashed by a knife – whether Edgecombe's or an associate's is unclear – requiring 17 stitches; and Keeler and Edgecombe went into hiding.[12]

'Opportunities Now For The Brave' ran the optimistic headline on the *Sunday Telegraph*'s City pages, edited by Nigel Lawson, while 'Dad & I went to church' noted Lee in Shobrooke, Devon, adding alliteratively that 'paragon parson preached against worrying about

Cuba'. In the event, Sunday the 28th did turn out to be the day of relief, with news of a Russian climbdown coming around lunchtime. 'Just as we were having our dinner,' recorded Pat Scott in Barking, 'it was announced that Mr Kruskchof has agreed to withdraw rocket bases from Cuba.' The most cheering and clapping was in Trafalgar Square, where some 2,000 attending a 'Hands off Cuba' rally heard one left-wing Labour MP, Sydney Silverman, describe the American blockade as 'just a naked, brutal act of war' and praise the 'patience and restraint' of the Soviet leaders. All good mood music for the Liverpool Empire that evening, with the Beatles on the bill there for the first time. Afterwards, recalled an early camp follower, Bernie Boyle, they 'left through the stage door and had to walk to their van, and then suddenly people were running after them and I was running with them and they'd become *pop stars*'. But for one diarist, William Halle in Wandsworth, it was, notwithstanding the welcome news, a day for sombre reflection: 'I think the international tension over Cuba has got me down. Small wonder. The world seems in such a state of feverish evil that one pictures most men as devils. Hard to keep a calm front. It takes away the appetite and makes one weary.'[13]

Perhaps because of memories still fresh of the Suez Crisis six years earlier, British public opinion had been less supportive of the US than one might have expected. But in any case, it did not really matter, given that Britain played only a bit part in the unfolding drama. 'The Americans have borne the brunt,' reflected Vere Hodgson, living in Church Stretton, Shropshire, on the Monday. 'I was glad they did not consult us. We have had plenty of responsibility in the past. Let other people do it for a change.' For CND, the crisis marked a downward step, displaying the apparent irrelevance of whether Britain had the bomb or not. Yet irrespective of all that, it had been a week in which the Cuban missile crisis seared itself into the memory of the children of the 1940s:

I remember from school [Downside] lines of boys queuing for confession. *(William Nicholson, fourteen, future screenwriter and novelist)*

At Lancing one boy told me in complete seriousness that there was no point to doing our homework that night because we were all going to be dead tomorrow ... It was thinking about the divine futility of a world containing the means of its own obliteration which started my move away from the Christian faith. *(David Hare, fifteen, future playwright)*

While I sat on the snowy pebble beach watching the grim-grey sea in Brighton, America and Russia played chicken ... It was perfectly clear to me, and to others, that my world was very likely to end within forty-eight hours. *(Jenny Diski, fifteen, future writer)*

I remember walking to college [Ealing Art College] and thinking, 'This is the end of the world, I am going to die.' I was actually a little pissed off when nothing happened. *(Pete Townshend, seventeen, future rock star)*

We were all in London and I was scared. I was old enough to understand and I thought 'My God, we're all going to be nuked!' and we were sitting listening to the radio and I was fidgeting about and being very nervous and my father said, 'I'm beginning to feel ashamed of you. However frightened you may be – and it's natural to be frightened – you've jolly well got to face it with courage.' *(David Hart, eighteen, future Thatcherite fixer)*

Hart's father was 'Boy' Hart, a stockbroker-turned-merchant banker who was also a classic father of his generation: shy, undemonstrative, physically strong. And it is hard to imagine that when, after the crisis, the Home Office issued advice to potential survivors of a nuclear strike – to wear 'stout shoes' and not forget to take a 'travelling rug' in order to stay warm – he would have altogether approved of the implicit lack of stoicism.[14]

2

Audaciously Satirical

Over the next few, post-crisis weeks of autumn 1962, Tommy Watt was fined £150 instead of imprisonment for six months; Birmingham Corporation announced that it had purchased land to enable a proposed 'expressway' to run along the line of Aston's to-be-redeveloped High Street; *Dance News* was the first national publication to fully profile the Beatles ('these four gentlemen from Britain's beat capital, Liverpool, are a big threat to the big names in the instrumental and vocal world'); the *TLS* welcomed as 'a powerful weapon on behalf of the exceptionality of books' the decision by the Restrictive Practices Court that the Net Book Agreement (ensuring fixed prices) was not contrary to the public interest; *Dr Kildare*'s return earned an RI of 70, though some 'did wonder whether it was perhaps altogether advisable to depict scenes of an undeniably harrowing nature concerning child-birth in such highly dramatic terms'; *Boyfriend* told its teenage readers that 'men may have their masculinity, but girls have guile'; the East Riding smallholder Dennis Dee paid his first visit to a Chinese restaurant; 'v.g. in parts' was Jennie Hill's verdict on the Royal Variety Performance, while viewers generally praised Dickie Henderson, Eartha Kitt and the juggler Rudy Gardenas among others, whereas 'Cleo Laine, Mike and Bernie Winters, and Rosemary Clooney were particular targets for adverse comment'; Madge Martin in Oxford went to see *Last Year in Marienbad* ('quite incomprehensible ... can *anyone* tell me what it was all about?'); Julia Moseley at hospital in Winchester unexpectedly gave birth to twins ('the Sister on the postnatal ward felt a bit sorry for me that I hadn't known'); the opening of Carlisle's Fine Fare supermarket involved the Dagenham

Girl Pipers marching through the city streets before they formed a
guard of honour for star guest David Jacobs and then toured outlying housing estates; that evening (6 November), press night at
Stratford-on-Avon for Peter Brook's landmark production of *King
Lear* ('brings me closer to Lear [played by Paul Scofield] than I have
ever been,' declared Kenneth Tynan) coincided with Margot Fonteyn
dancing for the first time at Covent Garden with Rudolf Nureyev;
George Brown, the incumbent, comfortably defeated Harold Wilson
for the deputy leadership of the Labour Party; 58 per cent of the TV
audience for *Miss World*, compèred by Michael Aspel, were women;
also on BBC television, not only a stunning RI of 88 for Ken Russell's
film biography of Elgar ('exquisite' according to Anthony Heap,
'sheer magic' thought a housewife), but praise for David Dimbleby's
'considerate yet clear-cut manner' as question master on *Top of the
Form* for the somewhat 'nervous' team from Manchester High School
for Girls, altogether less 'confident, calm and collected' than their
opponents from Hutcheson Boys' Grammar School in Glasgow; as
the question came up in the Commons of the possible demolition of
Newcastle's Georgian jewel, a local Labour MP, Ernie Popplewell,
assured the House that 'to many people there is nothing of real outstanding architectural or historical value attached to Eldon Square'
and wondered whether the MP (Nicholas Ridley) raising the issue
realised 'how necessary it is that this re-planning should take place so
that Newcastle may attract industrialists to develop in the area'; the
Vauxhall Mirror informed assembly line workers in the huge plant at
Luton that their attitudes were soon to be studied by the Cambridge
sociologists David Lockwood and John Goldthorpe ('we believe',
they explained, 'that an important part of education deals with
what is happening in our society *today* – not just 1066 and all that');
Vere Hodgson went to hear John Betjeman read at Birmingham's
Barber Institute ('has the situation well in hand and his blunders
are nicely calculated'); at Cheltenham the 5-year-old Arkle (owned
by the Duchess of Westminster, trained in Ireland by Tom Dreaper,
ridden by Pat Taaffe) announced his readiness for the big time by
running away with the Honeybourne Chase for novices; *Dixon of
Dock Green* ('like an old welcome friend coming into the house
every Saturday') warned about the pitfalls of hire purchase, all too
liable to tempt a policeman to turn to crime; the *Sunday Telegraph*'s

film critic Alan Dent found himself reviewing a flavoursome trio of Bryan Forbes's *The L-Shaped Room* ('not since *A Taste of Honey* has one seen so much poetic and genuine emotion squeezed out of such squalid circumstances'), Ingmar Bergman's *Through A Glass Darkly* ('the genius would appear to be caricaturing himself'), and Disney's *In Search of the Castaways* (Hayley Mills's eyes 'now almost alarmingly large', Wilfrid Hyde-White 'endlessly twinkling'); 'the best first spy thriller for years,' reckoned Julian Symons about Len Deighton's *The IPCRESS File*, with its unnamed, unidealistic, off-the-peg-suit-wearing and generally un-Bondian agent 'who is on the right side but might at any moment move to the wrong one'; and Mr R. Stockting, owner of the Gillott Lodge Hotel, Edgbaston, protested against the 'preposterous and high-handed' decision by Birmingham Corporation (following a complaint by an Indian businessman) to exclude it from the city's official list of hotels. 'I do not take coloured guests because it is a small, compact hotel and in a family atmosphere such as we have, it would be embarrassing to us and to them,' he publicly insisted. 'Why has the corporation picked on me? There is a tremendous number of other hotels in Edgbaston which do not take coloured people.'[1]

That was reported on Wednesday 21 November. Two days later, Jean Rook, responsible for the *Yorkshire Post*'s 'Especially for Women' section, focused on family planning clinics and the contraceptive pill. 'This is not a subject,' she noted, 'which a woman will discuss over morning coffee – even with her closest friends, and the religious and moral implications are the responsibility of an individual conscience.' At this stage it was still a somewhat theoretical matter, given that at one probably not atypical clinic, no more than 70 out of some 4,000 patients had had the pill prescribed for them. 'These pills', a female doctor had told her, 'are only available to a few selected patients, whereas it is possible to buy other preventatives in a chemist, and the assistant is hardly likely to ask if you are married or not.' 'Obviously,' continued Rook herself, 'there is a tremendous need for these pills in such countries as India and China. It is debateable whether they were evolved primarily to help solve the world population problem or to help individual needs.' Not yet a fiery, opinionated columnist in her own right, she gave a last word to the head of a family planning clinic, judiciously declaring that the two problems were of equal importance, before adding: 'You must remember that it is our duty to help young couples to have a child, not to avoid having children.'

'Juke Box Jury [David Jacobs joined by a safety-first panel comprising Dora Bryan, Jean Metcalfe, Kenneth More and Bobby Vee], Dock Green, & then Man of the World [an ATV drama series, starring Craig Stevens as a world-renowned photographer on international assignments], such wonderful cameos, & photography, but I was in no mood for any more, & came gladly to my bed,' recorded Nella Last, elderly housewife in Barrow, next day. She would have needed that Saturday evening to stay up until 10.50 for the debut of the BBC's first intentionally satirical TV programme, *That Was The Week That Was*, soon generally known as *TW3*. 'A triumph, not over adversity, but of diversity,' recalled its producer, Ned Sherrin, about its hitherto unknown 23-year-old front man, David Frost. 'His curiously classless accent, sloppy charcoal suit and over-ambitious haircut concealed a man who had come into his kingdom at a bound.' The three and a half million viewers (well above what had been expected) could hardly have been more divided, resulting in an RI of 64. 'The majority liked it for being "witty and sophisticated", "brilliantly impudent", with an excellent cast, lively and versatile, entering into the spirit of the show admirably,' noted the audience research report. 'Only hope they can keep it up – we are still chuckling over some of the quips,' declared one viewer. 'Harwich for the continent, Paris for the incontinent. Will British Railways alter their slogan now?' A significant minority was wholly unamused. 'A dismal failure: the incessant "knocking" of the Government, of America, of the ITA [Independent Television Authority] and of Norrie Paramor [the record producer with a penchant for putting his own compositions on the B-sides of likely hits] I found not only unoriginal but positively distasteful. This programme was really sick!' And from another viewer: 'An insult to an intelligent person. It's the first time I have ever really wanted to smash my television set in anger. I will never watch this programme again – I can't afford a new set every week.' Press reaction to the efforts of Frost and his troupe (principally at this stage Bernard Levin, Millicent Martin, Willie Rushton, Lance Percival, Roy Kinnear and the cartoonist Timothy Birdsall) was also mixed: an enthusiastic review from the *Sunday Telegraph*'s Pat Williams ('brilliant ... adventurous both visually and in its material'); Dennis Potter in the *Daily Herald* welcoming a topical show written by people 'with chips rather than pips on their shoulders'; Peter Black in the *Daily Mail* semi-damning Frost as 'what you could call the first anti-personality on TV'; and Peter Green in the BBC's own magazine, the *Listener*, having serious reservations about this initial, 'much-publicised' outing. 'Anyone who stayed up in the hope of enjoying some ripe topical savagery, Continental-style, was doomed to severe disappointment; several of these satirical items raised laughs, but never a blister.' And altogether, Green called on it to 'shed that air of daring cosiness which bedevils British satire at its very roots'.[2]

Still, undeniably something was stirring, something was in the water, and so too next day with the third of 1962's Reith Lectures. The lecturer this year was G. M. (Morris) Carstairs, professor of psychological medicine at Edinburgh University; the overall title of his lectures was 'This Island Now', taken from the title of an Auden poem; and his theme this Sunday evening was 'Vicissitudes of Adolescence'. 'I believe,' he asserted, 'that we may be mistaken in our alarm – at times mounting almost to panic – over young people's sexual experimentation. Contraception is still regarded as something wicked, threatening to chastity, opening the way to unbridled licence. But is chastity the supreme moral virtue?' Apparently not: 'It seems to me that our young people are rapidly turning our own society into one in which sexual experience, with precautions against conception, is becoming accepted as a sensible preliminary to marriage; a preliminary which makes it more likely that marriage, when it comes, will be a mutually considerate and mutually satisfying partnership.' The effect was predictably explosive – the Catholic Marriage Advisory Council warning that 'if the personal relationship is judged to be entirely independent of procreation, this new emphasis can lead to irresponsibility and tragic consequences'; the Salvation Army viewing 'the increasing carelessness in this island concerning sexual relationships' as 'but another symptom of the general lowering of moral standards'; cross letters to the *Daily Telegraph*, including D. C. H. Michell of Tunbridge Wells complaining that the BBC did not have the right 'to invade the sanctity of our homes with special views on a subject so deeply affecting the lives, health and happiness of our young people' – but what about Home Service listeners as a whole? Predictably, 'the speaker's implied sanctioning of pre-marital sexual experience, his suggestion that charity rather than chastity was the supreme virtue, aroused considerable criticism as a possible dangerous lead to young people'; while as for 'his comparison with the uninhibited behaviour of adolescents in primitive societies', undoubtedly 'some' were 'perturbed at such statements being made on the air'. Yet at the same time, audience research made clear, the discussion by Carstairs of contemporary adolescence 'was generally found absorbing and challenging', with 'his "realistic and honest" approach often welcomed as a jolt to complacency and hypocrisy'.[3] The exact balance of opinion remains hard to establish. But crystal clear at the time was that, as with *TW3*, traditional norms and assumptions were now under challenge, perhaps under threat.

Few norms were more seemingly inviolable than English cricket's two-class system, until on Monday the 26th at Lord's the Advisory County Cricket Committee, made up of the first-class counties, decided by a clear majority to abolish amateur and professional status and instead to call all players cricketers – a decision to be passed on to MCC (Marylebone Cricket Club) for approval. Over the years, cricket's internal apartheid had always been essentially about social class, with all its attendant snobberies; the hypocrisy involved in 'shamateurism' (i.e. so-called amateurs effectively being paid), apparent enough in W. G. Grace's day, was now rank; and a fairly typical response to the decision was the *Daily Mail*'s, welcoming the end of 'humbug and the need for petty deception'. E. W. Swanton, the *Daily Telegraph*'s cricket correspondent and sometimes known as the Archbishop of Lord's, did not agree. After the news had reached him in a cable (laconically announcing 'Amateurs abolished') sent to Brisbane – where England, captained, of course, by a privately educated, Oxbridge amateur (Ted Dexter), were about to start an Ashes series – he wrote a heartfelt piece for his paper. The decision, he insisted, was 'not only unnecessary but deplorable'; cricket professionals were of their nature 'dependent', whereas 'the essence of leadership is independence'; the result was likely to be 'a somewhat colourless uniformity'; and given larger ongoing discussions about the future structure of the first-class game, this was the wrong time 'to introduce a classless society on the cricket field'. A classless society? Not quite, whether on or off the green turf; but even so, the decision marked the completion of a notable three-day hat-trick for change and modernity. In Brisbane itself, egalitarian-minded Australian colleagues were not wrong to plant on Swanton's desk in the press box what he wryly recalled as 'a wreath and a droll cartoon or two'.

Voting in a local election dominated that Monday evening's *Coronation Street*, with Leonard Swindley – self-important recent founder and chairman of the Property Owners and Small Trading Party – among those on the ballot; next day, the legendarily take-no-prisoners Dame Evelyn Sharp, permanent secretary at the Ministry of Housing and Local Government, was guest at a formal civic lunch in Plymouth, where she praised the rebuilt city ('the point is that you had a plan and carried through a magnificent conception'), while that evening Philip Larkin in Hull was an unimpressed observer at a Ted Hughes reading ('appallingly bad ... I felt quite embarrassed for him, poor sod'); over the next few days, as Swindley came comprehensively bottom of the poll, Leeds Corporation announced that their 1930s modernist showpiece of public housing, Quarry Hill Flats, was to be painted outside in pale pink, the go-ahead was given for Glasgow's Inner Ring Road (partly elevated, and likely to cut a swathe through Laurieston's classical tenements), and the December issue of the *Architectural Review* focused on the continuing destruction of London's Victoria Street, where already 'the redevelopment of the Stag Brewery site has created a new square of tall office blocks, just back from the original building line, that has effectively destroyed the feeling of the *rue corridor*'; on Saturday the 1st, Sheffield Wednesday went down tamely 0–2 at Ipswich Town (with the performance of the England international Peter Swan at centre half being deemed 'adequate' by one reporter, despite both goals being scored by the home centre forward), while *TW3* had its second iteration ('more loosening up, the audience more with it, David Frost employing a good line in suety mike manners', according to the critic G. W. Stonier); and next day, Harvey Holford in Lewes prison managed to delay his trial by falling over safety wire and fracturing his skull, *The Times*'s Midlands Correspondent filed a vivid report about major problems of decaying, overcrowded and insanitary housing for immigrants (in a Birmingham house, typically five or six families living in single rooms with few other amenities), and the Beatles ('Love Me Do' at no. 21, highest position so far) were at the Embassy Cinema in Peterborough as part of the support bill for Frank Ifield. '"The exciting Beatles" rock group quite frankly failed to excite me,' noted local critic Lyndon Whittaker. 'The drummer apparently thought that his job was to lead, not to provide rhythm. He made far too much noise and in their final number "Twist and Shout" it sounded as though everyone was trying to make more noise than the others.' And when the Lana Sisters, clad in pink, did their stuff, one man was heard to remark, 'much better than those Beatles'.[4]

Two days later, on Tuesday afternoon, there was a thickening fog in Chingford. 'I was surprised school didn't close,' recorded Judy Haines. 'Buses stopped running and only then were the poor kids from Woodford, Loughton and outlying parts allowed to go home.' So, too, in north London, where that evening Anthony Heap and his son went to the Century to see *Crooks Anonymous*, a British comedy. 'Home through the densest (visibility 5 yards) and filthiest fog I can recall since the deadly Smog descended on us exactly ten years ago' – it was as if the 1956 Clean Air Act had never been. Next day, a local paper published the personal credo of Newcastle's dominant politician, Councillor T. Dan Smith ('my belief is that the scientific advances of the Nuclear Age can produce an abundance of things essential to the liberation of man from personal deprivations'), before Derby that evening had its worst fog for at least a quarter of a century, as motorised crocodiles of cars were led by public-spirited pedestrians walking in the road and holding a handkerchief to show where the kerb edges lay. Heap, meanwhile, made his way 'through the continuing smog' to the Saville Theatre for the London first night of *Semi-Detached*. Written by David Turner, directed by Tony Richardson and set in a Birmingham suburb, this unsparing exposure of snobbery and hypocrisy now had the greatest actor of the day playing the central character Fred Midway, an insurance salesman of working-class origins in search of life's good things, including upward social mobility. 'What could have induced Sir Laurence Olivier to appear in this cheap and nasty and utterly worthless apology for a comedy?' wondered a baffled Heap, while one professional critic, Roger Gellert, was provoked into a pop at the great man himself: 'The crudity of the satire on the world of the kitchen-dinette correspondence-course culture and up-with-the-Jonesmanship is underlined by the patronising ineptness of Sir Laurence's stab at a Birmingham accent, which he treats like a quaint foreign language that no one else need be expected to know.' And he added that 'it's sad to see good young players like Eileen Atkins, James Bolam and John Thaw knee-deep in such muck'.

More inspiriting was the publication in the *Listener* on Thursday morning of Jenny Joseph's 'Warning' (to be named in a BBC poll 35 years later as Britain's favourite post-war poem), but weather conditions were still appalling: blankets of fog covering much of the country; in Leeds, 30 acute respiratory cases admitted to hospital; in London, the poet Stephen Spender recording grimly that 'in fog I feel like a frozen gas main'. That evening, Heap stayed in to watch Terence Rattigan's 'taut, tense, enthralling' written-for-TV play, *Heart to Heart* (excellent RI of 82), but the 88-year-old Sir Winston Churchill gamely groped his way to a dinner at the Savoy, one of only 11 members of the Other Club to make it, and Roger Symon was among those at Westminster Abbey for the first London performance of Benjamin Britten's *War Requiem*. 'Sitting at the back of the Nave,' he recalled half a century later, 'the swirling mists up in the vault left a vivid impression, even enhancing the swooping soprano solo in Lacrimosa beautifully sung by Heather Harper.' 'Smog death toll is now 106' was the *Evening Standard*'s headline on Friday the 7th, with the paper reporting on a wave of thefts the previous night (including a mink coat worth £600 snatched from a dummy in the window of Swears and Wells in Kensington High Street), power cuts hitting many areas, four vessels colliding off Blackwall Point, and that morning the Boeing carrying the Duke of Norfolk, briefly taking time off from his duties as manager of the MCC tour of Australia, 'still circling' after already waiting two hours for a chance to land at London Airport.[5] But as Friday wore on, the pea souper at last cleared – and, six years after the Clean Air Act, the final great, days-long Dickensian fog, relic of an industrial age, was over.

Lady Violet Bonham Carter had braved the weather conditions on Wednesday by going to Lord ('Bob') Boothby's 'delightful flat' in Eaton Square. His political diagnosis, as summarised by her, was typically crisp: 'The Govt is sinking – beset by troubles on all sides – soaring Unemployment, now over ½ a million, which he thinks will reach the million mark, failing to get into the C.M. [Common Market], bungling everything it touches – riding for a tremendous fall at the next Election.' The PM himself, in his diary next day, would not have disputed the gloomy outlook. 'A very bad poll for Conservatives & esp. for me in D. Mail Gallup Poll,' noted Macmillan. 'This is partly

the result of the really hysterical talk about unemployment both in
Press [including a powerful *Daily Mirror* special issue the previous
Friday] and on Radio & TV.' By late 1962, few in the Westminster
village doubted the electoral runes, with Anthony Howard (now at
the very height of his powers as the *New Statesman*'s political commentator) reflecting shortly before Christmas that the Labour Party
'accepts as a matter of simple, factual conviction that Mr Gaitskell
will be travelling triumphantly to Buckingham Palace in probably less than a year's time'. What to do? Certainly it did not help
the Conservative cause that, on the last Saturday in November,
Macmillan had seemingly ignored the latest disastrous by-election
results (including Dorset South lost to Labour) and gone ahead with
three days of pheasant shooting at the country seat in Lanarkshire
of his foreign secretary, Lord Home. Potentially more helpful was
Reginald Maudling's clearly expansionary instincts at No. 11; while as
for the state of party organisation, that was the challenge for the previous chancellor, Selwyn Lloyd, now deputed to undertake a roving
enquiry across the country.

'It was agreed,' recorded the minutes of the initial meeting in
late October, 'that Mr Mount [the 23-year-old Ferdinand Mount,
working at the Conservative Research Department] should deal with
travelling arrangements, hotel bookings, etc. Mr Selwyn Lloyd said
he would like Mr Mount to travel with him all the time.' An early
stop, on 6 November, was in Birmingham, where chairmen, treasurers
and agents for the West Midlands Area had the chance to vent their
grumbles and those of party members:

No great rise in subscriptions could be expected unless the
Government produced more popular policies. (*Sir Theodore
Pritchard, Birmingham*)

Richer subscribers felt that the Government was hitting at them,
and were correspondingly reluctant to contribute. (*Lichfield and
Tamworth representative*)

There was a feeling that the country was being governed by the
civil servants who had a stranglehold on the Government. (*Mr Salt,
agent at Solihull South*)

The lack of emphasis on Conservative *principles* was very discouraging. *(Hall Green)*

MPs should go into the pubs on Saturday nights rather than holding cocktail parties for the converted. *(Oswestry representative)*

There were too many whist drives. *(Sutton Coldfield)*

What about a possible strategy of the party seeking to broaden its appeal and respond flexibly and imaginatively to a changing Britain? There, the West Midlands voices had little to offer, with just one exception: 'The Handsworth agent, 12% of whose electorate were coloured, hoped that a multi-racial note might occasionally be struck in propaganda.'[6]

*

No smog at West Point on the first Wednesday in December, as a former American secretary of state, Dean Acheson, explained to the military academy where an old ally stood in the great geopolitical game:

> Great Britain has lost an empire and has not yet found a role. The attempt to play a separate power role – that is, a role apart from Europe, a role based on a 'special relationship' with the United States, a role based on being the head of a 'Commonwealth' which has no political structure, or unity, or strength and enjoys a fragile and precarious economic relationship by means of the sterling area and preferences in the British market – this role is about to be played out.
>
> Great Britain, attempting to work alone and to be a broker between the United States and Russia, has seemed to conduct a policy as weak as its military power. Her Majesty's Government is now attempting, wisely in my opinion, to re-enter Europe, from which it was banished at the time of the Plantagenets, and the battle seems about as hard-fought as were those of an earlier day.

Reaction in the old country was predictable. The Institute of Directors (IoD) at once wrote to Macmillan, protesting against Acheson's 'calculated insult' to what it called the British nation, while over the next few days much of the press indulged in what Violet Bonham Carter called 'a ridiculous explosion of jingo rage'. Macmillan himself, privately reflecting that 'of course, Dean Acheson was always a conceited ass', sent a public reply to the IoD, in which – like so many British leaders after him – he had to ride two horses: playing to the patriotic gallery ('in so far as he appeared to denigrate the resolution and will of Britain and the British people, Mr Acheson has fallen into an error which has been made by quite a lot of people in the course of the last 400 years, including Philip of Spain, Louis XIV, Napoleon, the Kaiser and Hitler'), yet at the same time emphasising that it was 'the doctrine of interdependence which must be applied in the world today, if peace and prosperity are to be assured'. The *New Yorker*'s Mollie Panter-Downes, writing as usual for an American audience in her next 'Letter from London', reckoned Macmillan's reaction 'surprisingly prickly'; and, with the PM due to go shortly to the Château de Rambouillet to meet General de Gaulle, she wondered whether the government was 'showing signs of beginning to hedge on the urgent historical necessity of going into Europe'.

One former PM, Clement (now Earl) Attlee, refused to see that journey as a necessity at all. 'Mr Acheson has confused the Government of this country with Britain,' he wrote to *The Times* soon after the disobliging West Point speech. 'He has seen this Government, apparently indifferent to the interests of the Commonwealth, going cap in hand to certain Continental States begging to be allowed to join their Common Market. He has seen Mr Heath [Edward Heath, responsible as Lord Privy Seal for the ongoing negotiations in Brussels] return empty handed from the Continent. No wonder that he thinks Britain is down and out.' After a couple of brief paragraphs about how the appeasers of the 1930s had been followed by Churchill in 1940 and Britain's 'finest hour', Attlee finished in typically straightforward, economical fashion: 'It is time that the people of Britain should be given the opportunity of expressing their views before [the] Commonwealth is destroyed.' As ever, the great man was largely out of step with 'writers, scholars and intellectuals', their views elicited this month for an *Encounter* symposium, 'Going into Europe'. Among the majority Yeses were Nancy Mitford ('otherwise, may we not become a neglected appendage of North America?'), Leonard

Woolf, Harold Nicolson, T. S. Eliot (wanting 'close cultural relations with the countries of Western Europe'), Peregrine Worsthorne and Kingsley Amis (albeit noting that 'none of the countries of the Six interests me'); among the minority Noes were A. J. P. Taylor ('I prefer Nero to Adenauer or de Gaulle'), Marghanita Laski ('any Jew must hesitate before going in with Germany') and C. S. Lewis (wanting the localism of 'Wessex and Picardy, not "Britain" (a horrid word) and France'); while as for Harold Pinter, presumably in the absence of a response from Samuel Beckett, 'I have no interest in the matter and do not care what happens'.

There were probably moments for Macmillan at Rambouillet when he wished he had never gone down the European road, as for all his high-minded and sometimes emotional pleas (invoking 2,500 years of European civilisation and declaring that only if Europe was united could it stand up to the colossi of America, Russia and perhaps soon China) the General largely dug in his heels, not quite ruling out British membership of the Common Market but seemingly pushing it into the long grass. Not long afterwards, some private remarks of de Gaulle, made to his ministers, found their way into the press. 'We prefer the Britain of Macmillan to that of Labour [largely anti-Common Market] and would like to help him to stay in power. But what could I do, except sing to him Edith Piaf's song, *Ne Pleurez Pas, Milord*.'[7]

Macmillan himself by this time was at another summit, as he and Kennedy met at Nassau in the Bahamas to discuss nuclear matters. In essence, the American position was that they could no longer supply Britain with Skybolt missiles, as promised two years earlier to Macmillan by President Eisenhower, but were willing to sell Polaris ones – only, however, if overall control of their use was assigned to Nato. This, insisted Macmillan, was not good enough; and the upshot was a compromise by which, although still under the Nato umbrella, Britain reserved the right to use the warheads on British submarines autonomously in situations where 'Her Majesty's Government may decide that supreme national interests are at stake'. Quite apart from those hostile to nuclear weapons as such, not everyone at home was thrilled with the outcome. 'Yesterday's Press was quite good (except of course Lord Beaverbrook's),' noted Macmillan after arriving back on 23 December. 'Today's is *very* bad.' None more fuming than

Beaverbrook's *Sunday Express* (editor: John Junor). 'Our faces are not only wiped in the mud,' it declared about what it saw as a humiliating turn of events. 'We are also paying for the cost of the mud.' Vere Hodgson in Church Stretton tended broadly to agree. 'Poor Mr Macmillan has had a very difficult time with President Kennedy, and really I think the American government has not been quite fair with our government over the Skybolt,' she reflected on Boxing Day, adding that 'General de Gaulle is as difficult as ever' and then – seventeen years after the end of the war – drawing a larger moral: 'So after shedding our life's blood for freedom, and all the money we possessed, we are having to be pushed around by people who have not done so much. But their turn will come. It is the immutable Law of Life.'[8]

Also immutable, of course, were the economic facts of life – above all the fact that Britain in 1962 was a country experiencing palpable relative economic decline, with Macmillan's recently established exercise in corporatism, the National Economic Development Council ('Neddy'), unlikely to reverse that decline, especially given how the understandable fear of the trade unions that it was essentially a cover for incomes policy negated any desire they might have had to reach an agreement on reform and modernisation.

Over the years, few sectors would be more emblematic of decline than the British motorcycle industry, not helped by a newly uneven playing field: prior to the signing on 14 November of the Anglo-Japanese trade treaty, ending years of discrimination against Japanese goods in Britain, the British Cycle and Motor Cycle Association had complained strongly but unavailingly about the agreement giving most-favoured-nation treatment to Japanese motorcycles in the British market without corresponding treatment for British-made machines in Japan. Yet the uncomfortable larger truth was that much of the British motorcycle industry, including industry-leading, Birmingham-based BSA, was seemingly no longer capable, despite adequate financial muscle, of competing effectively with Japanese rivals. A few days earlier in November, at the Cycle and Motor Cycle Show at Earl's Court, where Alex Moulton had raised spirits by demonstrating his new small-wheeled, rubber-suspension bicycles ('one of the biggest moves in cycle design this century,' noted *The Times*), BSA's two new ultra-lightweight models on display were the Ariel Pixie and the BSA Beagle. 'These motor cycles were poor indeed by comparison with their Japanese counterparts and dealer reaction was somewhat scathing,' recalled BSA's Bert Hopwood in 1981 in his notably objective *Whatever Happened to the British Motorcycle Industry?*. 'The design and development work had been done "at the double" and the engine, in particular, was later dubbed by one or two of our top BSA dealers as "a first-class example of Mickey Mouse engineering". Production target dates simply could not be met and when the new models did, at last, trickle through, they gave so much trouble in the field that orders dried up and both models were withdrawn.' By the following summer, after only seven months of selling in Britain, Honda was claiming it had 40 per cent of the 50cc market; and the British business press was writing admiring, bittersweet articles about Honda's 'sophistications of production', with the contrast all too glaring.[9]

The other international treaty signed in November 1962, on the 29th, was by Britain and France for the joint development of what was expected to be the world's first supersonic airline. 'This slim, delta-winged aircraft,' reported *The Times*, 'will cut the Atlantic crossing time from seven and a half hours to about three hours.' The British government's share of the costs was estimated at £85 million; BOAC were expected to make their commercial judgement in about 1966 on whether or not to buy the aircraft; and no publicity was given to the absence in the agreement of a break-clause. French enthusiasm for the joint project had usually been greater than British since the two sides began talking in October 1959, but to a significant degree that had changed in recent months: 'modernisation' was ever more the aspirational language of the Macmillan government; whole-hearted commitment might help to persuade de Gaulle that the British were committed Europeans with technological expertise to offer; and Minister of Aviation since July was Macmillan's son-in-law, Julian Amery. A mixture of politics and technology now drove the case, with the Treasury decisively marginalised and Amery himself (nicely described in one study of the decision as 'ambitious, politically adroit, and a gambler') finding a helpful ally in his parliamentary secretary Basil de Ferranti, from a family which made electronic aviation equipment. 'Either none at all or a hell of a lot,' recalled Ferranti about the answer when he went to the Royal Aircraft Establishment at Farnborough to assess the project and ask about whether the plane would sell; while as for the overall attitude that Amery and he took in the weeks leading up to the signing: 'It is a gamble. But if we can do it with the French, it will halve the ante. So let's have a go.' Press reaction to the agreement, among experts anyway, was distinctly sceptical. The *Guardian*'s Leonard Beaton regretted how the essentially political 'European argument' had been used 'to silence both the timid and the more serious school of opinion which thinks supersonic passenger flying will be expensive and a nuisance'; and John Chappell's assessment in the *Daily Telegraph* had the headline 'The Big Gamble in the Air: An Anglo-French supersonic airliner by the 1970s is now almost certain. But who is going to buy it?' Another question, if lesser, was the name itself. 'It seems likely,' reckoned Beaton, 'that the aircraft will be called the Concorde, although the decision has not yet been taken. Apparently there has been unsuccessful search for an Anglo-French name equally good in either language.' And he added that at least one minister (Enoch Powell?) had objected to investing British millions into that final 'e' – but that 'with the European spirit abroad in Whitehall at the moment he decided to let it pass'.[10]

There was one other piece to the larger jigsaw this autumn. 'If we do not regard it as a major government responsibility to take this situation in hand and prevent two nations developing geographically, a poor north and a rich and overcrowded south,' the home secretary, Henry Brooke, warned the Cabinet in October, 'I am sure our successors will reproach us as we reproach the Victorians for complacency about slums and ugliness.' Two months later, against a background of rising unemployment, the urgency of the situation had only sharpened. 'The figures are expected to mount in the badly hit north after Christmas, which will not exactly be a season of good cheer in those areas, even though the usual spending spree will be going on in the prosperous south,' predicted Panter-Downes in her pre-Christmas round-up. 'The economic list of this island to the south-east, where the population and the capital are crowding in, has resulted in the cliché of the moment, about Britain's being split clean as a whistle into two halves, and in talk about the recurring pattern of the thirties, which to those of us old enough to remember them provides un-Christmassy emotions indeed.'

Between Brooke and Panter-Downes, the *Guardian* had run a series of five impressionistic articles by David Holden on the north–south divide. 'In one belief, at least, I have been confirmed,' he ended his first:

This is that rich or poor, for better or worse, the distinction between North and South still exists. Sometimes humorously, sometimes fancifully, sometimes resentfully, sometimes just factually, the differences still emerge. Deep down in the national fibre, on both sides of the North-South line, there is a lingering, atavistic conviction that – give or take a few miles here and there – the Wogs begin at the Trent.

Serious housing problems, neglected schools, struggling industries, population declining, a socially conformist and conservative tribalism, virtue too often lapsing into self-righteousness – Holden drew a generally downbeat picture of life on the northern side of the great divide. History's continuing legacy, he emphasised, was responsible for much:

The North is crippled with the burden of the industrial revolution to an extent that the South hardly begins to understand. Virtually the whole social capital of the northern towns, from the antiquated town halls of marble and millstone grit to the grimy schoolhouses among the streets of back-to-backs is of Victorian origin and desperately in need of renewal. The sheer mental depression that the sight of this decay induces is enough to deter most professional people in the South from ever settling in these towns – and, equally, to encourage the best local boys to get out and stay out as fast as they can.

Almost inevitably, whether then or now, any overall analysis of a country has to choose whether to privilege region or class. Holden at one point, in his article on the educational divide between north and south, noted that out of 27 schools which had been successful in winning open awards to Oxbridge in the past five years, only six were in the north, whereas 20 out of the remaining 21 were in the south (the other being in Birmingham). But what he omitted to add, observed Phyllis Willmott in a letter to the paper, was that all but two of those twenty-seven schools were public (i.e. private) schools – 'in other words, at least as far as entrance to Oxbridge is concerned, social class is of greater importance than the North-South distinction'.[11] She was surely right; and if social class does not quite trump everything, more often than not it trumps most things.

*

On 8 December, the day after the fog cleared, *The Economist* proposed
curing over-centralisation as well as the north–south divide by
moving the capital from London and creating a new, Brasilia-style one
at Marston Moor, between York and Leeds; Marian Raynham, an elderly diarist in Surbiton down with a bad cold and spending the day in
bed, lamented how people nowadays had 'no worthwhile possessions,
wear brass & glass jewellery like savages are pleased with, "work"! all
day, whizz around all week end in tinpan motor cars that don't last &
are not paid for'; a Third Programme talk on pop art noted that David
Hockney 'mingles graffiti and child art' and quoted him as recently
asserting, 'I paint what I like, when I like, and where I like'; and *TW3*,
third time out, entered squarely into the national psyche.

Items this Saturday evening included a depiction of Macmillan
having, as he complained to Kennedy on the hotline about Dean
Acheson, to spell out his own name; a variety of other hit jobs (at
the songwriter Lionel Bart, at the Roman Catholic Church, at
Reggie Maudling, and most memorably at the hotelier-cum-caterer
Charles Forte, grilled by Bernard Levin, whose consciously deployed
rudeness, here describing Forte's company to his face as 'lazy, inefficient, dishonest, dirty and unpleasant', was rapidly making him a
hate figure for middle England); and an instantly notorious sketch
about Roy Kinnear's open fly buttons. Amid newspaper headlines
about a plethora of complaints flooding into the BBC, what seems
to have happened over the next few days was a gathering sense that
here at last was a television programme willing to ignore stuffy norms
about what could and could not be said about the world at large. So
although on the Monday an editorial in the *Daily Telegraph* cautioned
that 'in a country such as Britain, tolerant to the point of faineance,
it may sometimes be easy to overdo the jibe at authority', letters next
day to the paper praised the 'adult and stimulating entertainment',
provoking admittedly a certain amount of squirming in the seat, but
also 'laughter and admiration'; by the following Saturday, Anthony
Heap was having 'to impatiently wait for the week's one bright spot
on television – the B.B.C.'s audaciously satirical late night revue',
while asking 'why oh why, can't they lay it on earlier than 10.30?'; and
it may have been at around this time that the young Ian Jack, growing

up in Fife, came home late on a Saturday night to find his father chort-
ling in front of their new television and saying to him, 'My, but these
boys are funny!' Surviving clips, as Matthew Engel has reflected,
only barely suggest what the fuss, what the impact, was all about.
'The programme had a raw edge and phenomenal energy. And the
point was that the staid BBC, which had only lately been respectfully
asking the prime minister if there was anything he wished to impart
to the nation, had now joined in and was knocking the politicians.
The nation was captivated and occasionally shocked by the audacity
[that word again] of it all.' In short: 'Anything seemed possible.' Yet
of course there were dissenters, not only the predictable ones. Phyllis
Willmott would recall the young and very left-wing future historian
Raphael Samuel stubbornly refusing to watch *TW3* when everyone
else was, saying that he wanted *real* conversation instead.[12] But for
most people even mildly questioning of Establishment assumptions,
so refreshing and sometimes eye-opening was it that that seemed a
more than fair exchange.

On Sunday the 9th, Sylvia Plath – with her two small children, but
without Ted Hughes – moved into her new home near Primrose Hill;
next day, Keith Joseph, having recently called on local authorities to
adopt higher densities for both planning and housing purposes, now
claimed in the Commons that his 'vision' was 'to reconcile the town
and its traffic, and create within the years to come, out of the squalor
and shapelessness of so much of the past, a new 20th century urbanity
worthy of the best in our history'; and on the 12th the *Architects'
Journal* publicised the London County Council's 'outline scheme
for providing housing for 25,000 people by the Thames Estuary' (i.e.
the future Thamesmead), Heap went to the Aldwych for the opening
London night of Peter Brook's *King Lear* ('with its bare stage and drab
leather costumes, rather too austerely abstract for my liking', though
Scofield 'awesomely majestic'), and Miss Jane Cain, the voice of 'Tim'
(the GPO's speaking clock) since 1935, handed over to the winner of
a 'Golden Voice' competition. 'I chose the safe roast turkey,' noted
Madge Martin next day in Oxford about going to 'the Chinese restaurant in Ship Street', whereas her husband Robert 'bravely tried a
strange Chinese dish, which *wasn't* so good!'; late morning on Friday
the 14th, Johnny Edgecombe, in a sleepless jealous rage intensified by
too many purple hearts, fired six shots at the door-lock of 17 Wimpole

Mews, home of the fashionable osteopath Stephen Ward and where Christine Keeler was holed up inside; Elvis's 'Return to Sender' now replaced Frank Ifield's 'Lovesick Blues' at the top of the charts, with 'Love Me Do' bumping along respectably enough at 19; Barbara Pym, in W.H. Smith in Fleet Street on Saturday, thought to herself, 'I'm just a tired-looking middle-aged woman to all those (mostly young) people yet I have had quite a life and written (or rather published) six novels which have been praised in the highest circles'; at a ceremonial dinner at Coventry that evening, it was a time for out-and-out paternalism as clocks were awarded to employees with over twenty-five years' service at the leading engineering firm Alfred Herbert ('we are all parts of one team,' urged the chairman, Colonel C. W. Clark, DSO, OBE, MC, 'so let us work together with goodwill and not kick the ball through our own goal'); *TW3* went through its paces ('a down-to-earth, nobody-is-safe attitude,' declared one viewer, though the Manchester doctor Hugh Selbourne thought it 'much watered down in the face of critics'); and on Monday afternoon, *Blue Peter* got its first pet, a brown-and-white mongrel puppy called Petra, which soon afterwards would die of distemper and have to be discreetly replaced without young viewers being any the wiser.[13]

Wednesday the 19th saw the formal opening of the latest stretch of the M6 (the accompanying brochure passing swiftly over Trentham gravel pit, but extolling the 'attractive rolling country between Whitgreave and Beech which opens up new vistas of Staffordshire which will be new and pleasantly surprising to many people'); 'I have come to police to tell you about my homosexual relations with Jeremy Thorpe, who is a Liberal MP, because these relations have caused me so much purgatory and I am afraid it might happen to someone else,' began a voluntary statement made at Chelsea police station by Norman Josiffe (later Scott); 'I'm having a ball here,' Keith Richards told his aunt Patty, 'I live in my friend's flat in Chelsea most of the time and we are starting to make the music business quite profitable'; the Friday issue of the *Smethwick Telephone* included the prospective Conservative candidate, Peter Griffiths, telling constituents that 'my party is against allowing a concentration of coloured people in any particular area'; and that evening between 8 and 9.20 the Haines family listened to a play (*Unman, Wittering and Zigo*) on the Third by Giles Cooper, set in a school. 'It turned out to be very cruel, and not humorous as I had thought when I suggested it,' Judy regretfully noted. 'I was relieved when it was over.' The *Sunday Times*'s John Russell Taylor for one would not have been surprised by this dusty reaction to the experimental, writing next day to Kenneth Clark that 'the public longs to hear from you that modern art doesn't really count and they can safely disregard it'. Saturday evening was of course *TW3* – 'good, but for that ill-mannered Bernard Levin,' reckoned 18-year-old Veronica Lee in Crediton, adding that she liked Frost, 'clever without being a boor' – but in retrospect perhaps the most resonant event was at the Singers' Club Christmas party at the Pindar of Wakefield pub in King's Cross. The 21-year-old Bob Dylan (peaked cap, sheepskin jacket, almost unknown, over in England to take part in a BBC TV play) sang a number or two, as the politically and musically intolerant main man of the British folk revival, Ewan MacColl, looked on quizzically.[14]

Sunday was Sunday, with almost all shops shut even just two days before Christmas; and William Halle, taking a walk from Wandsworth to Piccadilly in search of a chemist selling codeine, found 'a nearly empty Piccadilly Circus, the few people blue with cold, the underground dark and mysteriously deserted'. Blue indeed. 'Life here is very burdensome,' complained the experimental composer Cornelius Cardew, on holiday in Dartmoor. 'Stella is furious with the cold, and consequently refuses to consider sex, though this is a fast way to warmth.' Cold, too, in Shipley, Yorkshire, where Sidney Jackson noted that the weather was 'again bitter', with 'the barometer higher than I have ever known it', and next day flatly recorded, 'still bitterly cold.' 'Is it still possible amid this ghastly racket of "Xmas",' C. S. Lewis in non-meteorological vein now asked J. R. R. Tolkien, 'to exchange greetings for the Feast of the Nativity?' Neither man this Monday evening would probably have enjoyed BBC TV's *A Christmas Carol*, an opera with music by Edwin Coleman, receiving an RI of 43 and variously described by viewers as 'weird' and 'modern' and 'off-key', with 'not a single tuneful aria of any length'. Or as a less than gruntled fitter put it: 'Fancy messing up a traditional story with that awful music. Spoilt my Christmas Eve.' But at least for adults there was comfort from an Air Ministry spokesman, looking ahead to Christmas weather and predicting that 'there does not seem to be much more snow about'.[15]

'Bitter day' (Jackson), 'atrociously cold' (Heap), 'v. cold wind, hard frost' (Hill): the diarists on Christmas Day were of one accord, with Jennie Hill adding that, as part of the usual routine, she had watched the Queen's speech. 'V.g.' was her verdict; but despite its adroit use of Telstar ('the wise men of old followed a star: modern man has built one'), there was concern about ratings starting to slip. 'We can never rely on the Queen doing a much better performance than this Christmas,' reflected the BBC's Seymour de Lotbinière soon afterwards, with echoes of Lord Altrincham's controversial public criticisms some five years earlier. 'The text is however all important, and needs to be less stilted and more human if the Queen is to continue to command full attention as the years roll by.' When No. 10 raised this concern with the Palace, Sir Michael Adeane, the Queen's private secretary, had no doubts about the essential problem: 'Television [on which the Queen had been making her Christmas speech since 1957] has ruined the whole thing. The Queen is gay and relaxed beforehand, but in front of the cameras she freezes and there is nothing to be done about it.' On the day itself, she had been preceded on the BBC, by somewhat painful contrast, by *Max Bygraves invites you to Meet the Kids in hospital*, producing an RI of 83 and viewer comments like 'Lovely to see their little faces light up' and 'No gimmicks or "side" – just a big-hearted fellow who loves kids and people'.

For two poets it was a Christmas day of different types of misery. Plath and her children were given Christmas dinner and presents by kind friends in Camden Town, but beneath the surface cheerfulness she burst out despairingly at one point, 'Oh, my poor babies'; Larkin, at his mother's house in Loughborough with his sister and her family, found himself on heavy washing-up duties, being given the leftovers from tea for his supper, and having to play 'childish games' with his 15-year-old niece – 'honestly,' he reported to Monica Jones, 'I don't think I did anything I wanted ALL DAY except go to the lavatory'. Still, a less shattering experience than late that night befell the teenage Ian Addis, not so far away in Kettering. 'I stepped into the street outside our front door clutching my newly acquired Johnny Mathis LP, ironically entitled *Warm*, and promptly skidded on the frozen pavement,' he recalled. 'The record slipped from its sleeve and fell crashing to the ground, littering the gleaming slabs with pieces of black vinyl.'[16]

Boxing Day was the coldest for eighteen years, with snow falling almost everywhere and Marian Raynham in Surbiton wondering 'how the birds stand it'. Among other diarists and memoirists, Judy Haines, driven 'very cautiously' by husband John 'on treacherous roads', went to 'a wonderful performance' of *The Nutcracker* at the Royal Festival Hall, 'a magnificent place'; 14-year-old Roger Darlington in Manchester 'stayed at home and painted some further parts of my Fortress kit [having been given a Flying Fortress model kit] including the wings and fuselage'; 18-year-old Anton Rippon in Derby went at lunchtime with his girlfriend's father and uncle for the ritual five pints of Bass at a pub called the Douglas Bar, but known to everyone as 'Harry Leonard's' because of a pre-1914 Derby County footballer who had once run it; and 7-year-old Graham Brack in south-east London, all ready with scarf, gloves, balaclava and ballpoint pen, was bitterly disappointed to be told by his father that the snow meant there would be no Charlton Athletic match at The Valley that afternoon. One fixture that did go ahead was at Roker Park, where 42,000 saw Sunderland lose to Bury and the home side's prolific centre forward, Brian Clough, fatefully slip on the bone-hard pitch, leading to a collision with the goalkeeper and not only a broken leg but snapped cruciate ligaments – a career-ending injury. And Larkin? Partly no doubt to get away from the '*medieval*' cold in his mother's house ('the fire is all very well, but there needs solid accompaniment of two-bar heaters – and there's only one, awwrrghgh! only one'), he went for a walk in the snow. 'A young chap tried to give me a lift, but I declined, on the grounds that I was walking for exercise, at wch he broke into great guffaws of laughter: "Lovely! Jolly good!", slamming into gear, quite pleasantly though.'[17]

3

I Didn't Like to Ask

December 1962: exactly halfway between Clement Attlee's election victory in July 1945 and Margaret Thatcher's election victory in May 1979, bringing to power significantly different values and priorities. At the heart of the '1945' settlement had been the birth of the modern welfare state: in the round, a huge boon, the mark of a civilised society – but not necessarily beyond critical evaluation. By the early 1960s, a decade and a half old, what sort of shape was it in? How well was it doing its job? And how satisfied were its users?

Not everyone instinctively loved it. Conservative politicians, reflected Anthony Crosland broad-mindedly in 1962, were 'not necessarily less humanitarian' than Labour politicians like himself; but, rather, they happened to hold different views 'as to the proper role of the state, the desirable level of taxation, and the importance of private as opposed to collective responsibility'. The prevailing result, between roughly the mid-1940s and the mid-1970s, was what one historian of the welfare state, Rodney Lowe, would characterise as 'reluctant collectivism', involving on the part of mainstream Conservative politicians a degree of genuine acceptance of the limits of the free market, but also an undeniable degree of political realism. A key as well as intriguing figure by the early 1960s was Enoch Powell. Back in 1953 he had declared that 'the machinery of the welfare state was not helping the weak by its repression of the opportunities and independence of the strong'; five years later, he had been one of the Treasury ministers to resign in protest at what they saw as excessive government spending on social services; but now, as health minister, he was more circumspect, reminding his fellow Conservatives in an October

1961 lecture of the continuing truth that 'in politics it is more blessed not to take than to give'.

Instead, after a decade of Conservative rule in which the top rate of personal tax had never been below 88 per cent, it fell to the free-market Institute of Economic Affairs (IEA) to try to rein in the scope of the welfare state. In the same month as Powell's lecture, *Health through Choice* was the title of an IEA pamphlet, with the economist Dennis Lees urging government to 'move away from taxation and free services to private insurance and fees'; while in his preface, one of the IEA's co-founders, Arthur Seldon, noted not unfairly that 'until recently, much of the academic discussion of the principles under-lying the National Health Service has been conducted by sociologists who are not only philosophically inclined towards collective pro-vision, but also show little interest in the economic implications'. Certainly no sociologist, but instead a would-be Conservative polit-ician, was the youngish lawyer Geoffrey Howe, who earlier in 1961 had published an essay stating unequivocally that 'equality should never feature as an object of our social policy', reproaching Powell for his apparent acceptance of universal provision, and giving a low mark, too, to Keith Joseph ('plainly expects the State to go on making the basic provision for all of us for ever'). Instead, through a mixture of means testing, expanded private insurance and the use of education vouchers, he envisaged a much-reduced welfare state – one consistent with Seldon's view, cited approvingly, that the notion of permanently expanding social services was 'not ennobling but degrading'.[1] At this stage, Howe's was an obscure voice from the margins; but the lan-guage was pregnant as well as piquant.

The most respected, most morally upright voice of the welfare state, viewing the NHS in particular as (in John Vaizey's words) 'an attempt to put human needs before human greed', remained Richard Titmuss, professor of social administration at the London School of Economics (LSE) and by now in his mid-fifties. Yet far from Titmuss being an uncritical defender of the welfare state, no passage in a 1960 radio talk was more striking than this quasi-confessional *cri de coeur*:

Many of us must now admit that we put too much faith in the 1940s in the concept of universality as applied to social security. Mistakenly, it was linked with economic egalitarianism. Those who have benefited most are those who have needed it least. We are only just beginning to see that the problems of raising the level of living, the quality of education, housing, and medical care of the poorest third of the nation calls for an immense amount of social invent-iveness; the new institutional devices, new forms of co-operation, social control, ownership, and administration, and new ways of relating the citizen and consumer to services that intimately con-cern him. Social ideas may well be as important in Britain in the next half-century as technological innovation.

Nor was Titmuss any more cheerful two years later. 'It becomes clearer as we learn to distinguish between the promise of social legislation and its performance that the present generation has been mesmerised by the language of "The Welfare State,"' he reflected in *Income Distribution and Social Change*. 'It was assumed too readily after 1948 that all the answers had been found to the problems of health, education, social welfare and housing …'

Was part of the problem the very term itself? That had been Michael Young's belief as early as 1952, and by the end of the decade the campaigning, egalitarian-minded sociologist Peter Townsend tended to agree. 'Crushingly cold and complacent' was his verdict on the two fateful words: not only did they unhelpfully imply, he argued, 'a country which is soft and makes people soft'; but it was also pro-foundly unhelpful that 'in a country which is called a Welfare State there can be, in some strange way, no just causes left'.[2] No just causes left? That was debatable; while, in any case, he and Titmuss would surely have been in agreement that there existed no *juster* cause than effectively and humanely fighting Beveridge's famous five giant evils of want, disease, ignorance, squalor and idleness.

*

On the whole, and excepting certain pockets of the country, 'idleness' was regarded in the early 1960s as no longer one of those giants needing to be slain. If not quite a full-employment economy, it nearly was, with (apart from the odd blip) the unemployment rate at, or a little above, 2 per cent. What about 'want'? Anthony Crosland in his hugely influential *The Future of Socialism* (1956) had essentially

assumed that large-scale poverty had become a thing of the irredeemable past, while three years later Macmillan had won an election landslide on the back of 'never had it so good'. Yet in truth it was a myth,
an all-too-convenient myth, that poverty had been abolished; and at
the LSE in the early 1960s, a group of four strongly motivated people –
Titmuss, Townsend, Brian Abel-Smith and Tony Lynes – was already
starting to do the spadework that would eventually, by the middle of
the decade, result in the full-scale 'rediscovery of poverty'. Of course,
they were not alone. But without their dogged, unfashionable work,
sometimes referred to patronisingly in Whitehall as the work of 'the
skiffle group', that shape-shifting rediscovery might well have taken
quite a lot longer to happen.[3]

The year of uncomfortable truths starting to emerge about poverty's
disobliging non-disappearance was 1962. That spring, shortly after
the Cambridge economist-cum-sociologist Dorothy Wedderburn had
read a paper to the British Sociological Association (BSA) detailing
how there were many people in poverty not receiving National
Assistance, a widely read piece by Townsend in the New Statesman
not only claimed that at least seven million were living at below or
barely above subsistence rates, but argued that subsistence itself was
'an inadequate and misleading criterion of poverty' which needed to
be replaced 'by one of relative deprivation'. That autumn, even as
Titmuss launched his Income Distribution and Social Change with a
series of powerful New Statesman articles about continuing serious
inequality and the many ingenious means by which the rich preserved
their wealth, Townsend enlarged his thoughts on the meaning of
poverty:

Poverty is a dynamic, not a static, concept. Man is not a Robinson
Crusoe living on a desert island. He is a social animal entangled
in a web of relationships – at work and in family and community
– which exert complex and changing pressures to which he must
respond, as much in his consumption of goods and services as in
any other aspect of his behaviour. And there is no list of the absolute necessities of life to maintain even physical efficiency or health
which applies at any time and in any society, without reference to
the structure, organization, physical environment and available
resources of that society.

'Poverty,' in short, 'is not an absolute state. It is relative deprivation. Society itself is continuously changing and thrusting new obligations on its members. They, in turn, develop new needs. They are rich or poor according to their share of the resources that are available to all. This is true as much of nutritional as monetary or even educational resources.'

Wedderburn's particular focus, going back to a major survey she had conducted in 1959, was the elderly. Some 40 per cent of people over retirement age, she calculated on the basis of that survey, 'had resources up to or but little above National Assistance levels'; and she cited what struck her as a couple of not unrepresentative cases of poverty in old age:

This is a 74-year-old spinster. She worked until 65 as a companion and now lives in two furnished rooms for which she pays 18s 6d rent a week. This includes her light. She has a Retirement Pension of £2 10s and manages for the rest from her savings. These are under the mattress (as she showed me!) and amounted to £120. I asked her what she would do when that was gone and she said she would worry about that when it happened – perhaps the Lord would take her first.

I suggested to this couple that they should apply for National Assistance, but they wouldn't hear of it. He is 74 and worked past retiring age. So he has a pension of £4 10s a week, no other income and no assets. The rent in this tenement is 15s a week, but it must be a struggle for them to manage.

Later in 1962 itself, not long after Wedderburn had estimated in her paper to the BSA that some two and a half million old people were living on or around the poverty line, she and Townsend were the two principals in a new ambitious survey, involving a sample of well over four thousand people, of the aged in the welfare state. 'From our figures, on the most conservative basis,' noted Wedderburn in her part of their subsequent joint report, 'it still appears that in 1962, 1¾ million men and women aged 65 or over had total incomes of less than £4 a week, and 400,000 couples had total incomes of less than £6 a week.' Accordingly, 'whatever standards we care to take in making a comparison between the income of the elderly and the population generally, whether it be personal disposable per capita income, average earnings, or some other measure, we are left with this result: *the aged have income levels a half or more below the levels of the population generally.*' Also unmistakeable was the gender aspect, with Wedderburn again finding, as she had in her earlier survey, that in every respect – whether income-related (including pension payments) or assets-related – older women on their own tended to be financially worse off than either couples or single (including widowed) men. 'The differences are not due to sex as such,' she concluded, 'but to differences in employment experience, past and present ... For women, the crucial factors are the absence of employment experience, or employment experience at levels of income which rarely rise above half of their male counterparts.'[4]

What about the human aspect of the welfare state's commitment to combat want? In theory it was all a seamless, joined-up process – including on the one hand the provision of universal unemployment and sickness benefits (admittedly often inadequate) through the national insurance scheme; on the other, the provision to the out-and-out needy of additional, selective benefits (admittedly often frugal) through national assistance (which some 1.5 million people were receiving) – but *Casualties of the Welfare State* told a different story. This was Audrey Harvey's harrowing 1960 account, based on her experiences as a social worker in London's East End, of how the network of welfare agencies and social service departments was so administratively complex, and so bureaucratically organised, that one working-class family, facing sickness and unemployment, slipped helplessly into misery and despair. In his measured but sympathetic 1964 overview of the welfare state, David Marsh (professor of social science at Nottingham University) described the too often coldly impersonal approach of those administering national insurance, citing in some detail the case of a wife of a suddenly seriously injured husband applying for sickness benefit under the national insurance scheme. Not only was there the daunting form-filling ('requiring efforts of memory, knowledge of her husband's affairs, and a capacity to answer formal questions which would be beyond the powers of most people even if no shock had occurred'), but then the seemingly endless period, while her husband was still in hospital, during which 'contact between the Ministry and the insured person's wife was maintained by letters, form-filling, and occasional phone calls made by the wife to clear up ambiguities'. By contrast, Marsh went on, 'the National Assistance Board [NAB], whose officers were concerned with the same case, adopted a totally different approach in that contact was maintained by personal visits to the home and occasional requests for information'. Why the difference? Partly, he accepted, because of the NAB's considerable discretionary powers, not available to officers of the Ministry of Pensions and National Insurance; but he also noted that there had been 'tangible evidence' of an attempt by the NAB 'to make its officers aware of the nature of human and social problems, and of the principles involved in establishing good relationships between people'.

Yet perhaps that was too generous a verdict, given the continuing existence of the great take-up problem – including as many as one in three of the elderly failing to apply for national assistance despite being entitled to it. 'Ignorance, pride, a decision to "manage while we can"' were reasons given by Wedderburn, while Alan Deacon and Jonathan Bradshaw in their history of means testing flesh out the larger social context of the wartime atmosphere and attitudes beginning to fade by the 1960s:

> It was one thing for a claimant to have to tell the Board that he or she needed extra money for clothes or bedding when friends and neighbours were in a similar position and when the cause of the need was so obviously beyond the control of any one person. It was quite another to have to show worn clothing to a visiting officer when everyone else had 'never had it so good'. Moreover, the Assistance Board had been distinct from and obviously superior to the poor law, and after 1948 there were many pensioners who felt that it was humiliating to have to go to the same office as people they regarded as down and outs. These problems were exacerbated by the fact that facilities at many of the Board's offices were grossly inferior to those in national insurance offices, by the use of separate payment books for insurance and assistance, and by a range of other procedures which highlighted the difference between the two benefits.

Nor, according to Virginia Noble's 2009 study of the NAB in action between the late 1940s and mid-1960s, was that all. Her charge sheet includes administrators devising 'various forms of persuasion, coercion, and intimidation to compel women to look to estranged husbands, cohabitees, or, in some cases, other family members, for support'; administrators devising comparable deterrent strategies for unemployed men, involving in their case 'complicated machinery to reinforce a norm of masculinity centred on male breadwinning and autonomy'; and a key role given to local advisory subcommittees, with their deliberate shaming tactics typified by one in Surrey in 1961 'pointing out' to a man with five children and a serious back injury (which had kept him largely out of work for the previous three years) 'his moral obligations to his family' and urging 'that he should set an example to his children so that they would look up to him instead of having a father who was always unemployed'. David Vincent, in his history of poverty, convincingly argues in relation to national assistance that even by the 1960s there remained 'an underlying continuity of approach' with the pre-welfare state era. 'Most supervisors had been trained before 1948, and the executive officers under their control displayed sharply contrasting attitudes towards the deserving and undeserving amongst their clients. As with pre-war relieving officers, they retained extensive latitude in determining eligibility to benefit. Judgements about why a claimant had left a job or a husband were made with little charity and less expectation that they would be successfully challenged.'[5] Or in short, and despite so much having changed, Victorian values had never quite gone away.

New Frontiers for Social Security, aiming modestly at 'the abolition of the poverty that exists in the midst of plenty', was the title of Labour's policy document launched in April 1963 by Richard Crossman and aiming to fill a vacuum in government thinking. 'We are determined,' he told a press conference, 'to get what Beveridge never got – subsistence for everybody.' It was a document with essentially two main aspects: for the medium to long term, an attempt to close the huge gap between the two classes of pensioners (i.e. those with an occupational pension and those entirely dependent on a state pension), through a superannuation scheme leading in effect to half-pay pensions, a very different approach to the Beveridge principle of flat-rate contributions and flat-rate benefits; while for the short term, 'a special rescue operation' was proposed in the form of 'a quite novel kind of Income Guarantee which fixes a minimum income level and ensures that the necessary supplementary benefit will be paid as of right, and without investigation by the National Assistance Board, to everyone whose total income falls below that level'. Of particular symbolic resonance was that the mechanism for identifying those in need of that financial rescue would be through the existing system for calculating income tax, a mechanism viewed as having less of a 1930s-style stigma about it than other forms of means testing. Crossman himself, writing his regular 'Left of Centre' *Guardian* column a few days after the launch, not only made clear his intellectual debt to 'Titmuss and his young men', but stressed the giant leap forward from the assumptions of the Beveridge Report:

> Of course it is true that in the siege economy of 1942, with its rationing and fair shares in austerity, it did not seem nearly as outrageous as it does today to insist that, though earnings and standards of living differ so widely, everyone should receive the same minimum level of subsistence benefit in sickness, unemployment, and old age. Flat-rate equality remains acceptable so long as it is assumed that most people in a democratic community must always remain poor. It was because the trade union leaders were looking backwards at the mass unemployment and the mass poverty of the 1930s, and simply could not conceive what it would feel like to live in an expanding economy, that they accepted Beveridge so uncritically as their prophet, and permitted him to write his flat-rate concepts into the constitution of our postwar Welfare State.
>
> It has taken 18 years to break through this thought-barrier to a new and more human vision of how a democratic State should look after its casualties ...

'We really can,' he concluded optimistically, 'restore human dignity to those on State benefit, and abolish poverty in this country.'[6]

*

'It was dislike at first sight,' remembered Roy Hattersley three decades later:

> In those days, I worked for the Sheffield Regional Hospital Board and I was in London with a party of champion blood donors who were to receive their 'gold awards' from the minister of health.

The minister [from July 1960 to October 1963] was Enoch Powell, and he treated my Good Samaritans with a condescension which I found intolerable. Inevitably, they were entertained with a selection of Roman opinions on blood and bleeding. The translation was, in one sense, essential, for there was not one classical scholar amongst them. But it would not have been necessary if Mr Powell had resisted the temptation to use the original Latin.

No such dislike from the three-months-old *New Society*, when in January 1963 it ran an admiring profile of the 'brisk, purposeful and tough-minded' minister. It was full of praise for the 'shock tactics' – involving a series of quick, short, sharp campaigns – that Powell had deployed to try to humanise the NHS, especially in relation to such aspects of hospital life as 'relaxation of visiting hours, patients' hours of waking, noise in wards, access to children, benches in outpatient departments'; and as for his ten-year Hospital Plan launched with a great flourish a year earlier, it did not question Powell's own verdict that the Plan 'has not been seriously challenged from any responsible quarter'. Author of the piece was John MacGregor, a future Conservative minister.

His praise for Powell's humanising efforts – typified by the insistence that it was time to end the practice, established solely for the convenience of staff not patients, of the 5 a.m. wake-up – was entirely justified; but inevitably, the larger historical verdict on this complicated man's stewardship of the NHS has been more mixed. A general acknowledgement of his ambition, as in an October 1961 speech when he asserted that he wanted to get 'clean away from the long era of "make do and mend" in the hospital service', co-exists with scepticism about the intellectual foundations of his approach, above all the Hospital Plan, promising that ninety new hospitals, averaging 600 beds or more, would be completed (or at least begun) over the next ten years in England and Wales. Tony Cutler argues that Powell, along with his ministry officials and the Treasury, failed 'to understand the dynamics of acute hospital costs'; Glen O'Hara describes it as 'a remarkable document' which 'unfortunately' was 'deeply flawed', quoting a frank internal ministry memorandum about the 'absence of yardsticks for measuring either what standard of service is reasonable or what quantity of resources can reasonably be employed to provide any particular standard'; and Charles Webster, the most authoritative historian of the NHS, notes that 'in practice, despite grandiose publicity, the Hospital Plan was not a properly conceived planning exercise, and it involved in the short term only the most limited increase in capital expenditure'.[7]

What else? Conservative health ministers from 1951 onwards had done little to encourage the development of health centres, instinctively viewing those New Jerusalem symbols as unhealthily socialist, and Powell was no exception; while in early 1962, when the Royal College of Physicians published its first detailed report on the deadly effects of smoking, he declined to press the Cabinet to impose curbs on tobacco advertising. There was also, according to Harold Evans, editor at the time of the *Northern Echo*, the question of cervical cancer. In June 1963 his paper ran a series of detailed exposures showing that many women's lives could be saved through a national programme of smear tests, a campaign prompting MPs to submit parliamentary questions to Powell. 'They ran,' recalled Evans, 'into a brick wall. "I am advised" Powell intoned, "it would be premature to aim at a general application." How many more women had to die, we asked in the paper, before the minister acted on the evidence, already years old? He acknowledged that there had been 2,504 deaths in 1961, but every time the MPs came back the answer was always some variation of No.' Eventually, late that year, the health minister relented, requesting regional hospital boards to expand cytology services. 'It didn't represent a miraculous conversion. Powell had been replaced by Anthony Barber.'

Over the years, Evans also had Powell in his sights for another reason: the thalidomide story, which in the early 1970s he and his colleagues on the *Sunday Times* revealed in all its shocking detail. Yet even in 1962, following a sharp increase in 1960/61 in the number of abnormal births, it was starting to become recognised as a major human tragedy. 'A great national disaster,' the Labour MP Maurice Edelman called it that July, 'greater in its ramifications than any single train accident in the history of this country.' Yet when the same month Powell met Tory MPs, he told them that he had 'resisted any sentimental treatment of the situation'; and six months later, it was a similar approach when he met a delegation of affected parents:

> We called [remembered Christine Clark, the note-taking member of the delegation] for the setting up of a drug-testing centre to try to ensure that the tragedy would not be repeated. The minister was quite sharp and said that anyone who took so much as an aspirin put himself at risk. We then suggested a publicity campaign to warn against thalidomide that might still be in medicine cabinets. The minister said that this would be quite expensive and foolish; he refused to accept that there were any more thalidomide tablets around, and said the scheme was a 'scare-monger stunt' aimed at drawing publicity for our own purposes. Since the minister had told us that he had never seen a thalidomide victim, we suggested he visit a centre or meet a child at home. He rejected the idea. We asked him to issue a press statement that he had seen us and saying that the ministry would help wherever possible. He refused; there was no reason for the press to be brought into the matter, he said. The thing which struck me was that the minister expressed not one word of compassion or understanding. He astounded us by his coldness.

Unfeeling, too, was Powell's refusal to establish a public inquiry into the causes of the disaster – an 'intransigence', in Evans's words, which 'left the families with only one remedy, to sue the manufacturers (Distillers) for negligence', in turn condemning them and their children (including those 550 British thalidomide babies who survived beyond their first few months of life) 'to live in Bleak House legal torment', lasting until an eventual settlement in 1973.

The wretched story also had a larger significance. 'We published [in 1963] some early pictures in the *Northern Echo* of thalidomide infants at Chailey Heritage in Sussex, a hospital, home and school for disabled children,' remembered Evans. 'I expected an outpouring of sympathy. I was wrong. Most of the readers who wrote did so to protest that it was not right for "a family newspaper" to do this: "We don't want to know."' Perhaps not; yet in the context by the early 1960s of antibiotics reducing deaths from illegal abortions to almost zero, and the efforts of the Abortion Law Reform Association to legalise abortion seemingly stalling, it was the deformities inflicted by the thalidomide drug that quite suddenly persuaded middle-of-the-road, respectable opinion to stop worrying about the moral and societal implication of easy abortion. 'I'm sorry, but the ethical position is quite clear,' Trog in a *Private Eye* cartoon in 1962 had a pompous, pinstriped doctor condescendingly telling a young woman in distress. 'Thalidomide was a legal prescription, but what you suggest is an illegal operation.' Soon afterwards, a *Daily Mail*/NOP opinion poll found 80 per cent support for liberalising the abortion law in order to prevent major deformities at birth. In short, ruefully reflects the pro-life Catholic writer Mary Kenny about the thalidomide scandal, 'it was the secular version of an answer to prayer'.[8]

More generally, away from such controversial matters, one of the NHS's defining characteristics was how hierarchical an organisation it was. 'I was a junior house officer at the London Chest Hospital when Elizabeth Taylor developed the severe pneumonia that very nearly killed her,' recalled Peter Sonksen about a 1961 episode. 'She survived because of the excellent care given to her and demonstrated her gratitude by giving her consultant chest physician a yacht and a caravan. He rewarded his deputy, who had in fact done most of the work, with a pair of yellow socks with a large "R" on them. I heard this from my Senior Registrar, the beneficiary of new socks. He wasn't bitter but laughed it off ...' Yet at the same time, from the obituaries of some of the leading NHS figures of the time, it is hard not to be struck by the underlying idealism: Sir George Godber, for instance, forceful but also humane deputy CMO (chief medical officer) from 1950 to 1960, then CMO until 1973; Desmond Julian, cardiologist who in 1961 wrote an article for the *Lancet* which led to hospitals creating coronary care units for the first time; Neville Butler, a paediatrician who was one of the pioneers in longitudinal studies about the consequences of early childhood experience; Katharina Dalton, who qualified as a doctor on the day in 1948 the NHS began and over the years put the treatment of premenstrual syndrome (a term she coined in 1953) on the medical map; Ambrose King, the venereologist who did much to change his discipline from a 'Cinderella' speciality into a high-quality service; and the Kentish Town general practitioner Hugh Faulkner, who in his own idiosyncratic way ('idealistic, sometimes maddening, but always inspiring') preached the importance of the social context of health and eventually battered down the resistance of the BMA as well as many politicians to the concept of health centres, and more generally to primary care as a team effort.[9]

One doctor keeping a sceptical eye on everything by the early 1960s was Hugh Selbourne, a senior consultant physician to a group of hospitals around Manchester. 'Parkinson's Law is in operation throughout the Health Service,' recorded his diary in July 1962 after an afternoon of 'heavy Medical out-patients, with increasingly exacting patients, tiresome to a degree'; later that month, 'anti-coagulant clinic, 10.30 a.m., muddle and confusion'; and soon afterwards: 'Taking things easy. There is no point in self-destruction for the Manchester Regional Hospital Board, which is indifferent to my effort.' Would he have described himself as a fortunate man? The phrase was the title of John Berger's mid-1960s study (accompanied by wonderfully evocative Jean Mohr photographs) of John Sassall, a GP practising in rural Gloucestershire. 'A Fortunate Man is a memorial not just to this exceptional individual but to a way of practising medicine that has almost disappeared,' reflected Gavin Francis introducing the book's reissue in 2016. 'Sassall's approach to his practice is all-consuming – in today's culture of working-time-directives and the commercialisation of disease it would be almost impossible to sustain. Sassall has made a Faustian pact: he is rewarded with endless opportunities for experiencing the possibilities inherent in human lives, but at the cost of being subject to immense, and at times unbearable, pressures.' While as for the service Sassall provided to his local community, this is Berger's own key – and timeless – sentence: 'He is acknowledged as a good doctor because he meets the deep but unformulated expectation of the sick for a sense of fraternity.'[10]

Easily the fullest survey we have of general practice by around this time, especially as looked at from the point of view of patients, is that conducted by Ann Cartwright during the summer of 1964. Newcastle upon Tyne North, Sheffield Hillsborough, Ashton-under-Lyne, Luton, Southampton Test, Bristol South-East, Wandsworth Streatham, Kingston upon Thames, Nantwich, Worcester, Conwy and Cambridgeshire – these were the twelve diverse parliamentary constituencies (all but one of them in England) where a total of 1,397 people, selected at random from the electoral register, were interviewed in their homes. In her ensuing book, *Patients and their Doctors* (those doctors still much likelier to be male than female), Cartwright's main conclusions included:

- About a fifth of GP consultations were in the patients' homes. Only 2 per cent of patients felt their doctor was 'not so good' about always visiting when asked.
- Two-thirds thought that if they met their doctor in the street, he would know them by name.
- Ninety-three per cent felt their doctor was good about listening to what they had to say, 88 per cent that he was good about taking his time and not hurrying them, 75 per cent that he was good about explaining things to them fully.
- Twenty-eight per cent thought that, if they were worried about a personal problem not strictly medical, they might discuss it with their doctor.

Or, put another way, 'few people are directly critical of their doctor, most have confidence in his decisions and care, and many have a friendly and satisfying relationship with him'. 'These,' she declared, 'are the not inconsiderable achievements of general practice at the moment.' As for flaws, Cartwright pointed to the prevailing 'uncertainty about the doctor's role', which 'bedevils the relationship between general practice and hospital, hinders effective collaboration with local authority services and adversely affects the relationship between doctors and patients'; noted 'the absence of quality controls, incentives and any career structure'; regretted the lack of capital investment since 1948, especially with its negative knock-on effect on tests and investigations; and argued, perhaps the most telling point, that 'behind the satisfaction of most patients there lies an uncritical acceptance and lack of discrimination which is conducive to stagnation and apathy'.

A particular strength of Cartwright's study was, as with other reports from the Institute of Community Studies (still going strong in Bethnal Green a decade after being founded by Michael Young and Peter Willmott), the way it provided a range of intimate and often vivid voices from her respondents:

I like the way he acts if you need him. If you sent for him in the middle of the night he'd be right there, even with the top of his pyjamas tucked in his trousers and his carpet slippers still on. He doesn't waste any time at all.

He doesn't just rush you out. He says, 'Come in and have a cigarette. What's the trouble? Let yourself go.'

Now I'm approaching middle-age I'd like to talk to him about contraception and limiting the family. I don't mind talking to him, it's just getting round to it.

I'd like to ask him about my legs. I have thrombosis. All Dr— said was lots of aspirin and lead lotion, but other people seem to go to hospital and have different injections and so on. But you can't very well argue with a doctor. Mind you, I haven't said it *to* him.

The surgery is just a jumble – it's damned untidy. Probably under some of the junk there's quite a bit of equipment. But he can always find the tackle he wants from somewhere. But there's no showcases with gleaming instruments in them. The waiting room's a shocker – a great gap under the door you could back a barge under. The last time I went, there was a *little* electric fire. I'm not sure it's such a good thing to have a comfortable waiting room. I like a doctor's surgery to be a place to get into and get out of. So many people would sit there and talk about their ailments if it was too comfortable.

I'll take his failings first. When you're ill he'll come to see you and do his best for you. He'll promise to call again – but God know when. He's very remiss in following visits up unless there's real urgency. If you're ill, you're lying in bed fidgeting for him to come. He says, 'I'll call tomorrow or the next day'. It'll probably be three or four days before he does. Whether it's deliberate policy to keep you in bed longer I don't know … The surgery never opens at the time it's supposed to. Say I go down for 9.30 a.m. there's a few in – it might be quarter to eleven when he opens shop. Now what I like about him. Say I'm feeling ill and he prescribes something for me, I can go the next week and say, 'Look, your treatment hasn't done me a damn bit of good'. He won't take offence, he'll try something else. You can talk to him … He doesn't seem to have any system at all of cards or records, but by God, he can always remember what has happened in the past. He has a very good knowledge of his patients. If I went down tomorrow, when he'd sorted me out, he'd remember what my wife went for last time – and 'how was she now?' He's generally like this. He's always been very good to me.

'Sometimes of course,' this seasoned patient did admit, 'you come out saying "He's out of fettle today. He's taking no notice of me."'[11]

On the whole during these post-war years, however, critical attention on the NHS focused far less on general practice, far more on the hospitals. 'Provincial hospitals have been getting better,' observed the historian E. P. Thompson in 1987 after a stay in hospital. 'Gone are the stale airs of discipline and Poor Law that still lurked in the old Halifax General thirty years ago – and the accompanying religiosity which could victimise those who replied on an admission card that their religion was "none".' 'Hospital doctors,' he added, 'are becoming more courteous. This was commented on by fellow patients of my own age: "It's not like the old days – they talk to you now as if you was an equal." "You know that consultant? He really listens to what you says." There were also, in one of my wards, more women doctors than men – a distinct humanisation and a lessening of the oppressive sense of male professional hierarchy of the old days.'

One way and another, hospitals certainly impinged upon the collective memory, to judge by this retrospective collage about (in roughly chronological order) the early to mid-1960s:

I came to consciousness on the Maternity Ward, where the Crosshouses day was beginning. The regime was rigid: it wasn't only that temperatures, blood pressure, bed pans and medication were done on the dot, there were endless other rules. Hair-washing was strictly forbidden, even if you were well enough to walk to the bathroom; bathing was rationed; and make-up was frowned upon. Anything that might make you feel less wrecked and dirty was disallowed on principle, because Baby came first and by Crosshouses logic washing your hair was vanity, therefore traitorous to Maternity, morally unhygienic and dangerous. As a result, everyone had stiff, sweaty hair sticking out in tufts, some of it grey, for one of the offences several of these mothers had committed against order and decency was to go on having babies into their forties. By contrast the nurses, Sisters and Matron were as good as vestals, unmarried or at least childless, their baby worship was pure. They served the cause of motherhood selflessly, unlike the feckless women in their charge, who'd probably been thinking of sex, or failed to plan, and who didn't deserve babies ...

When Matron made her rounds, I said I didn't want to breast-feed, but luckily she wasn't listening, she'd spotted down the ward an enormity, a women with red nails. Marching smartly to the bedside she picked up the woman's hand and flung it back at her with disgust: 'We don't feed our babies on nail varnish!' she announced, looking around her in triumph, and sailed through the swing doors. *(Lorna Sage, after giving birth at Crosshouses Hospital, 'an ex-workhouse in the middle of nowhere on the road between Shrewsbury and Bridgenorth, a Victorian pile inherited by the National Health Service')*

No one who has ever visited such a ward can ever forget it. It was a heart-breaking experience. Though clean, the ward was large, gloomy and depressing, dominated at one end by a huge television. All the old people sat around or were propped up in bed ... Without wishing to disparage the kindness of those involved, the staff saw their task literally as feeding and putting to bed old people who in a sense had started to become children again. *(David Blunkett, visiting his grandfather in the geriatric ward of City General Hospital, Sheffield)*

Everyone tried to be as kind as possible, of course, the doctor came to see me and told me the baby had died of asphyxia. But he didn't give me many details, I still don't know whether she ever breathed, or whether she was already dead ... I never saw my baby. It wasn't suggested that I should, and I'd never have thought to ask to – it just wasn't done. I don't know what happened to her body ... Everyone tried to be sympathetic, but what I remember most was that no one would talk to me about it, and I did need to talk. *(Doreen Vickers, after giving birth to a stillborn daughter in a Home Counties hospital)*

Walking into the cancer ward felt like walking into a hospital from the Victorian age. There were at least forty men in that ward, old men with white hair, men around my dad's age – he was fifty-three then – and younger men. There was even a 14-year-old boy dying of leukaemia. All the patients lay in beds facing each other across a large ward with a high ceiling. As each became more ill, they were moved close to the door to save the doctors and nurses having to walk far. In his previous stays in this hospital, Dad had watched the drama of other men's failing health played out in bed moves as they'd been edged closer to the door. Finally they would end up in the bed right beside the door, where before long the curtain would be swished around the bed, and in the quiet half-light of night Dad would see the man's body carried out of the ward, freeing up the bed for the next doomed occupant. Terrified, he'd asked my mother to ask the nurses not to move him into the bed next to the door. She did ask but when we next visited, two days after he'd been admitted, that's where Dad was lying, hallucinating, saying things we couldn't make sense of. *(Richard Hines, visiting his dying father in the Royal Infirmary, Sheffield)*

As my labour progressed and the pain became excruciating no matter how furiously I drummed my fingers [as instructed at NCT classes], I screamed and swore and was petrified that such unexpected pain meant that something had gone terribly wrong. 'Do stop that noise Mrs Gardiner,' the male consultant said sharply. 'We've all had babies here.' *(Juliet Gardiner, giving birth in the Woolwich Memorial Hospital)*

In 1963 the 7-year-old John Lydon kept passing out, limp in his mother's arms, and was sent off to St Ann's Hospital in South Tottenham. There, after eventually being diagnosed with spinal meningitis, he spent a whole year. 'The hospital ward had about forty beds in it. Very old-fashioned. You see them in the old World War II movies. The metal-framed beds. It was kids of all ages. Nurses would bother you, and every six hours I had to have penicillin injections all over. They were particularly painful. Kids like me were scared of needles, and nurses did fuck all to alleviate that fear.'[12]

Children in hospitals were an understandably touchstone issue. As early as 1952, James and Joyce Robertson, closely associated with the child development specialist John Bowlby, had made the poignant film *A Two-Year-Old Goes to Hospital*, showing the effects on Laura (protest followed by despair followed by detachment) when separated from her mother for eight days while in hospital for a minor operation; and then in 1959 the Platt Report into

the welfare of children in hospital (coming out of an inquiry chaired
by Sir Harry Platt, chairman of the Royal College of Surgeons) had
strongly recommended frequent parental visits, especially important
in the early days of a child's stay. Yet as James Robertson showed in a
series of *Observer* articles in early 1961, action post-Platt was, albeit
with some exceptions, painfully slow. And, he noted, 'it is where
restrictions persist that parents complain of admission procedures
which intensify the child's distress; of children removed abruptly and
heard screaming in the distance while the mother is detained to fill in
forms; of uncalled-for interference with the children's comfort habits;
of the difficulty of getting information about the course of treatment,
and much else'. What should parents do? 'If the parents have conviction enough,' he asserted, 'they can simply ignore the out-dated
restrictions, go to their child's bedside and stay there'; though at the
same time he did accept that 'to break regulations might seem like
inciting a disturbance and not every parent could do it'.

Three years later, by 1964, the situation was (despite Enoch Powell's
laudable initiatives) not much better. Robertson reflected in *The Times*
that, because of 'the difficulty of changing long-established attitudes
and practices within the hospital professions', it might be necessary
'to wait for a change of generations before the [Platt] Report is fully
implemented'; the LSE's Annette Lawrence reckoned that in practice everything depended on the attitude of the sister in charge of a
ward; and a survey of twenty-one hospitals in the Birmingham area
revealed that only three had unrestricted visiting of children. Happily,
a heroine now began to emerge in the person of June Jolly, a recently
qualified graduate nurse who had also been influenced by Bowlby. She
was appalled to see the levels of distress of small children separated
during hospital stays from their parents, often only allowed to visit
once a week; and through the rest of the 1960s and into the 1970s she
would continue to push hard to speed up what sometimes felt like
glacial change. 'I still had to fight – theatres, anaesthetists, surgeons,
matrons,' she recalled. 'They didn't believe this mattered.'[13]

For those at life's other end, the dismal experience of David
Blunkett's grandfather seems to have been fairly typical. 'Dr [J. H.]
Sheldon minces no words in talking of primitive facilities, typical
Victorian workhouses, appalling fire risks, overcrowding, insani-
tary barrack-like buildings and degrading conditions for patients and

staff,' noted *The Economist* in 1961 about his report on medical services for old people in the Birmingham hospital region. Examples of his damning findings included:

It should be blown up and replaced. The odour of wet sheets in bags at the bottom of the backstairs permeates the whole building. Sadly lacking in most ordinary modern amenities, but ward sisters are dedicated and devoted. *(Selly Oak, K Block)*

Some of the old wards actually house sixty-four patients in four rows of beds. *(Summerfield)*

Overcrowded, toilets primitive, no sterilizing facilities. *(St Michael's)*

A typical Victorian workhouse. A misuse of words to call it a hospital. *(Shrub Hill)*

An institution which merely provides storage space for patients. *(The Beeches)*

Buildings inherited as slum property, and their only value would lie in preservation as a museum of social history. *(Burton Road)*

Later in 1961, the *Sunday Times* had this description of an unnamed north-country geriatric hospital:

The corridor's bare stone floor and unplastered brick walls stretch for 400 yards; they are dirty, dusty, and in winter very cold ...

The wards which now house 1,200 'chronic sick' old people lead off this corridor in three-storey blocks. There are no lifts. Every patient taken to a second- or third-storey ward – including those unconscious from the operating theatre – must be carried in a chair, up narrow stone stairs worn into crescents by a century of climbing feet.

The commode pans, and all bed-pans, are washed and left to soak in the patients' bath. They are then stacked beside the cleaner's bucket and pail, beneath a sink where crockery is washed. There is nowhere else to put them ...

In hospitals for all ages, an abiding, unresolved problem was food. In 1963 a random sample of 152 hospitals of all types found (as reported by *New Society*) that nearly half of prepared food sent to wards was left uneaten by patients; that standards of cleanliness and hygiene in food preparation and handling were poor; that 'a tendency to overcook vegetables and long delays in the service of meals caused nearly a complete loss of vitamin C in potatoes (cooked often for 1½ hours) and 75 per cent loss in green vegetables'; that 'there was a lack of variety and quality of food in large hospitals for acutely ill patients'; that 'the quality of meals in long-stay hospitals for the chronic sick was "extremely poor"'; and that in large hospitals, barely a third of patients described the standard of service as good. What about the experience of day visitors? 'Out-patient departments,' accurately noted Brian Inglis in 1964, 'have won, and earned, a reputation for being even drearier and more uncomfortable than station waiting-rooms; and waiting there usually is. Appointments systems, experience has shown, are quite easy to work; but few hospitals can be bothered with them.'[14]

Again (though in fact dating from earlier), it was Ann Cartwright who oversaw and then wrote up (*Human Relations and Hospital Care*) the fullest, most variegated survey: 739 interviews with people (almost two-thirds of them women) from different parts of England who had been hospital in-patients at some stage between October 1960 and March 1961. Seemingly, almost all had their distinctive experiences to relate, with here again just a flavour:

Well, there was one night – I suppose it comes to everybody. About the second night I became homesick and I began to snivel and cry to myself like. I thought nobody would hear, but a nurse came up and said, 'What's the matter dear?' I said, 'I can't help it, but I'm homesick', and she bent down and put her arms right round me and gave me quite a hug and said, 'Don't worry, everyone gets like that. We all feel like that. Now go to sleep and you'll feel better in the morning.' And I did. Now, wasn't that kind?

There was one man there who'd had a leg amputated because of gangrene and he used to call for a bed-pan and several times they didn't come. Sister said he could hold himself. Then he did it in the bed, 'It's not my fault, it's not my fault'. I think it used to worry him. One occasion I got out of bed and told a nurse and she said she'd only got one pair of hands, but she was only washing bottles at the time. The nurses didn't put themselves out.

If the nurses were sharp with any of the young mothers – well, I think they deserved it. You don't go in to be pampered, but to have your baby and get well again.

They were dressing the beds up every half-hour. They push you in like sausagemeat and bind you down so that when matron comes everything is beautiful. They're at the beds every flipping minute.

She [the ward sister] looked after you well, but she wasn't liked by the nurses. She was too dogmatic. She did show several of them up, which I felt quite unnecessary. It made us all feel uncomfortable.

There was one woman who'd had her breast removed and you could see all this terrible stuff draining into her bottle under her bed. I'll never drink Oxo again.

I learned indirectly the names of the tablets I was having. I gathered it was an understood thing that you didn't ask the doctor – they would take it amiss if you did. I wouldn't have had the audacity to ask sister in case of a snub. She might say, 'It's none of your business to know what you're having.' I don't know how sister and staff nurse would react if you asked them directly. It's a point I'm not sure about – whether you had a right to know.

I didn't like to ask. You can't get through to them [the doctors], you know – they seem a bit above you.

None of the doctors explained things – not like Emergency Ward 10.

I had a shock when they suddenly came to take me to the theatre. I'd already had three operations. The shock was so great I fainted. The sister was very nice about it. In fact, everyone was very apologetic, because they all thought the other one had told me.

Cartwright's accompanying data included some key findings: two-fifths of the sample entirely enthusiastic about their hospital stay;

two-fifths mainly but not wholly positive; and one-fifth mainly critical; a direct correlation between how early they were woken each
day and how critical they were of the nurses; women, especially those
who had been in maternity wards, likelier to complain about lack of
privacy, but overall only a smallish minority (13 per cent) doing so;
three-fifths of interviewees reporting some degree of difficulty in
getting information; and one-fifth saying that, in this respect, they
had not found any of the doctors helpful.

'The Best Hospital Service We Have' was the deliberately ambiguous
title of Cartwright's short but powerful concluding chapter. There,
she touched upon not only 'the poor and outmoded conditions in
many hospitals today', but also 'attitudes of condescension' on the
part of 'consultants who regard the time they keep patients waiting as
of little or no importance' and of matrons 'whose heralded entrance
to the ward must not be sullied by the sight of untidy beds or patients
eating'. Of course, she did not deny that these and other criticisms,
including the frequent lack of joined-up care (between hospital and
GPs, between hospital and welfare services), 'need to be seen against
a background of general satisfaction'. Yet the fact remained, to her
evident frustration, that 'some patients seem to accept low standards
without criticism':

> Their tolerance arises partly from a sense of gratitude and appreci-
> ation. The hospital service is surrounded by a halo, which has been
> acquired through the care given by individual members of the hos-
> pital staff. It is ironic that the professional integrity of doctors and
> nurses who work under difficulties encourages complacency about
> the hospital service among both patients and public, and discourages
> demands for improvements and greater expenditure on the hospital
> service. In a National Health Service, public opinion could and
> should be a potent weapon for incentive and improvement.

In short, as Cartwright ended her study with a sentiment that Michael
Young for one would have wholly endorsed, 'the public needs to rec-
ognize that the interests of both patients and staff can be served by
informed criticism and demands for improvements'.[15]

How well in general was the NHS doing by its adolescent years?
Specifically, how well was it doing in its implicit pledge to provide

effective and universal healthcare across the social classes? 'We have learned from fifteen years' experience of the Health Service that the higher income groups know how to make better use of the Service,' was Richard Titmuss's sceptical verdict at the time. 'They tend to receive more specialist attention; occupy more of the beds in the better equipped and staffed hospitals; receive more elective surgery; have better maternity care...' Then in 1980, the definitive report by Sir Douglas Black on health inequalities found that whereas death rates among middle-class professionals had declined by some 20 per cent between 1950 and 1970, those of manual workers had in the same period stayed roughly the same. A complex question, inevitably, involving lifestyle habits and choices among much else – but the fact is that Charles Webster has shown in some detail how, in the distribution of resources, the NHS during its early decades 'tended to mirror and perpetuate the accumulated idiosyncrasies and inequalities in health-care provision contained in the inherited system, which in the main reflected deep-seated patterns in the distribution of wealth, which had determined that those sections of community experiencing the greatest problems of ill health were provided with the worst health services'. It was not until 1964 that a detailed internal mechanism for more equitable resource provision (including dentists as well as GPs and hospitals) began to be developed; and accordingly, 'although the NHS had laudable consequences from the perspective of the poor, the historic north-south divide in social welfare and health care remained very much in evidence'.

Class inequalities in healthcare played out within as well across regions: for instance, a study of adults who died in Bristol between October 1962 and September 1963 found that whereas 24 per cent in social classes I and II (i.e. professional and intermediate, as in the registrar-general's five-part definition of social class) had not been referred to hospital for either investigation or treatment, this rose to 36 per cent in the case of class V (unskilled manual workers). How much did it matter that whereas by around this time some 80 per cent of doctors came from social classes I and II, about 80 per cent of their patients came from social classes III (skilled manual workers), IV (partly skilled manual workers) and V? 'There is often a clash of norms when two cultures interact,' reflected the sociologist Josephine Klein in her 1965 *Samples from English Cultures*, 'and this clash is likely to be accompanied by ill-feeling, particularly when one culture imposes norms of behaviour on the other in the self-confident assurance that where the two differ, the other is wrong.' It is impossible to quantify the consequences of this clash in terms of outcomes; but at the very least, it hardly helped.

A final snapshot of the mainstream 'physical' NHS concerns a different sort of inequality. Nancy Robertson, like her husband a wheelchair-user (in her case having had polio as a teenager), recalled her experience at a London hospital in 1962:

We were delighted when we found out I was pregnant, but no one I encountered during my visits to the antenatal clinic seemed remotely joyful or enthusiastic about what we were doing. My consultant was extremely dismissive – I was obviously concerned about how the birth would be and so on, but she just wouldn't discuss it at all. I told her I'd had a spinal fusion because of my polio, which meant my spinal cord had been fused together, but she said that wouldn't affect my ability to give birth at all.

I was already in hospital when my waters broke, and I was sent straight to the delivery ward as the consultant had said I could expect a very quick labour. But two days later nothing had happened, and I was in a lot of pain. Eventually a registrar came in and examined me, and asked what the scar was on my back. When I said it was a spinal fusion he was shocked: 'You'll never have your baby naturally in a month of Sundays if you've had a spinal fusion,' he said. 'Why didn't you tell us before?'

Jeremy was born by caesarean later that day – they didn't even bother to tell Andrew, my husband, what was happening. I was taken back to a room on my own and left there – no one suggested taking me to see the baby, who was in an incubator because he'd become distressed during the long labour. It wasn't until three days later that I got to see Jeremy – the consultant asked me why I wasn't eating, and I said I was too worried about my baby to eat. So eventually they brought him in to me. No one seemed to have thought that I might have been worried about him, which of course I was, desperately. I thought there must be something wrong with him and that was why they were keeping him away from me. In fact, he was perfect.

Looking back, what I remember most about my pregnancy and Jeremy's birth was the complete lack of support and friendliness.

Even after he was born, I don't remember anyone saying isn't this great, you've got a lovely baby. They just said things like 'but however will you cope?' Even after 33 years, it can still make me angry to think about it. But the wonderful joy of having a child of our own, of course, transcended all the hurt and anger.[16]

*

'A place of calm and lightness, set in beautiful gardens maintained by the patients,' remembers Ken Worpole about visiting his father, a patient in the 1950s in Runwell Hospital, a large mental asylum near Wickford in Essex. 'I subsequently found out that it was designed on a parkland-villa system of low-rise buildings, with patients organized into smaller residential groups, and was run with great dedication by medical staff who supported the ideals of the therapeutic community movement.' But Runwell, built in the 1930s, was almost certainly a post-war exception in evoking warm memories: most asylums were still housed in grim Victorian buildings, and over the years they would become a byword for human misery.

Take just a few examples. Elsewhere in Essex, at Severalls near Colchester ('a big red-brick building like a barracks, where men and women were segregated in separate wings, sometimes for decades, wearing hospital-issue clothes and having no say on what happened to them'), Diana Gittins's oral history has revealed a raft of horror stories, including fatal lobotomies on women and doctors experimenting on patients with new drugs before they knew what the doses should be; when in 1952 the Labour politician Alice Bacon visited Menston Mental Hospital (High Royds Hospital from 1963) near her Leeds constituency, she found 'over 500 patients in the hospital over sixty-five years of age, many of them bedridden and not requiring any mental attention at all'; incarcerated at Menston between 1953 and 1961, after a schizophrenia diagnosis, was a recent young Nigerian immigrant, David Oluwale, whose treatment of electro-convulsive therapy (ECT) and Largactil left him slow and twitchy, walking with a shuffle rather than a swing; a fellow patient at Menston recalled being sedated for ECT as 'like going to the gas chamber, you walked in and saw this horrendous cap that they put on your head and this bed that they asked you to lie on and the injection, to this day I can taste and smell it, and that was to me horrific'; Diana Melly's memory of having ECT at Banstead Hospital in 1958 was that 'not only was the treatment painful, but you came round with a splitting headache and no short-term memory'; and that same year, the troubled New Zealand writer Janet Frame took a look at Friern Mental Hospital (originally called Colney Hatch Lunatic Asylum) – 'tall, of grey stone, menacing, like an old workhouse or prison' – before, with a sense of 'rising panic', she turned back.

In 1958/9, the huge asylum at 'Northtown', in reality either Rainhill Mental Hospital near St Helen's or Prestwich Mental Hospital in Greater Manchester, was the subject of a detailed case study by Kathleen Jones and Roy Sidebotham (both based at Manchester University). At the hospital's heart, with 'the "asylum" atmosphere of locked doors, long stone corridors, and large bare wards containing a hundred or more patients, most of them actively demanding', was The Annexe:

> This block, which is devoted exclusively to the care of long-stay patients, is the biggest in the hospital. It houses 1,700 patients, male and female, in wards which stem off from a rigidly straight main corridor. A visitor may stand at one end, and look down successive receding arches to the door at the far end, exactly a quarter of a mile away. Every bed is occupied, and there are very few discharges except by death, so that the population is very nearly static.

Other observations included that 'it is quicker to give a patient ECT than to make an attempt at understanding his personal problems – one takes only a few minutes, while the other would take several hours of personal interviewing a week'; and that the patients' committee was stopped after it had 'developed a group entity of its own which became set in opposition against the staff – as one doctor said, "It was at us the whole time, agitating."' Jones and Sidebotham concluded (in their 1962 book, *Mental Hospitals at Work*) soberly enough:

> The medical staff is small and, with notable exceptions, not highly trained; at the same time, the laboratory and technical services are very good. These factors taken in conjunction make it inevitable that the orientation of the hospital should be an organic one, physical methods of treatment being used in almost all cases.

Facilities and amenities which depend for their success on capital equipment operate at a high level of efficiency. What Northtown cannot do is to personalize those services for the individual patient.

They also sent students to observe the hospital at work. After acknowledging how hard-pressed the staff were ('all the time there was the sense of pressure to get things done, the bed to be made, meals to be served, always something'), one reflected: 'What I felt to be lacking was a fundamental attitude of respect towards patients, the idea that they are adult human beings.'[17]

In fact, by the early 1960s a fundamental shift in the provision of mental healthcare was in progress: away from the increasingly dreaded large institutions, and towards the greater development of mental health services in the community. The Mental Health Act of 1959 had already pointed in this direction – including setting out the powers of local authorities to provide such things as residential hostels and centres for training and occupation – before in March 1961, in a speech given at Church Hall, Westminster, to the National Association of Mental Health, the health minister sought to call time on a whole era. 'There they stand,' declared Powell, 'isolated, majestic, imperious, brooded over by the gigantic water-tower and chimney combined, rising unmistakeable and daunting out of the countryside – the asylums which our forefathers built with such immense solidity.' Speaking of setting 'the torch to the funeral pyre' of these too often inhumane places, he added that 'if we err, it is our duty to err on the side of ruthlessness'. The impact was understandably instant and profound. 'We all sat up, looked at each other and wondered what had happened,' recalled one member of the audience. 'Because we'd been struggling for years to get the idea of community care and the eventual closure of mental hospitals on the map, and here it was offered to us on a plate.'

What lay behind the new policy? Explanations have tended to centre on two elements: the emergence in the mid-1950s of new psychotropic, mood-altering drug treatments (especially chlorpromazine, marketed as Largactil) which made it more possible to reduce in-patient numbers; and public opinion becoming somewhat more sympathetic to the mentally ill, especially after BBC TV's 1957 series *The Hurt Mind*. However, the detailed analysis of the historian Simon

Goodwin suggests that the crux was instead the increasingly manifest unsuitability of the large mental hospitals themselves, overcrowded and in a serious state of disrepair. Even so, for one sceptical contemporary observer, Kathleen Jones, the explanation was simple enough. The widespread desire to get rid of mental hospitals, she argued in her 1962 book with Sidebotham, was based partly on 'the fear motive buried deep in the national subconscious', and partly on 'the financial motive' – with both of those motives 'generally unacknowledged'. And indeed, within a few months of Powell's dramatic announcement, this very determined woman, daughter of a lorry driver and a dinner lady and brought up on a large London council estate, was campaigning vigorously not only that the closure of large psychiatric institutions (which with 'all but the grimmest Victorian shells can be made habitable with some money and a great deal of imagination') was in effect an asset-stripping exercise, but that to return mental-health patients to local authorities in large numbers, with inadequate funding, no research base and no staff retraining, was potentially disastrous – a campaign which apparently led to Powell sending her handwritten letters expressing his annoyance.[18]

'What some hope will one day exist is suddenly thought by many to exist already,' an equally sceptical Richard Titmuss told the conference at Church House the day after Powell's 'water-tower' speech:

> All kinds of wild and unlovely weeds are changed, by statutory magic and comforting appellation, into the most attractive flowers that bloom not just in the Spring, but all the year round ... And what of the everlasting cottage-garden trailer, 'community care'? Does it now conjure up a sense of warmth and human kindness, essentially personal and comforting, as loving as the wild flowers so enchantingly described by Lawrence in *Lady Chatterley's Lover*?

Almost everything, he insisted, depended on adequate resources; but as even the instinctively loyal *Sunday Telegraph* pointed out later in 1961, the problem was that the minister was 'assuming' in his pronouncement 'a massive framework of psychiatric service and community aid organized by local authorities and financed by ratepayers', which unfortunately 'does not exist'. Neither Powell nor his prime minister was deterred: a commitment to community care was formally embedded in the January 1962 Hospital Plan, while two months later Macmillan insisted that 'it is now recognised that care within the community is often the most effective, especially, of course, for the mentally ill'. Financial muscle, though, remained notable by its absence. 'The general impression is of extreme unevenness,' concluded Edinburgh University's F. M. Martin in his 1964 overview of community mental care, noting the many parts of the country with not just a shortage of qualified staff (especially psychiatric social workers), but also a lack of 'sheltered employment, short-stay hostels, social clubs, supervised lodgings'; while the same year, it was estimated that some 25,000 elderly people in mental hospitals (almost a fifth of the resident population there) could be released – being 'no more than eccentric, confused, forgetful, or just plain deaf' – if the envisaged special residential community homes were actually in place.[19]

As for the mental hospitals themselves, their number of patients was slowly declining, yet it would be many years before any asylums were finally closed. And as in the 1950s, so in the mid-1960s was the odd feel-good story – such as the calmly enlightened, not overly medicated treatment at Banstead Hospital of the adolescent Philip Adams when sectioned with a diagnosis of schizophrenia after assaulting a police officer – heavily outweighed by the continuing negatives. Three-fifths of wards providing 'dismal surroundings' for the patient, little indication of 'quickly integrating the hospital population with the outside community', staff (in short supply anyway) who were 'badly paid, have too little training and are mixed in quality' – such was Peter Townsend's charge sheet in 1964 following an LSE survey of twenty-six randomly selected mental hospitals, before he went on:

> Perhaps the most crushing indictment of mental hospitals is their disrespect for individual identity. Personal possessions are often non-existent. Dormitories allow little comfort or privacy. There is little variety in meals or the manner of their serving. Ill-fitting and cheaply made hospital clothes hang from human frames which are further derided by clumsy uniform haircuts. Small wonder that internecine warfare rages over apparently trivial issues like the ownership of carrier bags or the right to sit on a particular chair – which are all that are left to the patients.

Worst of all was 'the smell of neglect'; and Townsend memorably described that odour as 'the sweet but slightly rotting smell of an assortment of bewildered human beings who exist in claustrophobic proximity like wrinkling apples spaced fractionally apart in a dark cupboard'.[20]

One psychiatrist, far more than any other, entered the general conversation in the 1960s with his distinctive take on the subject of mental illness. *Sanity, Madness and the Family* was the title of R. D. Laing's 1964 study which (co-authored with his fellow Scot, Aaron Esterson) was based on a series of taped interviews with eleven patients, all of them young women, who had been authoritatively diagnosed as schizophrenic. Crucially, and in all possible combinations, these interviews also included parents and relatives of those patients. 'Vivid, direct, gripping' would many years later be Hilary Mantel's description of the book, recalling how the experience of reading it at a single sitting one afternoon in 1973 made her realise that she had already seen enough of the world (including, as a law student on a placement with the probation service, the world of Manchester high-rise estates) to become a writer herself. Mantel felt at the time, and continued to feel in 2008, sympathetic to Laing's repudiation of mental distress as an essentially biological phenomenon:

He didn't, as some claimed, accuse parents of making their children schizophrenic; he interrogated the whole idea of schizophrenia as a clinical entity. He was exceptionally alive to language and gestures, to the layers of meaning in every utterance; alive, also, to power play, to conscious and unconscious manipulation. He had seen the pain, terror and desolation of madness. He did not glamorise it or claim it didn't exist. He and his co-workers [including others at the Tavistock as well as Esterson] suggested that the way some families worked could generate psychotic behaviour in one member, who was selected, more or less unconsciously, to bear the brunt of family dysfunction …

  In Laing's families there is always a version behind the version. There are truths one member is allowed to air, that another member is forbidden to utter. The weakest finds him or herself in a lose-lose situation, unable to please, locked in a circuit of invalidation. Madness may, in some circumstances, seem a strategy for survival …

In the course of the recorded conversations, their families trip and contradict them [the patients]. The interviewer records their signals – winks, smirks, nods – and how, when the 'mad' member protests, they say: 'What, me? I didn't do anything.' Barefaced lies are countenanced, as being for the patient's own good. Left is right, up is down, and, often enough, your mother's your sister, and your father's not your father ...

'*We believe*,' Laing and Esterson wrote in italics as the final sentence of their introduction, '*that the shift of point of view that these descriptions both embody and demand has a historical significance no less radical than the shift from a demonological to a clinical viewpoint three hundred years ago.*' And later in 1964, giving a paper on 'What is Schizophrenia?' at the first International Congress of Social Psychiatry, Laing made an equally bold and compelling claim, one that chimed with an emerging counter-culture instinctively resistant to Whiggish claims and assumptions of ameliorating progress:

> Perhaps we will learn to accord to so-called schizophrenics who have come back to us, perhaps after years, no less respect than the often no less confused explorers of the Renaissance. If the human race survives, future men will, I suspect, look back on our enlightened epoch as a veritable age of Darkness ... They will see that what we call 'schizophrenia' was one of the forms in which, often through quite ordinary people, the light began to break through the cracks in our all-too-closed minds.[21]

*

'The personal social services are one of the most ill-defined, neglected and yet vital parts of the welfare state,' argued Rodney Lowe in 1993 in his clear-eyed survey of the post-war welfare state, adding that 'the term covers essentially the residual services provided by, or through, local government for groups such as the elderly, the physically and mentally handicapped, children and "problem families".' Why 'neglected'? For the 1945–75 period, he gave three main reasons: lack of a clear professional identity; lack, too, of political weight, in part through being the responsibility of local rather than central government; and a widespread presumption that, ultimately, these were matters not to be resolved by government (of whatever sort), but instead by families and or charity. That said, things were starting to change somewhat by the early 1960s, partly with the shift in these areas (as in mental illness) towards community care, as formally laid out by Powell's Ministry of Health in a White Paper on the subject in April 1963.

In theory it all sounded positive, including an expansion of local services and facilities for mothers and young children, for the elderly and for those with disabilities; but the verdict soon afterwards of David Marsh, in his Penguin Special *The Future of the Welfare State*, was scathing:

> All that this 'plan' shows is the numbers of staff of various kinds which each local authority thinks it will need in the next ten years. We cannot be sure that these figures are no more than a guess, or, even more likely, were not just 'thought up' for sending to the Ministry, and in any case no attempt is made by the Ministry to reconcile the very obvious differences in the figures supplied by roughly comparable authorities. Nor is any indication given of the extent to which it is believed that these numbers of specialized personnel will in fact be capable of providing 'health and welfare services' for the nation and on the basis of national standards.

Moreover, the fundamental question of funding, in effect involving a significant transfer of money from central to local government, remained a very real problem. It did begin to increase during the first half of the 1960s, but even by 1966 only 1.7 per cent of public expenditure was apportioned to the personal social services. Perhaps it was inevitable. 'I should feel it right to make almost any sacrifice rather than agree to any scaling down of the announced hospital building programme,' was the unequivocal priority of Powell himself probably as early as 1961; and the Treasury, its control over public expenditure always a cause close to Powell's heart, was reassured when in 1962 the permanent secretary at the Ministry of Health agreed to 'keep down the growth of the local health and welfare programme to maintain the hospital programme'.[22]

Yet whatever the larger financial constraints, the rise of the social worker was by now irresistible. 'During the last twenty years,'

observed Titmuss in 1965, 'whenever the British people have identified and investigated a social problem, there has followed a national
call for more social work and more trained social workers.' What did
they do? And what were the qualifications needed? *New Society*'s
six-part series 'A Day in Social Work' in early 1963 – about the hospital almoner; the psychiatric social worker; the probation officer; the
child-care officer; the youth employment officer; the youth worker –
helped in very broad terms to answer the first question, while the
second had been the subject of Eileen Younghusband's exhaustive
official report in 1959. Essentially, she called for an expansion of both
numbers and training, amounting in sum to the professionalisation
of social work. Implementation was patchy over the next few years,
not helped by Treasury stinginess, but gradually it began to happen,
including the establishment of the National Institute for Social Work
Training. By the mid-1960s, few were doubting the general direction
of travel. 'Only when we have far more trained social workers will
it be possible to have a family service with nation-wide coverage,'
declared Jim Northcott in his 1964 Penguin Special making the case
for Labour, 'and only then can we end the present sad emphasis on
picking up the bits of damaged lives and broken families after the
harm has been done, and concentrate instead on providing help before
it is too late and people have already cracked under the strain.'

Barbara Wootton, life peer and one of the great experts in social
administration, was almost certainly still unconvinced. 'Daddy
Knows Best' had been the ironic title for her largely critical response
to the Younghusband Report, with her particular ire provoked by its
definition of casework as 'a personal service provided by qualified
workers for individuals who require skilled assistance in resolving
some material, emotional or character problem'; and in her view, the
change from pre-war days (when 'bountiful members of the upper
classes distributed charitable gifts to the poor') had been 'more
apparent than real':

> The old-style social worker was a superior person because he came
> from a superior class and enjoyed a superior income. His modern
> counterpart adopts a pose of hardly less superiority on account
> of his 'professional skill' in dealing with other people's 'material,
> emotional or character problems'. Thus you pay your money and

you take your choice; but for my part, if I had to be patronized by either, I think I would rather have it from the rich than from anyone tainted with what Virginia Woolf has so aptly called 'the peculiar repulsiveness of those who dabble their fingers self-approvingly in the stuff of other people's souls.' What makes these attitudes particularly distasteful, moreover, is the fact that, whilst strenuously protesting that their work no longer has any old-fashioned 'class' basis, social workers actually learn their trade by practising on the poor: I have never known the practical casework arranged in social work training courses to be carried out in well-to-do residential districts ... People do not talk about 'dealing with the emotional or character problems' of those whom they believe to be their equals. High-falutin' talk about maladjustment is thus largely a smoke-screen to hide the fact that social work is still essentially a service designed for, and administered to, people in inferior social or economic positions ...

'As between sane adults,' concluded Wootton, 'no social worker has any professional title whatever to respect on account of his superior understanding of "human needs, motivation and behaviour"; or for his superior skill in dealing with the basic problems of human life.' And accordingly, her strong preference was that instead they should concentrate on the more humdrum, but more useful, task of helping people to access and negotiate 'the complicated social services of the so-called Welfare State', which 'so seldom work out in practice as they appear on paper'.

She should perhaps have cut some slack. 'I'm full of self-doubt about the rightness of my decisions,' a child-care officer in Buckinghamshire told a sociologist in about 1961. 'How can I be sure I'm making the right ones? It might make a difference if I were religious, but I'm not.' Another, similarly self-aware, mentioned the inherent difficulty of working for a local authority: 'There's a certain priggishness of outlook. Standards are too rigid, too bourgeois.' It was also often draining work, even in the affluent Home Counties. 'Our officers are carrying impossible caseloads,' noted a few years later the annual report for Hertfordshire Children's Department, adding that 'they are working longer hours at tremendous pressure and some of them, particularly the younger ones, are almost at breaking point'.[23]

As for children themselves in local authority care in the early 1960s, roughly 46 per cent (in England and Wales) were boarded out with foster parents, while most of the rest were in local authority homes – where a 1967 national inquiry showed staff (largely unqualified, and nearly two-thirds of whom were single women) working punishingly long hours. A very particular type of children's home was the remand home, possibly typified by Glasgow's fairly brutal Larchgrove Remand Home, doubling also as a detention centre, where the juvenile delinquent Jimmy Boyle (born 1944) spent time. 'Discipline reigned supreme,' he recalled, with punishments ranging 'from extra scrubbing of floors to being locked in solitary, or to corporal punishment taking the form of a thick leather strap over the buttocks.' The task of youth workers was to keep teenagers on the approximately straight and narrow – a task that Mary Morse explored in her compelling study, *The Unattached*, of three young social workers in the early 1960s doing their best, among (in the blurb's words) 'the bored, the apathetic, the rebellious, and the defiant', in three different towns. For all their efforts at trying, under concealed identities, to get close to these adolescents and make a positive difference, they largely failed. Or at the very least, noted Morse, 'there can be no legitimate claims to have brought about dramatic "cures" or reforms in any individual's way of life'. And the underlying fact remained about 'the unattached' that 'their own resentment blocked many from any adult help that may have been available'.

For those with disabilities, whether physical or mental or both, welfare services were still largely inadequate. This was a case partly of resources, but also approach. 'The enormous frustrations and isolation of handicap were too often dealt with by bright reassurance or incitement to "grin and bear it",' remembered Younghusband two decades later about how social workers in the late 1950s tackled physical disability. 'Most of the work was undertaken by welfare officers with other duties. They made preliminary visits to assess needs, including the type of services required. They then arranged for these services and kept in touch, though rarely in relation to a thorough assessment of the person in his family and social circumstances.' And she quoted an experienced investigator: 'Although one could observe their genuine enthusiasm in gathering new knowledge and developing a new service, there was the danger of failing to see the handicapped person and his family and of concentrating instead on the handicap itself.' According to Younghusband's account, welfare services for the physically disabled did then improve somewhat – albeit the Seebohm Report of 1968, referring to the mid-1960s, made it clear that much was still in need of urgent development; while it was not until the dogged Labour MP Alf Morris managed to push through what became the Chronically Sick and Disabled Persons Act of 1970, four years before he became Britain's first minister for disabled people, that local authorities were actually *obliged* to help their disabled residents.[24]

Progress, too, was slow for those with mental disabilities (but not actually kept in institutions), until two key breakthroughs: first, Jack Tizard's 1964 book *Community Services for the Mentally Handicapped*, showing on the basis of rigorous research (including about employability) how small-scale community care was the most practical as well as humane way of providing care; and second, as relentlessly lobbied for by Judy Fryd (founder of Mencap, originally called the Association of Parents of Backward Children), the Education (Handicapped Children) Act of 1971. Until that legislation, noted an obituary, parents struggling to cope with children with learning disabilities had had to find and pay for private education for their children: 'If they were unable to do so, they had to live with the disabilities and the disruption they caused to family life 24 hours a day. The only alternative was to have a child certified as mentally defective, in which case he or she would be confined to an NHS "sub-normality" hospital, where facilities were sparse and the patients were given little to do other than shuffle around the grounds.'[25]

Also left on life's margins, more often than not during the 1960s, were the old. 'Their needs had been traditionally neglected by government, other than through the payment of pensions,' reckoned Lowe in his overview of the welfare state. 'They had also tended to be neglected by social workers, in part because – with the near-certainty of constant deterioration and the absolute certainty of only one "cure" – the work was regarded as thankless.' Ahead of 1971 legislation which made a wider range of domiciliary care mandatory for local authorities, probably the most detailed survey was the Townsend/Wedderburn one in 1962/3. Three specific findings, noted Townsend, were that only a minority of the elderly who needed particular services were actually receiving them; that 'many of those receiving certain services – particularly the hearing aid, home help and meals services – are not getting all the help they might from the services in question'; and third, that 'the services are not properly co-ordinated'. 'Some of the deficiencies in the Welfare State,' concluded Townsend, 'are larger than even the sternest critics have dared suggest':

> Not only is there strong evidence for [the need for] a major expansion, in particular, of home help services, aids for disability and sheltered housing. There is also evidence that because of old people's diffidence total needs may have been underestimated. Some of our analyses by social class have suggested that needs are partly a function of expectations, and many old people are reluctant to confess their loss of independence or demand the services they appear to need. But there are indications, at least among middle and working-class people who are beginning to have contacts with professional services such as chiropody services, that the traditional reserve and tight-lipped self-sufficiency of old people in Britain is not nearly as rigid as it has been. There is greater readiness to see the social services as a means rather than as an obstacle to independence.

It is, of course, impossible to know for sure just how much of a psychological shift in this direction was taking place. One of those involved in the survey was Jeremy Tunstall, who in 1964 wrote of how 'again and again one comes up against the failure of those who provide services for old people to break successfully through this barrier of proud inhibition, of reluctance to participate'. For the young poet Dom Moraes, the crux was a loss of respect, a situation in which old people were increasingly 'looked upon by younger people as being none of their business'. In an Islington pub in 1963, he talked to some young men (dressed in 'appalling and expensive clothes'):

> They put forward a fairly clear point of view about old people. Old people, they said, well, they got a bit in the way when they were at home. There wasn't the time in life to be talking to them and humouring them all day. Also, it cost a lot to keep them. They didn't mind them, of course, there had to be old people, hadn't there? It was like listening to anti-Semites trying to be subtle ...

There is no possible meeting ground between the generations. The old have in many cases abdicated, half humbly, half proudly, not only from the world of the young, but from the world as it is.

At least one mercy would soon be at hand. Around the time of that pub conversation, Cicely Saunders, an experienced nurse who was also a qualified doctor, was finding a suitable location at Sydenham, south-east London; and four years later, St Christopher's Hospice, a world pioneer, received its first patient. By 1970 the NHS was contributing two-thirds of the running costs; and in 2005 she herself, suffering from inoperable cancer, would die there.[26]

What about residential care for those unable to go on living at home? Many of the elderly, noted Tunstall, 'say explicitly that the local old people's home is just the workhouse with a new name'; and indeed, 33.4 per cent of the beds in institutions offering residential accommodation in 1960 were former Public Assistance units (with local authorities providing a further 32.4 per cent of newer accommodation, voluntary and religious bodies some 24 per cent, and private, profit-making institutions some 10 per cent). It was a former Poor Law workhouse, now under local authority management, which Townsend visited in 1957:

The first impression was grim and sombre. A high wall surrounded some tall Victorian buildings, and the entrance lay under a forbidding arch with a porter's lodge at one side. The asphalt yards were broken up by a few beds of flowers but there was no garden worthy of the name. Several hundred residents were housed in large rooms on three floors. Dormitories were overcrowded, with ten or twenty iron-framed beds close together, no floor covering and little furniture other than ramshackle lockers. The day-rooms were bleak and uninviting. In one of them sat forty men in high-backed Windsor chairs, staring straight ahead or down at the floor. They seemed oblivious of what was going on around them. The sun was shining outside but no one was looking that way. Some were seated in readiness at the bare tables even though the midday meal was not to be served for over an hour. Watery-eyed and feeble, they looked suspiciously at our troupe of observers and then returned to their self-imposed contemplation. They wore shapeless tweed suits and carpet slippers or boots. Several wore caps. Life seemed to have drained from them, all but the dregs ...

As I walked round the building and discussed the daily routines, it seemed the staff took the attitude that the old people had surrendered any claims to privacy. The residents were washed and dressed and conveniently arranged in chairs and beds – almost as if they were made ready for a daily inspection. An attendant was always present in the bathroom, irrespective of old people's capacity to bath themselves. The lavatories could not be locked and there were large spaces at the top and bottom of the doors. The matron swung open one door and unfortunately it revealed a blind old woman installed on the w.c. She made no apology. In a dormitory she turned back the sheets covering one woman to show a deformed leg – again without apology or explanation ...

That visit was the genesis for *The Last Refuge*: Townsend's monumental study, published in November 1962 complete with the author's own vivid photographs, of old people's homes – a study based on visits to 173 institutions in England and Wales, with the bulk of the interviews done by Townsend himself. He found little to praise, typified by his comments on local authority homes (of which well over a thousand had been opened since the war): 'deficient' toilet facilities in many of them; 'nearly two-thirds of the residents sleep in rooms in which there are at least three beds'; 'too few lifts'; bedroom furniture 'twice as plentiful as in the old workhouses', though still 'in three-fifths of the Homes it falls below a modest standard'; staffing shortages in three-fifths of the Homes; two-fifths of matrons 'somewhat authoritarian in their attitude to residents' (including one reflecting that she could not talk to any of them 'for more than two minutes on end with any interest'); and 'comparatively few of the residents form friendships with others', being 'often discouraged from helping one another', so that 'a large minority lead a self-contained existence'.

Townsend's book made a distinct stir: on the day of publication, a *Times* editorial endorsed his recommendations for (in the paper's words) 'more sheltered housing in the form of one-roomed flatlets, for preventive and after-care services, and for family help services'; while soon afterwards, praising how it combined 'the impact of a Dickensian novel with the detachment of social science', Richard

Crossman in his *New Statesman* review called it 'the first book published since 1945 which really tests the pretensions on which the welfare state was based and the proud claims which its architects made for it' – with the resulting salutary revelation being that 'this welfare state conceals and fosters much senselessly cruel mishandling of old people'. Townsend himself, near the end, reflected more broadly on 'the uneven quality' he had found of 'the relationships between old people and welfare officers, matrons, nurses, attendants, relatives, friends and neighbours':

> One chastening lesson which can be learned by studying the difficulties of any particular group in the population is that social progress cannot be measured only in terms of legislative achievements and administrative regulations. History text-books tend to be dominated by the dramas of high politics. This or that reform is conceived by an individual or a pressure group and is taken up by the government or one of the opposition parties. A famous battle is waged and won and a new law is laid on the statute book. A giant step is taken, so it is suggested, along the road of progress.
>
> But usually this is only the formal acknowledgement, or anticipation, of change. People, and the conditions within which they act, change more slowly. New meanings that may be given to the terms 'public responsibility', 'tolerance', 'respect', 'need' and 'understanding' have to be taught not only to the new generation going through a country's schools and universities, but also to the older generations who were brought up to treat these terms very differently.

'Social reforms', accordingly, 'are only as good as the individuals who put them into practice or as the means they are given to put them into practice.'[27]

*

Another of Beveridge's evil giants was squalor. 'In spite of all we have done,' Keith Joseph told Cabinet colleagues in October 1962, 'housing is still desperately short in many places; hundreds of thousands of families are living in slums, many more in houses grossly ill-equipped.' 'Most people it is true,' he went on, 'are better housed today than ever before; but this only sharpens the contrast with the rest.' Housing, in short, was 'a source of bitter and constant criticism of the Government – from all directions'.

Certainly there was evidence of a renewed focus on the issue: in March that year, publication of the results of a large-scale 1960 survey demonstrating conclusively that 'the problem of obsolescent housing extends well beyond the 850,000 dwellings recorded as unfit'; in the summer, Stanley Alderson's Penguin Special on housing, pointing up the current serious housing shortage, as well as widespread dissatisfaction with existing housing; and, shortly after Joseph's urgent message to his colleagues, the housing expert David Donnison revealing that his own survey in March of well over three thousand households had shown one-fifth still without hot water supply and a quarter not even having a share in a bath. Most of the squalor was in privately rented housing, but for a mixture of reasons, including rent decontrols following the 1957 Rent Act and slum clearance programmes, this was a sector in decline: down from 36 per cent of housing tenure in 1956 to 26 per cent five years later, with Donnison commenting that it was mainly the old 'who are left behind in the massive and continuing flight from private rented property'. Instead, the primary public-policy focus for a better housing future was on building more council housing, which after the great push in the immediate post-war period had from the late 1950s been somewhat neglected, to such an extent that in 1961 only 98,466 houses were built in the public sector, compared to 170,366 for owner-occupiers. Even so, 27 per cent of housing tenure that year was in the public rented sector (over double the proportion at the end of the war); and the assumption, shared alike by Joseph and almost all activators, was that that percentage would continue to rise, not least with the help of new industrial building methods.[28]

The other widely held assumption about public housing was that this was now, unequivocally, the age of the high-rise. The figures for public housing approvals in England and Wales were striking enough – some 6,000 high-rise dwellings in 1956; 17,000 in 1961; 35,000 in 1964 – while in Scotland they were even more so, as high-rise flats as a proportion of approvals doubled from 12.1 per cent in 1960 to 24.6 per cent by 1964. Why this sudden burst? Clearly it owed something to the tempting existence between 1956 and 1966 of subsidies from central to local government for inner-city redevelopment, with a subsidy structure favouring height. But, as Patrick Dunleavy showed in his magisterial 1981 analysis, it was also a story of architects, planners and local politicians coming together in a very closed, technocratic process, far more susceptible to the influence of big construction firms than to any manifestations of public opinion. One such firm was Wates, which in 1962 ran an advertisement appealing directly to harassed planners and housing managers:

HOUSING PROBLEMS GIVING YOU GREEN-BELT BLUES?

Don't pack your overspill population off outside your conurbation; put them up at home by putting homes in a high block. Wates will show you designs up to 20 storeys high, which can be modified as necessary to meet your own special needs. Working in close collaboration with your experts, Wates will do the whole job for you; from preliminary survey to final coat of paint. For this they quote a firm price, inclusive of fees and charges from which final rents can be calculated before you begin. So, don't send people packing because your supply of land is low; send for Wates and build high.

Perhaps just as powerful a factor was something more intangible. 'High rise was the fashion,' an informant from the Ministry of Housing told Dunleavy about the way in which in the 1960s most of the big provincial cities followed London's example by going skywards. 'It was just an image. They didn't do any of the arithmetic. They just said, "Well, they're doing high rise. We'd like some high rise."'

Did public debate play, either way, any significant role? Not really, according to Dunleavy. 'Interest and pressure groups opposed to high-rise or putting forward the "consumer" interests of public housing clients secured little coverage'; local newspapers featured instead 'a lot of reportage of tower block opening ceremonies and "ultra-modern skyscraper flats" but little or no independent discussion of the issues involved'; and generally, 'the debate on high-rise before 1968 [year of the Ronan Point disaster], as well as being selective, restricted to the decision-makers' media, largely inspired by production interests, and quite markedly one-sided, was a low-level one.' Just occasionally, though, a dissenting local politician did break cover, as on Leeds City

Council's housing committee in June 1964 in the context of plans to demolish the much-loved prefab bungalows, with their well-tended gardens, on the Beckett Park Estate:

> Perhaps it would not be out of place for somebody in this chamber [declared Councillor Vyvyan Cardno] to question the rightness of these multi-storey flats. I know that both sides of the chamber are proud of them. I know that various visits are made to Germany and America and great enthusiasm is brought back about the value and the beauty and the wonderful effect of these large multi-storey flats. But the people who have been living in homes and gardens – I don't mean people who are being removed from slum properties, but the people who have spent up to the last 20 years in delightful little houses and gardens. To them it is a nightmare. And anyone can – as we all do – visit people in these houses. We visit these houses; we meet the people in the gardens, and we meet them outside their houses and inside their houses, with the doors open. You canvass a block of flats; you go up the stone stairs, and you meet locked doors; and a face comes round the door rather like a slug from around a stone.

'That,' she insisted, 'is what these people know, and it is a horror and an increasing horror to these people.'[29]

The dominant visual effect, and largely malign social consequences, can inevitably lead to tower-block exaggeration. In fact, even at high-rise's peak, the great majority (more than 90 per cent) of the housing stock owned and managed by local authorities was *not* high-rise. More generally, across the range of building types, who by the early to mid-1960s were the occupants of council housing? Overwhelmingly, even more than in privately rented housing, they were working class. 'Wealthy council tenants are a rarity,' noted Donnison. 'Only 7 per cent of the chief wage earners in our sample of council houses had a weekly "take home pay" of more than £15 a week, and only 1 per cent claimed to bring home more than £20 a week.' And he added that his survey had revealed among council tenants 'a smaller proportion of high incomes than we found in any other group of households'. Council tenants were also, by the process known under the ugly term 'residualisation', getting poorer relative to society as a whole: whereas in 1953 their median income was roughly the same as the overall median income, ten years later the proportion with lower-than-average incomes had increased significantly. As for their other characteristics, they tended – again overwhelmingly – to be local in background and white in skin. Housing-allocation policies did in some respects vary between local authorities, but the strong bias was not only towards insisting on several years' residence in the district before being allowed on the waiting list, but also in favour of existing tenants, as typified by Woolwich Borough Council's 'sons and daughters' scheme which prioritised tenants' grown-up children when properties became vacant. While as for the question of race, evidence suggests that, prior anyway to race relations legislation in 1968, non-white people seldom registered for council properties, assuming not implausibly that their eligibility would be questioned – and probably resented – if they did so.

The fullest, most textured contemporary survey of how all this played out is James Tucker's *Honourable Estates* (1966), largely based on immersive research in around 1964 across a range of local authorities. At one point, visiting a 'problem family' living in a dilapidated three-bedroom council house (over 100 years old, no hot water, no bathroom), he asked the wife (comparatively lively, unlike her 'lethargic' if 'genial' husband) how they came to be in such primitive accommodation. 'When you apply for a council house you get an interview,' she explained. 'If your husband is getting less than £10 a week you are put into one of these houses.' 'This,' reflected Tucker, 'was the grading machine in operation', essentially reflecting a system – not everywhere, but too often – in which concentrating problem families on a particular part of an estate amounted to what he called an 'unambiguous act of segregation'. In effect, as with the provision of national assistance, it was a reprise of that fundamental Victorian distinction between the deserving and the undeserving poor – a distinction which as enacted in the 1960s on the quite recently built Llanrumney Estate on the eastern rim of Cardiff was responsible for much mutual ill-feeling. 'The temperature reached boiling point when snobbery and class distinctions were mentioned,' observed a reporter for the *South Wales Echo*, shortly before Tucker paid his visit. 'If three words could start a riot in Llanrumney, those are the words. Llanrumney is divided against itself. The top end versus bottom end battle began again ...' 'Class distinctions,' reflected Tucker himself, 'do not require any solid differences to sustain them. There does not need to be real superiority or inferiority, say of job and income and education. The imagined can become the real. It looked to me as if this was happening at Llanrumney.' And he cited the example of the estate's youth club, where three teenage girls 'spoke with genial contempt about the bottom of the estate', while 'the one girl who came from the bottom took it all with a resigned smile'. 'It is,' he concluded, 'rather frightening.'[30]

Whether on behalf of the respectable or the less respectable, the management of mass council housing, by the housing departments of local authorities, tended to be an exercise in a rather authoritarian paternalism. In Glasgow for instance, according to one historian, the department was, right up to the end of the 1960s, 'still using methods of discipline and terror' recognisable from the nineteenth century, including the widespread use of warrant sales and evictions; and Charles Johnstone adds that there was little or no belief that tenants could 'organise their own lives' satisfactorily. In a more humdrum, day-to-day way, probably fairly typical were some of the 'conditions of tenancy' as they applied to living in the early 1960s in a council property in Lancaster: no dogs (let alone 'hens, rabbits, pigeons, pigs or livestock') without the permission of the Housing Committee; no second-hand furniture to be taken into the house without being properly fumigated; and the tenant 'not to carry on in the house any trade, profession or business, and shall not affix any professional notice or advertisement to the structure of the house or exhibit such a notice within the curtilage or boundary wall or fence, unless the prior consent in writing of the Corporation has been obtained.' 'Many councils are admirable landlords,' reckoned Jim Northcott in his 1964 *Why Labour?* Penguin Special, 'but some have a reputation for petty interference with tenants over such things as colour of front doors, height of hedges, hanging out of washing, installation of television aerials, playing of musical instruments, and whether you can keep a budgie but not a cat, or vice versa'; while Alderson in his Penguin Special a couple of years earlier reflected how in the long run 'power employed paternalistically provokes far greater resentment than power employed selfishly or even antagonistically'. For the time being, moreover, relatively few council estates had vigorous tenant associations, or sometimes indeed any tenant association. 'Before the late 1960s,' according to the housing historian Peter Shapely, 'tenants remained a largely passive group.' Or as Alison Ravetz strikingly puts it about the broader implications of that passivity: 'As an attempt by one class to provide an improved environment and culture for another class, council housing at best accommodated existing working-class culture: it did not renew it.'[31]

Given that the rented market was steadily drying up, and that the possible 'third way' of housing associations or housing co-operatives were both still well short of attaining a critical mass (though 1963 did see the start of the Notting Hill Housing Trust, founded by the Rev. Bruce Kenrick), the major alternative to being a council tenant was increasingly that of owner-occupation.[32] Against a long-run background of home ownership's share of overall housing tenure steadily rising – 26 per cent in 1945; 34 per cent in 1956; 42 per cent in 1961; 47 per cent five years later (by when the private rented sector was down to 19 per cent, ten percentage points less than the public rented) – Tucker on his travels round council estates heard a range of views:

People come and live here, and as they improve they go off and buy their own house ... We would have bought a house, too. Most people would, surely. Ninety per cent would on this estate. (*A market gardener and his wife on the Sunrising estate, Looe, Cornwall*)

I can't see that anyone who could afford to buy would stay on a council estate. (*Cleansing department worker on Buddle Estate, Exeter*)

I think there's a certain amount of snobbishness in the attitude of private owners towards us. They look down on you because you live in a council house. But what they should realise is that it is force of circumstances. Council tenants would like to better themselves, but they don't have the chance. We're here because we have to be. (*Retired railwayman in Abingdon Road, Erdington, Birmingham*)

If the social security had been what it is now, we wouldn't have hesitated to buy. You can't go wrong. But I never knew when I would be out of work. (*Brewery worker at Highbridge Road, Burnham*)

I wouldn't think of buying a house. My husband has had three periods of unemployment since we came to this house five and a half years ago. *(Wife of a dye sinker at Leighton Road, Gleadless Valley, Sheffield)*

We wouldn't think of buying. My husband has had T.B. and we don't go in for any big debts. We go along quietly, leading a happy life. That's how we like it. We couldn't do that if we had a debt of £2,000 or £3,000 over us. We just pay out the rent every week. *(Middle-aged woman in a prefab at Bordesley Green East, Birmingham)*

'It is unusual, though that is all, to come across council tenants who would not prefer to be owner-occupiers, possibly of council-built property [often only a marginal possibility at this stage, long before Margaret Thatcher's 'right to buy'], but more often of a house away from municipal estates,' was Tucker's sober enough overall conclusion. And he diagnosed a twofold motive, applicable in varying degrees: on the one hand, the desire to live in a property appreciating in value; on the other hand, the desire to take 'a leap upward in social standing', including an appetite on the part of 'the majority' of council tenants (but not the overwhelming majority) 'to accept the cares of ownership as the price of advancement'. His impressionistic findings were broadly consistent with John Cullingworth's 1960 survey of council tenants in Lancaster, revealing that 54 per cent preferred to own – but preferably not a council house, with less than a third of those would-be owner-occupiers saying that they would buy their existing council house even if it was 'offered at a fair price'.

Of course, one way and another, owner-occupation would continue over the ensuing decades to be the main direction of travel. And there was perhaps something emblematic about Joseph McGann, who worked in a copper factory as a quality control inspector and in 1960 became the first mortgage holder in his family's history when he bought for £700 a small terraced house in Birstall Road, Liverpool 6:

It had [recalled his son Stephen] three modest bedrooms up a steep flight of stairs, a cramped living room, a front parlour, and a tiny kitchen that ran out into a back yard with an outside toilet. Away from the fireplace, and in the days before central heating, the house was freezing – a cold that penetrated the sheets and misted the windows, congesting our chests and stealing our breath. But it was ours. Our little piece of the world.[33]

*

Finally, in this welfare tour some twenty years on from Beveridge, the evil of 'ignorance' as the provision of state education sought to rid the nation's children of that unfortunate condition. In various ways, not least the supply of adequate resources to enable that effective provision, it remained very much a work in progress.

The continuing shortage of resources was at the heart of a March 1963 letter to the *New Statesman* signed by all members of staff at Longslade Grammar School, Leicester; and they demanded that the government 'show us by a drastic re-thinking of its priorities that there is no longer any justice in the suspicion, often voiced, that state education is never treated with genuine urgency by our rulers because it is tacitly regarded as being, in effect, education "for other people's children."' Or as a letter-writer to *The Times* put it a few weeks later – about the undeniable if uncomfortable fact that 'education in public [i.e. private] schools is better because the teachers are generally better and there are more of them in relation to the number of boys than in other schools', and that 'this is so because the public schools can pay more' – this was unlikely to change until such time as Cabinet ministers actively wanted state schools to be 'excellent' and were 'prepared to send their sons to them'. Gallup that spring may have found 58 per cent satisfied with the education of their children (daughters as well as sons), and only 16 per cent dissatisfied; but that autumn, the findings of the Newsom Report (*Half Our Future*) amounted to a damning indictment of the failure of much of the secondary school system to give pupils the chance of realising their full potential. 'The educational experience of the electorate will still be something like this,' wrote *New Society* in April 1964, summing matters up in two pithy, incontrovertible sentences: 'Nothing until the age of five, a class of about 40 until eleven, either no thought of secondary education or rejection by the eleven-plus, a class of about 30 until fifteen and nothing much – certainly nothing full-time – thereafter. Most of them will emerge from this experience with a precarious adequacy in reading, writing and simple arithmetic.' Some improvements, yes, conceded the magazine, including the fact that whereas in the 1959 general election barely a fifth of first-time voters had stayed at school beyond the compulsory age of fifteen, this time round the proportion would be well over a quarter; yet, in the main, 'ignorance' still king.[34]

Material resources – the basic day-to-day environment – were at their most limited in primary schools. In 1963 an official survey of primaries in England and Wales found only 28 per cent having all their lavatories inside the main building and only 22 per cent having specialist rooms for all their activities. Other figures were equally damning: no warm water in 6,101 of these primaries; no central heating in 5,815; no kitchens in 4,647; no staffroom in 8,750; a 'seriously sub-standard' site for 9,211; children dining in classrooms in 2,288 – altogether, it was a toughening-up experience for other people's children and their largely undervalued, underpaid teachers. What about the teaching itself? Progressive, child-centred methods were undoubtedly on the rise by the early 1960s – encouraged by Ministry of Education pronouncements in the late 1950s that a primary school was 'no longer a mere machine for giving lessons', and instead 'a social unit concerned with the all-round developments of boys and girls', and that the deepest focus should be on 'children as children' – but a mixture of demographic pressures (directly affecting class sizes) and 11-plus pressures meant, quite apart from any other motives, that traditional methods were not easily relinquished.

As for primary schools and the bigger socio-economic picture, two books, both published in 1964 but based on earlier research, were in their own way game-changers. The first, James Douglas's longitudinal study *The Home and the School* based on some 5,000 children born in one week in March 1946, revealed that a middle-class child at a primary school was far likelier to pass the 11-plus than was an equally bright working-class child. For Douglas, writing two years after a survey had shown that only 4 per cent of junior schools rejected streaming and that 85 per cent of teachers still favoured it, the villain of the piece was unmistakeable:

> Children who come from well-kept homes and who are themselves clean, well-clothed and shod, stand a greater chance of being put in the upper streams than their measured ability would seem to justify.

Once there they are likely to stay and to improve in performance in succeeding years. This is in striking contrast to the deterioration noticed in those children of similar initial measured ability who were placed in the lower streams. In this way the validity of the initial selection appears to be confirmed by the subsequent performance of the children, and an element of rigidity is introduced early into the primary school system.

The other book, called simply *Streaming*, was by Brian Jackson. He argued passionately not only that 'streaming reflects social background, privilege, accident and handicaps', thereby perpetuating long-run inequalities, but also that, in terms of the intrinsic education, those primary schools operating on an unstreamed basis helped bright and less bright alike through a friendly atmosphere of co-operation in which children helped each other out and teachers were able to pay attention to individual needs and abilities. Both books made a considerable impact; perhaps not least on Lady (Bridget) Plowden, appointed in August 1963 by the education secretary, the liberal-minded Edward Boyle, to chair an inquiry into the state of primary schooling.[35]

At state secondary level in the early 1960s, just under a quarter of pupils in England (but over a third in Wales) had passed the 11-plus and were at a grammar school. There, as likely as not at a boys' grammar, the prevailing ethos was (recall the obituarists of Francis Scott) one of 'the gentlemanly amateur', as 'a pre-war generation of schoolmasters, motivated more by love of subject than by desire to educate the young, was everywhere in senior posts'. That certainly applied to the school where Scott arrived in 1962:

Stockport Grammar already had a highly distinguished academic record, but much of its pedagogic, administrative and financial thinking evoked a bygone era. The progressive emphasis on child-centred education was seen as psychological claptrap and flogging with a bamboo cane was regarded as a useful deterrent. Caps were worn by all pupils and academic gowns by all masters – the latter to protect themselves against chalk dust and the inadequacies of nineteenth-century heating arrangements (when Scott arrived, there was a fireplace in each classroom). Direct involvement of parents was not encouraged. The teaching staff was paid monthly by cheque and the ancillary staff fortnightly in cash. There were not departmental budgets – those who shouted loudest got most. The conclusion of teaching periods was announced by the ringing of a Dickensian handbell ...

It was not an ethos which suited the future educational sociologist Stephen Ball. From a skilled working-class background, and having got through the 11-plus, he had gone the previous year to Bishopshalt Grammar School, Uxbridge, second-tier in academic achievement but first-tier in keeping up traditions:

Adrift in an alien world of gowns, masters, Latin and cross-country running. Michael Cornes and I were the only working-class boys in our year ... The other boys, none of whom very often acknowledged my existence, were almost without exception, it seemed, the sons of lawyers, doctors or stockbrokers. The teaching was dull, didactic and repetitive. Talk, board writing and snap questions. I was now a 'fish out of water', frightened, isolated, and very ill at ease ... Much out-of-lesson time I spent in the wood-panelled library reading Sherlock Holmes – I am not sure why, but it was an escape from the immediate exclusions of the all too real world of Latin grammar and algebra. I assumed the mantle of school failure by the end of the first week. Much of my time at home was spent struggling with gnomic homework tasks, which made little sense to me and for which my parents were unable to give much practical help. Even my facility with words now seemed inadequate. My practical sense had no purchase on this world of middle-class taste, entitlement and easy accomplishment. I was lonely, unhappy and increasingly alienated.

In the event, because of a change in his father's work, Ball moved after a year to a different grammar school – one with mercifully 'a more mixed demographic', though 'my relation to grammar schooling remained strained, to say the least, for several years to come'; and he adds that albeit he did at last have an inspirational teacher in sixth form (having been allowed to enter it 'on probation'), 'most of my grammar school teachers could not teach their way out of a wet paper bag'. Eventually, at university, he encountered *Education and the Working Class*, the classic study (published in 1962) by Brian

Jackson and Dennis Marsden of the emotional roller-coaster of 88 working-class children (and their parents) who had passed through the grammar schools of Huddersfield since the 1944 Education Act. 'It was about me, about my life, my experience, my successes and failures, my struggles. It dealt with inequality in a nuanced but visceral way. It was grounded in mundane struggles and compromises, in the aspirations, failures, complexities and pain of real lives. I decided that this was what I wanted to do with my life – do sociology – tackle inequality through research and make it intolerable.' Soon afterwards, still an undergraduate, he read Colin Lacey's newly published *Hightown Grammar* (1970), based on an ethnographic study between 1962 and 1965 of Salford Grammar School: 'Again this was a book that captured the processes of schooling, of exclusion, differentiation, normalization, to which I had been subjected. I was enthralled and outraged.'

For Lacey himself, somewhere near the heart of his study was how by the early 1960s the school had become, locally speaking, 'the focus of "meritocratic" competition for qualifications which were themselves passports to a new world of employment', with the great majority of boys there having parents 'who had not themselves been to grammar schools, but who were very conscious of the advantages that a successful grammar school career could bring'. Accordingly, 'Hightown' and other grammars 'became the *means* by which parents could satisfy their career aspirations for their children. The education they offered was only rarely an end in itself. Knowledge for its own sake remained an unrealised ideal ... Parents and their children became centrally concerned with examination success as the key to life-chance allocation. Teachers therefore became saddled with and constrained by the narrower and specific task of achieving examination success.' Of course, these exam machines did not always succeed. Streaming, based to a significant degree on social class, was as prevalent as in primary schools; 'early leaving' remained a very real problem, especially if working-class parents wanted an immediate boost to family income; and as many as a third of grammar-school pupils failed even to secure three O levels.[36] Still, it was all relative, and undoubtedly in the course of the 1960s a grammar-school elite was starting to emerge potentially capable, at least on paper, of challenging the entrenched private-school elite.

Yet for every pupil at a grammar school, there were in most areas at least three or four who had failed (or not even taken) the 11-plus and thereby found themselves at a secondary modern. Perhaps inevitably, we know so much less about their experiences. Stereotypes are easy – of sink schools, of blackboard jungles, of factory fodder, of little in the curriculum that was academically challenging – but the truth was more complicated, as valuably shown by Dick Stroud's pioneering narrative overview (*The Secondary Mod*, 2021), an overview informed by his own experience of attending around this time a secondary modern in London's East End. Regional variations alone were considerable: for instance, in the north-east barely a quarter of secondary moderns having fifth forms, whereas in the south-east some seven-tenths had.

Even so, the stereotypes are not based on nothing. 'Ninety per cent of the work in a secondary modern school is control and discipline,' bleakly asserted Richard Farley in his 1960 treatise for teachers, *Secondary Modern Discipline*. 'The lesson content is, or should be, fairly simple, but if you don't carry out certain checks, then your lessons will be a fiasco. It is wise to keep a check on your cupboards – if you have any – for cupboards are fair game for any curious malcontent, so keep them locked.' Two years later, John Webb, who had attended a secondary modern himself, wrote a sociological essay depicting life there as, on the boys' side, 'almost a guerrilla war against the teacher's standards – a ragged, intermittent fight to be oneself by being spontaneous and irrepressible and by breaking rules', each bout usually ending with 'the ritual caning and telling-off'. And in the mid-1960s, it was Salford again under investigation, this time a secondary modern called 'Lumley', as the sociologist David Hargreaves portrayed a world of appropriately respectful upper-stream boys (in effect bought off by staff manipulation of such things as examination entry and job opportunity) and lower-stream boys for whom staff–pupil conflict was the daily defining reality:

We see clearly [noted a reviewer] the way in which the lower-stream boys find ever new ways of expressing their protests, to which the staff, guided by their values and expectations, rise predictably. Thus Clint, the leader of the delinquent group, says 'I'm going to get my hair flicking up', Derek says 'I'm going to let mine grow too', and the others follow. The situation rapidly escalates; the Headmaster refuses to let boys with long hair have time off to visit future employers; a teacher canes six long-haired boys on one day whilst another begins cutting boys' hair (notably only the low-status ones) ...

The heavyweight report on secondary moderns was John Newsom's *Half Our Future*, published in October 1963 shortly before the Robbins Report on higher education. A significant part of its value lay in its exposure of a continuing serious shortfall in physical and human resources – two-thirds with no reasonable room set aside for a library; more than half with no provision for any kind of music; one-third with no proper science laboratory; two-thirds with no gymnasium; playing fields sited well away from the school; large class sizes; high staff turnover – while more generally it went a long way to justify the *Daily Mirror*'s take next day: 'Too much young talent is being wasted in the classrooms ... the sense of failure must be banished from the secondary modern schools ... All this adds up to educational justice and a fair start in life for EVERY CHILD. Instead of a fairer start for some than for others.'

What, though, was the underlying *purpose* of secondary moderns? 'In the idealistic period of the 1940s it was hoped that in the new schools, freed from the constraint of external examinations, there would be the opportunity to develop a new type of education, enjoying parity of esteem with the academic and specialized curriculum of the grammar school, but of a completely different kind,' reflected the sociologist Olive Banks in 1963, reviewing William Taylor's *The Secondary Modern School*. 'The reality, of course, has been quite otherwise,' she went on, 'and Dr Taylor describes the process by which the secondary modern school has repudiated these aims in favour of work that enables it to contract in to the system of examination, competition and success.' Pressures of the labour market, parental scepticism about 'parity of esteem' with the grammars, teachers with an educational background naturally predisposing them in favour of the grammar school curriculum, and a natural desire to redress the increasingly publicised errors of the 11-plus selection procedure had all contributed.[37] And too often, Banks hardly needed to add, the result was the worst of both worlds.

The age of the comp, meanwhile, was almost ready to dawn, even though as late as 1965 comprehensive schools in England and Wales were still only educating 8.5 per cent of the total maintained secondary school population (compared to 4.7 per cent in 1960), with the great majority of the others continuing to go to either grammars or secondary moderns. The key players, in an 'activator' sense anyway, were on the one hand the local education authorities, with 92 out of 129 English LEAs having by the end of 1963 initiated plans to end selection at eleven; and on the other hand, Edward Boyle, who as the Conservative education secretary from July 1962 not only largely ensured that his ministry did not block such plans, but began the difficult task of telling his party that a mixture of the discredited 11-plus system, the rising creed of equality of opportunity and the apparent success of the first generation of comprehensives meant that it could no longer die in the ditch against quickening structural change. 'My own public remarks on this subject since I became a Minister,' he informed a sufficiently compliant Macmillan in July 1963, 'have deliberately implied that we do not, as a Party, regard separate grammar and modern schools as the right and usual way of organising secondary education'; and three months later, his preface to Newsom famously declared that 'the essential point is that all children should have an equal opportunity of acquiring intelligence, and developing their talents and abilities to the full'. Also that October, at its party conference, Labour committed itself 'to set up a universal system of comprehensive education and to abolish the 11-plus', by 'converting permissive into compulsory legislation' – even though, for the time being, the party's leadership preferred to talk about 'grammar schools for all' rather than a process of comprehensivisation as such.[38] Things generally during the second half of the 1950s and into the very early 1960s had been rumbling away in an anti-selection direction, at least on the left; but one way and another, this was the time when the plates truly began to shift.

Yet the question remains: how well did parents, and public opinion generally, manage during this historic shift to keep up with the activators? For the historian Peter Mandler, however, it was less a question of them keeping up with the activators (especially in the form of the LEAs), but instead the other way round. 'A massive social movement' is his characterisation of what was under way by the early 1960s – a movement which, in his account, directly led to local authorities, such as both Manchester and Liverpool in 1963, making decisive moves towards comprehensivisation. But in truth, for all his psychologically persuasive argument about everyday users of the welfare state – 'No-one was suggesting that there should be good hospitals for some and average hospitals for others; why was this choice offered to parents in secondary schooling?' – his evidence for the existence of this movement is, for these years anyway, somewhat thin; and although he downplays the findings of the principal pollster on the subject, Mark Abrams, as being unduly affected by what he calls Abrams' 'growing personal pessimism about the cultural tendencies of mass society', a particularly striking Abrams poll that he ignores is the one from summer 1962, revealing that only 10 per cent of Labour voters, and 11 per cent of Conservative voters, were critical of the 11-plus.[39]

The definitive account still awaits; but, generally, it does seem reasonably clear that, in degrees of parental engagement with matters of education, there was a big class difference:

> The middle-class parents [wrote James Douglas in 1964 in *The Home and the School*] take more interest in their children's progress at school than the manual working-class parents do, and they become relatively more interested as their children grow older. They visit the schools more frequently to find out how their children are getting on with their work, and when they do so are more likely to see the Head as well as the class teacher, whereas the manual working-class parents are usually content to see the class teacher only. But the most striking difference is that many middle-class fathers visit the schools to discuss their children's progress, whereas manual working-class fathers seldom do so.

That finding was consistent with the experience of Michael Young. 'The progress made in the schools in the last 25 years towards more freedom, less rigid discipline, more child-centred study, did not seem to have been matched in the understanding of parents – or at any rate of working-class parents,' ran the press report of an address he gave (also in 1964, in his capacity as chairman of the Advisory Centre for Education) about the problem of apathetic parents and

the desirability of a welfare service of 'education visitors' to maintain contacts with parents throughout their children's schooling. The
overall take of Elizabeth Roberts, based on her oral history of largely
working-class Barrow, Lancaster and Preston, is probably about right
concerning attitudes to the value of formal education: 'A few parents
were overtly hostile to the whole system, many were indifferent,
and a growing minority very enthusiastic.' By contrast, the default
position of most middle-class parents was almost certainly not one
of passive fatalism; and for them, if one of their children failed the
11-plus and they were unwilling or unable to go private, the prospect of that child going to the local secondary modern was a deeply
unattractive one. The continuing invidiousness (let alone unfairness)
of that exam, the poor reputation of secondary moderns, the shortage
in many areas of grammar-school places, the helpful fact that many
of the first generation of comprehensives were built in new suburban
areas lacking secondary provision: at this point anyway, as Boyle
realised, the word 'comprehensive' was not necessarily such a loaded
one to trepidatious, Conservative-voting, middle-class ears. And it
was perhaps unsurprising that the pro-comprehensive Confederation
for the Advancement of State Education (CASE), formed in 1962 as
a national organisation out of a range of local pressure groups, was
largely middle class in composition – though quite possibly with
the more idealistic herbivores heavily outnumbering the more self-
interested carnivores.

Ultimately, this was an issue about social class. 'It has served to
revitalise the abhorrent class structure in the country,' J. H. Morris
of Market Drayton wrote in July 1963 to his local paper about the
iniquities of the 11-plus, supporting Salop County Council's recent
contested decision to close the town's grammar school (est. 1555) and
convert the secondary modern into a comprehensive. 'People from the
status-seeking middle class,' Morris went on, 'aspire to send their children to the Grammar School, while the working man has his lack of
opportunity re-emphasised in the Modern School.' Or as G. Hickman
of Ironbridge crisply put it: 'Market Drayton, wake up and be bold!
The days of snobbery are numbered!' But at the same time, it was also
an issue about geography and gender: geography because of the very
uneven distribution of grammar schools, gender because girls had
to score higher marks than boys to qualify for entry into grammars,

a bias compounded by the fact that, when it came to staying on at
school for those with five or more O levels, ten boys did so compared
to every eight girls. In the early 1960s, calculated the great educational
historian Brian Simon, 'the opportunity to reach full-time higher education [itself heavily biased on the supply side towards men] for a
middle-class boy living in Cardiganshire was roughly 160 times as
great as that for a working-class girl living in West Ham'.[40] All told,
it was a system, predicated essentially on Rab Butler's 1944 Act, no
longer fit for purpose – *if* that purpose was, within the state system, a
fair shake for all.

*

'The welfare state,' remarked Kingsley Amis in 1957, 'is notoriously
unpopular with intellectuals.' What about the populace as a whole by
the early 1960s? *The Long Struggle* was a BBC TV documentary in
October 1962, narrated by Malcolm Muggeridge and charting the rise
of the welfare state. 'We hear quite enough of the past every time we
talk to the older people, without having TV hark back to it,' grumbled
a farm worker. 'One gets fed up hearing how badly they were off and
how lucky we are today.' That, though, was a distinctly minority reaction. 'Certainly demonstrated the fantastic changes over the years –
gradual in themselves but in aggregate quite staggering,' said a factory
manager; and another more typical viewer was glad 'to be reminded
of the long struggle and fight which we all take for granted today'.
More generally, feelings about the welfare state do seem to have been
largely positive. In around 1960, interviews with 144 people of varying
backgrounds found widely contrasting levels of knowledge (including
a strong tendency to equate the welfare state with the NHS), 'considerable ignorance and confusion' about the financing of the social services, the majority thinking that 'the community' had really benefited
from those services, and two-fifths wanting 'more stringent enquiry'
into people receiving benefits, especially national assistance; in 1961 a
survey (*Family Needs and Social Services*) undertaken by Abrams for
Political and Economic Planning (PEP), mainly seeking the views of
mothers, found high percentages from different social classes wanting
the government to spend the same or more; and in 1962 an opinion
poll relating specifically to the NHS found 89 per cent satisfied and

only 11 per cent dissatisfied, rising to 13 per cent among the 'lower class'.[41]

Even so, there were limits to the popular enthusiasm: in 1963 a national survey conducted by Mass-Observation of some two thousand 'male heads of households', including appreciably more Labour than Conservative voters, asked whether they would like the welfare services to go on growing as incomes grew, with bigger contributions, or would prefer other methods. Significantly, and even allowing for the fact that the survey had been commissioned by the Institute of Economic Affairs, the percentages of those *not* in favour of extending state provision were considerable: notably, 47 per cent in the case of education, 57 per cent in the case of health. Relevant here are the conclusions of Phyllis Willmott, compiling in the mid-1960s her pioneering *Consumer's Guide to the British Social Services*, first published in 1967 as a Pelican Original. A committed supporter of the welfare state, but in an impressively clear-eyed, non-doctrinaire way, she acknowledged a serious 'unevenness in distribution and quality of services'; reckoned that 'almost everywhere a lot remains to be done in improving information', especially on the part of hospitals and local authorities; and then made her central charge:

> It is fashionable to argue that one can 'as a consumer' complain about social services which prove unsatisfactory, just as with any other 'service'. Theoretically, this may be unanswerable. In practice it is often not so easy. In the ordinary way, behind the consumer's complaint lies a very powerful sanction – his freedom to take his custom elsewhere. Too often, when using the social services, there is no such freedom of choice – other than the crude one of 'take it, or leave it.'

Still, she noted hopefully on her final page, 'there is a growing awareness within the social services that they must be tailored more closely to the needs of those who use them'.[42]

To end with, a trio of 1962/3 glimpses. Starting with that young couple in Huddersfield, talking to Brian Jackson just as the Cuban Missile Crisis was about to unfold. 'I'll tell you what is different,' the wife declared about what had changed since the old days. 'There aren't so many poor people about now. And the ones that there are,

I think it's their own fault really, in't it nowadays? The only people I feel sorry for are the old aged pensioners. I'm really sorry for them. I think something ought to be done about them.' Who, asked Jackson, *were* the people on National Assistance? The same answer (almost wholly inaccurate) came back from each of them: mainly West Indian immigrants. A few months later, a University of Liverpool survey into the impoverished inhabitants of rundown, inner-city 'Crown Street' found that the prevailing attitude towards the welfare state was one of seeming indifference, with apparently relatively little use being made of its services. One of the more articulate interviewees, living in Mount Vernon Street, was a 58-year-old widower who had worked as a stores labourer in the docks. Did he need to know more himself about the availability of different services? 'Not particularly.' Should they be more widely known? 'Yes – for people who don't know.' How was this to be done? 'There are some very ignorant people who can't even read – it's very difficult to know how to help these people unless by visiting.' The last glimpse is of signing-on day at a local Labour Exchange, as described in May 1963 by G. Zambardi of London N5:

> The hall was crowded – eight queues for eight boxes. There were perhaps 60 to 80 men there, young and old, including West Indians, Scotsmen and Irishmen. A policeman was on duty. There were numerous delays. Names were mispronounced and the clerks were unhelpful. Thick fingers grasped pencils awkwardly. One tall West Indian in a cap and long coat, holding an attaché case, was sent from queue to queue: no clerk spared him a moment. At the counter, one man paused looking for the line and turned over the form – it was blank. The clerk shouted out that he was stupid, but did not venture to help him. He found the line, effectively humiliated. Do the clerks resent the presence of the unemployed or are they just desperately overworked?[43]

4

No Warmth Anywhere

'Back to work in morning through still falling snow, which had lain to a thickness of three inches overnight and continues to fall throughout most of the day,' recorded Anthony Heap on Thursday, 27 December. He and his fellow diarists now had their wintry theme, as 1962 gave way to 1963:

> More bitter, unrelenting cold. Skating on Lister Park lake [Bradford] for the third day. (*Sidney Jackson, Shipley, 28 December*)

> Still bitterly cold. (*Sidney Jackson, 29 December*)

> A foot of snow has fallen in the night! (*Judy Haines, Chingford, 30 December*)

> A wondrous heavy fall of snow awaited my stupefied gaze this morning. My steps have disappeared and the dustbins have tall cones on them ... Went out into Kensington Gardens. An eerie white snow waste effect with dark figures moving on it. Children sliding on toboggans and tin trays. (*William Halle, Wandsworth, 30 December*)

> An overnight blizzard sweeps the southern counties, leaves London under a further six inches deep coating of snow and causes the worst chaos on the roads for at least fifteen years. (*Anthony Heap, 30 December*)

Snow everywhere still & bitterly cold. *(Grace Taylor, Ruislip, 31 December)*

Horribly cold and gloomy. Blizzard unabated, the country snowbound. Watched old film of the Marx Brothers, 'A Night in Casablanca', and read book catalogues into the New Year. *(Hugh Selbourne, Manchester, 31 December)*

How is it possible to believe that we have crossed into a new year when the same deep eiderdown of whiteness lies feet deep over everything and more, *more* snow is falling from the sky? *(Frances Partridge, Lambourn, 1 January)*

Thick snow everywhere and much hardship caused by drifts cutting people off. Helicopters coming to their rescue. There have been some deaths, too. *(Judy Haines, 1 January)*

Went to wash hair but bitter cold makes drying impossible. *(Gladys Langford, Islington, 2 January)*

A job keeping the pigs warm. *(Dennis Dee, near Beverley, 2 January)*

We love our placid, warm 'tuck-in' with bottles and electric blanket, in the afternoon. The only time we get really warm in the whole day. *(Madge Martin, Oxford, 2 January)*

Big blizzard again threatened at end of day. Snow again accompanied by a high wind. Hope it won't cause more hazardous drifts. Spent lots of time looking through literature on Australia. *(Henry Woodley, Overcombe, near Weymouth, 2 January)*

Still freezing hard with no forecast of a let up. *(Grace Taylor, 3 January)*

The weather was not responsible for every misadventure. 'With a sickening crash,' noted Henry St John that first Thursday of the new year, 'someone fell out of a packed Piccadilly line train at Earls Court station this evening straight on to the crowded platform, and a shout of "Idiot!" went up.' Across the country as a whole, even as

the *Daily Mirror* dared to dream of summer by launching its afford-
able, family-oriented and immediately popular dinghy (designed by
Barry Bucknell) at the London International Boat Show, the dominant fact was wintry and indisputable: that whereas 90 per cent
of Swedish homes, and 60 per cent of American homes, had central heating, in British homes the figure was only a miserable 3.5
per cent. 'We are having something more like an American winter
than we've had for nearly a century,' C. S. Lewis in Headington,
Oxford, reflected on the 2nd to an American friend, 'and as we are
not prepared for it (v. little central heating, no snow-ploughs, etc)
it hits us v. hard.'[1]

'We already have a large following in the London area,' Brian Jones –
holed up with Mick Jagger and Keith Richards in frozen squalor in
Edith Grove, SW10 – wrote on the 2nd hopefully if not entirely accurately to the BBC in search of an audition for *Jazz Club*, 'and in view of
the vast increase of interest in Rhythm and Blues in Britain, an exceptionally good future has been predicted for us by many people.' Next
evening, the return on BBC television of *Steptoe and Son*, written by
Ray Galton and Alan Simpson, was immediately followed, over on
ITV, by the start of Tony Hancock's new series, alas not written by
Galton and Simpson after the comedian's disastrous decision to ditch
them. 'For a stretch he was gloriously himself,' reckoned the critic
G. W. Stonier, but 'at other times he seemed lost, putting a face on
it'; Nella Last in Barrow thought the script (by Terry Nation) 'rather
weak', with too much 'of the old slap stick type'; and another diarist,
Avril James in Birmingham, felt unrewarded by going to a friend's
house specially to watch it: 'not all that gd'. Over the coming weeks,
Hancock's ratings and critical stock would fall precipitately, in piquant
contrast to those of *Steptoe*. The experimental novelist B. S. Johnson,
doubling as a cultural conservative, was, however, unconvinced by
the rag-and-bone men of Oil Drum Lane. 'Objectionable almost to
the point of disgust,' he wrote later in January, viewing the whole
set-up as an insult to the working class. 'Many people say the show
is so "natural" and "realistic", but how many totters do they know?'
Instead, he championed ITV's Arthur Haynes, 'truly vulgar in that he
is in touch with and appeals to the common people'. Indeed, with the
eleventh series of *The Arthur Haynes Show* (Johnny Speight the main
scriptwriter) having started recently, he more than anyone was the

people's comedian: argumentative, combative, even belligerent – the working man with no doubts about his worth.

On Saturday the 5th at the Manor Place Baths in Elephant and Castle, and displaying his mastery of the revolutionary new art of loop spin, 15-year-old Chester Barnes (from Forest Gate) became the youngest ever English table tennis champion; 'the freakish weather has put the dustmen completely out of their routine,' noted Phyllis Willmott in north London on Sunday; next day in Ruislip, Grace Taylor's washing froze solid ('never seen it so stiff'), while in Barking the TV reception for Pat Scott was both flickering and noisy ('it must be ice on the aerial'), unfortunate for the debut of single-topic, tabloid-of-the-air *World in Action*; 'I never remember such cruelly cold weather since 1929, when the Isis froze over,' reckoned Madge Martin on the 9th, even as power cuts meant that Sylvia Plath began writing, she told an editor, 'by candlelight with cold fingers, a sinister return to Dickensian conditions'; and Lady Violet Bonham Carter let herself go: 'Arctic frost continues & there are electricity cuts from a "Go Slow" among electrical workers – a really brutal act in this weather. We have not suffered but the Hospitals have, in some cases with dire results. *This* is what makes the T.U.'s so widely unpopular …' 'Brian and I rather put off by lack of volume due to work to rule in power station,' noted Keith Richards, in his briefly kept diary, about the Stones at the Marquee on Thursday the 10th; but that same evening – while Veronica Lee 'watched Steptoe which is brilliant and so sad and Hancock which isn't as good', the former disturbing some by featuring Albert eating a jar of pickled onions in the bath – nothing stopped a crush outside the Warner in Leicester Square for the prem-iere of the Cliff Richard film *Summer Holiday*. 'I have never seen anything quite so frenzied,' said a Warner Pathé spokesman, adding that 'the teenagers got too excited', while Cliff himself was forced to retreat to a nearby flat. Neatly enough, at this moment of zenith for the old order, the breakthrough Beatles single, 'Please Please Me', was released the next day, appraised by Keith Fordyce in the *NME* as 'a really enjoyable platter, full of beat, vigour and vitality'.[2]

Distinctly unpleased that Friday were Anthony Heap ('the tempera-ture hasn't risen more than two or three degrees above freezing point since Christmas and every night always well below it'), Madge Martin ('our two lavatories have frozen, the most uncomfortable thing that

can happen') and Grace Taylor ('colder than ever – will it ever end?').
For Noël Coward next day, it was a case of good riddance to Blighty
as he travelled to Southampton to board the *Queen Mary* ('two hours
of purgatory in an unheated train on which was served the most
disgusting breakfast ... I am becoming sick of general "commonness",
sick of ugly voices, sick of bad manners and teenagers and debased
values') – a journey which passed through Surbiton, where Marian
Raynham was in similar mood: 'It's bitterly cold today. Worse than
ever. Power not out, but light went dim this a.m. Men working to
rule. What they will do for more money, putting everyone's lives in
jeopardy.' No let-up on Sunday the 13th. 'The snow and ice have been
so thick here that it has even become an ordeal to go to the shops
two or three hundred yards away.' (J. G. Farrell in Earl's Court.) 'The
weather I find loathsome. Winter seems to be stretching out, like the
F. A. [i.e. football] season, till summer is a pale childhood memory. It
depresses me: my sap sinks right down.' (Philip Larkin in Hull.) 'Very
cold, snow everywhere. Too cold to be outside for long. A job keeping
the pigs warm.' (Dennis Dee on his East Riding smallholding.) And
that evening, a combination of the Arctic weather, the go-slow and the
still hugely popular *Sunday Night at the London Palladium* proved all
too much for the electricity grid, leading to a blackout over large parts
of the south of England.[3]

Power cuts or no power cuts, urban redevelopment continued
apace. To dip almost randomly into the press during the first half
of January: for Blackburn, the latest iteration of plans for wholesale central-area redevelopment, to be bounded by a ring road; for
Nechells Green in Birmingham, approaching completion of the first
of the city's five 'neighbourhood centres', dominated by blocks of
flats; for Chelsea, following the demolition of the old barracks, their
newly completed replacement, including two identical 15-storey
point blocks (one per battalion for married soldiers and their families); for the Old Kent Road, Camberwell, plans by the London
County Council (LCC) for eight 19-storey blocks of flats (the central
area to include 'a private garden for old people'); and for the Elephant
and Castle, not only work in progress on a 25-storey block of flats
intended to be London's highest residential building, not only Erno
Goldfinger's recently built Alexander Fleming House (three parallel
blocks of office buildings for the Ministry of Health), and not only

the just finished London College of Printing ('crudely designed,' according to the architectural critic J. M. Richards), but also the destruction of the Trocadero Cinema and the imminent construction of the (in Richards's words) 'somewhat experimental covered shopping centre on the eastern side', in relation to which 'much will depend both on its functional success and its architectural quality'. Or take New Malden, an unremarkable, mainly inter-war outer London suburb between Wimbledon and Kingston. 'It is an exciting scheme which will at last provide a focal point for the town,' declared the *Surrey Comet* about the developers' plans for the station area that Malden Council was about to recommend to central government:

> On the station side of Malden Road there will be an open square with a tower-shaped office block 15 storeys high as well as a four-storey block of shops and offices which will also contain a banqueting hall. On the other side of the road there will be another 15-storey office block with ground-floor shops including a supermarket and suite of offices. In Grafton Road there will be a service garage and multi-storey car park. A similar car park – four storeys high – will be built in Dukes Avenue. These car parks will cater for people working in the new buildings.

Good for local employment and high-street footfall, undeniably; but of the destruction of a perfectly pleasant, intimate area, of the unrivalled concrete ugliness of the car parks, of the harsh and sometimes frightening wind-tunnel effect, and of the general soullessness, not even a hint of anticipation.

The *Surrey Comet*'s blessing appeared on the same day, Saturday the 12th, as the most controversial item yet on *TW3*. 'Very good tonight,' noted Hugh Selbourne, 'but blasphemous effort by David Frost on comparative religion.' This was the programme's 'Consumer Guide to Religion', a Frost monologue based on the premise that some of the world's leading religions could be subjected to a *Which?*-style analysis – whether Judaism ('membership of the oldest club in the world') or the Roman Catholic Church ('the confessional mechanism is standard; it operates as an added safety-factor to correct running mistakes, making Salvation almost foolproof') or Protestantism or Islam or Buddhism, not to mention the secular religion of Communism ('its chief prophet appears to have no background in the industry at all'). Best buy, judged Frost, was the Church of England, 'a jolly good little faith for a very moderate outlay'. Immediate telephonic response to the BBC was a record 246 complaints: 'I do not think it says much for the people who want this form of humour, or those who dispense it,' commented next day the Bishop of Leicester; but among the Viewing Panel, opinion was 'more or less evenly divided' as 'trepidation' and 'glee' cancelled each other out. Overall by this time, *TW3* was being watched by some 15 per cent of the population (as usual, excluding the under-fives), roughly double what it had started with, with the most common demographic among those eight million or so viewers being middle-class men aged 30–49. 'The vast majority have rejoiced in the programme's wit and "hard-hitting" satire,' reckoned audience research soon afterwards about *TW3*'s faithful. 'Bernard Levin [recently criticised by the *Observer*'s Mervyn Jones for the 'sag in tempo' as he 'works up steam for his ponderous tirades'] evokes the most mixed response, but the rest of the team usually comes in for particular praise, as does the production's presentation, and its so appropriate "casual air." '

As it happened, in the same week as the 'Consumer Guide', Levin was asked to contribute to the controversy about *The Black and White Minstrel Show*. Some sixteen and a half million regular viewers of the TV show, the stage version at the Victoria Palace now extended (having already run for three years) to August, the three albums totalling over half a million sales – but Bernard Braden had recently predicted on ITV that sooner or later the BBC would have to drop it 'on the grounds of taste', adding sardonically that 'the George Mitchell Singers will all have to take jobs as bus conductors, underground porters and hospital orderlies'. 'I simply do not see what people criticise,' responded the TV show's producer, George Inns. 'Blacking-up is equivalent to clowns' make-up and it is all surely traditional entertainment. The show is pure fantasy like golliwogs. So what is wrong? It has nothing whatever to do with undermining the Negro. The word "n—" has never been used in the programme.' This was cue for a music magazine to elicit some wider views. In the minority corner was George Melly, comparing the show to 'bear-baiting and throwing people to the lions'; in the majority corner were Acker Bilk ('I can't see anything offensive ... If there are enough people who dislike it, I suggest they all get together and get black people to dress up as whites'), Pete

Murray ('it may well be offensive to coloured people, but I've always regarded it as innocuous'), David Jacobs ('I don't find it in the least distasteful – any criticism of the show is absurd'), and Cleo Laine ('I do not object'). And Levin? 'I have never seen it.'[4]

The day after *TW3*'s take on the life spiritual, and up against *Sunday Night at the London Palladium* as well as a partial blackout, the BBC's Sunday evening play was Evan Jones's written-for-TV *The Madhouse on Castle Street*. It was set in a boarding house, where one of the lodgers (played by David Warner) had locked himself in, declaring he would stay there until he died. The critics were generally positive – 'searching reflections on Life with a big L and eloquent turns of phrase'; 'I thought it claimed the status of a not-too-poor relation to *The Cocktail Party*' – including praise for Philip Saville's 'polished and cunning' production. But viewers as a whole, not so much: an RI of 36, far below the recent average of 64 for televised plays, and 'deadbeat drivel' and 'a true nut house' as typical comments. As for the cast, one critic, the *Listener*'s Derek Hill, had a kindish word for the 'young American folk-singer' who 'sat around playing and singing attractively, if a little incomprehensibly'. Again, the panel was less enamoured. 'The artist who bore the brunt of viewers' displeasure was the guitar-playing "hobo", whose presence, it seemed, was as inexplicable as his song was incomprehensible,' noted audience research, quoting a couple of responses. 'That was a long trip from America for all that boy did – I never heard a word.' And: 'I hope Bob Dylan is on the next plane back to America. And stays there. What a ludicrous waste of money – and irresponsible.' The hobo himself, before he obliged, was interviewed by a music journalist:

London, Dylan thinks, is dead. If he could buy it and take it to Philadelphia, it would 'absorb life from the flow of things there. But it's your land so I can't do anything about it, and I don't believe in coming here and taking what's there, sucking the blood out of your land, so to speak. I've met lots of nice people here but some of them are superior, way out on top, looking down their long noses at you.' 'Patronising?' I suggested. 'That's the word,' said Bob.

'I knew then,' he would recall about his London experience, 'what it is like to be a Negro.'[5]

On Monday the 14th, even as negotiations about British membership of the European Economic Community were restarting in Brussels after the Christmas break, General de Gaulle held a press conference at the Elysée Palace. His dominant theme was 'insular' Britain's unsuitability, for the time being anyway, to join the club. 'She is maritime, she is linked through her exchanges, her markets, her supply lines to the most diverse and often the distant countries; she pursues essentially industrial and commercial activities, and only slightly agricultural ones.' Still more damaging in his eyes was Britain's reluctance to prioritise Europe ('without restriction, without reserve, and in preference to anything else'), meaning that if Britain joined she would be a 'Trojan horse' for America, given the long-standing special relationship. Ultimately, and most strikingly (especially in retrospect), it was on de Gaulle's part a *cultural* judgement about British exceptionalism: 'In her daily life, her habits and traditions are very special and very original.' Even though the signs had been already apparent, and even though negotiations would continue in Brussels for another fortnight, de Gaulle's pronouncements amounted to a bombshell. 'For Mr Macmillan, it looks like the end of the road,' pronounced the *New Statesman* with equal loftiness. 'He had gambled on redeeming everything by a triumphal entry into Europe ...' Even if not literally the end of the road for Macmillan, it was unmistakably a hammer blow for the PM and his party. 'Europe was to be our *deus ex machina*,' Sir Michael Fraser, in charge of the Conservative Party's research department, reflected a year or two later. 'It was to create a new contemporary political argument with insular Socialism; dish the Liberals by stealing their clothes; give us something *new* after 12–13 years; act as a catalyst of modernisation; give us a new place in the international sun. It was Macmillan's ace, and de Gaulle trumped it.'

At this point, according to Gallup, 50 per cent of British voters were in favour of joining the Common Market and 36 per cent were opposed. The Sunday after de Gaulle had spoken, Kingsley Amis – still just about seeing himself as a Labour-voting man of the left, and until recently pro-joining – set out in the *Observer* his case against. Reasons included the fact that 'nastier things, in the political sphere, have happened within living memory in all the countries of the Six, except possibly Luxembourg, than Britain has seen for much longer';

the lack of something tangible in Europe to identify with ('if it is a common human need to belong to some super-family, some large close-knit group, then the nation-State is the only one currently available'); and the language question. 'There is no substitute for the peculiar, immediate intimacy which a common *native* language confers. For this reason, if for no other, British eyes and ears should be turned towards the English-speaking world.' And, 'in her conversations with this world, I hope Britain will retain her British accent'. Amis's final-paragraph, semi-radical flourish – citing Orwell's line about Britain being like a family, but with the wrong members in charge, and wanting something to be done about it – did not fool Larkin. 'Thought I was reading the *Express* this morning for a minute,' he told Monica Jones. 'It would all read more stirringly,' he added about his by now only semi-friend, 'if he weren't off to Majorca & U.S. *sine die*, if I may venture on a foreign tongue.'[6]

*

The four days after the General's *démarche* on Monday the 14th were a cold, dismal and anxious time:

> Street lights failed thanks to the electrician strikers. They ought to be stoned or hunted down like the poor dumb beasts used for blood sports. *(Gladys Langford)*

> Drive impassable. Very few taps or lavatories working. Deluges impending when there is a thaw. *(Evelyn Waugh)*

> Mr Gaitskill [i.e. Hugh Gaitskell] is in hospital & it was announced tonight that his condition is very serious. He has a virus infection & isn't responding to treatment. *(Pat Scott)*

> LONGEST COLD SPELL FOR OVER 70 YEARS. *(Grace Taylor)*

> Mr Gaitskill is now gravely ill & there doesn't seem to be a lot of hope for him, even with all the treatment & help he is having. *(Pat Scott)*

The snow in the streets is solid, packed and very hard and dirty, with rubbish gathering in the gutters. There's no warmth anywhere, only coldness. The tubes are always late and it's chaos. *(Kate Paul, Earl's Court)*

Mr Gaitskill – no improvement. *(Pat Scott)*

Egg output dropping. Van won't start. Ordered a Battery Charger. £4. *(Dennis Dee)*

A blizzard again in the evening. Mr Gaitskill is having an artificial kidney machine to help him but although it is clearing the poison from his blood his heart is very weak. *(Pat Scott)*

The Archers – I feel I'd like to know *why* Ned Larkin is out of the cast – & why Jack Archer changed his wife – a change for the better – pity he couldn't swap precious but moronic girls! ... I began to watch Bonanza. I didn't like it ... Not good news about poor Mr Gaitskill: he seems in a much worse way than reported. *(Nella Last)*

Nine doctors are fighting to save his life. He remains cheerful. *(Judy Haines)*

Felt lousy today – throat still sore. Now a gale blowing. Bill home a bit early again (6.25). Mr Gaitskell died tonight. Bill bought a LARGE JAR OF BOVRIL! *(Grace Taylor)*

The Labour leader was indeed dead – the announcement made on BBC television that Friday evening, the 18th, as Robert Dougall was reading the 9.15 news. 'A lamentable end to a promising career,' reflected Hugh Selbourne, 'and the probable next Prime Minister.' Undone by lupus erythematosus (a rare disease of the immune system), and dying in the Middlesex, he was only 56.[7]

Not everyone grieved. 'Gaitskell died at 9.10 p.m.,' recorded at 11.30 that night an unsentimental Marian Raynham in Surbiton. 'They certainly kept on about him & his bulletins. One would think he was the King. I never thought much of him.' Within Labour, such over the years had been the bitterness between Gaitskellites and Bevanites that the hostile assessment by arch-Bevanite Michael Foot in the next issue of *Tribune* – accusing Gaitskell of lacking the 'supreme quality of political imagination', defined by Foot as 'combined imaginative sympathy, wisdom and power' – would have surprised few; while exactly a week after his death, at the Anarchist Ball at Fulham Town Hall, Diana Melly was shocked to see an anarchist get up on stage and declare, 'The only good politician is a dead one'. These, though, were the outliers. Among diarists, the reactions of Last ('very saddened') and Heap ('never have I been so saddened by the death of a polit-ician') were much more typical; even in the right-wing press, the *Daily Express*'s George Gale wrote of 'Gaitskell's greatness', the *Daily Telegraph* declared that 'there was nothing of envy or malice any-where in his nature'; and *TW3* included a 'particularly appreciated' tribute by Bernard Levin which, said one viewer, was 'much more personal and sincere than that by Mr Macmillan earlier in the evening' and showed, according to a previously anti-Levin viewer, 'a much nicer side to this young man's character.' Inevitably, grief was uncon-fined among the younger Gaitskellites, for all their recent dismay about his opposition to British entry to the Common Market. On the night itself, Anthony Crosland paid a spontaneous, heartfelt tribute on TV: 'He was a leader. You had complete confidence in him. You trusted him. You knew absolutely where you were with him, and of how many other politicians in Britain at the moment could you say the same? Most of the others are dwarfs and pigmies beside him …' 'I find Hugh's death almost totally shattering,' Roy Jenkins (in the States) wrote a few days later to Bill Rodgers (future fellow member of the SDP's 'Gang of Four'). 'Politics apart, I really adored him, and find the thought of coming back to an England without him almost unassimilable. It is rather as though an H-bomb had fallen in one's absence.' And Brian Walden, a lecturer at the newish Keele University but keen to become an MP, took to his bed for five days.[8]

What would be the long-term consequences? 'His mission was to cure the party of ideological self-indulgence, of its ambivalence about power, of speaking to itself instead of to ordinary people with ordinary needs,' reflected Peter Pulzer in 1988 about what he saw as Labour's failure during the intervening 25 years to fulfil Gaitskell's legacy. 'He wanted to make it what it had been once before, from 1940 to 1951: what Willy Brandt [the great German social democratic politician] was to call *politikfähig* – willing and able to accept responsibility.' It was in essence, added Pulzer, 'a vision of how politics should be conducted, a high-minded, rather intellectual, possibly slightly priggish approach in which you said what you meant, came clean with the electorate and worked for clear-cut decisions.' Was Gaitskell, then, the great lost prime minister? Roy Jenkins' answer in 1973, the tenth anniversary, was broadly affirmative:

> He had purpose and direction, courage and humanity. He was a man for raising the sights of politics, he clashed on great issues. He avoided the petty bitterness of personal jealousy. He could raise a banner which men were proud to follow, but he never perverted his leadership ability: it was infused by sense and humour, and by a desire to change the world, not for his own satisfaction, but so that people might more enjoy living in it. He was rarely obsessed either by politics or by himself.

Yet quite apart from matters of policy, of 'right' and 'left', one is tempted to wonder. Jenkins, before his compelling encomium, noted how his hero could 'become too emotionally committed to an over-rational position which, once he had thought it rigorously through, he believed must be the final answer'; Gaitskell himself acknowledged to a political journalist in 1959 that he was 'a rationalist' who did not like to think that people voted as they did 'because something appeals to their subconscious'; and Denis Healey, far from unsympathetic in the main, would recall him as 'hopelessly intellectual in his approach' and cite the famous Dean Rusk aphorism that (in Healey's words) 'the difference between academic life and the government is the difference between arguing to a conclusion and arguing to a decision'.[9] Perhaps ultimately this product of Winchester College was too much of a Wykehamist? But if so, a Wykehamist who believed, like Gladstone, that the highest duty of a politician in a democracy is to educate – rather than bamboozle – the electorate.

In January 1963 itself, amid the shock and the sorrow, what next? 'I find it difficult,' the philosopher Isaiah Berlin wrote on Monday the 21st to an old friend, 'to conceive a government under Mr Brown – still more so under Mr Wilson.' Yet, realistically, that was the choice which Labour MPs now had to make.

Favourite at the outset was probably George Brown (forty-eight), deputy leader and most plausible candidate of the right. The son of a Lambeth lorry driver, his background was authentically working class; his patron and inspiration, as he moved upwards through the Transport and General Workers' Union before becoming MP for Belper in 1945, was the great Ernest Bevin; he had, noted Mollie Panter-Downes just after Gaitskell's death, 'a tough, warm-hearted, and certainly likeable personality' as well as 'a foghorn voice'; while David Marquand would recall 'a marvellous capacity to cut to the heart of a complex problem' and how 'on his day' he 'could carry a Labour audience to heights that none of his contemporaries could match'. But there were two serious problems. The first was that Brown's mixture of egotism, class consciousness and intellectual inferiority complex alienated him from middle-class 'Hampstead' Gaitskellites, some of them snobbish in their own different way; the other problem, more fundamental, was his unpredictability, his capacity for blazing rows and erratic behaviour, especially when fuelled (as was increasingly often the case) by drink. 'Like the immortal Jemima, when he was good he was very, very good, but when he was bad he was horrid,' remarked Healey many years later, and undoubtedly that was true. 'His impetuosity, lack of tact and self-discipline are difficult to reconcile with the role of a party leader,' was how the *Observer* towards the end of January put it more circumspectly. Next day, writing his diary, Macmillan casually dismissed Brown as 'a buffoon'; but, in truth, he was a far more interesting and substantial figure than that.[10]

'Able but dangerous' was Macmillan's verdict on Harold Wilson, the 46-year-old shadow foreign secretary who, via grammar school and a brilliant academic career at Oxford, had transcended his lower-middle-class Huddersfield origins and become in 1947, as President of the Board of Trade, one of the youngest-ever Cabinet ministers. 'He is undoubtedly the superior brain, the sharper, more supple political performer, and the more experienced of the two main contenders,' observed Panter-Downes. 'His House of Commons speeches are often brilliant and cruelly funny.' For Violet Bonham Carter, 'Brown v Wilson' presented 'a harsh choice between an often (though not always) drunken boor – rude, clumsy, devoid of finesse or subtlety, but an honest & loyal man – & a *very* able, clever, experienced but universally distrusted one, of proven disloyalty'. 'One *might* I suppose,' she added, 'have some affection for Brown, one cd. have nothing but distaste, dislike & mistrust for Wilson.' For one Gaitskellite, Anthony Crosland, it was an entirely unpalatable choice between 'a crook and a drunk'.

What had Wilson done to deserve this reputation of being a politician without principle? An explanation would come half a century later from Roy Hattersley, in 1963 not yet an MP but a Sheffield city councillor who, two years earlier, had listened to a senior Labour politician, Richard Crossman, excoriate Wilson at length for his duplicity and treachery. His explanation focuses on two key episodes (from 1954 and 1960 respectively) that loomed large in tribal memory:

> Wilson had endorsed Aneurin Bevan's denunciation of the American-led South East Asia Treaty Organisation, and then – when his hero had resigned from the frontbench in protest – taken the vacant place in the shadow cabinet. He had supported the Nato nuclear alliance, but when Hugh Gaitskell promised to 'fight and fight again' to save Labour from unilateralism, Wilson had challenged him for the leadership on the grounds that party opinion must be respected. There was a rational justification for both decisions. But, in the emotional hothouse of the parliamentary Labour party, reason took second place to visceral loyalty.
>
> The suspicion of dishonesty was increased by Wilson's publicised life-style. No one doubted his intellectual distinction but his professed love of HP Sauce – like his enthusiasm for tinned, rather than smoked, salmon – seemed hard to reconcile with his years of dinners at Oxford high tables.

Hattersley himself came in the fullness of time to realise that Wilson was far from a politician without principle, but that instead he was 'what used to be called "a good Labour man" – instinctively the enemy of privilege and certain that improvement in the lives of the disadvantaged and the dispossessed depended on the success of the Labour party'. Possessing an ultimately moral outlook, owing much to his solid Yorkshire childhood of chapel, football and Boy Scouts, he was someone with little or no interest in ideas for their own sake and was instinctively suspicious of Crosland-style social liberalism.[11] Whether for a country still in most ways deeply conservative, or for a party badly in need of the agile skills of a unifier, it was not necessarily such a poor match.

During the three weeks after Gaitskell's death, things swung decisively Wilson's way. Brown's supporters surrendered to the temptation of strong-arm tactics, often counter-productive; Brown himself in his direct dealings with Labour MPs tended to be too noisy, too aggressive, whereas Wilson stayed calmly and deliberately above the fray, allowing the impression to settle that he was of the centre-left rather than the outright left – an impression strengthened by Brown unwisely accepting publicly that whoever was the loser would serve under the winner; and, most crucially of all, many Gaitskellites found themselves unable in practice to commit to Brown, despite their close agreement on policy matters, and instead looked to an alternative candidate of the right, even if that candidate stood no realistic chance of winning. This was the shadow chancellor, James Callaghan, at fifty older than either Brown or Wilson but possessing less political standing. In effect, the right was now split. Callaghan, much encouraged by Crosland and naturally keen on his own behalf to lay down a marker, announced his candidacy not long before nominations closed at the end of January; the *Guardian* on 1 February gave him the paper's endorsement; and six days later, the result of the first ballot (115 votes for Wilson, 88 for Brown, 41 for Callaghan) made it almost certain that Wilson would win conclusively in the second round. 'What do you think went wrong?' Brown the day after that first ballot asked the well-known right-wing Labour MP Woodrow Wyatt. 'The trouble is, George, you are quite rude to people when you're drunk.' To which Brown riposted: 'What makes them think I'm only rude to them because I'm drunk?'[12]

*

Labour's internal drama was not the only show in town. Back on 19 January, the Beatles mimed to 'Please Please Me' for their *Thank Your Lucky Stars* debut, near the bottom of a bill which included Acker Bilk, Petula Clark, Alma Cogan and Frankie Vaughan; later that Saturday evening, Martin Carthy, Robin Williamson and Bert Jansch all played at the Troubadour in Earl's Court; and in Hull, the poet was preoccupied with his electric blanket. 'I have,' he informed

Monica Jones, 'this sluggish *Dreamland*, 3 heats of wch one uses only the hottest of course, *no* thermostat which means that when you come in at 11.10 pm as I did last night, you can't get it hot for 12 midnight, whereas a thermostat-controlled one [not unsurprisingly, sold out] would do so.' Two days later, the Queen inspected the 100 racing pigeons in her pigeon lofts, recently transferred from Sandringham to the King's Lynn back garden of Leonard Rush, self-employed carpenter and joiner as well as well-known pigeon-fancier; that evening, *Coronation Street*'s black bus conductor Johnny Alexander (played by Thomas Baptiste) made his third and final appearance, losing his job as a result of lies by the racially abusive Len Fairclough; and the Third Programme broadcast Ted Hughes' radio play *Difficulties of a Bridegroom* about the symbolic death of his marriage to Sylvia Plath – a play described by Plath's biographer Heather Clark as 'misogynistic' and 'infamous'. 'The milk was frozen at school and home,' noted on the 22nd a 9-year-old diarist, Diana Rendall, living in Tunbridge Wells; 'longest cold spell since 1947,' recorded Dennis Dee; a third diarist, Hugh Selbourne, mentioned that his son David had been telling him about 'a fellow called Booth in Hay-on-Wye, who has an antiquarian book collection worth inspecting'; and a fourth, Keith Richards, was 'stopped by cops' on his way back to Edith Grove from a misfiring gig in Ealing: 'Frisked. Moaning bastards.' That same Tuesday, members of Bradford City Council had a long and emotive discussion about the future of the Leeds Road Wash-house, the proposed demolition of which – in order to be replaced by a purpose-built launderette – had the previous week provoked some 250 people (almost entirely women) to turn out on a snowy, frosty night in order to object. Arguing strongly for refurbishment, Alderman D. Black, a veteran on the Council, emphasised that 'a wash-house cleaned, boiled and dried clothes perfectly', whereas 'a launderette did not' – that in fact it was 'just the easy way out'. The wash-house (situated in an area full of cramped, back-to-back houses) may have been 'an out-of-date, worn-out building' (as another councillor, not unsympathetic to the protesters, pointed out); but clearly, for the working-class women who for many years had used it, it did the business – especially with its drying racks – and in this respect anyway there was little or no appetite for the age of automation.[13]

'Still no better weather forecast – spent until 11.35 getting coal, trying to light the fire etc – fed up to the teeth,' complained Grace Taylor in Ruislip next day; but for Surbiton and Kingston Folk Club, a notable Wednesday as rapidly rising membership (from 500 to over 1,000 in the past year) saw them have an opening session in their new premises at Surbiton's Assembly Rooms. Thursday evening was round four of Hancock versus *Steptoe*: the former sadly 'at half-cock again' (the critic Mervyn Jones), while in 'Sixty-Five Today' Harold overrode Albert's wish for a few pints in the Skinner's Arms followed by a plate of egg and chips, and instead took him out to an upmarket Chinese restaurant – an unhappy experience for both of them, but rich viewing. On Friday the 25th, Judy Haines's fishmonger in Chingford 'used h.w. bottle between serving', *Melody Maker* pondered the merits ('unbelievably bad, and doesn't even swing') of a new single called 'The Bossa Nova' by 'zany deejay Jimmy Savile', and in Darwen the Beatles were the main attraction at a dance held by the Baptist Youth Club at the town's Co-operative Hall. Greater fame for them next morning, with their first appearance on the Light Programme's *Saturday Club*, main BBC outlet for pop music, and for Haines a satisfactory afternoon making up for a protracted blackout earlier on: 'John and I went to Leytonia, Leyton, to pick up our repaired Pye radio. It sounded fine. They have found nothing wrong with medium wave, but corrected VHF. At Chingford – John's razor at last repaired! Good.' That day saw a widespread thaw, temporary as it turned out, but anyway too late to allow a return to football action. Instead it was the debut of the Pools Panel: five 'experts' (mainly retired players), plus pioneer aviator Lord Brabazon of Tara in the chair, deciding – for the benefit of the nearly seven million people who had sent in their football pools coupons – the hypothetical outcome of the afternoon's notional fixtures. Amid considerable publicity for their endeavours, scepticism was rife. 'I don't think it's at all fair,' Mrs Doris Posner, a London Transport worker living in Stepney, told the *Evening Standard*. 'I want nothing to do with it, and as far as I can see the Pools people are upset at not being able to get their money.' Phillip Borley, a lorry driver from SW9, agreed: 'What rubbish. If the so-called experts are as clever as the Pools promotors pretend, they'd be entering winning lines themselves.' But Major H. H. H. James, a City director living in Woking, took a broader view: 'It's a very odd way to decide who shall be winners, but I will be sending my coupon in.'[14]

Sunday was an important day for Sylvia Plath. *The Bell Jar* had recently appeared (under the pseudonym Victoria Lucas) to generally positive reviews – 'a clever first novel, and first feminine novel I've read in the Salinger mood' was the welcome praise from the *New Statesman*'s Robert Taubman, albeit in a review taking in four other novels, including Harold Robbins's *The Carpetbaggers* – but the key one in her mind was Anthony Burgess's in the *Observer*. Again there was the problem of the five-novels umbrella review, with only a single paragraph devoted to Plath's; and though Burgess was perfectly nice (the characterisation 'economical but full', the style 'careful without being either laboured or pretentious'), what his review was not was exciting. If a disappointment for Plath, perhaps more of a wrench that day for E. P. Thompson, who resigned as chairman of the *New Left Review* editorial board. 'His disagreements with the direction of the review were now substantial' recorded the minutes, and accordingly he 'wished to be free to form new political connections'. A memo to the board soon afterwards from the magazine's editor, the young and ultra-cerebral Perry Anderson, sought to reassure – promising 'a socialist humanism that is politically as well as intellectually relevant' – but the reality was that the *NLR* was unlikely ever to recapture the original British New Left spirit of 1956, a spirit simultaneously empirical, generous and as local as it was international. It was a spirit that may not have been entirely saddened when de Gaulle on Tuesday the 29th gave his expected definitive *Non* to Britain's application to join the Common Market, causing the collapse of the negotiations in Brussels and Edward Heath's dignified return home. How to respond? Obviously with a show of instant defiance; and according to one critic, Cliff Michelmore's *Tonight* 'caught the prevailing mood exactly' with 'a "Damn you, France!" pastiche in Augustan couplets'.[15]

A new, non-Georgian – and definitely anti-Victorian – urban environment continued to take shape. 'The Bull Ring Centre will be the largest and most comprehensive shopping centre under one roof in Europe, with a total floor area of about 23 acres,' trumpeted the *Birmingham Mail* at the end of January, adding that 'the method of construction is reinforced concrete throughout'. Whereas Birmingham's ancient Bull Ring market had what another local paper called soon afterwards 'no clearly defined limits' and thus 'a haphazard, inconsequential charm about it', its multi-storey successor – now under construction, including a massive new Market Hall – was likely to be short on informality, with Laing the developers announcing in February that it was going to recruit its own security force 'for the protection of public and traders'. Some 250 miles north, Glasgow Corporation had approved by this time plans not only for an inner ring road (some of it well above ground level) to encircle the central square mile of the city, but for 29 comprehensive development schemes, mainly within the ring road. Important backing, just before Christmas, had come from Scotland's minister of state, Lord Craigton, declaring war on 'dingy and poky offices, dirty alleys, cramped warehouses and traffic and pedestrians warring to the death'; while outside the ring road, the previous year had already seen an ever-more intensive pace of blocks of high-rise flats going up. Or take Sheffield, to which in mid-February the trade magazine *Site and Plant* devoted a special issue, hard on the heels of an ITV documentary, *A Roof over Our Heads*, 'a heartbreaking tour of the city's worst slums, of the long wait on the housing list, the soot and the overcrowding'. 'Commentator Bill Grundy,' added the magazine, 'had praise for the city's daring housing developments, particularly Park Hill, where community spirit is encouraged. At the conclusion of the programme he predicted: "Even in Sheffield, where a valiant and far-reaching housing programme is being pursued, it seems the position in 1980 will be even worse than it is today."' The need for action was undeniable, but what sort of action? Phyllis Willmott in early February attended an Architectural Association dinner-cum-discussion, including about the right relationship between needs and wants. 'Someone,' she noted, 'said one can't go on asking people what they want – they may want what they don't need.'[16]

The last day of January was 11-plus Thursday for 9,000 schoolchildren in Manchester competing for 1,500 grammar school places ('I have not known of any child in the last five years who should have gone to the grammar and has not,' one primary head in Ancoats reassured parents); an MCC committee meeting at Lord's unanimously confirmed the abolition of amateur status in county cricket and thus the long-overdue end of the invidious two-class system; cheering up the troops after the General's *Non*, the chancellor Reginald

Maudling gave an optimistic TV interview marking him out as a post-Macmillan contender for the top job ('that slow charm and twinkling teddy-bear manner,' thought the *Listener*'s Peter Green, 'mask a formidable mind, which moves like lightning and has little patience with abstractions'); *The Bed Sitting-Room* by Spike Milligan and John Antrobus, a black farce about a group of nuclear survivors in 29 Scum Terrace, Paddington, after World War Three, had its London premiere at the Mermaid – not to the taste ('Goonery Too Extravagant') of the *Daily Telegraph*'s W. A. Darlington, though he found relief 'when the actors paused and the band, the Temperance Seven, took over'; and Vere Hodgson in Church Stretton 'struggled through falling snow' to a performance of *The Messiah* by the Ludlow Choral Society ('it was nice to plod back home and get a cup of hot Bovril!'). For the Beatles, going into February with 'Please Please Me' poised for the big time at no. 16, a memorable two days: an *NME* feature (John remarking that they had aimed this single 'straight at the hit parade'); an unenthusiastic *Daily Mail* piece by the poet Adrian Mitchell, calling it 'almost incoherent except for its solid, battering beat'; an enthusiastic *Evening Standard* profile by Maureen Cleave (John's 'upper lip brutal in a devastating way', George 'handsome, whimsical and untidy', Paul with 'a round baby face', Ringo 'ugly but cute'); and that Saturday evening, the foursome were walking back to happiness at the Gaumont Cinema in Bradford for the start of their first package tour, headlined by sixteen-year-old Helen Shapiro and with comedian Dave Allen as MC.[17]

Earlier on Saturday, as a result of Brabazon publicly declaring that 'all pools are a gamble but a panel picking the results week after week is abusing the situation', the Pools Panel had a new chairman in the person of poet and man-of-letters Sir Alan Herbert. Although described by one paper as 'satirist "A. P. H."', he was not really in the mould of *TW3*, which that evening featured a sketch attaining instant notoriety. 'The Royal Barge is, as it were, sinking,' intoned Frost in a plausible imitation of Richard Dimbleby. 'The sleek, royal-blue hull of the Barge is sliding gracefully, almost regally, beneath the waters of the Pool of London … And now the Queen, smiling radiantly, is swimming for her life. Her Majesty is wearing a silk ensemble in canary yellow.' 'A fairly large number of viewers,' reported BBC audience research, 'disapproved strongly, regarding it as being in very bad taste, almost ruining the whole show. An equal number apparently thought it one of the funniest items and felt David Frost was exactly right as the "Royal Commentator".' A weekend, too, of more signifi-cant protest: for greater use and recognition of the Welsh language, a lengthy sit-down protest on Trefechan Bridge in Aberystwyth, bringing the town to a near-standstill; and for the cause of humanity, albeit uncomfortable for some on the left, Cyril Connolly's laudatory *Sunday Times* review of *One Day in the Life of Ivan Denisovich* ('an astonishing tour de force, as if Orwell's cart-horse Boxer had written *Animal Farm*') marking the arrival in the West of Alexander Solzhenitsyn as a major literary and moral figure.

It was also the weekend of the birth, on Saturday the 2nd in his family's small house in Liverpool, of the future actor Stephen McGann. 'The midwife was called. By the time the woman had struggled on her bicycle through drifted snow her mood was less than charitable. My mum told me that she was grumpy throughout my delivery.' That, though, was a fairly undramatic episode of the Big Freeze, cer-tainly compared to national grid breakdowns, or near-apocalypse for Bradwell nuclear power station in Essex when the cooling system froze, or severe water shortages when frost shattered water mains, or mass evacuation by helicopter of 283 workers from Fylingdales early warning defence station on the North York moors, or cross-Channel ferries having to dodge blocks of ice.[18]

Stoicism, according to Panter-Downes in late January, was gener-ally the order of the day – especially in the countryside, where people 'have dourly got into the rhythm of being snowed in, digging out, and being snowed in again'. 'In 1963, as we trudged through the snow to school in South Wales,' recalled John Harnedy almost half a century later, 'there was no thought of the school closing, or parents keeping us at home for the day. But there was an additional aspect that today would be equally unimaginable – we did so wearing short trousers throughout winter.' The memories of Anton Rippon, working as an 18-year-old at W.H. Smith in Loughborough but still living in Derby, are less benign, especially about the journey back and the change of trains 'at a station in the middle of nowhere, called Trent': 'Night after night I'd find myself sitting shivering on a porter's barrow, with no one for company. I'd arrive back at the Midland station at getting on for 10 p.m., walk home to Gerard Street through the freezing fog, sliding around on icy pavements as I went, and then set off again well before dawn to repeat the whole horrible process. I have never been so utterly miserable in my entire life.' Misery, too, for the quite recently widowed Frances Partridge. 'A new waft of snow, biting cold winds, and slippery pavements,' she recorded at the start of February. 'It is more somehow than one "bargained" for. It has driven me back into the socket of my own resources as a sledgehammer drives a stake into soft earth, and I have an uneasy feeling that the pressure put on those resources is pounding them into grey powdery ash.' As for Sylvia Plath, this cruel winter, involving all sorts of inconveniences and problems in her new London home, was hardly helpful to her state of mind, though she did write admiringly of how more generally in Primrose Hill 'we were all mucking in together, as in the Blitz'. Barbara Pym, still making in early February a few final revisions to her new novel before sending it hopefully to Cape, related to a friend abroad a somehow quintessentially English snatch of conversation. Mrs Parry-Chivers, wife of the vicar of St Lawrence the Martyr, Brondesbury: 'How are you off for candles, dear?' Pym: 'Oh, all right, thank you, and we haven't had any total blackouts yet.' Mrs P-C: 'Well, don't forget there's plenty of candles in the church, dear – I should take some if I were you.'[19]

'The thaw is over, more snow and temperatures low,' recorded Macmillan on Monday the 4th after returning from abroad. 'I'm afraid this is going to put us back a lot. Our affairs are not properly arranged for cold weather, so I fear that there will be further falls in production and employment.' The same day, Macmillan was informed that his secretary of state for war, John ('Jack') Profumo, was likely to be accused soon by the *Sunday Pictorial* (the Sunday version of the *Daily Mirror*) of having badly compromised both himself and national security: specifically, of having had an affair with the model Christine Keeler (who had celebrated her twenty-first birthday on the 2nd), at the very time she had also been having one with a Soviet naval attaché, Yevgeny Ivanov. Profumo had already strenuously denied the allegation to senior colleagues and now continued to do so. As it happened, this Monday also saw further fallout from the long-running Vassall affair. The previous October, John Vassall had been sentenced to eighteen years' imprisonment for having abused his trust as a civil servant by spying for the Soviet Union; soon afterwards, a junior minister, Thomas ('Tam') Galbraith, had resigned following lurid press rumours and innuendos about the nature of his relationship with Vassall. Macmillan had reluctantly set up a tribunal, under Lord Radcliffe, to examine the whole Vassall story; and now, on 4 February, two journalists – the *Daily Mail*'s Brendan Mulholland and the *Daily Sketch*'s Reginald Foster – were given sentences of six months and three months respectively for having refused to disclose to the Radcliffe Tribunal their sources of information. One way and another, the unmistakeable whiff in the air was of puritanical hypocrisy. 'The papers are full of this Vassall enquiry,' Kenneth Williams had noted a few weeks earlier, before going on bitterly enough: 'The reporters giving evidence all talk about homosexual intrigue & hint at dark secrets in high places. All the muck raking is going on. To no advantage. Homosexuality in itself is no vice, a law which makes it one is evil.'[20]

Veronica Lee on Tuesday the 5th arrived in Nottingham for a university interview ('a huge, frightening place', but 'the people I asked were kind and helpful'), Dennis Dee's wife went to Withernsea and 'bought a bath and sink for £4 15s from the knocked down Pre-Fabs', and William Halle took a walk 'in the snow waste of Kensington Gardens': 'The round pond solid with ice with snow on top, making it indistinguishable from land. People walking on it. Some men in Wellingtons were nearby beside a charcoal brazier and a handcart such as one does not often see nowadays.' *Z-Cars* the following evening secured an RI of 71, but also some sharp criticism. 'It is distressing to witness the continued rudeness of the Police, especially Barlow,' declared a bank official. 'Are there no good manners in the North?' And a housewife sincerely hoped that it *was* acting: 'Such a collection of scowling, bawling boors I've never met. Can this be authentic as so many say? Heaven forbid – I would not dare to ask any one of them the time.' Home deliveries mattered more than ever during adverse weather, but in Chingford it proved a distinctly problematic Thursday:

> The baker [noted Haines] flew off this morning, leaving sponge, sponge cakes and large loaf I did not want. I saw van draw up and was waiting, purse in hand, to pay him, as usual, and for a small loaf and plain flour I had mentioned in the week.
>
> Milkman's deputy nearly escaped, too. I went out to him. Mind you roads had been tricky, but it's hardly a day off for milkman if his job is only half done.

The working-class writer Jack Common, originally from the north-east, was living by this time in a cottage in Newport Pagnell. 'Hope you've survived the Great Frost,' he wrote the same day to friends. 'We're still carrying water. This I get mostly from the Tory Club, of which luckily I'm not a member so cannot buy beer, otherwise my pails of water would cost me dear.' Were those Buckinghamshire Conservatives worried by the news this evening that Harold Wilson was now in pole position to lead Labour into the next general election? Wilson himself, the Labour left's only candidate, quietly savoured the moment over supper with a handful of friends. But suddenly he said, invoking the politician who had died in 1960 and symbolised in the eyes of many the party's very soul, 'There is one toast we must drink, to the man who is not here, the man who should have done it, Nye Bevan.'[21]

*

The boy from Huddersfield made good, *Z-Cars*, the Beatles about to explode – this was seemingly the 'northern moment'; and, appropriately enough, Labour's first ballot coincided with the release of Lindsay Anderson's powerful film version of David Storey's 1960 novel, *This Sporting Life*, about a coal miner turned rugby league player. Set in the Yorkshire town of 'Primstone' (Wakefield), Richard Harris played Frank Machin (Arthur Machin in the novel), Rachel Roberts was his widowed landlady, and one critic, Penelope Gilliatt, reckoned she had 'never seen an English picture that gave such expression to the violence and the capacity for pain that there is in the English character'. Of all the British New Wave films – starting with *Room at the Top* in 1959 – it was the most unremittingly bleak, almost impossible to imagine having been made in colour. 'A bleak Northern affair,' Anderson himself called it at the time, 'of powerful, inarticulate emotions frustrated or deformed by puritanism and inhibition. The background rough and hard: no room here for charm or sentimental proletarianism.' No charm, no sentimentality – and, perhaps predictably, it bombed at the box office.

At this point, the part of the north where most national attention was focused was undoubtedly the north-east. 'With each passing week, the news got grimmer,' recalled Harold Evans, then editor of the Darlington-based *Northern Echo*, about the rapidly worsening situation in the course of 1962:

> The last shipbuilding yard on the Tees closed; so did Darlington's railway workshops. We hammered away at the piecemeal, short-term, and incoherent government policies for the region. We emphasized the crucial interaction between the economy and the environment. You couldn't walk in the shadow of the giant pit heaps without wondering why everyone had not fled long ago: skilled labour migrated south all the time. The vile winter of 1962–3, the worst in living memory, exposed the inadequacy of the road system, giant snow-drifts cut off thousands of people for days. The effect on the local economy was devastating; nearly 90,000 were unemployed.

By early 1963, the national unemployment rate was approaching 4 per cent, but more like 7 per cent in the north-east; Macmillan decided to give the pugnacious Tory politician Lord Hailsham particular responsibility for the region; and he duly spent the first week of February on a fact-finding tour. 'Tom Little, our veteran chief reporter in Newcastle, had seen officials come and go and testified that not since Winston Churchill visited the region during the war had a minister of the Crown seemed so seriously possessed by the urgency of his mission,' Evans also remembered. 'Hailsham defined it as "lifting the quality of life at all levels". He was shocked by the dereliction. He drove through South Durham and thought much of it should be pulled down. Lights blazed into the night in his Newcastle headquarters as he worked himself and his team from 8 a.m. into the small hours.' But Hailsham also – foolishly – spent most of his tour wearing a cloth cap, viewed locally as a ridiculous gimmick and even, fairly or unfairly, as condescending; and it prompted the song 'Little Cloth Cap' by the Newcastle folk singer Alex Glasgow, with its opening line, 'If you ever go to Tyneside, let me give you some advice'.

No hint of condescension the following week when the BBC showed Jack Ashley's evocative and moving documentary, *Waiting for Work*, about life in West Hartlepool, where one in nine of the town's working population were signing on twice a week at the Labour Exchange. 'You start to think you're a sort of parasite, living on the backs of your fellow-men,' said one of those unemployed; another sequence showed a couple living on one meal a day and chopping up the furniture for firewood; while another had this response from an unemployed man (suit and tie, early middle age) to Ashley's question about why he didn't go south for work:

Why don't I go down south? Why *should* I go down south? This is my home town, and this is where I'll live, and this is where I've been brought up, and this is where I've been working since I left school, and this is where I'm prepared to stop. The streets of London aren't lined with gold, there's money here when it comes, and I'm going to be prepared to stop here and wait till a job arises. If I did go south, it would mean running two homes, because I wouldn't think of taking the wife and the children down south, because this is their home as well as mine, and this is where the wife's parents is, and my parents, and therefore going down south wouldn't solve anything as far as I'm concerned.

In short, and stated more as plain, incontrovertible fact than as defiance, 'This is where I'm staying.'[22]

Another Tory politician out in the sticks this winter (though in his case his more natural habitat) was Selwyn Lloyd, continuing to investigate the state of party organisation. 'We travelled mostly by train,' recalled Ferdinand Mount, his bagman. At each station, the forewarned stationmaster was there to greet them. 'Sometimes he would be wearing a bowler hat or a buttonhole. At Crewe Junction he was wearing a bowler hat *and* a red carnation. I had been transported into a half-vanished world.' They stayed at hotels which 'hadn't been done up for years' – hotels like the Black Boy at Nottingham, the Blossoms at Chester, the Midland at Manchester, the Adelphi at Liverpool, the Station Hotel at Newcastle – where they dined each evening on 'the prawn cocktail and the tournedos Rossini and the rusty claret and the ancient camembert served from an enormous sideboard carved with motifs of local legends'. Next morning, often in 'the chilly function room' of the town hall, 'every local businessman worth his salt' would turn out to make mainly supportive and respectful noises:

There they were, straight out of the pages of J. B. Priestley, well advanced in middle age for the most part, with waistcoats and watch chains, wool merchants in Bradford, steelmen in Swansea, carpet makers in Kidderminster, fireworks manufacturers in Halifax – these last a couple of brothers or perhaps cousins who wore identical brown suits and who both sported brown bowler hats. And as we drove through the narrow rainswept Pennine valleys and over the Derbyshire Dales and across the Welsh valleys, we caught glimpses of their works, huge grimy piles, some with broken windows and rags stuffed in them but still operational because we could see the lights through the grimy panes, and when we stopped to look at the map we could hear the hum of the machines. They were cheerful and spoke in their local accents, without any attempt to sound posh, but now and then I thought they seemed a bit gloomy underneath, as though they knew their day was going. They were all still making things but their margins were melting like butter in the sun under competition from the Continent and the Far East.

To Mount himself, 'reared on the soft slopes of Salisbury Plain and gently watered at Eton and Oxford', this was 'a new world, more strange and entrancing than my first sight of Italy or Greece'.

Even so, this was not a tour which encompassed many average voters, and certainly not the inhabitants under the sociological microscope in Liverpool University's 'Crown Street' survey. Living alone at 75 Bamber Street, and paying rent of 27s 5d a week, the sixty-six-year-old widower there was just about surviving as a self-employed hawker ('cloths & brushes, from a suitcase') plying his trade 'anywhere, mainly city'. On the day of Gaitskell's death, his visitor made a full inspection of his living conditions and domestic circumstances. Exterior: 'Very dilapidated. Curtains at the windows but dirty. Steps to front door very worn. Terrace house.' Interior: 'Living Room cum bedroom dark and very depressing. Newspaper on table.' Furnishings: 'Very meagre. Only the necessities. Mr B sleeps in his living room as the rest of the house is so damp. It looked like a camp bed with very dirty bedding. A fire was laid but not lighted despite the awful cold.' Pets: 'An Alsatian dog sat on the bed during the interview. Mr B also has two cats which perched on the table and drank out of what appeared to be Mr B's own utensils.' General appearance of household: 'Very depressing house despite its animals.' Finally, Mr B:

Keeps to himself and does not bother with the neighbours. He has relatives in Bootle and Manchester but does not bother with them. He spent Xmas on his own. He does not know when he is too old to look after himself and seems anxious to work as long as possible to keep independent. Says he's very healthy because of his outdoors life. Mr B asked me to look upstairs. The house is in a shocking condition. There is a big hole in the bedroom ceiling where it has rained in. The bathroom is also unusable.[23]

*

The week ending Saturday, 9 February saw not only the Oxford Union vote 1,039 to 427 in favour of admitting female undergraduates as full members ('the start of a new and more progressive era,' according to the male president), but 'Please Please Me' make its big jump in the charts (up to no. 3); while on the 9th itself, the cold as miserable as ever, a '*very* blank' Churchill suddenly came to life during his lunch with Bonham Carter when he called de Gaulle a 'dirty beast', the Irish and English rugby union teams played out an attritional 0–0 draw in Dublin, new temporary chairman of the Pools Panel was former air ace Group Captain Douglas Bader ('I must be frank old chap,' he told a journalist, 'I don't know a thing about soccer – rugby's my game'), and the BBC repeated Ted Hughes's radio play. Main two events on Sunday were the explosion at Liverpool Corporation's reservoir at Tryweryn near Bala in North Wales – a spectacular protest by Welsh nationalists, successfully blowing up a transformer – and Arthur Koestler's accusatory state-of-the-nation piece ('When the Daydreaming had to Stop') in the *Observer*, setting out the facts of economic decline (for instance, France's GNP increasing by 7 per cent in 1962, Britain's by less than 2 per cent), declaring that 'the British working class has become an immensely powerful, non-competitive enclave in our competitive society', and seeing 'the breaking down of anachronistic class barriers' as 'the most urgent task confronting British patriotism':

The first decisive step towards a true democracy is to provide equal educational opportunities for all. This alone would enable the nation to speak the same language – both in the metaphorical and in the literal sense. Does that imply that the public school system ought to go? I am sorry to say it – yes. I am not such a fool or such a barbarian as to underestimate what the system has done to make the nation great. But its function is fulfilled; and unequal educational opportunities, placing privilege before merit, is the original sin which tears a nation apart and delivers it to the rule, not of a meritocracy, but of a mediocracy.

Next day, Monday the 11th, the *Financial Times* celebrated its seventy-fifth birthday on a more hopeful note (welcoming the emergence of a society that would be 'diverse, tolerant, sceptical and curious'), but at 23 Fitzroy Road all hope gone: there that morning, turning on the gas taps of her kitchen oven, Sylvia Plath committed suicide. Her biographer Heather Clark claims, perhaps not implausibly, that the immediate factor pushing her over the edge was her fear of where her doctor, the trusted Dr John Horder, might be about to send her, at a time when she could not afford private treatment: 'In America, free psychiatric care meant substandard care: the dreaded state hospital of her nightmares. Sylvia would have feared "Dickensian" psychiatric treatment in England even more than she had in America, which had a comparatively more progressive approach toward mental illness ...'[24]

A couple of miles away this Monday, in Abbey Road, the Beatles managed in a single 11-hour session, under George Martin's firm but sympathetic stewardship, to record all 14 tracks of their first LP – a marathon session which culminated shortly before midnight with John, his voice ravaged by a heavy cold and bad sore throat (despite the best efforts of Zubes lozenges), somehow managing to belt out an immortal version of 'Twist and Shout'. Next day, taking a continuing break from the package tour, it was nevertheless back on the road, playing first at the Azena Ballroom in Gleadless, Sheffield, and then, later that evening, two half-hour sets at the Astoria Ballroom in Oldham. 'The show was absolute pandemonium,' remembered the Astoria's head of security, George Shore (in charge of nine bouncers and doormen), 'with lots of screaming from the girls, many of whom tried to get as close as possible to the stage, and at one point myself and a colleague had to push them back using a microphone stand as a barrier. At the conclusion of the performance lots of girls did not want to leave, preferring to hang around in the hope of an autograph.

We even tried the fire alarm routine but this met with only limited success.' One of those teenage girls, Susan Fallows (fourteen), would recall how all the screaming made the music almost inaudible; another, Madeleine Everett (sixteen), how Paul vigorously shook his head, especially on 'Please Please Me'; a third, Maureen Jones (sixteen), how people were screaming the names of the group – and how amazed she was to find herself joining in with them.[25]

On Wednesday, the latest Charles Parker radio ballad ('On the Edge', about life as an adolescent) contrasted what he saw as the 'honesty' and 'solid foundations' of folk-song on the one hand, the 'shifting sands of pop-song sycophancy' on the other; photographs appeared of Britain's new tallest building, the Co-operative Insurance Society's 26-storey head office in Manchester; and Jorge Luis Borges arrived to give a lecture, announcing that in England he felt 'a great strength', that 'you are not a people for show' and 'do not need theories, ideologies, revolutions, proclamations'. Next day, the 14th, Wilson comfortably won the second ballot (144 votes to Brown's 103) and became Labour leader. 'A great shot in the arm,' reflected Anthony Wedgwood Benn, 'and opens up all sorts of possibilities for the Party.' Friday's *NME* announced 'to be rich and famous' (John), 'to popularise our sound' (Paul), 'to fulfil all group's hopes' (George) and 'to get to the top' (Ringo) as the respective professional ambitions of the foursome; 'yet another cold spell makes its perishing advent,' noted Anthony Heap on the Saturday; and doing the honours this week for the Pools Panel was Sir Gerald Nabarro, colourful and handlebar-moustached Tory MP. Next day the *Sunday Times* launched its 'Insight' pages, intended to give greater analytical depth to its news coverage, while in the *Observer* a review of Alan Day's *Roads* (the LSE economist wanting a 'hexagonal network of motorways in cities') jostled alongside four of Plath's last poems and a note by Al Alvarez about how in her final burst of creativity she had been 'systematically probing that narrow, violent area between the viable and the impossible, between experience which can be transmuted into poetry and that which is overwhelming', the sum representing 'a totally new breakthrough in modern verse'.[26]

For all too many survivors of two world wars and the inter-war slump, these were weeks as horrible in their way as any in their lifetimes. 'Startling Plight of Old People: Living Alone Without Food

Or Heat' was the headline in the most recent *Surrey Comet*. 'Behind the facades of some of Surbiton's Victorian houses, once so imposing, many old people living alone in single rooms have suffered bitterly,' noted the accompanying report. 'In arctic conditions some have been without heating and even food.' Some indeed, it added, had had to survive solely on their two meals a week from the Red Cross. And it quoted Mrs Eakins, welfare officer of the Red Cross's local division: 'The two sides of Surbiton seem to be prosperity and absolute poverty. So many people go out to work all day, and they don't bother about their next-door neighbours.'

The debating motion on Monday the 18th at Roundhay High School in Leeds was 'This house believes that wedlock is padlock' – overwhelmingly defeated; 'just a little more snow to make sure the records of bad weather are really broken,' noted on Tuesday a wholesale grocery manager, Frederick Ward, living near Bristol; next day, while Pat Scott in Barking took her children to see *Summer Holiday* ('both want to see it again', with Susan crying 'when we came out & all the way down the road'), a letter to an architectural magazine daringly suggested that, when it came to making architectural judgements, 'a housing scheme must ultimately be observed through the eyes of the people who live there, a school through the eyes of the staff and pupils'; 'Halifax football ground open for skating,' recorded Gladys Hague on Thursday; 'sadly more snow again, think it's never going to stop,' complained another Yorkshire diarist, Dennis Dee, on Friday; a junior minister, Charles Fletcher-Cooke, resigned following invidious press attention to the story of a handsome 18-year-old delinquent, Anthony Turner, being arrested for speeding while driving Fletcher-Cooke's Austin Princess without either driving licence or insurance; and 'Please Please Me' was by now perched equal top with Frank Ifield's 'The Wayward Wind'. Over the weekend, with enough football matches being played to mean no Pools Panel, 'lousy songs' was the verdict of Martin Phillips, a grammar schoolboy living in Watford, on the seven British possibles being showcased for the Eurovision Song Contest, with 'Say Wonderful Things' sung by Ronnie Carroll the chosen one; a trip to the Establishment club in Soho got Virginia Ironside, just nineteen, thinking gloomy thoughts ('How awful to marry someone who says "Great!" and "Swinging" now, which as it were is O.K., and to find that when they were forty they were still croaking out "Great" and "Swinging" '); and thirty-odd punters turned up at the Crawdaddy Club in Richmond's Station Hotel to see the Rolling Stones begin their Sunday night residency. Monday was as ever *Panorama*, an item on army recruiting prompting one critic to refer to 'the slippery-eel charm of Mr John Profumo when hard-pressed by his interviewer'; but for another critic, the animal-loving J. R. Ackerley living in Putney, it was humans per se who got him down. 'The poor birds have been absolutely frantic,' he lamented to a friend, 'and how stupid people are about them, throwing out their stale bread into the ice and snow, but in slices or hunks, not troubling to crumble it, so that the famished creatures have not been able to break and eat it.'[27]

London's East End was *en fête* on Tuesday the 26th for the world premiere of Joan Littlewood's locally set film, *Sparrows Can't Sing*. No Princess Margaret, down with flu, but Lord Snowdon showed up; and for the film's co-star, Barbara Windsor, thousands of people lining the Mile End Road, cheering and waving flags, as she arrived at the ABC Cinema in a Rolls-Royce. Afterwards, the cast and guests, including Lord Effingham, repaired to the nearby Kentucky Club (props: Reggie and Ronnie Kray). The film itself was admired from the start for its vivid depiction, impressionistic rather than documentary, of a rapidly changing East End – wastelands where once there had been houses; high-rise blocks of flats starting to take their place; a heavy-handed if well-intentioned bureaucracy in charge of the new dwellings – but critics were sharply divided about its portrait of the almost entirely working-class residents, though all of them seemingly taking for granted the domestic violence played for laughs. The film that 'took the East End out of the zoo', with Cockneys 'neither patronized nor deified', reckoned the *New Statesman*'s John Coleman, and Penelope Gilliatt essentially agreed, calling it 'tough-minded, instinctive and very reviving'; but for the *Listener*'s Eric Rhode ('the inhabitants are fantastics') and the *Sunday Telegraph*'s Philip Oakes, sentimental and even patronising was precisely what *Sparrows* was. 'It is based on the premise that Cockneys are Characters; all Cockneys, that is,' wrote Oakes. 'They are vital, salty, ribald, rowdy: forever gossiping, boozing and brawling. The life force hisses from their loveable pores. This is the brighter side to the myth which insists that all northerners are stolid and dour. As a folk legend it still has currency. The sad thing is that Joan

Littlewood, of all people, should give it her blessing.' Critical unan-
imity, though, on the performances of the two leads, with Coleman
acclaiming as 'stunning' both James Booth as 'the sexy, strutting sailor'
and Windsor as his 'tiny hotsy-totsy missus'.[28] The East End conquered,
the cinematic world, it now seemed, was their oyster.

Both a debut and a swansong the following evening, Wednesday the
27th: the debut was Alf Ramsey's, in charge of the England football
team for the first time, as it crashed 5–2 to France on a frozen, snow-
covered pitch in Paris; the swansong was *Bucknell's House*, thirty-
ninth and final episode of the Ealing-based series in which Barry
Bucknell, in the admiring words of *Radio Times*, 'totally transformed
a dilapidated crumbling Victorian house', converting it into 'two
homes – modern, labour-saving and attractive'. Or as an obituarist
would put it with the benefit of 40 years of hindsight, 'five and a half
million watched such unappealing features as Victorian fireplaces,
panelled doors and cornices give way to plywood, melamine and
headache-inducing wallcoverings'. Later that evening, at 9.30, two
politicians found themselves in direct competition, with Edward
Heath on the Home Service's *Frankly Speaking* and Harold Wilson
on television giving a party political broadcast. Neither performance was an out-and-out triumph – 'Mr Heath, alas, is not one of our
prominent self-revealers', displaying 'extreme caution in framing his
utterances', regretted one critic, while Wilson according to Crossman
was 'verbose and ham-handed' – but for the moment the force was
clearly with the Labour leader. Anthony Howard offered an analysis
of the broadcast that went way beyond presentation:

> The remarks about scientists, the call for a release of national energy,
> even the criticism of the present set-up in the nation's boardrooms
> all appear to have one purpose – to identify the Labour party with
> the next great social break-through in Britain, the moment when
> the employed executives, the white-coat brigade, even the drawing
> board planners decide that if they do the work, they might just as
> well have power and control as well …
>
> In a real sense he is the personal mascot of just the social revolu-
> tion that the Labour party now needs to mobilize. Call it 'the revolt
> of the grammar school,' 'of the technocrats' or anything else – the
> implication remains the same.

A general election was due to be held by autumn 1964 at the latest, and in the course of February the sociologist-cum-market-researcher Mark Abrams conducted a telling survey on the subject of 'Choosing the Next Prime Minister: Ability versus Birth'. It asked 1,433 electors in Tory-held marginals whether their preference would be for a railway porter's son who had got a scholarship to Bristol University before going into the war as a private and being promoted to captain, or instead for a PM from the more familiar mould of Eton, Oxford and the Guards (which just happened to be Macmillan's background). Overall, somewhat over half preferred the former, one-third the latter; and, perhaps counter-intuitively in a society with a still strong deferential streak, the further down the social scale among the respondents, the stronger the preference for ability over birth.[29]

February ended with early salvoes in Edinburgh of the soon-to-be-notorious divorce case of Margaret, Duchess of Argyll; March began with 'Please Please Me' sitting in splendid isolation at the top of the *NME* singles chart; and by Sunday the 3rd, Frances Partridge in Belgravia was detecting 'spring perhaps in the air, the sound of gentle hopeful twittering'. Elsewhere over the weekend, Dee in the East Riding was having trouble with his sows ('one has killed 6, another has only 7 left'); the press was announcing Manchester Corporation's imminent first factory-built block of flats (four 13-storey blocks at working-class, cotton-manufacturing Heywood); Jennie Hill near Winchester was having a good Saturday evening's viewing ('V.G. "Dixon of Dock Green", & also V.G. film "Dangerous Moonlight", with Anton Walbrook. Made me v. sad.'); the first investment column by emerging financial whizz-kid Jim Slater ('Capitalist' as carefully chosen pseudonym) appeared in the *Sunday Telegraph* ('my object is not to try and crystal-gaze into the future, but rather to spot anomalies on the basis of existing information before the market does'); the conscientious Judy Haines 'went for a drive with John at "Pick of Pops" time, 4 o'c, and located Granada, East Ham, scene of Pam's birthday treat with Janice and Sheila' (i.e. to see the Beatles there the following Saturday); and 21-year-old blues and rock fan Martin Easterbrook, having spotted a smallish ad in the musical press for R&B at the Crawdaddy, travelled to Richmond with fellow members of his Wembley-based football team 'to see what it was all about' and was 'immediately mesmerised': 'For the first time I heard and saw an English band not only do incredible versions of standards by blues masters such as Muddy Waters, Jimmy Reed, Bo Diddley, Slim Harpo, but the group were somehow making the sound authentic and perhaps more exciting than the originals. All this from six white guys [Mick, Keith, Brian, Bill, Charlie, plus Ian Stewart on piano] who might have lived next door to me …'[30]

On Monday, the daytime temperature in London was up to 54° Fahrenheit as Heap celebrated ('so cheering!') the capital's 'belated first breath of spring'; on Tuesday, snow tumuli were crumbling in the Essex countryside ('ditches are streams, streams brooks, the brook a river, the river a chain of moving lakes,' recorded the peregrine-watching J. A. Baker); while in Shipley, noted Sidney Jackson, 'a most welcome thaw started in real earnest'. Not so far away, in Keighley, a similarly welcome turn of events for Gladys Hague, who on Wednesday the 6th recorded simply and gratefully that 'today we have seen our lawn first time since Christmas'. After ten weeks of precious memories for children but little cheer for adults – 'people are having to economise on food owing to their heavy fuel bills this winter' was Frederick Ward's explanation the day before for grocery wholesalers like himself 'finding trade very poor' – the Big Freeze was officially over. 'Quite lovely,' reflected Madge Martin in Oxford that Wednesday, 'to be able to stroll, hatless, and in a suit, only, to the hairdresser in the morning.' Though as ever, still quite chilly in Cambridge, where that evening the 22-year-old Kenneth Clarke, known for his views against allowing in women, was elected president of the Cambridge Union. 'The fact that Oxford has admitted them,' he told The Times, 'does not impress me at all.'[31]

5

Closing the Stations with Beautiful Names

On Thursday, 7 March, following the House of Lords ruling against appeal, 'The Silent Men' (the *Mail*'s Mulholland, the *Sketch*'s Foster) were taken to Brixton Prison to begin their sentences – not brilliant timing, as it turned out, for the government to antagonise the whole of Fleet Street. Next day, driving a lime-green Ford Anglia (sign on the roof declaring 'Job No 1'), the Lord Mayor of Liverpool formally opened Ford's Halewood plant, situated on the city's southern out-skirts and manned by deliberately 'green labour', the majority of new recruits being unfamiliar with factory work; the *Salford City Reporter* announced the closure of W. T. Ellison & Co., the country's leading manufacturer of turnstiles; Dennis Dee solemnly recorded 'first day of N.H. [National Hunt] racing since 20th December 1962'; the Martins went to London ('at last a day in town') for their annual inspection of the Ideal Homes Exhibition at Olympia ('very much the same mixture of awful taste in furniture, etc, and fascinating exhibitions'); Jennie Hill watched the new vicar's wife, Mrs Payne, put out 'her first wash' but then fail to retrieve even as it clouded over ('she didn't take the clothes in till after dark, & steadily raining!!'); and *The Birth of a Private Man*, featuring Tony Garnett as a student follower of CND racked by doubts, concluded David Mercer's ambitious, increasingly didactic trilogy (starting over a year earlier with *Where the Difference Begins*) about current and recent socialist generations, with this final slice marking, noted one critic, 'the BBC drama department's first big fling under the management of Mr Sydney Newman', a prize recruit from ITV. Saturday saw the decision to wind up Pegasus, the upstanding amateur football club for Oxbridge graduates which had had its salad days in the early 1950s; that most professional of politicians, Harold Wilson, in his element as he took Granada TV's cameras on a tour of places from his youth, needing little encouragement to bring out from his wallet a cherished photograph of the 1922 Huddersfield Town team; and Pam Haines and friends at East Ham for the start of the Beatles' second package tour (headlined at the start by the American singers Tommy Roe and Chris Montez, but not for long). ' "Fabulous" show,' recorded Judy about the girls' reaction, 'but surprising how "rotten" most of the items were nevertheless! Funny.'[1]

John Bloom on Monday the 11th ran a full-page ad in the *Daily Mirror* for his sparkling new twin tub, Rolls Rapide; that evening a new Cambridge Union poll, initiated by the undergraduate Angus Calder, failed to produce the required two-thirds majority for admitting women; Jennie Hill next day turned her neighbourly gaze on the vicar himself ('out early *pruning* & *what* a mess he made of it ... poor shrubs look terrible!'), before on the Wednesday doing some polishing at the church and meeting his wife ('v. pleasant but working class, alas'); and on Thursday, while proceedings in the Argyll divorce case were adjourned pending judgement (the press not yet allowed to publish juicy details), the *Vauxhall Mirror*'s regular Q&A session with one of the workers in the Luton plant focused this month on Ken Perry from the trim shop:

What luxury item should be a standard fitting in every home? – 36-24-36!

If you won £1,000 what would be your first purchase? – I'd buy some new records to play on the nightshift!

If you could change jobs what would you like to do? – Be a Managing Director – then I could earn as much as my wife seems to think I do now.

What is your most valued possession? – My home.

If TV viewing were restricted to one programme per person? – Sportsview.

Is there any TV personality you positively loathe? – Yes. Malcolm Muggeridge.

Next day, the 15th, the Profumo story at last began to inch into something like mainstream public view. Christine Keeler the day before had failed to appear at the Old Bailey trial of Johnny Edgecombe (about to receive a seven-year sentence for possessing a firearm with intent to endanger life); and this morning, the *Daily Express*'s front page virtually juxtaposed 'WAR MINISTER SHOCK' (a splash story claiming that 'for personal reasons' the Defence Secretary, John Profumo, wanted to resign) with 'VANISHED: Old Bailey witness' (featuring a large photo of Keeler in model pose). 'Woman this time, thank God, not boys,' reflected a weary Macmillan, waiting to see how the story, increasingly the subject of Westminster and clubland gossip, developed. A brief lull on Saturday the 16th – instead, 20-year-old Oxford undergraduate James Higgins (first grammar school boy to become secretary of Christ Church's JCR) sent down for having had a woman in his room overnight; another Oxford undergraduate, the blond-haired Richard Sharp, who was also England's fly half and captain as well as former head boy of Blundell's (definitely not a grammar school), scoring against Scotland, and in front of the PM, the most elegant of all Twickenham tries – before the *News of the World* joined the party with a front-page photo of a smiling, bikini-clad Keeler, whose friends were 'rich, powerful, household names'. Mercer again in the evening, this time with a black farce, *For Tea on Sunday*, receiving an almost unbeatably low RI of 28. 'Another working-class writer falling over himself,' reckoned John Fowles, 'to prove the beastly futility of the middle classes, of money, of intellect; and the excellence of poetry, madness (irrationality) and genius. As if the equation was as simple as that.' Few couples more old-style middle class than the Martins, who in Oxford on Monday went to the town hall for a 'Freedom from Hunger' lunch. 'One gave what an ordinary lunch would cost – or more (we gave £1) – for a cheese roll, with no butter, & a cup of coffee, with *one* lump of sugar,' noted Madge. 'A good idea – but I think we might have had butter!'[2]

Dramatists like Mercer may not have been everyone's cup of tea, but the BBC under Hugh Carleton Greene's adventurous but pragmatic leadership was on a roll: traditionally well behind ITV, it was now level pegging in share of audience (that 88 per cent of the population able and willing to receive television), with each channel during the first quarter of 1963 viewed for 8.6 hours per week per viewer. Of course, most of the old ITV faithfuls still had large core audiences; but in a comparison of the first six weeks of 1963 with the first six weeks of 1961, *The Dickie Henderson Show* (a song-and-dance sitcom) was down from 35 per cent of the total adult population to 24 per cent, the comedy *Bootsie and Snudge* down from 36 to 27, and the game shows *Double Your Money* and *Take Your Pick* down respectively from 36 to 27 and 38 to 31. A report on a typical week, in early-to-mid-March, found the balance of viewing shifting from ITV to BBC 'with each step up the age scale'; viewers generally, but women especially, tending to desert BBC in the second half of the evening; and, entirely predictably, middle-class adults preferring BBC more often than working-class adults did. During the first half of the evening, up to 9 p.m., almost twice as many children watched ITV as BBC; but five BBC programmes primarily for adults did find particular favour with them – *Wagon Train* (Sun, 5.20), *Wells Fargo* (Mon, 6.25), *The Lucy Show* (Mon, 8), *Laramie* (Sat, 7.15) and *The Rag Trade* (Sat, 8), all but one of which were American imports. While as for high-profile programmes this week in direct competition with each other, decisive victories were scored one apiece: over twice as many viewers for ITV's *Coronation Street* as for BBC's *What's My Line?*; but over twice as many viewers for BBC's *Z-Cars* as for ITV's *Rawhide*.

What about the still cosy near-monopoly that was BBC radio? Main attention this spring focused on two programmes. The first was *Today*, with January–March figures revealing that 123 people were listening to the radio between 7 and 9 a.m. for every 100 a year earlier. 'With audiences approaching the two-million mark,' noted audience research, 'this five-days-a-week early morning miscellany [then much shorter than now] has obviously become part of the pattern of their life for many Home Service listeners'; individual reactions included 'not too taxing for the early hour' and 'for variety, entertainment and amusement it is hard to beat', plus a satisfied nod to Jack de Manio's 'dry humour'. The other programme was the Light's long-running weekday afternoon soap, *The Dales* (having been *Mrs Dale's Diary* from January 1948 to February 1962). There, 13 months after its move from a London suburb to a more industrial setting, a further facelift saw the experienced actor Charles Simon take over the role of Dr Jim Dale and the one-time famous film star Jessie Matthews become Mrs Dale, still endlessly fussy and 'rather worried' about her husband. A report a few weeks later found broad approval for the new voices, apart from some older listeners regretting that their 'dear friends' could never be replaced; but an Appreciation Index of only 51, mainly because of 'mixed feelings' about the scripts, including complaints that the serial was 'no longer a family story' and that 'too many "unlikely outsiders" were being introduced, with their "unpleasant quarrels"'. Even so, 'what was seen as a policy of change-over to more dramatic events was widely liked'.[3]

The new pairing was first heard on Monday the 18th, the same day that Madge Martin had her austere lunch – and the day before a remarkable trio of emblematic events.

Starting on this Tuesday with the heavily trailed publication of *Honest to God.* 'I believe we are being called, over the years ahead, to far more than a restating of traditional orthodoxy in modern terms,' declared John Robinson, Bishop of Woolwich, in his preface. 'Indeed, if our defence of the Faith is limited to this, we shall find in all likelihood that we have lost out to all but a tiny religious remnant. A much more radical recasting, I would judge, is demanded, in the process of which the most fundamental categories of our theology – of God, of the supernatural, and of religion itself – must go into the melting.' That melting, over his next 130 or so immediately iconoclastic paperback pages, included a thorough repudiation (drawing heavily on Tillich and Bonhoeffer) of conventional, supernaturalist pictures of a God 'out there'; a discussion of Christ's purpose culminating in the statement that 'the Christian community exists, not to promote a new religion, but simply to be the embodiment of his new being as love'; and, particularly provocative to the moral majority coming from an Anglican bishop who had been a defence witness for Penguin in the 1960 *Lady Chatterley* trial and was known to be opposed to the death penalty and nuclear weapons, a chapter on 'The New Morality' which insisted that 'nothing can of itself always be labelled as "wrong"', specifically citing divorce and pre-marital sex.

On publication day itself, the first print run of 6,000 copies sold out at once, while two days later Robinson was on *This Week* being questioned by Kenneth Harris. The following Sunday, the papers were full of the story: the Bishop of Pontefract calling it a 'dangerous book' likely to 'cause a great deal of pain to faithful Christians who may not possess the bishop's intellectual approach to theological matters'; the conservative commentator T. E. Utley demanding that the Church of England overcome its accustomed horror of heresy-hunting and instead refuse to tolerate 'an Anglican bishop who does not believe in God'; the philosopher A. J. Ayer, on behalf of explicit unbelievers, patronisingly condescending ('it seems to me he is coming round to a position a number of us have held for some time'); and C. S. Lewis, on behalf of lay Christians, barely any less patronising: 'We have long abandoned belief in a God who sits on a throne in a localised heaven. We call that belief anthropomorphism, and it was officially condemned before our time. There is something about this in Gibbon.' None of which condescension did anything to dull the book's impact, and that Sunday the Rev. David Edwards, managing director of the Student Christian Movement (SCM) Press, took the opportunity of preaching a sermon in Westminster Abbey defending Robinson to announce that they had ordered 40,000 more copies from the printers and expected to sell a total of at least 100,000.[4]

Back on Tuesday the 19th, not a great day, though she did not yet know it, for another author, as it happened a very faithful, middle-of-the-road Anglican. 'Dear Miss Pym,' wrote Wren Howard of the publishers Jonathan Cape, 'I feel that I must first warn you that this is a difficult letter to write.' He went on to explain that although he and his colleagues had read 'not without pleasure and interest' the typescript of her novel *An Unsuitable Attachment*, they had 'unanimously reached the sad conclusion that in present conditions we could not sell a sufficient number of copies to cover costs, let alone make any profit'. Those conditions included higher production costs and 'the disappearance of Smith's Circulating Libraries and the reduction in Boots' Libraries', as well as 'the steady decline in the sales of novels in Commonwealth markets'. For Pym herself, whose previous six novels (going back to *Some Tame Gazelle* in 1950) had all been published by Cape, it was a shattering blow when she received Howard's letter the next day; and almost from the start, once she had begun digesting the news, she realised that ultimately it was not really about economics, but instead about how her type of novel no longer chimed with the spirit of the age. 'Like Jane Austen,' one admirer, Alexander McCall Smith, has reflected, 'Pym painted her pictures on a small square of ivory, and covered much the same territory as did her better-known predecessor: the details of smallish lives led in places that could only be in England. Neither used a megaphone; neither said much about the great issues of their time.' 'I was not altogether surprised,' she herself wrote to a sympathetic Philip Larkin some weeks after the rejection letter, 'because several other Cape authors have been similarly treated – I don't know whether you have heard any murmur of the distant rumblings in 30 Bedford Square as the new regime gets to work with axe and bull-dozer, but the Cape list is now certainly different from what it was and naturally one hopes that Jonathan is turning in his grave.'⁵ Running the show there by this time was Tom Maschler: young, dynamic, macho, with literary tastes wholly different from Pym's (and indeed Larkin's); and in spring 1963 he was about to publish *The Collector* – first novel by a very un-Pym-like novelist, the 35-year-old John Fowles, and for which big bucks were already starting to come in from America. Pym herself was about to turn fifty; other publishers also rejected the novel; and, though she gamely kept on writing, these were now the wilderness years.

The Long, Long Trail: Soldiers' Songs of the First World War, a radio documentary by Charles Chilton heard the previous autumn on Armistice Day by Joan Littlewood's partner Gerry Raffles, was the inspiration for the third event this Tuesday – opening night of Theatre Workshop's latest production at Theatre Royal, Stratford, in the East End, barely three weeks after the semi-triumph of *Sparrows*. 'Her work was witty, skilful, vulgar and populist but not patronising,' Richard Eyre would write about Littlewood after her death in 2002. 'In *Oh What a Lovely War* [the comma and exclamation mark came with the 1969 film] she successfully brought together the traditions of popular entertainment – music hall – with the aims of propaganda. It sought to inform and to entertain, and it broke your heart in the pro-cess.' Attacking with equal vigour the generals (above all Haig) and the armaments industry, it had an unashamedly palpable design. 'In 1960, an American military research team fed all the facts of World War One into the computers they use to plan World War Three,' ran an accompanying programme note. 'They reached the conclusion that the 1914–18 war was impossible and couldn't have happened. There could not have been so many blunders nor so many casualties. Will there be a computer left to analyse World War Three?'

Most of the reviews were highly positive, including in the three upmarket Sundays: not only warm words from Harold Hobson ('the piece is stamped with originality, with entertainment and pathos, with the true life of the theatre') and Alan Brien ('a funny, moving and disturbing show'), but Kenneth Tynan declaring that 'when the annals of our theatre in the middle years of the twentieth century come to be written, one name will lead all the rest: that of Joan Littlewood'. There was, of course, the odd grumbler. Bamber Gascoigne's laudatory review in the *Spectator* ('the effect is superbly bitter-sweet') prompted one reader to register that the admittedly 'brilliant' production had 'nauseated' him ('the whole extravaganza is based on a crude and inaccurate "class conflict" interpretation'); while the *Daily Telegraph*'s satirical columnist 'Peter Simple' (Michael Wharton) reflected, in his obstinately conservative way, that Littlewood was being 'very ungrateful' to object so strongly to the First World War, which had been, he argued, the making of her and 'fashionable Left-wing theatre' generally:

> It was the suicidal clash of the great European nations, the death of their best men in millions, which laid the world open to the professional revolutionaries, gave them their first great base of operations in Russia, sapped the self-confidence of European civilisation, prepared the way for the collapse of authority, the decay of patriotism, the rage for meaningless change, the self-hatred and self-mockery of our present society.
>
> Because of the First World War, followed inevitably by the Second, we now have an England where, by the operation of a natural law, Joan Littlewood and her colleagues have become famous, esteemed, and even influential.

'What on earth,' in short, 'is she complaining about?'

Another, more pressing question was whether the production would transfer to a larger, more commercial theatre. 'I hope,' wrote Tynan, 'success will not doom her present troupe to the fate that immobilised its predecessors: indefinite incarceration in the dreaded West End.' Littlewood herself, though, was prepared to take the risk, there was no shortage of willing West End theatres, and the only question was whether Lord Cobbold (former governor of the Bank of England who now as Lord Chamberlain was responsible for theatrical censorship) would be prepared to allow the transfer without insisting on major changes. One evening, possibly more in the course of duty than pleasure, he accompanied Princess Margaret to Stratford. 'What you said here tonight, Miss Littlewood, should have been said a long time ago,' Margaret declared afterwards as she congratulated the cast, before adding, 'Don't you agree, Lord Cobbold?' To which he could only reply, 'Yes, ma'am,' prompting the aside from Littlewood to a nearby cast member, 'That's our permission'.[6]

On Thursday, 21 March, the Profumo story came fully into plain sight. Shortly before midnight – after the Harvey Holford 'Blue Gardenia' murder trial had belatedly opened that morning, and after Tommy Steele had starred in the first night of the Wells-inspired musical *Half a Sixpence* ('cuts a likeable enough figure as the guileless Kipps', thought Heap) – the Labour MP George Wigg, memorably characterised by Julian Critchley as 'a tall, donkey-eared, long-faced, lugubrious old rogue with more chips than Harry Ramsden', stood up in the Commons; there, exercising parliamentary privilege, he challenged the home secretary, Henry Brooke, to deny rumours concerning Keeler (her present whereabouts still a much-publicised mystery) and a government minister. The immediate upshot, in the small hours of the 22nd, was a hastily convened meeting, in which Profumo, given the choice by colleagues of public denial or resignation, chose the former. Some versions of the episode claim that he was still so stupefied – having taken a heavy dose of sleeping pills before being abruptly woken up – that it was not a thought-out decision on his part; but 'at the time,' recalled one of those present, the solicitor-general Peter Rawlinson, 'I did not gain any impression of drowsiness.' Either way, reflects Profumo's son David, 'my father made a very poor decision and stuck to his story'. He returned home to Chester Terrace at about five in the morning, to find a note from his wife, the former film star Valerie Hobson, reassuringly declaring that 'for eight wonderful years I have borne your name – but *never* have I looked forward to doing so as I shall from now on'.

'Minister and Model – Probe Demand by MPs' was the *Mirror*'s headline on Friday, as the debut Beatles album hit the shops and Profumo himself engaged in an adroit rearguard action: first, at 11 a.m. in the Commons, a personal statement, heard in silence, in which he admitted he had been 'on friendly terms' with Keeler but adamantly insisted there had been 'no impropriety whatsoever', so that accordingly 'I shall not hesitate to issue writs for libel and slander if scandalous allegations are made or repeated outside the House';

then in the afternoon, in the company of his wife and the Queen Mother, a visit to the races at Sandown Park; and in the evening, a fundraising dinner-dance at Quaglino's in aid of the Hatch End Conservative Association, as he and Valerie danced to 'The Green Leaves of Summer'. Job apparently done, prompting Macmillan privately to exonerate him ('Profumo has behaved foolishly and indiscreetly, but not wickedly') and the novelist Pamela Hansford Johnson to reflect that 'it is hard to be hounded as that poor chap is being for – if true – something basically *absurd*'. Indeed, that evening's main political storm was at a different dinner-dance, a formal civic one at Bishop's Stortford. Among those seated at top table were the rather pompous local Tory MP, Sir Derek Walker-Smith, and the prospective Labour candidate, a distinctly under-dressed, 27-year-old Dennis Potter. Walker-Smith proposed the first toast, in a way which Potter found intolerably patronising and complacent. 'Dennis said to me, out of the corner of his mouth, "I'm going to have a go at him",' recalled his agent's wife. 'Well, when it was his turn, he took the rise – I can remember him referring to Walker-Smith's "sonorous Victorian tones". At first, this caused quite a bit of laughter at the top table, until everyone saw Walker-Smith's reaction. And then the laughter froze, as if somebody had thrown a switch.' At which point the guests started, in disgust at Potter, to bang their cutlery against their plates, and the evening ended with some verbal but not quite actual fisticuffs.[7]

The papers on Saturday morning seemed to accept Profumo's statement, with the *Guardian* even declaring that it was 'the end of the story, and few, even among Mr Profumo's opponents, will be sorry'. The main exception was the Tory-supporting *Daily Sketch*, which kept up newsroom morale by running the banner headline 'Lucky John Profumo' in apparent connection with his bet on the 10–1 winner of the 3.30 at Sandown Park. As for the diarists, they as ever had other, non-Westminster concerns. 'Bitterly cold, still,' lamented Madge Martin in Oxford. 'Oh, *when* will Spring come? Scarcely a bud, yet.' The middle-aged grocery manager Frederick Ward spent most of the day in his Mangotsfield garden ('the first rows of peas, carrots, and parsnips are in and I am aching from my shoulders downwards'), Veronica Lee in rural Devon noted that 'Oxford won the Boat Race, but Ronnie Carroll didn't win the Eurovision thing', and Judy Haines's daughters went to an evening party. 'So glad girls wore their latest skirts and tops instead of slacks. The trend is slacks, but there's a time and place for them.' Still, Westminster-wise there was always *TW3*, focusing this Saturday night on the unbending and reactionary home secretary. 'This is Your Life – Henry Brooke,' announced Frost, opening something approximating to the famous red book and going through some of Brooke's more illiberal decisions since assuming the office the previous summer, culminating in recently sending back to Nigeria – and, quite likely, execution there – the exiled opposition leader, Chief Anthony Enahoro. The final word went to Brooke himself, as played by Willie Rushton: 'Just shows. If you're Home Secretary you can get away with murder!'

Next morning the *Observer* declared that 'this country would benefit if people made less fuss about the private lives of Ministers', but the not quite so high-minded *News of the World* was unconvinced that the story was dead, revealing that Christine Keeler had been tracked down to Spain; John Fowles took a Sunday walk round Hackney ('extraordinary how absolutely free of the middle-class the area is … all the boys, almost all the boys, in sharp suits …'); next day, the *Liverpool Echo* reported the development and planning committee's approval in principle for Graeme Shankland's latest 'three multi-million pound schemes for a complete and dramatic redevelopment of the greater part of the heart of Liverpool', a report complete with the headline 'MANY BUILDINGS MAY VANISH'; *Panorama* that evening interviewed Wigg, who concentrated on the security aspect (because of Ivanov, and however bogus he himself knew it to be); on Tuesday, the *Liverpool Daily Post* gave its full backing to Shankland ('a breadth of vision and imagination … Liverpool now has the immense opportunity of showing the way to the rest of Britain'), while the *Daily Express* splashed on the Keeler interview ('presumably if I had been fifty-two and a housewife in Surbiton there would have been none of this trouble') given in Madrid; in his trial at Lewes, Harvey Holford reiterated his claim that his wife Christine had provoked him by announcing that she wanted to go and live with John Bloom; Bradford City Council decided against spending £800 on a Sickert painting ('dark and unattractive,' argued Alderman Wilson, adding that 'perhaps Sickert was going through an experimental stage'); and that evening, Stephen Ward – the society osteopath who in 1961 had introduced Keeler to both Profumo and Ivanov, and who had been mentioned by Wigg in his television interview – went to see Wigg at the Commons, with a view to giving him more accurate information about Ivanov. A fateful moment: news of the meeting rapidly leaked to the government, resulting next day in Brooke deciding to launch a thorough police investigation into Ward. Because he wanted to discredit Ward's version of events, should Ward go public? Or even to scare him into silence? At least as possible, suggests Richard Davenport-Hines in his definitive account of the Profumo scandal, is that Brooke was aware of pimping allegations about Ward and felt a strong sense of moral disgust. 'At this time, when a growing number of people feel free to do anything not specifically condemned by Act, we should be slow to loosen up,' he had said soon after becoming home secretary, and he had meant it.[8] But whatever the motives, Ward was now a marked man.

Tony Hancock's increasingly dismal, low-ratings series came to a merciful end on Thursday evening, shortly before the showing on ITV of Harold Pinter's *The Lover*, itself coinciding with Keeler's late-night arrival at London Airport, where she needed a police escort to help her through; Holford next day was found guilty of manslaughter, but not murder, and given a three-year sentence; Henry St John on Saturday, waiting to have his hair cut on Acton High Street, noted the barber telling a customer that 'he thought that in the future Australia might be the only English land left', with 'the folk here speaking "Pakistan and Jamaican"'; and that afternoon at Aintree, the Grand National was won by Ayala, rank outsider owned by a rather different sort of barber, the flamboyant, self-promoting hair stylist 'Teasy Weasy' Raymond. March ended with the Archbishop of Canterbury, Michael Ramsey, appearing on ATV's *About Religion* to speak publicly for the first time about *Honest to God* ('really a caricature of the ordinary Christian's view of God'); Albert Finney, Andy Stewart and the Red Army Choir among those bringing down the curtain on the Glasgow Empire (in its day the great music-hall venue outside London); and Margaret Drabble's first novel, *A Summer Bird-Cage*, receiving praise in all the serious Sundays, including perhaps improbably from Simon Raven ('an intelligent, sly, prying kind of book, bristling with spikey, quasi-moral comments on human foibles and behaviour … she holds one to every word'). But it was another critic, Walter Allen in that week's *New Statesman*, who in one sense anyway really nailed it, acclaiming the 23-year-old for having written something 'very close to the grain of immediate contemporary life'.

So it was: Cadbury's milk chocolate in sixpenny blocks, the letter-punching machine on the railway platform, a formal bouquet of lilies 'with no Constance Spryery about them', the faux working-class clothes of the Wykehamist actor John ('rather fancies himself in jeans, open-necked shirts, and coal-heaver's jackets with leather patches on the back'), Sarah the heroine's glancing observation that 'the days are over, thank God, when a woman justifies her existence by marrying', her disdain at a female friend for wearing a plastic rain-coat, small children still able to play in the street, Sarah being grateful for her wooden-handled cutlery gift being 'not like that deformed and embryonic Swedish stuff', Sarah on a cold day going out with her black stockings on ('which I very rarely do as I resent having "Beatnik" and other insults shouted at me in the street'), her older sister's kitchen 'not in any way modern or streamlined, but very olde-worldy, with pestles and mortars and jars of herbs and copper pans' (giving 'the impression of French country cooking'), a tiny Italian coffee bar in Covent Garden ('Espresso machines and plants in pots, and a menu with Spaghetti Bolognese, 3s 6d; Veal Escalope, 5s 6d; Goulash, 4s 6d') – in short, a particular slice of life from Britain in 1963, by a writer whose ambivalent take on modernity and progress only added to the resonance.[9]

*

'What do you think of Beeching?' Larkin asked Monica Jones on 28 March, the day after the publication of the almost instantly famous/infamous report on the drastic reshaping of Britain's railway system. ' "I remember Adlestrop",' he added, 'takes on a new meaning, not to mention *Sunny Prestatyn*.' Beeching was Dr Richard Beeching: a classic meritocrat (father a journalist, mother a teacher), he was a physicist by training, and had become technical director of ICI (Imperial Chemical Industries) at the age of forty, before being chosen in 1961 by transport secretary Ernest Marples to try to turn round the heavily loss-making British Railways; and when Anthony Sampson (researching *Anatomy of Britain*) interviewed him soon afterwards, he had found him 'one of the most reassuring of all the administrators I talked to', giving 'the impression above all of a striking intellectual honesty'.

A third of the rail network to be closed and ripped up, many lines to remain open for freight only, a total of 2,363 stations and halts to be closed, all of this to happen over a seven-year period – such were his report's main recommendations. That Wednesday morning he gave a press conference at BR's headquarters next to Marylebone station. 'There is a great emotional upsurge every time we propose to close a service,' he observed about closures already announced during his chairmanship, 'but a week afterwards it all dies away. This time it may take a little longer.' The passionately pro-roads Marples took a similar line at his own press conference later in the day, before adding, 'but I think when they get on the bus it will all be forgotten'. That evening, the critic Peter Green watched both men on television. First, on *Tonight* (which included melancholic verses read by Derek Hart beginning 'They're closing the stations with beautiful names,/ Appledore and Chasewater and Saffron Walden'), 'a bland but rebarbative Mr Marples' had 'recourse to pruning metaphors', while when 'pressed by Kenneth Allsop over the dangers of road-congestion if too many passenger lines should go, he promised that the roads would be developed to cope with extra traffic'; later, on *Panorama*'s 'Railway Special', the doctor was 'shunted about between two economists, one telepundit, the Shadow Minister of Labour, the General Secretary of the N.U.R. [Sidney Greene of the National Union of Railwaymen], and thirty twitching commuters without any apparent damage to his massive self-confidence'.[10]

Next morning, 'STORM EXPECTED OVER BEECHING PLAN' was the *Guardian*'s not too controversial prediction, and at a local level that certainly proved the case. To give just two examples. 'SUFFOLK WILL BE HARD HIT UNDER THE BEECHING AXE' immediately proclaimed the *East Anglian Daily Times*, reporting that if the East Suffolk line from Ipswich to Lowestoft and the Stour Valley branch line were both closed, many Suffolk towns would lose their passenger service, including Aldeburgh, Beccles, Leiston and Saxmundham. Protests were rightly anticipated; and so too in west Wales, where the *Cambrian News*'s banner headline said it all:

TERRIBLE! DISTRESSING! CALAMITOUS! TRAGIC! INIQUITOUS! SOUL-LESS! CARMARTHEN LINE TO CLOSE

'The errors in Dr Beeching's grand strategy of railway economy,' declared the Mayor of Lampeter (the Rev. F. J. T. David), 'are illustrated in the proposed closure of the railway link between Carmarthen and Caernarvon. This creation of a strategic gap in communications is an error such as the ancient Romans at their worst, would never have made.' And, deploying an unusual adjective probably somewhere on the damning side of neutral, he added about Beeching: 'His computer imagination ought to be fed with more accurate details and more plentiful information. If the future method of transport is to be by road, then we must move with the times, but where are the roads?'

In fact, during the days and weeks following publication, there were surprisingly many largely positive voices to be heard. In Scotland, for example, despite the devastation likely to be wrought there (almost half the route miles lost, no passenger trains north-east of Aberdeen, or from Edinburgh through the Borders), the chairman of the Scottish Council (Development and Industry), Lord Polwarth, praised Beeching for 'a thorough-going piece of work' that 'one could not help admire', while Glasgow's Lord Provost, Jean Roberts, welcomed the prospect of station closures as a fine opportunity to build car parks. Among supportive letters to the press (itself broadly supportive), three stood out on Saturday the 30th. Peter Crichton of Naunton, Gloucestershire, compared Beeching's appearance on television to that of 'a giant among pygmies', as his 'simple and gentle logic' exposed 'the muddled thinking of London University dons and professional economists'; Patrick Morrison of Campden Hill Towers, W11, hailed the report as 'a splendid boost for the spirit', hopefully marking the moment when 'people are realizing that we are entitled only to what we can afford'; and the tough-minded, unsentimental historian Correlli Barnett (writing from East Carleton, Norfolk) was even more ambitious in his turning-point aspirations:

British Railways in their present state are surely a microcosm of Great Britain herself. That is, the basic shape of deployment is mid-Victorian, although random alteration and modernisation has been going on for years. Equally, British mental attitudes are like those of the pre-Beeching railways – traditional, unquestioning, rather than radical and analytical.

Is it not therefore time – in fact already late by 50 years – for us to do a Beeching on Great Britain as a whole? Should we not coldly analyse every aspect of our national deployment and our national institutions, and then ruthlessly replan to fit our true needs and opportunities?

Among commentators, the *Sunday Times*'s William Rees-Mogg predictably agreed with the plan's main thrust ('No Choice But Beeching'), but less predictable backing came from the north-eastern novelist Sid Chaplin. 'One thing is so obvious that it shrieks,' he wrote in June in his recently started 'Northern Accent' column in the *Guardian*. 'In an age of skyways and motorways the railways have gone on as if things were still the same as in 1900; maintaining thousands of miles of track that were best left to the grass and, in the process, footing a wages bill that of simple necessity cannot be justified. All that Dr Beeching wants to do is to put this right before the entire system becomes a vast and costly museum.'

What about the PM? At least one of his biographers (D. R. Thorpe) is puzzled that Macmillan ('a railway man through and through') gave the report his full backing, as did the government generally. The answer surely lies in the various leaflets that his party rapidly began to distribute, seeking to explain the plan in simple, straightforward language. Each leaflet carried in bold type the slogan 'Conservatives believe in modernizing Britain' – a slogan widely assumed to be the seductive message of the moment. Or as the Duke of Devonshire, Macmillan's nephew as well as ministerial colleague, put it to the annual dinner of the Traders' Road Transport Association, the Beeching report was a 'symbol of the future'; and he anticipated that future historians would look upon it as 'a first clarion call on which we stopped resting on the laurels of the industrial revolution to look forward to new industrial ideals'.[11]

In truth, though, even some of those broadly supportive had their doubts. 'Dr Beeching has shown brilliantly how the railways may be made to pay,' maintained *The Times*, but it still wanted a fuller assessment of 'the social cost' involved; much the same with the

Guardian, finding 'the economic argument' to be 'conclusive', while at the same time uneasy about not only 'the social consequences' but also 'the rather dogmatic thrusting tones of the report – the tones of Dr Beeching himself'; and the *Daily Telegraph* called on Marples to 'ensure that every closed branch line and abandoned stopping service is replaced by adequate road transport'. While among the letter-writing oppositionists, the poet and critic William Empson, living in Sheffield, warned that over-dependence on cars left the country potentially at the mercy of 'suppliers of petrol and rubber' and that therefore 'to destroy thousands of miles of irreplaceable track would be madness'; the cricket writer and commentator John Arlott, living in Alresford, worried about the bad-weather implications ('the closure of many rural lines will throw both the present regular train-travellers, and those who prefer not to hazard their lives, on to roads in their most dangerous state'); and H. B. Paten, living near Peterborough, 'sincerely hoped' that the government would 'insist that the trackways even after the removal of the sleepers and the rails are kept in being if any of the present railway systems are in fact closed', given that 'in 50 years' time those railways may again be wanted'. Particularly cogent were the thoughts of Vere Hodgson. Although relieved that Church Stretton was spared, she saw the bigger picture. 'He has analysed it all out, but what has he done to popularise the railways, to draw people to them, in a word to make them pay!' she wrote to friends in May. 'Not a bit ... He is just closing them, and with the small feeding lines closing how will the big lines get on? I am deeply disturbed ...'

Elsewhere, the rail unions launched a campaign of resistance, John Betjeman spoke up for them, prominent Scots declared that if the closures went ahead this would result in the worst of all Highlands clearances – and Harold Wilson gave an impression of greater commitment to stopping or reversing closures than was actually justified by what he said. For all his 'background knowledge, combined with his debating nimbleness and his flair for phrase,' noted Anthony Howard after the Labour leader had spoken in the Commons debate at the end of April, he did not 'even appear to attempt ... to formulate and forge a coherent and convincing transport policy for the opposition to offer as an alternative to Beeching'. That evening, although the government's theoretical majority of about 100 fell to 75, the Commons approved in principle the Beeching plan; and it was now clear that only a future Labour government could prevent that plan from coming substantially into being.[12]

That did not happen, and in the course of the rest of the decade most but not all of the March 1963 recommendations were duly implemented, resulting in the closure of some 4,000 miles of railways and 2,000 stations. Necessarily brutal surgery? Or horribly and arrogantly short-sighted, knowing the price of everything and the value of nothing?

A notably articulate defender, writing in 1990, was Nicholas Faith, railway enthusiast as well as financial journalist. Beeching, he insisted, was 'the only man since the War with the vision and managerial and intellectual equipment to provide Britain with an efficient railway system attuned to the country's social and economic needs'; Beeching had 'sought to separate the railways' economic and social purposes, with society – the taxpayer – picking up the tab for uneconomic but socially useful services'; and the case underlying his report had been 'simplicity itself':

When he arrived, he was staggered by the complete absence of factual information and financial awareness. On analysis he showed that half BR's 7,000 stations produced a mere two per cent of the traffic. At a time when car ownership was still increasing [in fact doubling in the course of the 1960s, up from almost five million cars to almost ten million cars], it was ridiculous to suppose that the surplus 3,500, many of which had been superfluous even before the advent of the motor car, could be worth preserving. But his restructuring plans to cut at least a third of BR's tracks and stations, designed not as a firm blueprint but as a statement enabling the public interest to be weighed in financial terms (itself then a revolutionary concept), were greeted inevitably with hysterical opposition.

So, too, in more academic vein, the historian Charles Loft. 'While the Beeching Report was clearly an attempt to reduce the railway deficit, it was not a knee-jerk response to it,' he concluded in 2003. 'Based on the idea that nationalised boards should be set clear targets, that the funding of social services should be the responsibility of accountable ministers and that the transport infrastructure should reflect future requirements, the report was a genuine exercise in modernisation, part of Whitehall's coming to terms with the new responsibilities that the creation of a nationalised sector placed upon it.'

Yet all that said, the overall verdict on the Beeching Report and its consequences has undeniably been more negative than positive. 'So many regrettable things – the glut of out-of-town malls, motorway gridlock, road rage, carbon pollution, the crazy commuting endured by millions, the death of the High Street and rural communities – stem from that day in 1963 when this ICI physicist with no railways expertise presented his report,' declared *The Times*'s Richard Morrison in 2013 (the fiftieth anniversary), a baleful list most readers probably agreed with. 'For the residents of Leicester, many of whom did not have motorcars and still relied on public transport, the impact was serious,' more soberly noted Ben Beazley in his 2006 post-war history of the city. 'The loss of services to the east coast constituted a body-blow to the holiday trade in places such as Skegness and Mablethorpe, which relied on a large percentage of their 400,000 yearly visitors arriving by train.'

Two specific surveys of the consequences have stood out. In 1980, ten case studies of closed lines found that 'although travel by train after closure was still possible for journeys on the regional or national network, much less use was made of this network', and that conse-quently British Rail (as it was called from 1965 until privatisation) 'lost patronage on the main network'. Moreover, a high proportion of former users of closed lines had tended to transfer their journeys to car rather than to the replacement bus service. Then in 2018, research by the LSE-based Centre for Economic Performance scrutinised the 20 per cent of places most exposed to rail cuts between the 1950s and the 1980s, with, of course, the 'Beeching Axe' at the epicentre of those cuts. The correlations were striking: markedly less population growth than in those areas of the country least exposed to rail cuts; a brain drain of young and skilled workers; an ageing population. Nor did it help those areas that they had done least well from the motorway expansion programme taking place at the same time as the Beeching cuts. While for the country as a whole, noted the report, the effect was to make many cross-country rail journeys increasingly difficult without going through London, in turn helping to make the economy ever more London-centric. The upshot of all this, concludes one eco-nomic commentator (Larry Elliott), was that once-thriving industrial towns (as opposed to cities) increasingly were – and increasingly felt – left behind. Or in other words, it is not too much of a stretch to view the Beeching Report as a significant contributory factor to the Brexit vote fifty-three years afterwards.

Especially, it is tempting to argue, if one adds in the emotional element. Forty-seven per cent of voters may have told Gallup in May 1963 that Beeching was doing a good job, as opposed to 30 per cent who said he was doing a bad one – but it was that 30 per cent who tended to have the much stronger feelings about railways. 'Letters about the Beeching plan pour in,' noted the *Daily Telegraph* only three days after publication. 'In many there is a note of genuine fear, even of terror. Pictures are drawn of remote districts entirely cut off, as though by some natural calamity, to wither and die.' That spring and summer, Frank Ferneyhaugh, working on the PR side for British Railways, was charged with the task of going around the country and explaining the Beeching Plan:

> In giving many talks, I was surprised at the range of knowledge people had of the railways, their keen interest in steam locomotives and how much the local railway station meant to them. Many quoted youthful anecdotes ('I well remember …') about trains and stations and seemed far more interested in the nostalgic past than in the technological future. The whole subject seemed to be charged with sentiment and emotion of considerable depth …

Nostalgia indeed, an emotion unerringly tapped into by 'Slow Train', the song of lament by Michael Flanders and Donald Swann which formed part of *At the Drop of Another Hat* that autumn and namechecked such doomed stations as Kirby Muxloe, Blandford Forum, Chorlton-cum-Hardy ('no churns, no porter, no cat on a seat'), Dogdyke, Tumby Woodside, Trouble House Halt and Windmill End.

A lost England, condemned to oblivion by a heartless technocrat, abetted over the years by successive generations of short-sighted politicians and faceless, number-crunching bureaucrats: it duly became a settled narrative, but was there also some measure of guilt involved? 'Perhaps,' wondered Ian Jack half a century after Beeching's report, 'he became a bogeyman because at some unconscious level people recognised that he was their fault – if they'd used the railways more, he would not have been necessary. A displaced self-hatred.

Or perhaps it was much simpler – his irritating moustache, his huge salary (over twice that of the PM), his know-it-all style.'[13] Put another way, the forces of modernity, including rapidly expanding car owner-ship, were seemingly irresistible; most people welcomed at least some of that modernity while still feeling uneasy about it; and, whatever the larger rights and wrongs of the issue, those people demonising Beeching often included the most assiduous of car users.

*

April began seismically enough – all protests rejected as *Watch With Mother* moved from early afternoon to 10.45 a.m. so that the BBC's only television channel was available for horseracing – but Monday the 1st was just another day in the tightly structured, prep-and-exam-oriented, grammar-school world of 15-year-old Martin Phillips, son of a civil servant and living in Watford:

> In the morning it was fairly sunny. In English we read whilst Benton marked our books, after learning that on Saturday, our U-16 Cross-Country team had won 14–28. In Maths we continued with the Velocity problems, and had a stinking one set for homework. In German Jack was working, so we all had a pretty good muck-around. In Latin we marked the Homework, & I did not do too badly, for once. Mucked around, playing Kingi at dinnertime, and at 1.30, after going in the Library, went with Al Shepherd to room 11 for the French Exchange meeting [about an Easter holiday trip to France starting later in the week]. In Physics I felt dead tired, so, I felt like doing hardly any work, which is precisely what I did do. In French we had our readers, which we continued reading. Went home with Bernie, and did in fact get home at about 4.55. Watched 'Blue Peter', and 'Bonehead', and then at 6.5 we had tea of kippers etc., and from 6.20 I continued my homework until 5 to 7. Then, until 7.30 I watched 'All Our Yesterdays'. Then I did my French, and at 8.25 I went to bed, & listened to the play [Simon Raven's *The Doomsday School*, set in a prep school], until 10, & then the news. Finally I fell asleep at about 10.50.

'Had breakfast at about 7.45, & I managed to do the Maths before then,' began his entry for Tuesday:

Got down to Bernie's at 8.30. Arrived at school at about 8.50. In English we talked about the sonnets, & that punk Benton asked if we could write one for prep. In Maths we started a new thing, concerning Velocity. In German we had to do a stinking exercise, & Hoppy was absent for History. Did my French, & played Kingi, Waterfall got a real punky shot in at me. Then talked to Al about buying some of his records during Latin as Matty was away, and no master was present. In P.E. we had a game of Pirates, and in French we were asked questions about our reader, which we also continued reading. Went home with Bernie & the Mob, & had my hair cut. Got out of the barbers at 10 to 5, and waited till gone 5 for that whiff Myles to turn up with his records, but the bum did not. Eventually went home, & arrived at 6'ish. Watched 'Tuesday Rendezvous', Tommy Roe & John Leyton being the guests. Then had a meal of fish-cakes, & a hot-cross bun, and cheese & then after all this I had my hair washed. Gran came round & brought me an apple & some sweets, & said goodbye, before I go to France. At the same time (6.30), dad took mum off to her Art class. Finished off my prep and watched 'Compact' with Jo [younger sister], and then the first of a new series on I.T.V., called 'Crane', with Patrick Allen. Then at 9.10 went to bed. At 9.30 till 10 I listened to 'My Word', the Quiz programme. Heard a little of the News. Fell asleep at 10.40.

Kingi as usual during the dinner break on Wednesday. 'Waterfall again got me really hard, but during the morning I had managed to get in some really good pokes at him.'

It was also Budget Day. 'Shambling in in a crumpled blue double-breasted suit,' wrote Anthony Howard about Reginald Maudling, 'he managed somehow to look the least tense man in the place.' A fluent speech followed ('both in manner and matter delighted the Government benches and won reluctant admiration from the Opposition,' noted Macmillan), before that evening his 15-minute explanation to the nation received an RI of 72, 'considerably above the average (62) for Budget broadcasts televised by Chancellors of the Exchequer during the last five years'. 'That Mr Maudling was factual and did not waste time on "political platitudes" was a point noted in his favour,' added the report, 'and agreeable traits such as an absence of "swank" and patronage ("doesn't talk at you") and an easy manner did not go unremarked.'

As for the Budget itself, a further injection of £270 million into the economy, adding to the £150 million since the autumn, confirmed his growth-minded instincts, very welcome to his boss, who would have liked even more. 'Though not nearly so sensational as expected,' observed Anthony Heap, 'Chancellor Maudling's "Expansion" Budget certainly makes some fairly generous cuts in taxation.' Significantly, rather than plumping, as some colleagues wanted, for a 6d or even 9d cut in the standard rate of income tax, Maudling chose instead to increase allowances, thereby particularly benefiting those on low incomes just above the tax threshold – in his biographer's words, 'a redistributive tax cut when there were strong arguments being made for a less egalitarian choice'. That decision reflected his genuinely progressive values, but it also had a more pragmatic motive: in essence, the calculation-cum-hope that, in return for this carefully targeted fiscal give-away, the trade unions would co-operate with his declared ambition to restrain growth in incomes to around 3 per cent, which understandably he saw as vital if his slogan of 'expansion without inflation' was going to be fulfilled. 'This is a bold and imaginative gamble on Mr Maudling's part,' commented the *Sunday Telegraph*'s City editor, Nigel Lawson. 'May it be successful. But I can't help wondering whether it was really wise to stake so much on something so elusive and – in present circumstances – Utopian as an incomes policy.'

Maudling's other potentially exposed flank concerned sterling. Almost from the day the previous summer he had moved into No. 11, he had been under pressure from the Bank of England to recognise that going too hard and too fast for domestic growth was liable to precipitate a balance-of-payments crisis and thereby jeopardise sterling's international position; but Maudling, partly perhaps because of poor personal chemistry between himself and governor Cromer, remained unmoved, instead stating breezily in his Budget speech, 'I absolutely reject the proposition that a vigorous economy and a strong position for sterling are incompatible.' The Bank may have been nationalised in 1946, but relations between it and expansion-minded, democratically elected politicians remained no less potentially charged than back in Montagu Norman's day.[14]

On Friday the 5th – as *Private Eye* had on its cover a photo of Profumo perched on a bed ('And if Private Eye prints a picture of <u>me</u>

on a bed – I'LL SUE THEM!'); as Brigid Brophy warmly reviewed Ian Fleming's *On Her Majesty's Secret Service* ('I can't share the high-brow disapproval of Bond'); and as Frederick Ward in Mangotsfield reflected on council notices proposing to change 'our part of Heath Walk' to Heath Road ('for various reasons, including snobbery, we don't like this and I believe we shall all protest') – the Tory back-bencher Sir Gerald Nabarro mused aloud on *Any Questions?* about the underlying difficulty of building a multi-racial society:

> The problem in Little Rock, Arkansas, or in Notting Hill Gate, or in Rhodesia, is one and the same. And it is a problem which has afflicted the white races and the civilising influences in the world, and the white races are the civilising influences in the world, and has been the same for hundreds of years. It is white versus black. That is all. And if anybody disagrees with that, I say to them straight away, if they are a parent, here in England: would you be happy if your blonde, blue-eyed daughter, aged 21, the apple of her father's eye, came home with a great big buck n— and said: 'I am going to marry this man'? And you had a prospect of some coffee-coloured grandchildren. That is the problem. It is a fundamental problem. It is an ethnic problem …

Controversy and censure immediately followed, but Nabarro remained adamant that despite his choice of words he was devoid of racial prejudice.

Next Monday, Sid Chaplin's first 'Northern Accent' column appeared (arguing that the north could not just rely on help from central government and needed to take a long hard look at its 'amen-ities' and general environment as well as its employment prospects), Henry Brooke as home secretary barred the American comedian Lenny Bruce (landed at London Airport, due to appear for his second season at the Establishment club in Soho) from entering the country ('not in the public interest'), Tony Hancock's *The Punch and Judy Man* went on general release (critical near-unanimity about a promising start before sadly petering out), and Judy Haines and her husband were at the Ambassadors to see Agatha Christie's *The Mousetrap*, by this time running for over ten years. 'Wore black dress for theatre and feathers hat. Since John considered white coat "exotic", I wore green and felt fine.' Profumo on the 11th was awarded damages of £50 from the English distributors of a rumour-repeating Italian magazine; protestors demonstrated on Saturday at the site of RSG-6, a secret – but recently exposed by Nicolas Walter and other Spies for Peace – government headquarters near Reading in the event of nuclear war; the *Sunday Pictorial* marked Easter Sunday by changing its name to the *Sunday Mirror*; Lenny Bruce for the second time in quick succession was deported back to the US, this time after spending the night at Harlington police station near the airport, where waking up late meant he missed the 1s 10d breakfast brought in by a police officer; the Oxford under-graduate Alan Macfarlane was in the Cotswolds ('the mystery of the old fir-forests and the eternal rivers, of the startled rabbits and the whirr of the pheasant,' he wrote to his girlfriend, 'is as real as the brassy women and frightened rabbitty-men who patronise Burford pubs, fear in their eyes, money wedged in their pockets, tiredness on their brows and a Jaguar outside'); and on Easter Monday, as David Frost submitted to Roy Plomley's less than forensic inter-rogation on *Desert Island Discs* (an interview prompting 'frequent accusations' from the listeners' panel of 'conceit, smugness and immaturity' on the castaway's part), Pat Scott's parents 'went up to Whitehall & along Embankment & met up with the [ban-the-bomb] Aldermaston Marchers'. 'They were,' she noted, 'both disgusted with their behaviour but were glad they had had an opportunity to see them for themselves. Mum said they look much worse – dirtier and beatnicy than when on T.V.'[15]

Christine Keeler's friend and rival Mandy Rice-Davies was by now securing her share of national attention, including the *Daily Sketch* on Tuesday the 16th giving the story of her life with Stephen Ward; two days later, the working-class writer Jack Common lamented that he was 'battling on a losing hand', being 'harassed by competition from clever young men new out of the universities their honours thick upon them'; the centenary edition of *Wisden Cricketers' Almanack* appeared on Friday, but not in time to mention C. L. R. James's recently published *Beyond a Boundary*, landmark study and perfect cue for the West Indian tourists about to arrive; Philip French's first *Observer* film review was on Sunday, a dismissive appraisal of *The Small World of Sammy Lee* ('so another opportunity of taking an

honest look at the London underworld is lost: fings are still unfortunately what they used to be in the British cinema'); C. S. Lewis next
day confided his intention to stay silent henceforth about 'Bishop
Robinson's book' ('I should find it hard to write of such a man with
charity, nor do I want to increase his publicity'); and on the evening
of Tuesday the 23rd, as Rice-Davies was being arrested on a minor,
patently trumped-up charge to enable the police to question her about
Ward, Noël Coward was doing his trusted-confidant turn at dinner
with the Queen Mother and her younger daughter. 'Poor Tony and
Princess M. are really upset about their bad Press. I tried to comfort
them as well as I could.'

Wednesday belonged to another couple, Princess Alexandra and
Angus Ogilvy:

Rang Mrs Bradley, who came just before 11.0 to watch on T.V. It
was excellent & Richard Dimbleby compered superbly as usual.
(*Jennie Hill*)

It was glorious – & we sat glued to the set [a friend's], eating vast
amounts of sandwiches … All very moving and beautiful, the bride
simply lovely, the bridegroom a handsome Scot. I always love most
the Windsor-Greys, which draw the glass coach back from the
Abbey. Sturdy and meek, with bowed heads, and tossing manes.
(*Madge Martin*)

How much we enjoyed it. I like her young man very much. A strong
face. Like all Scotsmen he had nothing to apologise for least of all
himself. He looked proud of his beautiful bride, but it was a pride
that had nothing to do with her being a princess. She looked very
beautiful. Nothing modern about her … Some of the side bits of the
commentary were delicious. We saw the Queen tread on the toes of
the King of Norway and give her profuse apologies to him. (*Vere
Hodgson*)

Listened on radio. Very nice. Just as bride was coming down the
aisle, potato man came, had to come then. 4 lbs washed potatoes
6/6. I get them once a fortnight and a few from my green grocer.
I said 'aren't they ever going down in price.' (*Marian Raynham*)

Did ironing and then suggested to Pam we take 38 bus to London and see what we can see ... Heard cheering but, at back of crowd on Duke of York steps, saw nothing but the crowds, boy scouts, policemen and some flags. However, I was happy to be there, and not cadging a view of someone's tele. We enjoyed our lunch at 'The Egg and I,' Haymarket. *(Judy Haines)*

Overall, almost half the entire population watched the wedding, with five out of every six doing so on BBC. 'Complete satisfaction,' recorded BBC's audience research about the RI of 89, 'was the usual reaction to Richard Dimbleby's commentary. Once again viewers felt he had handled a Royal occasion as only he could.'[16]

Thursday saw the publication at last of Radcliffe's report on the Vassall affair, predictably clearing the government, condemning the press, and describing Vassall himself as 'a bit of a miss' and 'addicted to homosexual practices from youth', albeit not obviously detectable as a homosexual; on Friday, as *Double Your Money*'s Hughie Green opened Ilford's first furniture supermarket, Archbishop Ramsey published a 5,000-word booklet seeking a degree of common ground with *Honest to God* ('we need to see if there are some who are helped by thinking not about God above us in heaven, or even God around and near, but about the deep-down meaning of human life in terms of love'), though still critical of Robinson's approach to matters of morality and also insistent, unlike Robinson, about the validity of prayer wholly detached from everyday matters ('there is ever an urgent place for *withdrawal* in the Christian life, far beyond what the new school of thought realises or allows'); Saturday was the start of the cricket season ('gorgeous day – really warm – nice to be back at Lord's,' noted a grateful female diarist in Chelsea); and next day the *Sunday Mirror*, following on from Radcliffe, treated its readers to an exposé on the still indispensable subject of 'How to Spot a Potential Homo'.

April for the Beatles was another relentless, unstoppable, eight-days-a-week sort of month. At Stowe, an audience of public schoolboys, all wearing ties; at Buxton Pavilion Gardens, an 'utterly electric' atmosphere (remembers Rodney Hylton-Potts), 'every boy there wanted to be and sing like a Beatle, every girl wanted to be a Beatles' girl'; at Kilburn's Gaumont State Cinema, 'fantastic, I've never known anything like it,' the verdict of harassed manager Ron

Stoten, who, reported the *Kilburn Times*, 'had spent an exhausting evening trying to hold back hundreds of hysterical teenagers'; at the Co-operative Hall in Middleton, Lancashire, 'raw, almost hysterical enthusiasm hit you in the face as you walked in,' noted a local journalist; on Easter Monday, a performance at the Bridge Hotel in Tenbury Wells, Worcestershire, the day before their BBC TV debut (on *The 625 Show*); three days later, the 18th, not only the emblematic Fiona Adams photo (jumping exuberantly into a bomb crater on the corner of Euston Road and Gower Street), but taking part that evening in *Swinging Sound '63* at the Royal Albert Hall, with George Melly deputed to introduce them ('the moment I went on I was met by a solid wall of screams – in the end I just gestured into the stairwell, mouthed "The Beatles" and walked off'); at the Empire Pool, Wembley, on the afternoon of Sunday the 21st, the penultimate act – second only to Cliff Richard and the Shadows – in a spectacular fourteen-act, 'poll winners' bill put on by the *NME*; and, by the end of the month, poised to go to no. 1 with their new single, 'From Me To You'. The record it displaced was the jaunty 'How Do You Do It?' by Gerry and the Pacemakers: also from Liverpool, also managed by Brian Epstein, also with George Martin as producer. The distinctive sound of Merseybeat had, in other words, arrived nationally and was now at the start of its 1963 moment; but almost as portentous in retrospect were developments in Richmond, Surrey. There, the Beatles went on Easter Sunday to see the Rolling Stones play; a week later, the self-confident 19-year-old publicist Andrew Loog Oldham was in the audience, where he (as David Hepworth nicely puts it) 'smelled oestrogen in the air'; and from early May he was their manager. 'His first move,' recalls Bill Wyman, 'was to smarten us up by making us wear *uniforms*,' as he kitted them out in Carnaby Street with black jeans, black roll-neck sweaters and black Spanish boots with Cuban heels. 'It's obvious to me now,' adds Wyman, 'that in trying to smarten us up, Andrew was attempting to make us look like the Beatles.'[17]

No let-up this spring in the pace of physical change, actual and prospective. 'Euston Station is in chaos,' noted one diarist, an RAF officer, on Maundy Thursday. 'Plans to rebuild the whole area are well under way and it may be beneficial when a new glass and chrome structure replaces Victorian solidity.' Elsewhere in London during

April, the capital's newest and highest-yet skyscraper, the 34-storey Millbank Tower (also known as the Vickers Tower), was opened; so, too, was the crude and brash London Hilton, its design rejected by the London County Council and the Royal Fine Art Commission, but according to one dismayed architectural commentator 'they were both overruled by tasteless, insensitive thugs at the Ministry of Housing', itself reputedly 'browbeaten' by 'the dollar-hungry Board of Trade'; while the day of the royal wedding was the opportunity for Profumo to announce the impending demolition of Knightsbridge Barracks. In Glasgow, the city's status as the high-rise champion of Europe was confirmed by the Corporation's detailed plans for the Cranhill housing scheme with three 19-storey blocks at its centre ('play space for small children will be provided and the whole site will be landscaped'); and in Manchester, the Corporation announced a new policy, to the effect that if slum-clearance tenants twice refused the offer of new housing, then they would be compulsorily evicted. 'There does not seem to be any alternative,' Councillor Wilfred Shaw, chairman of the Housing Committee, explained. 'Refusals are prolonging the clearance of slum areas and we have to take some steps if we are to attain the target figure.' Not many slums in Kingston upon Thames, but instead headlines of 'A Blueprint For Progress: Master Plan Reshapes Town Centre: Expansion The Theme'. 'The plan,' noted the *Surrey Comet*, 'envisages many more shops, all set in traffic-free pedestrian precincts; many more offices in tower blocks, a final total of 10,000 parking spaces; a completely new road system ...' An accompanying editorial did not deny that 'Kingston people' would have 'mixed feelings', especially as 'many houses, shops and other properties, including two cinemas, are scheduled for demolition'; but 'what the critics must remember is the vital necessity to face up to the demands of the times ...'[18]

The exhibition of Kingston's master plan opened on 27 April, the same day that *TW3* ended, after five months, its first series. It had been an eventful last few weeks. On Saturday the 6th, a one-off guest, Frankie Howerd, shamelessly stole the show, a seasoned pro among callow and rather smug university-educated satirists; a week later, a parody of *Honest to God*, turning on God's whereabouts, prompted plenty of protests; and on the 20th the husband of Agnes Burnelle, whose one-woman show at the Duchess Theatre had recently been panned by Bernard Levin in his capacity as the *Daily Mail*'s theatre critic, came out of the audience and, with 'a couple of swinging punches' (Heap's words), knocked him down – just as Levin was 'about to debate with a group of nuclear disarmers'. On the 27th itself, the star was Millicent Martin, not only delivering a monologue as a Keeler-style model ('I was on first-name terms with top politicians and we often had discussions which went on far into the night'), but singing a song knocking *The Black and White Minstrel Show*.

'T.W.T.W.T.W. ended tonight,' noted Veronica Lee. 'I feel quite glad as most of it now is rather boring dirty jokes. Some of it is still amusing and I suppose I shall miss having something to watch on Saturday evenings.' Next day in the Sunday papers, praise from the *Observer* for its bravery ('powerful interests have been affronted – organised religion, royal flummery, the CND leadership, Macmillan, Harold Wilson, Grimond [the Liberal leader Jo Grimond] and the press, including the tough-tactics "populars", have all been sent up with impartiality') contrasted sharply with the *People*'s 'Man of the People' denouncing Frost & co. as 'a bunch of juvenile clowns whose antics would not have got beyond a fifth form rag in any decent grammar school'. The programme's regular viewers among the BBC's Viewing Panel were now asked what they had liked and disliked about the series. 'Those taking part seemed to be enjoying themselves all the time', 'it was informed' and 'it gave me a good laugh' were the three most positive factors, well ahead of 'it took the mickey out of politicians and statesmen'; most negative were 'it was often coarse', 'it joked about religion and sacred things' and 'it was often just silly', all of them ahead of 'it went too far in poking fun'. As for the Panel as a whole, regular viewers awarded *TW3* an overall RI of 83, occasional viewers gave it 49 – and those who had at most only barely watched it settled for a disapprobatory 25.[19]

Destination for Tory ministers this last weekend in April was Chequers, for a summit meeting to attempt to chart the way ahead against a background of a rather stagnant economy, largely disheartening opinion polls, vigorous forty-something opponents in Wilson and Grimond, and the near-septuagenarian Macmillan publicly declaring his intention to lead his party into the next election. The fullest account we have of the proceedings – foreign affairs on Saturday evening, domestic policy on Sunday morning and afternoon – suggests mainly 'shallow and intellectually limited' contributions by those present, with one of the few exceptions being Enoch Powell, increasingly unhappy about the government's attachment to the seemingly invincible verities of economic planning. Another malcontent was the postmaster-general Reginald Bevins, from a working-class Liverpool background. 'Most of them seemed obsessed by material values,' he wrote two years later about his colleagues that Sunday. 'I felt that they did not understand that the younger voters were deserting the Conservative Party because it was so preoccupied with materialism, with easy money, with big business, to the exclusion of what, for want of a better word, I will call idealism. One or two of us said so, but we might have been speaking a foreign language.' But what sort of idealism exactly did he have in mind? The idealism of those Young Conservatives who earlier in the month had assembled in London and enthusiastically applauded those speakers who 'roundly condemned "eyewash" and demanded a complete ban on immigrants'? 'It was in this debate,' continued the report, 'that speaker after speaker fell into the pitfall of the rhetorical question. "Do we ostracise the Irish?" asked one. "Yes," roared the massed delegates. "Are we animals?" pleaded another. From the floor of the house a "Woof, woof" answered him.' At Chequers itself, whatever the intellectual lacunae, the discussions were undoubtedly well oiled. Three bottles of gin, five of whisky, five of white Burgundy (Macon la Chapelle 1957), two of champagne (Perrier Jouet NV), four of sherry, eight of claret (divided between Ch. Latour 1957 and Ch. Haut Bages Liberal 1952), one each of dry martini and brandy (Choice Old Cognac No. 6) – such was the record kept by the formidable housekeeper, Kathleen Hill; and when they all gathered in front of Lord Hailsham's camera for the group photo – twenty-two white men – the mood was palpably relaxed and cheerful, though perhaps slightly tighter smiles from Powell and Profumo than most of the others.

By the early 1960s a key aspect of a more planned approach to the economy was regional aid, which under Treasury pressure had virtually disappeared from the agenda during most of the 1950s. The 1960 Distribution of Industry Act in effect gave the green light to a new era of financial aid from central government seeking to combat areas (such as Scotland and the north-east) of higher-than-average unemployment and lower-than-average growth; major car manufacturers were encouraged that year to announce expansion in the development areas; Macmillan himself was chairing by the end of 1962 an informal steering committee designed to tackle short-term regional unemployment; in January 1963 he of course gave the north-east its own minister in the person of Hailsham; and Maudling's Budget three months later included a special carrot for the development areas, namely a generous tax write-off ('free depreciation') on investment there.

So it was a kind of apotheosis when on 2 May the Duke of Edinburgh formally opened the Linwood plant, 12 miles outside Glasgow, which had been built by Coventry-based Rootes Brothers with generous government subsidy in order to manufacture the Hillman Imp – their belated shot at cracking the highly competitive small-car market, in particular challenging the BMC's Mini. In an industry with distinctly mixed labour relations, might Linwood prove a shining light? 'Working conditions, as one would expect in a new factory, are very good,' wrote a broadly hopeful Kenneth Dodd in next day's *Guardian*:

> Workshops are spacious, trimly painted, well ventilated and heated. Amenities include a welfare block, housing a works surgery, toilets, showers, and locker accommodation for each worker; a self-service works canteen – it really deserves the name 'restaurant'; another for the [office] staff; and what Rootes call a waitress-service dining-room for those who can pay a little more. Perhaps another way of describing executives.

Richard West was unconvinced, with his reportage focusing less on the factory itself than on the newly created town to service it. 'The planning and building of Linwood are at best drab and at worst disgraceful,' he observed soon afterwards in the *Sunday Times*:

> The houses and blocks of flats seem to be scattered about in higgledy-piggledy fashion. The shops, not yet built, have been sited with small thought for convenience. Communal buildings, if any, will have to be built in the old village of Linwood. There is now no possibility of developing any community within each estate. Most scandalous of all, several houses have been built within a few yards of the giant electricity pylons that span the plain.

Asked what he thought of the way Linwood was being built, Geoffrey Rootes replied: 'Perhaps I'd better be careful what I say. But I think some of the architecture could be more imaginative than it is.' He can say *that* again. The houses and blocks of flats in concrete and pebbledash cannot even be called uniform in their ugliness. The juxtaposition of flat and gabled roofs serves to bring out the worst in each style of building. Almost every detail is horrible. The lampposts along the street look like men with broken necks after a hanging ...

West finished by drawing a painful contrast with Wolfsburg, the 'beautifully laid out' Volkswagen town in West Germany. 'Why could the same thing not be done in Scotland? It is no use saying that the Germans are cleverer than we are, or work harder. Perhaps it is just that they care.'[20]

One regional quirk – though perhaps not entirely an outlier – by spring 1963 was the Bristol Omnibus Company's continuing refusal to employ non-white bus crews. 'The advent of coloured crews would mean a gradual falling off of white staff,' the general manager, Ian Patey, told the press at the start of May after three young West Indian men, joining forces with the college-educated youth worker and supply teacher Paul Stephenson (himself of partially West African background), had initiated a bus boycott in the city, inspired by the famous Montgomery Bus Boycott of 1955 in Alabama after Rosa Parks had refused to give up her seat. 'It is true,' Patey continued, 'that London Transport employ a large coloured staff. They even have recruiting offices in Jamaica, and they subsidise the fares to Britain of their new coloured employees. As a result of this, the amount of white labour dwindles steadily on the London Underground. You won't get a white man in London to admit it, but which of them will join a service where they may find themselves working under a coloured foreman?' 'I understand that in London,' he added without providing any evidence, 'coloured men have become arrogant and rude, after they have been employed for some months.'

The upshot after a tense week – involving national attention, strong support for the boycott from local students, and a well-judged intervention by the famous ex-cricketer Sir Learie Constantine, now High Commissioner for Trinidad and Tobago – was an assurance by the company that it would no longer maintain a colour bar. Not everyone emerged with credit that week. In ascending order of discredit: Frank Worrell, captain of the West Indian cricket team which happened to be playing in Bristol during the boycott and who announced that 'we do not want to be involved in political matters'; the Bishop of Bristol, who not only blamed the trouble on 'an unrepresentative' group of West Indians, but failed to state explicitly that the colour bar was wrong and should go; the city's bus drivers and conductors, reported as 'nearly 100 per cent' behind the colour bar and typified by driver Ted Neale's comment that 'as a regular churchman I see few coloured people attending any church, but I see plenty leaving the bingo halls'; the Transport and General Workers' Union (T&G), which over the years had tacitly connived with local colour bars and whose regional secretary, Ron Nethercott, publicly accused Stephenson of being 'irresponsible and dishonest'; and elements of the great British public. 'From all over the country,' the seasoned reporter Claud Cockburn noted soon afterwards, 'fanatical individuals and organisations wrote to trade union and other bodies in Bristol expressing the most violent hatred of coloured people and urging Bristol to "stand firm against the black invasion."' What about the people of Bristol as a whole? The letters page of the local *Evening Post* suggests opinion fairly evenly split, with a reader from The Mall in Clifton – 'This is and always has been a white man's country ...' – neatly countered by one from Tynte Avenue in Hartcliffe: 'Edward Colston, famous in this city, was a slave trader. He split up loved ones. Families never saw one another after he passed their way. We should be grateful that these dark people should work with us.'[21]

The boycott was still in place when, the day after the West Indian fast bowler Charlie Griffith (eight for 23) had routed Gloucestershire, John Fowles had his long-awaited moment in the critical spotlight as the three heavies reviewed *The Collector* (its ultra-symbolic jacket design by Tom Adams featuring a lock of hair, a large old-fashioned key and a butterfly). The *Sunday Telegraph*'s Elizabeth Coxhead acclaimed it as an 'astonishing little novel'; in the *Observer*, a rather less enthusiastic Simon Raven – privately dismissed by Fowles himself as an 'egregiously dilettante "man of letters"' who 'would manage to make *War and Peace* sound rather ordinary' – thought it 'something above the average' with 'some cunningly worked suspense'; and in the *Sunday Times*, a large photo of Fowles accompanied a dream review. 'With John Fowles's first novel,' began Julian Jebb, 'we can welcome a new writer of real originality; a writer who, with a single book, establishes himself as an artist of great imaginative power.' Jebb ended by comparing *The Collector*'s 'authenticity and constructural brilliance' to a thriller by Patrick Hamilton, its 'moral implications' and 'imaginative use of language' to William Golding's *Lord of the Flies*.[22] In short, Maschler's chosen man had arrived.

*

'Max Miller, the great priapic God of Flashness dies,' recorded John Osborne on 8 May after the passing of the last of the great music-hall comedians, in his Brighton home the night before. 'As old John Betjeman says, an English genius as pure gold as Dickens or Shakespeare – or Betjeman come to that. Max's last words: "Oh, Mum," to his wife.' That Wednesday the 'Cheeky Chappie' might have enjoyed the revelations coming out of the Court of Session in Edinburgh, where Lord Wheatley, granting a divorce to the Duke of Argyll on the grounds of his wife's adultery, described the Duchess as 'a completely promiscuous woman whose sexual appetite could only be satisfied with a number of men'. Wheatley himself was teetotal and Jesuit-educated; and his 40,000-word ruling, taking three hours to read out, seemingly delighted in not only the details of the Duchess's diary (probably falsified) suggesting she had committed adultery with 88 men, but also a series of Polaroid snaps showing her pleasuring a man (the instantly infamous 'headless man') whose face was not shown. 'It was,' reflected Ben Macintyre in 2019, 'one of the first public slut-shamings in Britain, a combination of new technology, sweaty public fascination and mass-media hype that is grimly familiar in our own age'; and through the summer of 1963, the case of 'the Dirty Duchess' proved second only to Profumo and friends in its consumption of lurid and speculative tabloid column inches. All a world away from how things were properly done. 'It was very nice of you to come and give me your support at our "Topping Out" party at Lombard Street today,' Edwin MacAlpine (construction magnate, racehorse breeder, about to be knighted) wrote from 80 Park Lane on the 8th to William Donald, deputy chairman of Midland Bank. 'I wonder whether I can

persuade you and your wife to join us in our family box to see the
Oaks at Epsom on the 31st May? We race under extremely comfortable conditions and you will find one or two old friends in the party
as well as meet some new ones.'

Next day, while the Queen opened yet another strikingly tall
building (New Zealand House) in central London, was local
elections day: a strong trend towards Labour and away from the
Tories, with a notable exception in Smethwick, where gangs of children were organised to chant, 'If you want a n— neighbour, vote
Labour'. Henry St John spent the morning of Saturday the 11th in
Soho – 'at one pornographic shop in Little Newport Court, I could
not get near the magazines', he grumbled, being 'hemmed in by men
all wearing raincoats' – while later that day, even as Gyles Brandreth
noted regretfully that 'things are not going well for Mr Macmillan
and people are calling Mr Wilson "the British President Kennedy"'
(in the context of Kennedy and Wilson having their first meeting at
the White House), it was a triumph at Stamford Bridge for a rather
different forty-something operator. This was the 48-year-old Stanley
Matthews, playing for visiting Stoke City. Early on, when Chelsea's
Ron Harris, some thirty years the maestro's junior, bundled into him,
Matthews gave (in Brian Glanville's words) 'a look of shocked displeasure which put him in his place for the rest of the game'; Stoke
won 1–0; and at the end, 'squashed against the big men' in a vast
crowd of more than 66,000, 12-year-old Alan Johnson 'struggled to
get out in one piece'.[23]

Two days later, Lieutenant Richard Vaughan, the last National
Service army officer, arrived home from Germany to be demobilised;
a brace for Jimmy Greaves on Wednesday, as Tottenham Hotspur
demolished Atlético Madrid 5–1 at Rotterdam in the European
Cup Winners' Cup and thereby became the first British club to lift a
European trophy; next day at Holloway Comprehensive School, the
14-year-old Laurence Marks heard a song called 'I Saw Her Standing
There' coming out of the sixth-form common room and was so unable
to get it out of his head ('I really haven't heard anything like it before
and when I go home later I will ask my friends who The Beetles are')
that he started writing a diary; Henry Brooke on the 17th rejected a
suggestion by Conservative councillors at Smethwick that immigrants

unemployed continuously for six months should be sent home; Britain's first National Nature Week began next day, its relevance heightened by Rachel Carson's recent, well-publicised *Silent Spring*; Marks's new favourites began their third package tour that Saturday evening at the Adelphi Cinema in Slough ('we sat nicely in our seats until they came on stage, when we stood and screamed our heads off and could hear hardly anything!' recalls Liz Taylor, then four-teen); a Sunday paper interviewed *Vogue*'s first black model, Althea August from Martinique, who 'finds no prejudice among the English models, but senses a colour bar in the outside London air'; a run on sugar, accompanied by soaring sugar prices, had Judy Haines next day complaining ('may the mice descend upon it') about hoarding; Gladys Hague that evening in Keighley was 'lucky enough to get inside along with 2,000 more' to hear the legendary missionary Gladys Aylward speak, with 'about 1,000 outside the building'; Wednesday the 22nd, with the first full round of the Gillette Cup, marked the coming of one-day cricket, with even E. W. Swanton, unerring voice of the Establishment, happy to accept that 'there is no doubt that the idea has caught on'; and at some point this month, a shift was detected at Aberfan's Tip 7.[24]

Behind the scenes, things were moving on in Profumoland. 'I have placed before the Home Secretary certain facts of the relation-ship between Miss Keeler and Mr Profumo, since it is obvious now that my efforts to conceal these facts in the interests of Mr Profumo and the Government had made it appear that I myself have some-thing to hide – which I do not,' declared Stephen Ward (under inten-sive police investigation and increasingly agitated) on the 21st in a statement to the press. 'The result has been that I have been persecuted in a number of ways, causing damage not only to myself but to my friends and patients – a state of affairs which I propose to tolerate no longer.' Newspapers, however, for the moment declined to publish. Ward had also written to Wilson, who the following evening was due, along with Brown, Callaghan and others, to see senior trade union figures, including Frank Cousins, general secretary of the T&G. 'Harold's information from Dr Ward was that the whole thing as put up by Profumo was untrue etc & that he could no longer keep quiet,' recorded Cousins about the meeting at St Ermin's Hotel:

There were security issues involved in addition to the moral ones. Harold had made this all known to Macmillan but no action had been taken ... Harold made it clear that the press (Political) knew of the new situation but were not prepared to publish anything because (a) They were still scared of the prison sentences which had been imposed on the two journalists in the Vassall case & (b) there had been a *stop* put on this news. George Brown, who did not agree there should be suppression of this news, phoned the Daily Mirror to whom he is a parliamentary & industrial adviser but was told they knew about it but had received instructions from their top man [presumably Cecil King] not to publish anything of this *unless he gave personal instructions*. This did not materialise.

'So much,' commented Cousins, 'for the *freedom* of the *Press*.' And he added that 'we shall see how this develops, particularly as Harold & George feel this is sufficient to cause the fall of the Government.'

Later in the week, the new issue of *Melody Maker* had Graham Nash of the Manchester-based Hollies, first single just out, mulling over the bigger pop scene: 'The trend towards groups from the provinces becoming popular? Yes, it might turn into a bit of a bandwagon.' Saturday the 25th was Cup Final day (a comfortable 3–1 win for Manchester United over Leicester City), later than usual because of the Big Freeze but as ever the *only* domestic match in the entire season going out live on TV. 'On the [Merseyside] estate where I grew up,' recalls Frank Cottrell-Boyce, 'every window would have its curtains half drawn on the day to keep the sun off the screen.' Bonus that afternoon for ITV viewers was a rematch in the burgeoning rivalry between the wrestlers Mick McManus and Jackie ('Mr TV') Pallo, a grudge encounter rooted in genuine animosity. That evening, the Fab Four were at Sheffield City Hall. 'I remember the great Roy Orbison, alone on the stage, dressed all in black, winning over the audience, but nothing prepared me for the uproar when the Beatles appeared,' remembers Brian Clay. 'I spent most of the set watching the people around me in disbelief. I wrote in my diary "like a Roman orgy with screaming twisting girls" ... but I was convinced: they were magic.' Next day, the artist Keith Vaughan took the train from London to Leeds. 'Not a bad looking lot all round,' he scribbled. 'Solid, reliable. No talking. No women or children. Businessmen. Several take saccharin out of pocket phials. Watching the waist line.' Penultimate stop was Wakefield: 'Victorian brickwork. Solid, graceless, but very fine. Design conscious. Colour and shape of each brick carefully considered. Expressive and human. Feeling of the North. Sense of a different country. Crude and dirty but warm-blooded.' On Tuesday in Surbiton, Marian Raynham's daughter went 'to the Mills circus just down the road on the Athelstan recreation ground', her mother adding that 'the well known clown Coco was there walking around giving out road safety leaflets to the children'. And on Wednesday the 29th, two sporting events: in Bratislava, a 4–2 win for Alf Ramsey's England over Czechoslovakia, with Bobby Moore captain for the first time; in Epsom, the Derby, won by the French horse Relko, though the *Daily Express* did its best to restore national morale by claiming vigorously that he had been doped.[25]

'What is privacy?' asked the sociologist Margaret Willis in the *Architects' Journal* on the 29th, the first of a three-part survey which, based on interviews with people living in houses and flats in Greater London, found that whereas middle-class dwellers saw that elusive commodity more in terms of internal privacy – 'a room of one's own' – the strongest desire of working-class dwellers was not to be interfered with. 'I like to be left on my own when I want to,' explained a younger working-class woman, 'and I don't like to be interfered with in any way – people always coming round, although I do like to be friendly with them. No one interferes with me, we don't make a nuisance of ourselves for them to interfere.' 'Nosy parkers', as the phrase went, were a particular working-class bugbear; and, of course, living on an estate full of flats literally heightened the chances of being overlooked in an intrusive way from flats in the block opposite. 'I don't care to be overlooked by anyone,' said an older working-class man. 'Not nice to feel you're overlooked by friends or anyone. All times, I'd like to be absolutely private.' Generally, moreover, noted Willis, 'living in flats seems to increase the opportunities for knowing other people's business'; and in her concluding remarks, she argued that whereas the middle class enjoyed the huge advantage of choosing where they wanted to live, much of the working class was in an insecure, transitional state, 'increasingly being uprooted from established communities where relationships were ready-made, such as the extended family and workmates, and allocated a particular house on a council estate with no choice where neighbours are concerned'. 'As a result,' she went on, 'living near other people, especially in flats where there are larger numbers, often results in a "keep myself to myself" attitude which can lead to loneliness, or a feeling of resignation, "of putting up with it", or an active discontent …'. Willis ended by posing 'the question for the future' – namely, 'whether the community feeling of the slum street or the industrial areas of the north will eventually revive?' – but at this point was reluctant to make a prediction.

Few places in more rapid and total transition than the Gorbals. There in May, for the Light Programme's *Radio Newsreel*, Jameson Clark interviewed a housewife:

Mrs Devine, how long did you live in the old Gorbals, what was known as the slum Gorbals?
Fifty-five years – for forty-seven years in the same house.
What has happened to that house now?
It has been demolished.
How do you feel about the change from the old to the new?
It's really marvellous, but oh, I loved the old – and I loved all the people in the old Gorbals.
And you notice a tremendous difference in your new surroundings?
Yes, there is a big difference. In fact it is a whole new way of life. When you look at it, now, you wonder how you lived in the old conditions so long. But, of course, our hearts were there and we could not leave it.

'Many of the buildings are old and over-crowded, but at one time they were the homes of the well-to-do,' reflected Clark as, from high up in one of the new multi-storey blocks of flats, he looked down on the old Gorbals. 'And you can still see streets of dignified, stone-fronted, four-storeyed terraces, such as you would find in Edinburgh, or indeed the smarter parts of Glasgow itself on the other side of the river. But, in the redevelopment of the Gorbals, even these houses are going. Soon the Gorbals as we used to know it will be no more.'

Probably all change in Kingston, too, where on 30 May a public meeting was held at the Guildhall to discuss the plan for comprehensively redeveloping the town centre. Lionel Hill of East Molesey, in a recently published letter of protest, had called it 'incredibly bad', bearing 'all the stamp of the modern planners' preoccupation with four things: fast motor roads, car parks, shopping centres and office blocks'. 'A town built on this concept,' declared Hill, 'can have no soul, no civic pride and no history.' In another letter, Roy Plomley (born and brought up in Kingston) had flatly called the plan 'ruthless and tasteless … a monument to greed and commercialism'. Now it was the turn of some 400 locals to have their say in person. 'Not one spectator from the floor,' reported the *Surrey Comet*, 'had a good word to say about it, many were strongly critical and, from their applause, most people were right behind the critics.' Crucially, though, the criticism that was aired was seldom broad-based. Instead, 'speaker after speaker rose to bring up points of detail and to ask what the local authorities were doing to safeguard individual interests', often those of shopkeepers simply wanting to carry on their business undisturbed.[26] That was a national pattern, not just in Kingston; and, to use Rousseau's terms, all those expressions of individual will meant that more often than not the general will could safely be ignored.

None of which, to put it mildly, was on the minds of Profumo and the drama's other principals during the closing days of May. By the 29th, after Wilson had been to see Macmillan on what the latter disdainfully called 'a fishing expedition' and had subsequently sent him evidence purporting to show that Ward represented a security risk, the PM had reluctantly agreed to set up an inquiry under the Lord Chancellor, Lord Dilhorne. 'He is clearly not going to leave this alone,' reflected Macmillan next day about the Labour leader. 'He hopes, under pretence of security, to rake up a "sex" scandal, and to involve ministers, and members of "the upper classes" in a tremendous row, wh. will injure the "establishment". Wilson, himself a blackmailing type, is *absolutely* untrustworthy. No one has ever trusted him without being betrayed.' At which point, Parliament broke up for Whitsun; and on Friday the 31st, skipping the debut of ITV's new variety show *Stars and Garters* (Ray Martine as mildly risqué Cockney-Jewish host, Kathy Kirby and Vince Hill as regulars), John and Valerie Profumo caught a flight to Venice for a holiday, staying at the Cipriani.

That evening, over a Bellini cocktail, the minister confessed to his wife about the true nature of his relationship with Keeler; early on Saturday morning, the message came from London – accounts differ as to whether from Dilhorne himself or via the chief whip, Martin

Redmayne – that his game was up and he had to return at once to face the music; the opening this weekend of *British Painting in the Sixties* (older artists displayed at the Tate, younger artists at the Whitechapel) was the peg for a major feature in the *Sunday Times Colour Magazine* (text by David Sylvester, photographs by Snowdon), including a walk-on part for David Hockney ('as bright and stylish a Pop artist as there is') in a gold lamé jacket; and on a warm Whit Monday, as Pope John XXIII slowly died and the *Golden Arrow* brought the Profumos back to town, a bus conductor called Austin Finn noted 'a quiet day indeed' on the 84 'with most people and cars out of London', the annual procession of churches through the centre of Manchester saw a significantly reduced turnout (partly because of two long-established congregations having been virtually wiped out by slum-clearance programmes), the Beatles played at the Woolwich Granada ('lots of people,' recalled Ann Finch, 'were throwing jelly babies at the stage because one of the Beatles [George] had said it was his favourite sweet'), and returning motorists from seaside resorts wondered about the efficiency of the free market. 'Tea is the traditional British beverage, but why is it that one can hardly ever get a "cuppa" in an evening when travelling on the road?' asked 'Thirsty' of Beeston in Notts. 'One can get ice cream, soft drinks, beer, etc. But to ask for a "cuppa" is like asking for gold after 6 p.m.'[27]

Next day, as Profumo confessed to colleagues that he had lied in his personal statement to the Commons and now accordingly had no alternative but to step down as both minister and MP – 'I have been guilty of a grave misdemeanour … I cannot tell you of my deep remorse for the embarrassment I have caused,' he wrote to Macmillan – the Light Programme ran at teatime the first of a weekly series, *Pop Go the Beatles*, with plenty of humorous chat as well as music (including 'The Hippy Hippy Shake'). At the Old Bailey on Wednesday the 5th, where 'Lucky' Gordon was accused of having in April attacked Christine Keeler with intent to do her grievous bodily harm, witness of the day was Keeler herself, arriving in a chauffeur-driven Rolls-Royce and emphatically denying that she had ever been pregnant by him; elsewhere in London, the Profumos' 7-year-old son David was whisked away from school (Hill House, inevitably), as the family in their ice-blue Jag fled to friends in the country, ahead of the resignation letter going public that evening; and in Doncaster, an invited audience of 350 watched Douglas Bader roll the inaugural 'golden ball' down one of the twenty-six polished lanes to mark the opening of the Excel Bowl, another step in the rapid rise of tenpin bowling, a pastime now with over a quarter of a million regular players.

'We settled to The Archers & then Coronation Street,' faithfully recorded Nella Last in Barrow:

> Tonight was impossible on B.B.C. [i.e. poor reception] but Z Cars just playing enough for my husband to watch. I felt my head bad enough without further eye strain. I'd have liked to see [on ITV] The Runaway Bus [a 1954 comedy-thriller starring Frankie Howerd, Margaret Rutherford and Petula Clark], but it was from 8–9, then after the 9 o'clock news on till 9.45. The mood my husband was in, gave me a *'what's the use'* feeling. Sport came on [on the BBC] at 8.45, & I said as I began to set the breakfast table for morning, 'let's see if there is anything different on the news' [i.e. on ITV] – & heartily wished I hadn't, when the really shattering news about the Profumo-Keeler case came on. I felt a sadness as I came to bed. Such a *fool* of a man – he looks one anyway, but for a man of his breed & education to feel so 'above' the law & conduct of ordinary respon-sible people, was tragi-comic ... Poor Valerie Hobson – so gay & charming, few men would have strayed – especially to a little alley cat, who seemed to have preferred coloured men ...

'I don't feel sorry for him because he was able to be Christine Keeler's sex partner, and that is a fantasy I have every time I see a photograph of her,' was the understandably different reaction of another diarist, 14-year-old schoolboy Laurence Marks. But in Oxford the news apparently passed Madge Martin by. Instead, her preoccupation that night was 'a violent thunderstorm', coming first in the late evening and again in the small hours. Twice, in a state of some terror, she had to take refuge on her cellar steps; but with 'book, hot bottles and rug', plus 'ear-plugs which help a lot', she managed to get through.[28]

6

One Vast Leer

From Thursday, 6 June, the day after Profumo's resignation, it was open season, as the popular press gave blanket coverage – sometimes factual, very often less so – to the story.

Chapman Pincher in that day's *Express* revealed what Profumo had said to him shortly after the March denial ('who is going to believe Christine Keeler's word against mine?'), but it was the *Mirror* which stole much of the thunder with its front-page editorial, headed 'The Big Lie':

> God knows, he was never a good Minister: it seems now that he is not a very important man. But there is guilt in many a human heart, and skeletons in many cupboards.
> The question is:
> **What the hell is going on in this country?**
> All power corrupts – and the Tories have been in power for nearly twelve years. They are certainly enduring their full quota of fallen idols, whited sepulchres, and off-white morals.

That afternoon, Selwyn Lloyd's report on Conservative Party organisation was published and barely noticed; that evening, BBC TV's *Gallery* had a discussion on 'Politics, Morals, and Morale' which included the *Sunday Telegraph*'s Peregrine Worsthorne. 'Worsthorne suggested,' noted a watching Anthony Burgess, 'that private moral slackness was an aspect of that insouciance which comes from a party's being long in office, and perhaps could not be separated from a deeper, more dangerous slackness. The call-girl cult could be seen as

an unworthy flower of a suspect and lopsided affluence.' Surprisingly
few diarists had anything to say at this stage about the turn of events,
but an exception was 18-year-old Veronica Lee. 'I feel rather sorry
for Mr Profumo but the Keeler sounds foul,' she reflected. 'What
aggravates me is that the press have known for ages but aren't allowed
to tell the public because of libel laws.'[1]

'Very ordinary,' reckoned *Melody Maker*'s guest reviewer, Craig
Douglas, about the debut Rolling Stones single, 'Come On', released
on the 7th, with the singer adding helpfully that 'if there were a
Liverpool accent it might get somewhere'; on another page, Cliff
Richard, whose 'Lucky Lips' had stalled at no. 4 and was now on
its way down, declared defiantly about his next choice of single
that 'I'm certainly not going to be "beatled" into making a disc
for the sake of it'; 'the Keeler business,' observed Lee this Friday,
'seems to be getting more and more smirchy,' while Larkin confined
himself to the comment, 'what a set!', and Malcolm Muggeridge
remarked on *Any Questions?* that most men had committed adultery some time in their lives, thereby earning a fierce rebuke from
a fellow panellist for his 'disgraceful abuse of free speech'; Stephen
Ward was arrested on Saturday, hottest day of the year so far, and
charged with living off immoral earnings; the unfailingly sanctimo-
nious Conservative backbencher John Cordle, speaking at a church
fête in Oxfordshire, insisted that 'men who choose to live in adultery,
men who are homosexual or men whose moral influence is against
the highest interests of the nation ought not to be appointed to serve
our Queen and country'; next day the *Sunday Mirror*, printing Lewis
Morley's instantly iconic photograph of a naked Keeler straddling
a cheap studio chair, was rivalled only by the *News of the World*
running 'Confessions of Christine' ('I never used to think of Jack as a
Minister ... I liked Jack as a MAN'); the American ambassador David
Bruce, updating Washington, discounted accusations of Macmillan
having colluded with Profumo in foisting a lie on Parliament, but
could not acquit him of 'a remarkably credulous lack of sophistication'; Evelyn Waugh on the Monday was unconvinced there was a
scandal at all ('poor Profumo – an Italian, jew, freemason – had an
affair with a prostitute' and 'every paper pretends to be horrified'),
while Frances Partridge observed that in her circle everyone was
'very light-hearted' about the whole thing because 'the *only* serious

casualty is likely to be the Conservative Party'; Tuesday the 11th saw *The Times*, in a leader written by the editor Sir William Haley, pronounce unequivocally that 'IT *IS* A MORAL ISSUE', arguing that a decade of Conservative rule, appealing to 'immediate self-interest', had 'brought the nation psychologically and spiritually to a low ebb'; and next day the *Telegraph* called the party 'a shambles', while Bishop Mervyn Stockwood spoke publicly of 'the smell of corruption in high places, of evil practices, and of a repudiation of the simple decencies and the basic values'.

The Times's letters page on Thursday had general backing for Haley ('there must,' declared Helen Downing of Thames Ditton, Surrey, 'be countless ordinary people like myself glad to see your paper taking a stand for what is right'), several papers reported Enoch Powell as thinking of resigning, perhaps even of leading a Cabinet revolt against Macmillan, and Larkin, after detailing how he now called his lunchtime cigarette 'Profumos ... for the hell of a stink', admitted to Monica Jones that 'actually' he was 'rather sick of it all'; that evening on television, in an emotionally charged performance, Lord Hailsham told Robert McKenzie (or 'young McKenzie' as he persistently called him) that 'a great party is not to be brought down because of a squalid affair between a woman of easy virtue and a proved liar', a liar who had 'lied to his friends, lied to his family, lied to his colleagues, lied to the House of Commons'; at its 'lowest point since 1945' was the *Telegraph*'s estimate on Friday of Conservative morale, but the following afternoon, at a Norfolk fête, Powell made supportive noises of the PM ('personal honour and integrity ... absolutely unsullied and untouched'); and on Sunday, while Nella Last reflected on her husband's as well as her own behalf that 'neither of us like any "pop" singers, not excepting Frank Ifield', the *Sunday Times*'s William Rees-Mogg implicitly disavowed the Haley line: 'It is the job of government to govern, to make decisions of State on matters of essential policy. In the end even a scandal has to be brought back into proportion; the life of Britain does not really pass through the loins of one red-headed girl.'[2]

'Bread has gone up today making it 1/1½ per loaf!' grumbled Jennie Hill on Monday the 17th – yet for once the main focus of most people's attention was not the local and the quotidian, but instead (notwithstanding the absence of live – or indeed recorded – TV or radio coverage) the House of Commons, scene of what the *Telegraph* that morning anticipated as 'the most momentous debate since the war'. 'The scramble for every nook and cranny of seating accommodation in the House was so phenomenal,' recorded the *New Yorker*'s Mollie Panter-Downes, 'that journalists lucky enough to get a coveted pass often shared it with a confrere. Many of the visitors in the Strangers' Gallery, told by the attendants of the unusual special ruling that if they left for a cup of tea they would not be allowed back, because of the press of MPs' wives and others waiting in the hope of seat, chose to remain, riveted in fascination and cramp, peering down from the packed narrow benches for the full six and a half hours of the debate.' The subject, of course, was the Profumo affair; and the charge against Macmillan and his government was that they had handled it both feebly and foolishly.

Wilson made the case with, in Panter-Downes' words, 'a carefully low-toned, destructive, and effective speech'. Mainly he focused on the security aspect, as he accused Macmillan of 'gambling' with national security through his negligence in challenging and uncovering Profumo's lies. But towards the end he made a larger case, arguing that the scandal had in all its seediness exposed a government which was to all appearances 'a diseased excrescence, a corrupted and poisoned appendix of a small and unrepresentative section of society that makes no contribution to what Britain is, still less what Britain can be'. Macmillan for his part – 'tired but dignified,' as John Biffen recalled – explained at some length how in the spring he simply 'could not believe that a man would be so foolish, even if so wicked, not only to lie to colleagues in the House, but be prepared to issue a writ in respect of a libel which he must know to be true'. What about Profumo's infamous 'Darling' letter to Keeler? And Profumo's assurance to fellow ministers, in turn passed on to the PM, that in the circles in which he and his wife moved it was not a term of any great significance? 'I believe,' said Macmillan, 'that that might be accepted,' adding with unintended bathos, 'I do not live among young people fairly widely'.

There were two other notable speeches. The first came from the Conservative backbencher Nigel Birch, who had resigned from Macmillan's government five years earlier in protest against the PM's high-spending instincts and now had the chance to stick the knife in. It was time, he declared in his deceptively laconic speaking style, for Macmillan 'to make way for a much younger colleague'; and, to a stunned House, he quoted Browning's line, 'Never glad confident morning again!'. At which point, recalled another Conservative backbencher, Julian Critchley, Macmillan turned towards Birch, 'his face contorted with pain and anger'. The other speech – much less reported or remembered, and delivered after Macmillan had left the chamber, 'head more bowed, shuffle even more pronounced than usual, white as a ghost', according to the political journalist David Watt – was by Ben Parkin, Labour MP for North Paddington. 'Is no one in the House today going to say a word of compassion for the poor little slut who is at the centre of all this?' he asked. 'I think of five men in a room in the middle of the night discussing how they can make it appear that the word "Darling" is not compromising in any way, when surely we need a little compassion to consider how these wretches get into the state that they do.' Soon afterwards, the House divided, 27 Conservative MPs abstained, and the government's majority was cut from 93 to 69. 'Macmillan will probably resign in the Summer,' noted Hugh Selbourne flatly. 'Gross incompetence.' Kenneth Preston in Keighley agreed ('I cannot see how he can possibly stay'), while a third diarist, Sussex farmer Bert Weibel, took a broader pot shot: 'Saw PROFUMO Debate on Television [probably as covered on that evening's *Panorama*]. A smelly show indeed!'[3]

'Premier Likely To Resign Soon' was the *Telegraph*'s headline on Tuesday the 18th, but an Australian visitor, Donald Balfour, was unconcerned as he spent much of the afternoon 'tramping along alleys, lanes, and streets in the Borough of Stepney, East London, in an area bounded by Royal Mint Street and Whitechapel Road':

> I was amazed [he continued in his diary] at the evidence of the wartime bombing which still exists. I came across the shells of many warehouses, shops, houses, and churches, blackened and boarded up. Looking through gaps in the walls, or through broken windows, I could see charred timber, piles of rubble, and other debris. In the houses one could see smashed furniture and the skeletons of beds and settees.
>
> And generally, growing up through all this mess were green ferns and weeds of all descriptions ...

That evening, a highly partisan crowd of 55,000, including Elizabeth Taylor and Richard Burton in front-row seats, were at Wembley Stadium (still called the Empire Stadium) to watch Bellingham's finest. British heavyweight champion Henry Cooper was taking on the boastful young Cassius Clay, who had trained for the fight at the Territorial Army Drill Hall in Shepherd's Bush, dismissed his opponent as 'a tramp, a bum and a cripple', and was 4–1 on favourite as he entered the ring wearing a stage-prop crown. Advance publicity had been huge, and – with no live TV coverage – some sixteen million tuned in to the Light Programme, where according to subsequent audience research they found Simon Smith's commentary 'vivid', while W. Barrington Dalby 'was said to have given his usual calm, shrewd and concise summaries'. Smith described the imperishable moment:

> ... Just seconds left of this fourth round and it's Clay poking out one, two left hands ... Now he gets a good left-hander from Cooper in return ... They were both into Clay's face ... Clay tries to get back with a left hook ... Oh, Clay is down ... Cooper has felled him ... A beautiful punch ... The bell goes ... Clay has been dropped by a beautiful punch from Cooper ... Come in Barry ...

The bell had rescued Clay from his Waterloo, and in the next round Cooper's badly cut eye ended the fight. 'Cooper had lost,' reported *The Times*'s boxing correspondent, 'but he had won thousands of hearts'; and the instant legend of the left hook that was 'Enry's 'Ammer would only grow and grow. The following evening's *Sportsview* showed the fight: a predictably high RI of 72, but 'several viewers accused Harry Carpenter of being too obviously "pro-British"'.

Phyllis Willmott reflected that Wednesday on how even her sociologist husband Peter ('who has the lowest interest of anyone I know in the trivia of human intrigues') had been wholly consumed by 'the Profumo business', which she nicely characterised as 'so oddly a gigantic national gossip' and thus having the effect of 'uniting all people, parties and otherwise divided interests into a sense of being involved in a family scandal'; a new element in the national conversation was the Palace's admission that 14-year-old Charles, incarcerated at Gordonstoun, had in a rare moment of freedom gone into a pub in

Stornoway and drunk cherry brandy; while that evening, as Carpenter banged the patriotic drum and Sir Keith Joseph delivered a party political broadcast (poor RI of 49, with 'cold and mechanical manner' and 'stuffed shirt' among the reactions), Bill Naughton's *Alfie* had its first theatrical outing at the Mermaid – with John Neville in the title role and one of the amorous Cockney spiv's 'birds' played by Glenda Jackson, praised by the *Guardian*'s Gerard Fay for her 'particularly strong' performance. The *Telegraph* on Thursday published a poll of Conservative MPs showing Maudling as their easily preferred option should Macmillan feel impelled to step down; *Oh What a Lovely War* transferred that evening to Wyndham's (Heap bemoaning how 'all officers are automatically depicted as venal, stupid or callous', whereas 'all common soldiers are, of course, good-hearted exploited working class victims of the "system"'); and on Friday the 21st, as Vere Hodgson in Shropshire offered to friends her take on what had been going on (Profumo 'a wretched individual', Ivanov 'a Russian perhaps spy', Keeler 'a professional prostitute', Ward 'a NASTY PIECE OF WORK'), as Macmillan tried to call a temporary halt to the story by announcing that he had asked the Master of the Rolls, Lord Denning, to hold a judicial inquiry, and as the jaunty 'I Like It' by Gerry and the Pacemakers displaced 'From Me To You' at the top of the charts, the second day of the Lord's Test saw Ted Dexter's thrilling, counter-attacking innings of 70 against the West Indian fast bowlers. 'The magisterially defiant cameo represented the last sneering fling of Empire,' Frank Keating would reckon in hindsight. 'Crack! went Dexter's blade. Crackle! went the throng as all London stopped for an hour.'[4]

Over the weekend, Macmillan put on a brave face at the annual summer fête in his Bromley constituency ('they will not break my spirit,' he promised about 'the recent problems'), the first woman in space (Russian textile factory worker and amateur parachutist Valentina Tereshkova) returned to earth, Crossman pondered a recent meeting with Captain Robert Maxwell ('a Czech Jew with perfect knowledge of Russian, who owns the Pergamon Press, who runs a Rolls Royce, who owns the Manor House at Headington, and who everybody detests but nobody can fault'), C. S. Lewis told the *Sunday Times* that 'I only started reading the Profumo case half way through so I'm a bit vague about the plot', the *Sunday Mirror* had Malcolm Muggeridge rejoicing in 'The Slow, Sure Death of the Upper Classes' (which in his view had 'always been given to lying, fornication, corrupt practices and, doubtless as a result of the public school system, sodomy'), and the PM spent part of the sabbath writing a self-justifying letter to the Queen. 'I had of course no idea of the strange underworld in which other people, alas, besides Mr Profumo have allowed themselves to become entrapped,' he admitted at one point. 'We do not know the precise role that Dr Ward has played, but I begin to suspect in all these wild accusations against many people, Ministers and others, something in the nature of a plot to destroy the established system.' He ended, though, on a hopeful note: 'All these are very distressing affairs. But I am confident that they can be overcome and that when Your Majesty looks back upon them, in the course of what I trust may be a very long and successful reign, they will appear no more than the irritations which have, from time to time, been of concern to Your Majesty's predecessors.'

Two days later, at St John's Wood, the cricket reached its climax in front of an enthralled, nail-biting crowd. In the course of the Test, a quartet of high-quality writers recognised in the composition of that crowd a slice of social history. 'At Waterloo and Trafalgar Square the Underground train begins to fill,' noted V. S. Naipaul before play on the first day. 'Young men in tweed jackets, carrying mackintoshes and holdalls. Older men in City black, carrying umbrellas. At every station the crowd grows. Whole families now, equipped as for a rainy camping weekend. And more than a sprinkling of West Indians.' That same day, Alan Ross observed the sartorial contrast between on the one hand 'the foppish old MCC dandies, with their button-holes to match their complexions', and on the other hand 'the razor-sharp Shaftesbury Avenue-shirted West Indians'. Naipaul and Ross were there every day, but Colin MacInnes was present just for the last day, Tuesday the 25th, as rain prevented play until mid-afternoon:

To the west, cossetted in mackintoshes, sat the members, like senators at some Roman spectacle. To the east, the Caribbean contingent were massed enthusiastically as if preparing for some Birmingham or Little Rock. The displaced clergy wandered purposefully, very gentlemanly chaps mingled with gnarled provincials and hearties from the tavern, and dotted here and there were rare members of the sorority of female fans. 'If a woman was hard pressed for a man,' one of them said to me, 'this might not be a bad spot to look around in.'

The fourth in-person people watcher was the *New Statesman*'s Commonwealth correspondent. 'During one rain interval,' wrote John Hatch, 'the crowd outside the Tavern was a patchwork of black and white, and the singing was being conducted jointly from upturned beer crates by an Englishman and a West Indian. When the coloured conductor jumped down the whole crowd, parsons, businessmen, MCC ties and Caribbean gaudy shirts, all joined in "For he's a jolly good fellow".'

Once play resumed, and the tension ratcheted up, the commentator John Arlott became 'so excited that,' noted the listening Kenneth Preston, 'he said that at every ball some of the spectators got up and wriggled about as if they had "pants in their ants"'. Veronica Lee in Devon would have sympathised: 'The Test Match was never so exciting. I nearly had five fits. It ended in a draw, but we only needed six runs to win and only had broken-armed Cowdrey at the wicket.' In Chingford, Judy Haines's husband could apparently bear it no more, but right at the end she 'rushed to bottom of garden with transistor for John to hear the last ball'. Altogether, in her words, the 'most thrilling' of draws. But life of course went on, and the next paragraph of her diary, written up that evening, said much in its understated way: 'The girls are swotting for exams, John is quietly reading, and I am depressed.'[5]

Three leaders were in action on Wednesday. Macmillan as university chancellor was in Oxford, including for the Encaenia Garden Party at Balliol ('poor man,' noted Madge Martin who saw him close up, 'he looked tired, after the horrid time he's been through'); Wilson, with Labour by now some twenty points ahead in the opinion polls, delivered a party political broadcast ('excellent' according to the often-hard-to-please Hugh Selbourne); and President Kennedy declared himself a Berliner. Apart from the release of *Tom Jones* (starring Albert Finney) and an adaptation at the Criterion of Iris Murdoch's *A Severed Head* ('performances all over the place,' according to one critic, but Paul Eddington getting it 'right' as 'the analyst, sleek, moist-eyed and gravely smug'), the next few days were mainly about the old firm of Beatles + Profumo et al. Already on Wednesday night, in their Newcastle hotel room after performing at the city's Majestic Ballroom, John and Paul had written 'She Loves You'; Friday night at the Queen's Hall in Leeds proved a particularly tough gig for the stewards, one of them bitten on his arm by a girl as the Beatles played; the latest *Melody Maker* had the group giving a unanimous thumbs-up ('it's gear' from John the ultimate compliment) to Rolf Harris's new single, 'I Know a Man'; and early on Saturday evening, their appearance on ABC television's *Lucky Stars* (summer title of *Thank Your Lucky Stars*) overlapped for ten minutes with John being on *Juke Box Jury*, where his negativity about the new releases helped to ensure that the jury, including Katie Boyle and Caroline Maudling (daughter of Reggie), voted all but Elvis's 'Devil in Disguise' a miss. On the other front, Stephen Ward's committal hearing began on Friday the 28th at Marylebone Magistrates' Court, with both Keeler ('in an off-white suit') and Rice-Davies ('in a black coat, flowery hat and white gloves') giving evidence on the opening day. The last two sentences of the *Guardian*'s report packed a punch: 'Miss Rice-Davies said that for some time she had lived with a Mr Peter Rachman, but after his death in October 1962 had gone to live with Ward at Wimpole Mews. In his flat she had intercourse with an Indian doctor and with Lord Astor.' Bill Astor, married to the former model Bronwen Pugh, was the owner of the Cliveden estate where two years earlier Ward had brought Profumo and Keeler together; and in court next day, Ward's counsel challenged Rice-Davies, 'Do you know Lord Astor has made a statement to the police saying that these allegations of yours are absolutely untrue?', to which she replied (in the quote of the year, against strong competition), 'He would, wouldn't he?'. For Judy Haines, it was all becoming a bit too much. 'Papers contain much "sex" in the Dr Stephen Ward case, which I find sickening,' she reflected on Sunday. 'It blares out of the radio, too. It doesn't help one to bring up wholesome girls and boys.'[6]

July began with the Soviet spy Kim Philby being publicly iden-tified as 'The Third Man' (thereby creating another easy target for anti-Establishment rhetoric), the Beatles recording 'She Loves You', and Pat Scott in Barking changing her washing powder ('I've used Omo for 6–7 years but lately my hands have been dry so I'm trying

Fairy Snow for a while'); on Wednesday the 3rd, as Ward was granted bail ahead of his trial at the Old Bailey, Larkin shared with Monica Jones the latest joke going round the Senior Common Room at Hull ('Christine Keeler's newspaper order? – one *Mail*, one *Observer*, and as many *Times* as possible'); next day, on a stretch of the A34 at Hall Green, Birmingham, the transport minister Ernest Marples launched a new generation of non-motorway road signs, as British public signage continued to move steadily lower case; that evening, just before Harry Secombe opened in the musical *Pickwick* ('bright' but 'feeble' in Philip Hope-Wallace's broadly cool appraisal), 19-year-old Virginia Ironside went to drinks with Lord Lichfield (twenty-four, just out of the Grenadier Guards, 'a shirt open to his waist and a gold chain and tight trousers and full of energy and efficiency'); and on Friday, Terence Conran's new furniture factory was opened at Thetford in Norfolk, Gyles Brandreth entered national consciousness with a solemn letter in the *Spectator* about politics and morals, the redesigned *Smethwick Telephone* included correspondents praising attempts by the Conservative councillor Donald Finney to 'clean up' the more immigrant parts of the town ('are we so unchristian because we demand decent living and cleanliness in Smethwick?'), and another Donald was in Smith Square, Westminster, looking at 'the empty shell' of St John's, destroyed by the Luftwaffe almost a quarter of a century earlier. 'It was,' recorded the Australian visitor Donald Balfour, 'a forlorn sight – moss, weeds, and grass growing through the cracks in the now unused steps, the grounds a mass of weeds and shrubs run wild. The church nothing but blackened walls and empty windows.' Hugh Selbourne was in Birmingham that weekend. 'Great developments,' he noted after a car tour of the city centre, 'but it appears from what I am told that Birmingham is a conservative stronghold, with much aggressive ill-humour towards coloured people. (That is, shits and fascists.)'[7]

A new front now opened up in the scandal-ridden summer. Rice-Davies during Ward's committal hearing had talked a little of her relationship with Peter Rachman – a 'very rich man' – and of her suicide attempt after his sudden death the previous autumn. 'The life and times of Peter Rachman' was the title of the *Sunday Times*'s lengthy investigative piece (under the 'Insight' banner, and largely written by Ron Hall) this Sunday the 7th; and it revealed how in the slums of west

London (Paddington, Bayswater, North Kensington, Notting Hill) this son of a Polish dentist had slickly exploited racial tensions to make a large fortune for himself as a ruthless landlord and property racketeer. Further articles in the paper followed, including on the 21st on 'The Technique of Rachmanism', probably the coining of that term. For the tabloid press, it was the latest irresistible story, with the three highest circulation Sundays (*News of the World*, *People*, *Sunday Mirror*) adding the wholly fictitious twist that Rachman's empire extended also to brothels and prostitutes. As for the by now reliably sensationalist *Daily Mirror*, it did not shy away on the 15th from linking Ward (still awaiting trial) to Rachman ('sinister slum landlord and vice king') through the former's friendship with Rice-Davies, 'the whoring pal of Christine Keeler'. That evening, *Panorama* sought to focus on the housing aspect of Rachman's legacy; but, noted one disappointed TV critic, 'many people were too frightened to appear in this programme'.

Monday the 8th was also the start for the Beatles of a week at the 'jam-packed' Winter Gardens in Margate, with supporting acts including Billy J. Kramer & the Dakotas, the 'wisecracking' Derek Roy, the 'glamorous and shapely' Lana Sisters, and the Pan Yue Jen troupe of Oriental balancing and manipulation entertainers; on Tuesday, while the thinking dog Fred Basset had his first 'walkies' in the *Daily Mail*, King Paul and Queen Frederika of the Hellenes began a four-day visit, to be met by hundreds of demonstrators in Whitehall protesting vigorously against the detention of political prisoners in Greece, thereby prompting mass arrests; next day, as Cardiff diarist Frank Lewis ate out at the Bear in the mid-Glamorgan village of Llanharry ('a piece of roasted banana on a chicken surprised me'), Bill Oddie took most of the plaudits ('a talented, chubby all-rounder') in the Cambridge Footlights Revue, *Cambridge Circus*, at the New Arts, though 'the quintessential public school prefect, John Cleese, is hardly less droll'; on Thursday, in the absence of council leader T. Dan Smith, Newcastle's Housing Committee voted 9–1 in favour of a public inquiry to investigate the circumstances of the personally advantageous contract which Smith had negotiated in 1962 with the building firm Crudens to erect three multi-storey blocks of flats; the same day, another demonstration against the Greek royals, this time outside Claridge's, involved an arrest on trumped-up charges by the Met's high-profile resident tough, the war hero Harry Challenor – a stitch-up that soon went wrong, leading to (or perhaps accelerating) Challenor's breakdown and subsequent diagnosis of 'paranoid schizophrenia'; and on Friday, the latest poll of Conservative MPs showed painfully little enthusiasm for Macmillan carrying on and Smethwick's would-be Conservative MP, Peter Griffiths, declared that the children's controversial chant during the local elections had been merely 'a reflection of what their parents think'. This was also the terrible day when, on her way to a jive club in Gorton, Manchester, 16-year-old Pauline Reade went missing – first of the victims of Ian Brady and Myra Hindley.[8]

For Macmillan in his dog days, a weekend house party at Petworth ('Isaiah [Berlin] cheered the PM one evening, and [Peter] Quennell didn't do too badly,' reported Ann Fleming to Evelyn Waugh, 'but otherwise the PM was glum unless anecdoting on 1914, 15, 16, or merry tales of dukes in clubs, at home, on grouse moors etc'); for the Stones, the start of a national profile, that Saturday evening not only playing for the first time outside London (at the Alcove Club in Middlesbrough) but appearing, pre-recorded, on *Lucky Stars*. It was in its way a chrysalis moment: under Andrew Loog Oldham's orders, still sartorially in a 'showbiz' tradition ('matching black trousers and black and white houndstooth jackets with velvet collars,' notes Jagger's biographer Christopher Sandford); but already enough their own men to have longer-than-usual hair, causing compère Pete Murray to make an on-air joke about a delegation from the hairdressers' union wanting to see them – and a deluge of complaints from people who, in Bill Wyman's words, 'objected to our long hair and what they obviously regarded as our menacing sexuality'. In effect, as the penny about the group's USP gradually began to drop with their manager, it was the beginning of the Stones as the anti-Beatles. Pointing in broadly the same direction – at the end of a day in which Patricia Highsmith had taken stock of her temporary home in Aldeburgh ('only one tobacconist sells Philip Morris') – was BBC TV's Sunday evening programme on 'Sex and Family Life'. In it the medical biologist Dr Alex Comfort – watched by a Shropshire teacher, Mary Whitehouse, among others – caused a storm by boldly declaring that society had come to the view that 'chastity is no more a virtue than malnutrition', as well as talking freely about such unmentionables as rubber and contraception.

Over the following week, Vere Hodgson reflected sadly on 'poor Mr Macmillan' ('he seems too unworldly to cope with people as they are today'); the annual conference of the Royal Institute of British Architects opened at Sheffield (ending with a triumphal tour of the completed Park Hill scheme); speech day at Manchester Grammar School saw the high master urging the city's local authority to think twice about dispensing with its successful grammar schools ('the case for such "wholesale action" is far from proven and the result may well be both to divide us even further and to deprive us, at a crucial moment, of young men and women capable and objective enough to carry further the evolution we all desire'); and a detailed survey of London's seven main termini (excluding Euston, under 'hectic transformation') over some twenty-four fairly typical hours found Paddington best for access, Victoria marked by disorderly queues and triple-banked taxis, station porters generally helpful (but confusion on both sides about tipping protocol), service at left-luggage offices 'prompt but curt', adequate ticket offices, better-than-expected punctuality of trains, patchy levels of information, waiting rooms that to a greater or lesser extent were 'relics of Dickensian squalor', *snackerie anglaise* the norm when it came to refreshments (St Pancras the most hygienic), and lavatories and washing facilities ranging from 'spotless' at Liverpool Street to 'dirty' at Waterloo. Overall, concluded Christopher Martin (a member of the Liberal Party's Transport Committee), 'though there was much detail to praise, the overwhelming impression is that nobody really cares enough about what happens to the passenger on the other side of the buffers'.

Saturday night was music night – Donald Balfour at the Proms (Sir Malcolm Sargent 'resplendent in white tie and tails, bronzed, and with smooth, jet-black hair'), David Roberts of Aberystwyth at the Ritz Ballroom, Rhyl to catch the Beatles ('smartly dressed in jackets and ties') – before Noël Coward on Sunday the 21st contemplated 'the squalid Ward case' (about to start for real at the Old Bailey) and 'those miserable little tarts Christine Keeler and Mandy Rice-Davies': 'They have both, apparently, been given vast sums for their sordid life stories. I *do* know what the world's coming to and that's a fact. It's coming to complete moral and mental disintegration ...' Who was to blame? 'Most of the vulgarity,' concluded Coward, was attributable to the press – especially, he added, in the context of 'a troubled world' at a time when 'the yellow and black tides are rising'.[9]

＊

'Affluence and the British Class Structure', by the Cambridge sociologists John Goldthorpe and David Lockwood, was the lead article in this month's *Sociological Review*. In essence it questioned what had become, after Labour's crushing election defeat in 1959, the almost instantly fashionable 'embourgeoisement' theory – that, in other words, a rising standard of living was making large chunks of the country's manual wage workers increasingly middle class in their identity and values, and thus increasingly likely to vote Conservative. The sociological underpinning of this theory had, according to Goldthorpe and Lockwood, relied too heavily on patterns of consumption, with not enough attention paid to questions of work and social activity. 'It does not appear to have occurred to those who argue that the worker is being merged into the middle class that this implies that within communities, neighbourhoods and associations long-standing social barriers are being broken down and that manual workers and their families are being accepted as equals into status groups from which they, or their kind, were previously excluded.' Was that, they asked, in fact the case? Probably not, they reckoned, given that 'a variety of studies carried out in different parts of Britain over the last ten years or so have pointed to a marked degree of status segregation in housing, in informal neighbourhood relations, in friendship groups, in the membership of local clubs, societies and organisations and so on' – status segregation, moreover, in which 'in all cases the division between manual and non-manual workers and their families has proved to be one of the most salient'. What, however, the two Cambridge men failed to mention was that their own study – which would become known and celebrated as the Affluent Worker study – was now, this summer of 1963, in full swing.

Their principal focus was the booming town of Luton, above all the giant Vauxhall car plant, where they and their research team interviewed between them well over 150 married male workers (aged 21–46), usually including 'home' interviews with wives present as well as 'work' interviews. The result was a sociological goldmine, not least on occasion the running commentary provided by the interviewers in their write-ups. At one home, where the wife had 'sat silently for most of the time, looking foolish', and had been 'fairly dismayed when asked a question and embarrassed when husband started telling her to speak up', but did at one point dare to say that 'she found it very dull and lonely being at home all the time' (without children or social life), the husband was 'not upset by this and just continued to assume that women didn't want to work and no self-respecting man would allow them to'. Or take this passage about another couple's home:

> The living room wallpaper was tasteless, dirty and badly faded. There was a wooden-armed three-piece suite, which had shabby-looking loose covers. The table was covered by a floral, plastic cloth. There was a 17″ television set which was, at first, left on while I interviewed him, until he asked me if I wanted it off. There were no books, pictures etc. The husband still had his working clothes on, jeans and boots. The wife was cleanly, but not fashionably dressed in blouse and loose skirt. The two older children were clean, and well-dressed. Tea was brought in on a tray but sugared, ready to drink, by his wife. Some cake was put on a plate, but never eaten, as it was never handed around.

In an exercise generating not far short of a quarter of a million words, inevitably some interviews were more rewarding than others. A trio gives something of the overall flavour.

Starting with a worker in his late thirties ('a big man with black hair brushed straight back from his forehead and greased down') who after the war had worked in a garage in Tenby, South Wales, before marrying a Luton girl:

> Have you ever thought of leaving your present job at Vauxhall? – Always worked on engines – worked on engines during war; quite happy doing engines.
> What it is that keeps you here? – Decent money and decent standard of living. Security. Been charge-hand for eight years.

A Conservative voter ('I believe they're giving a fair share to all'), and not a member of a trade union, he had no problem with there being different canteens for managers, office workers and shop-floor workers: 'Can't have canteens open to everyone – depends on the clothes they wear. It's common sense. Secondly you can't have workers mixing with the management too much.' What about social life?

'We're home-birds – don't go out much,' answered his wife ('seemed a tasteful woman') in their newish, 'very well-furnished' house about ten minutes' walk from the centre of town. More generally, what sort of people did they feel completely at ease with? 'People who've had same upbringing I've had,' she replied; 'people who speak the same language, who're interested in the same things,' he replied. Any people they felt awkward with? 'Haven't a lot of time for Scottish people,' he responded. 'Can't get on with the blackies very much. They seem to have a bee in their bonnet about us and that's it. You try to get on with them, but I think they feel you're trying to patronise them.'

The next interviewee was probably more of a floating voter (taking at home the right-wing *Daily Sketch* and the left-wing *Sunday Mirror*), but expecting Labour, if they won the next election, to do better than the Conservatives over unemployment. 'Shipbuilding and things like that. It's a devil when Britain has to go abroad to get ships built.' In answer to questions, his wife expressed her dislike for the 'snooty kind of person' ('always makes you feel they're better than you … usually better off too'), while as for him: 'Like to be with people who mix … Don't like people you work with who snub you on the street. And trouble-makers, drunks in a pub.' Why did he prefer to have as friends people with a similar background and outlook? 'People who go out and like to enjoy themselves. Don't stir up trouble. I like good mixers myself. People you know pretty well and have some things in common.' – 'What kind?' – 'Well, go in pub and have game of darts.' Then came, the crux of the session, the specific question of class:

Do you think it's inevitable that there should be different classes, or do you think it would be possible not to have them? – Always been like that. Been like that for years now.

Well, what are the reasons for the resistance of classes? – I think it's in the way they're brought up. Tend to follow their parents. It's true for most.

Do you think it's a good thing or a bad thing? – Don't see anything wrong with it. If they want to live the way they choose, I don't see why they shouldn't.

What is it that makes you think like this? – The way the lower classes react to the top class; and the way they react to the

lower classes. They just don't make friends easy. Just go their
own ways.

Do you think the classes are going to stay much the same in the
future, or are there likely to be changes? – Stop much the same.
Been like that for years. Be like that for years to come.

'Can't explain it to you very well,' he added. 'But that's my own
opinion.'

The final snapshot was of a couple who had moved to Luton from
Glasgow:

Wife was originally from Dublin – large, motherly, deep voice.
Husband quiet except on the subject of the ruling classes, let his
wife take the initiative often – when they disagreed there was no
disputing. He seemed tired, very devoted to the children. Wife
obviously very devoted to him. Eight-year-old daughter sat on
her father's knee through interview. Friendly, cheerful atmosphere – good working-class Catholics, absolutely no bourgeois
traces. Tiny house in seedy street near town centre – small rooms,
lino floors, landlady furniture. Religious pictures. An enormous
tea was pressed on me – huge cups of strong black tea, the milk in
the bottle handled separately. I was given a plate with seven slices
of cake and a dozen biscuits on it and was expected to eat it all.
They told me they would be happier in Glasgow – or Dublin –
Luton very unfriendly – you didn't leave your doors unlocked and
have the neighbours slipping in and out. All the same I'd say they
enjoyed life.

Why, asked the interviewer, had they made the move? 'For the
money,' she replied. 'No other reason, we just hadn't enough money.
Otherwise there's nothing else in Luton.' To which he added: 'I'd
rather have Glasgow but it's no use if you can't have a decent living.
£8 5s a week I was on and I was one of the lucky ones. Not a friendly
place, Luton.' Next up was the feeling-at-ease question:

Husband. Just ordinary people are the ones I'm most at ease
with. Just working-class people. You get some friendlier than
others.

Wife. Not in Luton, none of them are friendly here. They don't
want the Scotch or Irish here. Doesn't worry Bill [husband], he
goes down to have a pint and just takes people as he finds them.
Husband. The people I work with, they're all right.

In the class section, it was just Bill who fielded the questions, including
one perhaps awkward moment with the interviewer:

What classes are there? – You've got the untouchables, you've got
the middle class and you've got the workers. There's three more
or less.
Who do you mean by the untouchables? – All them big business men.
Anybody else? – No, I don't think so.
Who is in the middle class? – They're the ones who think they're
something but they're not.
I don't quite understand. – They think they have a lot of authority,
which is wrong, they haven't. If they've a good position they
think they're the cheese.
How else would you describe them? – They're the type who
wouldn't help a drowning man.
Who is in the working class? – We're all in the working class, –
I hope. (*Sideways glance at me.*)
How else would you describe the working class? – I mean the
ordinary working man, I know you get some bad ones but not
on the whole, not the majority.
How is the working class different from the middle class? – It comes
in snobbery, some are a lot of snobs aren't they?

Unsurprisingly, the couple were staunch Labour voters. 'As far as
I can see,' he declared, 'it's the only party that would give the worker
a chance to get the benefit of his work and sweat and labour.' To
which she added that 'Labour will bring down [i.e. in price] a lot of
things such as sweets'. And he then had the last, emphatic word: 'The
other party just treat you as slaves. I thought they got rid of slaves
years ago.'

By 1967, in the lead article of the pioneer issue of *Sociology* (sub-
titled *The Journal of the British Sociological Association*), Goldthorpe,
Lockwood and their colleagues were able to present the essence of

their conclusions about the validity or otherwise of the *embourgeoise-ment* thesis:

> A study of what might be regarded as a critical sample of affluent workers reveals little evidence of changes in the direction of 'middle-classness'. In order to achieve a high level of income, many of these men must experience greater deprivation in their working lives than do most white-collar employees; they also differ from the latter in having little chance of occupational advancement. In their home lives, they are largely 'privatized'. They no longer share in trad-itional patterns of working-class sociability, yet few have adopted middle-class life-styles and fewer still have become assimilated into middle-class society. Finally, these workers are found to be at least as strong in their support of the Labour Party as manual workers in the country generally.

In due course, there followed from Goldthorpe et al. a three-volume study of *The Affluent Worker*, full of statistical matter but sadly shorn of the original fieldwork's human texture – almost certainly a delib-erate repudiation of the far more accessible (and ultimately helpful) approach taken by Michael Young and Peter Willmott in their classic 1957 study, *Family and Kinship in East London*.

In recent years, historians have started to go back to the field-work and test the Goldthorpe/Lockwood conclusions. According to Selina Todd in *The People* (2014), they have stood up well, above all the central finding that affluence in the early 1960s was *not* destroying the working class; and on the basis of the interviews, she notes how most of the Vauxhall car workers saw Britain as a class-based society, viewed the working class as the class that had to work for whatever it got, saw the prospect of moving social class as not only hard but often undesirable, and were (in her words) 'acutely conscious that they and their relatives had not had the chances avail-able to wealthier people'. By contrast, the focus of Jon Lawrence in *Me Me Me?* (2019) is more on what the Luton fieldwork reveals about 'community' and suchlike in the early to mid-1960s in this and presumably similar booming parts of southern England. Here, he finds a perhaps predictably mixed picture: for example, many wanting to move out of Luton's sprawling new council estates and acquire their own homes, but others (especially if they had come from London) appreciating the friendliness to be found on those estates; or, again, a distinctly mixed cluster of attitudes about non-white migration to the town. Overall, in his notably nuanced reading of the transcripts, Lawrence seems to be struck by change at least as much as by continuity:

> Perhaps the clearest indication that the meanings attached to home life were changing in the 1960s was the vogue for home improvement – or 'DIY' as it came to be known. We have heard Bob Green [pseudonym for an interviewee] complaining that, unlike in Suffolk [where he had come from], Luton people seemed to do nothing but work or redecorate, and sure enough we do often find interviewers commenting that the house they are visiting is in a state of upheaval thanks to some ambitious DIY project. They also frequently comment on the 'garish' contemporary colour schemes favoured by Luton's affluent workers, including one where every wall had a different coloured wallpaper and another with a 'terrifying granite-wall motif on wallpaper over fireplace'. They also called on a number of homes where the family were in the midst of more radical DIY alterations, either building an extension or knocking through their downstairs rooms to create a large living space.

So, still working class by self-identification, by broad values, but a rather different working-class way of life, pointing to a future with a somewhat richer palette – less culturally conservative, more lifestyle individualistic.

Yet, of course, if Luton was (in Lawrence's words) 'the epitome of the emerging high-speed mobile society', the fact remained that, for the time being anyway, the overwhelming majority of the British working class continued to live – in the Midlands, in the north, in South Wales, in industrial Scotland – in very different sorts of places.[10]

*

The *Daily Mail*'s annual Sand Design Contest began on Monday, 22 July at selected holiday resorts around the coast – Bognor Regis,

Bridlington, Broadstairs, Bude, Burnham-on-Sea, Colwyn Bay, Cromer, Filey, Llandudno, Mablethorpe, Minehead (Butlin's Camp), Morecambe, Rhyl, Sandown (Isle of Wight), St Annes-on-Sea, Southport, Tenby, Weston-super-Mare – for boys and girls aged six to fourteen. 'Competitors will be able to build any sort of design they like – a castle, house, lighthouse, harbour, monument, boat, car – in fact, anything that takes their fancy,' the paper had announced earlier in the summer. 'The only conditions are that the design must be *built* on the sand and not just drawn *in* the sand, and the work must be completed in 1½ hours at the most.' As for decoration, only materials found on the beach in their natural state, such as pebbles, pieces of rock, shells, seaweed, etc., would be permitted. 'Match-sticks, string, old cigarette cartons, and lolly sticks will *not* be allowed.'

Also starting at Weston-super-Mare this day, even more excitingly, was a week of the Beatles, performing twice daily at the Odeon. Still on the bill were the Lana Sisters ('good to have at least one all-female act in the show,' commented the local paper's entertainment correspondent); here the old-fashioned variety spot was filled by husband-and-wife team Tommy Wallis & Beryl, whose set (including xylophone, vibes, saxophone and trumpet) won 'a tremendous reception' as they finished their act with 'a phenomenal drum solo, lasting fully five minutes'; and also on the bill were Gerry and the Pacemakers, with Gerry's 'dynamic personality of a Tommy Steele' radiating 'right through his group's happy, all-action performance'. But inevitably, it was another, and even more publicised, 'singing combination from Liverpool' who stole the show:

The girls screamed with delight as 'Please Please Me' and 'From Me To You' were performed – as precisely, incidentally, as on the actual records – but it was the Beatles' latest hit parade offering, 'Twist and Shout', which really brought the house down.

Well before the end of this number, hundreds of twisting teenagers had progressed from the edge of their seats to within feet of where the Beatles were performing. Two wildly excited youths scaled the barrier on to the stage to shake hands with each member of the quartet – Paul McCartney, John Lennon, George Harrison and Ringo Starr – and the curtain finally went down with the teenagers still howling for more.

Surnames of that Merseyside combo still for the moment necessary for readers of the *Weston Mercury and Somersetshire Herald*? But if so, not for much longer.

Elsewhere this Monday, Donald Balfour in NW8 had a pleasant day in the sunshine at Lord's, where the tourists were watched by fellow West Indians displaying 'a keen knowledge of the game' and 'a delightful sense of humour'; Keith Joseph in SW1 took the brunt of Labour's Rachmanism-focused attack in an emergency housing debate and announced an inquiry into London housing, to be chaired by the leading company lawyer Sir Milner Holland; and the Old Bailey in EC4 was the scene for the opening day of the trial of Stephen Ward. There, people had queued all night to get into the tiny public gallery, while that morning hundreds jostled outside the main entrance in the hope of getting a glimpse of the witnesses – one above all. 'She was a pitiful spectacle, sitting in terrified dignity, her face covered with a pancake make-up which levels out the natural toning of the skin, and her determination to make a good show levelling her features to the flatness of a mask,' wrote Rebecca West about Keeler as, exposed to 'one vast leer', she sat trapped in her car. 'First, the photographers surrounded her, then they fell away, and their place was taken by women, mostly old or in late middle-age, and they were without exception ill-favoured and unkempt, and elderly men of the unprosperous sort. Their cries and boos expressed the purest envy.'[11]

Ward himself faced three charges of living off immoral earnings; and two of procuring. After Mervyn Griffith-Jones (unsuccessful prosecutor of *Lady Chatterley's Lover* three years earlier) had made a lengthy opening speech for the Crown – full of 'innuendo, posturing, and distortion' (Richard Davenport-Hines), including 'a righteous wallow in indignation' – Keeler was called to give evidence. At least two male observers were gripped: the *Daily Mirror*'s Donald Zek by how 'the voluptuous lips, slightly parted over protruding teeth, extend from high cheekbones, a slash of red against the sallow skin'; and Ludovic Kennedy by her 'animal' appeal ('long slender legs … mass of copper hair … high cheekbones … hint of Red Indian blood'), before her voice (that of 'any little shop girl, lacking style and distinction') and details of her early life (living in Staines before going to Slough, 'no two towns in Britain less happily named') robbed him of all 'romantic notions'. In the evidence itself, while itemising the men she had had sex with, she angrily denied that she had ever been a prostitute; and when asked what proportion of money received from men she then gave to Ward while she was staying with him at Wimpole Mews, she replied, 'Well, I usually owed him more than I ever made. I only gave him half of that.' That evening, Mandy Rice-Davies ('drinking champagne from a bottle and surrounded by photographers') but not Keeler was present at a press preview in a Bloomsbury gallery of portrait sketches by Ward, including of Prince Philip, Princess Margaret, Ivanov, Lord Astor and Rice-Davies herself. 'A genuine, if tiny, talent' was Terence Mullaly's verdict in the *Telegraph*; while the paper's detailed court report of day one would have as its main headline, 'Christine Keeler talks about her conscience', in seemingly sarcastic reference to her assertion that she had 'told the whole truth' at the earlier trial of 'Lucky' Gordon.

The Ward trial continued over the rest of the week, but at the High Court in Aberdeen the trial of 21-year-old Harry Burnett, accused of murdering merchant seaman Thomas Guyan, started on Tuesday and ended on Thursday. The defence did not deny the act, essentially a *crime passionnel*; but the strong psychiatric evidence it brought for diminished responsibility was essentially laughed out of court, leading to the jury returning a majority verdict (13-2) of capital murder. 'The choice was whether this man was mad or bad,' remarked afterwards the foreman (a headmaster in his day job). 'I see boys like this every day who are just bad.' Back in the Old Bailey, over these four days, Rice-Davies ('a hard, cat-like little face, but a very pretty one,' noted Kennedy, describing her as 'in turns pert, cool, innocent, tearful, giggly') said that she had been under police pressure to give evidence at the magistrates' court and denied that Ward, for all that he was 'a depraved and immoral man', had ever influenced her to sleep with anyone; Vickie Barrett ('a little whey-faced blonde') gave dubious evidence making out Ward as (Kennedy's words again) 'a ponce, a pimp, a professional brothel-keeper'; and Ward himself gave evidence ('one had heard of his charm and personality, and now one was experiencing them ... a voice of quite extraordinary power, richness and resonance'), denying the charges and at one point, provoked by the relentless Griffith-Jones, banging the side of the witness box and shouting out, 'Any little tart from the streets can come forward in this court and say I am lying', adding that 'apart from this case I am considered to be a truthful person'. 'If he is sentenced,' reflected the young novelist J. G. Farrell on the Friday, 'it will be a gross miscarriage of justice and he'll be the victim of bourgeois morality.'[12]

Elsewhere this week, Keith Joseph undertook a two and a half hour coach tour of Liverpool housing, stopping off every now and then. Outside a house in Upper Canning Street, Toxteth, where six families had only one lavatory between them, Mrs Patricia Jones (thirty-one) told the minister that she and her seaman husband and their five children were living in one room with no gas or sink. Also briefly in Liverpool, on his way to Ireland, was Balfour, who found 'most depressing' the last stretch of his journey from London:

> Smoke hung everywhere and everything was grimy. The train ran close to row after row of terraced houses with absolutely no front yard and room at the back for a small shed and nothing else. Not a sign of a tree or a shrub anywhere. The skyline just a mass of chimney pots.
>
> Mixed in with all this were factories, filthy with the dust and smoke of many years, piles of slag, heaps of rubbish. Altogether a horrible sight.

In Smethwick, Griffiths expressed himself 'tired' of Labour's talk of a colour bar ('I have found no colour bar in Smethwick but I have found on every hand a "squalor" bar as people seek to protect their homes and families'); in Moscow, the Russian, American and British negotiators initialled the Limited Nuclear Test Ban Treaty (formally signed 11 days later), a further blow to CND's apparent relevance; and in the *New Statesman*, Francis Newton (aka Eric Hobsbawm) warned that the incipient folk-song boom, involving all too often 'the public appearance of the relatively incompetent amateur', would further encourage 'that decline in professional and craft standards which is the most dangerous aspect of pop music today'. Play of the week was Barry Reckord's *Skyvers* at the Royal Court, depicting the largely incoherent and inarticulate rage, racism and sexism of a group of south London boys (an all-white cast, including David Hemmings) in their last few days at a sink school, with a mutual contempt between the teachers and the taught, as the former resign themselves to being able to offer nothing more than 'gym and football and free milk'.

An utterly different world at Benenden, where (it had recently been announced) Princess Anne was due to go. 'Of course,' thundered regretfully the egalitarian-minded educationist Brian Jackson, 'it is not only the Royal Family that keeps aloof from State schools: our whole governing group does – not merely Cabinet Ministers but Labour politicians as well, and even Ministry of Education officials and chairmen of local authority education committees. Who can be sharp about the Royal Family when Labour politicians will not "risk" their child's having one year in a State infants' school, ostensibly in case it affects his preparation for Winchester?' Yet inevitably, he concluded in a *Guardian* piece aimed squarely at that paper's well-meaning, progressive-minded readers, the decision to send the princess to her 'expensive private school' would only 'crystallise the feeling that State schools – even the best – are in the end only schools for other people's children'.

One such reader was presumably Ann Hales-Tooke of Cambridge, who on Saturday the 27th riposted to Jackson by not only claiming that Princess Anne going to boarding school represented 'an enormous step forward compared to her mother's upbringing', but confidently predicting that 'no doubt Princess Anne's children will go as a matter of course to a State day school'; that evening on ITV, at peak viewing time, *Big Night Out* made its debut, with the knockabout comedy double act Mike and Bernie Winters as compères; next day, the *Sunday Telegraph* sought to dial down what it saw as the current national moral obsession ('in our concentration on sex we may forget other forces with even greater potentialities for the corruption of character'); on Monday the architect Sir Basil Spence defended to journalists his design for the new Knightsbridge Barracks, angrily jabbing at his model with a rolled umbrella as he called the proposed tower block 'a mere tiddler' at 275 feet high and generally launching a counter-attack against the London County Council's objections; while over at the Old Bailey, Griffith-Jones in his closing speech insisted that the 'evil' of Ward went 'very deep'.[13]

Tuesday the 30th, hottest day of the year so far, began with an *FT* item about Robert Maxwell opening a new bookshop in Oxford ('spurning mere books, he talked enthusiastically of "information systems"'), but most attention was on EC4, where – hours after the Court of Criminal Appeal had set aside Gordon's conviction, thereby enabling Griffith-Jones in the rest of his final address to cast further doubt upon Keeler's truthfulness as a witness, including her denial of being a prostitute – the judge, the puritanical Sir Archie Marshall, began his summing-up. In it, he directed the jury to the effect that the activities of both Keeler and Rice-Davies came within the legal definition of prostitution; and more than one observer, including Kennedy, was struck by how he confined himself to 'a flat matter-of-fact voice' when pointing out things in Ward's favour, whereas 'his voice and bearing became brighter, livelier' when dealing with matters that told against the defendant. After the court rose, Ward retreated as usual to the Chelsea flat of Noel Howard-Jones, a staunch ally; and that night, in response to an urgent phone call, the journalist Tom Mangold, with whom he had become friendly, came to see him there. 'I think I know which way the jury will go tomorrow,' the chain-smoking Ward told Mangold. 'It's not a pleasant thought, Tom. I'll tell you frankly, I don't think I'm going to be able to do time for these offences. It's not prison that worries me, it's taking the blame, being the victim of a witch-hunt. And my friends – Tom, not one of them stood by me. How could every one of them let me down?'

Next morning, having taken thirty-five grains of barbiturate, he was found in a deep coma by Howard-Jones. An ambulance took him to St Stephen's Hospital in Fulham Road ('Victorian institutional at its worst, five-storey barrack blocks of dirty brick,' noted a journalist), where he remained unconscious. Later that morning, at the Old Bailey, no word of sympathy from Mr Justice Marshall, who continued his marathon summing-up, including an implicit endorsement of Vickie Barrett's damning evidence. ('Am I misrepresenting Barrett when I say she answered her questions quietly and straightforwardly?'). A mile or two away, in Broadcasting House, the BBC's chairman, Sir Arthur fforde, found a note on his desk from a secretary: 'A Mrs Whitehouse phoned. She was extremely forceful and wants very much to come and see you ...' Marshall eventually finished at around 2.30, and the jury (11 men and one woman) retired to consider their verdict. They were still doing so when at 6.22, in the Lord Chancellor's office, Anthony Wedgwood Benn handed in a document disclaiming the title Lord Stansgate. Over two and a half years earlier, his father's death had meant that he had had to give up his Bristol seat; the Peerage Bill, almost entirely his own work and allowing voluntary renunciation of a hereditary peerage, had at six o'clock received the royal assent; and the expectation was of an almost immediate uncontested by-election to enable him to return to the Commons. At the Old Bailey, shortly after seven, the jury at last delivered its verdict to a weary court: that Ward was guilty of living on the immoral earnings of Keeler and Rice-Davies. The judge announced that he would delay sentencing until Ward was well enough to be present. That evening in Tottenham Court Road, a huge crowd gathered outside the Dominion for the British premiere of *Cleopatra*, treated by the BBC (noted a disapproving TV critic) 'as if it were the event of the century'. No-shows from Elizabeth Taylor and Richard Burton; but definitely present was Mandy Rice-Davies, ready as ever to field reporters' questions. 'Whatever he has done or admitted,' she said of the condemned one, 'he never deserved to get into this awful mess.'[14]

'Guilty' was the *Daily Mirror*'s satisfied headline on Thursday, 1 August, with its celebrated columnist 'Cassandra' (William Connor) observing on an inside page that those foolish enough to send flowers to St Stephen's were offering garlands to depravity; in Newcastle, the City Council voted 40–18 (wholly along party lines) against an inquiry into Smith and the Crudens contract; in the Commons, Joseph found himself, following pressure from colleagues (Iain Macleod in particular), having to row back from his commitment to absorb the tiny county of Rutland into Leicestershire; and on late-afternoon television, the BBC's *Pinky and Perky: The Pop-In*, with the piglet puppets being watched by 21 per cent of the population even though a repeat, comfortably outgunning ITV's *Criss Cross Quiz* (10 per cent). On Friday, as Ward's condition continued to worsen, Virginia Graham put her friend Joyce Grenfell (on tour in Australia) in the picture. 'Great efforts are being made to revive him, so that he can be put in prison,' she reported. However: 'Ward is obviously going to die & suddenly everybody seems a bit sorry for him! I think the whole thing got well out of proportion.' Ward did indeed die, on Saturday afternoon, aged fifty. 'He had been stretched too far upon the "rack of this rough world"', reflected Pamela Hansford Johnson, '& death is too high a price to pay for goatishness in the service of the rich.'

The new issue of *Melody Maker* had four young men pondering time and change:

I'm sure in four years' time we won't be so popular. I just consider myself a lucky layabout from Liverpool who has had some
success. *(John)*

All our fans in the [Cavern] club, the ones we all knew personally, we
don't see them anymore, not since the big fan club got going. *(Paul)*

Sometimes, on concerts now, I start to think too much about
playing, or my mind's on something else, and the audience can see
I'm not enjoying myself. You can't kid them. You have to grin away
all the time. *(George)*

It can't last forever, I know that. I'm saving like mad. Never want
to work for anybody else. When things get rough, I want enough
money to buy my own business. Definitely. *(Ringo)*

That evening of Saturday, 3 August, would, as it happened, be the last
time the Beatles played at the Cavern. More than 500 fans (over double
the legal capacity) crammed in; acts preceding them included such
local attractions as the Escorts, the Merseybeats, the Road Runners,
Johnny Ringo and the Colts, and Faron's Flamingos; things became so
sweaty that condensation was soon running down the walls, onto the
stage; and mid-way through the headliners' set, water got into the electrical system, causing a power outage. At which point, time-bendingly
enough, Paul performed an acoustic version of his song 'When I'm
Sixty-Four'.[15] The world at large would have to wait almost another
four years to hear it; and one weak but well-intentioned man would
never hear it at all, let alone make it to that landmark age.

*

There were few signs of the affluent worker in Salford. Ewan
MacColl's 'Dirty Old Town', it had experienced over the past decade
successive waves of slum clearance and redevelopment, increasingly
often involving high-rise blocks of flats. The sociologist Dennis
Marsden, with his wife Pat and their two small children, moved in
summer 1963 to 2 Davenham House, Salford 3 in order to undertake
a 'slum and rehousing' study. Marsden never formally wrote up his

findings, before long moving to the new University of Essex, but the fieldwork suggests a difficult experience; and that between the three principal actors involved – the residents; the authorities; the sociologist – there was little meeting of minds.

It was not, though, that the authorities were wholly unsympathetic to the human situation. 'People are caught in a cleft stick,' a housing manager told Marsden early on, highlighting the contrast between low-density, low-rise situated further out (notably the new estates at Little Hulton, seven miles from the centre of Salford) and new blocks of high-rise flats in the more central area. 'They don't want to overspill, except young ones who go with children, and they don't want flats (except, curiously enough, the top floor).' Or as an assistant planning officer crisply put it soon afterwards: 'Everybody wants houses, few want to leave Salford.' The flat-dwellers also almost certainly wanted gas, as used by the great majority of Salfordians, but the new flats were all-electric. Still, an assistant to the borough engineer reassured Marsden, 'they seem to accept it as part of a new way of life'. Perhaps the most insightful of his informants was a female housing inspector, talking eloquently about the 'loneliness of the old people in these high flats':

> They find it very quiet after sitting at their doors, living in a street. They can be very isolated … I've been on at the housing manager to do something about it, but [*lowering her voice*] the trouble is that that's the welfare department's job [*pulling a face*] and my boss says that he wouldn't want to trespass on their ground. But meanwhile the old people aren't getting to know one another, and the time to do something was when they first moved in, before they had time to settle into a rut. They are going to do something now, they're starting an over-sixties' club, but by this time it will all be too late.

'I don't like high flat blocks, nobody does,' she added. 'What they really want is a house, but all the houses are so far out …'

At one point during his stay, Marsden went as an observer (not asked to contribute) to a Salford Council joint meeting on housing estates, attended by members (mainly Labour) of the housing, education, parks, welfare, road safety and health committees:

Nobody had any doubt that 'community spirit' should be fostered, that it was going, that the community centres would foster 'community spirit', that the two sorts of 'community spirit' were the same, that the community spirit might not be schismatic. There was no evidence that anyone present had ever read a sociological study of rehousing (except Dr Burn), no suggestion of finding out what people 'want' or that people's wants – if indeed they could be found out – were not common knowledge and identical with those of the council, or they ought to be. There was the feeling that these community centres were for the specific estates upon which they were situated. It was apparently not incongruous to them that, having despatched the Ellor Street residents [in the centre of Salford] to the corners of Salford and Little Hulton, they should talk about Ellor Street community spirit as though it was an attribute of something which still existed (the razed area of ground even) which could be regenerated by putting suitable buildings on the old site and filling them with 'similar' people.

One of the councillors (Peter Grimshaw, chairman of Salford Labour Party, 'very sure of himself') especially vexed Marsden. 'He thought the trouble with the flats wasn't in any way the flats themselves but the fault of the council who hadn't "educated" the people into wanting the flats. When this generation of flat-dwelling children had grown up they would accept the flats. He didn't think there was the possibility that flat-dwelling in these flats was unpleasant in itself.'

Marsden himself certainly did not much enjoy the experience of living on Salford's Trinity Estate in a block of flats, itemising in a later report the isolation, the noise of neighbours above and below whom one didn't get to know, the bleak staircases, and so on. Not long after moving in, he started keeping a diary of the broader Trinity experience:

10 August, going that Saturday evening to the Bird in Hand pub. The tap room was inhospitable with cold lino tiles. In it were a large group of men ranging in age from early twenties to sixty, playing a card game with very fast hands (bragg? some sort of 3 card game) for small wagers. Lots of swearing, particularly from a man with deformed wrists. Lots of good-natured abuse, and once a very

earnest inquiry on a hand to see if it was honest. Another game, of
darts, going on ...

This is not a room to stop in. A large number of empty glasses and
bottles showed where men had been in that evening and left. Both
the darts game and the cards game had rapidly shifting participants.
Someone would come in, give a greeting, talk for a while to the
players or to one of the loose fringe of observers, become a player,
and leave. The man with deformed hands was going to leave at ten.
'Ah've got somebody to see. We might get t'leg over tonight where
we're going' ...

All were smartly dressed, some with open collars – no cloth
caps here ...

11 August. In the evening the rhythm of the estate. Groups of
boys and groups of girls set off with an aura of transistor music
surrounding each group. The odd 'mam' headsquare off and rollers
out, setting off to the pub, hurling severe warnings to her sons as she
went. Later the wave of returning groups. The teenagers shouting or
moaning 'rock' songs, the older people singing ballads, or shouting,
lots of sexual innuendoes, hundreds of 'goodnights'. Either pub
hours are late or the law is slack.

Friday, 16 August. Forgot to put down for Wednesday that I was
followed by a gang of kids across the rectory space, with the leader
shouting 'bearded nit'.

12 September. Corporation workman having an awful time
cutting the grass. Small ginger-haired girl lying down in his path,
standing, running just before him, grabbing hold and pushing. Man
(or rather boy) reduced in the end to clouting her, since nothing else
would make her shift.

13 September. On the central avenue the usual comments from
the younger teenagers when they saw me, 'Jesus Christ Almighty.'
The older ones were completely indifferent to me, discussing motor
bikes. The younger ones, boys and girls, were trying to squash
altogether on the concrete seat, far too many of them. While in the
shadows a group of old people were looking at them helplessly con-
templating intervention ... 'I'm just about fed up with the noise ...'
'But if you say anything to them all you get is cheek. It's no use, etc,
etc.' Half an hour later the same business was still going on, the old
people standing at another doorway now.

A few days later, he pondered how 'illnesses present a social problem', in the context of Pat almost certainly catching a cold from their son's friend Tony, who 'still comes sniffing, sneezing and wiping his nose on the back of his hand, playing with Daniel's toys'. 'We have,' he went on, 'the urge and need to be on good terms with neighbours, but no more so than the average communally minded neighbour. Do we let Tony in or declare him persona non grata until his cold is better, which it appears never will be.'

Pervading much of Marsden's Trinity fieldwork is a sense of discontent. 'We thought the [ground floor] flat was marvellous at first,' a 35-year-old mother of two told him:

> We couldn't rush down here fast enough, but I wouldn't have a flat again. I wouldn't move out of here unless to go into a house. When I first came here I used to wake up in the morning and I used to have a terrible headache. It was as though there was something pressing on my head. It was these ceilings and the idea of people living upstairs. I used to feel they were going to fall down on me ...

As for television, she went on, 'it's taken all our family life away. Before we got TV, after tea we used to sit down and play with the kids. We used to get the dominos out and the ludo ... And then you get arguments about which channel to watch.' Also unhappy was an elderly lady with grown-up children. 'You don't get good neighbours now,' she declared to Pat (likewise keeping a diary). 'To me a good neighbour is someone who'll help you out when you're ill. You get none of that round here.' A last word on neighbourliness or the lack of it went to a tough-minded but baffled elderly widow:

> It never bothered me, because I never neighboured anyway, but people just aren't as neighbourly any more. Yes, there were rough families, and bad families, but even so they seemed to have a sort of fellow-feeling for the people round about. Not now, though. The people just want to keep to themselves and have nothing to do with the others. I think television's a lot to blame; when people sit glued to a television set all night they soon lose interest in other things. The people must be worse than they used to; there's more crime.

I can't understand it; people are being given more money, better houses, better opportunities …[16]

*

' "The People" placard stated: "Christine Keeler a shameless slut exposed," so I bought a copy (5d),' noted Henry St John on 4 August. His pay-off included descriptions of her as 'an empty-headed trollop, skilled only at using her body to bewitch and betray', who 'smoked marijuana and loved orgies', rarely washed, had soiled underwear, and 'boasted of picking up down-and-outs in the street and taking one of the scruffiest of them to sleep with her'. In short, 'if you want your house turned into a brothel, with coloured layabouts all over the place, drug orgies and all that jazz, accept Miss Keeler as a tenant'. Philip Larkin's downmarket reading that Sunday was the *News of the World*, which opted to attack Keeler's friend, his body barely cold. 'I still feel a bit sorry for Ward,' he told Monica Jones. 'I don't think any proper evidence was brought against him, & in any case he has "paid the final entrance fee" … No doubt he was a disagreeable person – the *N of the W* tried to make him sound so – I am perhaps being over-sensitive.'

It was a Bank Holiday weekend of jazz festivals. At Smethwick, complained 'Old Square' to the local paper, Lightwood's Park was taken over by 'beatniks and bearded weirdies' listening to 'the ear-splitting dischords that pass for modern music'; while at Cleethorpes, two of the performers, Acker Bilk and George Melly, found themselves in conversation. 'Acker told me how strongly he felt about Ward's suicide,' related Melly in a letter to the *Guardian* some ten days later. ' "Fall guy" was the expression he used, and his indignation was expressed in his usual rich and forthright idiom.' Melly then mentioned to Bilk about a wreath that he and others were intending to send to Ward's funeral, a wreath that would carry the message, 'To Stephen Ward, a victim of British hypocrisy'. 'So enthusiastic was he,' went on Melly's account, 'that he offered to pay for the whole thing and suggested that the words "Hard luck, mate," should be added to the message.' In the event, after press reports about Acker's proposed involvement had reached his brother-cum-manager David Bilk, his name was withdrawn; but the wreath of 600 white roses, with accompanying message, for Ward's funeral (held very privately at Mortlake

Crematorium on the afternoon of Friday the 9th) was still sent by such notable, if more predictable, writers, artists and others as Peter Blake, Alex Comfort, Fenella Fielding, Doris Lessing, Joan Littlewood, Christopher Logue, Adrian Mitchell, Edna O'Brien, John Osborne, Alan Sillitoe, Kenneth Tynan, Arnold Wesker and Angus Wilson, as well as Melly himself.

Next day, an editorial in the *Guardian*, far from saluting the wreath, praised Acker Bilk for his 'wisdom and discretion' in withdrawing his name, called Ward 'the victim of his own impulses which led him into many squalid sorts of crime, not all of them mentioned on the official charge sheet', and declared flatly that 'there ought to be no support for any myth about his being a "martyr" and nothing but contempt for those who try to encourage such a myth'. Letters of protest rapidly poured in. 'A scapegoat was found, and the Establishment has closed its ranks around his body,' insisted Tynan in response to the paper's 'oddly unhinged' editorial; Melly made clear that there was no reason to believe that Acker Bilk had changed his original views; C. S. Forbes of Kensington called it 'the most vicious obituary ever written in a reputable newspaper'; and from 121 Broadhurst Gardens in West Hampstead, Eric Thompson quoted classic liberal doctrine ('there must remain a realm of private morality and immorality which is, in brief and crude terms, not the law's business') before declaring: 'The alarming feature of this case is not the conduct of Dr Ward: it is the way in which justice has so signally failed to be seen to be done. The widespread suspicion of political manipulation of the police and judiciary – however unfounded – is the real threat to our institutions.'[17] However unfounded ... And there, indeed, matters more or less rested, pending Lord Denning's verdict on whether, *inter alia*, such suspicions were founded or otherwise.

The world somehow staggered on during these late-summer weeks. In the early hours of Thursday the 8th, the Cheddington train robbery (as it was sedately called before rapidly transmuting into the much-glamorised Great Train Robbery) involved the Glasgow–London mail train being halted in Buckinghamshire, the driver Jack Mills being hit over the head with an iron bar and permanently injured, and a gang of 15 men getting away with £2,631,684 in used banknotes; early evening on Friday, hours after Ward's funeral and

coming on ITV immediately after *Emergency-Ward 10*, the genial
Keith Fordyce presented the first *Ready, Steady, Go!* (slogan: 'The
Weekend Starts Here!'), with a line-up of Brian Poole and the
Tremeloes (their hit version of 'Twist and Shout'), Billy Fury, Chris
Barber, Pat Boone, and Miss X (Lionel Blair's sister Joyce, performing
topical 'Christine') in front of a live and active teenage audience,
the whole thing instantly prompting one teenage viewer, Laurence
Marks, to acclaim it as 'the best pop television programme I have ever
watched'; on Sunday, while the *News of the World* ran an exception-
ally nasty obituary of Ward ('utterly depraved man ... a central figure
of evil ... a coward'), the *People* exposed a former player called Jimmy
Gauld as the mastermind behind an emerging football match-fixing
scandal; later that day, at the National Jazz and Blues Festival held in
Richmond, it was a case again of unfortunate Acker as his youthful
audience abruptly deserted him en masse once they heard the Rolling
Stones strike up in a nearby marquee; on Thursday the 15th, Harry
Burnett was hanged in Aberdeen (the gallows only built the previous
year), *Billy Liar* opened at the Warner in Leicester Square, and the
Stratford-on-Avon by-election, following Profumo's departure from
the Commons, produced a sharply reduced Conservative majority –
with 22-year-old singer Screaming Lord Sutch (top hat, black tie, tails
and white gloves, all of them oversized) securing just the 209 votes
for the newly formed National Teenagers Party and its policy of
reducing the voting age from twenty-one to eighteen; the following
week, Peter Hall brought his triumphant Stratford production of *The
Wars of the Roses* (four Shakespeare plays turned into a trilogy) to the
Aldwych, the new commoner was returned (in the event not entirely
unopposed) for Bristol South East, the England manager Alf Ramsey
('a compact, urbane man who speaks slowly and picks his words
adroitly') predicted in a press conference at a London hotel that his
team would win the 1966 World Cup, an adaptation at the New Arts
of Anthony Powell's *Afternoon Men* got mixed reviews ('a firm, controlled, inbred performance by James Fox as the weedy, wet hero,'
thought Alan Brien, but 'the girls – Imogen Hassall, Georgina Ward
and Pauline Boty – are more attractive to look at than interesting to
listen to'), James Baldwin appeared on *This Week* ('doesn't he speak
English well?' remarked Veronica Lee's mother), the Beatles released
'She Loves You' – and the Stones, fresh from Brian Jones telling *NME*

about their increasingly luxurious hair that 'we see no reason why we should cut it off to conform', destroyed the competition on the third outing of *Ready, Steady, Go!* 'Tonight they make Jet Harris and Tony Meehan look like they have arrived in the prehistoric age,' recorded Marks. 'The Rolling Stones are dressed in leather waistcoats, white shirts and dark ties, but their hair is the longest of any group around. They play their new record "Come On" and I would buy it if I could afford it.'[18]

The final Test of the series was by now under way at The Oval. On Saturday the 24th, allowed up on my own from Salisbury and unutterably thrilled by the whole experience, I sat in a packed crowd next to a friendly West Indian man as the English batting once again flattered to deceive; on Monday, in front of another full house estimated by *Wisden* as two-thirds West Indian, the match finished in a decisive victory for the visitors. 'The only people seemingly blind and deaf to this predestination,' observed John Fowles in the 'six-bob' seats, 'are those in the pavilion and the members' stands.' They 'sit up there,' he went on, 'layered row after row of pink jelly-babies, togas off and club ties on, looking utterly out of sympathy with everyone else all round the ground ... They sit there, morosely clapping, taking their Caribbean medicine with the bitterest of old-school faces.' Whereas:

Down in the crowd one has the reality, the placid white and the vital brown mixing, laughing, shouting, carried away in the currents of joy and jokes that ripple round and round the field. I find myself surrounded by English and West Indians in about equal proportions. Only one person seems out of place, a middle-aged and middle-class Englishman whose looks become grimmer and grimmer ...

The middle-aged Englishman who wants England to win snaps at a young ted listening to the commentary on his transistor. 'For God's sake turn that damn thing off.' The West Indians around us rush to the ted's defence. 'You listen, boy, you listen. You do just what you like.' The transistor gets louder, there's a gurgle of laughter, and the killjoy sits out the rest of the match with a permanent scowl on his puritan face.

By late afternoon it was almost over. 'It ceases to be cricket, it changes effervescently into a religious experience, a lovely joy. It is intense for the last few moments of the match, this communion, this white love of the brown, this brown love of the white, this equality.' Next day, a mass meeting of 500 bus workers in Bristol finally agreed to end the colour bar there; and on Wednesday the 28th, to complete a sequence of hope, Martin Luther King declared in Washington DC that he had a dream.

Eight days later, as Keeler was being arrested and charged with perjury and conspiracy to obstruct the course of justice, Macmillan reflected on who in the fullness of time should succeed him ('it needs a man with vision & moral strength – Hailsham, not Maudling'); on the Saturday (7 September), Ted Dexter's Sussex defeated Worcestershire in the first Gillette Cup Final amidst a raucous, football-style atmosphere at Lord's, prompting E. W. Swanton to comment warily that 'everyone seemed to be "with it"'; Harold Wilson's speech in Glasgow next day included a personal commitment to starting a 'university of the air'; *Outlook Europe* on BBC TV on Monday had a liberal-minded French reporter being dismayed by the illiberal views he had heard in Smethwick ('I don't mind foreigners, mind you, but I can't stand darkies ... They smell ... They're a lower class than we ...'); next weekend, Jo Grimond told the Liberals gathered at Brighton of his intention to march his troops 'toward the sound of gunfire', seventeen-year-old George Best made his nerveless debut for Manchester United against West Bromwich Albion in front of 50,043 spectators at Old Trafford ('like dog shit, he got everywhere,' recalled the opposing full back), the Last Night of the Proms did its annual televised stuff ('I always turn the volume up full blast and just sit there singing and cheering with the audience,' said a shorthand typist), on Sunday afternoon it was the turn at the Royal Albert Hall for the 'Great Pop Prom' (Beatles and Stones both appearing, Alan Freeman the MC), and Robert Harling in the *Sunday Times* acclaimed John le Carré's *The Spy Who Came In From The Cold* as 'the real thing' in the genre of suspense fiction, the work of 'a rare and disturbing writer' – break-through moment for the former Eton teacher. On Tuesday the 17th, as Raghbir Singh, a Sikh, became Bristol's first non-white bus conductor, Patrick Gordon Walker held a press conference in Smethwick, calling the recent TV coverage of his constituency overstated but conceding 'a little bit of Fascist trouble' in relation to immigration; the following Monday, it was the Albert Hall again, this time for Keith Joseph to address a mass meeting of London local government officers ahead of the amalgamation of London boroughs, with the attending Anthony Heap finding the minister 'amiable but vague'; the same day, Lord Gosford, chairman of the British Road Federation, opened the six-ways Aston underpass in Birmingham, declaring as he did so, 'Take the motor vehicle away and the city will surely die'; and on Tuesday the 24th, Jeremy Sandford made his first TV splash with a revealing documentary about life below stairs – overworked and underpaid – in the Savoy Hotel, transmitted despite the Savoy's best legal efforts to block it.[19]

Diarists and others recorded some of the rhythms of daily life post-Ward, pre-Denning. Soon after Patrick Anderson, a lecturer-cum-reviewer of late middle age had moved into an Essex village near Halstead, the milkman from a nearby farm called in, leaving behind 'little blue and white paper collars to fit the empties – *Another Pinta Please*'. For many, of course, during August and early September anyway, it was holiday time. 'The most terrible place, full of funfair-type amusements, rock shops, bingo halls, etc', where 'everyone looked as bored as I felt' was Veronica Lee's disaffected take on Great Yarmouth; 17-year-old Kathleen Perry, from Barrow, was on holiday in Blackpool and went to the Russ Conway Show ('saw Russ at stage door, he was very sarcastic to his fans & would not give autographs but I still like him'); and the journalist Geoffrey Moorhouse dipped a toe at Southend-on-Sea, where 'you don't hear much apart from East End voices', stalls every few yards along the prom sold cockles and jellied eels, and crowds thronged 'its chambers of horrors, its deafening arcades (which have all gone to Bingo) and its amusement park in the Kursaal'. Dominant sound during the early weeks was 'Sweets for My Sweet' by the Searchers (another Merseybeat group), but from late August it was 'She Loves You' all the way. Joy Davis was on a family holiday in Cornwall, teaming up with a girl cousin of the same age, when they realised to their consternation that the new Beatles single was about to come out:

> Fortunately [she recalled years later], a catering assistant we had befriended in the hotel was a fellow fan and told us where we could find a record shop – 30 miles away. We pestered my uncle to take us, but he was somewhat reluctant, sensibly pointing out that we would

be unable to play the disc until we got home ... He failed to appreciate that for two teenage girls consumed by Beatlemania [the word itself about to be coined], it didn't matter that we couldn't play it. To keep the peace, he agreed to take us to the shop, on the proviso that we behaved impeccably for the remainder of the holiday. We agreed, of course.

So, on the release day, we bought our copies, and when we returned to the hotel clutching our precious vinyl, we found a note slipped under our door, from our fellow fan, to say she had the evening off, and if we went to her room in the staff annexe, she would let us play the disc on her Dansette. What followed was a great evening listening to the Fab Four, eating cakes she had got from the hotel's afternoon tea service selection and quaffing West Country cider ...

Pop Go the Beatles was still weekly on the radio: on 10 September some 19 per cent of all twelve to fourteen year olds listened to it; a fortnight later, as the series ended, the proportion was over 27 per cent. New arrival on the small screen was *Marriage Lines*, a good-natured sitcom making the names of both Richard Briers and Prunella Scales. The critics naturally loathed it ('a trivial, stale, inept bore,' thought the *New Statesman*'s Francis Hope); equally naturally, viewer comments on the first episode included 'good light entertainment for a tired businessman on a Friday evening' and 'how nice to have an *English* comedy series like this'.

A highlight for Judy Haines these weeks was her husband John buying a Pye Black Box stereo record player ('it is really wonderful, and lovely to look at'), but for most of the time for most people, like any other time of the year and including for Judy herself, life was real, life was earnest. 'Started my 5th year at the Xaverian College,' solemnly noted 15-year-old Roger Darlington in Fallowfield, Manchester. 'THE year – the G.C.E. year.' *The Times* responded to heightened concern about the state of London housing by describing in graphic detail a house in which 'a young girl near to tears' was living in a 'pitifully small room' with her husband: no water except for a cold tap in the backyard three flights down; the only lavatory for the house's eleven people 'too filthy to use'; shared cooking facilities; an infestation of rats; and 'the walls so ridden with bugs and beetles that the girl was afraid to replace the ancient wall-paper which helped to some extent to keep them from crawling into the room'. In Southall, the sight in highly 'respectable' Palgrave Avenue of Indians looking over a house for sale prompted a prominent local Conservative, Mrs Penn, to form a Palgrave Avenue Residents' Association, successfully petitioning the council to prevent the house falling into non-white hands, that rapidly transmuted into a Southall Residents' Association. None of this sort of thing surfaced in Donald Balfour's diary, but the visiting Australian was struck by the industrial grimness of Glasgow ('dense smoke, really thick') and the approach from Rochdale into Manchester ('everywhere chimneys are to be seen belching out black smoke which settles all over the place'). One Saturday, as he and his wife travelled around London on a 'Go as you please' ticket, they got off a bus at Aldgate in search of sustenance, encountering there a somehow quintessential English experience:

Ordered some chicken soup, but after five minutes were told that chicken soup was off.

Didn't fancy the other soups, so went to the next course. The menu showed that plaice was off, so we asked for Dover Sole. Asked whether we wanted salad with it, at no extra cost, we said no.

After ten minutes the waitress came back to announce that they couldn't find the sole. When I expressed disappointment that the sole was off I was told that it wasn't off, they just couldn't find it! But the plaice was nice, I was assured. We pointed out that the menu indicated that plaice was off. We were assured that plaice was on.

So we ordered that, and for good measure, by now being quite hungry, asked for salad with it. The waitress informed us that salad was extra with plaice. By now we were confused, so decided no salad.

'Anyway,' he concluded, 'the plaice proved to be nice.'[20]

On the evening of Wednesday, 25 September, around the time of the first outing of ITV's new sitcom *Our Man at St Mark's* (Leslie Phillips as the vicar, Joan Hickson as loyal but overbearing housekeeper), queues started to lengthen outside Her Majesty's Stationery Office in Kingsway. 'There was,' remembered taxi driver David Morris, 'a scene of utter chaos':

> The Kingsway tramway was being converted to the road under-pass from Waterloo Bridge, and there was scaffolding in the exit to the tunnel. Men, all men, were clambering precariously on the scaffolding, the street was packed, spilling into the road and blocking the traffic, with people waiting for the doors to open. There was an air of mild hysteria as everyone tried to get a copy of the report to enjoy the titillating bits ...

In answer to a question from a TV reporter, a man replied that he had come along because he was a life-long admirer of Lord Denning. Finally, at 12.30 a.m., his report was officially released: a young Oxford undergraduate from East Finchley, buying eight copies at 7s 6d each, the first to be served; 4,000 copies sold in the first hour; and some 100,000 copies within a week.

Overall, apart from criticising Macmillan and his colleagues for a certain gullibility in failing to take seriously enough the rumours about Profumo's adultery, Denning exonerated the government. In relation to Keeler, the Master of the Rolls declared that back in February the *News of the World*'s photograph of her in 'the slightest of swimming garbs' had been sufficient for most people to be able to 'infer' her 'avocation', i.e. that she was a prostitute; in relation to Ward, he drew a relentlessly and pruriently hostile portrait of him as (in Davenport-Hines's words) 'a repugnant, irredeemable wretch ... almost as a white slaver'. Despite the overall whitewash, some of the Conservative-supporting but no longer pro-Macmillan press made a decent stab on Thursday morning at embarrassing the PM – 'Premier Failed' (*Telegraph*); 'Mac Blamed' (*Sketch*) – while the *Mirror* targeted Denning, observing that 'public doubts and worries about morality in high places are left unanswered'. On the whole, though, the general mood that day seems to have been one of flatness, of a feeling that a fitfully compelling but ultimately discreditable episode had come to an end. Still, for schoolboys anyway (and perhaps not only them), curiosity did not abate instantly. Among them, 14-year-old Laurence Marks:

Fans clapping for the Beatles at the Globe Theatre. Stockton-on-Tees, 22 November 1963.

Mods and Rockers by the seaside. Margate, 17 May 1964.

Holiday scene. Brighton, 1 July 1963.

English athlete Ann Packer, a PE teacher at Coombe County Secondary School for Girls. She won gold and silver medals while representing Great Britain at the 1964 Tokyo Olympics. New Malden, 2 November 1964.

Demolition of the old clock tower.
Blackburn, 30 December 1964.

A view of the lights in Lord Street. Liverpool, 22 November 1962.

Postman and postwoman having a picnic. Norfolk, 1964.

A busy street on a rainy day. Smethwick, 1964.

Queen Elizabeth II visits the Bull Ring market. Birmingham, 24 May 1963.

Labour Party poster starring Harold Wilson. London, January 1964.

Fans crowd the street outside the London Pavilion ahead of the premiere of the Beatles' first feature-length film, *A Hard Day's Night*. London, 6 July 1964.

Cheers from West Indian spectators after an England wicket falls. The Oval, London, 24 August 1963.

Battersea smog over rooftops. London, 7 December 1962.

Tottenham Hotspur footballers Terry Dyson, John Hollowbread, Jimmy Greaves, Dave Mackay, John White and Freddie Sharpe celebrate at their annual Christmas party at the canteen at White Hart Lane. London, 18 December 1962.

At the end of our double maths lesson, Hogg tells me that Wildman, whose dad is a solicitor, has a copy of the government report published last week with all the dirty bits in it. We meet in the biology lab and it's true, Wildman does have a copy of the Denning Report. It is too thick to read in the time we have because we know that if we are caught with this report we could be expelled. I can see that Christine Keeler is called a 'Call Girl' and I don't know what this means.

'Please sir, what's a call girl?' I ask our history master later this afternoon. He whacks me round the head and asks me where I heard that expression? I tell him in the Denning Report and he whacks me round the head for a second time. I think he is just jealous that I have seen a copy and he hasn't ...

That was on Thursday. And next day:

I ask Wildman if I can read his copy of Lord Denning's Report and he says 'yes', but in exchange for a bar of Topic from the tuck shop. I take it to the library ... but there's nothing sexy in it at all. It's in four parts and I turn all the pages to see if Lord Denning tells us what went on between John Profumo and Christine Keeler, as Hogg said it would, but there's nothing really. Who cares 'Where Lies the Responsibility?' I want to know all about what Christine Keeler did and how she did it and to who. I'd be better off reading the News of the World, which we're not allowed to at school.[21]

7

Under Our Noses

There were moments in 1963 when Britain was seemingly on the verge of a nervous breakdown, or worse. Even with a quarter of the year still to go, it was clear that two narratives had been neatly complementing each other: one of deep and perhaps irreversible economic-cum-geopolitical decline; the other of deep and perhaps irreversible moral and spiritual decline.

'SUICIDE OF A NATION?', *Encounter*'s special issue that July, was largely about the first, including 'Amateurs and Gentlemen, or the Cult of Incompetence' (Goronwy Rees), 'The Comforts of Stagnation' (Michael Shanks), 'Taboo on Expertise' (Austen Albu) and 'The Tragedy of Being Clever' (John Vaizey on education, arguing that 'the degree to which social class has limited the development of talent can hardly be exaggerated'). 'Each time I return to England from abroad,' declared Malcolm Muggeridge in the lead piece ('England, Whose England?'), 'the country seems a little more run down than when I went away; its streets a little shabbier, its railway carriages and restaurants a little dingier; the editorial pretensions of the newspapers a little emptier, and the vainglorious rhetoric of its politicians a little more fatuous.' At which point the Fat Controller might have nodded his shiny, balding head. 'Not only we as railways, but the whole nation has to choose whether it is going to see things clearly and then grapple with the difficulties which result from reshaping, or not,' Dr Beeching a few weeks earlier had told 400 Glasgow businessmen gathered at an Institute of Directors luncheon. 'We are at the point where we decide whether to go on pretending that we continue the pattern which was fine at the beginning of this century, or even in the 19th century, or whether we are going to look at it squarely and reshape the industry of the country so that we compete in the world.' He ended on a barely optimistic note: 'I think we shall make the right choice, but we make very heavy weather in the process.'

The other narrative had of course at its heart the juiciest scandal of a scandal-ridden year. 'The Denning Report is out, and everyone has been agog,' Vere Hodgson in Shropshire relayed to friends abroad soon after publication. 'We still read about Mr Profumo's conduct with a sort of GASP ... The general result is that Christine Keeler who has had lovers galore comes out richer with a fortune. The Wages of Sin are shekels and shekels ... and shekels.' For one thoroughly jaundiced observer, the two narratives were effectively a single tale of woe. 'What did they die for?', wondered Noël Coward earlier in September after attending a ' "Battle of Britain" dinner':

> I came away from that gentle, touching, tatty little party with a heavy and sad heart. The England those boys died for has disappeared. Our history, except for stupid, squalid, social scandals, is over ...
>
> We are now beset by the 'clever ones,' all the cheap, frightened people. The young men who are angry and mediocre, the playwrights who can see nothing but defeat and who have no pride, no know-ledge of the past, no reverence for our lovely heritage, nothing but a sick kowtowing to fear of death. Perhaps – just perhaps – someone will rise up and say, 'This isn't good enough.' There is still the basic English character to hold on to.

'I despise the young,' he concluded – those young who 'see no quality in our great past and who spit, with phoney, left-wing distain, on all that we, as a race, have contributed to the living world.'[1]

Over half a century on, and whatever one's take on moral decline or otherwise, it is hard to make out a revisionist case for the Profumo scandal as an uplifting passage in our island story. A minister who lied first to colleagues, then to Parliament, before getting off quite lightly; the popular press on a prurient, sensationalist, conscience-free ram-page; a young woman exploited and trashed; a scapegoat identified and entrapped; a show trial at the Old Bailey; a life ended early; the whitewash of a report.

What did the public make of it all? Questioned by Gallup towards the end of June, more than half declared themselves 'horrified', wanted the private lives of ministers to be 'above reproach', and thought that the affair would have 'a serious effect on our reputation abroad'; later in the summer, Gallup found 85 per cent disapproving 'of newspapers paying large sums to people like Christine Keeler to publish their stories'. Somewhat more relaxed, to judge by research undertaken in London during October, were working-class Conservatives. The main target of any moral censure was Keeler ('She was only out to make money, wasn't she, from whoever she could go to bed with, and I think she wanted a damn good tanning. Somebody ought to put her over their knee and wallop her. After all, he's a married man ...'); while as for Profumo, the predominant view was that what he did in his private life was up to him ('Nature will have its way, whichever way you look at it ... If he wants all the women in the world, let him have 'em!'), but that he was wrong to have lied ('A liar is worse than a thief, and once a man is a liar, he's always a liar, to my idea'). So, too, broadly speaking, with a local poll (including some of Profumo's constituents) taken by the *Banbury Guardian*: overwhelming condemnation of the former minister for having lied in the Commons, but otherwise little sense of shock, with any blame for what he had done behind closed doors coming almost entirely from the middle-aged or elderly. Among them, 'Mrs D. M. England' of '1 Council Houses, Town Hill': 'I expect my MP to lead a blameless life, and this is dreadful. I cannot forgive him ...'[2] Overall, then, a mixed picture, but with the only national survey suggesting that the British were not yet *quite* ready, in the matter of politicians and morals, to go entirely Gallic.

What if anything, over and above significantly undermining the authority of Macmillan and his government, was the episode's legacy? For David Frost, writing 30 years later on behalf of 'the TW3 gang and *Private Eye* and the rest', it was 'as if the Profumo affair had been the test case':

Was Britain in fact led by men of honour, and were we all just teenaged sneerers seeking to erode all that was fine and good in our green and pleasant land? The Profumo affair, however illogically, seemed to prove everything.

For years we had had a growing suspicion that the Old Order, while preaching stern Old Morality to its subjects, had been enjoying private passage-creeping on a basis that made even the New Morality look austere by comparison. Now the Establishment had been caught with its pants down and, unable to hide, was standing red-faced as everyone else fell about laughing. Game, set and match to satire!

More recently, Richard Davenport-Hines tends (albeit less enthusiastically) to agree, depicting the Profumo affair as not only 'a body-blow to Macmillan's government', but 'the death-blow of an England that was deferential and discreet'. 'That summer,' he asserts, 'inaugurated the raucous period when authority figures were denied respect even when they deserved it ... Traditional notions of deference had been weakening for years, but after June 1963 they became mortally sick. Authority – however disinterested, well-qualified and experienced – was increasingly greeted with suspicion rather than trust. Respect and deference, even when merited, were increasingly seen as a species of snobbery.' For Anthony Wedgwood Benn at the time, a week after Profumo's resignation, the moment marked unmistakeably 'the decay of the old British Establishment'; and the day before the trial began of that hypocritical Establishment's chosen victim, Mollie Panter-Downes reflected that 'it is ironic that Miss Keeler and her friends have been made to appear not as purveyors of pleasure but almost as high moralists and puritanical reformers, asking the startled country to look through the doors they have in unexpected ways helped to open on various aspects of British life, all unflattering'.

Yet did anyone imagine that at this point an embarrassed Establishment – almost entirely white and male, with many coming from the same families (as shown by the famous blue chart in Anthony Sampson's 1962 *Anatomy of Britain*) – would simply fold its tent and slink away? That the monarchy would suddenly stop being a semi-religious organisation? That Whitehall would suddenly stop being wrapped in secrecy, with the idea of explanation viewed as almost unpatriotic? That Britain would suddenly become a land of genuine meritocracy and equality of opportunity? Take the City of London: 1963 may have been the year that saw the start in London of the Eurobond market, in effect a new international capital market, with the still only barely trusted outsider Siegmund Warburg a key pioneer figure; but the City as a whole remained determinedly insular, cartel-ridden and nepotistic, a clubbish place of short working days and long alcoholic lunches. 'When I came out of the office in the evening,' recalled Martin Gordon (who joined Warburgs in 1963), 'the only other people I would ever see would be Japanese bankers.'[3] A world, in short, of entitled gentlemanly capitalism: utterly reliable in its own terms, but very seldom seeing a bigger picture.

Critics of the Establishment had little doubt, structurally speaking, about the identity of the prime guilty party. 'No one visiting a public [i.e. private] school can fail to be struck by the continuity of these isolated communities,' Sampson had already noted in *Anatomy*. 'They roll on with their Latin jokes, their founders' prayers, their fags and private languages, still perpetuating vestigial aspects of a Victorian world.' In his 1963 study *The British Political Elite*, W. L. Guttsman lamented how nearly all Conservative MPs, and a significant minority of Labour MPs, had been educated at fee-paying boarding schools, meaning that 'a majority of the membership of the House of Commons lacked during some of the most formative years of their lives any contact with those outside the circle of the upper or the upper middle class' – in effect, 'a barrier to democracy'. A notably strong critique was Elizabeth Young's in the 'Suicide' issue of *Encounter*. She explained how, because of financially superior resources invested in his education, 'a moderately intelligent boy has a better chance of getting to a university (and particularly to Oxford or Cambridge) from the better public schools than from all but a handful of State schools'; and how this particular form of education provided many other unfair advantages, above all through personal connection. The unavoidable remedy, she concluded, was integration:

One need not take very seriously the argument that a comprehensive fee-less system is an intolerable infringement of an Englishman's freedom to spend his money as he likes. The Englishman gave up his freedom to buy his way to heaven centuries ago; he gave up his right to buy himself a commission in the army, to buy himself a private bill of divorcement, and each time gained more freedom than

he lost. These things were and are too important to be left to the
chance ownership of money.

It is now in education that the buyable element is cancerous on
the system as a whole, just as indulgencies and scandalous officers
were in their day. Education, which used to be a class luxury, is now
a necessity for the whole of our society.

Ted Hughes presumably agreed. In a searing piece ('The Rat under the
Bowler') written for an American magazine later in the year, he laid
into the snobbery of the British ruling class, as imbibed at their 'big
expensive Public Schools' and as most eloquently revealed by the way
that class talked: 'The aloof, condescending superiority, the dry for-
mality, the implicit contempt, the routine thought and extinction of
feeling – above all, that pistol-shot, policing quality. It is a voice for a
purpose, an instrument.' That purpose, he added, was to elicit 'instant
obedience and fear'.

Was, then, a moment at hand? The Attlee government had missed
a clear earlier moment, but perhaps it was not too late? The Liberal
Party's 1,600 delegates, meeting that September in Brighton for
their annual conference, certainly thought the tide of history was
now running one way. 'The public schools,' noted Panter-Downes,
'came in for scathing attacks from all sides as "the kindergarten of the
Establishment" – not, as many speakers hastened to point out, because
they do not provide a first-rate liberal education but because they seg-
regate their pupils for life in what one member of the Executive (who
spoke with some experience, having been educated at two of the segre-
gating establishments – Eton for a brief spell and then Prince Charles's
school, Gordonstoun) described as "the Old Boy net of privilege"'.
What about the libertarian argument? 'A lady in a lampshade hat who
said something mild about parents being possibly allowed to pay
for the education of their choice was heckled with cheerful shouts
of "Tory!," after which the assembly voted to bring all independent
schools into the state system.'

A fine dream in a hierarchical, status-ridden society … And seemingly few places as status-ridden, with every worldly nuance counting,
as largely working-class Birkenhead, where Paul O'Grady grew up.
His mother, he admits, 'could be a bit of a snob', and her particular ire
was directed at the woman who ran the local newsagent-cum-grocer's:

Eileen Henshaw liked to adopt a superior attitude, the sort she imagined befitted a grocer's wife. My mother said she was common and that she gave herself airs above her station. She [Eileen] was forever bragging about her son's scholastic achievements and the fact that he went to a grammar school. 'The teachers reckon the way he's going on it'll be head boy for him in a few years,' she'd say to my mother as she sliced into a lump of Cheshire cheese with a length of wire. 'He's a child prodigal,' she'd add, picking crumbs of cheese off the board and chewing on them, smiling pityingly all the while over the counter at me.

'Common cow,' my mother would say on her way home, 'you'd think she ran Harrods instead of a shitty backstreet midden.'

The denouement came in early September 1963, after the parents of 8-year-old Paul (his father a blue-collar worker for Shell Oil at Ellesmere Port) had managed to scrape together the funds to ensure a memorable triumph:

My mother took me to school, but not without paying a visit to Henshaw's first to show off her very own child prodigy.

'I see they've arrested that Christine Keeler for perjury,' Eileen said as we came into the shop, looking up from the *Daily Mirror* that was spread out before her on the counter.

'I'm not interested in the affairs of trollops,' my mother replied curtly. 'I'll just take a *Woman's Own*, please, something to read on the bus.'

'And where are you off to then?' Eileen asked, looking at me and pulling a face as if she'd just discovered dogshit on the floor.

'School,' my mother replied before I could speak. 'It's his first day of term ... at St Anselm's College.' She savoured the words. 'It's two buses, you know, but worth the journey seeing how it's the best boys' school in Birkenhead.'

Eileen, resenting the implication that her own little darling's school might be somewhat inferior to the omnipotent St Anselm's, took the gloves off and unsheathed her claws.

'Isn't that a fee-paying school?' she asked, her face a picture of innocence.

'That's right,' my ma replied airily, as if money were no object.

'Then let's hope they don't have to wait as long for their money as I do for the paper bill,' Eileen crowed.

My mother remained cool in the face of such heavy gunfire.

'Oh, thanks for reminding me,' she said sweetly. 'I've had such a lot on my mind, what with Paul's new school, that I completely forgot about the trivial little things like the paper bill.'

'I think I was the only child that morning who went to school on the bus,' adds O'Grady. 'All the other kids were dropped off by Mummy or Daddy in the car.'[4]

*

Kingsley Amis breaking free from Cambridge ('in England one is supposed to be a writer about Britain in the '50s and '60s') and heading to Majorca; Henry Miller's *Tropic of Cancer* managing to get through first the DPP's relevant department ('public opinion has become much more liberal in the thirty years since the book was written,' reflected its reader, Michael Evelyn) and then the scrutiny of Mervyn Griffith-Jones ('an unpleasant and disgusting book') before being published by John Calder; young Tom Maschler's brutal ditching of the quietly and humorously observant domestic novelist Barbara Pym; the breakthrough novels, almost wholly non-domestic, for Fowles and le Carré – altogether, one way and another, it is not difficult to make out a literary-based case for 1963 as a turning-point year.

Two other writers retrospectively clinched the deal: most famously, in 'Annus Mirabilis' written four years later, Larkin with his iden-tification of 1963 as the year that 'sexual intercourse began', albeit 'rather late' for the middle-aged poet himself; and then, in 1975, Malcolm Bradbury in his brilliant, zeitgeist-capturing novel *The History Man*, relating how in that 'crucial summer, crucial for them, of 1963' a young northern couple, Howard and Barbara Kirk – both of them from 'more or less puritanical homes ... Chapel families ... a mood of self-denial and deliberately chosen inhibition' – broke free, 'making love in parks, smoking pot at parties, going up on the moors and running with their clothes off through the wind, buying stereo equipment, taking trips to London, rubbing margarine on each other in bed, going on demos'. It was also the start of an academic career for the 25-year-old Howard, as he secured a temporary assistant lecture-ship in sociology at Leeds:

> When the new academic year came around in the autumn, and Howard began teaching for the very first time, he found that the events of the summer had given him the gift for bringing a passionate fervour into the subject, making him want to teach it as it had never been taught before. He took his classes to the law courts, and lectured them in the corridors, until the noise became so great that he was asked to leave. He went with them and they all spent the night in a Salvation Army hostel, to know at first hand. He got into demography and social psychology, and took a Wright Mills reformist approach to the field. He found himself deeper into the academic sub-culture, the lifestyle of his fellow-lecturers and especially of his fellow-sociologists. He talked very seriously and solemnly about theoretical matters. He took to wearing the black leather jackets that most of his colleagues, for some reason, affected.

Bradbury knew of what he wrote. 'There were many new beards in 1963; Howard's was one of them.'[5]

No mention by him, though, of the Beatles, nor indeed of the rise more generally by 1963 of popular youth culture. The key material circumstances behind this rise are not difficult to identify: on the one hand, full employment and seemingly ever-expanding teenage spending power; on the other hand, the end of National Service giving young males a more protracted adolescence. But perhaps harder to be precise about is exactly why it was the Beatles who enjoyed such a phenomenally steep ascent, in turn cementing the broader culture. Not being Cliff Richard surely helped. 'At heart these teenage ravers are as square as the Huggets and wouldn't have minded having Her Glorious Majesty Anna Neagle coming along to chaperone,' noted in March one acerbic film critic (Raymond Durgnat) about 'Cliff and his chums clowning agreeably' in *Summer Holiday*, while later in the year John Lennon was tactlessly unequivocal about the great British pop star of the early sixties: 'We've always *hated* him. He was every-thing we hated in pop.' Cliff for his part repaid the compliment. 'All they've done is revert to rock'n' roll,' he disapprovingly informed the *Daily Mirror*. 'We've [i.e. Cliff and the Shadows] played the whole thing down, the screaming and the raving. The Beatles have stoked the whole thing up again ... Their stuff is real homemade music.'

Of course, the Beatles at this particular moment in time had a lot else going for them. 'This working-class explosion was all happening, and we were very much part of it,' Paul McCartney recalled three decades later. 'Making it okay to be common ... we were the wacky chappies from up north.' It was high time, more broadly, for a dose of irreverent informality. 'The Beatles changed everything,' remembered Muriel Young, co-host (with Shaw Taylor) of Radio Luxembourg's *Dance Party*, taped in front of a live audience at EMI's Manchester Square studio and on which the Beatles often appeared. 'Before them I used to do all my announcing in cocktail frocks and things, but after the Beatles you could wear any casual outfit you wanted.' What about sex? 'Just as the Northern Wave films spoke about sex frankly, so did the Beatles,' reflects Travis Elborough. 'The standard conventions of "Love" in song were adhered to, tiresomely on occasion, but there was an honesty that had been rare in British pop before them. The first LP opens with the unambiguously sexual "I Saw Her Standing There".' Towards the end of 1963, a psychiatrist called Dixon Scott made a decent stab at digging deeper into the appeal:

> We admire [their] freshness and innocence so much that it's almost like giving birth. Older generations look at them in wonder, thinking 'This is what we have given birth to: how marvellous they should have gone so far so soon.' With the younger fans, the girls, the adoration is mostly the old story of mass hysteria at a given time. A lot of the feeling among the girls is phoney. But it would not have taken on the magnitude it has if there had not been the need to release sexual urges ...
>
> There's no getting away from it – a revolution is taking place under our noses. It amounts to sexual freedom with a sense of responsibility and honesty. The fans recognise the honesty that shines from the Beatles. While other pop stars have thought in artificial terms of reaching out to their audience, the Beatles are giving honestly as well as receiving.

'The songs were somehow so moving,' was how, her voice breathless with emotion and especially remembering 'All My Loving', Jessica

Chappell would put it half a century later, about seeing them at Sheffield City Hall in her mid-teens. 'It was wonderful. I didn't scream. I just loved them, I was "Beatle barmy". We fancied them like mad, and, I don't know, we just thought they were amazing.' So they were, but their phenomenal rise also represented an astonishing achievement by Brian Epstein. His 'quiet overhaul after he became their manager kept their abrasive life force intact inside a subtly codified front of tidy, polite charm,' reflects Ian Penman. 'The Beatles' class, accent and sex appeal weren't glossed away, but finessed for a world beyond the raucous, claustrophobic clubs they were used to.' They were, in short, 'both deeply ordinary, and something entirely new.'[6]

Rapidly networked after its debut in August, the TV programme that spread the new youth culture across the country was Rediffusion's *Ready, Steady, Go!*. Going out early evening on Fridays, from a basement studio in Kingsway, central London, it was a path-breaking show (utterly different in feel from staid, formulaic *Thank Your Lucky Stars* fronted by Brian Matthew) in which spontaneity was everything. 'We never got it right,' recalls Vicki Wickham, its young editor. 'Every week a camera would mow down a dancer or someone would miss their cue. But because the show was live, it was an absolute must-see. The camerawork set the bar for music on TV: we'd get closeups of the girls dancing, all really sexily. Cathy and I chose the crowd by going to clubs and picking people we thought looked great and could dance.' 'Cathy' was Cathy McGowan, a 19-year-old typist from Tooting when she was originally chosen, just ahead of Annie Nightingale, to be one of the youthful co-presenters alongside the venerable, 34-year-old Keith Fordyce. What, Rediffusion's Elkan Allan asked the two girls in the tie-breaker, mattered most to teenagers. Sex or music or fashion? 'Fashion', unerringly answered McGowan; and in the course of that autumn, making a series of appearances although not formally co-presenting until December, she started to become an icon of the age. 'This one-time secretary with the impracticably long fringe, the curtains of dark hair which were constantly flicked back, the breathless voice and a vocabulary seemingly composed of two words, "smashing" and "fabulous" ("fab" for short),' wrote the fashion journalist Prudence Glynn in 1968. 'What was remarkable about her,' reckons Bob Stanley, 'was how unremarkable she was – she was cool and attractive, but the kind of girl that you could meet in any British town; tall, slim and deeply knowledgeable about fashion, but not unreachable.' As early as October 1963, with the programme barely two months old, the *Daily Sketch* was interviewing 'with-it Cathy' and giving considerable space to her opinions:

> Politicians, clergymen, welfare workers, teachers, – they often seem to us like a lot of silly kids. And if there's one subject they get mixed up about more often than any other, it's this one – the Teenager of Today. They'll say, for example, that Britain's teenagers are becoming more Americanised every day.
>
> They couldn't be more wrong. Just now it's great to be as English as you can get. And if you're from the North of England, like Liverpool, that's even better still … At one time, some kids would pretend that their father were a doctor or a solicitor to impress their friends. Now they're more likely to boast that their Dad works in the meat market or on the roads, particularly if they really do some dull desk job. Teenagers who come from wealthy homes are always trying like mad to prove that they're working-class.

'What We Think of Adults' was the title of her think-piece, and at last the generational traffic was two-way.[7]

Naturally, there was no shortage in 1963 of '1963' moments and markers. Take just the two dozen or so. 'The girls at Freddie's school go on strike because of the school ban on high heels,' May Marlor in Derbyshire recording in relation to her teacher husband; Cambridge University, thanks to senior proctor Ralph Bennett, at last moving to abolish the requirement for students to wear gowns in the streets after dark; the programme for *Oh What a Lovely War* at Wyndham's announcing that the National Anthem 'will only be played in the presence of Royalty or Heads of State'; when the Scala Cinema in Oxford's Walton Street played 'God Save the Queen' after a showing of Wajda's *Ashes and Diamonds*, the new undergraduate Tariq Ali 'thoughtlessly' standing up ('as I used to in Lahore when the national anthem was played'), only to be 'greeted with a uniform chant from the row behind, "Sit down, you fascist!"'; Clifford Williams's RSC production at Stratford of *The Comedy of Errors* instantly famed for how, starting uniformly grey, the scene gradually turned (a scarlet feather, a striking ruff, an absurd hat) into a carnival of colour; BBC TV's new Sunday evening drama slot, *First Night*, from September showcasing new plays by Alun Owen and Arnold Wesker among others, but heavily attacked by the press for sordidness and generally too much 'kitchen-sink-ness'; at Granada, the young director Michael Grigsby making a sympathetic documentary on *Unmarried Mothers*; two American books published in Britain to considerable impact – Helen Gurley Brown's *Sex and the Single Girl* ('is there anything particularly attractive about a 34-year-old virgin?') and Betty Friedan's more radical *The Feminine Mystique* about the plight of suburban housewives (Katharine Whitehorn reflecting how 'she shows pretty conclusively that it is not the drive to independence that has done damage to these American women, but the increasing compulsion to concentrate on getting a man rather than becoming a human being'); Esmé Langley, a lesbian disguised as a middle-aged single mother, gathering together the first meeting of the circumspectly named Minorities Research Group, in effect a lesbian mutual-support club, thereafter coming together monthly at the Shakespeare's Head just behind Liberty's; Toni & Guy hairdressing salons, the creation of Giuseppe ('Toni') Mascolo, starting to appear; Valium arriving in Britain; suicide ceasing to be a crime; creatively talented northerners Ossie Clark and Celia Birtwell (dress designs from him, fabrics from her) now ensconced in London; Jeff Banks, 20-year-old son of an Ebbw Vale sheet-metal worker, opening Cobblers, a boutique in Blackheath, sold out on the first day; Modesty Blaise, strip-cartoon heroine, starting her long run in the *Evening Standard*; Raymond Hawkey's cover for the Pan paperback of Ian Fleming's *Thunderball*, featuring bullet holes cut into the Brian Duffy photograph of a girl's back; the Royal Academy's Summer Exhibition including, for the first time, pop art; debut solo shows including the painter Patrick Procktor at the Redfern (John Berger struck by how 'the figures look as though they have been painted fast: as though the image on the canvas clothed the figure only an instant before and is still crackling like a nylon garment as it is pulled off') and the sculptor John Wragg at the Hanover ('long swaying stalks, gnarled and knotted roots, bare rib-cases, and suggestions of human torsos that have turned to plants', according to *The Times*); not a critic in sight, but many teachers as baffled as their pupils, as the School Mathematics Project (aka the New

Maths) began to spread its wings; pioneering, too, Sybil Marshall's influential *An Experiment in Education*, describing on the basis of her Fenland experience how to bring out the inherent creativity of primary-school children; Robin Pedley, from humble Leicester University, writing a Pelican Original on *The Comprehensive School* (their purpose stirringly defined as 'the forging of a communal culture by the pursuit of quality with equality, by the education of their pupils in and for democracy, and by the creation of happy, vigorous, local communities in which the school is the focus of social and educational life') which over the rest of the decade would go through five reprints or new editions; the era ending on BBC TV of on-screen continuity announcers (tasteful bowl of flowers, appropriate dress for time of day), to be replaced by a spinning globe; the subversive puppet fox Basil Brush, created by Ivan Owen, quickly finding early fame on Rediffusion's *The Three Scampis*; and in Canterbury, the Kent batsman Peter Richardson, son of a Herefordshire farmer, daring to play a practical joke on an unamused E. W. Swanton, as he successfully complained to the umpire (in on the joke) about a booming noise coming from the commentary position above the sight screen – a well-worked gag, leaving the Archbishop of Lord's to ponder sadly less deferential times.[8]

What is *the* '1963' film? Sadly, not quite *Sparrows Can't Sing*, just a bit too sentimental; nor *Heavens Above!*, a Boulting Brothers satire on Church of England self-righteous hypocrisy, but as Penelope Gilliatt rightly noted, 'there's nothing in it that wouldn't make a curate chortle'; and definitely not *It's All Happening*, a feel-good vehicle for Tommy Steele, with others in attendance including Russ Conway, Marion Ryan, Shane Fenton and the Fentones, and most of the regulars from *The Black and White Minstrel Show*. A much more plausible contender, released in November after delays, is Joseph Losey's *The Servant*, with screenplay by Harold Pinter. It was, Losey reflected after finishing it, 'about the destructiveness of trying to live by obsolete and false standards ... a film about people for whom servility is a way of life'. Undeniably, it was – even though filming was completed several months before the Profumo scandal broke – of its moment. 'This year, 1963, was the first year of rumours, doubts, suspicion and scandal about public figures,' the critic Alexander Walker would observe. '*The Servant* managed to capture a state of change

... It exposed the arrogant, self-indulgent corruption of a privileged class ...' Also in the lists are Lindsay Anderson's *This Sporting Life* and John Schlesinger's *Billy Liar*, with the latter's location filming in fast-changing Bradford a particularly compelling mixture of the old and the new. A five-minute sequence, twenty-five minutes in, stands out: Billy (Tom Courtenay) and his friend (played by Rodney Bewes) taking the piss out of the sententious and aged local establishment; Julie Christie, in her first major role, swinging her handbag down the drab northern street, against a background of traffic and demolition; the cheesy comedian, up from London, opening a new supermarket, with the last shot being of a line of trolleys. The most perceptive reviewer at the time was Philip Oakes, calling the film 'a farewell note to the provinces, written by the ones [Keith Waterhouse and Willis Hall, both originally from Leeds] who got away, and dedicated to those who didn't'. And he went on:

> Their script is a detailed survey of a cultural barren, with every blemish carefully noted, every slag-heap ringed with relish. It is a catalogue of prejudice, intolerance, prudishness, and parochialism: universal horrors, to be sure, but at their grimmest north of the Trent. Men who stay there, it suggests, go mad, or take refuge in dreams. No one can be blamed for showing a clean pair of heels.

But, of course, Billy fails to get away, fails to catch that train to London leaving at five minutes after midnight; and Oakes praised Schlesinger for having transcended the original novel-cum-play by giving the whole thing 'a tender irony, which soars now and then into fantasy, but which never, never blunders into farce'.

Yet ultimately, the palm goes to Tony Richardson's *Tom Jones*, released in late June. John Osborne wrote the screenplay (based on the Henry Fielding novel), Albert Finney starred, and it was made by Woodfall Films, hitherto best known for such sober, more social-realist fare as *The Entertainer*, *A Taste of Honey* and *The Loneliness of the Long Distance Runner*. 'We thought it was time,' remarked Richardson, 'we made a really uncommitted film. No social significance for once, no contemporary problems to lay bare. Just a lot of colourful, sexy fun.' In terms of box office – a huge international hit – the formula worked a treat; and Mollie Panter-Downes was far

from alone in praising 'a great, sprawling, boisterous film that is out
to unbutton the elegant embroidered waistcoat in which such elaborate productions usually encase the eighteenth century, and show
it dirty, cruel, yahooish, leching, and guzzling, as well as stylish'.
Nevertheless, after some four or five very notable 'New Wave' years,
it undeniably marked a sea-change away from social comment and
towards escapism. Did Richardson himself regret in retrospect his key
role in that sea-change? Here, his autobiography is silent. But perhaps he took comfort from the *Observer*'s review at the time. 'The
truth that marks most of the relationships and incidents in the film,
the charity, the energy and the brutality, come from Fielding, and
seem moreover related to something enduring in the English character,' claimed Philip French. 'So oddly enough, therefore, *Tom Jones*
appears more generally, socially relevant than earlier Woodfall films,
despite their more obvious superficial contemporaneity.'[9]

Overall, few close observers in 1963 denied that the country's switch
was set at 'on' rather than 'off'. As early as March, *Time* magazine's
man in London had no doubt what the big new preoccupation was:

> On the island where the subject has long been taboo in polite society,
> sex has exploded into the national consciousness and national
> headlines. 'Are We Going Sex Crazy?' asks the *Daily Herald*. 'Is
> Chastity Outmoded?' asks a school magazine for teenagers. 'Are
> Virgins Obsolete?' is the question posed by the solemn *New
> Statesman*. The answers vary but one thing is clear: Britain is being
> bombarded with a barrage of frankness about sex.

That three-letter word was never the PM's favourite, least of all this
particular year; instead, a diary entry in May saw Macmillan in pessimistic vein characterising the British public as seemingly 'more and
more cynical and satirical':

> I read a most depressing account, based on question and answer,
> of what the young intelligentsia are supposed to be thinking. The
> number questioned was 7,000 or so; the questions very detailed and
> very well devised. Religion, morality, patriotism, honour, all these
> are at a discount. Envy (although concealed) is a strong emotion,
> and a rather doleful highbrow concept of a good time.

A day later, and shortly before his own premature death, *Private Eye*'s cartoonist Timothy Birdsall, a star also of *TW3*, put his finishing touches to a double-page spread called 'Britain Gets Wythe Itte, 1963'. 'A nightmarish panorama depicting contemporary England in the style of an eighteenth-century cartoon of debauchery and moral collapse' was the subsequent description by Christopher Booker (co-founder of *Private Eye*, but by July 1963 no longer on the editorial board):

> Against a backdrop of towering office blocks, a huge crowd carrying such banners as 'Hang the Queers' was gathered in Trafalgar Square to watch the public figures of the day, each uttering a street cry such as 'Come ye and stare at ye breasts of a duchesse!', 'Come buy my sweet pornographie, pictures of ye famous lovinge me!'. A placard proclaimed a debate between two bishops on 'Is There A God?', while the Royal Family were posed on a fairground platform, alongside the sign 'Get Snapped With The Royals'. Over it all flew helicopters showering advertising and free gifts with the cry 'Buy Something Today. Buy Anything Today. It Doesn't Matter What But Buy Itte'. The Prime Minister looked on and declaimed 'Looke around ye my people! See what happiness I have brought ye' ...

As for the future author of *The History Man*, he was on the '1963' case even at the time:

> The formality of BBC official language [wrote Malcolm Bradbury in a magazine article that summer] used to be one of great reassurance; it spoke of order, like guards on trains. Now, in a wave of informality, even the news is changing. The names of contributors to newsreels are frequently mentioned (personal), announcers cough regularly and carefully do not, as they easily can, switch the cough out (informal), the opinions of people in the street are canvassed, though they frequently have none (democratic), and interviewers are aggressive and sometimes even offensive (vernacular). So, personal, informal, democratic and vernacular, becomes the new common speech for all things.

No such set-piece analysis or statements from an older novelist, Sid Chaplin. In September, after wryly defining 'self-sufficiency' as 'the means to get out and away and return in time for a favourite television programme', he wrote in the *Guardian* of how 'I have been struck in my wanderings this summer by degrees of social isolation; the aged sitting with their parcels on park benches; the holiday-makers sitting in cars, apart from each other as well as the folk of the countryside, who seem equally disinclined to fraternise.' And Chaplin noted that 'a couple of American poets who had walked the length and breadth of the United Kingdom told me that they were not impressed by our traditional English reticence. They thought it had gone to seed in a barren self-sufficiency.' In short, he wondered: 'Are we contracting out of community?'[10]

Or putting the question another way, was the rise of individualism the master story of 1963? If so, it was not, of course, a trend that started this year – a report in 1962 by the Central Office of Information, partly based on the 1961 census, had already confidently predicted that 'more people will want to move into an outer suburban life, buy cars, educate their children longer, suffer their surgical illnesses in private rooms of hospitals, spend evenings staring at television, spend more, gamble more, buy more washing machines on hire purchase, take holidays in Italy, lay their own parquet floors, and so on' – but perhaps 1963 represented some kind of inflection point? Take a trio of emblematic items: the Beeching Report brutally amputating the rail network and gladdening the car-cum-road lobby; the ad of the elegant woman in evening dress ('After Eight wafer-thin mints have the same effect on me as camellias and candlelight – they make me feel expensive, pampered and gay'); and another woman, another outfit, but this time a skirt and tunic by the already semi-iconic fashion designer Mary Quant that eventually found its way to the V&A's Quant exhibition in 2019, with a small label recording the owner's memory of wearing it in 1963 ('I felt like the bee's knees'). One well-qualified witness had no doubts about the larger state of play by the end of 1963. 'The society-based dogma of the Fifties had been discredited; the individual-based Sixties were getting into full swing,' reckoned David Frost in semi-sceptical middle age. ' "Do your bit" was no longer the motto. Now it was "Do your thing".'

And the politics of it all? The historian Brian Brivati has argued cogently that, in the face of widely perceived relative economic decline, there were only two possible pragmatic responses: either statist (emphasising state action and the key role of the developmental state) or individualist (emphasising the free market and wanting to take the state out of the economy) – a time-honoured conflict of approaches, but especially critical in an era of palpable decline. For the moment, both main parties seemed to be firmly wedded to the more statist, corporatist approach. Yet it has been the cardinal insight of the great American sociologist Robert Putnam that cultural shifts come chronologically *before* political-cum-economic; and on both sides of the herring pond, the shift was under way from a more 'we' to a more 'I' society.[11]

As ever, one can exaggerate the pace of social change. 'There was a pub, on the corner of Silver and Wandsworth Road, that wouldn't serve blacks at all,' recalled Alan Maycock about living in Clapham in 1963 (soon after arriving from Barbados), adding that 'there was another which wouldn't allow them in the saloon bar'; Leo Abse's parliamentary attempt to rationalise and civilise the divorce process was defeated by the Christian lobby, though later in the year the Archbishop of Canterbury did agree to set up a committee on the emotive subject; the Newsom Report on secondary school educa- tion made it clear that sex instruction was to be given on the basis of 'chastity before marriage and fidelity within it'; a survey conducted at 96 grammar schools found that 55.8 per cent of sixth-form girls (though only 28.6 per cent of sixth-form boys) agreed with the proposition that pre-marital sexual intercourse was 'always wrong'; a *Daily Mirror* editorial in October warned against pre-marital sex becoming normalised ('one of the oldest lessons about love outside marriage and couldn't-care-less morals is that it is the woman who always pays'); the pill remained for the most part only available to married women, with the number of UK users still barely 50,000; a minister, Denzil Freeth, abruptly stepped down after morality's grand inquisitor, Lord Denning, had informed Macmillan 'that Mr Freeth did, three years ago, go to a party of a homosexual character and that he participated in homosexual conduct'; the hardback of Harold Robbins's *The Carpetbaggers* sold 200,000 copies, up to half of them at W.H. Smith, but only after the publisher Anthony Blond had taken out the four-letter words and softened the 'explicit' passages in order to ensure that Smiths were prepared to sell it; winner of the competition to become the new voice of the speaking clock was Pat

Simmons, whose refined, cut-glass, thoroughly non-demotic accent (albeit coming from someone who lived in East Ham her whole life) would be regularly likened to the Queen's. Or take the two leading soaps and their often deeply normative followers. A detailed BBC report into the Listening Panel's reactions to *The Archers*, now 12 years old, found dislike of Philip Archer for behaving like a 'spoilt boy', of Lilian Archer for being too self-centred, of Joan Hood for having 'too many moods and complexes'; while a widespread criticism of life as evoked in Ambridge was that there were simply too many 'emotional crises'. Among viewers of *Coronation Street*, no appetite either for confronting the ultimate emotional crisis: there, the scene was filmed of the factory girl Sheila Birtles, crossed in love, committing suicide by taking an overdose of aspirin and then gassing herself – but ahead of intended transmission, word got out to the press, a predictable outcry followed and a hastily rewritten storyline had Dennis Tanner smashing a window in order to get in and bring her round.[12]

It is impossible to gauge precisely where the historical balance lies. Harry Hopkins, writing in 1963, observed that though 'the English may still consume vastly more suet pudding than *apfelstrudel*', nevertheless for the social historian '*apfelstrudel* may embody the *zeitgeist* in a way that roly-poly may not'. A suggestive thought, but is he right? After all, notions of a zeitgeist only get one so far if, at any particular time, the majority of actual flesh-and-blood people, some of them inconveniently old, are in practice obstinately declining in their daily behaviour to follow the reputed spirit of the time. In July the *Smethwick Telephone & Warley Courier* featured a front-page story about two unmarried sisters – Mary Ward (ninety-eight), born when Lord Palmerston was prime minister, and Florrie Ward (eighty-nine) – living together at 50 Park Hill Road and still doing most of the household chores, including cooking: 'Sample lunch: mackerel, fresh peas, potatoes, stewed apple and cornflour blancmange.'

It was probably later this much-mythologised summer that a 17-year-old would-be journalist, Robert Fisk, arrived in Newcastle:

It was a city of heavy, black, 19th-century buildings, a spider's web of iron bridges and smouldering steam locomotives, the air thick with coal smoke and red haze from the steel works at Consett. The news editor of the *Evening Chronicle*, John Brownlee, did his best to cheer me up. 'You'll be in our Blyth office, Bob, a bustling little coal town on the coast with plenty of life and lots of news.' Brownlee was in estate-agent mode. Blyth was a down-at-heel collier harbour, smothered in the dust of doomed mines and a thousand coal fires. The slagheaps glowed red at night, the dying shipyards were bankrupt, pools of vomit lay splashed over the pavements outside the 'Blyth and Tyne' and two dozen other pubs and clubs every Sunday morning. Even in summer, a kind of North Sea mildew settled over the town, a damp, cold cloth mixed with coal smoke that smothered all who lived there.

In 2001, looking back on his youthful year or two on the *Chronicle* before he went to university, Fisk returned to Blyth and met up with Jim Harland, the town's senior reporter back in 1963. The older man proceeded to tell Fisk 'much that I had not known when I worked there':

The town clerk who had been such a classical scholar had been on the make. The police chief had been in the habit of ringing up landlords in the early hours of the morning for a drink, forcing them to open their pubs at 6 am for the local, newly off-duty, cops. 'No, we didn't write this,' Harland said. 'These people fed us. They'd help us. The policeman who'd want an early morning drink would also tip us off on stories. We had to talk to everyone, the town clerk, the police, the fire brigade ... Then there was child abuse. There was a lot of it here. A terrible thing. But the social services wouldn't talk to us. They said all their enquiries were confidential, that we didn't have the right to know what they had learnt. And so child abuse went on. I only realised the state of things when a cricketer I knew made a comment about his daughters and I realised it was a common thing. But we accepted the "privacy" of the social services. And in court, we reported "indecency with a minor". Those were the words we used.'

'We reported the closure of Blyth's mines,' reflected Fisk himself afterwards, 'but we rarely asked why the mines had to die':

We watched Blyth decay. We reported its death. In my cub reporter days, we watched its last moments as a coal-and-ship city. But we didn't scratch the black, caked soot off the walls of Newcastle and ask why Britain's prime ministers allowed the centre of the Industrial Revolution to go to the grave. Harland agreed that there was a culture of 'acceptance' of authority. We didn't challenge the police or the council – or the social services. They may not have been our friends. But we needed them. We respected them, in an odd sort of way. They were the 'chiefs', the 'bosses' ...[13]

*

Although poorly covered by the local press, not least when it came to digging deep into motives and rewards, few aspects of 1963 were more '1963' than the built environment, both present and prospective. Two new books – *London 2000* by 31-year-old geographer and town planner Peter Hall; *New Towns for Old* by Newcastle's city planning officer, Wilfred Burns – simultaneously caught the prevailing mood and pointed the way ahead.

London 2000, recalled a 2014 obituary of Hall, 'argued that London and the south-east should be comprehensively rebuilt, with vast areas of the inner cities bulldozed and replaced by blocks of flats, winding streets by a rectilinear system of motorways and on-ramps, and pedestrians segregated from traffic by walkways in the sky. Detroit, the spiritual home of the motor car, was his guiding light.' That overview was slightly unfair, given that Hall's picture of inner-city Brixton in 37 years' time was a mixture of the old (including its market under the railway arches) and the new. Or as Michael Young noted in his review at the time: 'The terraced houses have been rehabilitated and modernised; their road pattern broken up and sealed from the main traffic streams. On a pedestrian deck above are new shops and offices and a higher education campus.' Young's take on Hall's treatise was broadly favourable – both men sharing a commitment to urbanism – while characteristically reflecting that 'people only come into this book in the last chapter'. 'The more perfect the plan [resting in Hall's case very much on better transport], the more deadly it could be – unless it allows for the unexpected, unless it allows people to make their own still life out of earshot of the motorways, above all, unless it allows for the muddle which people will always create,' added Young, very much in the spirit of Jane Jacobs. 'It will be a great planner who will plan for disorder in the midst of order. It will be a great planner who will let people plan rather than be planned.'

The same critique was true in spades of Burns, for whom the post-war process of urban renewal was still only just getting going. 'With our continually rising standard of living,' he declared, 'the housing redevelopment problem cannot be said to end with the clearance of the slums. Vast areas of mid and late Victorian housing are now outdated even though not always physically outworn.' The lesson he took from existing redevelopment schemes was plain –'we should be looking towards the creation of new types of environment where vertical segregation is the basis of design' – and he had little patience with the inconvenient finding of Margaret Willis that two-thirds of people living in London flats would have preferred to be in a house with a garden. 'The situation,' he insisted about the unpopularity of flats, 'will no doubt change in the future as ways of living change and people are able to lead fuller lives'; while he was adamant that 'old people' in particular 'can be happy in a tall block of flats'. There was, though, one human factor which gave Burns a serious headache. After asserting that 'in a huge city, it is a fairly common observation that the dwellers in a slum area are almost a separate race of people, with different values, aspirations and ways of living', he went on in a passage that over the years acquired justifiable notoriety:

One result of slum clearance is that a considerable movement of people takes place over long distances with devastating effect on the social groupings built up over the years. But, one might argue, this is a good thing when we are dealing with people who have no initiative or civic pride. The task, surely, is to break up such groupings even though the people seem to be satisfied with their miserable environment and seem to enjoy an extrovert social life in their own locality.

'He was,' asserted *Town Planning Review*'s warm obituary of Burns in 1984, 'a man with a vision for what might be: not for design or for the visual appearance of cities, but for making cities work in such a way that brings benefit to people. He was a man who could use opportunities, Newcastle being his personal creative showpiece ...'

Most of the features of that showpiece – involving a major new shopping centre, new office blocks, a cultural plaza, the upgrading of an inner ring road to motorway status, and the destruction of the Royal Arcade and much of Eldon Square, the city's twin jewels from the Georgian era – were set out in Burns's 1963 *Development Plan*, building on his interim plan of two years earlier. At the public inquiry in October into the demolition of Eldon Square, the ineffectual opposition mainly came from small local traders, with such bodies as the Northern Architectural Association or the Northumberland and Newcastle Society (the main local amenity body) conspicuous by their silence.[14] Elsewhere, across Britain's cities and towns in 1963, it was a largely similar story: out with the old, in with the new, the modern, the future.

In Birmingham, for instance, the cylindrical office block that would be the Rotunda continued to rise irresistibly alongside the new Bull Ring shopping development that was taking shape; Bristol's summer included the Rownham fountain being removed and its attendant trees cut down, the demolition of the Mayor's Baths in Clarence Road and the Georgian house on the corner of Ashley Road and Picton Street, and the sale of fittings from the once resplendent Empire Theatre; Burnley's deputy town clerk told a public inquiry into the town's development plan (a new shopping centre and market at the heart of it) that 'to reject the council's realistic proposals would be to condemn the town to a long period of obsolescence and leave it like a patchwork quilt'; Derby's plan for an inner ring road, announced in July, would lead to the creation of St Alkmund's Way, involving the destruction of the city's only Georgian square, St Alkmund's Church Yard, as well as the church itself; newly planned Comprehensive Development Areas (CDAs) for Glasgow included the transformation of residential, rundown Cowcaddens into a mixture of an industrial zone and high-rise housing, while for the city as a whole the Highway Plan was completed, comprising three ring roads as well as radial motorways and expressways; Graeme Shankland continued to produce reports aimed at the future transformation of central Liverpool, 'spearhead of a combined attack on a slum environment'; in London, in addition to such familiar future landmarks as the Hilton Hotel, Millbank Tower and Centre Point being completed or under way, Catford's new joy was the brutalist Eros House brought to it by Owen Luder, plans were approved for Goldfinger's equally brutalist 26-storey Balfron Tower in Poplar, and Kenneth Williams checked out the Square Mile ('it's fantastic what's going on in the City – they're cleaning St Paul's! and all behind there now are new buildings going up'); under construction in Manchester, on the site of warehouses destroyed in the war, was Piccadilly Plaza, coolly appraised by Clare Hartwell four decades later ('a huge commercial superblock consisting of three buildings linked by a podium, more exciting than architecturally valuable ... it completely fails to take any account of its surroundings, but the sheer confidence and scale impress'); the proposals by Sir Robert Matthew and Percy Johnson-Marshall for the comprehensive redevelopment of central Salford, including six large tower blocks, were warmly greeted by Walter Bor (a leading planner, now working with Shankland in Liverpool) as having 'aimed at an exceptionally high standard of environment in terms of living, shopping and civic administration to replace a nineteenth-century twilight area of obsolete housing'; Shrewsbury's general market hall was bulldozed ('quaintly hideous, with a great tower, built in brick in the Italianate style, it was quite inefficient, yet given another five years and it would surely have been "listed" with the aid of the Victorian Society,' noted a relieved architectural critic), to be replaced by a charmless creation in concrete; and Worcester, some forty miles down the Severn, was declared by Ian Nairn and Kenneth Browne to be 'in real peril':

> This most subtle and complex of cathedral cities, with a flavour that is sometimes more Italian than English, is menaced by a fearful combination of insensitive local planning and crude developers' schemes. Insensitivity in driving a boulevard called Deansway from bridge to cathedral; in allowing housing to creep down towards the best distant view, from the south-west; in providing lunatic setbacks to what was a close-built street; in permitting old buildings to be cut down to size in the High Street ...

'See it quickly,' they despairingly concluded, 'before Worcester is ripped apart.'[15]

It is too easy – too tempting indeed – to slide into a cartoon version of all this. A necessary corrective is Otto Saumarez Smith's *Boom Cities* (2019), where he focuses especially on the leading architect-planners of the day, including Lionel Brett as well as Burns, Shankland and Bor, a rather different breed from the out-and-out architects like Goldfinger, Basil Spence and Alison and Peter Smithson. The motives of these architect-planners were, he emphasises in his nuanced study, honourable and well-intentioned; they did not entirely ignore the conservation aspect; and the twin assumptions underwriting their plans, namely of economic growth continuing and mass affluence spreading, were in the early 1960s not irrational. Saumarez Smith also brings out the extent to which politicians from across the parties vied with each other in projecting the urban future as a seemingly blank page to be filled with the rewards of material and technological progress. Just as Anthony Crosland wanted in 1962 'complete physical rehabilitation' for northern cities, so Macmillan's transport minister, the incorrigibly upbeat Ernest Marples, declared in 1963 that 'the old Roman concept of a road, a pavement and a building – the way we have been building for over a thousand years – is now outdated'. Local politicians likewise competed in advancing for their own particular patches the claims of radical urban renewal to meet the moment. None more so by this time than T. Dan Smith:

> In Newcastle I wanted to see [he recalled in 1970] the creation of a 20th-century equivalent of [John] Dobson's masterpiece, and its integration into the historic framework of the city. If this could be achieved, I felt, then our regional capital would become the outstanding provincial city in the country. The method of development, as I saw it, was to make good existing deficiencies by a new central area redevelopment … I was determined that Newcastle would not accept just any architect whom the developer might wish to impose on it. I felt it wrong that when a city was beginning to take care to ensure that its public buildings were of the highest standard and best design, it should show less concern about its central redevelopment. The best of our national and international architects were to be commissioned.

'*Paris doit épouser son siècle*,' was how Paul Delouvrier, urbanist and prefect of the Seine, perfectly expressed in 1963 the western world's prevailing zeitgeist, here the inescapable word.

Seemingly entirely sympathetic to it were two young urbanists before they came to view things differently. 'You see,' explained twenty-four-year-old Ray Gosling to a journalist about the sorry state of Nottingham, 'a shambles where it shouldn't be – a city ripe and ready to develop and move into the 1960s, but swimming in its own slime'; while a future doyen of oral history, Paul Thompson, was positively euphoric about Shankland's plans for Liverpool: 'Two years ago the prospects for this tangled and decayed city centre seemed nothing but congested disintegration. Now it can look forward to one of the finest urban environments in Europe, repeopled by the new housing, its shopping centre and traffic system planned for the motor age.' Among the high priests of modernity and immaculate progressive taste was the architect Sir Leslie Martin, former chief architect of the London County Council but by 1963 professor of architecture at Cambridge while simultaneously conducting a private practice at Shalford Mill, Great Shalford, in association with Colin St John Wilson among others. 'Sir L. lives in a converted mill of great size & altitude, with companion-way ladders instead of stairs & bags of split levels – all in natural woods in natural colours and decorated by the occasional mobile or Ethiopian devil-mask or stuffed owl,' reported an instinctively sceptical Philip Larkin after a visit in July 1963 to discuss the next stage of Hull University's library extension. 'I longed for the occasional plush bunny rabbit or Present from Clacton kept because someone liked it …'[16]

It was, of course, still full steam ahead in 1963 for slum clearance and high-rise public housing to replace those slums. 'We have got to get the people out,' declared Sir Maxwell Entwistle, Conservative leader of Liverpool City Council, as he and Keith Joseph gazed one July morning at the slums of Pakington Street in the Edge Hill district. 'We must start thinking in terms of whole areas, and not just a few streets.' As for the building process, industrialised methods were rapidly, after a lengthy gestation period, becoming a realistic possibility. 'There can be little doubt,' Sheffield's architect-planner J. L. Womersley noted earlier that month, 'but that we are on the verge of a vast upsurge in our production of dwellings because of the greatly increased use of mechanisation and of factory-made building components'; and in October, at his party conference, Joseph's claim that housing output would reach an unprecedented 400,000 homes a year as a result of industrialisation gained him a standing ovation.

Whether in terms of mass housing or city-centre redevelopment, a truly profound transformation was taking place, especially across the great Victorian cities. 'In all this work of recreating Sheffield you can't overestimate the impression that Womersley is making,' Roy Hattersley told the largely pro-modernist *Architects' Journal* in July 1963, as the Royal Institute of British Architects gathered for their annual conference, this year in the city increasingly renowned for its Park Hill ('streets in the sky') housing scheme. 'We started late,' went on the 30-year-old local councillor, 'so now we're going faster. We are right behind him and we want to see the full expansion of his ingenuity.' The same issue of the magazine featured the members of one of Sheffield's working men's clubs – the Amalgamated Engineering Union Club, in Stanley Place – talking to a visitor:

How did they feel about the tall flats that are replacing the terraces of small houses which once crept all over the Sheffield hills?

'The flats are fine – Womersley a good chap; he's doing a good job,' said Ted Scott.

'Have you seen Park Hill? Have you been round inside?' Tommy Blagg broke in. 'There are all sorts of communal provisions there, you know. It's splendid. Really. And it's keeping people near in, near their work. Go up and see Gleadless Valley – it's a magnificent job up there. All the same, all this rebuilding and rehousing, we're losing some of our sense of community ...'

Notwithstanding poignant farewells to rundown but long-lived-in family homes (a situation heartrendingly caught towards the end of Basil Dearden's crime drama *A Place to Go*, set in Bethnal Green and released in July), many of the new flat-dwellers were still travelling hopefully. Among them, Rosina Vaughan and her husband Jim: both in their late sixties, they had lived for many years as private tenants at 92 Ryland Street in Birmingham's Ladywood district; but number 92 was one of a row due to be demolished under a slum clearance order, and in summer 1963 they moved into a flat on the third floor of a new eight-storey council block. Three months on, she explained touchingly to a local journalist her very mixed emotions, almost certainly far from unrepresentative, especially of older people:

We are lucky. Avery House isn't just a box. It looks like a smart hotel, and the Council have left the trees and the grass.

Looking out of the living-room I can see the little shops where I still go for most of the groceries. There are the children swarming over those huge logs in the adventure playground. Bless them, they get a bit noisy, but they are better off there than mine were in the yard …

I had to get rid of a lot of things when we moved. I gave some away and left the tin bath behind. It was an old friend. Every Saturday morning for years we had to heat the water in saucepans and plonk 'old tinnie' in front of the fire. Now I just turn on a tap in the bathroom.

I walk round looking at all these modern things and the toilet. That one in the yard was terrible to clean. We had known for two years that we were moving, so we put a bit by. It wasn't much, but we have been able to buy a new bedroom wardrobe, a rug chest and a few other odd things. Our son bought us an electric bell.

Just like getting married again, said my husband, bless him. He retired from the railway after 49 years' service. I had a little job at one time. Now we live pretty quietly. Funny … we miss making up the old fire. No crackle, no smoke. I suppose we'll get used to it.

There is central heating in the flats and electric fires. We have had the fire bar on but haven't needed the heating yet. Waiting for the first electricity bill makes you think twice. There is an electric drying motor in the kitchen cupboard, but I haven't used that either. The washing dries well on top of the roof when the weather's good. It is much cleaner than the yard.

There is plenty of cupboard space in the flats and one specially ventilated for food. Just fancy me with a stainless steel draining-board.

We were a bit worried about the new rent when we moved in. More than twice as much as the old house. We had a chat with the Council man and decided that we could manage by going carefully.

Cleaning is easy at the moment. Even the walls up the stairs have a special plastic surface that looks like black and white wallpaper. The wood on the stairs is a reddish-brown and shiny; good enough to stroke.

My daughter-in-law says she would like to live here. She thinks Dad and I look better since we moved out of Ryland Street. I have always kept pretty well and active. Now I can go for a stroll round the grass down there.

The neighbours are all here ... Lol, Lily Ashley, Jack Stokes and Mrs Stapleton, but we seem more shut away from them. I miss the odd cup of tea.

It was certainly a dark little world we lived in down there around the yard in Ryland Street. There are no mice or dustbins here. Everything goes into the disposal unit.

'We got quite used to the old life there,' Rosina ended. 'But even at 68 we are not too old to enjoy our new life – third floor up in the "square."'[17]

Among the more thoughtful activators in relation to Britain's dramatically changing built environment, trying to see the big picture and make sense of it all, two 1963 voices stood out: those of Wyndham Thomas (director of the Town and Country Planning Association) and Lionel Brett (the architect-planner who in October inherited the title of Viscount Esher). Thomas, who had grown up in a mining community, was on the attack that spring against what he saw as the insufferable arrogance of the sociologists and architects:

Most sociologists look at these places as they do at goldfish bowls; and manifest the same rapport with the inhabitants of either. How else could they be so sloppily sentimental on the one hand and so infuriatingly patronising on the other?

Too many, though not all, architects are also making patronising assumptions from a standpoint of even more massive ignorance. For instance, they seem determined to force face-to-face contacts on tenants of public housing the moment they step out of doors. It may be said that these architects, and sociologists who encourage them, sincerely feel this is socially desirable. But I have not heard or read one who has convinced me that he is not concerned above and before all else with the visual result, with a self-induced euphoria of 'impact, drama and excitement'.

Where is the one who admits his ignorance of the inner fabric of the lives of his prospective tenants: who respects their dignity and regards them as his equals; and who then approaches his task with genuine humility? ...

As for Brett, an attractive man with a strongly developed sense of public duty, his poignant fate by this time was to be wrestling with the modernist dream: unable to let it go, yet already knowing in his heart that it was starting in reality to turn into at best a semi-nightmare. A major piece by him that July in the *Architectural Review* included this 'stingingly accurate parody' (Saumarez Smith) of developer-speak:

> Skyscraper flats, spacious shopping malls and a drive-in bank are among the features proposed. New retail premises will line a landscaped pedestrian piazza and motorists will find ample accommodation in the multi-storey garages adjacent to the Inner Ring Road. Conveniently grouped with a Civic Hall and Public Library, the new Council Offices will take the form of an 11-storey tower block rising from a podium. The historic Chequers Inn, part of which dates back to the fifteenth-century, will be preserved and incorporated in the new development.

'The heart sinks,' added Brett for himself, 'even though this is what we asked for, more or less.' What was the alternative? Brett's piece was titled 'Doing Without Utopia'; and while insisting that 'a Luddite orgy of machine-bashing is hardly ever the answer', he called for an end to 'the cocky tone' and 'the failure to define and achieve liveability in our new housing projects', and an acceptance of the Jane Jacobs dictum that 'the City cannot be a work of art'. 'In the end,' he concluded humbly enough, 'we have to find our way through to the far side of our inadequacies.'

The article clearly represented, even if only implicitly, some kind of moment of catharsis, of painful self-examination. But perhaps, in what was an overwhelmingly male world, Brett should have listened harder, four years earlier, to a woman's voice, that of the housing consultant Elizabeth Denby. Both she and Brett were members of the Society for the Promotion of Urban Renewal (SPUR); and in 1959 she wrote a paper for it which ideally would have been pinned above the desks of every activator – whether planner or architect or politician or sociologist or commentator – during the ensuing decade:

> 'Comprehensive redevelopment' is the generally accepted method of regenerating a dilapidated or worn-out area. This policy seems to

me to be short-sighted as well as wrong. All British towns are the growth of centuries. They enshrine local history. They represent the activities, successes, hopes and failures, work and play of the citizens for many generations. The result is 'flavour and character', though neither the flavour nor the character may appeal at first sight to any but the citizens themselves. Thus shipbuilding, the cotton, the pottery, the mining towns give a very different impression to a visitor when he visits them by himself than when he is shown around by some old resident. There is of course no doubt whatever that many very large areas of British industrial development need regenerating, but it is my strong conviction that this must be done sensitively *with* and not *for* or *against* the citizens themselves.[18]

8

With It

'I lunched at Lyon's to see a bit of life, and finished my shopping in Walthamstow on the way home,' recorded Judy Haines on Friday, 27 September, the day after the Denning Report. 'Glad to be out of snobby, hard-hearted Chingford for a while. I am rather unfair, as most people have given me something for the refugees [from Bechuanaland], but some were horribly callous.' Saturday afternoon included sport good and sport bad – in horseracing, two winners apiece at Newbury for fierce rivals Scobie Breasley and Lester Piggott as they continued to joust for champion jockey; in rugby league, an after-match punch-up at Warrington following racial insults by a home player directed at two Halifax players, just as some forty miles away at Keighley the black Wigan winger Billy Boston was coming under verbal abuse as he left the field and having sods thrown at him – while that evening it was *TW3* versus *The Avengers*, both returning for the autumn. Labour politicians, gathered in the TV lounge of the Royal Hotel, Scarborough, ahead of their annual conference, unhesitatingly chose the more topical show.

'I sat quietly in the corner, watching the enthusiastic reaction,' recalled Robin Day. 'Barbara Castle was one, and Tony Greenwood was another. They revelled in the pillorying and abuse of the Tory government. This provoked shrieks of delighted laughter.' 'Not a single anti-Labour joke was made,' noted Anthony Wedgwood Benn, also in the room, 'and even I wondered if it had gone too far.' Among viewers generally, though Hugh Selbourne enjoyed the 'splendid satire' and Bernard Levin taking on the morally censorious Tory backbencher Sir Cyril Osborne, an RI (Reaction Index) of 57, a full 15 points down on the average for the first series, suggested work to be done to recapture the glory days; among the critics, negative verdicts by Francis Hope ('either under-rehearsed or spoiled by attacks of nervousness') and Anthony Burgess ('the tone is that of a clever and liberally controlled school magazine') contributed to a feeling that the suits at Television Centre were out to tame the programme; and Kenneth Tynan privately thought it 'tedious beyond belief'.

But over on ITV, this was the moment of real take-off for *The Avengers* – arguably, television's comparable escapist moment to *Tom Jones* on the big screen. 'A new craze took over the nation's Saturday nights,' remembered Christopher Booker about this autumn. 'The show aroused particular excitement through Miss Blackman's "kinky" black leather costumes.' Few more besotted, and allowed after extensive negotiations to stay up late, than eight-year-old Paul O'Grady. 'I lived for *The Avengers*. John Steed [Patrick Macnee] with his bowler and brolly at the ready and his cavalier attitude to life, and Cathy Gale [Blackman] the ice-cool anthropologist who chucked men over her shoulder with a flick of her wrist, touched a nerve ...' The most widely celebrated return, however, was on Sunday. 'Glad the Minstrels are back,' declared one viewer. 'They can't do anything wrong for our family.' And another viewer: 'Thoroughly enjoyable entertainment, and wholesome to boot. The dancing is a joy to watch and the music is gay, tuneful and singable.' Later that evening, Nella Last in Barrow watched and admired ballet dancers on *Sunday Night at the London Palladium* (Bruce Forsyth back in charge after three years away, Billy Fury topping the bill). 'I felt wryly how values – all of them very queerly "twisted" nowadays – to think of a "pop" singer, at best a moth round a candle, should ever, even by the keenest agent, be considered to hold precedence,' she reflected. 'I wonder what all the jangling "Liverpool sound" youths will do shortly – they & the kitchen sink type of play & film have lasted longer than I thought.'[1]

On Monday, as the globe logo made its debut on BBC television and Mick Jagger formally notified the Kent Education Committee that he was ending his studies at the London School of Economics ('I have been offered a really excellent opportunity in the entertainment world'), Sidney Jackson and his wife Marie arrived in Eastbourne. 'We put up at York House Hotel, on the promenade, a place which accommodates 150,' noted the keeper of Bradford's Cartwright Hall Museum:

> We expected it to be like the Kenilworth and other hotels, where meals are served between certain times, and one goes in when convenient. Instead, we discovered that the place was a giant boarding house, with everyone assembled at the sound of a gong and trooping into the dining room. This type of holiday is foreign to us, and we, especially I, were soon very uncomfortable, for the type of guest was such that we didn't fit. We are so accustomed to being with people interested in archaeology or geology that a mixed crowd like this disturbs us.

That evening at Cheltenham, the literary festival (one of the very few in the country) began with a panel event on the current state of literature. Among the audience of five or six hundred, 'two types predominated,' reported the Oxford philosopher Anthony Quinton. Namely, 'substantial elderly couples in warm, well-made clothing, brought in by a sense of not too painful duty, and plenty of the lithe untidy girls in black trousers who spring out of the ground whenever any sort of cultural trumpet is sounded'. Chair was 'a comparatively taciturn' J. B. Priestley, while participants included Iris Murdoch, her husband John Bayley, and Bayley's New College contemporary John Fowles, making his first major appearance on the in-person literary scene. 'The marriage must surely be *hors de lit*, one of affection only,' reckoned Fowles afterwards. 'She is prim, rather schoolmarmishly precise, with (she implies) slightly daring opinions. "I love Italy," she advances, coyly, like an ugly schoolgirl presenting flowers.' Fowles himself got into the national press by declaring that prospective novelists in Britain were receiving less and less encouragement to continue their careers. 'If a first novel sells 1,500 copies it is acclaimed as a success; in America, the figure is around 4,500,' he pointed out. 'What clearer indication of the public's apathy towards literature can you have? Television and other mass media are having undeniably a serious effect on influencing the public away from the world of books and inducing a lower intellectual standard.' Two other writers, meeting on Tuesday the 1st, might have nodded their heads. 'I went to London,' Philip Larkin told his mother, 'where I handed in my final version of *The Whitsun Weddings* to Faber's and had a short talk with T. S. Eliot.'[2]

That October morning, in Scarborough's Spa Hall, the reliably evocative Mollie Panter-Downes watched Harold Wilson – 'the stocky gray shape with its scholarly round shoulders; the small, neat baby features arranged around the watchful eyes; the pipe; the dry voice, with its occasional gritty broadening of vowels' – give an instantly celebrated speech:

His theme was that the Labour Party would bring science and technology out of their neglected back room and put them under the state's wing, in the front line of a scientific revolution that will change Britain out of recognition and help to fight poverty and starvation in the world – the old idealistic note that never fails to light up the Party ... His courage and gamble lay in asking these rows and rows of intently listening, often elderly, work-marked rank-and-filers, who have so often damaged Labour in the public mind at past conferences with their bitter, trivial squabbles over abandoning an inch of their hard-won traditional ground or rewriting a line of sacred, outdated dogma, to take a mighty flying leap off the Scarborough ground and project themselves like stout missiles into an unimaginably changed future. What was more, this future was to be made magical by science, which to many of those present no doubt had mostly, and fearfully, been tied up with the potential to destroy. Now the men in white coats were to be the deliverers, and the conference clasped the idea as though everybody had streamed to the meeting thinking of little else. Mr Wilson spoke of plans for producing more and better-paid scientists, for keeping them in this country when we have them, and for making higher education generally possible for thousands more children by a program of new universities and a 'university of the air,' in which students could enrol by sitting down at their radio or television set. All this, naturally, was greatly applauded, but in the section of his speech that dealt with the coming age of automation he told the trade unions roundly that they would have to scrap some of their old traditions and practices where they restricted the wheels, and, to a party in which 'redundancy' is a wicked word, he spoke of the late nineteen-seventies, when ten million new jobs would be needed here. The next fifteen years, he warned, would bring more startling revolutionary changes than the whole two hundred years of the industrial revolution, and grizzled old trade unionists who had long resisted any changes at all could be seen getting to their feet and smiting their calluses together as enthusiastically as though they had just been shown their places on the barricades.

Two particular passages stood out. In one, he created a defining image of the whole era by invoking how a new Britain would be forged by Labour in 'the white heat' of the scientific-cum-technological revolution which was under way; in the other, citing how 'even the MCC has abolished the distinction between amateurs and professionals', he demanded an end to Britain's class-based rigidities in which 'in science and industry we are content to remain a nation of Gentlemen in a world of Players'.

Next day the press was almost universally laudatory, while even Macmillan privately conceded that it had been 'a very brilliant & effective "key-note" speech' which would 'have a wide appeal & be difficult to answer'. '*All* the difficulties are swept under the carpet,' he went on, 'and a "new vision" is developed in a Jack Kennedy sort of style. It was excellently done, if fundamentally dishonest.' Yet for the most powerful trade unionist of the time, the left-wing Frank Cousins, the day had a disquieting aspect. Following a recent conversation with Wilson, in which in effect the two men had agreed that a future Labour government would need to establish a dynamic department devoted to economic planning in order to act as a counterweight to Treasury institutional conservatism, he now had a quiet chat in his car with the shadow chancellor, Jim Callaghan. 'Some of his views were shattering,' recorded Cousins. 'Talks of a wealth tax without understanding its implications or its extent. Assumes one cannot limit dividends or profits but can limit wages. Doesn't accept that NEDC should be a planning body with teeth ... Eventually recognises that we are not talking same language.' Cousins hardly needed to add that, if 'white heat' was ever going to become a reality, then a lingua franca was likely to be helpful.

'It was – I now confess – not the vision of slide rules and valve-driven computers that inspired me,' recalled Roy Hattersley about his leader's conference speech. 'I was moved by Wilson's apparent determination to turn Britain's back on the class system which had prejudiced the national prospect for so long.' As it happened, this Tuesday at Scarborough also saw a debate on the historically vexed issue of public schools. Two years earlier the party's policy statement, *Signpost for the Sixties*, had advocated 'integration' of the two systems, declaring that 'the nation should now take the decision to end the social inequalities and educational anomalies arising from the existence of the highly influential and privileged private sector of education, outside the State system'. Now, barely a fortnight after the Liberals had voted to bring all private schools into the state system, Labour considered and voted on an amendment maintaining that 'certain essential social objectives of educational policy cannot be achieved without abolishing the private sector of education'. How in practice would 'abolition' be different from 'integration'? Did 'abolition' mean the physical bulldozing of Eton, Harrow, et al.? Or ending them as places of education? Or what? Sadly, for all the passion engendered – including Eton and Slough's prospective parliamentary candidate, Joan Lestor, urging all those who claimed to be Labour supporters to stop sending their children to private schools – relatively little light was shed, apart perhaps from Eirene White asserting on behalf of the party's executive that 'abolition' was too negative a word and that the aim instead should be to transform places like Eton into what she called 'a very real asset to the educational system'. In the event, in a block vote in which the big trade unions brought their numbers to bear, 'abolition' was seen off by a landslide 5,202,000 votes to 1,088,000. A telling postscript to the episode came the following week, when an unpublished poll taken by Gallup found that Labour's conference had made a favourable impression on public opinion on all issues except two – one of which was, in the words of Wedgwood Benn after ferreting out the information, 'our decision not to abolish private education'.[3]

Larkin, on a bookshops tour for library purposes, spent that Tuesday night in Southampton, staying at 'the worst, very firm's-representative hotel, 10% service charge & shoes not cleaned (I did them on the curtains) & D. Telegraph not got'; Judy Haines on Wednesday paid '8/- lb for steak', but 'John didn't enjoy it, and sprouts were hard'; Macmillan returned to No. 10 after a three-year refurbishment ('I am very glad to be back'); Leeds City Council discussed vandalism in its parks ('one is sometimes told,' mulled aloud Alderman Mrs Pearce, 'that if only we provided enough playing-fields for these boys we should not have so much vandalism, and I sometimes wonder if that is absolutely correct, when I tell you that in Cross Flatts Park the boys have even destroyed some of the goalposts'); the deputy headmaster of Court Lees Approved School for Boys in South Godstone, Surrey (the largest of these schools where courts sent young offenders), ordered six superior canes from a tutelage supply company (Eric E. Wildman) in Chingford; *At the Drop of Another Hat* opened at the Haymarket ('The English the English the English are best/I wouldn't give tuppence for all of the rest'); John Bloom announced on Thursday that Rolls Razor would be giving away a fan heater with each of its washing machines; at Cheltenham's continuing literary festival, the RSC's Diana Rigg talked that afternoon about acting as a career, with Fowles in the chair silently appraising her ('charming and frank ... a flat face with a snub nose, but beautiful brown and eager eyes'); Kenneth Preston in Keighley finished reading both the Denning Report ('gives one or two peeps into some cess-pools') and Angus Wilson's 1961 novel *The Old Men at the Zoo* ('indecent in places ... not an admirable person in the lot ... I am afraid we are living in a sick age and it is far from pleasant'); Anthony Heap relished the first night of *A Funny Thing Happened on the Way to the Forum* ('as wildly funny and joyously uninhibited as any straight farce I can recall', with Frankie Howerd's a 'comic performance of wondrous richness and ripeness'); the Beatles starred on Friday evening's *Ready, Steady, Go!*, with Dusty Springfield reading out letters from fans ('Hello, gorgeous Paul ... please ask [him] if he plucks his well-shaped eyebrows? They're absolutely beautiful ...'); the Beatles top of the bill, too, for the fifth anniversary edition of *Saturday Club* – probably not distracting the John Hilton Bureau (in its troubleshooting role for the *News of the World*) as it wrote pointedly to Rolls Razor's service director that 'we still seem to be handling a great many failures of understanding or liaison, or whatever it is, between your customers who are also our readers and your firm'; hooliganism in the news that evening, as Liverpool fans wrecked ten of the 11 coaches of the return football special from Birmingham, while in Glasgow a city councillor described as 'semi-savage' the behaviour of teenagers damaging seats during two shows by the Beatles; a weekend poll in Luton (a marginal seat where a by-election was due in early November) revealed that a majority of both Conservative and Labour voters (67 and 52 per cent respectively) wanted entry conditions for immigrants to be made harder; Gyles Brandreth noted on Sunday without comment that 'the nation is gripped by Beatlemania – "She loves you – yeah, yeah, yeah" etc', with the single by now four straight weeks at no. 1; *The Times* on Monday reported that Pain's Hill Cottage in Cobham, once the home of Matthew Arnold, had been demolished, with more than twenty new homes to be built on the site; detailed plans were announced the same day for Oxford's inner relief road, to run directly across fourteenth-century Christchurch Meadow in a tree-lined cutting deep enough to conceal a double-decker bus; that night, the PM's prostate flared up, only hours after he had at last definitively decided to stay in office and fight the next election, due by October 1964; and on Tuesday the 8th, as most of the Cabinet travelled to Blackpool ahead of their party conference, Haines accurately summarised the dramatic turn of events in London: 'Nation startled at sudden news that Prime Minister, Mr Macmillan, has to undergo an operation for prostate gland trouble, and of his admission to King Edward VII Hospital, Marylebone, at 9 p.m.'[4]

It was possibly that Tuesday, but certainly by Wednesday, Macmillan decided to resign. For many years it would be widely assumed that he had – incorrectly – believed himself to be fatally ill, but a recent authoritative biographer, D. R. Thorpe, is adamant that he knew his condition to be benign. Either way, even though the PM did not want the news to be made public until Thursday, his chancellor, Reggie Maudling, called it right when, popping into the Treasury on his way to Euston and Blackpool, he remarked to his permanent secretary that 'the rat race is on'. The obvious successor, and current *de facto* deputy PM, was Rab Butler, thwarted by Macmillan for the leadership almost seven years earlier; he now successfully insisted that he stand in for Macmillan and on Saturday afternoon make the leader's speech at the closing rally in Blackpool. As for the laid-back Maudling, so widely favoured during much of the summer to be the next PM, he arrived in Blackpool later on Wednesday to find a series of meetings and TV interviews immediately lined up for him, only to tell his disappointed PPS that 'there's a really good fish bar up the coast and I really have to visit'. Instead, almost all the noise at this stage came from the nakedly ambitious Lord Hailsham, free as a result of the recent Peerage Act to revert to commoner status as Quintin Hogg. 'Get on the Hog's back while there's still time' was Julian Amery's gravelly-voiced advice that evening to anyone who would listen; but even at this early stage there was an image problem, with Benn probably not alone in finding 'odious' the sight on television of 'a man in the grip of suppressed hysteria, smirking and protesting loyalty to Macmillan'.

Also on TV this day (though only in London and the north) was a BBC documentary on *The Mersey Sound*, geographically not so far from the Tory grandees in Blackpool's Imperial Hotel (filling the place, recalled Ferdinand Mount, with 'the strong aroma of Trumper's Bay Rum hair oil'), but culturally a world away. 'Light and fast yet packed with significance, it gave you a strong contemporary feeling,' thought one critic, Maurice Richardson. 'The degree of Beatlemania [that word again, this time in print], with fans sleeping under Beatles' windows and sending them jelly babies by the ton, seemed to be fairly acute.' As for the Beatles themselves, added Richardson, they 'made a distinctly agreeable impression. They weren't exactly modest, but they were quite free from megalomania and perfectly prepared to face the possibility of a short reign before oblivion set in.' Anthony Burgess, somewhat to his surprise, was also favourably struck. 'I have normally only to see a photograph of the Beatles to start shivering with ague', but here they 'emerged as decent, not very bright, working lads, aware of the transience of fame in their field, even rather frightened of the orgiastic transports their music brings about'. Indeed, he went on, it was those teenage (or even younger) 'transports' that were the real problem: 'What, in God's name, are we going to do about these children, with their screechings as in orgasm, their distorted faces, their claws, their cutting-off of the higher senses? The Lord of the Flies grins, a pig's head on a stick.'[5]

On Thursday afternoon the foreign secretary, Lord Home, read out to assembled delegates the PM's message that he was stepping down, at which point (in Simon Heffer's words) 'near hysteria gripped the conference'; that evening, Home's sister-in-law, Lavinia Mynors, 'turned on the wireless, as Alec's goings on at Blackpool hold our interest'; 15-year-old grammar schoolboy Roger Darlington in Manchester 'managed to watch the "Saint" but the homework was pouring upon me like a black tidal wave'; the second James Bond film, *From Russia With Love*, had its premiere; Hailsham, having already offended decency by being seen feeding his infant daughter in the lobby of the Imperial, further compounded the offence by prompting an unseemly outburst of enthusiasm as he announced, as a dramatic coda to a speech at a fringe event, that he was forthwith renouncing his peerage; next day's papers had more about the battle for the succession than about Macmillan's legacy, though the *FT* did speculate that 'in the long retrospective history, perhaps, to have set Britain on the path which leads to Europe will appear his most lasting claim to greatness'; Ladbroke's amid considerable publicity inaugurated the Tory Leadership Stakes, starting with Butler as 5–4 favourite, Hailsham at 7–4, Maudling at 6–1 and Home at 16–1; in the conference hall at Blackpool, a competent but flatly delivered speech by Maudling ('left the mute stuck in his trumpet,' thought *The Times*) was much less positively received than Home's, in which he self-deprecatingly offered a prize 'to any newspaperman who can find any clue in my speech that this is Lord Home's bid for the leadership'; Winston Churchill's son Randolph, a fierce Hailsham supporter, was asked by Robin Day on TV about the possibility of Home getting the big prize and replied, 'That's a lot of rot'; and Larkin, dismissing Hailsham as a 'posturing ass', unenthusiastically reckoned Butler 'least bad' of the candidates.

'Lord Home May Be Compromise Choice' was the *FT's* headline on Saturday morning; a columnist in the *Oldham Chronicle* speculated that John Bloom, with his plan to give away some 60,000 fan heaters over the next few weeks, might be on 'the slippery road' towards bankruptcy; Butler's address that afternoon was even more underwhelming than Maudling's the day before, his delivery not helped by learning just before that Home was indeed willing to throw his hat in the ring; at Kempton Park, Breasley extended his lead over Piggott to four ('brilliant jockeyship,' conceded the patrician racing correspondent Richard Baerlein, but 'a near thing and could not have done the horse much good'); and in Mangotsfield, half an hour after that race, the big issue of the autumn was at last resolved. 'The question for weeks has been, shall I be able to cut the lawn before winter?' noted Frederick Ward. 'The odd dry day has not been sufficient. At 4.30 this afternoon after hot summer sunshine and a warm breeze the grass and ground beneath were just dry enough. We worked ourselves to a standstill and the garden is almost finished until the spring.'[6]

'IT'S STILL ANYONE'S GUESS' was the *Sunday Mirror*'s take on the Tory leadership stakes, as speculation ran rife in the Sunday press about a contest seemingly all about personalities rather than policy. The foreign secretary's was by now the name on several lips, with Ian Waller in the *Sunday Telegraph* calling Home 'the compromise and universally acceptable but reluctant candidate' and Wilfred Sendall in the *News of the World* even expressing his belief that 'the Earl of Home can become Prime Minister if he wants to', given the strength of 'stop Quintin' sentiment in parts of the Cabinet. Elsewhere in what was still comfortably the highest-circulation paper, Randolph Churchill did his best to stem the pro-Home tide. 'Lord Home could hardly with decency come downstairs from the House of Lords 48 hours after Lord Hailsham had given the lead,' he argued hopefully. 'He would be branded a copy-cat. A thing which no Scottish nobleman would like to be called.' At this point, as sensible an overview as any was that in the diary of the 15-year-old Brandreth. Butler's 'moment', he reckoned, had 'passed'; Hailsham had been 'photographed kissing babies, eating candyfloss and distributing badges marked Q for Quintin – not the behaviour we expect from a Tory statesman'; while as for Home, 'emerging as the unexpected favourite', he 'may have a lisp and a face like a skull (think of an albino version of the Green Mekon in Dan Dare in the *Eagle*!), but he is a gentleman to his fingertips and I reckon could turn out to be our man'.

That evening, 15 million viewers tuned in to *Sunday Night at the London Palladium* to watch the Beatles top the bill. Going out live, after the Palladium itself had been besieged all day by chanting fans (they and George equally oblivious to Ravi Shankar giving a concert that afternoon at the Royal Festival Hall), it was the moment which marked the official start of 'Beatlemania' – especially once the mass-circulation papers, next morning, ran as hard as they possibly could with somewhat exaggerated stories of riots and suchlike. 'Screaming girls launched themselves against the police – sending helmets flying and constables reeling,' reported the *Daily Herald* about the scenes after the show. 'Police vans sealed off the front of the theatre so that the Beatles could be smuggled out.' Or as the *Daily Mail* headline put it: 'This Beatlemania: Beatles Flee in Fantastic Palladium Siege.' In short, this was the moment when, to quote the pioneer Beatles biographer Hunter Davies, 'the Beatles stopped being simply an interesting pop music story and became front-page hard *news* in every national newspaper'.[7]

John Boorman that Monday was filming in Swindon for a TV documentary about the local football club to be shown in December. After morning training, two of the players, Ernie Hunt and Mike Summerbee, play football with children in the street of back to backs (virtually devoid of cars) where Hunt was born, before they go into a local shop, where the banter is of Oxo and 'man appeal'. Altogether, *Six Days to Saturday* evokes a world of still strong and traditional localism, albeit with – two years after the abolition of the maximum wage for professional footballers – just a hint of unease. 'They can never really relax,' Boorman's commentary says at one point about the players. 'They are known and watched. They are the focus of pride for an industrial city of 92,000 ... The men of Pressed Steel, of Plessey's, of the locomotive yards admire their prowess, resent their freedom and high wages.' Localism, too, in Durham, where the Duke of Edinburgh opened the new county hall, featuring a 30-foot mural by the Pitman painter Norman Cornish, still a working miner but already renowned for his portrayal of working-class life in and around his home town of Spennymoor. As for the Westminster village, as Macmillan formally triggered the process of sounding opinion in the party, latest odds had Home's shortening to 6–1, but Butler and Hailsham still firm favourites. 'The party in the Country,' Macmillan privately reflected, 'wants Hogg; the Parly Party wants Maudling or Butler; the Cabinet wants Butler.' And he conceded that 'the "draft Home" movement' was 'in reality a "Keep Out Butler" movement', of which there was no keener member than the outgoing PM himself. Across the aisle, there was seemingly little anxiety at this stage about the possibility of Home emerging as the compromise choice able to unite the warring Butlerites and Hailshamites. 'He will be a dud when it comes to exciting the electorate,' confidently predicted Benn, 'and Wilson will make rings round him.'

Macmillan, still in hospital, spent much of Tuesday the 15th dictating the first draft of a memorandum he intended to give to the Queen later in the week, once various soundings had helped to identify whom he was going to recommend to succeed him. By far his warmest words were reserved for Home, not only 'a man who represents the old, governing class at its best', but 'a popular, delightful man' who 'would make an effective chief'. Warm sentiments, too, for David Attenborough, whose *Attenborough and Animals* on Wednesday afternoon received an RI of 84, way above the average (61) for children's programmes. 'I liked this very very much,' said a girl in the four-to-seven age group. 'I liked the music when the little armadillo ran away. I think David Attenborough is nice and I like his voice.' Back on the main beat, the news of the day was the opinion poll in the *Daily Express*, showing Butler backed by almost two-fifths of the electorate (whether Tory supporters or not), with the rest of the field trailing well behind; and in the evening, Kenneth Preston noted that a successor was likely to be announced on Friday. 'I wonder,' he added, 'what sort of a struggle is going on in secret.'[8]

In secret indeed, amid swirling rumours, and Thursday proved to be decision day, albeit with the public still kept in the dark. 'The remarkable and to me unexpected result,' Macmillan recorded in his diary about the party's collective view as brought to him at hospital that morning by various trusted intermediaries, 'was a *preponderant first* choice for Lord Home (except in the constituencies, who hardly knew he was a serious candidate but agreed that he would be universally acceptable if *drafted*)':

> There were *strong pro*-Butlerites; but equally violent *anti*. There were strong – very strong – *pro*-Hailsham – but very violent *anti*. On Maudling the feelings were not so strong in either direction.
>
> In Cabinet, ten for Home; three for Butler; four for Maudling; two for Hailsham. Among three hundred M.P.s consulted, the largest group (not by much, but significant) were *pro*-Home. But, again, no one against. In Lords, two to one for Home. The constituencies were about sixty per cent for Hailsham; forty per cent for Butler, with *strong* opposition feelings to both.

Macmillan added that he had been reassured by the two key party officials he had seen, both of them close to the Tory heartlands, that 'everyone would rally round Home'. Home himself got the news that afternoon from Macmillan on the telephone; and in due course, Lavinia Mynors was also in the know. 'This evening,' recorded Home's sister-in-law, 'Lady Home rang up to say that they were for it, and if I could come by a wireless at one tomorrow, we should hear as much. She said that the Principal in all this was in tremendous form, and they were all right but breathless.'

How would Butler, still in the public mind the likeliest successor, react? In the course of Thursday night, four leading members of the Cabinet – Hailsham, Maudling, Enoch Powell and Iain Macleod – handed Butler what Macleod at the time called a 'golden ball in Rab's lap' and what Powell retrospectively called 'a loaded revolver': this was the assurance from all four that they were willing to serve under him, should Butler for his part refuse to serve under Home and thereby render a Home premiership untenable. 'Don your armour, dear Rab!' urged Hailsham in a late-night phone call. 'You must fight, dear Rab! There is still time.' But Butler, only sixty-one but in body an old man, feebly replied, 'I take note of your remarks, but now I really must doze off.' Next morning, even if *The Times* went out on a limb with 'THE QUEEN MAY SEND FOR MR BUTLER TODAY', most of the papers perceived that things were swinging Home's way – though Home himself was much disconcerted to hear about the potential cabal against him and had to be talked round by Macmillan from completely stepping away. Later that morning, Macmillan in his hospital bed received the Queen ('she came in alone,' he noted, 'with a firm step, and those brightly shining eyes which are her chief beauty'); he read out to her the final draft of his memorandum, recommending Home; shortly after noon, Home was on his way to the Palace, where the Queen asked him to try to form an administration; and the waiting world was duly informed to this effect on the Home Service's one o'clock news (appropriately preceding *Pick of the Week*). In the course of the rest of Friday, though Macleod and Powell categorically refused to serve under Home, there were no such refusals from Hailsham, Maudling and – most crucially – Butler. 'It was not in his character to do so,' reflects John Campbell in his study of the rivalry between Butler and Macmillan. 'Home was an old friend, and an honourable man whom it was impossible to dislike, whatever he [Butler] thought of Macmillan's machinations. Above all he would not split the party.' Among diarists, Judy Haines expressed regret ('our family is very sympathetic') for his having been 'overlooked the second time', but the main focus was on the almost certain next PM. 'First reaction of most people was incredulity,' privately noted William Kirkman, *The*

Times's Africa correspondent, adding that it was 'a deplorable choice'. Kenneth Preston, by contrast, was open-minded enough to listen on the radio that evening to 'a long assessment' of Home, finding that he came across as 'a very sound man', indeed 'one without personal ambition'.[9]

The following morning, once it was confirmed that none of the three big-hitters was prepared to block him, the 14th Earl of Home was free to go to the Palace and kiss hands – thereby becoming, albeit briefly given his declared intention to renounce his peerage and seek to become an MP, the first peer to occupy No. 10 since Lord Salisbury in 1902. 'I hope now,' he told a cheering crowd in Downing Street on his return from the Palace, 'that everyone on this fine Saturday morning can forget about politics except me.' Over the rest of the day, while he unsuccessfully tried to persuade Powell and Macleod to change their minds, his wish was dutifully followed: the radio reporting (in Preston's words) 'tremendous crowds at the motor-show, queues of I don't know how many deep and all traffic round Earl's Court at a standstill'; at Newmarket, two winners for Piggott (one involving an objection after he had been beaten by a neck) seeing him draw level with Breasley; at Swindon's County Ground, Boorman's cameras recording a thumping 5–0 home win over Leyton Orient; and at Anfield, the Kop for the first time singing 'You'll Never Walk Alone', as the emotive single by Gerry and the Pacemakers rapidly climbed the charts.

That evening, speaking in Manchester, Harold Wilson went on the attack against the third Etonian PM in a row:

What can anyone bred and reared in this sheltered and aristocratic background know of the problems of ordinary families? What can they know of housing problems, of getting a house, of the Rent Act, of the problem of keeping up mortgage payments, of the cost of travelling to work, of the problem of running the home at times of sickness, of providing for aged relatives, of simply making ends meet?

On education, what can they know of the agonies of the 11-plus, or of finding a room to do homework – for in the case of Britain's new Prime Minister the question of which school he would go to was settled two hundred years before he was born ...

This is a counter-revolution. After half a century of democratic advance, of social revolution, of rising expectations, the whole process has ground to a halt with a 14th Earl …

On the attack, too, with at least as much genuine anger, were the *TW3* crowd. Their second series had so far been relatively low-impact, but now Christopher Booker wrote an inspired set piece, in which Frost (frock coat and pointed black beard) delivered, rather poorly, Disraeli's message to the new PM:

Your acceptance of the Queen's commission to form an administration has proved and will prove an unmitigated catastrophe for the Conservative party, the Constitution, for the nation and for yourself. The art of statesmanship consists as much in foreseeing as in doing. You, my Lord, in your sixty years have foreseen nothing. As you yourself have confessed in the past – you lack many of the basic qualifications for political leadership at this time. You know little of economics, little of all the manifold, complex needs of a country that has become tired in a technological age, and nothing of the lives of the ordinary people who must now, without consent, submit as your subjects. You have foreseen nothing; you are qualified to do only – nothing.

The programme ended with Frost, back in normal wear, making an even-handed crack: 'And so there is the choice for the electorate – on the one hand Lord Home and on the other Mr Harold Wilson: Dull Alec versus Smart Alec.' But, as complaints immediately flooded the BBC switchboard, viewers had no doubt about whom the main thrust was targeted at.

The fight for the Tory leadership was over, but the question remained: had it been a fair fight? Bill Deedes wryly recalled, three decades later, his lunchtime conversation on the crucial Thursday with Martin Redmayne, responsible on Macmillan's behalf for canvassing the views of Conservative MPs and junior ministers:

The Chief Whip called me into his official residence at 12 Downing Street, gave me a glass of sherry and revealed the Conservative party's choice, stressing that no one else in the Cabinet yet knew. He emphasized that this was the fruit of the fullest 'processes' ever;

that Home was first in his own right – by a margin. He also led
the 'alternatives', and had fewer 'objections' than anyone else ... By
every count it seemed, there had been the widest canvass ever made,
and Home came out top; and this despite the fact that some did not
think he was in the field at all.

The combined activities of Redmayne and Lord Dilhorne (responsible for polling the Cabinet) have subsequently found little favour
with historians. Notably, Andrew Denham and Mark Garnett in their
biography of Keith Joseph, and Lewis Baston in his biography of
Maudling, have revealed in some detail how inaccurate – and biased
towards Home – the figures were that they gave to Macmillan. Yet
perhaps it was not quite a stitch-up? Arguably, the most revealing five
words of the whole saga were pronounced as early as the summer, amid
intensifying speculation about Macmillan's future. 'The chaps won't
have you': such, directly to Butler's face, was the discouraging view
of John Morrison, for the past eight years the all-powerful chairman
of the 1922 Committee of Conservative backbenchers. Ultimately –
for all their respect, even admiration, for him – the reflective, fatal-
istic, feline Rab was not *their* kind of chap. Ian Gilmour in his history
of the Conservative Party memorably criticised the choice of Home
over Butler or Hailsham or Maudling as self-indulgent: 'It was as if
an army had chosen a very popular officer from the reserve to be its
Commander-in-Chief, even though it knew he was unlikely ever to
win a major battle.' Such at the time was the view of one Conservative-
supporting, battle-hardened member of the House of Lords. 'What do
you want: the best PM or a man to win the election?' responded Field
Marshal Lord Montgomery when asked during the canvassing process
for his preference. 'We want both,' came back the reply. 'You can't
have that,' insisted Monty. 'Home'd make the best PM, Hailsham's
the best man to win the election.'[10] But Home it was, and the election
would come soon enough to test the conventional wisdom that the
age of deference and gentlemanly amateurism was conclusively over.

On Monday the 21st – the day after he had been adopted as
Conservative candidate for the conveniently available Kinross and
West Perthshire by-election due on 7 November – the new PM gave
interviews on both television channels. 'As far as the 14th Earl is
concerned,' he riposted when Kenneth Harris on ITV brought up

Wilson's charge, 'I suppose Mr Wilson, when you come to think of it, is the 14th Mr Wilson. I don't really see why criticism should centre on this. If all men are equal – well, that's a very good doctrine. But are we to say that all men are equal except peers? And nobody can be Prime Minister because he happens to be an earl?' Panter-Downes for one was impressed by Home's 'abounding self-confidence, crisp authority, and humor', the last quality reminding her in 'a dry, waspish' way of Clement Attlee, 'who used to be a master of the deflating sentence'; and when Wilson was interviewed the following evening, she noted how he was 'carefully polite' in his references to Home – or, as Randolph Churchill put it, 'very much on his best behaviour' as he 'abandoned his anti-feudal attack'.

This Tuesday evening was first night of the National Theatre's opening production: necessarily at the Old Vic, with its own physical home still many years away; and Sir Laurence Olivier chose to open the NT's account with an uncut *Hamlet*, with Peter O'Toole (star of David Lean's recent *Lawrence of Arabia*) seeking to recreate the role in which he had made such a stir a few years earlier in rep at Bristol. A star-studded audience also included Anthony Heap. 'A mordantly long and wearisomely drawn out evening,' he recorded about a performance which started at 6.40 and ended at 11.25, adding that 'much of the acting leaves much to be desired'. He made a semi-exception for O'Toole – a 'lightweight' Hamlet, but still 'the best, as well as the most human, of the younger Hamlets of our time' – whereas 'Derek Jacobi's Laertes and Robert Stephens' Horatio were scarcely more than adequate', and understandably no word for the spear-carriers, among them Michael Gambon. Reviews generally were so-so; but at last, after 115 years of delays and shilly-shallying, a great venture was under way.[11]

*

Next day, Wednesday the 23rd, was also another date for the history books, with the publication of the keenly awaited Robbins Report on higher education. Robbins was the 65-year-old economist Lord (Lionel) Robbins; and his key helpmate was the statistician Claus Moser, responsible for the detailed research revealing a prospective rise in the number of applicants, in turn leading to the cardinal principle of the report that 'all young persons qualified by ability and attainment to pursue a full-time course in higher education should have the opportunity to do so'. 'The cost,' commented an admiring obituary of Robbins in the very different climate of the mid-1980s, 'was no bar: taxation might have to be raised, but that was always possible if the value of education as an investment was recognized.' Specifics of the report included: doubling, as a minimum, the proportion of eighteen year olds in higher education by 1980; creating six new universities; and extending university status to, among others, CATs (Colleges of Advanced Technology) and SISTERs (Special Institutions for Scientific and Technical Education and Research). Crucially, Robbins envisaged the pool of qualified applicants to higher education as far from static, declaring that 'if there is to be talk of a pool of ability, it must be of a pool which surpasses the widow's cruse in the Old Testament, in that when more is taken for higher education in one generation more will tend to be available in the next'. Equally crucially, and especially striking coming from someone who as an economist was very much on the free-market side, Robbins insisted that a university education was a *public* good. 'Excellence is not,' he emphasised, 'something that can be bought any day in the market.' And he added that 'the essential aim of a first degree was not to impart a utilitarian body of knowledge', but instead 'to teach the student how to think'.[12]

In response to the report, the government almost immediately agreed that it would 'seek to accelerate' university expansion; while on the part of the universities themselves, the near-euphoric reaction was epitomised soon afterwards by the sight at Hull of (noted Larkin) 'the VC handing out copies of Robbins at his sherry'. The right-wing press was not quite so happy. 'The Robbins rate of expansion, for all the potency with which it is argued and all the acclaim of which it is assured, is not,' insisted *The Times*, 'proof against the criticism that it would work to dilute academic standards in the universities' – an implicit nod to Kingsley Amis's mordant prediction three years earlier that 'MORE will mean WORSE'. On a different tack, the *Daily Telegraph* wondered whether producing a greater number of 'higher-educated people' was 'what the nation's society and economy require': 'The committee's plan will mean in the end that 15 per cent of the working population will have completed full-time education.

This is a thought more awesome than attractive.' 'Is this,' immediately riposted the *Daily Mirror*, 'the old outlook that college education is only for the privileged few?'

But, of course, the truth was that, even if the Robbins proposals were fully implemented, it was still only going to be a relatively small proportion of eighteen year olds (indeed around 15 per cent at the very most) who went to university. And an especially pertinent early critique came from not the right but the left, in the person of Peter Townsend, by now professor of sociology at the newly established University of Essex. 'If we devote more of the extra resources of future years to "higher" than to other education, so that a larger but still small minority may have education after 18,' he wrote to *The Times* about the danger of choosing the wrong educational and social priorities, 'we may create a larger professional class and even further enhance professional and educational prestige – without doing much to improve social communication and understanding.' 'Fundamentally,' he went on, 'there is a naked choice between the principles of privilege and of equality':

> Those who believe that professional and managerial people deserve higher pay will also believe that higher education should have priority over the primary and secondary schools. More equality of opportunity cannot be obtained without much greater equality of incomes. The two are linked. Many professional and managerial people are, in relation to manual workers, paid too much. University professors are paid too much. Some of those at the lower end of the university teaching hierarchy may, it is true, deserve more. But too much attention is being paid to the argument about keeping up with the overpaid members of other professions and with members of the same professions abroad. By institutionalizing wide income differentials we are institutionalizing privilege – and this affects the whole educational and social system.

'Nearly everyone agrees that universities should be expanded,' Townsend accepted in conclusion; but at the same time, he understandably doubted 'whether a majority of the people of this country would prefer to see the greater part of our extra resources for education devoted to squeezing a larger minority through them rather than to abolishing over-crowded classes and drab facilities in the schools.'[13]

Townsend's Essex was one of the seven new English 'plateglass' universities – East Anglia, Kent, Lancaster, Sussex, Warwick and York the others – which opened between 1961 and 1965, having been planned well before Robbins got to work. Their emphasis was often on breadth as much as depth of study, with Sussex the exemplar. 'Its founders spoke of "a new map of learning" whose watchword was "interdisciplinarity",' recalled Stephen Medcalf. 'Its central hypothesis was that in an age when all existing disciplines were becoming, on the one hand so complex that it was increasingly difficult to master any one, and yet on the other increasingly interdependent, the best place to set a student was at the borders of two or even three disciplines or areas of study.' What about intake? The conventional wisdom was that it was significantly broader than at older universities, but in practice that seems to have been the case more in terms of gender (where the popularity of their arts subjects helped to push the proportion of women in the overall university population up from 24 per cent in 1958 to 28 per cent ten years later) than of social class. In the Reith Lectures that he gave a few weeks after the Robbins Report, Essex's vice-chancellor, Albert Sloman, talked boosterishly of how 'students *now* come from all sections of the community, *many* from homes with no tradition or culture or learning'; but three years later, the first detailed study made at one of the new universities (East Anglia) found working-class students to be less well represented there than in the general university population. Nor, again contrary to certain assumptions, were the early intakes at the new universities particularly radical in outlook or unconventional in behaviour. 'Except for a few grumpy beatnik types, the students are remarkably well-dressed and kempt: you see few beards, anoraks or ban-the-bomb badges,' reported a palpably disappointed Richard West in his July 1963 profile of Sussex. 'At one Friday evening dance, a good third of the men wore dinner jackets.' Even so, he ended on an upbeat note: 'More than any other university that I have visited, Sussex gives a feeling of intellectual excitement and enthusiasm. Without the drabness of Redbrick or the affectation of Oxbridge, it must be a fine place indeed at which to study. It is the best thing that has happened to Brighton since the wicked Prince Regent chose the town for his orgies.'

At Sussex and the others, permanent buildings gradually through the rest of the decade followed the students. 'In a few years' time the new universities will doubtless each look very different, but at the moment they are curiously similar,' reflected Paul Thompson in 1965, assessing the architectural state of play:

> Nearly always the elements are the same: the park outside a cathedral town, the old mansion, the grand plan. Contractors' cranes peer above the crowns of elms, oaks and beeches in a nobly landscaped park, which is to be further enhanced by a great new lake, said to be the easiest way of providing drainage or disposing of the site rubble. The old house has been converted for administration and teaching until the first permanent buildings are ready, and in its entrance hall is displayed an impressive balsa-wood model of the university in 1985, when its population will be 5,000 or 10,000. If these models are realised there is no doubt that they will be the grandest architectural schemes produced by this country in the early 1960s ...

Thompson on a quickfire tour was favourably impressed by Basil Spence's buildings at Sussex ('convey an air of quality, of modernity blended with traditional dignity, of an expensive experiment'); unimpressed by Lord Holford's designs for Kent ('lumpish blocks arranged in repetitive squares, depressingly reminiscent of the pseudo-modern architecture favoured by the universities until the late 1950s'); and most struck by Kenneth Capon's futuristic plan for Essex, as forged in close tandem with Sloman and given the go-ahead in June 1963:

> In spite of being set in the open country outside the market town of Colchester, it aims at a dense city character. A steep valley divides the site, with a chain of lakes at its head. Lower down, the valley is spanned by a giant podium, so that traffic can be confined to the chasm below, with the teaching buildings above forming a series of enclosed pedestrian squares. The scale of these buildings, with irregular white slotted concrete sides, is very impressive. On the valley sides the first residential tower is rising in purple brick, very like a point block in a dense city housing estate ...

In 1963 itself, however, the university building to catch the moment was not at one of the new universities, but instead at Leicester, one of the so-called 'redbricks', those non-Oxbridge universities largely built in the nineteenth century. 'The main architectural

themes are two,' the *Guardian*'s architectural critic Diana Rowntree
explained about the new engineering building by James Stirling
and James Gowan. 'One is the interplay between a 45deg. geometry superimposed upon a rectangular geometry. The other, the relation between the spreading horizontals and the tall tower. These
two themes recur incessantly throughout the building, hammering
the senses with the relentless energy of a Bach fugue.' And, after
acclaiming the building for its 'unique sense of penetration and
depth', with 'the conventional sense of gravity curiously absent',
she left her readers wondering – barely a fortnight before Wilson's
'white heat' speech – whether the effect of this architecture, deliberately looking back to the origins of the modern movement, would
be to produce 'a new generation of engineers disposed to narrow the
gap between art and science'. 'For myself,' she added, 'as I toured
the workshops I could see for the first time in my life how the study
of engineering could be a pleasure.'[14]

Little social cachet attached itself to going to a redbrick university like Leicester, perhaps even less once the new universities, certainly Sussex among them, started to become instantly fashionable.
'Many public school boys,' observed Anthony Sampson in his 1962
Anatomy, 'would rather go straight into business, into the services or
to a foreign university like McGill, Grenoble or Harvard, than go to
a Redbrick university: they prefer no degree to a Redbrick degree.'
But just in case any of his privately educated readers were eccentric
enough to want to go to one, he explained that there were 'different
layers of Redbrick': 'There are the big blackened city universities like
Manchester, Liverpool or Birmingham, where most students live in
digs on the outskirts and commute like office workers. There are the
superior provincials, like Edinburgh or Bristol, which have cleaner air
and a tradition of undergraduate spirit. And there is London, in an
extraordinarily shapeless class of its own, with three times as many
undergraduates as any other university ...'

Those from state schools comprised some 90 per cent of those
going to redbricks, where at one, Birmingham, the young novelist
David Lodge had been teaching since 1960. Years later, he would
offer a highly critical overview of that world. His retrospective
strictures included 'no instruction of new recruits on how to lecture
or teach smaller groups'; an 'unexamined consensus' when it came to

awarding different classes of degree; and a 'defective' appointments process, comprising a haphazard combination of references ('often unreliable and sometimes deceitful') and interviews ('too brief to really test the candidates'), predictably leading to 'some unfortunate appointments over the years'. Similarly critical in retrospect, but from a student perspective, was Veronica Lee, who in 1963 had started at Leeds on her nineteenth birthday, the day of the Denning Report. 'Many faculties, including sociology, were housed in very scruffy Victorian buildings which had been roughly partitioned up to make tutorial rooms, offices and so on,' she recalled. 'The university was gradually redeveloping and these houses were being closed down and left empty, prior to being knocked down. In my first term we often used these buildings to have parties in, burning furniture and even floorboards in the fireplaces.' That was bearable enough; so just about was being crammed into a small house with four other students and the landlady's family; but because of the unimaginative way it was taught, the sociology she had come to study largely failed over the three years to engage her:

> My fondness for the subject was not improved in the second year by having to do a whole paper on statistics for which I needed log tables, and I hadn't used those since O-level. I had chosen to do criminology and the sociology of the family for my special papers and I had hopes they would be interesting, but I was disappointed in them, particularly criminology. Noel Parry taught it but he often didn't turn up for lectures or tutorials and was badly prepared when he did. I was in a constant state of fury with him and developed a visceral hatred of him which centred on his full, moist lips and what I believed to be his inaccurate summaries of the facts. Miss Rowntree took us for the family, and although that was far more interesting I found her teaching rather dry. None of our lecturers was very inspiring.

What about redbrick students more generally? Across the Pennines, a survey in March 1963 of Manchester undergraduates revealed almost three-quarters of them to be middle class; Conservative and Labour level-pegging in voting intentions; and 54 per cent agreeing with the proposition that 'On balance, it's a good country', whereas only 26 per cent concurred with 'There are many things I would like to see changed' and a nugatory 14 per cent with 'What Britain needs is a classless society'. Still, almost half (45 per cent) did agree that 'The Government should take some steps to remove social inequalities'; and 21 per cent had the intellectual humility to tick the box, 'I do not know what to think'.[15]

Oxbridge remained a different world – a world where in 1961, noted Robbins, less than one-third of the male entrants came from maintained (i.e. wholly state) schools, with the rest coming from public schools (roughly 50 per cent of the intake) and direct-grant grammar schools. Was there selection bias at work? An Oxford historian, Michael Brock, argued not, claiming in a 1962 article that 'the public schools are favoured not by the people who operate the selection system but by the system itself and all that lies behind it':

> It is extremely complicated. 'To spot the right college,' one headmaster has said, 'calls for a combination of Old Moore, a racing tipster, and an electronic computer.' Suppose two boys of comparable ability, both fit to be commoners [i.e. as opposed to the less numerous scholars, who were in receipt of financial scholarships] at Oxford, one at a famous public school, the other at a two-stream maintained school. The first headmaster has candidates for Oxford every year and is known in several colleges. He is an expert on which college to approach and on how to play his cards. Spurred on by parents who will consider no university except Oxford or Cambridge, he makes persistent efforts to place his boy, and at last finds a college to take him.
>
> The second headmaster has not had a candidate for several years and has no Oxford contacts. He puts the boy in for Oxford once, and, when this fails, settles for a modern university. Indeed, to say that the 'selection system' favours the first headmaster is to put the case too narrowly. The second one may not give the system a chance: he may never enter his boy at all. He has no difficulty in spotting a potential Oxford scholar among his pupils; but he may have a good deal in spotting the potential commoner, and the boy's parents are unlikely to demand a shot at Oxford.

Even so, as a Manchester academic, W. J. M. Mackenzie, pointed out soon afterwards, an instinctive preference probably did come into it, with admissions tutors naturally vulnerable to 'top dressing skilfully applied by schoolmasters who specialise in discerning Oxford's taste'.

Either way, for the student once ensconced at Oxbridge, undisputed joint pinnacle of a far more hierarchical university structure than in most western countries, the daily advantages continued to be formidable (quite apart from all the post-graduation advantages of connection and suchlike bequeathed). Much of this advantage, as an appendix to Robbins set out in some detail, came down to resources: cumulatively, a picture of being taught by college tutors more highly qualified than their contemporaries at other British universities, more highly paid, enjoying better work accommodation, and – crucially – having more personal contact with their students. Oxbridge's mixture of intellectual excellence and social prestige inevitably had its demoralising effect on universities elsewhere; and when the Advisory Centre for Education, soon after Robbins, elicited replies from 238 lecturers across the British university system to an inquiry about which six universities, and in what order, they would advise for a student seeking to read their subject, the overall result was that on the specified subjects, Cambridge took 14 first places, Oxford took five, London took two – and no other university secured a first place.

What, if anything, was to be done? Perhaps the most thoughtful as well as knowledgeable educational commentator of the day was John Vaizey, who, in his 1962 Penguin Special, *Education for Tomorrow*, backed the idea that Oxford and Cambridge should move towards becoming primarily graduate universities. The prospect did not cause Vaizey, at this stage still a man of the left, to shed tears. 'Oxford and Cambridge are blessed with great beauty, long history, and a magnificent system of education; but new universities with good contemporary architecture in places like Brighton and Coventry, teaching new subjects in exciting ways, will certainly offer to the student a life as interesting as that which is offered by the banks of the Cam and the Isis.'[16]

*

The publication of the Robbins Report on 23 October coincided with Lord Home disclaiming for life all six of his hereditary peerages, as he instead became relatively plain Sir Alec Douglas-Home; next day, in a move which Wilson in his recent TV interview had described as 'verging on the unconstitutional', Parliament was prorogued until 12 November, the week after the PM's by-election; Peter Griffiths on Friday the 25th declared that he had seen white girls in Smethwick enter houses owned by Indians and warned that those girls (who were in fact social workers) were 'in moral danger'; that evening, while Judy Haines and her husband went to Sadler's Wells to see Rossini's comic opera *Count Ory* ('musical and entertaining ...I did enjoy a Banana Melba, Double Ripple, in the only interval'), Harry Worth returned to the small screen with *Here's Harry* ('only a small minority,' noted audience research, 'were strongly critical of a show they considered stupid and childish'); Sid Chaplin next day in his 'Northern Accent' column reflected on the soulless state of public parks ('the interminable black-letter bylaws, the excessively geometrical complex of asphalt pathways, the dreary ponds with their singularly uninteresting islands, and those grimly defensive bandstands'); Bo Diddley and the Rolling Stones were both on *Saturday Club*, with the great man paying behind the scenes the ultimate compliment ('You gonna outlast the Beatles because you play like *black dudes* ... If you don't be *bigger* than the Beatles, you gonna last *longer*'); and that evening's *TW3* was in the context of RIs for the second series still bumping along in the mid-to-high fifties, with 'something amiss' the general reaction, perhaps not helped by declining indignation about the Profumo affair. 'The present series had been "cleaned-up" a little (to which there was no noticeable objection) but the show's original freshness seemed to have staled'; 'some viewers thought that the Conservatives should be given a rest', i.e. as a target; and though Lance Percival's impersonations were 'considered a joy', typical criticisms of the cast as a whole included 'all too pleased with themselves' and 'behaved like students performing for students'.[17]

Sunday in Newcastle saw a stampede of 7,000 teenagers as the box office opened for tickets to see the Beatles the following month – girls trampled on, mass faintings, two gallons of sal volatile taken to the scene by ambulance men – before on the Monday a new candidate in the Kinross by-election appeared in the person of *TW3*'s (and *Private Eye*'s) Willie Rushton. 'Dressed for the moors in tweed and with a "rather sexy" scarlet silk handkerchief in his breast pocket,' noted the watching Christopher Driver, he 'insisted that his only reason for fighting the election was the "undemocratic skulduggery" which had attended it'. For the PM himself, in this heavily rural and rock-solid Tory constituency where seemingly everyone knew their place, it was not a challenging contest; but following events closely was a twelve-year-old Scottish schoolboy, Gordon Brown, particularly struck by Home's response when asked if he intended to buy a house in the constituency. No, replied Sir Alec, 'I have too many houses to live in already'.

This was also the week when the great trading stamps war really began to heat up, going beyond the small shops where it had so far been waged. 'The idea,' recalled Stephen Debenham about an aspect of shopping that became almost a way of life, 'was to collect several thousand of these stamps, given out "free" with most shop purchases, and stick them into a book. The books could then be exchanged at special warehouses for a mouth-watering variety of "free" gifts.' In one corner of the war were the big American players Sperry and Hutchinson, whose pink trading stamps were now being introduced into the Fine Fare supermarket chain; in the other corner were Green Shield, founded in 1958 by the British entrepreneur Richard Tompkins and now with both Tesco and Pricerite agreeing to participate. Fire and counter-fire were rapid. On Monday, teams of colourfully dressed salesgirls paraded the nation's High Streets with Day-Glo posters extolling the benefits of shopping at Fine Fare and thereby acquiring pink stamps; on Tuesday, the opening by Tommy Trinder of Tesco's second-largest supermarket, at Small Heath in Birmingham, was the occasion for the introduction of green stamps into the chain. 'Stamps are what housewives like and we are here to serve them,' Tesco's chairman, Jack Cohen, told the press after he and Trinder had done a cross-talk act on a hastily erected stage outside the front windows. 'They like change all the time and it is our job to serve them.'[18]

'What a shock on the Archers!' Larkin wrote to Monica Jones on Thursday evening. 'Did you hear it? Janet dead, Charles badly hurt ...' A shock indeed, not least to Judy Parfitt, who after reading about the car crash in the script had given a smothered scream and exclaimed 'My God! They've killed me!' The letters poured in. 'You've done it again,' said one. 'First it was Grace Archer [in 1955] and now Janet Tregorran. There's only one word for it – murder.' 'I didn't mind,' said another, 'when Grace bought it. Her voice always did drive me up the wall, but that nice nurse ...' Next day, Friday 1 November – as listeners recovered, as the *Herts Advertiser* reported that by the beginning of 1965 all gas produced by the Eastern Gas Board's Watford Division (including St Albans, Welwyn Garden City and Borehamwood) would be 'almost entirely non-poisonous', as 'You'll Never Walk Alone' went to no. 1 (just ahead of 'She Loves You', never out of the top three since early September) – the *NME* previewed the Royal Variety Performance, due to take place on Monday at the Prince of Wales Theatre. Those on the bill included 'old-stagers' Max Bygraves and Charlie Drake, *Steptoe and Son*'s Wilfrid Brambell and Harry H. Corbett, the full companies from the current West End productions *Half a Sixpence* and *Pickwick*, Dickie Henderson ('has prepared a new mickey-take twist routine'), 'lovely' Susan Maughan – and the Beatles. For them, reflected the magazine's Derek Johnson in the light of 12 out of the 19 acts being new to the annual high-profile event, 'it will seem particularly strange, for they will be without the mass teenage hysteria which invariably accompanies all their shows. But no doubt the distinguished audience will be fully aware of the group's accomplishments this year, and accord it the reception it deserves.'

'Beatlemania: It's happening everywhere – even in sedate Cheltenham' was the *Daily Herald*'s headline on Saturday morning after the group had begun their autumn tour there; an editorial in the *Daily Telegraph* pondered the phenomenon ('is there not something a bit frightening in whole masses of young people, all apparently so suggestible, so volatile and rudderless?') and despaired of how whereas 'the cultural tone of society is normally set by the leisured and moneyed classes', in the case of pop music 'professors, writers, intellectuals, bishops, all take care to be discreetly "with it", fully conversant and in sympathy with all that wells and throbs up from the slums beneath them'; and at Lingfield, a winner for Breasley, unlike Piggott's blank, extended the Australian's lead to four, with just four days' flat racing left. Next evening, BBC's latest 'First Night' play, Thomas Murphy's *Veronica* starring Billie Whitelaw, secured an RI of 59 that admittedly was above the average (55) for the six earlier 'First Night' plays but still prompted heartfelt groans from the Viewing Panel. 'Here we had another sick-minded heroine,' declared a teacher. 'How tired I am of them all. We have them among us in the entertainment world as it is, without writing plays about them. Don't you show-business people have any hidden depths or resources to turn to when things go wrong? Just the pill box and the psychiatrist, it seems.' Or as another panel member demanded more succinctly: 'Why, oh why, can't we have a good, honest, down-to-earth play on a Sunday night, about ordinary people – one that everyone can understand?'[19]

Next evening, as the Cambridge Union voted at last to admit women, it was an audience of evening dresses and black ties for the Royal Variety Performance in front of the Queen Mother, Princess Margaret and Lord Snowdon. Max Bygraves relaxing everyone early on with a singalong 'Hands'; two tap dancers; a Paraguayan folk group; pint-sized Charlie Drake doing his comedy routine with a tall, statuesque girl; wide-eyed and wholesome Susan Maughan promising to be faithful and thankful if she could only be Bobby's girl – such was the warm-up for the turn of the moment:

> The Liverpool lads [reported Andy Gray in that week's *NME*] were looking most immaculate in new black suits with high V-necks, and tiny lapels, and in white shirts and black ribbon ties. With hair brushed to a glossy sheen, The Beatles were powering their vocal-instrument way into 'From Me To You' as the curtains opened … with NOT A SCREAM!
>
> But this eerie phenomenon didn't put them off. The warm applause that greeted their appearance made up for it, and they increased their efforts to please. By the end, the acclaim staggered – and delighted – them. They pressed on with 'She Loves You' and ended with even greater applause.
>
> Then came the first burst of 'Scouse' humour. Paul McCartney announced he'd sing a number from 'The Music Man', which had been covered 'by our favourite American group – Sophie Tucker'. This got a big laugh, but the listeners soon stilled as Paul sang with complete audience silence 'Till There Was You', and most appealingly, too.
>
> John Lennon announced the last number with cheeky assurance as he asked the audience to join in 'Twist and Shout' by demanding: 'Would the people in the cheaper seats clap your hands, and the rest of you, if you'd just rattle your jewellery' – to get a big laugh.
>
> The Beatles then tore into the excitement-provoking 'Twist and Shout', and by the end of it the entire audience – Royal Party included – was asking for more!

In such a strictly timed show there could be no encores, but compere Dickie Henderson had to quieten the applause before the show could go on, quite a time after The Beatles had made their deep bows to the Royal box and audience.

To watch the show on YouTube is to realise how nervous they were, perhaps especially Paul; and to imagine Brian Epstein's relief as John decided to omit 'fucking' before 'jewellery' from his prepared patter. Dickie Henderson also had his words ready: 'Thank you, the Beatles. Aren't they fabulous? So successful, so young. Frightening.'

Over the next two hours or so, other acts included Joe Loss and his Orchestra (with Elvis Costello's father, Ross MacManus, as vocalist on 'If I Had a Hammer'); Pinky and Perky making a topical aside about 'green stamps' as they mimed to 'Speedy Gonzales'; Michael Flanders delivering a long riff about the dubious joys of flying (at a time when probably fewer than one in twenty had ever been on a plane); and Marlene Dietrich giving a stunning rendition of Pete Seeger's 'Where Have All the Flowers Gone?'. At the end, as all involved took to a crowded stage, Harry Secombe came forward, took off his bald Pickwickian pate, and then, saying 'I've got a joke, I've just thought of it', put it back on (back to front) in order to deliver his quip: 'The Beatles in 50 years' time.' Cue huge laughter from all, including the four young men – with in truth not all that long hair – standing just behind. Afterwards, reported a semi-reconciled *Daily Telegraph*, the royal party were presented to the undisputed show stealers. 'Princess Margaret told the four that she thought the show had been "great" and asked which town they would visit next. When they replied they would be going to Slough, Princess Margaret replied: "Yes. Slough, Slough, quick, quick, slow." '[20]

The Beatles and what they were taken to symbolise seemingly dominated everything this November. 'Fact is that Beatle People are everywhere,' announced the *Daily Mirror*, by now Britain's best-selling daily, on Tuesday the 5th:

From Wapping to Windsor. Aged seven to seventy. And it's plain to see why these four cheeky, energetic lads from Liverpool go down so big.

They're young, new. They're high-spirited, cheerful. What a change from the self-pitying moaners, crooning their lovelorn tunes from the tortured shallows of lukewarm hearts.

The Beatles are wacky. They wear their hair like a mop – but it's WASHED, it's super clean. So is their fresh young act. They don't have to rely on off-colour jokes about homos for their fun ...

Youngsters like the Beatles are doing a good turn for show business – and the rest of us – with their new sounds, new looks.

Good luck Beatles!

On Wednesday, a letter to the *Telegraph* from A. P. Garland of Medstead, Hants, praised the paper for its recent 'thoughtful' leader on the subject, surmised that 'there must be many like myself who know in our hearts that "it" is not worth being "with",' and declared, in relation to professors, writers, intellectuals and bishops, 'let us think for ourselves and be true to our own feelings'. The same day, a discussion on Leeds City Council about where to site the city's new abattoir, prompted a topical reference from Councillor George Addlestone of Osmondthorpe ward: 'We are at present, my Lord Mayor, being plagued with "The Beatles". Given fine weather in summer – and it is about time we got some fine weather – we will be plagued with this fly nuisance ...'

That evening – while the *Sunday Times*'s William Rees-Mogg told Lady Violet Bonham Carter at dinner that Wilson was a politician like Macmillan, both being 'adroit, skilful, ruthless, without personal loyalties, "fixers" & manoeuvrers & manipulators' – by-election candidates made their final appeals. 'There is no cause for the British people in 1963 to live colourless, drab, and uniform lives,' the PM told the people of Blair Drummond. 'We can be a happy people, enjoying prosperity, and using it morally and well.' Rushton for his part, speaking to a packed audience at Crieff, now suddenly switched tack: 'I came up here with only one intention – to make Home look silly. I have come to realise that the best way of doing this is to advise you to vote for the Liberal.' Thursday saw police seizing hundreds of copies from a Manchester bookshop of Mayflower's newly published uncensored paperback version of *Fanny Hill*, a move neatly coinciding with the decision of the BBC's Board of Governors to pull the plug by year end on *TW3*, with the fact that 1964 was going to be a general election year pretext as much as cause. The Luton by-election result came through at midnight, with Labour regaining a seat it had lost in 1950, while at noon on Friday the Kinross and West Perthshire result was a comfortable win for Sir Alec, over 9,000 votes ahead of the Liberal in second, and just the 45 votes for Rushton, who by this time had headed home. Soon afterwards, on Manchester's (though really Salford's) Castle Irwell racecourse, two winners for Piggott saw him close the gap to two, but with just a day to go; and in the latest weeklies, K. W. Gransden's *TLS* review of Mary McCarthy's *The Group* complained that 'we get pages on the fitting of a contraceptive, but in the end we know much more about Dottie's vagina than ever we do about Dottie'; in the same issue, Marghanita Laski criticised P. D. James's *A Mind to Murder* for having 'a far too perfect policeman, Superintendent Dalgleish'; and Eric Hobsbawm in the *New Statesman* damned with faint praise the Beatles as 'an agreeable bunch of kids', albeit 'in 20 years' time nothing of them will survive'.[21]

On Saturday afternoon at Castle Irwell, the course's last day (before property developers took over) after 276 years of racing, it was Scobie's title, one ahead of his never-say-die rival for the jockeys' championship. That evening, TV cameras were present at the Royal Albert Hall for the annual Festival of Remembrance. 'It was very well staged but one poses the question: "how many more years?"' wondered a middle-aged, diary-keeping RAF officer. 'Some of the faces are old and tired while all the younger elements there seem disembodied from the actual proceedings. A decade of overwhelming materialism, pop, and "climbing down" has had a marked success among all classes.' Sunday proved a red-letter day for some, not all. 'Got up to find John [her son] had been sick in bed again – awful mess,' recorded 39-year-old Betty Allen in Poulton-le-Fylde, Lancashire. 'David [her doctor husband] had been called out at 7 a.m. & was working all morning. I had to have a wash day. Dreadful wind & rain so none of us went to the War Memorial. David on call all day, so altogether it was a miserable day! Glad to get to bed!' Little better for Maud Smith (age uncertain) at 59 Victoria Road, Mablethorpe, Lincs: 'Rained. Cold, miserable day. Made Christmas Pudding.' The Beatles that evening had a date at the Birmingham Hippodrome, besieged by crowds of teenage girls who during their ten-hour wait were undeterred by heavy rain. 'The car in which the singing group travelled from London broke down on the M1 and they were over an hour late in arriving at Birmingham police headquarters,' reported *The Times*. 'There, after having tea with the police officers, they borrowed helmets and mackintoshes and drove to the theatre in the van preceded by decoy police cars. Before the crowd realised it, the gates of a yard near the stage door were opened, the van drove in and the gates were closed.' It would be simpler afterwards, the group and their minders knew, because the audience standing respectfully for the National Anthem would just give that minute's crucial breathing space to get away safely.[22]

But for most people this Sunday evening, it was the Beatles on the box, as ATV showed a virtually full recording of the previous Monday's Royal Variety Performance. Viewing figures were remarkable: over on BBC, just 4 per cent of the population watching a worthy play, *Do Me No Favours*, about an ex-convict's relapse after ten years; whereas on the other side, a 59 per cent share, with presumably an even higher proportion among teenagers. Nella Last in Barrow was among that majority and, though feeling feverish and sick, still performed her diarist duty:

> I did manage to make tea & watch 'Kidnapped', one of the high lights of the week, & then rested quietly till 'Command Performance'. Perhaps with not feeling well, I tended to be 'carping', but it *did* seem a dull 'dragging' programme – till Dickie Henderson began to compère. Other years we have been surprised by the 'speed' of performers – not so four songs by the Beatles, & the S American musick show. I wanted to see Harry Secombe as Mr Pickwick, but soon after 10.30 I began to feel the call of my warm, quiet bed.

Reactions to the Beatles from other diarists were predictably age-determined. A member of Tavistock Ladies' Luncheon Club, living in rural South Devon, found them 'disappointing', in contrast to 'otherwise a terrific evening's entertainment with Marlene Dietrich the highlight'; but among fifteen year olds, Brandreth's slightly grudging 'it has to be said they were very good' was supplemented by all-out enthusiasm from Roger Darlington ('fabulous') and Worthing's Diana Griffith (' "Royal Variety Show" fantab – Beatles – man, fantastic!').[23] When the credits eventually rolled on some fifteen million television sets – after Secombe's spontaneous gag, after the show's second rendition of the National Anthem, after Secombe had led the cast in three cheers for the Queen Mother and her daughter – the music playing over them left no doubt about whose triumphant evening it had been: come on baby now ...

PART TWO

9

Put Right Out of Gear

On Monday, 11 November, as Gerry and the Pacemakers settled into their third week at no. 1 with 'You'll Never Walk Alone', and the *Daily Mirror* began to step up media attention on Mods and Rockers ('How to Spot Them'), Henry St John astutely observed that 'the much publicised new fashion of high boots for women, reaching to a variable distance below the knees, continues to gain ground among younger women, more slowly than one would have suspected from reading newspapers or magazines'; next day Joe Meek (creator of 'Telstar') was especially fearful of his mother's reaction when the *Evening News* ran a story about the police having picked him up for importuning, Alan Ayckbourn's first distinctively 'Ayckbourn' play had its first night at Stoke-on-Trent's in-the-round Victoria Theatre (the local paper acclaiming *Mr Whatnot* as 'full of invention' with 'an endless stream of comic tricks'), and on the small screen it was the first round of *University Challenge*'s first final, between Leicester University (three men, one woman) and Balliol College, Oxford (four men); the Wednesday bombshell was the BBC's announcement that it was permanently taking off *TW3* at the end of the year, while that evening on BBC TV it was an RI of 31 for *Krapp's Last Tape*, even worse than the 32 for *Waiting for Godot* two years earlier. 'Over two-thirds of those supplying evidence thought the play excruciatingly dull and dreary to watch. They frequently described it as "pointless" and "repetitive" rubbish, with no visual appeal whatever, and a "cheerless" atmosphere.' More acceptably challenging was Joseph Losey's *The Servant*, premiered on the Thursday and winning high praise from Richard Mallett for the performances of Dirk Bogarde and James Fox, with *Punch*'s film critic adding that 'the girls [Wendy Craig and Sarah Miles] do well in their quite unemphasised corners of the narrative'; the latest *TLS* described Evelyn Waugh's *Basil Seal Rides Again* as 'a nasty little book' and had the evocative one-word headline 'Ugh ...' for its review by John Willett of William Burroughs's *Dead Fingers Talk* ('pure verbal masturbation ... air of pretentiousness ... a yawn is a yawn is a yawn, the reader soon comes to feel'); and political attention that day focused on the government's newly published plans for the north-east, envisaging a 'growth zone' stretching from Tyneside to Teesside and greeted by the *Northern Echo* as 'like a glimpse of spring'. Marjorie Proops in the *Mirror* on Friday the 15th welcomed *Which?*'s detailed report on contraceptives (27 types of sheath) on the grounds that 'it may make those "unofficial" users of contraceptives, the unmarrieds who slink into rubber goods shops, think twice before taking a chance'; Peter Griffiths the same day declared that 'decent, hardworking immigrants have been welcomed, but Smethwick folk will not sit quietly by and watch road after road turned into slums'; the Tory backbencher Gerald Nabarro on that evening's *Any Questions?* declined to mourn the imminent passing of *TW3*, not only 'utterly one-sided', but 'highly pornographic'; and Dr Alex Comfort's contribution to a BBC TV programme called *Men Tomorrow*, in which he defined a chivalrous boy as 'one who takes contraceptives with him when he goes to meet his girlfriend', seems to have been the specific spark for what would become Mary Whitehouse's Women of Britain Clean-Up TV Campaign. Over the weekend, the Police Federation protested against the Home Secretary's 'peculiar' decision to hold a public inquiry into the recent case of Sheffield Police using a rhinoceros whip to beat up three men being questioned in connection with breaking into a store; Sid Chaplin in his 'Northern Accent' column was sceptical about the chances of a genuine folk revival ('it is difficult to hard-sell the honest song the way they do the contemporary counterfeits') and dismissed the Merseyside Sound as having 'turned out to be only the slave trade getting a belated revenge on the port and the people'; C. S. Lewis gloomily predicted Labour coming to power in the next few months ('which I suppose means back to the old scheme of austerity for everyone and extravagance for the government'); Hugh Selbourne accidentally found himself watching *Juke Box Jury* ('astonishing rubbish'); Bernard Levin on *TW3* interrogated the washing-machine magnate John Bloom about his introduction of trading stamps (with Bloom, according to one viewer, winning the scrap); John Gross welcomed Nell Dunn's Battersea-set *Up the Junction* ('a kind of miniature Mayhew'); and the *Sunday Times* reckoned that, in a way unthinkable only five years earlier, soccer was 'clearly usurping the position of cricket as the sport which is socially "okay"'. On the Monday, recorded Judy Haines with satisfaction, 'Victor Value issuing King-Korn Stamps and starting us off with 120'; on the Tuesday, Field Marshal Montgomery called in the House of Lords for the reintroduction of National Service ('it may even result in the Beatles having to get their hair cut') and the *University Challenge* final had its second leg; on the Wednesday, Malcolm Bradbury dismissed Kingsley Amis's *One Fat Englishman* as 'an incomplete novel, a curiously irritating novel, and a more than slightly unpleasant one', Frederick Ward as manager of the Co-operative Wholesale Society's Bristol Grocery and Provisions Department confessed to himself that 'it is a job to keep one's mind off sugar' (in 1963 the most volatile of commodities), the Labour Party accepted the need for immigration controls, John Bingham (future 7th Earl of Lucan) married 'petite, gamine and elegant' Veronica Duncan at Holy Trinity Brompton, the local vicar urged pupils at Abbotsford County Secondary School for boys in Ashford, Middlesex, not to say when they left, 'Thank God it's over, now for the lolly', and England played at Wembley their first floodlit international (an 8–3 win over Northern Ireland); on the Thursday, as Labour decisively won the Dundee West by-election and Prince Philip in Aberystwyth received 'a Beatles welcome by nearly 200 women students', Ward noted that 'sugar has depressed me more today'; and next day, Friday the 22nd, Roy Strong's first curated exhibition ('The Winter Queen') opened at the National Portrait Gallery, the second Beatles album came out (*With The Beatles*, including Robert Freeman's moody cover photo of 'four white faces in a coal cellar'), the *Liverpool Daily Post* printed a photo of the pioneering, anti-hooligan fences behind the goals at Goodison Park ('EVERTON'S BARRIERS OF SHAME'), three chassis inspectors at the British Motor Corporation's Austin plant at Longbridge sent to the assistant works manager a nine-point letter setting out their rationale for a wage rise (reasons including 'tied to the tracks without slip men, we find it difficult to go to the toilet'), the architect Denys Lasdun was publicly given a free hand in designing the theatres on the South Bank for the National Theatre, the Duke and Duchess of Windsor arrived in London to do their Christmas shopping, plans were unveiled for a 40-acre shopping centre at Brent Cross 'with comparable shopping facilities to Knightsbridge and Oxford Street', a male diarist in 'fine & sunny' Hawkhurst, Kent 'secured loose trellis sections with dry earth round posts & re-tied wheelbarrow!', Madge Martin in Oxford went to the Scala (not staying to the end of the 'gloomy in the extreme' *Sweet Bird of Youth*), Grace Taylor in Ruislip 'did the house as usual', and in Dallas …[1]

Inexplicably, *Ready, Steady, Go!* was not yet fully networked – line-up that Friday evening in order of billing: Gerry and the Pacemakers, Freddie and the Dreamers, Kathy Kirby, Kenny Lynch, Rolling Stones – and among the variants was Granada's *Scene at 6.30*, fronted by Mike Scott. Five minutes into the programme, the telephone rang in the newsroom next to the studio – a tip-off from CBS in New York that President Kennedy had been shot. 'There was a rule that individual programme companies should never pre-empt ITN on big news,' recalled an obituary of Scott. 'Denis Forman, the senior Granada executive present, called ITN and was told they were not going to break into the schedules with the story until they had it from their own reporter in America. On the impulse Forman decided to go ahead, and Scott broke the news to northern viewers.' Then, over the next two and a bit hours, the broadcasting timeline seems to have been this:

7.05 or soon after Cliff Michelmore on BBC TV's *Tonight* gives news of the shooting. The programme continues.

7.15 Across the whole ITV network, *Take Your Pick* interrupted for a 'NEWSFLASH', with a solemn voice informing viewers about the shooting.

7.27 Newsflash on BBC TV. A numb-looking announcer repeats the words he has been given by telephone: 'We regret to announce that President Kennedy is dead.' The rest of *Tonight* abandoned, with instead for the next twenty or so minutes a mixture of revolving globe, solemn music and the occasional newsroom announcement.

7.30 News of death given on ITV, followed by two-minute silence and the start of *Emergency – Ward 10*.

7.38 BBC executives, seeing that ITV is going ahead with its soap, decide to revert shortly to normal programmes. An unlucky decision, subsequently much criticised.

7.40 *Emergency – Ward 10* abruptly halted, to be replaced by a piano recital (Bach and Chopin) by Joan Burns. No ads.

7.50 Starting five minutes late on BBC TV, *Here's Harry* with Harry Worth. Undeterred by the fact that he can only play (badly) 'The Bluebells of Scotland', Harry takes his fiddle along to an audition of the Woodbridge Municipal Orchestra – where he fails to recognise the honorary president, Max Jaffa ...

8.00 On ITV, the start of almost an hour of solemn music played by the Hallé Orchestra, interrupted by the occasional news-flash from Washington. No ads.

8.15 Five minutes late, start on BBC TV of *Dr Finlay's Casebook*.

8.40 BBC Light Programme. Announcer: 'Because of the news you've just heard about the assassination of President Kennedy we're not broadcasting our regular *Any Questions?* programme, but we are now going over to Wellington, in Somerset, for a few minutes to hear from the team and their question master, Freddie Grisewood.'

Over the past hour or so in Wellington itself, at a dinner in a local hotel with the wine flowing freely, there had been agitated discussion amongst the panellists about whether the programme in its usual format could conceivably go ahead in the tragic circumstances – with their mood turning increasingly rebellious, until word came from London that it would be a truncated, tribute-only broadcast. Accordingly, after mentioning that 'the audience here is standing at this moment as a gesture of sympathy for the American nation', Grisewood invited each member of the team 'to pay tribute to a very great man'. Starting with Lord ('Bob') Boothby, who after saying that Kennedy 'seemed to stand for all that is good and hopeful for the future of the world', continued with voice breaking and tears welling: 'This is a deadly blow from which we can, somehow I suppose, recover. He was a personal friend of mine. I knew him.' Conventional enough tributes were paid by Marghanita Laski and Wynford Vaughan Thomas, but the panellist in a delicate position was Michael Frayn, best known at this time as a satirist. 'I think his death,' he observed, 'is a reminder to people like myself and others who criticise governments, who criticise leaders, that in the long run, in the end, it is the men who lead who have to face the tough options.' After Grisewood had wrapped things up with the remark that 'there is obviously no more to be said at this moment', the announcer in Broadcasting House said that he would play music until nine o'clock. Back in Wellington, meanwhile, Boothby's fellow panellists were offering him shocked condolences, with apologies for not having known about their personal relationship. 'Well,' said a now cheerful, thoroughly composed Boothby, 'I didn't know him that well. I did a TV programme once with him in the States.'[2]

Inevitably, for one of the century's 'where were you when?' moments, almost all diarists (though not the solipsistic Henry St John) mentioned the shocking news. One of them, a musician living in south London, had gone up to Piccadilly and had 'high tea in original Lyons' before going to the Columbia for a double bill of *From Here to Eternity* and *You Can't Take It With You*, with the news being announced in the interval and everyone standing for a minute's silence; Sidney Jackson in Shipley heard 'the tragic news' on the radio, though reflecting that 'I never thought he was a friend to Britain – he had far too many family connections in Eire'; for Nella Last in Barrow, watching *Emergency – Ward 10* and looking forward to *Bonanza*, 'when the "stand by" for a News Flash came on, I said "must be something serious," & as conjectures filtered through my mind, dear knows why, I wondered if De Gaulle had been assassinated', with the actual news setting 'all my nerves jangling in bewildered unbelief'; Kenneth Johnson, a librarian in Letchworth Garden City and editor of *Hertfordshire Scout News*, was at a rehearsal for the Baldock Gang Show when he heard about the shooting and 'thought it was some sort of joke'; for the understandably preoccupied Frederick Ward, arriving for choir practice and being told the news, 'my thoughts went to the sugar market'; an anonymous teenager, living in St Albans, did mention the news, but only as a brief footnote to how her recent loss of virginity ('I'm not pure any more') had left her feeling 'tense' as well as 'guilty'; Anthony Heap in St Pancras was most concerned about 'tonight's television programmes put right out of gear', and Laurence Marks and his father in Finsbury Park had contrasting concerns. 'My dad thinks the Soviets killed the President and there will be another world war. I'm not worried about war, I'm worried whether the Arsenal–Blackpool match will be called off tomorrow.'[3]

Equally inevitably, that Friday evening features in many memoirs and recollections. Among already established or near-established public figures, Cliff Richard was in his newly acquired country pad in Essex, watching the TV set installed in his bathroom, when the news came through; Isaiah Berlin, about to give a lecture on Machiavelli at the University of Sussex, requested a quarter of an hour's grace to compose himself and drink two glasses of cold water, which did the trick; Melvyn Bragg and Hunter Davies were having supper in Soho's Arts Club when a waiter shouted out the news; Screaming Lord Sutch had just got to a gig in Cambridge when he heard the news on the radio and soon afterwards announced it at the concert – 'but it seemed so impossible and was so shocking it was a long time before the audience believed me'; and Ted Dexter had heard the news on his car radio before arriving late for his sister's dinner party at Tetbury, soon realised that no one else knew, and eventually stopped the party dead in its tracks by breaking into the conversation and asking portentously, 'Are any of you aware that President Kennedy was assassinated in Dallas today?' Among those still wholly 'unknown', seventeen-year-old John Bird in working-class Fulham had some hours of highly charged emotions, partly about the murdered Irish Catholic whom he strongly identified with, partly about the Australian model whose breasts were being unveiled at the drawing group in Parsons Green School he attended; 14-year-old Floella Benjamin in Penge was washing up when her sister Marmie, seated next door at her sewing machine with the TV on in the background, suddenly wailed with horror, 'They've killed a great man, they've killed a great man!'; 19-year-old Jimmy Boyle was in Glasgow's Barlinnie prison when a long-term inmate (allowed a radio) shouted out the news, but 'through the haze of the drugs [having recently received a parcel of purple hearts and sleepers] I thought it was some unreal dream that could never be true'; and 13-year-old Alan Johnson was with his three-piece band the Vampires, rehearsing a Beatles song in the cellar of fellow member Colin, when Colin's mum opened the door at the top of the stairs, gave the news, and 'our efforts to emulate the Beatles were immediately abandoned'.[4]

Perhaps the most piquant experience of all was that of Claire Tomalin, married to charismatic but unfaithful husband Nick and looking after three small children. When he rang from the *Sunday Times* to pass on the news and say that he was going to have to stay on late, her first reaction was not to do with a world tragedy, but to wonder if this was yet another cover story for one of his assignations. As so often, she would reflect in recalling that frozen-in-time moment, the micro trumps the macro.

What is surprisingly hard to find, whether in national or local newspapers, is as it were the mood on the street. A rare exception is Darlington, where the *Northern Echo*'s Stanley Hurwitz, after hearing that Kennedy had been shot and that they had sent for a priest, left the office and walked round the town, presumably notebook in hand:

The barmaid said: 'There has been another news flash – he's dead.'

It was still only 7.35 p.m. She was a grey-haired woman who put her hand to her lips: 'I've been feeling cold ever since I heard.'

The darts continued striking and sticking into the board. A young chap, a pint in his hand, said: 'As soon as I've finished this, I'm going home to press my uniform.'

A lot of people kept saying that sort of thing. A gulp at a pint and a thought for one's own skin: 'He's the most powerful man in the world. I just hope it wasn't a Commie who shot him.'

One old man in the street hung on to his pale principles: 'It's a shock – but there are two things I won't commit myself about – religion and politics.'

The blonde tripping down the street to the nightclub hadn't heard. She said: 'I don't know anything about politics, but he seemed a decent sort of chap – a nice man.'

A middle-aged couple was going to a party. The man said: 'If it had been in South America, or somewhere, I could understand it.'

The party would go on. Other parties would go on. A woman in evening dress said: 'It isn't quite the same as if it was one of our own Royal Family.'

In another public house the television was on, but instead of *Gunsmoke* [due to be shown on Tyne Tees TV between 8.0 and 8.55] there was symphony music, and no one complained. A game of dominoes rattled on beneath the sound.

Would there be a flare up? Would their own lives be disturbed by the shot that was fired at Dallas? Not one single person – and I spoke to perhaps 50 – said: 'How will it be with Jackie?'

Emotions ran unsurprisingly high in one port city. 'Shortly after the death of the President was announced on television,' noted the *Liverpool Daily Post*, 'one man suggested *Emergency Ward 10* should have been left on as the doctors might have been able to help. He was promptly lifted from his bar stool in a city pub by a left hook.'

The evening was not yet over. At the Globe Cinema in Stockton-on-Tees, hysteria was seemingly unabated as the Beatles performed; at a poetry and jazz concert at the King's Hall in Aberystwyth, after the manager had made the news announcement followed by a two-minute silence, the audience apparently, as recalled by the poet Dannie Abse, 'clapped all through' and 'laughed louder than any audience I had ever heard'; whereas at Hook Community Centre in Surrey, in a perform-ance by the local drama club of Derek Benfield's *Fish out of Water* (a comedy about 'fish-and-chip-eating, tea-loving Englishmen on holiday in Italy'), 'many laugh lines went by unnoticed by the audi-ence and only one person out of a cast of nine was word perfect'. Friday night was, of course, party night. At Cliff Richard's beano (the Dave Clark Five, the Shadows and Frank Ifield among those attending), the news 'changed the atmosphere because everybody was so shaken by it'; so, too, at a Chelsea soirée attended by 17-year-old party girl Kristina Reed, where 'the party ended early 'cos everyone was devastated'; by contrast, at a party of Leeds University students, Veronica Lee observed that 'quite a few men were disgruntled', appar-ently not because of the news, but instead 'because there wasn't really enough women'. In Oxford, a Keble College club dinner went ahead, though towards the end a whispered message to the Warden meant that he had to leave – on account, it transpired next day, of having been told of the death late that afternoon of his close friend C. S. Lewis. Elsewhere in Oxford, Madge Martin and her clergyman hus-band took the news from America as hard as anyone. 'Robert had his stomach trouble again, at night, poor dear,' she recorded. 'Of course I worried, and couldn't sleep at night. I think and think of poor gay young Mrs Kennedy.'[5]

Millions had been continuing to watch the box in the corner. The BBC pulled *The Dick Van Dyke Show* (due to start at 9.10), but did transmit *Britten at Fifty*, a birthday tribute to the composer which ended suitably enough with an extract from *The War Requiem*. There followed (shown on ITV as well) tributes to Kennedy by the three main party leaders, with a general consensus that Wilson took the honours, 'characteristically' dwelling (noted Violet Bonham Carter) on the late President's 'administrative efficiency & power'. On ITV, programmes broadly reverted to normal apart from a special edition of *This Week*, which took the risky decision to invite Wilson's deputy, the unpredictable George Brown. Already well-oiled by the time he arrived at Rediffusion's Kingsway studio, having been at a mayor's dinner in Shoreditch, he soon got involved, ahead of the live transmission, in a verbal barney with the understandably upset American actor Eli Wallach – a barney which would have led to fisticuffs had not Rediffusion's Milton Shulman (not yet a TV and theatre critic) managed to intervene. Then it was time for Brown, being interviewed by Kenneth Harris, to do his bit. 'At the first moment I saw that he was pissed and he was pretty awful,' recorded Richard Crossman soon afterwards. 'He jumped up and down and claimed a very intimate relationship with Kennedy. He said, "Jack Kennedy was one of my best friends," and I knew quite well that George had only seen him twice in his life, in formal interviews.' Brown then went on to say how he would have to go over to America to discuss things with 'Lyndon', the newly sworn-in president Lyndon Johnson. 'His rambling, inconclusive remarks indicated a remarkable insensitivity to the mood of the moment,' would be Shulman's recollection, while Anthony Wedgwood Benn put it succinctly at the time: 'He is a complete disgrace and one day it will all blow up.'[6]

Next day, Saturday the 23rd, the death of JFK cast a long but not invariable shadow. Take the contrasting evidence from a clutch of diarists:

On the radio heard continually about the Kennedy Assassination. (*Roger Darlington, schoolboy at a direct grant grammar in Manchester*)

This morning a lot of the girls are wearing black arm-bands that they must have made overnight. We had a special Assembly and stood in silence. Except for a couple of girls who kept blubbing loudly in the quad, everything everywhere is very quiet. Nobody knows what to say, except how terrible it is. Lessons as usual (Singing, French, Maths, Gym). *(Gyles Brandreth, schoolboy at Bedales, near Petersfield)*

We [Arsenal] beat Blackpool this afternoon 5–3. I take my usual spot behind the goal and from there I see eight goals that makes this game one of the best of the season. *(Laurence Marks)*

Everyone grieved about President Kennedy, the girls wore black sweaters at the hair dressers. *(London-based female music publicist)*

Thank Goodness my period started today – what a relief. *(The anonymous teenager, St Albans)*

51° Fahrenheit; weather fair. 8.34 a.m. I walked to Hammersmith Metropolitan Station, having coffee (9d) at Lyons'.

I proceeded to Shepherds Bush and at the market observing what looked like a few copies of 'Connoisseur's Choice' I asked to look through them. There were only 2 issues, both recent, and although I bought one (1/-) I did not want it.

I proceeded (1/-) to Acton Town and walked to my lodgings. Placard stated: 'Assassination. Midnight murder charge.' A newspaper seller said to another that papers should sell well throughout today. At the lavatory the woman gave me an Australian penny in my change, but I gave it her back. *(Henry St John)*

The papers full of the awful tragedy, and all the flags in Oxford – and I suppose everywhere – at half-mast. *(Madge Martin)*

Nearby at Oxford Town Hall, a junior minister, Margaret Thatcher, opened the Conservative bazaar, observing that Kennedy's death had been a salutary reminder that 'however great our mechanical achievements may be, the ultimate destiny of the world is in the hands of men and women'; at Westminster Cathedral, the requiem mass at 12.30 was described by Bonham Carter as '*most* moving – the vast Cathedral packed with people – mostly poor & humble bringing their children with them'; around the same time, at Headley in Hampshire, my mother and stepfather went to the village pub, saw long faces in the bar, and only then heard about what had happened; and at Ruyton-XI-Towns in rural Shropshire, captaining my prep school against our great rivals Packwood Haugh, my heart was not really in it as we went down to a tame 2–1 defeat.

'First of a new series of adventures in space and time' was how the *Daily Express* billed BBC TV's 25-minute offering at 5.15: in other words, the debut of *Dr Who*, as yet Dalek-free and starring William Hartnell in an episode called 'An Unearthly Child'. 'Tonight's new serial,' commented a retired naval officer, 'seemed to be a cross between Wells' Time Machine and a space-age Old Curiosity Shop, with a touch of Mack Sennett comedy.' 'Anyway,' he added, 'it was all good, clean fun and I look forward to meeting the nice Doctor's planetary friends next Saturday, whether it be in the ninth or ninety-ninth century A.D.' Not everyone on the Viewing Panel was so enamoured ('a police box with flashing beacon travelling through interstellar space – what clap trap!'), but an opening RI of 63 was perfectly respectable.

Yet it was in a truly parallel universe, one of unmitigated evil, that something terrible began to unfold while the programme was still on. 12-year-old John Kilbride was the oldest of seven children, living in a three-bedroom, red-brick house at 262 Smallshaw Lane, Ashton-under-Lyne, a largely working-class Lancashire textile and engineering town of some 50,000 people; that afternoon, he and three friends had been to the Pavilion Cinema to see Jack Palance as the son of Genghis Khan in *The Mongols* (an A-rated film, but a kind-hearted man had agreed to take them in); and afterwards, they had gone to the market square – over a hundred stalls lit up in the dark – to see if they could (in the words of Carol Ann Lee's poignant account) 'earn a few bob running errands'. 'I knew,' recalled John's younger brother Danny many years later, 'John and his mates used to help out there. They did it for spending money because most parents couldn't afford much – you were lucky if you got a packet of toffee. And there were quite a few of us, so it was hard for our parents. I used to give the biggest part of my paper money to my mum.' Soon after 5.30, having been last seen near the carpet dealer's stall, John was cajoled into a hired Ford Anglia for a lift home, with

Ian Brady and Myra Hindley saying his parents would be worried he was out so late, and promising him also a bottle of sherry. By nine o'clock he still had not returned home; his frantic mother, not having a phone, went to her sister's to call the police; and the search began for the second victim of the Moors Murderers.[7]

'The Kennedy assassination,' grumbled the single-minded Heap, 'continues to dominate the news today and upset scheduled television programmes.' Among the changes that Saturday evening were *Juke Box Jury* being replaced by a tribute programme fronted by Cliff Michelmore; and, several hours later, *TW3*'s own tribute, following a decision to jettison all that week's prepared satirical material. Barely nineteen minutes long in total, its notable moments included Millicent Martin singing 'In the Summer of His Years' (lyrics by Herbert Kretzner), an actor reading Bernard Levin's formal oration and Sybil Thorndike reciting Caryl Brahms's poem 'To Jackie', with all three items having been hastily written shortly before the programme went out live. Humphrey Carpenter in his account of the decade's satire boom quotes Paul Foot's unforgiving verdict ('sickeningly sycophantic') and argues that the whole thing was 'a belated attempt to save *TW3* from the scaffold'. This, though, seems overly cynical, not taking into sufficient account the high emotions running freely, not so different in kind from those after another sudden death thirty-four years later. Even Anthony Burgess reckoned, in his overview of how television had responded to the news from Dallas, that *TW3* 'achieved, out of dignity and simplicity, the most moving of all the tributes', albeit adding that 'one is not really carping if one deplores that saccharine ode "To Jackie"'. But it was Vere Hodgson who spoke for middle England. 'Something made me look in,' that middle-aged diarist, living in Church Stretton, wrote soon afterwards. 'I wondered what those irreverent vulgar young people would do on such an occasion. They were wonderful. Each one paid his tribute. So fresh, so sincere ... not a cliché nor a platitude among them. I was reduced to tears by the song the girl sang ...' In the programme itself, the last word went, of course, to a solemn-faced David Frost: 'It is a time for private thoughts. Good night.'[8]

*

This weekend coincided with the publication and early reception of one of the pivotal history books of the twentieth century. In August 1959 the 35-year-old New Left historian E. P. (Edward) Thompson had signed a contract to write a 60,000-word textbook on working-class politics from 1759 to 1921; four years later, in August 1963 in his Halifax study, he had written the preface to what had become not remotely a textbook, as well as largely confining itself to the period 1780 to 1832; and now *The Making of the English Working Class*, all 848 pages, was upon the world, published by Gollancz and costing 73s 6d.

Over half a century later, Thompson's much-quoted preface remains irresistible to quote from. 'The working class did not rise like the sun at an appointed time,' he declared about the book's title in his first paragraph. 'It was present at its own making.' As for the more contentious word 'class', he insisted that 'the notion of class entails the notion of historical relationship', that 'the finest-meshed sociological net cannot give us a pure specimen of class, any more than it can give us one of deference or of love', and that 'the relationship must always be embodied in real people and in a real context'. In short: 'Class is defined by men as they live their own history, and, in the end, this is its only definition.' Later, after identifying as his methodological enemies three particular 'prevailing orthodoxies' – 'the Fabian orthodoxy, in which the great majority of working people are seen as passive victims of *laissez faire*'; 'the orthodoxy of the empirical economic historians, in which working people are seen as a labour force, as migrants, or as the data for statistical series'; 'the "Pilgrim's Progress" orthodoxy, in which the period is ransacked for forerunners-pioneers of the Welfare State, progenitors of a Socialist Commonwealth, or (more recently) early exemplars of rational industrial relations' – there came the most celebrated sentence of Thompson's entire prodigious writing career: 'I am seeking to rescue the poor stockinger, the Luddite cropper, the "obsolete" hand-loom weaver, the "utopian" artisan, and even the deluded follower of Joanna Southcott, from the enormous condescension of posterity.'

Reviews over the next month or so were largely enthusiastic, with the three heavyweight appraisals coming from Richard Hoggart, Raymond Williams and Eric Hobsbawm, all to varying degrees men of the left. 'This scrupulous and humane book,' noted Hoggart in the

Observer (on 24 November), finding it a rare example of 'a scholarly book which not only sets out to examine events in great and qualified complexity but tries also to assess their human, their imaginative meaning'. Raymond Williams in the *Listener* was characteristically more guarded, though he did call it 'an active, valuing history' and praised its 'combination of attention to detailed structures of feeling with the necessarily generalizing nature of history'. The verdict that Thompson would surely have cared most about was that of Hobsbawm (who unlike Thompson had not broken with the Communist Party after the Soviet invasion of Hungary in 1956). It was with perhaps a certain implicit disparagement that he saw it as very much a book of the moment:

It reflects [wrote Hobsbawm in the *New Statesman*] not only the notable gifts of its author, but also a specific atmosphere – neo-Marxist – and a specific group – the New Left itself. The themes which run through it – working-class culture, a preoccupation with subjects recently opened up to scholarship such as riots and millennial movements – its markedly if non-professionally socio-logical approach, its sympathy with grass-roots radicalism, all place it firmly post-Suez ...

The final paragraph, too, had its grudging element:

Much of the interest of Mr Thompson's book lies in the details, which reveal an acute insight into pre-industrial patterns of life and their disruption, an admirable knowledge of the period and a romantic sympathy with the defeated heroes of historians. The author has long been known as a historian of striking gifts, though hampered by a lack of self-criticism from which this book also suffers. It is, for instance, excessively long without actually being comprehensive. Nevertheless it will become a landmark in the study of the British working class.[9]

Thompson and Hobsbawm: perhaps the rivalry was more imaginary than real; but over the next three or so decades, most young British historians knew instinctively which was their man.

Thompson's *Making* had, inevitably, its omissions. Surprisingly or otherwise, none of these early reviewers looked at the index and did the maths: some 246 readily identifiable men, but only nine women (one of them Charlotte Brontë, with Beatrice Webb another). Other absences included servants – 'the largest group of working people in Britain until the 1950s,' notes Selina Todd in her largely favourable fiftieth-anniversary tribute to the book – and the workers who did not choose to join those nascent trade unions so powerfully and pioneeringly described by Thompson. What, though, was *Making*'s long-term legacy? Three aspects perhaps stand out as giving it such resonance over the years. One was its strong sense of Englishness ('The Free-born Englishman' the evocative title of chapter 4), and English place, very often somewhere close to his Halifax base as an extra-mural lecturer in adult education for the University of Leeds – a particularism prompting Raphael Samuel to identify 'the local history library of Heckmondwike or Todmorden' as 'the Pennine crucible' for the book. Another aspect was Thompson's no-holds-barred rejection of the blessings of industrial capitalism, a rejection which, eight years on from his massive and very political biography of William Morris, placed him even more firmly in the long and honourable tradition of English romantic protest – soon to find its echoes in the counter-culture of the high sixties and beyond. The third aspect is brought out by the intellectual historian Stefan Collini, writing in 2005 in the context of how 'a triumphalist corporate capitalism operating within a consumerist facsimile of democracy holds undisputed sway, while it is more often the detritus of a debased postmodernism that clogs intellectual discussion in universities and on the Left':

> For Thompson, writing history involved an act of political imagination, so habitual as to be second nature, by which the daily pressures under which the poor lived, above all the pressures of economic exploitation and political harassment, were not buried by what he once called 'clumpish' terms, such as 'culture' and 'class', nor bathed in the rosy glow of the comfortable modern reader's nostalgia, but focussed in the most mundane details about the extent of the wasteland on which the Warwickshire cottager could run his pig, or about the number of days on which Cornish tin-miners supplemented their income by pilchard fishing, or about the wording of the by-law protecting the Northamptonshire labourers' 'liberty to cut rushes at Xmas and not after Candlemas'. This was

not the flaccid 'bringing the past alive' of middlebrow popular history, nor the sanitized 'heritage' of a tour of a country-house kitchen. It was a form of moral respect that took the trouble to itemize the precariousness of others' lives and to appreciate the kinds of courage and endurance needed to sustain them.

History, then, as 'a form of moral respect'; and it was not long after *Making* that 'history from below' began to flourish, including in the new universities, far from Oxbridge and where much of the book's early readership lay.

Back on that JFK weekend of November 1963, Hoggart in his review wondered briefly about what had happened to the working class in the century or more since Thompson's study ended. 'Many people assume that it has changed beyond recognition; others talk as though "the old spirit" is still to be found in every union branch and back street. Perhaps the truth lies somewhere in between.' It might have been that day, or certainly very soon afterwards, that the Labour politician Anthony Crosland was among those who gathered in a TV studio to discuss virtually that very question, 'Is There a Working Class?'. All the current talk of 'classlessness', he declared, was 'very superficial':

It exists on a certain level among the younger generation and everybody affects to like the Beatles. Upper-class and middle-class children will share great enthusiasms and all that – it's frightfully superficial. Below this there still are terrific accent differences. In five years' time all these people are going to separate out into different jobs and so on and I think much too much has been made of this [i.e. classlessness] in the last few years. It exists, but very much on the surface.

And right at the end of the discussion, Crosland sought to clinch his case by reaching for the comparative. 'There is still a difference between the barriers in this country and the barriers in most other countries,' he insisted. 'Practically, Swedes, or Germans, etc, don't mix in the evening any more than people do in Britain. Nevertheless the barriers are still quite different. The differences are not so marked. Here they would also be prevented by differences in way of life, accent ...'[10]

*

'Out of the shadows' was the title of Hoggart's review, and in a way that was what it felt like in the days and weeks after the first initial reaction to the awful news from Dallas. 'Everyone shocked and shopgirls in a dither, unable to give correct change,' wrote Kate Paul on Sunday the 24th in her Earl's Court diary, but already in Liverpool that day queues were a mile long for tickets for a pre-Christmas Beatles show, while that evening in Hull the 17-year-old Maureen Lipman had her Damascus moment. In the first half, from her balcony seat, she had viewed the screaming girls around her with a mixture of 'amusement and disdain'; but in the second half, John 'stepped forward to the mike, thighs straining against his shiny and confining suit, shook his locks, lowered his eyes', and started singing 'Money (That's What I Want)'. 'My Cornetto dangled. Sweat ran across my upper lip and down my virgin armpits. The screaming was increasing in volume and intensity. Someone was about to implode. I realised with an electric shock that the screaming someone was me.' Over the next three days, as normal life resumed, the *Daily Sketch* called on Everton to remove 'the hooligan barriers' at Goodison Park ('those who plead for cages and moats and barbed wire can weep in their beer, for the British football fan is showing he can correct the stormy situation of recent weeks in the good old British manner – by common sense'), Liverpool Council's Development and Planning Committee enthusiastically adopted Shankland's plan (in his own words, 'the biggest urban renewal planned in the whole of Europe'), QPR rejected at its AGM a takeover bid by John Bloom (his first major public setback), *University Challenge*'s first final ended with a win for Leicester University, Harold Wilson in the Commons confirmed (without explaining why) that Labour was no longer opposed to the principles of immigration control contained in the 1962 Commonwealth Immigrants Act, and Stoke-on-Trent's *Evening Sentinel* reported the continuing existence of a colour bar at the White Hart Inn in Burslem, where the licensee, Mr T. A. Evans, said that he was prepared to serve 'coloured people' in the bar and the snug, but not in the back room, where the juke box was kept.[11]

Wednesday the 27th also saw the publication of *Traffic in Towns*, the last of 1963's series of major reports, in this case by Professor

Colin Buchanan. An engineer by training, he had already previewed the report's essential subject and objective in a magazine article some weeks earlier. After declaring that urban planning was the 'only way to avoid future chaos', he had gone on: 'We have taken a bull into the china shop and to that old problem there are only two answers – shoot the bull, or, more creatively, build a new china shop specifically designed for bulls.' The bull was, of course, the motor car; and in the report itself, a surprise bestseller whose principal recommendations were broadly accepted at once by government, he and his team argued that, with the number of vehicles predicted to double in the next ten years, there needed to be two key things put in place in order to combine the maximum use of vehicles with tolerable living conditions in towns. The first was a primary road network, where necessary built to motorway standards and replacing the old street system; and the second, within that network, was a variety of 'environmental areas' in which the main criterion would be a pleasant milieu.

Immediate reaction, not least from the exuberantly pro-car transport minister Ernest Marples, tended to emphasise the first of those things. That evening's *Tonight*, noted Anthony Burgess, 'devoted itself almost entirely to the future of our towns under the stress of fast-increasing car ownership, and seemed to assume that the driver's view represented the norm (Cliff Michelmore drove into the studio with what I believe is known as insolent skill)'. 'GO-AHEAD FOR MOTOR AGE PLANNING' was the *Liverpool Daily Post*'s headline next morning, and over the years Buchanan himself came to believe that he had been badly misinterpreted, that the mistaken assumption about his report had been (as he put it in 1983) that it had offered 'a blueprint for the total reconstruction of towns and cities with traffic circulation at different levels, costing a fortune and not very nice to look at into the bargain'. This was perhaps on the whole broadly true, yet at least one exception at the time among commentators was John Morgan, who wrote in the *New Statesman* in praise of the report's unexpected 'humanism': 'In the great clearances it envisages, roads will not eat men. Equally, it is hostile to the "visual intrusion" of traffic in towns; the professor and his colleagues care when the architectural or historic appeal of towns and cities is disfigured.' It was, in short, a report which genuinely offered 'the chance of learning from the errors of the US and accommodating the motor car into a civilised town life'.[12]

Elsewhere in the weeklies, letters in the *TLS* applauding its take-down of William Burroughs appeared from Victor Gollancz and Edith Sitwell ('very right-minded,' she declared, adding that 'the public canonization of that insignificant, dirty little book *Lady Chatterley's Lover* was a signal to persons who wish to unload the filth in their minds on the British public'); in the context of *TW3*'s imminent demise, Richard Ingrams, recently established editor of *Private Eye*, took to the *Spectator* to make the case for the continuing need for 'the "satire" movement', arguing that Orwell's 'picture of class-ridden England has not changed', that 'the Prime Minister is still an asinine figure in knickerbockers firing off at the obsequious grouse', and that 'satire appeals to the young, and the young are the future'; while with the charts now dominated by British groups (eight of the top ten singles, 14 of the top 20, 20 of the top 30), the pop weeklies celebrated the release of the Beatles' fifth single, 'I Want to Hold Your Hand', its advance orders of a million about to propel it straight to no. 1. Around the same time, George Brown was using a party meeting to try to justify his worse-for-wear TV appearance the previous Friday ('acutely embarrassing,' noted Benn, 'and there was no comment, nor even grunts of sympathy from MPs there'), John Bloom was quickly trying to bounce back from his QPR reversal by taking over Golden Eagle Gifts (trading stamp subsidiary of Great Universal Stores), and Peter Griffiths was writing to the Ministry of Housing to suggest, on behalf of Smethwick's Tory councillors, a ten-year residential qualification for immigrants displaced from their homes by slum clearance ('if immigrants start to get a lot of council flats, there will be a riot'). But in retrospect, perhaps the most preg-nant moment from these late November days was a letter in the *FT* on Saturday the 30th. Against a background of the rapid concentra-tion in recent years of the brewing industry, including the death of many independent breweries, it came from an Uxbridge reader, Mr E. A. H. Cross, who identified this 'swallowing up' of small brew-eries by larger ones as the prime cause for the disastrous turn to keg beers – 'blown up,' in his words, 'out of sealed dustbins'; and he urged drinkers not only to complain to their MP if they could no longer find beer to their satisfaction in their local pub, but to suggest to that politician (assumed to be male) that he himself have 'some nice draught beer drawn from the wood'.[13] Eight years before the start of CAMRA (Campaign for the Revitalisation of Ale), it signalled, rather like all the increasingly flourishing steam railway preservation societies, a warning shot against the unquestioned joys of the modern.

Yet if the year drawing to a close had had a master theme to rival the rise of individualism, it was surely that of the desirability of antiquated 'amateurs' giving way to up-to-date 'professionals'. The first half of December did not disappoint. 'Mancroft Leaves Board', 'Lord Mancroft Silent on Resignation', 'Anti-Semitism Denied', 'Arabs Forced Resignation', '"Furore" over Mancroft', 'Norwich Directors Sit Till Midnight As Storm Grows', 'Britain Resents Arab Pressure', '"Job Back" Offer to Mancroft', 'Mancroft Not to Go Back', '2 Quit Board of Norwich Union' – such were among *Telegraph* headlines about the story of Arab states successfully pressuring the Norwich Union Insurance Company to sack from its London board a prominent Jewish businessman, Lord Mancroft. For Anthony Sampson, the whole episode exemplified less a residual anti-Semitism, more the hopeless amateurishness not only of the Norwich Union's board, but of much of the insurance industry generally. 'The most modest international contacts – even a brief visit to the Foreign Office or the Board of Trade beforehand – would have told them that their action was commercially daft,' he wrote in an *Observer* piece headlined 'Mancroft and the twilight of the amateurs'. 'Most companies,' he added, 'still perpetuate the nasty outmoded division between Gentlemen and Players. The young insurance recruit can be fairly certain that, however efficiently he works, he can never reach the board. He will be embroiled in a system which, whatever its first justification [about external directors protecting the public from misuse of funds], has now become an extension of privilege.' Sampson in his piece did not name names, but two years later, in his *Anatomy of Britain Today*, he did, characterising the main board at the time of the Mancroft affair as 'largely composed of Norfolk dignitaries': 'The president was Sir Robert Bignold, a 72-year-old Norfolk brewer and author of "Five Generations of the Bignold Family", and other directors included the Marquess of Townshend, the wealthy Norfolk landowner descended from Turnip Townshend, and the veteran diplomat Sir Hughe Knatchbull-Hugessen.' Not long after the episode, including an uncomfortable TV appearance, Sir Robert resigned as president and was succeeded by Desmond Longe – 'also,' in Sampson's nicely understated words, 'from an old Norfolk family, one of a parson's huge family'.

December's issue of *Encounter* had Katherine Whitehorn praising Mary McCarthy's *The Group* and Muriel Spark's *The Girls of Slender Means* for their wit and their sense of place and history, whereas *The Unicorn* provoked her to dismiss Iris Murdoch as 'a fantasist with no feet on the ground and no sense of humour', even suggesting that she switch to writing science fiction. Five years after her incisive if lofty contribution to the *Conviction* set of essays, there was clearly no social-realist, state-of-the-nation novel to be expected from that quarter. What about *Suicide of a Nation?*, edited by Arthur Koestler and in effect a revised version of *Encounter*'s special issue from the summer? 'We ought surely to have finished with the diagnosis by now and be getting on with the cure,' contended an impatient Norman Shrapnel, the *TLS*'s reviewer on 5 December, in implicit reproach to Sampson et al. 'Does anyone still need convincing about our snobbishness, amateurism, national introversion, unhealthy addiction to eld, failures of management and the rest of it? Or are we beginning to gloat over our symptoms and ailments like elderly ladies in the tea-room of some rather deteriorated spa? Would we be lost without them?' He perhaps had a case, to judge by John Calmann's account earlier in the week of being recently interviewed for a job on the *Daily Sketch*. It took place 'over the lunch table at the Ivy,' and at one point the editor Howard French (recalled by Ferdinand Mount as looking like 'Osbert Lancaster's Lord Littlehampton with droopy shoulders and a luxuriant grey moustache of the type seldom seen in England since the 1890s') observed to the young economic journalist: 'This country is being demoralized by people like the *New Statesman* crowd and the *Observer*. You know, Marghanita Laski.' Where then, in the eyes of those whose role in life was to pontificate solemnly on these matters, did hope lie? The *TLS* had no doubt. 'The relentless sound of the Liverpool beat filling the air today – the ramshot "yeah, yeah" of the Beatles – tells us of one direction in which the intellectuals' eyes are turned as the mid-1960s come on,' declared an editorial in the same issue as its review of *Suicide*. 'It is towards the hope of a new vitality, emotional and imaginative, springing up among the working class – or, to be more precise, among young working people who have begun to forget the idea of class, and to blend with the classless, cosmopolitan crowd that grows stronger and stronger in our big cities.' Or as the *Daily Mirror* put it more succinctly next day: 'You have to be a real sour square not to love the nutty, noisy, happy, handsome Beatles.'[14]

This Thursday the 5th and Friday the 6th coincided with the trial of the by now thoroughly unloved Christine Keeler. The accusation was that, at the Old Bailey trial in June of 'Lucky' Gordon for his assault on her, she had knowingly failed to give full disclosure about which witnesses had been present. Now, on the first day, her defence counsel Jeremy Hutchinson (who three years earlier had successfully acted for Penguin Books in the *Lady Chatterley* trial) sought but failed to get quashed the indictment of conspiring to obstruct the course of justice; and next morning, she was advised by Hutchinson that the jury was almost certain to find against her and that, in the interests of a shorter sentence, it would be sensible to plead guilty – advice which she accepted because, in the plausible words in 2021 of her son Seymour, 'she simply could not fight any more' and, having seen close up the scapegoating of Stephen Ward at his trial, 'knew that the system was against her'. That afternoon, before sentence was passed, Hutchinson invoked to the judge the time-honoured quality of mercy ('Ward is dead; Profumo is disgraced; and now I know that your Lordship will resist the temptation for what I might call society's pound of flesh'), even quoting Lord Denning ('let no one judge her too harshly'), but the result was still a nine months' prison sentence. Composed at that moment, and wearing lime-green, Keeler then 'burst into tears', reported the *Telegraph*, 'as she reached the bottom of the stairs leading from the court to the cells'. Years later, Hutchinson would remember talking with her during the trial: 'It was the voice of a person who had lived many years longer than her twenty-one years and who seemed to have grown entirely weary of life. It was a voice which had lost any joy in life.'

That Friday evening, as Keeler prepared to spend her first night in Holloway, political pundits were in agreement that a better-than-expected by-election result at Sudbury and Woodbridge pointed to a fighting chance for the Conservatives in the 1964 election; David Hockney, whose first solo show (*Paintings with People*) had just opened at the Kasmin Gallery, was basking in John Richardson's largely favourable *New Statesman* review ('dean of British Pop painters ... his gift for pinning down picturesque aspects of contemporary life in arresting, if somewhat whimsical images ...'); two British female singers were now in the Top Ten (Kathy Kirby – 'more curves than a Cresta Run,' according to one male pop columnist – with 'Secret Love' and Dusty Springfield with 'I Only Want To Be With You', her first solo single); Cathy McGowan was co-presenting *Ready, Steady, Go!* for the first time; less than a week after Cross's *FT* letter, the first formal meeting of the Society for the Preservation of Beers from the Wood was taking place at a pub in Epsom; and Frank Lewis, Cardiff's loner diarist, was at the New Theatre to see David Turner's *Semi-Detached*, with Steven Berkoff among the cast. 'Not all that good, but not bad,' he reckoned, before adding: 'I don't like all these middle-class women types you get in theatres – all these snooty-nicy-nice types. I don't like to think that theatres cater for *just* these types, – which it very often seems *is* the case.' For another diarist, Madge Martin in Oxford, one domestic issue now loomed above all else. 'At *last* succumbing,' she noted next day about her and her husband making arrangements to acquire a TV set, 'though both of us are a bit loath to do so.' Still, she went on, 'if we *are* selective, it may be quite fun to have'.[15] The die was cast – albeit too late, she might or might not have regretted, for a Beatles bonanza this particular Saturday.

First up on BBC's enterprising double bill was all four moptops on *Juke Box Jury*, running from 6.05 to 6.35 and viewed by 43 per cent of the population (compared to only 10 per cent for *Thank Your Lucky Stars* on the other side). An RI of 63 (seven above the average for *JBJ*), but audience research noted the entirely predictable 'wide disparity of opinion between the under- and over-thirties', with the former 'generally enthusiastic to a degree', whereas 'many' of the latter 'remarked that, with the possible exception of John Lennon, all four seemed incredibly inarticulate ... while in addition none was considered to be over-endowed with personality'. 'Fantab' was the reaction of 15-year-old Diana Griffith in West Worthing, but not 19-year-old Veronica Lee at Leeds University: 'They were quite moronic. To think of all the people crazy over them and slavishly following their every word.' The second half of the bill came at 8.10, a half-hour show *It's the Beatles!*, recorded (like *JBJ*) earlier that day at the Empire Theatre, Liverpool, in front of 2,500 members of the group's Northern Area Fan Club. This time an RI of 59, including 'tremendous enthusiasm' from the under-twenties though with some disgruntlement about too much focus on the screamers ('we wanted to watch the Beatles, not the stupid nits in the audience'). As for older viewers, the widespread feeling was summed up as 'likeable enough lads, with a youthful zest that was in itself infectious, but they could not really sing and had only a very limited repertoire'. 'Decidedly a nine-day wonder,' pronounced one. 'In eighteen months I think they will be "has-Beatles".' The day had a couple of piquant footnotes. One was a young, publicity-seeking Jeffrey Archer, closely involved with Oxfam's latest campaign to end world hunger, managing to get backstage at the Empire, hold out collecting tins to Paul, George and John, and thereby successfully achieve his *Daily Mail* photo op; the other concerned the Orchids, an all-girl group of Coventry teenagers (children of factory workers and the youngest only fourteen). They had recently been signed by Decca, instructed to pose in their full school uniforms for publicity photos, and had released their first single, the Motown-style 'Love Hit Me', a week earlier. It was among the new discs played on *Juke Box Jury*, but got dismissed out of hand by all the Beatles except Paul. At which point the three girls, sitting high up in the audience, were asked to stand up; the audience went 'Aaaahhh!'; and John said, 'I'll buy a hundred'. But it was too late, and in the event it never really quite happened for the Orchids, apart from appearing as a comic strip in *Judy*.

By chance that Saturday, the writer Nicholas Wollaston was in the middle of an eight-day stay in Liverpool, the only city on an English tour that had begun in August and so far taken in, *inter alia*, Skegness ('seven super jollidays' at Butlin's), Blyth ('a man's town'), Leek ('old-fashioned' the word he heard most often), Bridgwater ('a town of supreme normality') and Swanage ('a town of prep schools, run by pink-faced men in check jackets and striped ties'). Now, he gazed around him from a tugboat in the middle of the Mersey:

The liver birds perched on the tallest office building, the smudge of the [Anglican] Cathedral tower looking faintly Hindu in the distance, the funnels and masts behind the dock wall, the Gothic warehouses of Bootle, the gantries of Birkenhead, the stumps of the

New Brighton tower (Blackpool's rival that had to be felled because
it was unsafe), the Wallasey ferry and Irish packet and Canadian
liner and Liberian super-tanker forming their slow patterns across
the viscous surface – it looked pretty good.

But not so good close up, as much of the rest of his chapter portrayed
a city not only in almost childish thrall to the Beatles ('those masters
of monotony, archpriests of din ... before long as dead as the liver
birds'), but also in palpable decline. The visual evidence included
'the murk' hanging over the central area's grand nineteenth-century
buildings (typified by St George's Hall, 'so dirty, big and black that
one hardly believes it can be hollow'); the slums not far away ('the
world of bedroom slippers on the cobbles, of Z-cars and Oxo cubes
and Typhoo tea'); and the lack of good restaurants ('there are scores of
Chinese eating-places, but as almost everybody orders fish and chips
anyway, the food is as tawdry and inevitable as the crimson lanterns
and willow-pattern wallpaper'). Ultimately, argued Wollaston, the
problem was economic, embodied by, as someone at the Chamber
of Commerce told him regretfully, 'the decline of the small family
businesses – tramp owners, fruit brokers, oil seed merchants – that
had been passed from father to son since Liverpool's golden days and
that had handed on from one generation to the next more than just a
comfortable job and a loyal staff'. There was also, helping to explain
the city's 6 per cent unemployment rate, a fundamental structural
difficulty: on the one hand, a manufacturing base that was simultaneously too small (employing only about a third of the working population) and the wrong sort, with its key industries of soap, rubber
and chemicals employing only a small proportion of skilled workers;
on the other hand, an over-reliance on commerce, transport and distribution, so that 'when a Lancashire cotton mill closes down or a
company sells a couple of transatlantic liners or a merchant moves his
South American business to London, it affects Liverpool'. Apart from
the inherent vigour and vitality of the place and its people, Wollaston
saw just two hopeful signs. One was the huge new Ford plant on the
outskirts in Halewood; the other was the Shankland redevelopment
plan, perhaps capable of restoring 'a little of Liverpool's self-respect'.
His chapter ended where it had begun. 'They've seen a thing or two
in their time, but nothing to what's coming,' said the tugmaster as he

nodded across to the liver birds. To which the mate responded: 'It can't change Everton, skipper. They'll go on winning, like, whatever happens.'[16]

Three days later, and less than a week after Ian Nairn in the *Telegraph* had attacked as 'slum clearance run mad' the planned redevelopment of Gravesend's Wakefield Street area ('a cheerful hugger-mugger of cottages, corner shops and pubs, around the Georgian church where Princess Pocahontas is buried'), a two-day conference called 'People and Cities' began at Friends' House. Organised by the British Road Federation, it was clearly an attempt, in the immediate aftermath of Buchanan, to (in the *Guardian's* anticipatory words) 'press the Government to promote massive schemes for town-rebuilding and so reduce to the minimum the need for restricting traffic'. Marples, opening the proceedings, did not disappoint. 'We have to face the fact, whether we like it or not, that we have built our towns in entirely the wrong way for motor traffic,' he insisted. 'We want an entirely different type of town.' For Sir Geoffrey Crowther, former editor of *The Economist* and more recently chairman of the steering group on the Buchanan Report, the crux was 'to dis-invent suburbia' and, in the city centres, 'go upwards'; while Buchanan himself did not really at this point distance himself from Marples, arguing that the capital needed motorways comparable to those already planned for Glasgow and Liverpool. 'A motorway network in London would mean redevelopment of the most radical character,' ran his reported words. 'This was not impossible in physical terms, and if only the means and courage to do it could be found it would produce a metropolitan area of the most marvellous character.'

Others at the conference mainly spoke in the same sort of tenor, but a dissenting note came from Arthur Ling, Coventry's left-wing chief architect and planning officer. 'One thing that has struck me in this conference,' he observed about the conference's misleading name, 'is the few times that *people* have been mentioned. We have heard about planning for traffic, we have heard about planning for profit, but we have not heard enough about planning for people.' Yet which political party would prioritise the interests of 'people', especially those very many conservatively minded change-averse people who arguably comprised the majority? Perhaps not, despite their name, the Conservatives. 'The bold scale of modernist solutions,' notes

Otto Saumarez Smith, 'was a central element of what Tories took from modernism, as modernist planning would provide ever-greater sites for profitable redevelopment. The engagement with modernism went further than this, though: it was used to give form to the future envisioned by the Conservatives through the mantras of prosperity and affluence.'[17] While as for Labour, there was, on the national stage anyway, all still left to play for.

The conference was still taking place when Cecil Beaton visited the 'crowded' David Hockney exhibition and recorded Hockney himself ('yellow glasses, yellow dyed hair and exaggerated north-country accent') being accosted by 'an irate lady':

> In a loud voice she challenged him for drawing his nude women in such a distorted manner. 'Can you really imagine that is the way the arm comes out of the socket? Look at their bosoms – they're nowhere near where they should be. Have you ever seen a naked woman?' 'A dorn't knogh ars ah harve!' 'Well, I'll tell you the hips are not like that; the *entrejamb* starts here, not there. The thighs aren't flat like that, the buttocks aren't small and squashed and side-ways. Don't you realise that the rib cage runs down to the groin?' 'A dorn't knogh ars ahm unturusted!'

That evening, in another sign of seemingly renewed provincial confidence, the new, uncompromisingly modernist Nottingham Playhouse opened, with the artistic director John Neville (a major star of the Old Vic before his 1961 move to the East Midlands) taking the title role in *Coriolanus*. Next day, Thursday the 12th, a TV set was installed in the Martins' drawing room in Oxford – 'I expect we *shall* stretch a point sometimes, when there is anything *really* tempting' – and as early as Friday they cracked, watching 'the likeable comedian' Harry Worth. Two diarists then had very different Saturday evenings: in north London, Phyllis Willmott and her husband going to a dinner party and encountering a less-than-soulmate in the young novelist Antonia Byatt ('Oh my, she did prove vexatious to Petie & I ... The mixture of taking herself so seriously, and demanding entire attention, got on my nerves ...'); in Epsom, a ticketless teenager, Jacqui Graham, managing to persuade a 'darling DARLING doorman' to let her in to see the Rolling Stones. 'Got right to the front & wow! Leaning up on the stage gazing into the face of Mick and he looked at me – he did! Keith glanced once, Charlie never ...' Sunday saw the heavies give glowing reviews to Hockney ('something irresistibly fresh-faced' about his work, according to the *Observer*'s Nigel Gosling); Madge Martin on Monday watched *Top of the Form*; and on Tuesday, a depressed Frances Partridge, her lunch cancelled, went to the Empire in Leicester Square to see Garbo in *Ninotchka*. 'Perhaps that wasn't lowering but coming out into the so-called daylight was, and brushing past figures with drab pinched faces, and having a sandwich and a Bovril in an awful café where everyone looked as though they were just going to drown themselves and the waitresses worse – expressionless, gone under.'[18]

Earlier that day, at 8 a.m., two men had been hanged: 23-year-old Russell Pascoe at Bristol, 22-year-old Dennis Whitty at Winchester. Their crime was having brutally murdered – multiple stabbings, and beating with an iron bar – a reclusive farmer living on an isolated Cornish farm where it was believed that he kept large sums of money. Sitting with Pascoe in Bristol's Horfield Prison, the night before the execution, were two prison officers. One of them, Robert Douglas, would recall half a century later the scene in the warm and stuffy condemned cell, as the prison governor came in, accompanied by another man:

'How are you, Pascoe?' asks the governor.

'All right, sir,' he replies. The other man suddenly steps towards the prisoner, thrusts his hand out.

'How do you do, son?'

In a reflex action, Russell takes it. They shake. Ken and I glance at one another.

'I'm a, not so bad,' mumbles Russell, obviously thinking.

The governor and the man turn on their heels and leave. As the doors are locked, Ken and I unbutton our tunics again and sit down. But the mood has changed. Russell sits quietly for a minute.

'Who were that with the governor?'

Ken and I know. I've just had supper with him in the mess. 'I'm not sure,' Ken mutters, unconvincingly.

'I knows,' says Russell. 'That were the fucking hangman weren't it?'

I look at Ken. He shrugs.

'Aye, it was,' I say.

'I knew it. What's he want to shake hands with me for?'

'It's a thing Albert Pierrepoint used to do,' I say, and 'Harry Allen has carried it on. Probably makes him feel better or something.'

'If I'd twigged I wouldn't have took his hand. Fucker! Caught me on the hop!' He goes to the end of the cell and lies on his bed. A moment later he raises his head. 'They weighed me this afternoon, you know. So they know how far to drop me.'

Next morning, less than an hour after the deed had been done and having been assured by Allen that Pascoe had been 'good as gold' in his last moments, Douglas stepped out of the prison gates. 'It's a cold morning, with a weak, wintry sun. For a moment I stand on the cobbled streets in front of the gate and watch people go about their business. The demonstrators have gone. Buses lumber past with passengers reading their morning papers. I don't see anybody take as much as a glance at the prison.' Later in the week, one of Bristol's MPs wrote an article about what had happened. 'How soon before the gallows are banished to join the axe, the thumbscrew, and the rack in the museum of past horrors perpetrated by man on man?' asked Wedgwood Benn. 'Not long now,' he reckoned, looking ahead to the next general election and the influx of younger, more liberal-minded MPs. 'The year 1964 will almost certainly see the final end of capital punishment in Britain.'[19]

'Today,' noted Richard Crossman on Thursday the 19th, 'I've just done my Christmas shopping in the usual places, Hatchards in Piccadilly and Fortnum & Mason':

I brought the shopping home across St James's Park and when I was crossing the little bridge, I saw a sight which excited me more than anything I've seen for a very long time. It is just a year ago since I took Anne to New York and saw that beautiful view from Central Park across to the Plaza Hotel, with the ice-rink in front. Now here I was looking down towards the new War Office and behind it Whitehall Court. Suddenly this became one of those romantic views. On the left was that great new building, New Zealand House, at the bottom of the Haymarket. Then came the trees, and, in the background, a

fantastic arrangement, a fairy castle rising behind the modern structure. As I turned round to face Buckingham Palace, there was a cres-
cent moon and behind it the new brilliantly illuminated skyscraper. It
was really my first sight of the new London, with the old behind it.

And Crossman was 'reminded once again that, in some mysterious
way, in a living city the old and the new do blend together'. Next day,
the *Mirror* reported a headmistress declaring, 'I don't like the Beatles'
as she cancelled the rest of her school's Christmas show, and accompanying party, after four boys had dressed up as Beatles to mime to
their records and 300 girls had screamed as if it were the real thing;
27-year-old Sher Akram Khan, a Pakistani who since 1960 had been
living in Bradford and working as a four-loom operative on the night
shift of a Keighley mill, told the *Guardian*'s Geoffrey Moorhouse that
he had never been on the receiving end of racial discrimination, that
he was gradually adjusting to the ways of the West Riding, and that in
sum, 'I have a nice job here, and lots of friends, and I'm very happy';
and in Oxford, on her sixty-fourth birthday, Madge Martin opted to
watch Harry Worth on TV rather than go out 'in the freezing cold'
to carols at their church. That weekend, the first Dalek (at this stage
a 'sucker' arm only, resembling a sink plunger) appeared on *Dr Who*
and Gladys Langford found herself dreaming, six months after the
event, about 'Prince Charles & cherry brandy'; while on Christmas
Eve, it was curtain up at the Finsbury Park Astoria for the first night
of The Beatles' Christmas Show. 'I Want To Hold Your Hand' and
'She Loves You' were perched at nos 1 and 2 in the charts, another
northern sound was at no. 3 with 'You Were Made For Me' by Freddie
and the Dreamers, even Dora Bryan was getting in on the craze with
'All I Want For Christmas is A Beatle', and one way and another this
festive show (part panto-cum-revue, part rock 'n' roll, and supported
by fellow Liverpudlians Billy J. Kramer & the Dakotas and Cilla
Black) capped the year.[20]

'Surprised to find the church so empty,' noted the poet and travel
writer Patrick Anderson after attending Christmas Day morning
service in the Essex village near Braintree where he was temporarily
living. 'Only three or four choirboys, two singing maidens in blue
cassocks and floppy tricorn hats, one or two men.' As for the service
itself, having been shown to 'a box pew rather far up on the left':

Those of my fellow churchgoers whom I could glimpse looked so secure: tuned to a single settled expression. They sang. They prayed. They rose and they fell. Their singing was only faintly jolly, their prayers the whispered confidences of a businessman to his bank manager. Everything was in the best of taste ... I couldn't spot a teenager anywhere ...

On Boxing Day evening, in a beauty contest attended by more than 300 West Indians at a school in Smethwick, 19-year-old Pauline Dean, working locally as a secretary, was chosen as the West Indian 'Miss Midlands 1963'; next day, *The Times*'s anonymous music critic (William Mann) wrote appreciatively of how Lennon and McCartney in their songwriting 'think simultaneously of harmony and melody, so firmly are the major tonic sevenths and ninths built into their tunes, and the flat submediant key switches, so natural is the Aeolian cadence at the end of "Not a second time" (the chord progression which ends Mahler's *Song of the Earth*)'; on Saturday the 28th, after seventeen-year-old George Best in his second senior game for Manchester United had struck one watcher as 'a slight, dark, casual Irishman with lovely ball control and a fine feeling for the positional game', and after the now 15-year-old Laurence Marks had as usual watched *Juke Box Jury* ('one of tonight's jurors is Jimmy Savile, who always looks a bit weird to me'), it was a final outing for *TW3*, which according to one critic 'quietly expired on a note of fairly genial nostalgia', with most of the programme 'a recapitulation of outstanding items from past shows'; next day, Katherine Whitehorn's column in the *Observer* won long-lasting fame through its vigorous defence of 'the miserable, optimistic, misunderstood race of sluts' in daily domestic life ('Have you ever,' she challenged her female readers, 'taken anything back out of the dirty-clothes basket because it had become, relatively, the cleaner thing?'); and on New Year's Eve, it was Norman Wisdom's latest, *A Stitch in Time*, for Anthony Heap at the King's Cross Odeon ('a very accept-able and easily assimilated mixture of slapstick and sentiment with medical jokes galore'), a 'quiet evening at home' for Madge Martin ('some of the T.V. programmes are very good!'), and a pub in Corby, within sight of the blast furnaces of the huge steelworks and with nude photos pinned on the wall above his seat, for the just-arrived Nicholas Wollaston and a Cockney sitting on the other side to him:

The bar was packed full. There were people playing dominoes and darts, and young Scotch steelworkers smoking cigars with girls drinking Italian aperitifs. The divisions were not by class but by age-groups; one generation of men wore cloth caps and bicycle clips, another wore belted raincoats and trilbies, a third wore Beatle jackets and winkle-pickers. At a table in the middle were two thin boys in skin-tight jeans, with pale hunted faces and long cavalier ringlets, dirty copper-colour.

'The C.N.D. brigade,' said the Cockney. 'I bet there's many a girl'd like that hair.' He told me about everybody. The three women in the party over in the opposite corner were tarts, and at the far end of the bar was the ton-up crowd, in leather jackets and crash helmets; one of them got killed every month, racing his bike on the motorway. And there was a Scotsman leaning across a table of domino-players, being hearty and buying everybody drinks; actually, he was very frightened, for he had been involved in a court case with another man who had been sent to prison, while he himself had got off; the other man was due out soon, and this fellow was getting worried. The Cockney said there was a lot of funny business like that in Corby.

And in Holland Park, just before midnight, Benn arrived home, 'where the boys and Melissa were welcoming in the New Year, twisting and shouting'.[21]

10

I Shouldn't Like to Be Poor Again

Wollaston continued during the early months of 1964 his tour of England. He did not much enjoy the rest of his stay in Corby – in its public bars, the almost invariable 'gang of happy steelworkers bawling about dear old Glasgie toun'; in the town centre, 'a weird feeling of impermanence', with 'no Georgian houses, however disfigured, no Gothic churches, no narrow High Street splitting with traffic'; on the streets, 'girls pushing the smartest pixie-dressed babies over muddy pavements in the most terrific prams, young men in mock sheepskin streaming out of the technical college into the bowling-alley, shadowy characters in jeans and donkey jackets hailing taxis and speeding off to the far corners of nowhere' – and was happy to reach the north Cambridgeshire town of Wisbech with its 'air of solid, historic respectability'. There, 'life-sized pictures of the Beatles were pasted over the windows of the music shop in the market square, but inside one could also buy a clarinet or the piano sonatas of Scarlatti'; in the Mermaid in the market square, 'big weather-beaten men with pints of brown-and-mild' were 'playing dominoes for money', with 'only one or two women waiting for their husbands'; and at the Corn Exchange, with its Victorian cast-iron and glass roof, he watched the spectators watching an evening's wrestling ('"He don't want to marry you!" shouted somebody when the wrestlers were locked together like dogs'). No wrestling in Chertsey, deep in Surrey commuterland, which he reached on a packed early evening train from Waterloo (bowlers and briefcases on the rack, women having to stand because nobody offered them seats). As usual, it was pub life that got Wollaston's sociological juices going: in the lounge bar, with its 'frieze made of the tips of club ties pinned to a shelf of miniature liqueur bottles', a woman in trousers declaring how she despised the Americans ('they've brought every *vice* to this country') and a man looking forward to a day's golfing in Sunningdale ('eighteen holes in the morning, then a few beers, and nine in the afternoon'); while in the homelier public bar, where there was 'the same talk of cars, but of hire-purchase rather than dogs', and 'a generous barmaid who laughed at her own jokes', he watched a high-quality darts match between 'smart, hard women' (Glad, Phyl, Madge, Elaine) and 'smart, soft men' (Stan, Eddy, Don, Smiff). A day or two later, leaving this largely nondescript town in whose High Street cafés 'women in purple hats sit like beleaguered dowagers, gossiping over tea and scones, attended by sharp-voiced waitresses who have seen better days and like to take it out on their customers', he returned to London on a morning commuter train, with its 'familiar smell of pipe-smoke and newspapers', mainly the *Telegraph*, the *Express*, the *Mail*. 'At Addlestone I opened the door for a woman who was getting in, and both she and the other passengers gave me the sort of look ("Poor chap, he doesn't know the form") that I have come to expect.'

'"Top Pops" great,' recorded 15-year-old Diana Griffith on New Year's Day. It was the first *Top of the Pops*, going out live at 6.35 from a converted church in Manchester, as the Rolling Stones, Dusty Springfield, the Dave Clark Five, the Hollies and the Swinging Blue Jeans mimed to their latest hits. The presenter was thirty-seven-year-old Jimmy Savile – reasonably enough, given that the producer Johnnie Stewart had based the show's format on Savile's popular *Teen and Twenty Disc Club* on Radio Luxembourg. Audience Research revealed that among under-twenties, most found him 'lively, amusing and knowledgeable'; nor was it so different among over-twenties, where 'there were plenty who thought Jimmy Savile appropriately lively and gay'. Even so, those adults who disliked the programme (an overall RI of 62) largely did so because of his unusual appearance. 'What an odd-looking individual ... A cross between a Beatle and an Aldwych farce curate. Like a Presbyterian minister ... Like something from Dr Who ... Mutton dressed as lamb ... Presiding over the orgy like a Puritan clergyman resurrected from his own churchyard.' Over the next three Wednesdays it was the turn of 36-year-old Alan Freeman (from the previous Sunday the permanent presenter of *Pick of the Pops* on the Light Programme), 37-year-old David Jacobs and

38-year-old Pete Murray, before Savile returned to the helm on 29 January. This time, 'many' of the over-twenties 'found Jimmy Savile's manner and appearance disconcerting to a degree'. 'Is this Jimmy Savile sane?' wondered one viewer. 'I must say his most peculiar appearance and manner suggest otherwise. I couldn't understand a word of his "gabble", either.' As for the under-twenties, although he came in for some criticism ('a real nit', 'a proper twerp', 'a big idiotic nothing'), they found him only 'a minor irritant in an otherwise "altogether smashing" and "absolutely fab" show'. The programme itself (with 19-year-old local girl Samantha Juste, remembered after her death as 'tall, long-haired and beautiful', responsible for dropping the needle on each record) was by now rapidly establishing itself as a fixture in the TV schedules. 'An audience of youngsters twisting and jiving to canned favourites,' noted *Punch*'s Bernard Hollowood not unbenignly soon afterwards. 'A lot of the music is British, most of it is based on solid, elementary jazz rhythms, and it all makes the nippers extremely happy.'[1]

In the wider pop scene across these early months of the year, it was – notwithstanding massive hits for the Dave Clark Five ('Glad All Over', 'Bits and Pieces'), the Searchers ('Needles and Pins'), the Bachelors ('Diane') and Cilla Black ('Anyone Who Had A Heart'), and not to mention the Detours becoming the Who, as well as Ray Davies and his combo appearing on 1 February for the first time as the Kinks at a thinly attended Oxford Town Hall – really all about the Beatles versus the Stones, as the gap between their public images became ever wider.

The Beatles, following their triumph at the Royal Variety Performance, were now being positively embraced by the Establishment. One minister, Bill Deedes, publicly applauded their 'work, skill, sweat'; his boss, Sir Alec Douglas-Home, made a nod to their path-breaking US tour as he called them 'our best exports' and 'a useful contribution to the Balance of Payments'; and the Duke of Edinburgh, when asked how he regarded 'Beatlemania', replied that 'these blokes are helping people to enjoy themselves', as opposed to 'fighting and stealing'. The incentive for their fellow northerner Harold Wilson to get in on the act was clear, and he sought to persuade EMI's chairman, Sir Joseph Lockwood, that as 'a fellow Merseysider' (a partial truth at best) he would be the ideal person, at the upcoming

Variety Club Awards at the Dorchester Hotel on 19 March, to crown them as the 'Show Business Personalities of 1963'. Lockwood agreed; the photo op was duly secured; and John reputedly quipped as he looked at his gong, 'Thanks for the Purple Hearts, Harold'. But no show-biz gongs, let alone a knighthood, yet in the offing for the Stones. 'They look like boys that any self-respecting mum would lock in the bathroom,' declared the *Daily Express* at the end of February; 'a bunch of right 'erberts!' a middle-aged London taxi-driver told an enquiring music journalist; and five days before the Beatles were anointed in Park Lane, *Melody Maker*'s full-length profile had the headline 'WOULD YOU LET YOUR SISTER GO WITH A ROLLING STONE?' – a headline carefully fed to the paper by their ever-enterprising manager Andrew Loog Oldham, as the *MM* duly obliged by including some appropriate details and quotes. 'I don't see why we shouldn't grow our hair as long as we like,' said Brian Jones, before Mick conceded 'I don't bathe every day' and Bill Wyman chipped in, 'I know!'. 'Young fans,' reflected Ray Coleman, 'now realise that their elders groan with horror at the Rolling Stones. So their loyalty is unswerving.' A week later, the *Evening Standard*'s Maureen Cleave responded with 'WOULD YOU LET YOUR DAUGHTER MARRY A ROLLING STONE?' and offered a clear-eyed take. She described Loog Oldham as 'passionately devoted to their scruffy image'; noted that Jones was planning to move to Belgravia and live next door to Lady Dartmouth; and, indeed, gave the last word to the one with 'floppy yellow hair', her favourite in the group. 'We're quite clean really,' confided Jones to her. 'What we want to do is bring a lot of pleasure to people. Thereby earning a bomb!'[2]

It was the northerners, though, who were by early 1964 truly part of the national furniture. 'I wish the girls had won without picking up easy marks on the Beatles,' lamented Hollowood in *Punch* after Brownhills High School for Girls had defeated 'the male grammarians of Hull' in the recent final of TV's *Top of the Form*. 'It seemed grossly unfair for boys to be familiar with the nomenclature of this booming group ... The boys were routed here and the girls answered with smirking, contemptuous certainty.' Soon afterwards, the retired teacher Gladys Langford had a dream-cum-nightmare about being back at her old school 'brilliantly lit & crammed with teen-agers, girls fashionably & showily dressed, all boys with "Beatles" hideous hair styles'; another diarist, Judy Haines, approvingly called them 'good ambassadors' for their tour of the States; the novelist Sid Chaplin welcomed them as an example of 'the English', after 'nearly half a century of silence', at last 'opening their mouths and letting it rip again'; and in Bromyard, Herefordshire, 99-year-old Anne Hill, about to bring up her century, had her moment in the spotlight. 'She enjoys reading, but only "good" literature,' reported *Berrow's Worcester Journal*. 'She thinks the young people of today are too soft and would make better people if they had not so much done for them. Asked what she thought of the present "Liverpool Sound," she remarked that the Beatles made "a lot of noise about nothing!"'

The journalist and commentator Paul Johnson would not have disagreed. 'The Menace of Beatlism' was the title of his *New Statesman* piece a week later, as he inveighed against 'the new cult of youth' and the way in which the nation's leaders, 'bewildered by a rapidly changing society' and 'excessively fearful of becoming out of date', were 'increasingly turning to young people as guides and mentors'. 'Both TV channels,' he went on, 'now run weekly programmes in which popular records are played to teenagers and judged. While the music is performed, the cameras linger savagely over the faces of the audience. What a bottomless chasm of vacuity they reveal! The huge faces, bloated with cheap confectionary and smeared with chain-store makeup, the open, sagging mouths and glazed eyes, the broken stiletto heels ...' In short, 'those who flock round the Beatles, who scream themselves into hysteria, are the least fortunate of their generation, the dull, the idle, the failures'. A rather different perspective came from 19-year-old Virginia Ironside, whose first novel, *Chelsea Bird*, was soon to be published. 'I think intellectuals are frightened of the Beatles, they think brains will quite soon count for nothing,' she reflected privately after the 26-year-old journalist Anthony Haden-Guest had told her that 'frankly' the Beatles bored him stiff. 'They can't bear to think that someone who does the shake beautifully could be admired more than Robert Helpmann [the ballet dancer]. This is such a new, vital thing, I mean it really excites me, like abstract art excites the phonies, how they can't receive it with open arms, burning with curiosity and sheer ecstasy I don't know.'[3]

There was, of course, plenty of other popular culture going on that was aimed at a broader demographic. On the big screen, *The*

Leather Boys, focusing on a working-class marriage (Rita Tushingham as the manipulative Dot), represented a late flurry from the British New Wave of social realism, including a tentative depiction of a gay character and scenes filmed at the Ace, the notorious motorcyclists' café next to Brent railway bridge; *Zulu* had Stanley Baker holding Rorke's Drift, with his second-in-command played by the working-class Michael Caine ('slightly wrongly cast as an upper-class officer,' thought Penelope Gilliatt, 'but he does it very well'); and *Nothing But the Best*, with screenplay by Frederic Raphael, was a kind of satirical, metropolitan *Room at the Top* ('I had expected it to be more subtle,' noted Judy Haines, 'but it wasn't bad'). By this time the Haines household had a rented TV, from British Relay, after at least eight years without a set. The girls 'thrilled' with it, she recorded, as well as being 'good' for her husband John. So, too, in Barrow, where television (usually preceded by a dose of Ambridge) became seemingly ever-more central for Nella Last and her not always easy husband. 'We had the usual "Archers", Ward 10 & then Steptoe & Son,' she noted on a typical Tuesday evening. Or two days later, after *Double Your Money*: 'I *was* so pleased the 15 year old boy, so good on Ballet questions, took the £500 – whereas on hearing the £1,000 one he would have lost.' The old favourites largely continued to appeal: 'I would never willingly miss meeting my Dock Green friends, specially Dixon himself,' a postwoman told audience research. While of the new favourites, *The Avengers* won especial praise from the critic Francis Hope because of Honor Blackman: not only did she possess 'those important physical prerequisites (both of them)', but as the widowed anthropologist she had not on the whole become 'that all-time drag, a talking dumb blonde'. One diarist was more critical of the whole medium. 'We have, until a few minutes ago, been looking at a play on TV [Clive Exton's *Land of My Dreams*, with Michael Hordern playing a Jew-hating major with political ambitions],' wrote Phyllis Willmott on a Saturday evening in February. 'A lot of old rubbish as usual. An hour and fifteen minutes – never enough. Almost all TV stuff *written* for TV is a dreadful parody of life-in-earnest. Come to think of it probably no play I have seen – actually *written* for TV – has been memorable, let alone outstanding.'[4]

That March – a month after Philip Hope-Wallace had admired the 'skill and spirit' of 'a tall gangling Canadian called Donald

Sutherland' in a dramatic revue (*Spoon River*) at the Royal Court, and two months after A. S. Byatt's debut novel *The Shadow of a Sun* had received mixed reviews, with its 'maturity of vision and observation' reminding Richard Church of *Middlemarch*, but Isabel Quigly finding it 'long-winded and often just off the mark in social or spiritual accuracy' – the world of poetry saw an emblematic juxtaposition. 'It goes down like pure whimsy and then back-kicks like a sick mule' (George Melly, *Sunday Times*); 'the work of a strong, untutored, immensely self-confident mind' (*Vogue*); 'slight as it is, it is worth the attention of anyone who fears for the impoverishment of the English language and the British imagination' (*TLS*) – the praise as well as the sales (first print run of 50,000 copies immediately sold out) rained down for John Lennon's *In His Own Write*, described by the author himself as 'weird, off-beat and slightly sick'. No keener fan than Joyce Grenfell. 'John (Beatle) Lennon's nonsense poetry book is so wonderfully silly,' she told a friend on publication day, the 23rd. 'I dote on it but defy you to ask me why. It's crazy, man. Crazy. But I larf.' Given the book had been published by Jonathan Cape (where Tom Maschler was still editorial director), the phenomenon had a particular resonance for the discarded Barbara Pym, who even ahead of publication had observed tartly to Philip Larkin that 'that and Miss Bowen should give their list the variety it has seemed to need lately'. But if Larkin himself was not too bothered, that was understandable, for during March it became apparent that his new collection *The Whitsun Weddings* (published by Faber on 28 February) had moved him into the generally recognised top league, both reputationally and commercially. Within days of publication, two people on a train had asked him to sign copies ('the Ringo Starr of contemporary verse', he now dubbed himself); while in the *Listener*, John Betjeman described him as not only 'the John Clare of the building estates', but 'this unperturbed, unenvious and compassionate poet of doubt, common experience, and the search for truth'. 'He has certainly,' concluded the nation's favourite poet, 'closed the gap between poetry and the public which the experiments and obscurity of the last fifty years have done so much to widen.' A particular piquancy attached to the reaction of Pym's unwitting nemesis, another Maschler coup. 'Larkin, thank God, is an English poet, not just a poet in English,' reflected John Fowles in his diary. 'The lovely

dark dinginess of the English provinces, the backstreet blues, the pervasive palpable futility of existence. Larkin's characteristic "spine"
is: Things are bad; but (last stanza) not so bad as I've made them
seem. This is very English. The scorpion-tail in our pessimism.'⁵

Different readers, different books. 'Mim [Miriam] & I,' recorded
somewhat unexpectedly in February the 54-year-old Frederick Ward,
'are kept busy a few minutes each evening "oohing" and "ahing" over
Miller's "Tropic of Cancer" and the "Karma Sutra". The descriptions
in the first are as crude as I have read, but not unknown.' About the
same time, the Queen Mother was in hospital recovering from a colos-
tomy. 'It was a truly enjoyable experience,' she told Cecil Beaton soon
after leaving, 'apart from the fact that kind people sent me modern
novels to read, and they were so loathsome, & so perfectly horrible,
that I felt quite sick with distaste.' 'I think,' she added, 'that we must
be living through a moment of bad taste in many forms of art, &
I hope that the English will revolt soon.' The real frontier of the limits
of taste, though, was increasingly television, featuring between late
January and mid-March a series of *causes célèbres*. In Roger Smith's
Catherine, the first play directed by Kenneth (not yet Ken) Loach
for the BBC, a singer played by Tony Selby approached a divorced
woman (Kika Markham) in a bar and asked, 'Do you charver?', said in
such a way that even those ignorant of slang could work out it meant,
'Do you fuck?'; a David Turner play, *Trevor*, had a young married
couple talking frankly to each other about their sex problems; another
play, an adaptation of James Hanley's novel *Say Nothing* directed by
Philip Saville, had what Sheila Hancock recalled as 'some off-screen
huffing and puffing noises depicting sexual intercourse', provoking
in turn 'a leader in the *Express* the next day and dozens of letters';
a Sunday evening religious affairs programme, *Meeting Point: What
Kind of Loving?*, had a psychiatrist telling Joan Bakewell that 'it is no
longer absolutely necessary for a girl to be a virgin when she comes
to marriage – in fact, some men prefer that she should not be'; and
on ITV's *This Week*, investigating erotic books and films, a sequence
included Pamela Green performing a striptease, the first time a naked
woman had appeared on British TV. Mary Whitehouse, teaching in
a large Shropshire secondary modern, was by now on the march.
Three days after the 'charver' episode, she and her friend Norah
Buckland, a vicar's wife in the Potteries, launched on behalf of 'The

Women of Britain' a manifesto condemning 'the propaganda of dis-belief, doubt and dirt that the BBC projects into millions of homes through the television screen', and calling on the Corporation instead to show programmes 'which build character instead of destroying it, and encourage and sustain faith in God and bring Him back to the heart of the family and national life'. Over the next two months, they distributed leaflets and spoke to the press, with preparations in train for a big meeting at Birmingham Town Hall to launch nationally their Clean-Up T.V. Campaign.[6]

Two trials during these months also contributed to the shaping of a certain climate of moral panic – a leitmotif for the rest of the decade and beyond. One, held in February at Bow Street in front of the Chief Metropolitan Magistrate, Sir Robert Blundell, turned on whether Ralph Gold, proprietor of the Magic Shop in Tottenham Court Road, had been in contravention of the 1959 Obscene Publications Act through his decision to sell the recently published cheap paper-back edition of the unexpurgated *Fanny Hill*. With the publishers (Mayflower Books) underwriting the defence, Jeremy Hutchinson argued that the true place of this eighteenth-century erotic novel lay 'in the history of literature and not in the history of smut'; the pros-ecution for its part emphasised an atypical scene involving flagella-tion; and Sir Robert, reportedly with 'scarcely a minute for reflection', found against the bookseller. The line had held – to the relief of Peregrine Worsthorne, concerned about the danger of a widely avail-able edition persuading its male readers that 'erotic excitement' was 'a civilised and even innocent experience which it is perfectly proper to enjoy' – but few imagined it would for much longer. The other trial, starting in Aylesbury in January and lasting much longer, was of those responsible for the previous summer's Great Train Robbery and enjoying by this time almost film-star status. Early on, the per-manently injured driver of the Glasgow–London express, Jack Mills, gave a vivid account of the brutal iron-bar attack on him; five weeks in, Arthur Hopcraft described 'the public gallery still full, mornings and afternoons, as it has been from the start', the ten defendants 'all spruce, all attentive', the 20 counsel 'identically pink of face', the moments of humour mainly unintentional, the general 'grinding of detail'; and by 27 March, Maundy Thursday, the all-male jury was at last poised to give its verdicts.

'Because of a football match at Stamford Bridge this evening,' lamented Henry St John one Wednesday in January, 'I did not get home [Acton] until 7.18 p.m., after standing for 33 minutes at St James's Park before I could get in a train, and getting out of it at Victoria because the crush, and halting in the tunnel, with men lighting more cigarettes with all windows shut, was unbearable.' The sporting social divide remained seemingly as strong as ever. 'Of course, they're a bit slow off the mark' was the judgement on the Fen people made around this time by the clerk of the Wisbech and Marshland Rural District Council, an outsider himself. 'Let me put it like this,' he added to Wollaston, 'they're soccer players rather than rugger players'; and it went without saying that he meant union, not league. Still, even as hooliganism was starting to take hold as football's biggest problem – 'I hope this is the last time I have to drive a football special,' declared Harold Griffiths after the 'worst' journey of his 43 years on the railways, as Manchester United fans returning from a Cup match in Southampton pulled the communication cord at least fifty times – the intelligentsia was continuing its stealthy embrace of the people's game. Defences 'repeatedly cracked open like unpricked roasting chestnuts', Stanley Matthews still able to 'bring order out of chaos with absolute authority', John Ritchie 'a good centre-forward in the classic Lawton-Lofthouse build': all part of the first match report (Stoke City v Portsmouth) for the *Observer* by B. S. Johnson, admittedly someone who had served his time on the terraces of Stamford Bridge. Elsewhere these months there was no doubt about the identity of the racing car and racehorse of the moment. In late January, after a Mini-Cooper driven by Paddy Hopkirk had won the Monte Carlo Rally, their reward was to squeeze on to a revolving stage in order to feature in a comedy sketch on *Sunday Night at the London Palladium*, with Bruce Forsyth and watched by some twenty million; then, on a Saturday some five weeks later (7 March), the 'unbeatable' English champion Mill House, in search of a second successive Cheltenham Gold Cup, met his match from Ireland. 'Our wildest dreams came true this afternoon,' reported John Lawrence, 'as Mill House and Arkle rose together at the second last. Then, as Arkle swept irresistibly away a thousand arguments were settled – and we who watched stood hats in hand, lifted clean out of ourselves by the finest racing spectacle I ever saw or hoped to see.' A legend had been born. 'I have never seen at Cheltenham, or anywhere else, enthusiasm to equal the welcome Arkle got today,' added Lawrence about the scene outside the winners' enclosure. 'Mobbed, patted and pushed on every side he walked calmly through the milling cheering crowd ...'

And the man of the moment? In February the veteran theatre director George Devine was asked about Lindsay Anderson's recent complaint that the London theatre-going public was still very conventional and middlebrow. 'The situation in the theatre is nearly always symptomatic of the political and economic situation at any time,' he judiciously replied. 'In the middle and late '50s there was a lot of political excitement in the air, but there's less so now. Both the major political parties look very much alike. People are busy making money, and good luck to them.' If being busy making money was indeed the prevailing zeitgeist, then prime candidate for the accolade was, at this very moment in time, surely the self-made, 32-year-old John Bloom. Having made a fortune selling cut-price washing machines, he had recently diversified into trading stamps, television rentals and Bulgarian package holidays; on 12 February, he and his wife celebrated their third wedding anniversary with a lavish, well-publicised party at Soho's Jack o' Clubs (including a performance by Davie Jones (the future David Bowie) & the King Bees, given an underwhelming reception by guests including Lord Thomson of Fleet, Lance Percival and Adam Faith); and a week before Easter he was the subject of a full-length profile ('The Electric Man') by Margaret Laing in the *Sunday Times* colour magazine. The cover showed Bloom at the wheel of his yacht, the 376-ton *Ariane III* complete with cinema and lift; Laing depicted him as an autocrat in business, working on hunches and finding it impossible to admit to mistakes; while he in return gave her good value in quotes. 'I shouldn't like to be poor again,' he declared, 'and I have taken all the precautions to see that I shan't be.' 'The people who are getting on in the world,' he insisted, 'are people who are prepared to work themselves and persevere', before condemning public schools for their 'breeding of the Establishment, which I think is diabolical'. She asked him if he wanted a knighthood. 'Not at the moment,' he replied, 'but I might when I'm 40.' While as for his obvious competitors as men of the moment: 'I like the Beatles because I think I'm the top of one sphere and they're top of another. There are a lot of similarities.'

'There is,' concluded an impressed Laing, 'scant danger that his rivals will catch this particular business man unawares.'[7]

In early 1964, as before and after, the spirit of the times remained tirelessly afoot in the sphere of urban demolition and redevelopment. 'In a quarter of a century, the old Gorbals will be nothing more than a fading memory,' confidently predicted – and, just as confidently, celebrated – the *Scottish Field* in March. 'Rotting tenements, crowded single-ends, noisome back courts, ill-lit alleyways – all will have gone. In their stead will be not just the blocks and clusters of high flats that are already such familiar landmarks, but spacious schools and playgrounds, rented unit factories, an entertainment building, a new commercial centre – welded by landscaping into a new environment bearing no least resemblance to the old.' Elsewhere, demolitions in Bristol included the Embassy Cinema, the Fry's 1902 building in All Saints Street, the Royal Exchange in Corn Street and Georgian houses in St Thomas Street, plus no last-minute reprieve for Shot Tower, the earliest extant brickwork in the city; under the wrecking ball in Salford was 'Chomlea', one of its few surviving stately homes; 'I suppose we have got to face up to progress,' reluctantly concluded Alderman William Bird about Worcester's latest development plan (two new ring roads, two new bridges, huge shopping centre, likely death-knell for many small and medium-sized shopkeepers and small businesses); while in the capital, the government was apparently intent on demolishing the sumptuous 'Renaissance Palace' (Foreign Office, Commonwealth Relations Office, Home Office, Old India Office) bequeathed by the Victorians, the Post Office Tower continued to rise ('like a petrified gusher,' thought Geoffrey Moorhouse from his Tottenham Court Road vantage point), and Mollie Panter-Downes referred just before Easter to 'the construction right in central London of great slabs of new office buildings, which seem to be going up all over the place this spring', with particular obloquy reserved for 'the ninety-foot block [the future Juxon House] that has started to rear its undistinguished head at the top of Ludgate Hill, where, it seems to many indignant Londoners, it will partly obstruct the pedestrians' approach view of the West Front of St Paul's Cathedral'. Not, it should be emphasised about this crucial strand of post-war history, that doing *nothing* was ever a realistic option. When Derek Worlock moved that March to the parish of St Mary and St Michael in Stepney, the future Catholic archbishop found within a quarter of a mile of the church, record his biographers, 'dosshouses and a brothel, derelict buildings, the remains of bombed houses where meths drinkers gathered, streets full of litter and debris'; and Worlock was amused to look across the road from all this mess and see a Tory poster, 'Don't let Labour ruin it'.

London in general was now a city in flux, with a significant trend starting to be observed. The key pioneer witness was the sociologist Ruth Glass. 'One by one,' she wrote in her introduction to the newly published *London: Aspects of Change* (assembled by UCL's Centre for Urban Studies),

> many of the working-class quarters of London have been invaded by the middle classes – upper and lower. Shabby, modest mews and cottages – two rooms up and two down – have been taken over, when their leases have expired, and have become elegant, expensive residences, larger Victorian houses, downgraded in an earlier or recent period – which were used as lodging houses or were otherwise in multiple occupation – have been upgraded once again ... Once this process of 'gentrification' starts in a district, it goes on rapidly until all or most of the original working-class occupiers are displaced, and the whole social character of the district is changed. There is very little left of the poorer enclaves of Hampstead and Chelsea: in those boroughs, the upper-middle-class take-over was consolidated some time ago. The invasion has since spread to Islington, Paddington, North Kensington – even to the 'shady' parts of Notting Hill – to Battersea, and to several other districts, north and south of the river. (The East End has so far been exempt.)

'Gentrification': this, as suggested by the inverted commas, was the term's first sighting. Glass herself saw it as 'an inevitable development, in view of the demographic, economic and political pressures to which London, and especially Central London, has been subjected'; but as to whether it was healthy or unhealthy, she was silent.[8]

Silence, too, from many about race, but not the increasingly high-profile champion of white-collar trade unionism, Clive Jenkins. 'The BBC's *Black and White Minstrel Show* is a revolting disgrace,' he declared at the start of the year in the left-wing *Tribune*. 'At a time

when the coloured peoples of the world are demanding their rights –
and their dignity – it is a cultural obscenity. Its black-face singers
mime with simian exaggeration. They recall the stereotypes of the
Ku-Klux-Klan.' 'Quaint but damaging rubbish' was how a week
later one reader, Douglas Harrison of Edinburgh, described Jenkins's
views. 'I dread to think what would happen if the *Daily Express* got
hold of it, for it is the completely wrong image of Socialists, exemplified by this article, of extremists who will find fault in anything,
that makes the cause of Socialism an object of ridicule with so many
people.'

The political crucible of the race question was undoubtedly
Smethwick, by now starting to receive national attention, albeit
patchy. In that West Midlands town – where around 6 to 7 per
cent of the population were non-white immigrants (over half of
them Indian, over a third of them West Indian) and where, noted
Geoffrey Moorhouse, 'most pubs exclude coloured people from
their lounge bars' and 'some barbers refuse to cut their hair' – the
general expectation was that the Conservatives would gain control in
the May local elections. Their most vocal figure was Peter Griffiths,
a primary school headmaster and prospective parliamentary candidate. 'Apparently the plight of English children held back by the
presence of non-English speaking children in a class doesn't bother
the immigrant leaders,' he wrote in January in his regular column
in the *Smethwick Telephone*. 'Well, it bothers the Smethwick Tories,
and our kids are going to get a square deal in spite of the combined
opposition of the Socialists and their immigrant friends.' Soon afterwards, the *Guardian*'s Dennis Barker asked him a series of pointed
questions:

> Would he have preferred the immigrants not to have come to
> Smethwick? – Yes indeed; the housing list was long enough as
> it was.
> Was he in favour of any sort of colour bar? – No, he had no colour
> bar at all, only a squalor bar.
> Would he like the immigrants to be driven out? – No, he would
> encourage them to go away.
> Was he a supporter of the policies of the South African Government
> on apartheid? – He would have to be on the spot to decide.

'I am very disturbed by the present political atmosphere in Smethwick,' a local vicar told *The Times*'s Midlands Correspondent (Brian Priestley) in March. 'The Conservatives will not let the colour question be forgotten. They are constantly talking about it ...' Priestley also interviewed Griffiths himself, asking him direct what he thought about his party's 'n— neighbour' slogan that had been circulated during 1963's municipal elections. 'I fully understand the feelings of the people who say it,' replied an unrepentant Griffiths. 'I would say it is exasperation, not fascism.'

What to do? A background paper this spring for the Labour Party's study group on Commonwealth immigrants wondered whether the answer lay in seeking greater integration through the growth of 'Friendship Councils', sponsored by local authorities and involving liaison officers; but the paper noted that 'few authorities outside London make effective efforts to integrate immigrants by these means', while even in London an authority like Lambeth was preferring to pin its hopes for integration on what that council called 'a natural process of absorption by the community'. 'Whilst this must necessarily be long-term,' continued Lambeth Borough Council's statement, 'it has the advantage that no charge can be laid at its door of discrimination between first and second-class citizens. Accordingly, no special activity for immigrants is promoted directly or sponsored.' What did Paul Stephenson, central figure of the Bristol bus strike, think? The only solution, he told a journalist, was to 'encourage' different racial groups 'to understand one another as people like themselves'. Yet as for the white woman who had told him the other day that she 'liked the West Indian cricketers and watched the Black and White Minstrels every week,' he (noted his interviewer) 'still doesn't know what the best reply is to a remark like that'.[9]

Other matters rumbled away or came to the surface during these months. The Ministry of Aviation chose Stansted in Essex as the site for London's future third airport, to the regret/relief of Luton and, a perhaps less obvious alternative, Foulness on the Essex bank of the Thames Estuary; a simultaneous announcement by the British and French governments theoretically opened the way to a railway tunnel under the Channel, a prospect receiving roughly 60 per cent public approval in Britain, though the *Daily Telegraph* saw 'no possibility of completion before the end of 1970'; an inquiry was set up following

Chapman Pincher's embarrassing revelations in the *Daily Express* that the defence manufacturers Ferranti had been seriously over-charging on its contract with government for Bloodhound missiles; BBC TV's *Death in the Morning* (Alan Whicker the reporter, Jack Gold the director) vividly showed Leicestershire's legendary Quorn Hunt in action, including from the fox's terrified perspective; the Corporation's decision to drop *Children's Hour* from the Home Service upset many nostalgic adults, but the figures were unarguable (some 24,000 listeners daily, compared to five million viewers for children's programmes on TV); in the same month that the Education Secretary, Sir Edward Boyle, overrode loud local objections and gave the go-ahead for Market Drayton Grammar School to go comprehensive from September 1965, the pro-comp Michael Young co-authored a lengthy analysis for the Fabian Society insisting how important it was 'not to rush' the whole process ('the issue does need a great deal of discussion and a great deal of preparation before that proposal which is best for a particular district can be confidently agreed'); an article in *Punch* by Elspeth Huxley – claiming that the policy of no corporal punishment at one of London's newest comprehensives, Risinghill School in Islington, meant that the pupils 'shout, yell, fight and make life impossible', including a torrent of 'four-letter words' directed at their teachers – generated considerable publicity; and Eton's new headmaster, Anthony Chevenix-Trench, reflected aloud that 'being known as an Old Etonian can be an embarrassment, a cross a boy has to bear probably for his life'.

These early months of 1964 were also when Hugh Cudlipp, editorial director of the IPC (International Publishing Corporation), sent a telegram to the leading trade unionist Frank Cousins, convalescing in Jamaica:

OFFICIAL RESULT OF TUC TALKS WITH IPC ABOUT FUTURE OF HERALD STOP FINANCE COMMITTEE MET AGAIN YESTERDAY AND ARE RECOMMENDING TO TUC GENERAL COUNCIL THAT HERALD BECOMES FREE ON PAYMENT SEVENTY-FIVE THOUSAND POUNDS STOP NEW RADICAL POPULAR NEWSPAPER CALLED THE SUN TO BE LAUNCHED IN AUTUMN STOP DO NOT BOTHER TO REPLY STOP I THOUGHT

YOU WOULD LIKE TO KNOW FINAL DECISION WHICH
IS OF COURSE THE RIGHT ONE FROM ALL POINTS OF
VIEW STOP

It was quite a moment. Some three years earlier, the IPC had reluctantly inherited the *Daily Herald*, traditionally the paper of the trade
union movement; the nature of its core readership (elderly, northern,
too working-class, not attractive to advertisers) had ensured continuing losses; and now Cudlipp and IPC's chairman, Cecil King,
had decided to throw the dice with a complete relaunch, including a
new name and, so it was hoped, a new readership. Or as the *Sunday
Times* put it a fortnight or so after Cudlipp's telegram, this bold move
represented 'the first chance anybody has had to tailor a daily newspaper, from scratch, to that great contemporary puzzle, the aspirant,
affluent, never-had-it-so-good, all-mod-con, technocratic and meritocratic young husband and wife'.[10]

Which way would these ripening sociological specimens vote in
1964's general election? 'In spite of everything,' noted Panter-Downes
in early February (with that 'everything' including Iain Macleod's
recent candid revelations in the *Spectator* about the cynical way in
which Harold Macmillan had manipulated the Tory succession
battle the previous autumn), 'one finds an astonishing number of
people who think that the Conservatives will get back as the next
Government by a narrow margin, because of (they say generally) a
cautious last-minute feeling that, man for man, the Conservatives
have the expertise necessary to handle the pressing international and
domestic problems better than Mr Wilson's team would.' Even so, the
conventional wisdom, fortified by opinion polls, remained that of the
Bank of England's deputy governor, Humphrey Mynors, referring in
a memo later in February to 'all parties assuming that the Socialists
win the election'.

That was certainly the assumption of Enoch Powell, who, having
declined to serve under Sir Alec Douglas-Home, was by now intent
on publicly laying the intellectual foundations for a very different
type of Conservatism from the interventionism-cum-corporatism
which had increasingly characterised the Macmillan era. In a speech
on 28 January to the National Liberal Forum in Caxton Hall, a speech
thereafter viewed by Powell himself as a turning point in his life, he

ridiculed as 'hocus pocus' the government's attempt to restrain pay and prices, asserting instead that 'wages, profits, prices are determined, always have been determined, and always will be determined, until we go communist, by the market – by supply and demand working through the market'; then following up five days later, in the *Sunday Telegraph*, he entrenched his position by insisting not only that an incomes policy would 'freeze the economic pattern for ever and stop all progress', but that the only economic law which mattered, when it came to distribution of incomes, was that of supply and demand – even in relation to such popular, well-thought-of groups as teachers and nurses. 'I don't know if this is old Toryism or new Conservatism,' he remarked soon afterwards at a press gallery lunch; but both of his major biographers (Robert Shepherd in 1996, Simon Heffer in 1998) would choose 'Powellism' as the chapter heading for this new phase of his career.

None of which mattered hugely at this stage to Harold Wilson, intensely preoccupied with the election due in either May or October (the PM as yet unable to make up his mind). Shortly before Easter, an electricity supply dispute, with the unions refusing to accept arbitration, had him urgently ringing Frank Cousins:

> He appeared [Cousins recorded] to be rather upset & said 'This is absolutely impossible. They will ruin our chance of winning an election, every time there is a power cut we shall lose 100,000 votes & I intend to issue a statement in the morning repudiating the bastards. I don't intend allowing them to throw away our prospects now.' I calmed him down a bit & suggested he shouldn't make any such statement unless he really wanted to lose the election.

Next day, after the TUC's general secretary, George Woodcock, had managed to broker a temporary solution (the time-honoured one of an inquiry), Cousins reflected on the episode:

> One conclusion I reached is that the Labour party are certainly suffering from pre-election jitters. Also they have certainly swallowed the Tory press view that close association with the unions damages *their* chances. Politics is a dirty game & I understand more all the time why George Woodcock despises politicians. Too many

of ours try to prove to the Tories that they are not really friends of
the unions. They don't realise their own danger or appreciate that
without the unions they are absolutely without power.

Labour and the unions: a crucial relationship now coming fully
into view.

The electorate for the moment kept its ultimate counsel, but
Mark Abrams towards the end of March tried to dig deeper than
opinion polls, with his detailed survey concentrating especially on
undecided voters in Conservative-held marginals. 'Half the sample,'
he found, 'say that in material terms they themselves have done
very well or fairly well in recent years; but 30 per cent said they had
experienced no gains and 20 per cent that they had fallen behind;
these are massive minorities in a population conditioned to a climate
of rising expectations.' Moreover, even though Labour as a whole
had made 'little progress' in convincing voters that it was 'the best
party for white-collar workers', Wilson himself was rated highly by
almost everyone 'for his awareness of the nation's problems, his personality, and his general alertness and vitality'. By contrast, when
undecided voters were asked to judge the qualities of ten leading
politicians (five Conservative, five Labour), Douglas-Home came
bottom of them all, scoring particularly poorly on 'such qualities
as thoughtful, up-to-date in his thinking, lively, good on television'.
What mattered most to the sample? Given a menu to choose from,
they opted for 'maintain full employment', 'hold down cost of living'
and 'modernisation of Britain' as their top three priorities; whereas
they attached 'little importance to an all-embracing incomes policy,
Government control of large private monopolies and the reduction
of economic inequalities'. Tellingly, a majority were 'still unable to
describe any single feature of Labour's educational policy', with the
party's commitment to abolish the 11-plus and private education
being recalled by only 4 per cent and 5 per cent respectively. As for
immigration, a 'large majority', whether Conservative or Labour or
undecided, 'approved strongly of restrictions on the entry of coloured immigrants to Britain', most often on the grounds that 'there
are not enough houses and not enough jobs "for our own people"'.
The third most common reason given was 'Britain overcrowded',
followed by 'Live on welfare state' (mainly Labour voters) and 'They

are dirty', 'Races do not mix' and 'They are dishonest' (in each case, mainly Conservative voters). Altogether, Abrams seems to have had little doubt where the next election was heading; and in an *Observer* article summarising his survey, he quoted the 'typical floater's viewpoint' as being encapsulated by the middle-aged wife of a male nurse on Teesside: 'We're just ordinary working-class people. I never bother about politics. I have heard the names of the men at the top of the parties, but I don't know anything about them – except Mr Wilson; he seems honest and sensible.'[11]

Few of the diarists bothered all that much about politics either. 'Fenwick sale – Mother here as usual – did the washing as usual – fed up again as usual – nothing dried as usual, so we go on,' despaired Grace Taylor in Ruislip one particularly grim day. Elsewhere during these months, Madge Martin in Oxford was watching TV when she 'should have been ironing'; Judy Haines in Chingford was wearing 'my black tights to get to Keep Fit, as others now do' and reflecting that 'black stockings were so "beatnik" at one time'; Kathleen Perry, a young woman from Barrow now working in London, was putting on false eyelashes ('look nice') and having her hair cut short at Frederick Stamp of Chelsea ('cost 5/6, quite nice'); Betty Allen in Poulton-le-Fylde was having a gas fire fitted ('looks very smart and gives out lots of warmth but goodness me, it seems bleak after a coal fire'); Veronica Lee in Leeds was reflecting about her boyfriend that 'I'm sure I would sleep with him if I weren't afraid of getting pregnant' (the contraceptive pill not yet widely available); and Henry St John in Acton was listening irritably to the birds outside 'singing before it was light this morning, uttering long piercing single notes'.

A relatively rare working-class (or, anyway, lower-middle-class) diarist was Pat Scott in Barking:

Went to 12 oclock Mass. In the afternoon children went to Odeon to see Norman Wisdom. The washing machine was serviced & guaranteed for another Year for £3. (*1 January*)

After dinner we all went to Odeon to see 'El Cid' with Charlton Heston & Sophia Loren. It was a marvellous film & well worth the headache I had all evening. I always get one so have to debate whether any film is worth it. This was. We don't often go together

[she, her husband Ted, 11-year-old Stephen and 8-year-old Susan].
It cost £1 which makes it a very expensive evening. *(11 January)*

Ted bought the children 'Fabulous'. It was 1/- but loads of pictures
of Beatles, so I suppose its worth it. *(14 January)*

Ted has nearly finished the cabinet. It will fit into recess with painted
doors & dark oak 'contact' top. *(19 January)*

Ted varnished fireplace. The colour has altered to terracotta & looks
much better. *(26 January)*

We took washing to new launderette in North St. Coin operated
Frigidaire. It cost 2s & 6d to dry it & its quite good. *(17 February)*

After dinner [on a Tuesday in half-term week] we went to The Rio
to see Peggy Mount & Miriam Karlin in Ladies Who Do. Not very
good. There was a long queue but we went in quickly. The children
stayed to see it again. *(18 February)*

Soon afterwards, life took a new and exciting turn. 'Ted has suggested –
after a bit of hinting – that he buys me a caravan,' she noted on 4 March.
'Partly to hire out & for our own use.' Then on the 5th: 'We have been
thinking more about the caravan ... I would like it at Shoeburyness or
Thorpe Bay, but anywhere in that area would really do.' And on the
7th, she and Ted went to a caravan site on Canvey Island, about a mile
from the beach, to look at a caravan for sale: 'Train straight through
to Benfleet and bus to Chambers Corner. It's a 10 min walk from
there. The camp is new – very clean & smart ... We think we'll have
it.' Next day they bought it, but the day of really taking possession
was Saturday the 21st. Stephen went to the Albert Hall 'to see World
Championships of Trampoline', but Pat and Ted took Susan along
with them to Canvey Island to inspect and start sorting out their new
possession. 'It was lovely when we got there although the ground was
4 or 5 inches under water. Ted put some planks down on top of bricks
to make a duckboard, the caravan was quite dry & we soon had lunch
ready. Then it started pouring & there was a bad storm right overhead.
We did some measuring up & got home about 7.30.'

Rainy, too, this Saturday in Burnley, where Nicholas Wollaston was on the final stop of his English tour. Throughout, it had been the tension between the old and the new – often, as in Wisbech, 'never quite sloughing off the old' yet 'never quite achieving the new' – that had most fascinated him; and it was no different in this still almost entirely monocultural Lancashire town of 81,000 people. In the key passage of his briefish account (the account of a somewhat sated, exhausted traveller), he made clear not just his expectation that sooner rather than later the modern was going to come out decisively on top, but that this was no cause for regret:

> Burnley has turned its back on itself. The mills are still there, but they are no longer the whole point of the place. Many of them have closed down, and others have been turned into something else. No smoke comes from the tall chimneys, roofs have collapsed and blackened windows have been broken, as though the cotton girls, before quitting, had hurled their clogs at them, pane by pane. The scum in the canals that run high along the hillsides is unruffled by barges, and though the shaft wheel of the coal mine in the middle of the town still turns, it turns without the old significance and without the old drama. Burnley was never a coal town, and now it is no longer even a cotton town. The modern factories round the edge – bungalows beside the tall old buildings, with neither the stature nor the style – making motor tyres and electric cookers, are more prosperous than the remaining cotton mills; the television aerials and giant floodlights above the football stadium are more symbolic on the skyline than the mill chimneys; the stucco houses with stained glass front doors creeping out of town are more significant than the old cottages, now waiting to be demolished. Clearance is in the air. Things aren't what they used to be in Burnley; and Burnley is mighty glad they aren't.[12]

*

An engineer from Fulham, a bookmaker from Clapham, a book-maker from Camberwell, a club proprietor from Islington, a painter from Dog Kennel Hill, East Dulwich, a 'silversmith and racing motorist' from Chelsea, a hairdresser from Putney, a managing clerk

from Whitchurch Hill, Oxon, a merchant seaman from Harringay –
all nine men, ages varying from twenty-eight to fifty, were found
guilty at Buckinghamshire Assizes at Aylesbury on 27 March (Good
Friday) of conspiring to stop a mail train, with seven found guilty of
taking part in the ambush. At this point (with only about £600,000
of the £2.6 million haul so far recovered), no verdict yet on Ronald
Arthur Biggs, a 34-year-old carpenter from Redhill, whose trial had
been delayed because of an irregularity. The same day, Glasgow's
David Gibson, described by the admiring historians of the tower
block as 'arguably the most remarkable of Western Europe's postwar
municipal housing leaders', died suddenly, 'the result of both chain-
smoking and sheer overwork'; and the Scotts were back in Canvey.
'We bought groceries in shop on site. The prices aren't much higher
than outside. Since last week the new toilets across the road had
been opened.' 'The Kings Country Club,' added Pat, 'is quite good.
We have to pay 5/- per year but its nice inside.' Next day, Simon
Dee played the first record ('Not Fade Away' by the Stones) on the
pioneer pirate radio station Radio Caroline, anchored three miles
off the Essex coast, just outside British territorial waters. The creation of an Irish maverick, Ronan O'Rahilly, it probably took its
name from his girlfriend Caroline Maudling, not only a columnist
('Travelling Teenager') in the *Daily Mail* but daughter of the chancellor of the exchequer, whose party was instinctively in favour of
challenging the BBC's monopoly. The Stones that Saturday night, in
fact the small hours of Sunday morning, played a memorable gig at
the Club Noreik in Tottenham – hugely overcrowded, 'a hot, smelly,
sticky, sweaty heat', Mick with his shirt off – but Easter Sunday itself
was, recorded Barbara Pym, the 'coldest since 1903' (though gratefully noting that her church in Queen's Park, NW6, 'is warm and full
of people'). A melancholy aspect to Easter Monday. In Blackburn,
the market square's last Easter Fair, before the centre of the town
was rendered almost unrecognisable; at her lodgings in Islington,
Gladys Langford 'very depressed from continued silence', longing
'most of all for death'; and at his lodgings in Acton, Henry St John
summarising an Easter chilly in every sense: 'Since Friday all meals
have been served in the kitchen, with the boiler fire unlit and no other
heating, and, at lunch times, the window open as well. The landlady
did not speak at any meal.'[13]

Easter at Clacton-on-Sea (nearest town to Radio Caroline) was less quiet. It had begun sedately enough – on the Saturday, a 3–1 win for Stowmarket over Tankards at the town's annual hockey festival, but the home town going down to Pickwickians by the same scoreline – before the real action began. ' "WILD ONES" INVADE SEASIDE – 97 ARRESTS' was the *Daily Mirror*'s front-page headline (with a nod to the 1953 Marlon Brando film) on the Monday, after an Easter Sunday to remember:

> The Wild Ones invaded a seaside town yesterday – 1,000 fighting, drinking, roaring, rampaging teenagers on scooters and motor-cycles. By last night, after a day of riots and battles with police, ninety-seven of them had been arrested.
>
> A desperate S.O.S. went out from police at Clacton, Essex, as leather-jacketed youths and girls attacked people in the streets, turned over parked cars, broke into beach huts, smashed windows, and fought with rival gangs.
>
> Police reinforcements from other Essex towns raced to the shattered resort, where fearful residents had locked themselves indoors.
>
> By this time the centre of Clacton was jammed with screaming teenagers …
>
> The crowd was broken up by police and police dogs. Several policemen were injured as the teenagers fought them …
>
> Worried mothers and fathers were beginning to arrive from the London area to bail out their sons and daughters.
>
> The harassed police were glad to see them go …
>
> Among incidents reported to the police were: **THE CLUB HOUSE** of the local bowling club was broken into and wrecked and liquor and cigarettes stolen.
>
> **PENNY-IN-THE-SLOT** weighing machines and 3d-a-time telescopes on the promenades were thrown into the sea.
>
> **PARKED** cars had panels kicked in and windows smashed …

Monday was less violent, apart from a fight after 'some 20 or 30 youths and girls,' reported the *Guardian*, had been 'refused service at a seafront cafeteria'; but at Margate 'a gang of 50 youths terrified holidaymakers when they ran wild through seafront shops and stalls and smashed up a jukebox in a coffee bar'.

Who were Clacton's unwelcome invaders? According to Mark Frankland's sober analysis the following weekend, based in part on evidence from the arrests, just over two-thirds were boys; around two-thirds were under eighteen; and about half came from south and east London, plus a sizeable minority from Harlow, Barking, Dagenham, Chingford and Romford ('many from new housing estates populated by ex-Londoners'). 'Contrary to the image that has almost spontaneously grown up of motor-cycle and motor-scooter riding hooligans,' added Frankland, 'it is likely that at least 500 of the boys and girls arrived by train. And the police say that the worst offenders from their point of view were the groups in cars and vans – "on a motor-scooter you get no sense of anonymous security," remarked a Clacton police officer.' 'Did most of the Easter invaders go to Clacton bent on making trouble,' wondered Frankland without providing an answer, 'or was it only a small group of them who were set on mischief?'

Across the country, one newly released record, about to hit no. 1 in the charts, was the sound of Easter 1964. 'In the middle of the floor is a record-player, a neat little box covered in white leatherette, it looks a bit like a vanity case,' recalls Viv Albertine about the pivotal evening she spent, as a nine year old, at the Muswell Hill house of her baby-sitter Kristina:

Flat paper squares with circles cut out of the middle are scattered around the floor. Kristina opens the lid of the record-player and takes a shiny liquorice-black disk out of one of the wrappers, puts it on the central spindle and carefully lowers a plastic arm into the grooves. There's a scratchy sound. I have no idea what's going to happen next.

Boys' voices leap out of the little speaker – 'Can't buy me love!'. No warning. No introduction. Straight into the room. It's the Beatles.

I don't move a muscle whilst the song plays. I don't want to miss one second of it. I listen with every fibre of my being. The voices are so alive. I love that they don't finish the word *love* – they give up on it halfway through and turn it into a grunt. The song careens along, only stopping once for a scream. I know what that scream means: *Wake up! We've arrived! We're changing the world!* I feel as if I've jammed my finger into an electricity socket, every part of me is fizzing.[14]

＊

With an individual potted plant from the gardens department sitting as usual in front of each member, Clacton-on-Sea Council began April by letting off steam. 'Animals, sub-humans, objects, scallywags, slimy and insignificant creatures' – such were some of its verdicts on the resort's recent Easter visitors. 'You have got to decide,' declared one councillor, Ernest Stanley, 'whether you want the decent sort of holidaymaker or not. They won't mix.' On Friday the 3rd, against a background of one in two of the British public wanting the offenders to be heavily punished, the *Any Questions?* panel was asked: 'Given a free hand, how would the team deal with the Mods and Rockers who smashed up Clacton last week-end?' Amid a generally punitive tone – with the Australian writer Russell Braddon insisting that 'the first thing to do is to smash up all their motorbikes so that they're irretrievably done in' – Frank Cousins struck a note of baffled concern: 'What sort of a system of society are we developing where youngsters feel that the only way to relieve boredom is to break things or to fight, or to have what they describe as a "punch-up", or a night out with "birds", as they described it?' Three days later, *Panorama* was on the case, though at least one viewer was dissatisfied with its treatment. 'Was it not coming dangerously near to fanning the flames to ask youngsters if they thought there would be another battle at Whitsuntide, and if they would take part in it?' wondered the *Sunday Times*'s Maurice Wiggin. 'There is a point at which reporting ceases to be reporting and starts to create the situation which is its business merely to report.' The Whitsun holiday was due in mid-May; but before then, in late April, Clacton Magistrates' Court began to dole out its punishment, mainly fines but jail for some. 'Shrunken young men, carefully dressed in neat dark suits with white shirts, looked clean as bank clerks,' noted Lena Jeger after watching one day's 'wretched' proceedings. 'Apparently they are all good boys at home – worried-looking fathers and respectable, sad-faced mothers repeated the phrase till it lost all meaning.' One such boy was 17-year-old Peter Sees, whose behaviour had taken two policemen and handcuffs to deal with. 'His father could not think how it had all happened. "I dunno. I dunno," he repeated in a misery of confusion.'[15]

April had started more generally with Enoch Powell writing three anonymous but easily identifiable articles for *The Times* outlining his political philosophy (including the assertion that 'the massive coloured immigration in the last decade' had 'inflicted social and political damage that will take decades to obliterate'); with Norman Swallow's documentary *A Wedding on Saturday* (about a young couple getting married in a Yorkshire mining village) as a relatively early exemplar of TV naturalism, with no voice-over or visible interviewer; and with the *Daily Telegraph*'s art critic Terence Mullaly condemning the Whitechapel Art Gallery's latest exhibition ('The New Generation', including David Hockney, Patrick Procktor and Patrick Caulfield) as 'an affront, with few parallels, to what is serious in contemporary British art'. Keith Vaughan, from a generation of artists no longer new, presumably agreed. 'After all one's thought and search and effort to make some sort of image which would embody the life of our time,' he reflected bitterly enough after a visit, 'it turns out that all that was really significant were toffee wrappers, liquorice allsorts and ton-up motor bikes.' Home Service listeners at 9.30 p.m. on Friday the 3rd heard the first outing of *I'm Sorry, I'll Read That Again* (Tim Brooke-Taylor, John Cleese, Bill Oddie), described by *Radio Times* as a 'diversion' and neatly summarised by Brooke-Taylor's obituarist as 'a cocktail of silly voices, awful puns and smutty humour'; two days later, the determinedly pro-youth Labour politician Tom Driberg boasted in a Sunday paper about how much he had been enjoying Radio Caroline ('this brain-liberating opiate', blessedly without 'ghastly "light" music or organ syrup'); and Kathleen Perry, after an Easter stay with her family in Barrow, returned to her flat in Adelaide Road near Swiss Cottage. 'Bad journey. Cases heavy. Arrived back in middle of power cut, everything black. My goldfish is dead.' Next day the *Evening News* hailed the Zombies as spearheading the 'St Albans sound', before a day of drama on Tuesday the 7th: the *Daily Mail* announced the imminent cull of up to ten characters on *Coronation Street*; Samuel Beckett's *Play*, with Robert Stephens, Rosemary Harris and Billie Whitelaw as the trio encased in urns and with their faces a mass of glue and porridge, had its first night at the Old Vic

(*The Times*'s verdict of 'motionless, impersonal and sterile' typical of largely unenthusiastic reviews); and Edna O'Brien's TV play *Three Piece Suite* (part of ATV's Love Story series), about a middle-aged charwoman's perpetually frustrated affair with an elderly working-class man, was greeted by one critic as 'genuinely sentimental without cloying'. A day to remember on Wednesday the 8th for Ronnie Biggs and John Bloom: for the former, the start of his trial at Aylesbury; for the latter, the publication in *Which?* of a detailed report on 22 brands of twin-tub washing machines, with little favour found for Bloom's directly sold Rolls Concorde De Luxe (which had recently replaced the Rolls Rapide De Luxe). Advertisements and sales booklets failing to make it clear either that this Rolls machine had no heater or that it held only 3½ lb of washing, the cost of a cotton wash the most expensive of all the brands, the spin-drying facility one of the poorest when it came to drying a full load – it was an extensive charge sheet, complete with the detail that the final price, after paying three years of instalments, was not the much-trumpeted 39 guineas but instead £83 1s, with a true interest rate of 23 per cent which was over twice that usually to be found in a shop or electricity board showroom. That evening, for an hour from 9.50 and stuffed with cigarette ads, a *Ready, Steady, Go!* special, live from the Wembley Pool and called *The Mod Ball*, was shown on ITV. 'My God, Manfred Mann, the Rolling Stones, Cilla Black, Billy J …,' noted Virginia Ironside. 'It really was rather nice.' Appropriate mood music for an anxious parent. 'You *must* sort out your personal scale of priorities,' Kenneth Allsop wrote next day to his teenage daughter Amanda about her apparent reluctance to work hard for her imminent O levels. 'You must tidy up what can be relegated as quite amusing, minor, occasional side pastimes – and by that I mean the Beatles, and pop records, and watching TV, and all the other alluring diversions …' It was the day of elections for the newly created Greater London Council (replacing the old London County Council); and even before the polls closed, Douglas-Home, justifiably fearing the worst for the Conservatives, announced that the general election would definitely not be until the autumn, his last pos-sible time. On the 10th the local press reported that, by an 11–1 vote, Salford Transport Committee had decided not to follow Manchester's example in seeking to ban smoking on the upper decks of buses; and two days later a major exposé in the *People* revealed that, back in December 1962, three Sheffield Wednesday players – Peter Swan, Tony Kay and David 'Bronco' Layne – had deliberately helped to lose a match at Ipswich in order to win bets on the fixed-odds pools. Prison and lengthy bans from football followed, with Swan's story an especially piquant might-have-been. In Alf Ramsey's mind he had been nailed on as England's centre half for the 1966 World Cup; but now, a door opened for Bobby Charlton's big brother, Jack.[16]

Reginald Maudling presented his second Budget on Tuesday the 14th. Given the considerable increase in public spending under his chancellorship, and given the economy was now growing at an unsustainable 6 per cent – Maudling's famous/infamous 'dash for growth' since the previous autumn – the underlying question was whether the touch on the brakes would be the heavier one that prudent economics dictated (to avoid boom turning at some point into bust) or the lighter one that political considerations dictated (an election only six months away). Maudling's biographer Lewis Baston broadly defends him, arguing that tax increases totalling some £100 million was, as election-year budgets from Conservative governments went, 'at the responsible end of the spectrum'. The contemporary verdict of the *Financial Times* was less sanguine. 'He has deliberately decided to gamble on the chance that things will go well in the months ahead,' it declared next day. Accordingly: 'In choosing to take a risk, he has incurred an even greater obligation to watch the progress of the economy closely in the months ahead and to take further restrictive action if ever it becomes clear that he has miscalculated.' Increasingly, the eyes of those on the inside track were on the UK's growing balance of payments deficit. 'The deficit in prospect for 1964/65 is over £800 million,' the government's economic adviser, Alec Cairncross, had privately warned in March, adding that 'the public has no inkling of this'.

Not yet an insider, but keeping as close a watch as he could manage, was Harold Wilson. Convinced as early as February that the Bank of England had been 'cooking the books', in the sense of deliberately obfuscating the country's true external situation, he had only with difficulty been persuaded not to go public with that allegation. He and the shadow chancellor, Jim Callaghan, were also convinced, noted the Bank's deputy governor around the same time, that 'the Conservatives are going to leave things in a pickle just to annoy their successors'. Essentially, the 'pickle' they feared inheriting was a continuing imports-led boom, a rapidly deteriorating balance of payments position, and accompanying pressure on the sterling reserves. Was devaluation the answer? Certainly not in the eyes of the Old Lady. 'The devaluation of the currency of a major trading nation may be a necessity,' a senior figure, Maurice Parsons, bluntly asserted in an April memo to the governor (Lord Cromer) and others, 'but only as a confession of ineptitude and irresponsibility.'[17] The time was fast approaching for Wilson, Callaghan and their economic advisers to do some very serious thinking on the subject.

The day after the Budget, it took the jury at Aylesbury ninety minutes to find Biggs guilty, the TV personality Lady Isobel Barnett gave a talk at Keighley's Temperance Hall (Gladys Hague finding her 'so charming & natural'), and some 47,000 were at Manchester City's Maine Road for a testimonial match for their beloved goalkeeper Bert Trautmann, once a German POW. Next day, 16 April, the first Rolling Stones album was released (the *NME* hailing its 'frenetic primal magnificence', but 'a stinker' according to the *Daily Herald*), Mr Justice Edmond Davies passed the stiffest possible sentences, including seven of them for 30 years, on those responsible for the Great Train Robbery, and the second series of *Our Man at St Mark's* began with Donald Sinden playing the vicar (Leslie Phillips deemed no longer suitable after the exposure of his affair, as a married man, with Caroline Mortimer). The BBC on the 17th broadcast from the City Varieties Theatre in Leeds the special edition of *The Good Old Days*, featuring Jimmy Edwards' rumbustious trombone act, that was its surprising entry for the Montreux television festival, with one puzzled critic 'haunted throughout by the feeling that I had seen it all too often'; while next day, not only did Bill Shankly's Liverpool win the First Division championship with a 5–0 thrashing of Arsenal at an exuberant Anfield (the watching Clement Freud beguiled by 'the swaying masses behind the goal singing "EE I ALLEY OH, we've got the best eleven in the land"'), but the city's four favourite sons appeared on *The Morecambe and Wise Show*, a relaxed affair which included Eric in a Beatle wig and collarless jacket screaming 'Yeah, yeah, yeah'.

The mood more downbeat at Worcester on Monday the 20th, as John Betjeman, speaking to a packed audience at the Shire Hall, revealed that the sponsors of James Lees-Milne's forthcoming *Shell Guide to Worcestershire* had expunged a critical passage about the city's redevelopment – including the assertion that 'Worcester was repeatedly sacked by the Romans, Danes, Saxons, Welsh and Roundheads, but never so thoroughly as it is being sacked by the vandals of our day' – before expressing his own equally heartfelt sentiments: 'We can all help by insisting on eyes and heart before money. What we see around is the barbarism treated by money.' And, sitting down, he cried, 'Long live Worcester!' A few days later the local paper begged to differ, declaring that 'the kind of criticism, which while lacking nothing in acerbity, offers no alternative except to leave things as they are, is neither helpful nor sensible'. As ever, the diarists this week had their own even more local preoccupations. On the Wednesday, Laurence Marks acquired the Rolling Stones LP, though was not allowed to play it on the radiogram at home ('my dad won't let me, he says it will contaminate his needle'); next day, Frederick Ward noted that a visit to Taunton had after all been worthwhile 'because it resulted in orders for about 1500 cases Canned Meat'; and 'Can't Buy Me Love' at last gave way at the top of the charts to Peter and Gordon's 'A World Without Love', a song mainly written by Paul (going out with Peter Asher's sister Jane) after John had mocked its opening line, 'Please lock me away'.[18]

By this time the third television channel had been launched, albeit in somewhat bathetic circumstances. 'In the grand opening of BBC 2,' noted Judy Haines on the 20th, 'there was a breakdown of electricity power caused by a fire at Battersea Power Station. Gerald Priestland was able to give us news [at 10 p.m.] from Alexandra Palace news room, but the West End was blacked out.' Accordingly, programmes on BBC 2 did not start for real until *Play School* on the 21st. 'Here's a house,' said the infinitely reassuring Brian Cant. 'Here's a door. Windows – one, two, three, four ... Ready to play? What's the day? It's Tuesday.' That evening, as BBC 1 launched its new sitcom series *Meet the Wife*, an immediately successful vehicle for Thora Hird as the socially aspirational wife of a north country plumber played by Freddie Frinton, the new channel simply showed the programmes it would have broadcast 24 hours earlier. Haines especially enjoyed brothers Tony and Dougie Gray plus inventor Bruce Lacey in *The Alberts' Channel Too* ('very funny taking off early tele'), while *Kiss Me Kate* was 'a good choice of musical on this 400th Anniversary Year of Shakespeare's birth'. Joyce Grenfell (a member of the Pilkington Committee which had paved the way for

BBC to have the third channel) also approved. 'Channel 2 was great fun,' she wrote next day to a friend. 'We saw fireworks to finish with and a news report at the end done in a direct but somehow fresh and young way! It was all very young but disciplined and intelligent. I'm full of hope for it.'

In the event, though, the early weeks were something of a struggle. Viewing figures stayed obstinately low, not helped by most TV sets having to be adapted to receive the new channel; while the initial 'seven faces of the week' concept of the channel's first chief of programmes, Michael Peacock, grouping each evening's output around a particular theme (e.g. leisure on Thursdays), proved sterile and unpopular. 'I've already lost count of the number of times I've been unfaithful to BBC-2,' declared the TV critic Maurice Richardson after less than a fortnight. 'It's not different enough to command total fidelity for more than a couple of hours at a stretch.' Another critic, Bernard Hollowood, disliked the 'contrived mateyness', contrasting it unfavourably to the announcers and newsreaders on BBC 1 and ITV, whose speech was 'friendly, unmannered, widely comprehensible and almost devoid of the tricks that pervade and perpetuate class distinctions'. In short, asserted a third critic, John Russell Taylor, after exactly a month, 'the general feeling seems to be that BBC-2 has fizzled considerably more than it has flared'; and he added that 'it has just never been excitingly, stimulatingly new'.[19]

Most viewers, anyway, simply preferred the old favourites on the established channels, including among them a particular Sunday evening favourite:

> Still nothing to beat the Black and White Minstrels for sheer entertainment all the way. *(Shop assistant)*

> Wonderful music and songs, great comedy, fabulous dresses and sets – and so slick too. This is one show I *never* miss. *(Journalist)*

> This really is grand entertainment and a great favourite of all here from the seven year old to Grandad. *(Motor driver)*

The uninhibited praise was for the show broadcast on 26 April – praise generating a hard-to-top RI of 87 and seemingly oblivious to the type of criticism ('I loathe the idea of Whites masquerading as Blacks in a charade dating back to a time when off-white pigmentation was thought to be funny') voiced by Hollowood a few days earlier. Also on the 26th, 'Two-Way Dream' was the *Observer*'s title for reportage by Donald Hinds – a 36-year-old Jamaican living in Brixton and working as a London Transport bus conductor – about the teenage children of West Indian immigrants. He focused on Winston, 14-year-old son of a Jamaican couple, the three of them living in two small rooms in Brixton (for which they paid a steep rent of £7 a week):

Outside Winston's school the wind is sharp as a razor. He stands, oversize but graceful, with some of his mates. They eat ice-cream as though it were their first meal of the day.

Winston: School's awright, I guess. They don't beat you.
Sam, a St Lucian: First day was a bit frightening. I was 11 and I'd just come over, but the English boys were real friendly. Ever'one tried to make me feel at home.
Joe, an English boy: Of course. We get on fine.
Winston: Aw, he just says that. Soon somebody'll come along and shout 'Who's for cawfee?' Remember last week? *(The dark faces scowl.)* Over Merton we was in the change room and these white kids comes up and shouted: 'Anyone for Kit-e-Kat?' So we had a feight.
Johnnie, a Grenadian: The teachers them is awright, but the kids them pick on you. Call you wogs. When you call them white wogs them jus' laugh and say that is one kind of wog and that is you.
Winston: Say things like we only grow up and live on National Assistance. You can't run to the teachers all the time 'cos you don't like to carry news.
Sam: Once I see a teacher telling off a white boy for calling a coloured boy names and then the teacher turn his head away and smile ...

A week later, the paper's industrial correspondent, Peter Dunn, surveyed the employment aspect of the British colour bar:

There were seventy cards advertising jobs recently in one of the Fine employment agency windows in Praed Street, near Paddington Station. 69 had typed at the bottom 'Regret no overseas applicants for this post.' A selection showed white preference for an insurance broker's office boy, a storeman 'age immaterial', litigation clerks, a publisher's book-keeper, a shipper's cable clerk, and a travel agent's typist.

Miss Betty Fishman, secretary of the agency, said the attitude of these employers was very widespread. 'We still have difficulty in placing the very good coloured applicants who have been in England many years. People who have been to university have to take ordinary run-of-the-mill jobs. One has to try to put them off as kindly as possible. Unless they have had three or four years' experience employers won't take them. The labour exchanges won't help them either, so how are they to get experience?'

Another London agency, the Brook Street Bureau, said it did its best but it was, after all, the employer who paid the fees. 'Some firms are very definite about not taking coloured people,' said one of the agency's offices. 'We put a little mark – a cross – on their cards so that we all know.'

Many of Dunn's employer interviewees dead-batted him, but the personnel manager at Harrods was more candid than most. 'We've many coloured workers but it's quite true that we haven't yet got them as sales assistants,' she told him. 'The management's view on the sales side is rather like, I believe, that of the Commissioner of the Metropolitan Police – anyone in direct contact with all customers must be acceptable to all customers.'

All the time, though not yet widely recognised despite the odd article in the national press, there loomed Smethwick. 'It is hard for adults to understand,' wrote G. F. on the 24th in the *Smethwick Telephone*, 'what good Smethwick Youth can hope to obtain in the campaign against colour prejudice by demonstrations, distribution of leaflets and pickets outside public houses, etc':

Help is certainly needed, but where prejudice exists, would it not be better to do something about the reason for it? The main cause is obvious – people do not like the way a large number of immigrant property owners allow their houses to look so awful.

It certainly cannot be called colour bar to want people and houses clean and tidy. If there is a colour bar anywhere it is of the coloured people's own creation.

Unfortunately, there are only a few who take any pride in their property and their neighbours do not complain. Others will not co-operate and tell you to 'keep your big mouth shut.' In cases like this, are we expected **not** to complain?

Municipal elections were due in early May, and top of the local Conservative Party's seven promises was 'Clean up Smethwick' (with 'Rebuild our Town with Sympathy and Understanding' as the penultimate one).[20]

Sympathy and understanding were in shortish supply as the rebuilding of Newcastle now prepared to move into full-action mode. 'While the rest of the country talks about the Buchanan Report, Newcastle's council have anticipated it,' declared Tom Baistow in the *Daily Herald* on 1 May. 'Excavators are tearing a deep trench through the heart of the city.' And he went on:

By the late seventies, it will carry Britain's most ambitious urban motorway system into a rebuilt multi-level city centre.

Newcastle is a pleasant shock for those from the south who picture the North-East as dying of population anaemia among rusty derricks and weed-grown pit-heaps.

From spectacular slum clearance to booming night life, the joint is jumping.

Plans for the new £80 million city centre included Sir Basil Spence designing 'a magnificent central library', Sir Robert Matthew (president of RIBA) designing 'the complex of skyscraper office blocks on stilts that will straddle the motorway', and the prominent Danish architect Arne Jacobsen designing 'a luxury hotel and the traffic-free shopping area'.

The title of Baistow's ultra-boosterish article was 'Mr Smith builds a new city'; and this was perhaps the moment when the Labour leader since 1960 of Newcastle City Council, T. Dan Smith, became a national figure. These were the years – the early to mid-1960s – of his remarkable heyday:

He twinkled, he made jokes, he broke stories, indeed he did everything to make the lives of young cub reporters – of which I was
one – more felicitous [recalled Lewis Chester]. And he was so smart.
This was something that everybody – even the Tories – recognised.
Indeed, Smith had few personal critics in those days. It was as if
everybody recognised that they had a man who was going places
and that his city, and indeed the whole of the north-east, was going
with him.

In a region that had been depressed for so long, Smith's mixture of high, wide and handsome plans and low, sometimes earthy
witticisms was the tonic that most felt was needed. He called
Newcastle 'the Athens of the north-east' and that went down a
treat ...

Tall and driven, 'Mr Newcastle' (as he was increasingly known) was
undeniably a force to be reckoned with. 'From the time of my arrival
[1960] in the House of Commons I was amazed at the deference
shown to Dan Smith by many members of the Northern Group of
Labour MPs,' remembered Blyth's Eddie Milne; and to fail to attend a
meeting arranged for him was 'almost a crime in the eyes of the leadership of the MPs for the North-East of England'. Nor could anyone
gainsay his ambitions for Tyneside, typified this spring by his row
with Newcastle United's directors, as he urged them to enlarge and
modernise St James' Park so that it was, in Smith's authoritative words
to Baistow, 'ready for the European Super League – it's coming soon,
you know'.

Almost tragically, though, the element of genuine if arguably
misdirected idealism went along with two fundamental flaws. The
first was venality. All he wanted, he once told a friend, was 'a fraction
of 1% of the contracts that are available to developers', as planning
controls were loosened, urban Britain was rebuilt and fortunes were
there to be made. But after his death in 1993, the verdict of local
historian David Byrne, in a far from wholly unsympathetic evalu-
ative obituary, was unsparing: 'Dan was as bent as a corkscrew, he
became rich on the skimmings of the municipal construction game.'
The other flaw was Smith's authoritarianism, an essentially anti-
democratic instinct going back to his youthful days as a Trotskyist. It
was a 'model of modernism,' reflected Beatrix Campbell after Smith's

passing, 'marked by an autocratic architecture – willies in the air – that celebrated *his* power':

> He claimed he was bringing Brasilia to Scotswood [i.e. the Scotswood Road area of classic working-class housing by 1964 largely razed to the ground and replaced by 15-storey tower blocks]. It was macho, it was megalomaniac, and it was inaccessible to alteration by an informed public. Indeed, participation by an *educated* rather than a merely *admiring* public would not have serviced the making of his myth. The photographs of Smith in the Sixties show him, like Faust in a trenchcoat hailing his brittle castles in the air, 'bestride the earth like a Colossus'.

Or as she damningly added, Smith 'gave the imprimatur of class to a political project *for* the people but was never troubled by the unruly presence *of* the people'.[21]

Also poised for a place in the nation's consciousness was the schoolteacher living in Claverley, near Wolverhampton. Ahead of her big moment, a rally to be held at Birmingham Town Hall on 5 May, how carefully had Mary Whitehouse been studying her postbag? If so, she might have pondered the contrast between two types of letter. The first, as exemplified by the *cri de coeur* sent in late April by Miss F. M. Arthur, was unambiguously in her corner. Congratulating Whitehouse on her initiative, the 67-year-old living in West Kirby on the Wirral sent a list of 'What I would like to see on Television':

> More travel films, especially with Johnny Morris in them.
> More documentaries, such as the one about Elgar.
> More films about animals, such as the lovely one about 'Greyfriar's Bobby', the old films about Lassie & Laddie, & dogs like Rin Tin Tin …
> Programmes of which I never tire are 'Dr Finlay's Casebook', 'This is your Life' (with Eamonn Andrews of course), Panorama, Dixon of Dock Green, Lucy, the Van Dyke Show, Mr. Worth, Eric Sykes & Hattie.
> Any programme with the Attenboroughs, Armand and Michaela, Terry Scott & Hugh Lloyd …

> I dislike Monitor & most of the Television plays, which are morbid, immoral & disgusting, with only an occasional exception. I never watched That Was the Week That Was. The first few mins. of the first programme was enough ...
>
> I *hate* Beatles & screaming teen-agers & put them off as soon as I can reach the T.V. knob. I know there are some good teen-agers – please let us see some occasionally just to cheer us up. Especially let us see more babies & small children to counteract the To-night programme which is getting more & more disgusting.

The other type of letter was not unsupportive, but wondered whether the campaign was concentrating its fire wholly in the right direction. In early April, for instance, a member of the Methodist Church in Potters Bar, where Whitehouse was due to speak shortly, detailed the advertising in the local press and the printing of posters, before going on: 'I must point out however that we do find it difficult to explain why the campaign is against B.B.C. T.V. and not I.T.V., of which there is a more universal condemnation.' A similar implicit warning came from Mrs Phyllis Adland of Godalming, Surrey. 'Many signatories have felt that we were being too hard on the B.B.C.,' she observed on 28 April (the same day as Miss Arthur's wish-list) while returning signatures to the campaign's manifesto that she had been gathering locally. 'The majority of programmes,' she went on, 'give great satisfaction for their wide range in catering to all tastes and backgrounds. We shall rightly be labelled a fanatical minority if we try to put the B.B.C. back into the long petticoats of a generation ago.' Instead, she argued, 'just let us concentrate on cleaning up the plays ...'.

The Birmingham meeting itself was (bar some heckling) a triumph, attended by some 1,500–2,000 people, overwhelmingly middle-aged women, many of them churchgoers and with messages of support read out from the conductor Adrian Boult, the actress Anna Neagle and various bishops. The TV clip which would survive for posterity was Whitehouse's attack on the BBC's latest satirical comedy show (*Between the Lines*) as 'the dirtiest programme that I have seen for a very long time'. But to judge by the notes for her speech, the main focus was indeed on the Corporation's drama output. 'Why are all the plays about the same thing?' she asked. 'Not interesting, they make you feel rotten and afraid of marriage in later life, wondering if you have picked the wrong person. I wish they would change the plays and put more feeling, good feeling, into them instead of hatred and wretchedness all the time.' She then broadened her case:

The young have always felt the necessity to revolt against the established ideas of their parents and within limited confines of their society, but until now the young, breaking their shell, have known that their elders would stand firm in the declaration of truth … But today, the path of anarchy and the jungle of doubt and confusion is being blazed by a few middle-aged intellectuals while the young cry out for discipline and security.

'There are those,' noted *The Times*'s Midlands Correspondent in his report on the rally, 'who will find it easy enough to laugh at the women who were here tonight.' 'Yet,' he went on, 'a good many of the speakers had experience as teachers or social workers who were seriously concerned with social questions in the field.' And he pointed out that such people, as exemplified by Whitehouse's ally Norah Buckland, were 'likely to know at least as much about the realities of social problems' as those authors of the plays now under such impassioned attack.[22]

Later that Tuesday evening, between 10.05 and 10.55, some of the ITV stations, but not all, showed a one-off *World in Action* special called *Seven Up!* 'We brought these children together,' explained the narrator in the introduction, 'because we wanted a glimpse of England in the year 2000. The shop steward and the executive of the year 2000 are now seven years old.' Over the next three-quarters of an hour, 14 seven year olds spoke candidly to an unseen interviewer, Paul Almond, the programme's director and co-creator. He was a Canadian, *World in Action*'s main man, Tim Hewat, was an Australian, and together they wanted to explore the impact of social class on British children's outlook and ambitions. The sample was found, under considerable time pressure, by a young Granada researcher, Michael Apted, who would later regret two aspects of his selection: the gender imbalance (ten boys, four girls); and the too blunt overall contrast between top and bottom of the social pecking order, with not enough representation of the in-between middle. But whatever the flaws – of what no one at this point conceived as a long-running series – some of the exchanges would pass into the collective memory:

Do you think it's important to fight? – Is it important to fight? Yes! The poshies … They're nuts. Just have to touch them, and they say, 'Oh! Oh! Oh!'. *(Tony, son of a porter at an East End butcher's shop)*

What are your plans for the future? – When I leave this school I'm down for Heathfield and Southover Manor, and then maybe I may want to go to university, but I don't know which one yet. *(Suzy, living with her parents and nanny in a flat overlooking Hyde Park and attending Lady Eden's, a fashionable day school)*

What do you think about rich people? – Well, not much … They think they can do everything but without you doing it as well, just because they're rich and they have to have people to do all their work and stuff. *(Symon, illegitimate son of a black father and a white mother, living in a children's home in Middlesex)*

What plans do you have for the future? – Well, I'll go into Africa and try and teach people who are not civilized to be more or less good. *(Bruce, at a highly disciplined boarding school in Hampshire)*

What are your plans for the future? – I'm going to work in Woolworth's. *(Lynn, living in her family's two-bedroom flat in the East End)*

Do you want to go to a university? – What does 'university' mean? *(Paul, son of separated parents, his father a tailor, and living in the same children's home as Symon)*

What plans do you have for the future? – When I leave this school, I go to Broadstairs, St Peter's Court. Then after that, I'm going to Charterhouse, and then after that to Trinity Hall, Cambridge. *(Andrew, son of a merchant banker and reader of the* Financial Times*)*

Why did you say you prefer living in town instead of in the country? – Because in the winter, if you live in the country, it would be just all wet, and there wouldn't be anything for miles around, and you'd get soaked if you tried to go out, and there's no shelter anywhere except in your own house. But in the town, you can go out on wet, wintry days. You can always find somewhere to shelter, 'cause there's lots of places. *(Neil, growing up in Woolton, the Liverpool suburb where Lennon and McCartney had first met seven years earlier)*

'Pure gold for the anthropologist, the sociologist, the market-researcher, and me,' declared an appreciative Maurice Wiggin in his review. 'What knocked me out was the unwavering conformity to social (and regional) patterns which I had vaguely thought obsolete. They all came out automatically true to their environment: they were already conditioned to become predictable members of instantly recognisable social groups.' In short, he wondered about the programme's message, 'it seemed to say that the social change everyone keeps talking about is a bit of an illusion … People may move a little more freely from class to class, or group to group if you don't like the word class; but within each group there is a strong group consciousness, with all that implies for good or ill.' '*Mutatis mutandis*,' Wiggin went on, 'this film could have been made forty-four years ago [1920], when I was seven, and it would have come out much the same.'[23]

The day after *Seven Up!* was Joe Orton's long-awaited moment, as *Entertaining Mr Sloane* had its first night at the Arts Theatre. 'In *Sloane*,' he reflected three years later about a time when the courts were still coming down hard on homosexual offences, 'I wrote a man who was interested in having sex with boys. I wanted him played [by Dudley Sutton] as if he was the most ordinary man in the world, and not as if the moment you wanted sex with boys, you had to put on earrings and scent.' Reviews were broadly positive – including John Mortimer (dialogue 'a skilled and highly formalised version of South Ruislip Mandarin') and Bernard Levin ('his talent is a real one, his naivety fresh, his artlessness genuine'), plus a rave from Harold Hobson ('the calculation is close, and the satire very funny') – but not the *Daily Telegraph*'s W. A. Darlington. Under the headline 'A REVOLTING LODGER'S SWAY', he began by declaring that 'not for a long time' had he 'disliked a play so much'; compared the experience of seeing it to 'snakes writhing round my feet'; and ended with a reference to 'the general degradation' of the whole thing.

Not that any of this impacted significantly, either way, on the population at large. Thursday the 7th saw Smethwick as one of the very few Conservative gains in the local elections across England; Vere Hodgson, up in London on Saturday to see Vanessa Redgrave ('glorious') in a matinée of *The Seagull*, had fish and chips beforehand at the Trafalgar in Villiers Street ('my surprise was great to find it was staffed entirely by Italians'); 'my slacks look good,' noted Judy Haines that evening; another diarist, Frank Ayliffe, working for the London millinery manufacturers Woolley, Sanders & Co., reflected sadly next day on how 'the millinery trade gets more and more depressed as hatlessness shows stronger'; the severely injured train driver Jack Mills was at last back at work on Monday the 11th, but only on 'light duties' preparing engines in the Crewe motive power depot; that lunchtime, the Rolling Stones were refused admission to the restaurant at Bristol's Grand Hotel on the grounds of unacceptable scruffiness ('I offered to provide a maroon tie and a lightweight fawn jacket for each of the members of the group,' said head waiter Dick Court, 'but they turned this down'); Anthony Heap, a confirmed hater of long hair on men, complained in his diary that 'the sight of these awful effeminate-looking youths is, in sooth, becoming as sickening as that of the sloppy couples one so frequently sees kissing and embracing in the street nowadays'; Prince Philip that evening, speaking at the Jewish Welfare Board dinner at the Savoy, warned against the dangers of the welfare state ('it generates the idea that you do not have to worry about your neighbour because somebody else is looking after him'); and in Chelsea, a sparkling reception marked the launch of 32-year-old Terence Conran's shape-shifting brainchild.[24]

11

My Husband Won't Do with Cheap Stuff

'There's a feeling, particularly among young shoppers, that they want to make shopping for the home an impulsive, gay affair,' Elizabeth Good had written in the *Sunday Times* the day before. 'If you don't shop in London, don't make the mistake of thinking Habitat or its campaign to make shopping fun is not eventually going to affect you,' she warned her more suspicious readers. 'The staff scream in anguish if you call it "that shop in Chelsea." And with good reason. That shop in Chelsea is just the first link of a plan for a chain of sixteen more stretching all over the country.' As to what was actually in the pioneer Habitat, standing on a curved corner at 77–79 Fulham Road (with South Kensington the nearest underground station), the *Financial Times*'s Sheila Black, virtually the only female journalist on the paper, gave the detailed, enthusiastic low-down the following Saturday in her weekly 'Shopping Guide':

It really does have the most tempting range of merchandise for any and every corner of a tasteful home, ancient or modern. Heavy porcelain cooking ware from France; deep, cushioned armchairs in cane by Corbusier, or upholstery with clean, elegant lines; scrubbable butchers' blocks for large kitchens or garden eating; fabrics, pots and pans, shopping baskets, teak chests and lovely deep-pile rugs for barefooted sybarites, to quote Habitat; miniature Thai oil lamps, and warm pine kitchen units; all these, and literally thousands more original, simple but sophisticated, wares from any country that makes them best will keep you walking around the shop wishing you had left the cheque book at home.

'But there is no need,' she helpfully added, 'to feel shy – they encourage browsing and have laid out everything for easy view. Hire purchase schemes exist for orders of £25 or over, but you can spend as little as a shilling or two on some things.'

Three and a half years after the appearance of Elizabeth David's groundbreaking *French Provincial Cooking*, and at a time when the middle class of London and the Home Counties were increasingly looking across the Channel for their summer holidays (often camping holidays), Terence Conran's new enterprise unerringly hit the spot, with its distinctive and seductive flavour of abroad:

> Its most famous early merchandise [recalls the historian Juliet Gardiner about shopping there in the early days] was undoubtedly the earthenware chicken brick, which was to become a symbol of what we imagined was a new domestic idiom of continental peasant cookery, using dried herbs and creating what was known as *jus* rather than making Bisto gravy to accompany every meat dish or add a ubiquitous flavour to mince. The shop's shelves were stocked to overflowing with wooden spoons, blue-striped butchers' aprons, rustic crockery, and glass storage jars for the pasta as spaghetti (other than Heinz or Crosse & Blackwell's in tins) was beginning to make its appearance in British kitchens ...

One way and another, the arrival of Habitat represented the richest of socio-cultural moments: a 'synthesis of urban minimalism and pastoral chic' that, in Joe Moran's words, 'allowed young professionals to live in the modern city while feeling reassuringly separate from its senior side'; a key aid to 'stripped, smooth and history-free' living (Jonathan Glancey) in newly gentrifying parts of the capital, as 'out went dusty cornices and dado-rails, Victorian fire-surrounds and panelled doors' and 'in came white paint, shag-pile rugs, bare floorboards and white plastic TVs', accompanied by 'bentwood chairs (Bauhaus via Conran) for the kitchen, French cooking pots, strings of garlic hanging from the walls and quarry tiles for the floor'; and altogether, as the shop's managing director, the former model Pagan Taylor, wryly acknowledged at the outset as being what Habitat aimed to do, the provision of 'instant good taste' – perhaps especially, she did not add, for those moving socially upwards and uncertain about lifestyle, about how to play things in the domestic sphere. Habitat also in its way represented something bigger than all that. 'In those strange, post-war years, people needed things,' Conran himself recalled in 1990, 'and by the early 1960s the need was satisfied. In the 1960s people started to want things.'[1] Need being replaced by want, and in turn, of course, by choice: the new individualism-cum-social-liberalism had found its first spiritual home.

A mecca, too, in its way, for all its flaws, was the phenomenon that Prince Philip opened two and a half weeks later, on the 29th, remarking at the ceremony that Birmingham City Council, by approving such a revolutionary design, had restored the nation's faith in local government. His host for the day at the formal unveiling of the newly built Bull Ring Centre was that council's Labour leader, Frank Price, who not long before as the city's planning chairman had been elected 'Mr Birmingham' in a poll conducted by the local *Evening Mail*; and as Roy Hattersley (about to become a Birmingham MP) would reflect 35 years later, 'his popularity was a recognition of the way in which he had demolished the city centre and replaced the noble Victorian buildings with a network of ring roads and underpasses'. Even so, whatever the state of local opinion (perhaps more ambivalent than Hattersley allows), external opinion seems to have been somewhat sceptical from the off about this shopping 'complex' (the word used at the time), with its 23 acres of shopping space, its five levels, its 15 exits, its 22 escalators, its 40 lifts, its spiral access path leading to it. 'The overriding impression is of sultry heat and of having lost one's way', with the whole thing creating the sense of a 'topographic vacuum,' noted on opening day the *Guardian*'s Diana Rowntree, normally welcoming the new in her architectural judgement; while in the *Daily Telegraph* a fortnight later, the also instantly lost Ann Steele did acknowledge the 'realisation of a planner's dream' – '100 shops, three department stores, two supermarkets, three public houses, one betting shop, four banks, nine restaurants and cafés', altogether amounting to 'a High Street for 40,000 shoppers at a time all under one four-acre roof' – but even so wrote of how 'as I travelled from level to level, up and down the escalators, along the noise-absorbent rubber flooring, trying to find my bearings, it looked to me a bit like a shopper's nightmare', indeed 'a fantasy of the future'. 'An army fortification within the city centre' were the damning words in 1965 of a

local Conservative councillor, but the truly scathing verdict awaited
Prince Philip's son in 1988. 'No charm, no human scale, no character
except arrogance' was how, on peak-time television, Prince Charles
described the Bull Ring; and barely a decade later, amid few tears, this
particular iteration of a historic space was demolished.[2]

Habitat and the Bull Ring, both born in May 1964: two very
different types of Aladdin's cave, but taken together symbolising the
start of the last major era of shopping before the arrival of the internet.[3]

*

By this time the two key trends in shopping – towards self-service
on the one hand, size on the other – were ever more mutually
reinforcing. Latest figures this spring indicated that the number of
supermarkets (usually defined as stores of not less than 2,000 square
feet of sales area, about the same size as a modern-day Tesco Express
or Sainsbury's Local and stocking both foods and other lines) was up
to some 1,250–1,300, compared to 996 at the end of 1962 and 367 at
the end of 1960; while in addition, there were at least 10,000 smaller
self-service stores. The logic was compelling. 'To convert a grocer's
shop to self-service today is often to double its volume of business,'
a keen-eyed observer, John Coldstream, pointed out in November
1962; and as specifically for supermarkets, he went on, it was not just
that they offered a range of products going way beyond the traditional local grocer's, but that they fitted in so well with other trends in
everyday life – including the growing numbers of married women in
paid employment (around one in three, and naturally drawn to once-
weekly, one-stop shopping), rapidly increasing car ownership (up
by 600,000 every year) with its obvious advantages for transporting
a big shopping load back home, and the ever-greater prevalence of
refrigerators (sales of around one million a year) making it possible to
keep food for longer periods. 'Best for less and it's all under one roof'
proclaimed a Tesco ad in 1966 publicising the opening in Llanelli of
a store of 5,400 square feet, 100 feet of refrigerated cabinets, eight
check-outs and sixty staff, as well as being open on Fridays until as
late as eight o'clock. Or, in short, a 'revolution which is making life
easier and happier for shoppers'.[4]

What about the overall retail picture? Three sets of share-of-trade figures (in percentages) for different types of outlet show the underlying trend:

	1957	1961	1966
Department stores	5	5	5
Multiple shops (including supermarkets, but excluding Co-ops)	24	27	32
Co-ops	12	10	9
Mail order	2	3	4
Independents	57	55	50

The multiples (or chains) up, the smaller shops down: it was going to happen anyway, but one controversial piece of legislation in 1964 undeniably consolidated and accelerated the process. This was the abolition of resale price maintenance – an issue long seen as a political hot potato because of its likely negative implications for small traders and shopkeepers if retail prices for the same items became a free-for-all. But in January, against the background of the government wanting to burnish its modernising credentials and RPM itself being steadily undermined in practice (especially by Tesco's aggressive, even brazen, discounting), the Cabinet narrowly agreed to go ahead. Tory back-bench opposition over the next few months, taking particular exception to the steamrollering tactics of Edward Heath (responsible as President of the Board of Trade for taking the bill through Parliament), was both bitter and considerable, culminating in the second reading in March when almost 50 MPs either voted against or abstained, the party's biggest revolt since 1940. Even Enoch Powell, for all his pro-market and pro-competition instincts, was a far from enthusiastic supporter of the measure, believing not only that it was too much of a one-off and should have been complemented by other liberal economic policies, but also that it was electorally dangerous, given that thousands of upset small shopkeepers would in daily conversation be sharing their unhappiness with their customers. The grocer's daughter, by contrast, did not doubt that abolition's time had come, albeit similarly nervous about the short-term political consequences. 'When small shopkeepers write and say: "I'm afraid it will put us out of business," I can only say that my father would have said the same thing ten years ago,' Margaret Thatcher told her Finchley constituents at a Golders Green Brains Trust in February. 'But resale price maintenance has virtually gone from the grocery trade, and opportunities for small shops have increased.'

The nervousness was understandable, if on the face of it overdone. With the major exception of the *Daily Express* (still a power in the land, read regularly by some 28 per cent of the population), the press was largely supportive of abolition; and a Gallup poll soon after Heath had announced his intention found 63 per cent in favour, against 18 per cent disapproving, on the understanding that this would enable shops to sell at prices below those fixed by manufacturers. Even so, there remained the human factor:

> My husband is an Ironmonger [began a listener's letter read out on *Woman's Hour* around the time of that poll], and has always been fair with his prices, but it is nice to know where you stand with your profits … We work very hard, many a time until one o'clock in the mornings, making out statements for small amounts, such as Paraffin Oil, nails and screws. After five years of working the business up, we have put our savings into the alterations needed around the shop, and were hoping to have a good heating system, so everyone can be pleasant to each other; also we wanted to raise the wage of a very good man we have working for us. How can we know what profits we have if customers ask for things cheaper, which they will, because they have seen it priced in a larger store, and they will travel almost any distance or wait for them if necessary, before paying a little extra. My husband said he will have to use a hammer and make bids for his goods, or take a shop in a high street, where 14,000 people pass through, instead of the area we are now in with a population of approximately 4,000.

Piquantly enough, Gallup also asked voters where they stood if abolition were to result in 'quite considerable hardship' for small shopkeepers. Faced by that scenario, 43 per cent were against abolition, only 39 per cent in favour. And though ultimately the lure of cheaper prices would trump human sympathies, the probability – though not certainty – is that abolition of RPM did later in the year inflict *some* electoral damage on the Conservatives.[5]

If abolition generally benefited the big beasts in the retail jungle, that did not mean they were all equally well placed to take advantage of the new, more competitive environment. Take a trio of those beasts. The dinosaur was undoubtedly the Co-operative movement, at the centre of which was the Co-operative Wholesale Society (CWS) and its many retail outlets (just over 5 per cent of all retail outlets). By this point it was in the middle of a long-term secular decline, as its share of the retail market fell by a massive one-third between 1957 and 1970. 'Tied to the geography of the tram rather than the bus or motor car' was the damning verdict of economic historian Sidney Pollard in his 1965 Fabian pamphlet, *The Co-operatives at the Crossroads*, adding that the Co-op's image was 'coloured by the drab and semi-derelict nature of their strongholds in the North'. Not based in the north, but deeply frustrated, was the diarist Frederick Ward, who in 1963 completed 40 years' service with the CWS. Lamenting in his year-end review the movement's continuing decline, he largely blamed weaknesses 'on the director and managerial level', including how 'petty jealousies and reputation building result in piecemeal efforts instead of concerted action'; while in April 1964 after a 'certainly unnecessary' meeting, he could not but reflect, 'What time and money the co-operative movement wastes in talking'. Six years earlier, Anthony Crosland's report had advocated wholesale change, in order to equip the Co-op for the emerging more affluent society. But because of deep-set institutional conservatism, allied to instinctive suspicions about affluence itself, that moment had been missed, never to return for many years to come.[6]

In their different ways, neither Marks & Spencer nor Tesco had any such qualms. The former's driving force was Simon (Lord) Marks, hands-on and visionary chairman from 1916 until his death in December 1964, reputedly while examining at head office in Baker Street a new line of merchandise. The last ten years of his life coincided with post-rationing, post-austerity; and Israel Sieff, his brother-in-law and close colleague, would in 1970 recall them as M & S's 'golden decade of profitability and expansion', as it grew to sell at least one-third of all the bras in the country, one-quarter of all the girdles, one-eighth of all the nylon stockings. 'More successfully than any other retailing business,' noted an admiring profile in 1962, 'M. & S., by establishing a quality mark [the brand name St Michael] which means something, have drawn into their net all kinds of fishes from all class groups; they have two peak sales times, once a week when the wages are paid, and once a month when the salary cheque rolls in.' That cross-class appeal did not yet apply at Tesco, for all that it was very visibly on the march, typified by the way in 1964 it moved into Salford, setting up four supermarkets there, including at the old Bijou Cinema in Broughton Road. *Its* supremo, brilliantly exploiting the coming to Britain of supermarkets and strongly focused on working-class customers, was the aggressively price-cutting, anti-RPM Jack Cohen – born 1898, founding Tesco in 1924, a classic story of the poor East End boy made good. *Pile It High, Sell It Cheap* would be the title of Cohen's authorised biography, published a year before his death in 1979; and for most of his life, the formula worked a treat.[7]

It was, for all the irresistible rise of the supermarket, still a very mixed shopping ecology. The small grocers may have left the main shopping centres to the multiples, commented Jane Ridley in March 1965 about their post-RPM fightback, but they had instead 're-settled into the suburbs, the side-streets and the outskirts'; and she pointed out that independent grocers, over 100,000 of them, continued to do 'more than half the country's grocery trade', with their sales of around £1,300 million a year well above the £830 million of 'all the multiple food shops put together'. For an especially resonant example of that mixed ecology, take Birmingham in 1964: yes, the shiny new, multiples-heavy Bull Ring, but not all that far out from the city centre, in Moseley's Woodbridge Road, a range of shops which included Mackinnon's self-service for groceries and provisions (billed in its ad as 'an Independent Enterprise'), Forss at No. 25 for 'Gowns, Knitwear & Hosiery', F. Lloyd at No. 27 for 'Choice Meat', Coopers Stores at No. 33 for 'Toys, Baby Linen, Ladies Wear, Gent's Wear, General Drapery', K. R. Hinton at No. 34 for 'Chocolates, Sweets, Wall's Ice Cream', Woodbridge Hardware at No. 35 ('Pink Paraffin, Garden Tools, Paints and Wallpaper, Hardboard, Everything Domestic, China, etc.'), Burton at No. 40 ('High Class Fruit & Vegetables') and Gabel's at No. 44A ('Kosher Meat and Poultry "Choice"'). Or take Tolworth in Surrey, just off the Kingston by-pass. There, a giant Fine Fare, proclaimed as the biggest supermarket in Europe, opened in 1964 below Richard Seifert's newly built, 21-storey Tolworth Tower; but nearby, on Tolworth Broadway, it was very much business as usual

at Beswick's furnishing store (where the shop fascia would bear the
telephone number 'ELM 6001' into the next century), even as Philip
Black, son of a House of Commons hairdresser, was running a very
local empire of Victor Towler shops (including for brightly lit lamps,
electrical fittings generally, black-and-white TV sets, wireless sets,
washing machines and, at No. 13, Dinky toys, Triang model railways,
rocking horses and dolls houses). The shopping ecology, in other
words, was shifting – but not necessarily quickly, and certainly not
necessarily at a uniform pace. 'A supermarket is already open in the
main street,' observed Nicholas Wollaston visiting Leek in autumn
1963, yet 'most of the ironmongers and greengrocers seem to have
resisted the advance of packaged goods and plastic display stands, and
have the same air of unchangeability, inside and out, as most of the
gaunt red-brick mills.'[8]

Even so, by this time an array of ultimately significant developments
was under way, albeit often wholly or partially below the radar: Ken
Morrison in 1962 opening the first Wm Morrison supermarket in a
disused cinema in Bradford's Thornton Road; the maverick young,
wheeler-dealing Ahmed Pochee starting in 1963 the first Oddbins
in a basement in Covent Garden's Henrietta Street; that same year,
the brothers Peter and Fred Asquith converting a disused cinema in
Castleford into a price-cutting supermarket, direct forerunner of the
start of Asda two years later; Trevor Storer, also in 1963, launching
Trevor Storer's Home Made Pies, the following year renamed Pukka
Pies, from his home in Oadby; the traders Noel Lister and Donald
Searle, who had previously specialised in government surplus goods,
coming together in 1964 to form Mullard Furniture Industries, the
future MFI; and the first Topshop, specifically geared to the teenage
market, making its debut the same year as a first-floor department
of Peter Robinson's Sheffield branch. Green shoots, too, in an
ex-chemist's shop in Abingdon Road, Kensington, where Barbara
Hulanicki and her husband Stephen Fitz-Simon opened in September
1964 a clothes shop called Biba – four months after the *Daily Mirror*'s
fashion editor Felicity Green had given a huge boost to Biba's Postal
Boutique (their original mail-order business) by enthusiastically
endorsing a Hulanicki-designed pink gingham dress, selling at £1 5s.

That had been on 4 May, exactly a week before the start of
Habitat; and the same month, *Vogue*'s regular shopping columnist

('Shop Hound') bravely ventured in quest of the latest in high-end shopping. In Liverpool she found Diana Fraser's clothes shop, 'one of the most charming new shops Hound visited on her country-wide search for what's new'; in Harrogate the shop ('black and white Georgian, with bow-shaped windows and Swedish lighting') recently opened by Pamela Swaine and Keith Sproull selling 'young and sophisticated clothes'; in Knutsford 'a bright new shop called Jill Killick', specialising in 'ravishing hats of every kind'; and even in Grimsby, a recently 'rebuilt and revivified' shop called Cavalcade, selling not only 'nothing but the best in all kinds of household goods', but also 'presents from all over the world'. 'Shop Hound Breaks New Ground', her column this month was eloquently titled: herald of a new phase dawning in the affluent society, a phase increasingly embracing the provinces, or anyway some select parts of them, as well as the capital.[9]

*

150 NEW SUPER STALLS
50 MODERN SHOPS
GIANT SUPERSTORE
HERE IS THE MODERN WAY TO DO YOUR SHOPPING!
Just imagine shopping in this beautiful new Rathbone Market, being served by old trusted friends who have served you so well before and have now modernised their shops and stalls to give you luxury shopping.
AT THE LOWEST POSSIBLE PRICES ANYWHERE IN THE COUNTRY

The full-page advertisement in the *East London Advertiser* was for the reopening in June 1963 of Canning Town's revamped market, running alongside Barking Road and in fact comprising 156 stalls and 32 shops. The Mayor of West Ham, Councillor Margaret Scott, did the honours, accompanied by 'television's "Buzzie Bee"', the comedian Arthur Askey. 'Arthur, dressed in a blue suit and red tie, stepped from the car and immediately kissed some of the old ladies nearby, who had been standing for over an hour to catch a glimpse of him.' And, after the ceremony, he had these words of approval-cum-reassurance: 'It's marvellous. Though it is a modern and clean market it still retains the atmosphere of the old. That is what people want. This is progress but it doesn't leave them behind.'

Of course, not everywhere was changing. To look at photographs taken in autumn 1964 of rows of small shops in different parts of Birmingham – Northfield's Bristol Road South, Small Heath's Green Lane, Nechells Green's Nechells Park Road, Cotteridge's Watford Road – is to see a visual composition that would have looked very familiar a decade or two earlier. Or take the St Ebbes district of Oxford, where the writer Brian Aldiss lived before 'the bulldozers moved in' in the mid-to-late 1960s:

> Those streets were still lit by gas. Few cars ever passed that way, cer-
> tainly the inhabitants of the little terraced houses did not own cars …
>
> I used to buy some food at an impoverished Co-op in Gas Street.
> It was the poorest of shops; you entered on to bare boards. The
> assistants, thin, stringy women of indeterminate age, would cut
> the traditional English quarter-pound of butter in two for you: an
> eighth of a pound was all some people could afford at one time.
> I also bought half-loaves of bread there. The Co-op understood
> poverty, and catered for it.[10]

The urban future, though, pointed irresistibly to the bespoke shopping centre – at this stage almost invariably located centrally, as opposed to American-style out-of-town, reflecting the fact that most people did not yet own a car. And though Birmingham's Bull Ring attracted the most attention, it was far from alone.

Certainly by the mid-point of the decade they were starting to pro-liferate, whether completed or under way and whether commercially viable or in danger of being a white elephant. In Bedford, the Greyfriars Shopping Centre was the site for the first Safeway designed-and-built supermarket (1963); in Blackburn, the shopping centre in the process of being built, in place of the demolished Victorian market hall, would be one of the relatively few to win praise from an architectural historian (Otto Saumarez Smith), for its 'almost constructivist, multidimen-sional quality, breaking up its massive scale with a picturesque massing … probably the first built English iteration of the avant-garde idea of a megastructure – the concept of building all the multiple functions of a city in a single building'; in Croydon, the Croydon Centre (1964, aka St George's Walk) would prove no match ('a desolate wind tunnel') for the much larger Whitgift Centre (Croydon's 'showpiece') just starting to be built; in Leeds, the Merrion Centre (1964) began as a precinct, but because of the wind factor was soon roofed over and converted into a mall (complete with such non-retail amenities as a bowling alley, a nightclub, a dance hall and a cinema), while elsewhere in the city, in the Crossgates district, the first authentic Arndale Centre was taking shape; in Lewisham, the Leegate Centre had opened in March 1963 with high hopes and no knowledge that half a century later it would be condemned as a 'ghost town'; in Margate, the Arlington Square development had been acclaimed in July 1963 by the *East Kent Times* as 'Britain's first "park and buy" shopping centre' ('Traffic problems no longer exist in this clean, fume-free piazza – you can be sure the children are safe. And you can do *all* the shopping here, with a supermarket and 50 shops to choose from ...'); and in Stockport, the concrete-and-steel Merseyway Shopping Precinct (1965) was helped by its site alongside the Mersey Square bus terminus and perhaps also by its tower with a numberless square white clock face. 'I liked it at the time because it seemed like something that might have featured in the shakily futuristic *Thunderbirds* puppet show on TV,' recalls Paul Morley (eight when it opened, and living on the outskirts of the town), though adding that 'as time has passed the buildings near it constructed a hundred years before have retained their overwhelming and future-minded power, and the clock has come to look cheap and plastic, like it runs on clockwork and the key has been lost'. 'It symbolises,' in short, 'a zealous, anxious 1960s, which bulldozed the finicky, embalming and hieratic Victorian and Edwardian past into oblivion but very soon started to look a little dated itself.'[11]

Only four shopping centres of that decade, though, would become as famous or infamous as the Bull Ring, all of them likewise now demolished. The first to be built was Sheffield's Castle Market, replacing an open street market and which by 1963, according to an architectural magazine, 'dominates the central shopping area'. It had few defenders over the years – even the usually pro-modernist Elain Harwood noting how despite being an 'ideal site' it showed how 'difficult' it was 'to make multi-level shopping centres work' – albeit Owen Hatherley has offered a striking, leftfield defence. 'Just as Park Hill [Sheffield's celebrated multi-storey housing development of the late 1950s] famously tried to replicate slum bustle in the sky, Castle Market recreates the teeming strangeness of an old market in a fearlessly Modernist form,' he declared in 2010. 'Its several levels are built into the sloping landscape, from a raised gallery outside to a fish market in the basement. Inside is a joyous mess of vintage sixties signage, sights, smells and visual chaos, soundtracked by a stall playing easy listening, full of old cafes where net curtains and Mondrian geometries make richly perverse bedfellows.' The Soda Fountain, the Riviera Snack Bar, the Roof-Top Café – all that, and 'a sweet shop using the same font as *The Prisoner*.' Few such joys at the Elephant & Castle Shopping Centre, opened in 1965 and damningly described two years later. 'Its location was ill-chosen,' wrote Oliver Marriott, 'access was difficult and the layout of the shops on three floors was inconvenient for those shoppers who penetrated the castle surrounded by its moat of traffic.'

The other two shopping centres, both by 1965 in the process of being constructed, were the work of the brutalist architect Owen Luder. 'An architectural orchestration in reinforced concrete that is the equivalent of Berlioz or the 1812 Overture: trumpets, double percussion, cannons, the lot,' acclaimed Ian Nairn soon after Portsmouth's Tricorn Centre had opened in 1966. 'This is every student's dream made visible, spiral staircases, heroically modelled facades, writhing compositions of cross-overs and pass-unders. Everything is going on all at once on about six different levels.' 'Flamboyance in Concrete' was the title of Nairn's euphoric appraisal; yet by 2001, three years before demolition, it had not only been voted Britain's most hated building in a Radio 4 poll, but described by Prince Charles as 'a mildewed lump of elephant droppings'. Luder's other notorious shopping centre was in Gateshead's Trinity Square (1967), a 12-storey concrete monster which included the multi-storey car park made internationally renowned not long afterwards in *Get Carter*. The whole complex, sometimes known as the Treaty Centre, was demolished in 2011; and three years later, Jonathan Meades wistfully recalled it and the Tricorn Centre as 'great monuments of an age', the latter-day equivalents of Stonehenge or Lincoln Cathedral.

It would obviously be absurd to condemn all post-war shopping centres as unfit for human purpose. But perhaps the underlying problem with too many of those conceived and built in the 1960s was that they were hubristic, that they failed to follow the more modest modernism – a soft brutalism as opposed to a hard brutalism – of the ones built in the 1950s in bombed-out cities like Plymouth and Coventry. Overall, it is hard to dispute the verdict of Colin Buchanan. 'I do not know one of these projects which is not a disappointment when visited,' he reflected in 1972 more in sorrow than in anger, 'and which does not fill one with regrets at the lack of quality in design and finishes, at the brashness and the stickers, at the loss of the sense of intimacy and services which the older shops provided, and even at the goods that are sold.'[12]

*

How much customer loyalty was there? 'I think the gentleman on Woman's Hour was very wrong in saying women don't know which shop sells goods at 2d and 3d cheaper,' an indignant listener wrote in after Alan Brien had rashly pronounced in January 1964 about female shoppers tending to stick with the shop they liked the best, irrespective of price. 'We do and we walk,' she went on. 'I know which shop I get my cheese from, my bacon from, my toilet rolls, my tea, and so on. If I go to the shop round the corner, I pay 11d more for coffee, so I walk to town.' It may have depended, to a degree anyway, on what kind of shop. The same year, Yvonne Trethewy, summarising the results of a survey conducted by the Research Institute for Consumer Affairs, found 'the overall impression' to be 'one of strong customer loyalty to a traditional-style butcher's shop', while at the same time observing that 'a butcher's shop may be chosen much more carefully than a grocer's or fruiterer's, presumably because meat is usually the centrepiece of a meal'. Certainly, a strong residual loyalty still attached to the Co-op, and in particular to the dividend, or 'divi', helpfully defined by Rachel Bowlby as 'a system of regular returns in proportion to customers' retail purchases whereby the surplus – what was not retained for running costs and reinvestment – was distributed among the members of a given local Co-op', with individual amounts 'calculated from stamps supplied at the time of the purchase and pasted into a book'. Dividend rates were falling, down by 1964 to an average of 9d (compared to 1s some five years earlier) of the total spent; but the evidence from Rosalind Watkiss Singleton's oral history of three Black Country communities (Pensnett, Sedgley and Tipton) is probably typical of many old-fashioned and socially conservative working-class areas. 'That was lovely that was,' fondly recalled one of her female interviewees about the divi; while another remembered how 'mother paid for my wedding [in 1963] out of her divi'.[13]

The other, newer way of attracting customer loyalty was through trading stamps, above all Green Shield stamps, which by the mid-to-late 1960s enjoyed some 80 per cent of the trading stamps market, not-withstanding competition from the American-financed Pink Stamps. In 1963, Green Shield's catalogue of what could be redeemed through its stamps (at one of its many 'gift houses') comprised 800 items; and that autumn, of course, the start of the great Stamps War saw Tesco in the green corner and a rival supermarket chain, Priceright, in the pink. Sainsbury's, supported by many smaller players and fearing that trading stamps would only serve to intensify competition in the grocery retail trade, stood out loudly and obdurately against all forms of stamps – but they were on a losing wicket, one that did not take sufficient account of human psychology. 'Trading stamps must be a boon to poorer people who otherwise could not afford the "gifts",' a reader declared in the *Leicester Mercury* in November 1963. 'It's all very well for people like Lord Sainsbury to try to stop trading stamps but he doesn't understand the plight of poor people and has never experienced the joyful day when the postman knocks to deliver the wonderful "free" frying pan.'[14]

There remained, especially in working-class districts full of small corner shops, the classic way of maintaining customer loyalty: namely, the provision of credit. 'We know that many housewives are blinded by the soft lights and sweet music approach of the supermarkets and the multiple stores, but I contend that their price-cutting is phoney and is intended just to lure the people in,' declared Thomas Lynch, president of the National Union of Small Shopkeepers, addressing in January 1963 more than a hundred shopkeepers from Burnley and district. And he went on: 'If the housewives of Britain want the little man because he is prepared to grant them credit facilities and listen to their troubles – if that is the pattern of retail distribution that they want – then we say it is only right and proper that the small shopkeepers should be allowed to stay in business.' Although the long-term forces were inexorably pitted against those small shopkeepers – the proportion of trade carried out by independent outlets declining from 100 per cent in 1800 to 65 per cent by 1939 and to 31 per cent by 1980 – Avram Taylor notes in his 2002 study of working-class credit and community that 'despite the decline in the numbers of small shops, the tradition of corner-shop credit has survived into the present, even if it is not as widespread as it used to be'. Of course, where 'tick' (i.e. paying later) stopped and 'saving' began could be a fine distinction, suggestive of different shades of working-class respectability or otherwise. Either, though, could be beneficial to the small shopkeeper's retention of loyalty, as Watkiss Singleton shows in her evocation of a way of life in the Black Country which not only had a distinct flavour of Arnold Bennett's Five Towns half a century earlier, but in some key essentials did not really start to change until the 1980s. For example, in all three of her small towns, 'virtually all butcher and corner shops provided customers with the facility to defray the expense of Christmas whilst simultaneously ensuring their own profits'; or take the way in which a drapery business in Dudley 'encouraged female customers to become agents by offering them discounted goods, with the onus upon agents to recruit clients from their immediate circle':

Mrs Jones explained the dynamics of the system – 'She asked around and got a group of women to pay a set amount each week for (say) eight weeks. She would need eight ladies to pay 1/- each. This meant that each week there was an 8/- voucher for Hawkins. A draw was made to decide the order of issue. People used to swap chances if they needed something urgently, people who were desperate for cash would "sell" their 8/- voucher for 7/-'. Throughout the period [1945–70], the author's mother, and other female family members, 'paid into Hawkins', through longstanding custom and loyalty to the local agent, whose husband was unable to work. In these instances, allegiance to shop-keepers or their intermediary, and acknowledgement of family custom were the over-riding decisive factors and deemed more important than personal preference. Other customers visited Hawkins personally to pay a weekly sum, which was entered onto a card and 'spent' on household linen at a later date. Although never purchasing 'on tick', Mrs Woolley's mother patronised Hawkins' shop, paying 'so much a week and when she'd got enough she'd have the stuff'.[15]

'More important than personal preference': it is a salutary reminder of – whatever the apparent prevailing zeitgeist – the continuing limits of individualism.

In general, moreover, though patterns of shopping by the mid-1960s undeniably were showing a significant degree of change, the forces of conservatism remained strong. 'There is some evidence that shopping once a week (or less often) is on the increase,' noted Elizabeth Gundrey in 1966, mainly on the basis of evidence a few years earlier. 'Those who shop most frequently tend to be D-E [i.e. social classes D and E] mothers of young children, in northern towns. The vast majority still walk or bus to the shops (only 1 per cent use a car). About a quarter of women have children in tow. Loyalty to the same grocer has fallen steeply, and most women patronise at least two.' The issue of shopping hours – strictly regulated by the 1950 Shops Act, including compulsory early closing on one weekday – was revealing. A survey in 1964 of 5,000 members of the Consumers' Association found four out of ten shoppers wanting shops to stay open until 10 p.m. at least once a week, with that proportion rising to six out of ten in the case of working women; but membership of the CA was overwhelmingly middle class, and two years later a broader survey conducted by Southern Television revealed that 82 per cent of shoppers (including 73 per cent of supermarket users) never made use of late-night shopping (permitted once a week), even though only 13 per cent had no late-night shopping in convenient reach. Nor is there all that much compelling evidence that shopping was becoming by this time a leisure activity, least of all an activity intrinsic to a happy, companionate marriage. When in around 1964 some 120 London housewives were asked whether they regarded shopping as 'a social occasion', a mere 8 per cent said that that was 'very much the case'; 28 per cent said that it was 'to some extent'; and 64 per cent were adamant that it was 'not at all'. Unsurprisingly, the same survey also demonstrated that it was 'rare' for husbands to go shopping with their wives. Little change there, and not much either in the memories of the historian Tony Judt, who for several years from 1966, living in Putney, 'worked variously as a deliverer of carpets, warehouse supplies, and domestic dry goods':

Looking back on my days ferrying groceries around south London, I am struck by how compact the orders were. A typical household would take no more than two small boxes a week. For everything else the housewife shopped daily at a neighbourhood greengrocer, dairy, butcher, or poulterer ... Bulk purchases made no sense: most people had tiny refrigerators, some had none at all. In my green Morris van, the grocer's family name proudly emblazoned on its side, I could carry up to two dozen orders at a go.

'Today,' he reflected in 2010, 'a typical outing to the mall would fill the little Morris with one household's weekly supplies.'[16]

Class, as ever, mattered. 'I can see now,' recalls another historian, John Benson, 'that during the late 1950s and 1960s, my mother believed firmly that shopping at department stores like Stones of Romford and Roomes of Upminster helped to confirm our family's highly prized lower middle-class identity.' A trio of female diarists help to flesh out the class/shopping relationship. One of them, Dennis Marsden's wife Pat, was a fascinated observer during their sociological sojourn in heavily working-class Salford. 'Went shopping to St. Stephen St.,' she recorded in September 1963:

Hardly any of the shops sell Heinz baby foods – and none sell strained veg, which I want at the moment. Best sellers are e.g. Co-op sells strained apples, egg custard, and apricot and rice ... Frank Lee had dozens of strained choc puddings and few strained apples and egg custard. Had a few junior dinners and broths. Says don't sell.

'I've noticed that a lot of people buy milk (sterilised) from the sweet shop,' she mentioned next day. 'I should think they don't have regular orders from a milkman ...' An utterly different world for Daphne Meryon, living in Emsworth and married to a naval commander. 'Hoping to find clothes for Gibraltar, but found the shops wholly uninspiring,' she noted in May 1964 (three days before Habitat's opening) after a trip to Chichester; while next day, in Portsmouth, 'I went dress-hunting in Knight and Lee'. Or later in the year, a month before Christmas:

Nonie and I both caught 9.5 train to Waterloo. She went to Speedwriting and I caught bus to A&N [the Army and Navy

Stores], where I had a good many things to do. Another to Sloane St to go to General Trading Company about picture framing, and to Bedding Centre, and then by underground to Bond St. Met Nonie outside Speedwriting at 1 p.m., had lunch together in a sordid Lyons, then spent afternoon Christmas shopping. She had to return to Speedwriting for an hour in the middle; I had cup of tea and collected my thoughts in Selfridges meanwhile ...

Somewhere in the middle of the social pecking order was Judy Haines in Chingford: keenly interested in shopping trends, while refreshingly open-minded about where she shopped:

Did my week-end shopping. I have less and less delivered – groceries, green groceries and now bread, but I managed. *(15 February 1963)*

Went shopping and came home loaded with groceries, green groceries, bread, cakes and fish and chips. Once I had all but fish and chips delivered. Prefer choosing quality and price. *(19 February 1963)*

Victor Value [the supermarket] redeemed my coupon for another thirty King Korn Stamps. Thirty also free last week and thirty next to purchasers of over 5/- worth of goods. Prices are cheaper than most, too. *(27 November 1963)*

There are many changes taking place in our shopping centre. Co-op has a new Self-Service look, opening 7th Feb with parcels of groceries free for customers spending at least £1. The Supermarket [Victor Value?] is doubling its size, having taken over Star Radio; Woolworth's is extending; Mayer's (Greengrocer) and Mount Sports have gone. Our new Betting Shop looks neglected. Silverthorn Café is now a Chinese Restaurant. I like Lyons for lunch lately. *(4 February 1964)*

I do enjoy buying vegetables, meat and groceries at the Co-op, since they have brought their shops up to date. My divi should be mounting ... *(6 March 1964)*[17]

It is possible to be a bit more scientific. 'Attitudes to Spending Money on Consumer Goods and Services: A small-scale psychological

survey' was the title of Emer Rodnight's survey for the Consumers'
Association, based on tape-recorded interviews in late 1964 with
shoppers who mainly went to Brixton or Peckham or Croydon. The
main findings were that 'a working-class woman who does not know
the right questions to ask or the relevant qualities to look for, is likely
to arrive at a final choice quickly and easily and feel happy that this
choice represents value for money even though, to a critical outside
observer, she may appear to have "thrown her money away"'; that
'the perceived ranges of choice in furniture showed much stronger
social class variations than were found in the field of large electrical
equipment'; that 'working-class respondents made a sharp distinction
between cheap unbranded furniture (which was thought to be the
most appropriate and sensible choice in certain sets of circumstances
and was not expected to last) and "quality" furniture, epitomised for
many working-class respondents by the brand name, G Plan, which
was regarded as a luxury buy and was expected to have a very long
life'; and that 'in the choosing of furniture even the most cautious
and careful working-class shopper tended to confine his investigation of quality to a thorough personal inspection of the price being
considered, whereas the middle-class respondent had a more analytic
approach and attempted to supplement whatever information might
be derived from a physical inspection, by asking detailed questions
about the identity and quality of the materials used in the manufacture
of the furniture'. Rodnight then quoted three working-class women,
aged between roughly twenty and forty-five:

I bought a three-piece suite because we had one very large room and
I'd had some heavy stuff in it – very difficult to clean underneath
and to push it around. I wanted one that took up less space in the
room also. There is one thing I don't like about the new one – the
tubular legs dig into the lino – which is very bad. I hadn't thought
of that at the time I bought it.

When we went to choose our furniture about six years ago – just
after marriage – we went into this shop – and my husband is one
of those people – he sees all this beautiful stuff [G Plan] – and it's
pricey. We'll have that, that and that he says, and before you know
it we've a bill for £400. Well I don't know – I thought we should
have had something different – because I knew there'd be children

along. I've got two now and you should see my furniture after five years – it's falling to pieces. But my husband won't do with cheap stuff. He's not practical. He didn't even think of where we were going to put it. We only have two rooms, yet we have this six-seater couch and six-place dining table – a great big thing. Well, we don't even have the room for it really.

They'll tell you anything that suits them in most shops. They're only interested in selling it to you. When things go wrong you go back to the shop but they don't really take any notice. They don't care because they've already got your money.

Predictably enough, none of the three were readers of *Which?*. By contrast, one middle-class male subscriber was discrimination itself:

One of the great advantages of shopping in London is that you can really go to town on an article, take the back off and look inside etc, in fact *really shop*, whereas in the small local shop someone wants to serve you as soon as you get inside the door. You feel hampered and restricted, and you can't really investigate the article satisfactorily.

While as for suburban furniture shops for the traditional working-class market, well, these were 'filled with cheap and nasty unbranded rubbish, flashy and pseudo furniture that you could never think of buying'.[18]

*

This was undoubtedly an age of ever-increasing consumption. The figures for volume of consumption in 1965 speak for themselves (on the basis that 1950, 15 years earlier, equals 100):

Food	125.7
Drink, tobacco	129.8
Clothing	135.4
Housing and maintenance	137.3
Furniture, household goods	142.4
Radio, electrical	281.4
Motor vehicles and fuel	694.1

By comparison, the equivalent figure for population by 1965 was only 108.5, in other words a much smaller rate of growth than for the seven categories of consumption. Of course, these overall figures masked significant regional differences – in Wales, for instance, only 23 per cent of households had a refrigerator, compared with 34 per cent across the UK – but the trend was all one-way, with its inevitable accompaniment a growing consumer movement. *Which?* itself (started in 1957 by the Consumers' Association and up by 1964 to almost half a million subscribers) continued rapidly to expand its readership; 1961 saw the start of the pioneer Oxford Consumers' Group; and by 1963 some 5,000 members made up almost 50 local consumer groups. Lying at the very heart of the movement's rationale at this stage was the provision of accurate, impartial information at a time of technological innovation rapidly increasing both the range and the complexity of available products. For Michael Young, questing and ever-restless patron saint of the movement, matters of everyday shopping were only part of what was at stake. 'Public and professional services need modernisation almost more than anything else,' he declared in May 1963 as he launched his latest brainchild, the Research Institute for Consumer Affairs. 'They are so liable to become flabby,' he went on. 'If a consumer is dissatisfied with his telephone service, or the state of his railway station, or the amenities of his public library, what can he do? He can't turn his custom over to a rival.' Estate agents, GPs, lawyers and accountants were all also in his sights; while as for the 'nineteenth-century attitude of many petty bureaucrats' towards the public, he argued that not only 'teachers still treat parents like children', but 'many officials take the attitude that people are trying to get money out of them by false pretences'.[19]

Yet for all its noble aims and growing sense of purpose, the consumer movement's potential was by the mid-1960s seriously hobbled by two fundamental problems. The first was its instinctive lack of sympathy for material consumption as such – as something crucial for self-identity, and increasingly to be enjoyed in a guilt-free way for its own sake. The emblematic figure here was Eirlys Roberts, editor of *Which?* for almost all its first 16 years and remembered on her death in 2008 as 'the mother of the modern consumer movement'. In earlier days she had worked for the UN relief agency in Albania and for the Treasury in the ultra-austere Cripps era; by the early 1960s she was living in a shabby Georgian house and driving a 10-year-old Morris Minor; and for all her personal charm, she was deeply anti-frivolous. The other problem was perhaps even more fundamental: that in a society which still overwhelmingly identified itself as working class – some 64 per cent, as opposed to 30 per cent identifying as middle class and 6 per cent having no class identity, according to 1964 electoral studies data – the consumer movement was almost irretrievably middle class in composition and outlook. 'It has still to reach the mass of wage earners,' noted Arthur Seldon (of the Institute of Economic Affairs) in 1963 about *Which?*; while, two years later, the trade magazine *Stores & Shops* revealed conclusively that only 30 per cent of *Which?*'s readership was lower middle class or skilled working class, and that 'the unskilled working class are hardly touched at all'. Around the same time, *New Society* quoted some responses by three very different London shopkeepers to what it called the 'consumer revolution'. 'Consumer groups have had a good and definite influence,' asserted the qualm-free manager of a supermarket in a posh Marylebone street. 'Our customers are more price-conscious and hygiene-conscious than ever.' An Italian greengrocer in St Pancras was less sure: '*Which?* What which? Consumer group? Never heard of them.' And last word went to a barrow woman in Leather Lane: 'Consumer groups? Don't make me laugh! Bargains, that's all these people want, all they ever wanted. Just bargains ... they're bloodthirsty!'[20]

There was little doubt about the prime commercial enemy of Young, Roberts, et al. 'Advertising is the main instrument for creating the larger market without which productive capacity cannot be planned on the optimum scale and, indeed, much existing capacity would quickly become redundant,' defensively insisted Lord (Alf) Robens, president of the Advertising Association as well as chairman of the National Coal Board, as he introduced in May 1964 the *Financial Times*'s 16-page supplement on advertising. 'To produce more,' he continued, 'we must sell more: good advertising is the key to successful selling. Britain needs good advertising men just as much as good production engineers ...' The key statistics for 1963 backed up his claim about the unavoidable if controversial importance of the advertising industry: total expenditure on advertising and sales promotion running at some £500 million a year (compared to some £300 million in 1956), with advertising as a percentage of national income being higher, at just over 2 per cent, than in any other developed economy except the USA. Within the total spend – of which three-fifths was devoted to consumer advertising and one-fifth to sales promotion activities – some 46 per cent went to the press, 17 per cent to television, 9 per cent to catalogues and suchlike, and 7 per cent to window displays. In 1964 that total spend jumped up further, to around £553 million. Which was, the English lecturer Frank Whitehead laconically noted, 'an amount which compares interestingly with a net expenditure of £545 million in the same year on all primary and secondary schools in England and Wales'.[21]

'Advertising,' reflected an only marginally less critical Anthony Sampson in 1965, 'has no direction, no centre, no obvious tycoon. It exists as a hectic go-between, between the two great wheels of industry and the public, taking a succession of quick and temporary decisions, existing from hand to mouth, and constantly surprised by its own existence and wealth.' In reality, it was itself increasingly an industry in its own right. By 1963 the Institute of Practitioners in Advertising had 272 member agencies, handling 92 per cent of all agency business and employing some 18,000 people. 'Still a young man's business,' a director of SH Benson, second only to J. Walter Thompson in market share, told the *FT* soon afterwards, noting 'the determination of some agencies to attract young graduates'. It was almost certainly time for an infusion of meritocracy. 'Contrary to the anti-advertising myth, the flower of the nation's young minds do not rush into the advertising business,' observed the young sociologist Jeremy Tunstall in a 1964 overview of 'the advertising man' (not a woman to be seen higher than secretarial level). 'In fact,' he went on, 'the low educational level of most advertising recruits is openly regarded as a chronic problem by leaders of the advertising business. I recently asked the personnel director of one the biggest London agencies how many holders of first-class degrees he had employed in the last ten years, and his answer was: "None".'

The most vivid depiction of the industry as it still was by the early 1960s, and to a large extent even in the mid-sixties, comes from Peter York:

> Advertising [he recalled in 2010] was not quite a gents' profession, not quite an art. But certainly it employed gentlefolk and artists.

The gentlefolk were mostly 'suits', the account-handler types who dealt with the clients and presented the work. The artists – visual and verbal ones, famously dreaming of their novels, film scripts and first Cork Street shows – did the work. An emerging group of researchers thought about consumers and their habits. And rather more pragmatic types – the media buyers – did the deals with media owners. All under one roof.

Set up like this, a 'big' London advertising agency would employ around 300 people in somewhere tolerably genteel, ideally Mayfair W1, or at least Mid-Town Holborn or Southampton Row – no raffish Soho or edgy Shoreditch then ...

They didn't lead on anything as grand as 'creativity'; that came later. Clients training it up to town from, say, Walton-on-Thames, might find that altogether too poncy a claim. Easy Modernity, meaning American-influenced new-as-tomorrow layouts, was on – as was *haute*-suburban elegance in illustrations and photographs and mild, 'well-written' humorous copy lines. The constantly cited conventional wisdom was that Brits were difficult to sell to in the full-throttle, balls-out American way; they needed to be charmed or amused into buying ...

'Just dig up any early-1960s fashion magazine,' he adds, 'and the advertising looks ten years behind the editorial. Dull. Formulaic.' According to York, the game-changing agency, bringing 'a new, sharper and distinctly British 1960s style to advertising,' was Collett Dickenson Pearce, founded as recently as 1960 and employing 'a mass of clever young people' – among them, David Puttnam, Alan Parker and (recruited in 1966) Charles Saatchi. One notably unimpressed observer of the whole scene was Wally Olins, who as a thirty-something advertising executive found his work, he would tell York many years later, 'very superficial and cosmetic and we didn't get to the heart of anything'. Instead, he came to believe that the future lay not with conventional advertising, nor with PR, nor even with design, but with branding; and in 1965, amid ill-disguised condescension from advertising people, he co-founded Wolff Olins, the pioneer brand consultancy.[22]

Whatever that larger story about to unfold, the press remained the staple platform, perhaps especially local newspapers and women's magazines. The emphasis in the former was often heavily on price alone, whereas the ads in a typical issue of *Woman* ('Every Wednesday') bore the stamp of the 'creative' arm of the advertising agency, as in these from March 1964:

K Personalities pamper hard-to-please feet

It's bliss to wear! Brilliant stretch elastic straps that stay where they're put all the time, on or off the shoulders! A beautifully low Scoop back that looks and feels simply sensational! Gentle control, care-free comfort, glamorous elegance ... 'Sheer heaven', the bra that magically follows your every move. It's heavenly!

How to prove that Spry-crust is lighter than pie-crust. *(You don't have to weigh it – just eat it!)*

Ill or tired LUCOZADE aids recovery

There's nothing to surpass the dairy-cream flavour and smooth consistency of Lurpak butter. Lurpak is butter supreme – well worth every penny of its price. Live better with Lurpak on your table ... **Probably the finest butter in the world**

KIWI – THE POLISH THAT DOES SO MUCH MORE THAN SHINE

Make a most delicious trifle with creamy-rich Carnation

Poly means everything for your hair

Brooke Bond P.G. Tips – tea you can really taste!

Maggi makes Minestrone in the true Italian style – a soup to make a meal!

Yes, Stork makes a cake so light – it's fantastic!

How to Relieve Tense Nervous Headaches? Nothing acts faster than ANADIN

BENGERS FOR A GOOD NIGHT'S SLEEP

So far so relatively staid; but it was on TV commercials that the advertising pace was now starting to pick up, helped by such luminaries as Lindsay Anderson directing ads for Rowntree's, Karel Reisz for Persil and Joseph Losey for Nimble Bread. 'To analyse the methods used by advertisers in this evanescent medium is peculiarly difficult,' reflected Frank Whitehead in 1964:

> Words are no longer the main channel of appeal, but have become only one adjunct among many – the visual setting, the personality of the actors, the camera angles on cutting, the background music, the catchy singing-jingle, the appeal of the puppet figures or the amusement contributed by the animated cartoon. There can be no doubt that the combined effect of these multiple resources makes an exceptionally powerful impact ... The preferred aim nowadays is to associate the product with pleasurable screen images and personalities rather than harp on fears and anxieties that may introduce a jarring note into the family viewing. Cigarette brands are linked, by the most tenuous of connexions, with idyllic rural or sporting scenes, photographed in sunlight which is unfailingly benign; while a bedtime drink has to be extolled to us, in rapt tones, because it provides 'a *happy* flavour at the end of each day' ...

Amid much dross ('Do you use it? Pepsodent?'), these were years that saw crafted half a dozen classics. Two in 1962: Leslie Crowther on behalf of Stork SB asking women in supermarkets to tell the difference and a gentle travelogue announcing 'We're Going Shell'. Two more in 1963: the upward social mobility promised by serving After Eights at a dinner party and William Franklyn whispering for the first time 'Shh ... you know who' to sell Schweppes Tonic Water. And two more in 1964: Esso's 'Put A Tiger In Your Tank' (zany car, cartoon tiger inside, jazzy music) and, the true immortal, 'Happiness Is ...' for Hamlet cigars. A man in bed with a broken leg in plaster, the cigar lit up, Bach's 'Air on the G String' playing in the background – it was the signature work of Collett Dickenson Pearce.[23]

There was the odd other legendary campaign. 'The "Persil Mum" television campaign must be the apotheosis of all "sell the sizzle as well as the steak" advertising, for this campaign sells the promise *beyond* the promise,' claimed J. Walter Thompson's advert for itself in the *FT*'s 1964 supplement. 'Here the promise is not only a modern washing powder, nor even the promise of extra whiteness it gives, but a visible expression of a woman's skill in caring for her children. Does it sound too far-fetched? In the most cut-throat consumer market in the country, Persil sales are nearly three times greater than their nearest rival.' Or take the campaign dreamed up by a left-leaning classical scholar, Will Camp, working for the Gas Council and charged in the early 1960s with overhauling the image of a fuel hitherto 'chiefly notable', in his own words, 'as a pitiful means of committing suicide in a lonely bedsit'. A single phrase did the trick. 'Two out of three housewives (and the Sunday help) use High Speed Gas for cooking', ran a typical ad in 1964. 'The third would, as well, if she knew how much easier life was for the other two!' High Speed Gas ... and by the mid-1960s it was gas rather than electricity which was becoming the fuel of choice for many of those households at last able to embrace the joys of central heating.[24]

Yet more broadly, how effective were advertising's dark arts? Most people at this stage were certainly prepared to give them their headspace: a 1961 survey showed 84 per cent approving of TV advertising; while in terms of class it was predictably the less numerous middle class who were less enthusiastic, with a survey five years later of London married couples finding among them a particular dislike for 'loud' and 'trivial' advertising jingles, whereas a typical working-class response was, 'The Milky Bar kid with glasses – I love the Milky Bar kid'. One contemporary observer, the *Daily Express*'s improbably left-wing consumer columnist Robert Millar, viewed adland's targets as putty in its hands. 'The vast majority of the British people remain confused and bewildered,' he argued in 1963 in his expressively titled *The Affluent Sheep*. 'They stick to habits formed in the past which have no relevance to conditions in the Sixties; they prefer traditional consumer goods and a pattern of spending more appropriate to the Thirties; they rely upon advertising and other biased sources of advice to an unhealthy extent. They remain virtually untouched by the technological revolution which is capable of transforming their lives.'

Perhaps he overdid the gloom. For as James Obelkevich, one of the relatively few historians of consumption, persuasively argues, not only has advertising been over the years no guarantee of success, but in practice 'most people's responses to advertising are not those of naïve and helpless victims'. Or as one discriminating viewer, Mrs B. Jeavers, put it in December 1965 in response to Oxo's latest TV ad (with Mary Holland still playing Katie the Oxo Mum): 'What good housewife would come in after a morning's shopping and crumble an Oxo cube to make gravy without washing her hands first? Urgh! Need I say more!'[25]

*

All this left the intelligentsia at large – not just Whitehead, Sampson and Millar – essentially unhappy. Back in October 1961, Michael Frayn had written a celebrated satirical piece in the *Guardian* about 'the Harvest Festival which CADCAR (the Congress of Advertising, Confidence, and Allied Racketeers) was holding in St Swiz's' ('We put our trust in Swiz,/ For only Swiz has Fiz' the opening lines of the first hymn), earning him a stiff rebuke from Mark Chapman-Walker, a director of the *News of the World* as well as Television Wales and West; while just over two years later, the young graphic designer Ken Garland, wearing an Afghan sheepskin waistcoat and forcing his way to the front of a meeting of the Society of Industrial Artists, told his colleagues (to strikingly enthusiastic applause) that he was fed up with them throwing away their talents on selling cat food, toothpaste, cigarettes and slimming powder, that such visual incontinence had reached 'a saturation point', and that 'the high-pitched scream of consumer selling' had become 'no more than sheer noise'. Given the inexorable socio-economic forces at play, were these sorts of protests any more than a feel-good exercise in pissing in the wind? Probably not. Yet at some level it is hard, over half a century on, not to sympathise with the feelings of Patrick Anderson, following a trip in September 1963 to Halstead, a small town in Essex's Colne Valley:

> Visits to a small and intermittently pretty English town are likely to induce reflections on the ugly uniformity of chain-stores, the reckless sacrifice of old buildings to the 'shopping precincts' of the developer, the lack of the personal note in the establishments one has to enter. Again and again the 'packs' of merchandise displayed remind one of the horrors of television advertising. Each product is labelled *new*, often because of the addition of some 'scientific' ingredient ...[26]

12

Completely Against any Radical Changes

'I first went to Europe on 13 May 1964,' recalled Margaret Atwood in 2005 about her trip as a 24-year-old would-be writer. First stop was England, and during her two months there she lived in a cheap Willesden Green boarding house (the dingy furnishings smelling of 'old, sad cigarette smoke'; the sheets 'not just damp and cold, they were wet'; the bathroom freezing) before being 'smuggled' into a South Kensington flat where a fellow Canadian was staying. As she packed in the sights, her outfit was far from cutting edge – skirts not jeans (which had 'not yet swept all before them'), 'grey-flannel jumpers with Peter-Pan-collared blouses', shoes functional rather than elegant 'rubber-soled suede items known as Hush Puppies' – though that did not prevent a series of men trying to pick her up in museums. Trips out of London included a bus tour of the Lake District (viewing the Lakes 'through fumes of cigar smoke and nausea'), but before she left for France, it was attempting to eat out in London on a tight budget which left the strongest impression:

> I made the mistake of trying a hamburger and a milkshake, but the English didn't yet have the concept: the former was fried in rancid lamb fat, the latter fortified with what tasted like ground-up chalk. The best places were the fish-and-chip shops, or, barring that, the cafés, where you could get eggs, sausages, chips, and peas, in any combination. Finally I ran into some fellow Canadians who'd been in England longer than I had, and who put me onto a Greek place in Soho, which actually had salads, a few reliable pubs, and the Lyons

Corner House on Trafalgar Square, which had a roast-beef all-you-can-eat for a set price.

Atwood also remembered her 'intermittently-bathed, cadaverous and/or dentally-challenged fellow passengers' as she took her first tube journey to Willesden Green on the Bakerloo line: a true glimpse of old England.

Elsewhere on Wednesday the 13th, as the *Coronation Street* cull got seriously under way with Martha Longhurst ('gossipy foil of Minnie Caldwell and Ena Sharples') suffering a fatal heart attack in the Rovers' snug, the recently ennobled Ted Willis, creator of *Dixon of Dock Green*, delighted the Lords by describing the cult of the Beatles as a 'cheap plastic substitute for culture', 'an act of worship of phoney idols' and 'a ritual pop-pill'; that night, Vere Hodgson took the sleeper from Paddington to Shrewsbury ('something of an adventure, as the tales of hooligans on trains were vivid in my mind,' but 'there were several carriages for LADIES ONLY', so 'all was well'); a by-election next day at Devizes saw the Tories defy the political weather by holding on ('a real set-back for our hopes,' noted Anthony Wedgwood Benn, with the autumn general election no longer looking so assuredly in the bag); John Holmstrom in the latest *New Statesman* had a pop of his own at TV's pop programmes (his vote for most-loathed DJ split between Alan Freeman 'with his roguish smirk' and Jimmy Savile 'with his platinum wig'; the performers on *Ready, Steady, Go!*, itself 'a snakepit of twisting teenagers', quizzed by 'an insufferably callow pair of teenage interviewers'; *Thank Your Lucky Stars* 'solemnly grandiose', as 'the singers thread their way through the gothick arches and loopholes of elaborate set-pieces, as though the grottos of some great plastic cathedral of Beat'); Pat Scott and family headed for the Whit weekend to Canvey Island, where on a 'scorching hot' Saturday they were all day on the beach ('only shell & shingle but clean & plenty of places for children to play'); in the afternoon, Nella Last and her hairdresser discussed *Coronation Street* ('we both hoped the odious Dennis Tanner was to go – and the unlikeable Hewet teenager [the wayward Lucille Hewitt]'); next day, Sunday, 17 May with the Whit heatwave continuing, surprise visitors at Willis's home in Chislehurst were the recently formed Yardbirds ('the Yardsticks', according to the *Daily Telegraph*'s report, and including a teenage

Eric Clapton), who played a brief set on the patio in an effort to show that pop music was not wholly worthless; and that afternoon, a sold-out Royal Festival Hall witnessed a performance which in its own way made the same point.

'Is Mr Bob Dylan a passing phenomenon or is he in the true line of creative folk artists?' asked *The Times* next morning about 'this 22-year-old minstrel from Minnesota with ruffled hair and insouciant manner' who, 'dressed in a leather jacket, jeans and boots', had 'sauntered almost apologetically on to the platform and, aided only by a harmonica hung round his neck and his guitar, entertained his young listeners with a programme of his own songs'. Dylan had been in England for over a week – an awkward appearance on *Tonight*, the obligatory interview with Maureen Cleave, up to Manchester to record three songs for ATV's *Hallelujah*, telling a music magazine that his Mayfair hotel 'isn't bad really', albeit 'the bar is the only place I'm allowed in without a tie' – but the main event was his debut English concert. Among relatively few reviewers present was the *New Statesman*'s 'Francis Newton', the Marxist historian Eric Hobsbawm. Amid 'a rapt Festival Hall, packed with carefully informal O and A-level dandies of both sexes between 16 and 22', the forty-six year old listened unimpressed to 'the nasal, flat, anti-rhetorical voice of a thin, child-faced chansonnier from the US, a cross between a curlier James Dean (minus death wish) and a politically conscious Holden Caulfield'. Hobsbawm's contempt was palpable: 'It's clear – especially from Dylan's fairly numerous bad verses – that he comes from that *Reader's Digest* mass civilisation which has atrophied not merely man's souls but also their language, confining the ordinary person to a mixture of stammering and cliché.' Nor, the final insult, was this 'political poetry for the young' even where the weekend's youthful action really lay. 'Dylan's vision,' he concluded, 'remains that of a minority: Mods and Rockers were absent from the Festival Hall.'[1]

*

Their absence was unsurprising. 'Brighton is packed with Rockers and Mods,' noted the actor Kenneth Williams that Whit Sunday, halfway through a 'doomed to disaster' Bank Holiday weekend by the sea. 'There were several fights & over 50 arrests. Lovely. I saw a great mass

of Mods by the Palace Pier, one boy of about 14 or 15 had a gash &
blood pouring all over his face.' Trouble had indeed kicked off on the
Sunday, and it continued next day, as the *Brighton & Hove Gazette*'s
Angela Browning recorded:

Elderly holidaymakers were jostled roughly aside as hundreds
of screaming Mods swept down from West Pier to congregate at
Madeira Drive.

Two hundred teenagers chased a 13-year-old boy across the
beach, hurling stones at him. Police managed to rescue the boy, who
was taken to hospital with a leg injury.

At the height of Monday morning's battle, between 2,000 and
3,000 crowded the Madeira Drive area.

Outnumbered by 10 to 1, Rockers were cornered at the Aquarium
by hoards of Mods. Stones, deckchairs and wastebins were hurled.
They escaped by jumping 20 feet from the terrace into the arms of
police ...

But shortly before 1 pm, Mods and Rockers regrouped near
the Palace Pier. Police horse Kim and dogs helped uniformed men
keep crowds moving as rival gangs chanted and jeered at each other,
attempting to stage a mass sit-down.

After hours of tension, hundreds of Mods and Rockers suddenly
broke into a stone-throwing afternoon battle by the pier. Thousands
of trippers watched from pier railings and the promenade as Mods
surged forward armed with stones and rubbish ...

The other main flashpoint over the weekend was Margate. 'Nothing
much happened today,' wrote ironically on Monday evening the
Daily Mail's celebrated 'colour' writer, Vincent Mulchrone, direct
from the Kent coast. 'An old dear roughed up. A couple of stabbings
on the sands. Oh, yes, and one of the blokes got a starter's pistol fired
up his hooter. Dead quiet reely.' 'And all this time,' he added about
a 100-strong pack of Mods stampeding the beach ('boys and girls
running, hand-in-hand, Chelsea boots with Cuban heels drumming
across the sands') and taking over a large part of it, 'the British public
("We want nothing to do with it, mate") either watched with anticipatory glee and safe-distance scorn from the prom, or remained
doggedly in their deck-chairs, looking as if nothing untoward was

happening'. Among the Rocker invaders, likewise forcibly making their presence felt and intermittently scrapping with the Mods, was a red-haired (beehive-style) 20-year-old London-based singer, Brigitte Bond. 'Lord, No!' she told a journalist soon afterwards when asked if she felt any remorse for the havoc. 'I shall never forget this Whitsun. It was much better than Clacton. The fights and the screaming just drove me crazy. Why? I like it, that's why. Isn't that a good enough reason?'

It was easy to exaggerate the extent of the weekend's violence and disorder – 'in reality,' notes Richard Weight in his authoritative history of the Mod phenomenon, 'the events were not riots but skirmishes' – but undoubtedly this was the cue for the latest wave of moral panic about British youth. 'These young thugs smashing seaside resorts on Bank Holidays are the curse of the Welfare State, so rich in money allowing them so much for clothes, cars, scooters & travelling,' reflected the septuagenarian Gladys Langford on the Monday. 'They need birchings or fire hoses turned on them & their transistors.' Next day the press, after a day or two of limbering up, gave it both barrels. 'LIVING FOR KICKS' was the *Daily Mirror*'s front-page headline, with a large photo showing a Mod putting his boot into a Rocker lying prostrate on the beach at Brighton; another paper of the left, the *Daily Herald*, wanted these 'yobs and roughnecks' to be shown that 'they are really a tiny minority up against a large, angry majority', preferably by means of the fire brigade turning its hoses on them 'the next time they set out to wreck a town, to trample over other people's lives and leisure'; and the *Daily Express*'s banner headline 'SAWDUST CAESARS' was a quote from the Margate magistrate Dr George Simpson, who the day before, sentencing offenders, had spoken of how 'these long-haired, mentally unstable petty little sawdust Caesars seem to find courage, like rats, by hunting only in packs'. It was a sentiment also quoted and endorsed by Anthony Heap. 'Since all they understand is violence, what they should be given, of course, is a taste of their own medicine in the form of a good flogging,' he wrote that Tuesday. 'Or better still, have exactly the same injury inflicted on them as they inflict on their victims ...' Yet the sad truth, he added, was that 'in this decadent and degenerate country, where there is always more concern and sympathy for criminals than their victims, such "unenlightened" justice would never do!'.[2]

But who actually were the Mods and the Rockers themselves? What was distinctive about their particular sub-cultures? And how representative were they of youth as a whole?

'The difference between Mods and Rockers is a class one,' confidently asserted the writer Wayland Young (Lord Kennet) even before the instantly notorious Whit weekend. 'Mods pursue high fashion, and have clean hair, moderate means of transport, and educational aspirations. Rockers pursue low (or outmoded) fashion, wear "Brylcreem," have spots and ton-up machines, live in slums, etc.' His class point was broadly true, with analysis of those arrested following the Margate disturbances showing that Rockers tended to be in unskilled manual work, whereas Mods were likelier to be from a skilled working-class or lower-middle-class background. Interviews conducted this spring with 100 Mods and 100 Rockers, in Brighton's coffee bars, dance halls and streets, revealed other differences: 62 per cent of Mods taking drugs, compared to 42 per cent of Rockers; 73 per cent of boy Mods saying that they had had sexual intercourse, compared to 60 per cent of boy Rockers; and 28 per cent of girl Mods claiming or admitting the same, compared to 12 per cent of girl Rockers.

The stylistic contrast between the two sub-cultures was, as Young suggested, acute. 'Rockers, with their greased-up hair and motor-cycle leathers, represented a thorough commitment to the past – albeit a past that dated back barely a decade to Marlon Brando in *The Wild One* and the prototype rock 'n' roll of Elvis's Sun records,' recalls Richard Williams. 'Mods, "modernists", were the future: neat, clean, cool, and aspiring to an air of affluence and Continental sophistication.' Or in the words of Stuart Jeffries, it was 'leather v mohair, biker boots v two-tone bowling shoes, Brando v Belmondo, white rock 'n' roll v black rhythm 'n' blues, Triumph v Vespa'. How numerous were they? We know that Mods congregated especially in London and the south, whereas Rockers had the north as their stronghold, though in both cases there were pockets of assertive enemy penetration; we know also that by this time the combined circulation of weekly magazines with a Mod character amounted to around half a million; but not much else. In all probability, self-identifying Mods and self-identifying Rockers represented, between them, only a minority of their peer group, but a distinctive and far from negligible minority. The Birdcage in Portsmouth, the Twisted Wheel in Manchester, the Sink in Liverpool, the Ricky Tick in Windsor, the Scene Club in Soho, the King Mojo in Sheffield (youthful entrepreneur Peter Stringfellow the main man), Wheels in Reading – these were among thriving Mod clubs in 1964 or soon after. One young Mod, 14-year-old Lesley Hornby living in Neasden, did not go to clubs but instead, every Saturday night, to enormous and packed dance halls, more often than not the Starlight Ballroom in Sudbury. 'We only danced with girls (except for the slow songs),' remembered Twiggy. 'You'd put your handbags in the middle and dance around them. On the stage there would be three or four fresh-faced boys with guitars and drums who were known as the group.' Already, though, it was fashion that mattered in outer north-west London at least as much as the music:

> Our Mod uniform was a long plastic mac, a brand known as Pakamac, worn over whatever was the thing to wear at the time. We used to freeze in them. But that wasn't important. You had to be 'with it'. You had to look the same. One Saturday night the group of seventeen- and eighteen-year-old girls who were the trend-setters were all wearing ankle-length skirts and granny blouses in chiffon with cameo brooches. If that was the look, we had to have it, and we did. The following week, armed with our pocket money, Jennifer [Read] and I went up to C&A on our quest and bought two chiffon blouses, one in royal blue (mine) and one in brown. The sleeves and the Peter Pan collars were see-through, but the rest was lined in satin. As for the skirts, they had to be made. So I bought two yards of tweed each, black and grey for me with a blue slub, and one with a brown slub for Jennifer. She couldn't sew so I had to do both. There was no way I'd have worn one on my own. The trouble was that Jennifer's mother wasn't as understanding as mine. She was not going to have Jennifer going out looking like that, she said. 'In case of what the neighbours might say.'

Accordingly, 'both skirts were kept at my house until D-Day, and the next Saturday night we set off, me in mine, Jennifer in an ordinary skirt, and she changed under her mac on the top of the bus. We were hysterical.'[3]

Against a background of youth more broadly apparently having its moment in the economic and demographic sun – huge, never-to-be-repeated demand for unskilled and semi-skilled labour; income of many young people almost doubling between 1958 and 1966; disposable weekly income of some £7 for teenagers in work, even after payment (roughly £3) for 'keep' at home; under twenty-fives (most of them baby boomers) comprising some two-fifths of the population – much sociological and other attention now focused on their attitudes, their way of life and whether they constituted a threat to the existing social and moral order. *Youth and the Social Order* was indeed the title of Frank Musgrove's Midlands-based 1964 study, where to his own surprise he found that the so-called 'failures' or 'rejected' in secondary modern schools, the majority in other words of the secondary school population, 'seemed to suffer far less doubt and uncertainty, and to identify themselves far more closely with the adult world', than did grammar-school pupils, 'beset' as the latter were by 'irreconcilable social demands'. The essential continuity between adolescence and adulthood was a theme, too, in John Barron Mays's *The Young Pretenders* (1965), arguing flatly that for 'the great majority' of teenagers the top priority was 'getting a good job with financial prospects'. Indeed, though accepting that 'there may be some grounds for criticising youth' (including 'hedonism, fecklessness, lack of ambition, complacency'), Mays insisted that 'there is obviously nothing like a moral landslide amongst the rising generation'; and he pointed to 'the increasing popularity of marriage' as 'one of the most surprising demographic facts of recent years'. In the same year, Michael Schofield's *The Sexual Behaviour of Young People*, based on a survey of unmarried adolescents of both sexes living in the south of England, similarly emphasised the underlying forces of social conservatism: barely one-third of the boys, and less than one-fifth of the girls, having had some sexual experience, in many cases falling short of full intercourse. A final survey in this sort of terrain was *Adolescents and Morality* (1966) by Emmanuel and May Eppel, a married couple who had investigated the key concerns of some 250 working-class adolescents (again, both sexes) who had left school and were attending day-release courses. 'The picture that has emerged of this group of young working people,' they concluded, 'is that most of them regard themselves as belonging to a generation handicapped by distorted stereotypes about their behaviour and moral standards', with the view being 'repeatedly expressed or implied' that 'the behaviour or a delinquent or antisocial fringe had unfortunately been extended to characterize their whole generation'. Accordingly, 'many traditional obligations to family, work, and society are accepted by these adolescents' – though the Eppels did add the telling rider, 'if they feel that they have some say in the choice'.[4]

What about the young and politics? On the basis of a series of large-scale National Opinion Polls (NOP) surveys conducted in the first half of 1964, together with their own interviews, Philip Abrams and Alan Little concluded soon afterwards that, despite the growth since the mid-1950s of a distinctive 'youth culture' (the inverted commas theirs), young voters – i.e. aged twenty-one to twenty-four – were not fundamentally different from the rest of the electorate in their attitude to politics. 'Both commitment and an appetite for change are alien to contemporary British youth,' insisted the two sociologists. 'They are for the most part "realistic" about British society, seeing it as class-ridden, exploited by speculators and trade unions, governed adequately rather than well, difficult if not impossible to change. And for the most part they adapt their expectations to this image, confining their interests and ambitions to a purely personal sphere; a happy marriage, friendship, success in a job, these are the values they cherish.' Abrams and Little also looked specifically at the section of the youthful electorate which had been educated to the age of eighteen or more, with a handful of interview quotes giving the flavour of what they called 'a philosophy of pragmatic complacency':

To make the electoral system fair would involve many difficulties – therefore it is wisely left as it is.

The advantages of the system [of British politics] must be greater than the disadvantages or it would not be kept.

As things stand at the moment it does not seem necessary to change the system. Very few, if any, complaints are made.

As with all British institutions it [local government] works and it works reasonably well.

Our monarchy is as good in essentials as it could possibly be and I am completely against any radical changes.

Our system is old and well-tried ... it would be a shame to clog up the wheels of a quite smoothly run country by changing.

'Withdrawal makes it possible,' nicely commented Abrams and Little, 'to combine social and institutional conservatism with a diffuse political irritation.'

It was also in 1964 that Philip's father, Mark Abrams, reached his latest findings on an old favourite, the teenage consumer. Contrary to most adult assumptions about the high spending power of teenagers, he pointed out that, although undeniably it was increasing, they were still responsible for only 6 per cent of all consumer expenditure; and he showed how their expenditure was concentrated on relatively few products – notably clothing and footwear (18.6 per cent of expenditure), cigarettes and tobacco (10.5 per cent), meals out and snacks (8.7 per cent), holidays (7.7 per cent), and alcoholic drink (6.4 per cent), with records and record players accounting for only 3.3 per cent and cinema admissions a paltry 1.7 per cent. As for class differences in income and expenditure, Abrams noted that they were 'comparatively small' for boys, whereas the working-class girl (with barely half as much to spend as the working-class boy) 'is much worse off than her middle-class sister'. 'The working-class teenage world,' he explained further, 'is one where boys outnumber eligible [i.e. unmarried] girls by almost 2 to 1; thus they have only a low scarcity value, and are prone to seek compensation for this in and through their greater spending power.'

The most detailed – and evocative – evidence we have of youth in early to mid-1960s quotidian action is in *Adolescent Boys of East London* (1966) by Peter Willmott (husband of Phyllis), another of the richly textured ethnographic studies coming out of the Institute of Community Studies which he had co-founded. 'The most casual observation in Bethnal Green confirms that, as in other places where adolescence has been studied, the boys are often in each other's company,' began a descriptive passage:

> They stand on street-corners in knots in the early evening, discussing the relative merits of West Ham United and Arsenal one minute, whistling after a pair of girls the next. Younger boys scuffle and race about in the yards of the red-brick blocks of buildings or sit talking on the low walls outside. Older boys speed along Bethnal Green Road three abreast on scooters, or tear through Victoria Park together on motor bikes, wearing silver crash helmets and black

leather jackets. An assembly of youths fills a local café, drinking Coca-Cola and playing at the pin-tables to the reverberating music of a giant juke-box. A dozen shout obscenities and push at each other as they leave the youth club at eleven o'clock at night.

Willmott's sample of 246 male adolescents (age range of fourteen to twenty) was intensively interviewed, often by relatively 'classless' young Australians or New Zealanders, in the summer of 1964. Some of his main conclusions included that 'the characteristic pattern' of sociability was 'to go about with one male friend or, more often, a small company of them'; that 'most expected to marry young'; that by their late teens most boys were starting to 'settle down' and increasingly to associate sex 'with love and with the idea of marriage'; that at around the same time, 'the familiar dispositions of the local sub-culture begin to take shape'; that the educational system was fundamentally flawed, with all Bethnal Green's schools being, to a greater or lesser extent, 'out of tune with the local community'; that 'for the majority of boys, the failures of secondary education are not made good in further education'; and that 'most boys are – perhaps surprisingly – content with their work'.

But the real pay dirt of Willmott's study were the diaries that, for a week in either July or October 1964, 36 of his sample compiled. Take half a dozen snippets:

I went with my mate Barry to take his dog out for a walk. We walked around and then went in the pub, the City of Paris, for a drink. Barry had mild and I had brown ales. Barry's dog went to the toilet up the curtain, but fortunately nobody noticed. After two drinks, we went home at 10 p.m. *(Fifteen year old)*

I came home from school and had my tea. My mum knocked a flowerpot off the window ledge and asked me to sweep it up for her. I took out the dust-pan and brush and started to clear up, but then my mate Arthur came along and he said I was a cissy to help my mum, so I stopped. I went with Arthur over the flats where he lives and we met our other mates. *(Fourteen year old)*

7.30 p.m. Went to the Regal with three of my mates. We sat behind some birds and tried to start talking to them. They kept on giggling and telling us to shut up ... When we came out [at 10.30] we walked along with them and mucked about. We went to where they lived. We said we might see them at the Regal again next Friday night. *(Fifteen year old)*

About 7.30 I put on a suit and went to my girl's house in Shoreditch. I took her out for a drink. We had a chat about what to do over the week-end and decided to go to the pictures on Saturday and over Regent's Park Sunday if it's nice. We left the pub when it shut, got to her house at about 11.30. I left at about midnight. *(Twenty year old)*

I had my tea, washed and left for my girl-friend's house, in Bow. When I arrived her mother let me in and told me to take a seat in the living-room. Christine (my girl) and I watched 'Sunday Night at the London Palladium'. Afterwards we went for a walk until about 10.30 p.m. when I took her home and said 'Good night' for about 20 minutes before leaving ... *(Eighteen year old)*

Arrived home at 5.30, had a wash and my tea and played records till 7.30. I had decided to have an evening in. I sat back and watched TV and then washed my hair. After that I had a cup of coffee and had an early night. *(Eighteen year old)*

One of the fuller, more descriptive entries was this by a fourteen year old:

I got up and had sausage, egg, bacon and tomatoes for breakfast and read the *Sunday Mirror*. Then my brother Wally knocked at the door. He asked me if I wanted to go fishing with him and June, my sister-in-law. I quickly got my boots on and went with them in their van. We got to Broxbourne at about 12.30 and Wally and me started fishing and June started getting the dinner with a calor gas cooker. We had sausage, egg and bacon again, after that a cup of hot orange and a piece of swiss roll. Then it started to rain. It poured down and we all got soaked, so we made for home. When we got back they came in and Mum made us a hot cup of tea. Then Wally and June went off home.

It was probably a different fourteen year old (anonymity strictly preserved) who gave this account of a usual sort of day at his secondary modern:

9 a.m. Started out for school. On the way I called for my mate Andy L. and we went together...

10.55 a.m. The milk bell went and me and my friend John B. gave out the milk cartons.

11 a.m. Me and three of my mates went into the toilets for a smoke ...

12.30 a.m. Went up the fish and chip shop with Andy. We had our dinner there and then went over the park for a walk ...

3 p.m. Had a fight in break with a boy called Stephen S. I got a busted mouth and I got the cane for fighting ...

4 p.m. School ended and I went up the café with my friends.

As for the world of work, this account by a fifteen year old, who had presumably only just left school, was fairly typical:

6.30 a.m. Was woken up by Mum with a cup of tea. After I had my tea I got up and got dressed and washed. I had egg and bacon for breakfast.

7.17 a.m. I was a bit late and had missed my usual bus, but a few minutes later another bus came along. I supposed Frank had caught the 7.15 bus.

7.29 a.m. Arrived in work just in time to clock in at 7.30.

7.30 a.m. I was not working with Albert. I was working with Gerry. We were making a balustrade. I had to cut up the bars.

10.17 a.m. Had tea break as usual.

10.30 a.m. Started work again.

12.30 p.m. Stopped for dinner, went to the café. After I had dinner I went to the park; sat in the park until 12.58. Gerry had the afternoon off because he had to go to hospital about his eyes, because he kept getting headaches.

1.00 p.m. Started work.

1.30 p.m. I finished cutting up the bars then I drilled them with a $^2/_{32}''$ drill.

3.00 p.m. Had another cup of tea.

3.12 p.m. Started work again.

3.30 p.m. Had finished drilling, started on tapping with a ¼" tap.

7.30 p.m. Finished work and went home with Frank on the bus.

8.00 p.m. Got home, had fish and chips for tea. I decided to get washed and dressed and go to the 'Beat Club'.

9.00 p.m. Arrived at the club. When I got in the club I saw a lot
of my mates, so I went with them. We talked about the group.
They said it was the worst group they had up there for a long time.
I agreed with them.

9.45 p.m. One of my mates, Roger, said, 'let's go over the fair', so
we went over the fair. When we got over there we saw some more
of our mates and they tagged along with us. We stood on the side of
the whip and listened to the records.

10.45 p.m. We all decided to go home.

11.00 p.m. Got in and had a cup of tea, then I went to bed at 11.45.

Each of the 36 boys was incentivised by Willmott's promise of a £2
payment on receipt of a completed diary: cheap, really, at the price.

It was all a world away from being a university student. The diary
of 19-year-old Veronica Lee in summer 1964, centring on herself and
her boyfriend Ricky near the end of their first year at Leeds, gives a
glimpse of what was still for the nation's youth a very minority way
of life: listening with friends to 'a super Bob Dylan L.P.'; a Sunday
afternoon spent reading the upmarket broadsheets ('a killing article
by Frayn on the fashion of bare breasts'); going to the cinema to see
Fellini's 'quite brilliant' 8½ ('I hadn't a clue what was fantasy and
what was reality but it didn't seem to matter'); and, once term had
finished, the two of them hitching to Exeter, involving ten lifts, 'coffee
in Newark and a drink in Warwick', and all going smoothly 'except
for Bristol where we had to walk a long way in the boiling sun'. But
a week later, staying with her parents in the sleepy Devon village of
Shobrooke, the undergrads had an experience which quite possibly
would have resonated with Veronica's fellow diarists in Bethnal Green:

Ricky came into my bed this morning and it was wonderful again.
Unfortunately we feel so unhappy about it. Rick doesn't want to
use contraceptives because he just isn't happy about it anyway and
I'm so afraid we have gone too far. It was a gloomy day. England
lost the Test Match very badly.[5]

*

On Whit Monday, after an afternoon's fishing with the children in
Canvey Island's Small Gains Creek, Pat Scott ended the family's

mini-holiday by taking 'children over to club to see the Johnny Saint & The Sinners Group': 'They were good – so they say – to me they sounded just like the others. Stephen got their autographs.' That same evening, Douglas Wilmer played Sherlock Holmes for the first time (a BBC adaptation of *The Adventure of the Speckled Band*); next day, Tuesday the 19th, the *Telegraph*'s 'Peter Simple' had a satirical pop at 'the new National Union of Dons' no longer accepting 'open adultery with each other's wives or affairs with their pupils' as cause for disciplinary action ('*Does he think that's satire?*' Hull University's librarian asked Monica Jones, 'cos iff he deos hes gott anuhter thikn comig, eh!'); in Wednesday's *Punch*, the radio critic Peter Dickinson noted approvingly of *Today*, still being fronted by Jack de Manio, that 'lately they have been devoting less of their time to total trivia – singing cats and the centenary of the inventor of cheese straws – and more to comment, fairly lightweight, on topicalities that might conceivably matter to someone somewhere'; at the weekend, Norah Buckland and Mary Whitehouse, on behalf of the Women of Britain Clean-Up T.V. Campaign, wrote to the BBC's director-general, Sir Hugh Carleton Greene, saying that they already had 150,000 signatories to their manifesto, that they were looking to him for leadership, and that 'we are not asking for censorship and we do not hanker after "The Old Days" but it is complete fallacy to suggest that the only alternative is a licence which is making its mark on the bodies, minds and characters of young and old alike'; on Monday evening, Anthony Wedgwood Benn and his wife Caroline, 'very discontented' as parents 'with the prospect of Westminster [i.e. Westminster School] for educational, social and political reasons', went as parents to talk with the headmaster of their nearby comprehensive, Holland Park School and, on being shown round, found it 'new and vigorous and active'; Tuesday the 26th saw the opening of the Merrion Centre, acclaimed by the *Yorkshire Evening Post* as the 'greatest commercial development in Leeds for more than a century'; and in Edinburgh next day, the General Assembly of the Church of Scotland formally rejected the petition for ordination presented by Miss Mary Lusk, assistant chaplain to Edinburgh University. 'It assumes that there is a certain definite and limited "place" which is to be given to women in the church,' she had a few days earlier told the all-male assembly about the Kirk's report on her petition. 'Whereas the truth is that we, together with you, fathers and brethren, are the church, and there can be no question of your prescribing for us an appropriate sphere.'[6]

That was not the only Scottish story. On 21 May – the day after a party of 26 senior boys from Buckie High School had finished a two-day tour of Aberdeen's factories ('After tea we set out for home, waving good-bye to every pretty girl that passed, and feeling sad at having to leave the big city,' wrote William McWhirr of IIIA) – the city's Medical Officer of Health, Dr Ian MacQueen, revealed that 12 people were in hospital with typhoid, though adding that there was no cause for alarm. Five days later the tally of confirmed cases was up to 81, with contaminated corned beef identified as the culprit; and on Saturday the 30th, with cases up to 155 confirmed and 44 suspected, MacQueen conceded under pressure at a press conference that Aberdeen was 'a sort of beleaguered city' and appealed to people not to leave or enter without good reason. 'I have eaten in the almost empty dining room of one of the city's largest hotels for the past two days,' noted next day the Sunday Times's Stephen Fay, albeit emphasising that 'though typhoid is the overwhelming subject of conversation', in the city there were 'no obvious signs of panic'. Another week or so of considerable disquiet followed, but from about the 5th the evidence was of a slowing trend in new cases, and by mid-June the city was being described as almost back to normal, with even a few sunbathers on the hitherto deserted beach. Had the whole episode been overhyped by the media, especially with its stress not only on the beleaguered, 'leper colony' aspect, but also on poor housing and sanitation having made Aberdeen ripe for a typhoid outbreak? That would certainly be the retrospective local view, as over the years the episode acquired its own mythology. Yet in any case, things could certainly have taken a worse turn. 'We expected people to die and they didn't,' recalled long afterwards Elizabeth Russell, a young house doctor working in the City Hospital when the first victims arrived. 'It was a mild organism. We were lucky. But it is apparently true that Aberdonians still wash their hands after going to the loo more than people anywhere else in the country.'[7]

Aberdeen's typhoid crisis was just getting critical when, on 29 May, Prince Philip did his ceremonial stuff at Birmingham's Bull Ring, though not without stopping at a winkle stall, hardly the acme of classless modernity. That evening's Any Questions? included the issue of pirate radio stations, with Enoch Powell sanguine about the BBC having its radio monopoly broken, but Labour's Richard Crossman in favour of keeping it, lest the alternative be 'the kind of local sound radio station which they have to suffer under in America'; *The Great War*, a 26-part series marking the fiftieth anniversary, began next evening on BBC 2, immediately becoming the new channel's crown jewel and prompting a housewife to report that she had 'already had requests from young teenage boys for permission to view regularly'; Scobie Breasley on 3 June won his first Derby at his thirteenth attempt, a masterpiece of patience ('I knew I had the race in my pocket') on Santa Claus, with Billy Fury's recently acquired colt, Anselmo, finishing fourth; next day at the Old Bailey, the jury found Detective Sergeant Harold Challenor to be insane and unfit to plead, having been accused of unlawful arrests, false statements and fabrication of evidence in the context of protests the previous summer about the visit of the King and Queen of Greece; and on around Friday the 5th, Virginia Ironside – whose first novel, *Chelsea Bird*, had recently been greeted by *Vogue* as a 'funny, quick and intelligent' portrait of 'the cool, finger-clicking clique' who made up 'the King's Road set' – went to a party in Camden Town given by Nicholas and Claire Tomalin, with guests including Kenneth Allsop, Marc Boxer, Michael Frayn, Jonathan Miller and Bamber Gascoigne. 'What was so depressing,' she recorded, 'was this vast group of successful journalists and things, all university educated, and all feeling GUILTY about being successful journalists and not writing books.' 'Why,' she went on, 'can't they just feel "How great it is to be a successful journalist, what fun it is, all this money, and jollity." Gawd I don't understand. The SHAME just oozed out of them. UGG.' Saturday as usual featured *Juke Box Jury*, with the panel (among them Diana Dors, Jessie Matthews and Charlie Drake) giving a thumbs-down to 'Liza Jane', debut single by David Jones & the King Bees, before Jones himself sportingly emerged from behind the screen to shake their hands; an hour or two later, at Holyport, near Maidenhead, Prince Philip's Rover collided with a Ford Popular driven by William Cooper, a 30-year-old machinist living at the nearby caravan site, but no one (including the Queen) was seriously injured; the following evening, Frankie Vaughan's last-minute replacement, the relatively unknown Irish singer Val Doonican, had an eight-minute slot on *Sunday Night at the London*

Palladium which transported him to instant stardom; and early on Monday the 8th, after serving some six months of her nine-month sentence, Holloway's most famous prisoner was released, an occasion for serious perturbation at a nearby boys' school:

> When I get into my classroom for register [recorded Laurence Marks in his diary], my form master Mr Gore asks where all the boys are? Why are there only six of you in the class? Gander shouts out they've gone to Holloway Prison, about a five minute walk away. Mr Gore asks why and Gander tells him that Christine Keeler is being released at nine o'clock. Mr Gore seems interested, but then who isn't interested in Christine Keeler? So he takes the remaining half dozen of us to the gates of the prison, a sort of school outing, and we actually see Christine Keeler coming through. Mind you, there is a really big crowd out into Camden Road. When the rest of our class sees Mr Gore they make a run for it. I bet they will all be put into detention this afternoon and made to write 100 times 'I mustn't have dirty dreams about Christine Keeler'.

'I wonder what happens to Christine Keeler now she is free again?' added Marks. 'I wish I had brought my Kodak camera with me to capture the moment.'[8]

The new month was also marked, on the 1st itself, by Vauxhall's new Ellesmere Port plant on Merseyside assembling its first Vauxhall cars – starting with the Vauxhall Viva, soon to establish itself as the great rival to the Ford Cortina in the market for mass-produced saloon cars. 'Remarkably light controls and a very flexible engine with strong low-speed torque makes it particularly attractive to women,' noted a few months later an appreciative motoring correspondent, 'and my wife drove it 610 miles in a day with no sign of fatigue.' Relatively few motoring writers, though, focused on the larger urban picture that Colin Buchanan had highlighted the previous autumn in his report on *Traffic in Towns*, an increasingly vexed relationship which, of course, included the problem of congestion. Back in 1962, the transport minister, Ernest Marples, had commissioned R. J. Smeed, deputy director of the British Road Research Laboratory, to study possible methods of charging for road use; and on 10 June the government belatedly and reluctantly published his report. '10s AN HOUR TO DRIVE

IN TOWN CENTRES' was the *Daily Telegraph*'s headline about the 'revolutionary road pricing system' advocated by Smeed, involving 'drivers paying through meters in their vehicles'. But with an autumn election looming, Marples now opted for the safety of the long grass. 'Road-pricing is a considerable time ahead, if it comes at all,' he told a press conference. A direct road-pricing system might, he added, be 'perfect in a perfect world'; but such would be the enforcement problems that really, he concluded, Smeed and his committee had posed more problems than they had solved. Marples himself was fully supported by his leader, with Sir Alec Douglas-Home apparently pledging to 'take a vow that, if we are re-elected, we will never again set up a study like this one'; while across the aisle there was little political appetite to be seen as the motorist's enemy at a time of steadily widening car ownership. Still, the problem of traffic congestion and cities being choked to death was unlikely to go away; and even the *Telegraph*, definitely the motorist's as well as the government's friend, conceded that 'the consequences of doing nothing could be far more frightening than the Smeed Report'.[9]

Smeed coincided with a notably highbrow television moment on the evening of Wednesday the 10th: at 9.45, the programmes on offer from the only three channels were *Bloomsday* (a dramatisation of James Joyce's *Ulysses*) on BBC 1, a dramatisation of H. G. Wells's *Ann Veronica* on BBC 2, and (as part of the *Men of Our Time* series) Malcolm Muggeridge's personal analysis of Stanley Baldwin on ITV. Yet it is salutary that *Bloomsday* received from viewers a dismal RI of 38, with comments such as 'a bore and an ordeal to sit through', 'too odd for my liking' and 'the poor actors doing their very best with such poor material'; while the fact that the day before the *Daily Mirror* had been trumpeting its all-time record circulation of over five million (which in practice meant that some fourteen million, more than a third of the adult population, were reading the paper) perhaps gave an added piquancy to the unrepeatable moment. Viewers this week were more positive (RI of 60) about BBC 2's deliberately informal late-night *Newsroom*, albeit at least one viewer disliking 'the short-sleeves and typewriters constantly in the background'. Dislike, too, elsewhere: from Ian Nairn in Thursday's *Listener* for the 'brutish blocks of flats' being put up in Liverpool to replace the slum terraces (Nairn predicting 'an urban population reacting in loveless

meaningless violence against the up-to-date but loveless environment'); from the critic Laurence Kitchin, giving a talk on Sunday on
the Third Programme for what he saw as an increasing pattern of gra-
tuitous violence in the arts ('the cinema, slowly becoming free from an
embargo on sex, behaves like a voyeur of violence, patently obsessed');
and from the *Mirror* on Monday for the racing driver Jack Sears, test-
driving on the M1 the day before his AC Cobra ('the very thought
of being passed at 183 mph on the public highway must give the
ordinary motorist the willies'). On the evening of Tuesday the 16th,
while the Morden Tower in Newcastle opened on Bloomsday itself
as a soon semi-legendary poetry centre (Pete Brown giving the first
reading), Veronica Lee and Ricky went to the Carlton in Leeds and
saw 'two terrible films – some ghastly, foolish American crap about
a "Yum-yum tree" and then an evil, perverted wicked film "Women
of the world"'. 'The cinema,' she went on, 'smelled very strongly of
tom-cats; there were double seats but we both started itching; there
were two queers sitting in front of us and then four police came in and
removed some youths.'

That same evening, not so many miles away, a truly terrible and evil
thing was happening. Keith Bennett, growing up in the Manchester
suburb of Longsight, had celebrated his twelfth birthday four days
earlier; but now, walking from home to his grandmother's nearby
house, he disappeared – abducted by Myra Hindley, who drove to
a layby on Saddleworth Moor, where Ian Brady sexually assaulted,
killed and buried him. Keith's mother Winnie would spend most of
the rest of her life, until her death in 2012, trying in vain to find his
body and give him a Christian burial.[10]

One issue not disappearing this summer was race; and as it
happened, it was on that Tuesday evening – a month or so after 'My
Boy Lollipop' by Millie (Small) introducing many listeners to Jamaican
bluebeat or ska, had peaked in the charts at no. 2 – that BBC 1 showed
Philip Donnellan's challenging documentary *The Colony*, about West
Indians in Birmingham. 'You can be walking with me, talking with
me, having a drink with me, or invite me to your house', a black man
tells a white man 34 minutes in. 'But the fact still remains you have a
little complex – that you're better than me.' An RI of 63, and though
(according to audience research) some viewers saw the programme
as 'another tiresome example of coloured people "complaining about

their lot when they are so well treated"', the majority welcomed it as 'a step towards the lifting of a barrier'. Was British opinion at last ready to embrace the prospect of becoming a multicultural society? Enoch Powell seemingly hoped so. 'The immigrants who have come already, or who are admitted in the future, *are* part of the community,' he wrote in the *Sunday Times* shortly before the documentary. 'Their most rapid and effective integration is in the interests of all.' Such was not the view of another Conservative politician. 'I do not wish to win by a majority of only two or three thousand,' declared Peter Griffiths in early July, looking ahead to the autumn election. 'There will be so much to do in the years ahead. Smethwick rejects the idea of being a multi-racial society. The Government must be told this.' The probability is that, when it came anyway to white working-class opinion, the Griffiths view chimed the more strongly. An attitude survey conducted in July in Islington, Tottenham and Edmonton, all of them at this stage heavily working-class districts, found that 91 per cent disapproved of mixed marriages. Or take this letter, sent in June by Wilfred Gardiner to a senior shop steward about what had been going on in an area ('the Trentham Paint Shop') of the British Motor Corporation's Austin works in Birmingham:

> For some time a certain grade of workers were promoted according to experiences to piece-work under a particular system, and all went well till my turn came around. First, stewards refused me, (reason) 'Being a coloured man the management won't accept you as a piece worker,' he said, 'And besides, the men won't work with you,' he continued. I then applied direct to the foreman; he in turn turned me down (reason) 'The unions won't accept it'; That's a matter of observation, I replied. He then told me to apply to the Personnel Department, a suggestion that was never offered to any of the fellows that were upgraded instead of me, and to think I was before them all. Finally the steward thought it best to leave the decision to the workers, a section of them who are obviously his supporters. They voted against having me to work with them, or for that matter any 'coloured' as they describe a West Indian.

'I cannot tell you in this letter,' concluded Gardiner, 'all that's being done against justice …'[11]

Natural justice at stake, too, at one of Oxford University's women's colleges, St Hilda's, where on Wednesday, 17 June formal consideration began of whether a pregnant undergraduate, Julia Ballam, would be allowed to return in October for her second year, with the governing body soon afterwards narrowly deciding (almost against precedent) that she could, provided she was married by then; on the 18th, the shadow chancellor, James Callaghan, called on Reginald Maudling and, over a whisky and soda, was assured that the economy was not overheating, even if the balance-of-payments situation was likely to become problematic; Madge Martin in Oxford went on Saturday to the Dragon School's fête in aid of a new swimming pool ('fun, well organised and gay, with John Betjeman arriving by helicopter to open it'), while Kenneth Williams at the Old Vic to see *Othello* was struck by Laurence Olivier's 'incredibly negroid' appearance; 'Beveridge was very costly,' the PM on the 22nd scribbled on a minute and wondered, if his party was re-elected, 'should we not impose our own scheme?'; next evening, Clement Attlee spoke to a group of youngish Labour MPs and, in Benn's words, 'wanted the public schools established as great Commonwealth and international schools to which people would come from all over the world'; *Punch*'s Bernard Hollowood noted with satisfaction on the 24th that 'it hasn't taken BBC 2 very long to rethink its policy, to cut out some of the dead wood and to realise that programmes for minorities need not *create* minorities'; Laurence Marks on Saturday the 27th had his first tantalising glimpse of Carnaby Street and its colourful clothes shops ('I can't get those bottle green, low slung trousers out of my mind, but at 39/11d I am going to have to'); and among those on the *Juke Box Jury* panel later that day was Jimmy Savile. 'More viewers than not,' recorded audience research, 'claim to have found both his manner and appearance "utterly repulsive" and more than once doubts were expressed of his sanity'; while even among the under-twenties 'his grotesque appearance and revolting behaviour was enough to put anybody off the programme, many declared'. 'I gather from photos,' reflected Iris Murdoch next day about the Rolling Stones, 'that they carry ambiguity of appearance to lengths which might satisfy even me'; on Monday the 29th, even as Jane Asher, 'the doctor's daughter with a Beatle boyfriend', told the *Daily Mirror* that 'class doesn't matter any more', the archetypally proletarian Stan Ogden made his debut on

Coronation Street; and that same evening Joe Orton's *Entertaining Mr Sloane* began its West End run at Wyndham's, thereby moving centre stage as a theatrical *cause célèbre*. 'One of the most repellent plays I've ever seen,' thought Anthony Heap, being 'neither funny nor horrifying, but revolting and tedious at the same time'; though this time round, the *Telegraph*'s W. A Darlington was a little kinder ('I was held throughout'), albeit still finding the characters 'shameless and repulsive in the extreme'.[12]

On 1 July, the young Kathleen Perry and a girlfriend 'went for a walk down the Strand & had flap-jacks in a Golden Egg Restaurant'; the new issue of the *Railway Magazine* reported that 15 platelayers working on Glasgow's Pollokshields to Eglinton Street line had been issued with 'a new kind of illuminous safety jacket which shines in half-light conditions' – a first sighting, perhaps in the world, of high-visibility vests; 'I would like to be thought of as a great Englishman,' John Osborne told July's *Vogue*, adding that 'to try to deny one's nationality is like trying to deny one's eyes'; and around this time, the Mothers' Union revealed that in only two out of 13 dioceses were there television-watching groups in favour of the Clean-Up TV Campaign, with those dissenting members especially critical of the passage in the campaign's manifesto accusing BBC television of 'pouring into millions of homes the propaganda of disbelief, doubt and dirt'. Presumably all 13 dioceses shuddered on Saturday the 4th, as the Rolling Stones took over *Juke Box Jury*, voted every record a miss, exuded a sullen indifference and generally (according to the *Daily Mail*) 'scandalized millions of parents'; the same day in Salford, less than five weeks after the demolition of the old Lord Egerton pub, a single-storey prefabricated pub in its place was officially opened; at Braziers Park in the Chilterns, a weekend conference organised by the poet Jeff Nuttall for the purpose of plotting to overthrow 'the system', and with attendees including R. D. Laing, the writer Clancy Sigal and the editor of *Peace News*, Tom McGrath, descended into anarchy, largely thanks to the destructive tendencies of the Scottish novelist Alexander Trocchi; on Monday, the *FT* endorsed Maudling's 'determination that "go" on this occasion should not be followed by a "stop"', while warning against 'growth' proving 'a sloppy synonym for expanding faster than the economy can manage'; a trio of those responsible for the Great Train Robbery, including a fit-looking

Ronnie Biggs, began their appeals against their lengthy sentences; BBC
2 unveiled its latest youthful offering, *The Beat Room*, including this
week the Animals (their 'House of the Rising Sun' poised to go briefly
to no. 1) and Lulu & the Luvvers; and Julia Ballam's mother sent off
a letter to the Principal of St Hilda's, Miss Kathleen Major: 'She is
now married & seems confident that she can cope if she returns at this
Michaelmas Term. It is up to her to do her best, from now on.'[13]

That evening, 12,000 Beatles fans (as well as some Stones fans,
with scuffles duly breaking out) gathered as near as they could
to Leicester Square's London Pavilion Cinema for the premiere,
attended by Princess Margaret, of *A Hard Day's Night*. Directed
by Richard Lester (an American), and with screenplay by Alun
Owen (a Liverpudlian), the black and white film's fast-paced mixture of social realism, humour, poignancy and surrealism made
a sharp contrast with Cliff Richard's recently released, family-
oriented offering: *Wonderful Life*, with its (in the words of cultural
historian Andrew Roberts) 'Canary Island locations, Techniscope
colour and elaborate Hollywood-style choreography', together
with an 'ultimate deference of the young protagonists to middle-
aged authority' which 'made the film look about as fashionable as an
Austin A60 Cambridge'. The crucial, much-cited moment in *A Hard
Day's Night* is when the foursome find themselves sharing a railway
carriage with a middle-aged, bowler-hatted man oozing southern
middle-classness. The initial aggro comes from him (including per-
emptorily closing the compartment window), at which point the
mockery begins. 'I fought the war for your sort,' he says indignantly,
to which Ringo instantly ripostes, 'I bet you're sorry you won!'.
Reviews were largely positive (Penelope Gilliatt hailing 'the first
film in England that has anything like the urgency and dash of an
English popular daily at its best'), though *The Times*'s anonymous
critic could not resist a patronising pat on the head ('the illustrious
four come over agreeably enough as genuine personalities, if hardly
yet as actors'). Four days later, on Friday the 10th, the film had its
northern premiere. 'THE NIGHT OF 100,000 SCREAMS' was the
Liverpool Daily Post's headline, as the Beatles returned home to mass
hysteria after seven months' absence and John called it 'the proudest
moment of our lives'. Within a couple of weeks the single had gone

to no. 1, supplanting the Stones's 'It's All Over Now', and the film was being shown everywhere. 'To this day I think my happiest memory is the night my sister Jackie took me on the 36 bus to the [Peckham] Odeon,' recalled Gary Oldman half a century later about his 6-year-old self. 'I remember clearly waiting in line, then sitting in the audience in that lovely old cinema singing along to all the Beatles songs. Jackie had the album so I knew all the lyrics. I think I was wearing short trousers and a sweater my mother knitted for me. At one point Jackie had to shush me because I was singing so loudly ... I didn't have a care in the world.'[14]

'St Catherine's is pretty ghastly,' wrote James Lees-Milne on Tuesday, 7 July about the 'rough, grim and cold' feel of Oxford's newest (and architecturally much-acclaimed) college. 'The undergraduates' bed-sitting rooms have their outer walls entirely of glass,' he added. 'Shoddiness, shoddiness is the hallmark of all the work in this beastly building.' A few days later, Cecil Beaton struck a similarly disenchanted note, though as much about the old as the new. 'Leeds, Sheffield, the smoking chimneys, wires, derricks, cranes,' he recorded about his recent motoring tour of northern England. 'The clustered villages on slopes of moors, the drab symmetry of slum roads, dark brick walls, mauve-painted doors. The young men of the towns are "beat" in appearance. The population doomed to live here and not liking it any more than I do.' Almost certainly, neither Lees-Milne nor Beaton would have reacted favourably to the boosterish optimism of *Housing in Britain*, a futuristic survey published this week by the Town and Country Planning Association (TCPA). 'A dream home for every family is on its way,' declared the *Evening News*'s enthusiastic summary. 'Millions of families within the next 40 years will have two homes and two cars. And the working week will be cut to only 24 hours – to produce the new leisured class.' Two specific developments, in addition to greater leisure, apparently held the key to future domestic bliss. One, the more predictable, was 'revolutionary labour-saving gadgets and equipment': 'Most families by 2002 will take the luxuries of today for granted. Housewives will at last be emancipated from the kitchen sink and housework drudgery. Rooms will vacuum-clean themselves, food will be prepared and housework done for them. All they do is flick a switch.' The other envisaged development was also technology-based, namely the provision of extra space as and when required:

> You need an extra room – just move the soundproof room partitions around! If you are having a party – take them down and stack them in the garden!
>
> Work on producing these do-it-yourself walls cheaply has already started.
>
> Says the survey: 'By 1982 it is likely that many houses will be built as shells containing the floors and staircase, with traditional internal walls around a bathroom and toilet only. The remaining areas and bedrooms will be left as clear space to be subdivided by the occupier.'
>
> And it may be possible to alter the size of your home by the same method in future ...

The TCPA's crystal ball could detect only one significant flaw. 'The breadwinner of the future is going to have to spend a greater proportion of his income on providing this luxury living.' And accordingly, 'he will be paying a bigger mortgage over a longer period, and putting down a smaller deposit'.[15]

No joy on the 8th for Biggs et al., as the Court of Criminal Appeal upheld the 30-year prison sentences; that evening, Stan Ogden's wife, the more aspirational Hilda (three plaster ducks rising up her living-room 'muriel'), made her belated *Coronation Street* debut, having been delayed by a technicians' strike; on Saturday evening, as those trying to see the Stones at Bridlington's Spa Royal Hall were only allowed in if they were wearing 'orthodox dress' as opposed to jeans or leather jackets, Hughie Green's *Opportunity Knocks*, briefly on ITV in 1956, now returned there for the long haul. Next afternoon, Henry St John, on holiday in Essex, caught a bus from 'thronged' Clacton back to his hotel in Dovercourt and inadvertently sat next to 'a youth, chewing, wearing a tee shirt, imitation black leather jacket and jeans, in a back pocket of which was a coloured comic postcard, with a suggestive "joke" referring to pubic hair'; and the nation digested the front-page story in that day's *Sunday Mirror*. 'PEER AND A GANGSTER: YARD PROBE' was the headline, with the story below claiming that police were investigating an alleged homosexual relationship between a 'prominent peer and a leading thug in the London underworld', though naming neither. Who was the peer? A 'household name', according to the *Mirror*; and the rumour-mill soon lit on Lord Boothby, one-time Conservative private secretary to Churchill and now – as on the evening of Kennedy's death – a leading media personality. As for the unidentified thug, alleged to be involved in a West End protection racket, the guesswork was less confident, for neither Ronnie Kray nor his East End twin Reggie were yet notorious.[16]

Beyond the Fringe, but with none of the original cast, was on at Brighton's Theatre Royal all the following week. David Hare was among a group of Lancing College sixth-formers escorted to it by their inspirational English teacher Donald Bancroft, 'a short, pugnacious Northerner'. The young Hare was astonished when, coming out of the theatre, Bancroft took 'violent exception' to the Peter Cook sketch 'Aftermyth of War', parodying a whole genre of British stiff-upper-lip films about the Second World War. 'Walking away down the street, Donald was puffing at his pipe, saying that the evening was an insult to the brave men and women who had sacrificed their lives for a generation which was now rewarding them with nothing more than mockery and ingratitude.' A 'bewildered' Hare sought to counter him, insisting that the satire was aimed not at the military as such but at 'the ridiculous myths that had been propagated by their phlegmatic misrepresentation in countless bad films and television series since 1945', that in truth it had been 'six years of slaughter and violence', and that it was 'high time' to start seeing the difference between fiction and reality. 'Donald turned to me, unforgiving, still missing the point. "I doubt if you lot would have done any better ..."' The soaps, meanwhile, rolled on: in Tuesday's *Emergency – Ward 10*, a scene in which Dr Giles Farmer was due to kiss and embrace a black female surgeon, Louise Mahler, was excised at the last minute; in Wednesday's *Coronation Street*, no wedding bells for Leonard Swindley (played by Arthur Lowe), with Emily Nugent being afflicted by moral doubts and backing out, also at the last minute. Harold Wilson that same evening gave a TV interview in which he looked ahead Kennedy-style to Labour's first 100 days in power; on Thursday, hottest day of the year so far, a one-day postal strike was part of more protracted industrial action; later on, the Beatles and Dusty Springfield starred on *Top Gear*, BBC radio's new late-night pop offering; next day, 17

July, another pirate radio station, Radio Invicta, launched; and in the course of that Friday, the John Bloom empire collapsed.[17]

*

The writing had been clearly on the wall since the spring. In May, the announcement of very disappointing results for 1963, the share price sharply down, sales of Rolls Razor washing machines a mere 6,504 for the month; in early June, the company's chairman, the Conservative MP Richard Reader Harris, announcing that 'profits so far this year are considerably lower'; and in early July, the announcement at Rolls Razor's annual meeting (held as usual at the company's Cricklewood headquarters) that all five of the non-executive directors, including Reader Harris, were resigning in the interests of 'economy', given the somewhat 'strained' liquid position. Amid all this, on 8 June, Bloom himself starred in the first of a Rediffusion series called *The Young Tigers* about what made a man or woman successful before reaching the age of thirty. 'They're not going to obliterate me – I'm going to be one up on them,' insisted this son of a poor Polish tailor in the East End about the continuing challenge of 'beating the other man who started up with a lot more than me'; and added boldly that he now had 'enough to live comfortably until I'm 432'. Barely a month later, on the hot and humid 17 July, the denouement came, as a board meeting – with Bloom himself absent in Bulgaria, heart of his troubled package-holiday business, but almost certainly in the know – decided there was no alternative but voluntary liquidation. The news was delivered to the Stock Exchange shortly before dealings stopped for the day at 3.30, prompting sell-at-any-price dealers to break into a run to crowd around the jobbers handling Rolls Razor shares. 'The end of Mr John Bloom's direct sales empire,' observed one journalist in a first draft of history, 'has proved as dramatic as its ascent to prominence from the late 1950s.'[18]

A week later, in perhaps the most insightful of the torrent of instant analysis, John Cobb of the *Investors Chronicle* reckoned that Bloom had badly miscalculated on three main fronts: underestimating 'the impact that bad personal publicity had had on his business relationships' (including, Cobb did not add, in the City, still instinctively anti-Semitic and where Rolls Razor's merchant bank, Kleinwort Benson, did not greatly stir itself to mount a rescue); underestimating, too, 'the vigour with which other washing machine manufacturers, selling through normal channels, were prepared to fight back'; and, having 'ridden the crest of the wave with his twin-tub washing machines when they supplanted the separate washing machine and spin dryer', then failing to 'jump in soon enough with a fully automatic machine' – a failure that one business historian, T. A. B. Corley, soon afterwards attributed to inadequate market research. Cobb perhaps underplayed Bloom's increasingly kamikaze pricing policy, with prices lowered to a point where they could not hope to cover costs; but he did, quite rightly, bring out the human factor: 'Bloom needed men capable of overriding his own ego when prudence made it necessary. He failed to find them.'

For the *New Statesman*, in an editorial the week after his fall, the whole Bloom phenomenon had essentially been 'a suitable moral tale to append to 13 years of Tory rule':

Here was an ambitious young man who grew up in the Opportunity State and absorbed its atmosphere of unrestrained commercialism almost in the schoolroom. He had been taught to believe that the best employment for agile brains was to make a million before you were 30 – preferably on a tax-free capital gains basis – and he did it. Having done so, he was then presented by the press and television as a contemporary success-symbol, a love-hate figure inspiring rival emotions of admiration and envy.

Was that the sum of it? Not really, according anyway to Ralph Harris of the free-market Institute of Economic Affairs. That same week, in a letter to *The Times*, he claimed that Bloom's 'invasion – and widening – of the washing machine market' had 'demonstrated how new enterprise can transform an established industry that had allowed costs and prices to get out of hand', that in short he had been 'the victim of his own success in driving competitors to modernise their methods' – a view which Lord Sainsbury, arch-opponent of RPM-busters like Bloom, dismissed next day as more suitable for the pages of *Punch*. Six years later, surveying the decade that had just finished, Bernard Levin would side with Harris, praising Bloom as 'a young and brilliant businessman' who had 'burst violently and cheerfully into the traditional washing-machine market'. So, too, his largely positive obituaries in

2019, one noting that he had 'transformed the way the British buy and sell electrical goods, paving the way for the high-street discount stores of today', while in the process 'effectively abolishing', especially for his relentlessly targeted market of working mothers and newly-weds, 'the drudgery of the old-fashioned "washday"'. Yet perhaps Bloom's greatest virtue was, for all the conspicuous consumption and self-publicising flamboyance, not taking himself too seriously. Or as he put it in 1969, leaving the Old Bailey after eventually being found guilty of making misleading statements to shareholders, 'My biggest mistake was that I was too cocky.'[19]

In July 1964 itself, just as Bloom's star was being extinguished, another's was on its upwards trajectory. 'Since I started operations on March 1 1963, the F.T.-Actuaries All-share index has risen by 9 p.c.,' noted 'Capitalist' in the *Sunday Telegraph* at the start of the month. 'The shares in my portfolio have, during the same period, appreciated by 75 p.c. measured at middle market prices and after all buying costs.' The writer was Jim Slater, not above – it emerged subsequently – either buying the relevant shares shortly before tipping them in his monthly column, or selling them soon afterwards. For Slater himself, 35-year-old son of a sales manager, this was a pivotal time: that spring he had left his post as deputy sales director at Leyland Motors in order to start an investment advisory business; and now, in July, not only did he complete his first asset-stripping exercise, taking control of a 'shell' company called H. Lottery, but he changed its name to Slater, Walker & Co., with Walker being the equally ambitious, equally financially driven (in his case a thriving insurance broking business), and similarly lower-middle-class Conservative politician Peter Walker, in effect a semi-sleeping partner. 'Walker could bring to a partnership with Slater not only valuable contacts in the City, and a considerable experience of the intricacies of raising money, but also a reputation as a thrusting young politician whose name would add lustre to the board of Slater's latest brainchild,' reflected Slater's formidably investigative biographer Charles Raw in 1977. 'For Walker's part, he was no doubt not averse to having his name coupled with Slater's in the title of the new venture: an image of a go-ahead entrepreneur assorted well with the political gospel that he preached.'[20] Together they represented the future – or at the least, one very secular, very unsentimental version of it.

13

Enough to be Going on With

The widespread assumption this summer was that Labour, for a long time ahead in the opinion polls, was poised at last to return to power for the first time since 1951. Many of those 13 years in the political wilderness had been dominated by the running battle between the 'left-wing' traditionalists and the 'right-wing' revisionists, with Aneurin Bevan and Hugh Gaitskell as their respective leaders until their deaths in 1960 and 1963. Harold Wilson's achievement, since becoming party leader in February 1963, had been to consolidate the rather precarious truce of the early 1960s between these two main factions within the party. By summer 1964, what mattered most was not so much Labour's internal state of play, but instead whether it was a party – taken as a whole – ready to face the challenges of government. This is not to deny that the two questions were intimately related, with Wilson himself more keenly aware of that than anyone. 'You must understand,' he had told friends on the left (his historic home) shortly after succeeding Gaitskell, 'that I am running a Bolshevik Revolution with a Tsarist Shadow Cabinet.'[1] A neat trick, deployed by a deft hand. But party management alone was not – and could never be – enough.

*

'A lotus island of easy, tolerant ways, bathed in the golden glow of an imperial sunset' had been Michael Shanks's description of Britain in 1961 in his hugely influential *The Stagnant Society*. A year later, Anthony Sampson's *Anatomy of Britain* had offered broadly the same damning portrait – that of a country potentially in a state of irreversible economic

decline, certainly relative to other comparable economies. The invidiousness was increased by the way in which, across the developed economies in the first half of the 1960s, targets for growth suddenly seemed
all-important, especially after the newly founded OECD [Organisation
for Economic Co-operation and Development] had in 1961 adopted
growth as the goal of all economic policy, with full employment no
longer being considered as a sufficient end in its own right. In fact,
Britain's annual rate of growth between 1957 and 1965 of 3.2 per cent
represented the economy's fastest period of growth since 1870; but the
problem was that rival economies were growing appreciably faster – to
such an extent that Labour, in its election manifesto, would be able to
claim that 'if we had only kept up with the rest of Western Europe since
1951, our national income in 1964 would be one-third more than it is'
and 'we should have available an extra £8,000 million of goods and services to meet Britain's problems and to raise living standards'. Naturally,
the further claim was that, in sharp contrast to the failed 'stop-go' policies of Conservative governments during those 13 years, a Labour
government would be able to reverse this relative decline, essentially
through deeply and permanently modernising the economy. 'Defeatism
will vanish with the advent of a Labour Government,' declared Wilson
in his major January 1964 speech at Swansea on economic policy. And
invoking 'the pioneers of space travel', he insisted that only Labour was
capable of providing the necessary 'thrust' which would ensure that, at
last, Britain could banish 'the idea that the world owes us a living and
that we can muddle on in an amateurish way'.[2]

Coming three months after his immediately celebrated conference speech at Scarborough about how the new Britain was going
to be 'forged' by Labour in 'the white heat' of 'the scientific revolution', Wilson's reference to 'space travel' was no accident. Getting
more scientists, keeping them in Britain, applying the fruits of their
research more 'purposively' to British industry – such were Wilson's
Scarborough specifics as he warmed to this theme. The historian
David Edgerton has persuasively argued that Britain in the early
1960s was in reality *already* 'the scientific and technological power-
house of Western Europe', with R&D spending 'significantly higher
than in any capitalist country other than the USA'; but crucially, that
was not what was widely believed at the time, so that to a large extent,
in terms of public perception, Wilson was kicking at an apparently

open door, especially given science's meritocratic, non-Establishment connotations. Among his instant converts was Frank Cousins, leader of the biggest trade union, the Transport and General Workers' Union (T&G). 'I think it is a great thing that we are taking science as our main theme,' he asserted later that day, enthusiastically calling it 'a vision with its working clothes on' as he looked ahead to 'a new social order with science as its background'. In July 1964, Wilson offered Cousins the new position of Minister of Technology should Labour win the coming election, an offer Cousins soon afterwards accepted. It was an appointment, reflected William Rees-Mogg three decades later, which unmistakeably revealed that Wilson 'could not be serious' about technological development. 'No one less suitable for that purpose than Frank Cousins could have been found; the appointment was merely a manoeuvre to keep the support of left-wing trade unions.'

Yet perhaps that is to underestimate Wilson's genuine commitment to regenerating Britain by encouraging and stimulating new technology. His father was an industrial chemist; at Oxford, as a youthful would-be economist, he had focused on the pace of technological change; through the 1950s, he had consistently attacked the Tories for their lack of scientific grasp; and in 1960, telling his party's conference that 'socialism must be harnessed to science and science to socialism', he had declared that 'the world into which we are moving is a world characterized by a scientific revolution beyond the dreams of a generation ago'.[3] In short, in this area anyway, he was a visionary as well as a political realist; and, whether inside or outside his party, it was a vision of widespread appeal.

The other central pillar of what a Labour-run economy would in theory look like was also taking shape by summer 1964. Economic planning had been largely marginalised in Labour thinking during the 1950s, especially on the part of centre-right revisionists like Anthony Crosland, whose *The Future of Socialism* (1956) had argued that, in the context of full employment and the Welfare State, there was little need to go beyond Keynesian demand management of the economy. But the 'declinism' of the early 1960s – to which Macmillan's government responded by setting up the corporatist National Economic Development Council ('Neddy'), seeking mutually beneficial engagement between employers and unions – changed everything, with planning moving to the core of the Labour approach. 'The problems we are facing underline the need for effective economic planning covering industrial policy, financial policy, and the application of science to industry,' insisted Wilson in his Swansea speech. 'This is why,' he went on, 'we have been thinking in terms of a Ministry of Economic Planning, under a senior Minister, to ensure that an effective national plan is worked out for production, exports, imports, capital investment, and industrial training and technological research.' In short, 'what Neddy has begun, this Ministry must carry through to completion, with effective powers for the job.'

Wilson was indeed by now thinking in such terms, having in effect bought into the 'productionist' argument that unless the Treasury's powers were significantly reduced, then it would be impossible to have an effective growth-oriented economy – as opposed to one in which the brakes were slammed on at the faintest sign of domestic inflation or trouble in the foreign exchange markets. By the time the election was only a few months away, three things were clear: that the new ministry would be known as the Department of Economic Affairs (DEA); that George Brown, Labour's deputy leader, was lined up to be the minister in charge; and that central government was going to play a much more active role than in the case of Neddy, though it was as yet uncertain whether that role would be French-style *dirigiste* planning or more a case of so-called 'indicative' planning – the latter being planning (to quote the economic historian Jim Tomlinson) 'whose prime purpose was educational: to demonstrate the benefits of future expansion, and by that very demonstration hope to motivate its achievement'. Either way, would it work? Even in 1963, the shrewd and experienced economist-cum-banker-cum-public-servant Sir Eric Roll, having been approached to be the putative DEA's permanent secretary, was sceptical, telling Brown that a department lacking control over the three main instruments of economic policy – interest rates, the exchange rate and the Budget – was unlikely to get the better of the Treasury, controlling all three; while, for all his intended recruitment of gifted outsiders, much would depend on the gifted but flawed Brown himself.[4]

A palpable sense of excitement, not to mention controversy and discord, for the most part no longer extended to the time-honoured question (Clause Four and all that) of public ownership. By the mid-1960s, the focus on the issue was, in intention anyway, predominantly technocratic: how could the nationalised industries, controlling some 40 per cent of the national total of fixed capital, best serve Labour's ambition to be the party of permanent growth? Tellingly, the long-standing commitment to renationalise the iron and steel industry – a commitment at the very most only tepidly supported by the electorate – was more than just a tactical sop to Labour's potentially disgruntled left wing; it also had a genuine economic rationale, including a belief that restoring the industry to public ownership would, among other benefits, reduce the need for steel imports, enable the development of larger and more modern steel plants, and stimulate greater technical innovation; while more generally, as Wilson had told curious readers of the *New York Times* only a fortnight or so before his 'white heat' speech, the whole matter of nationalisation was something to be flexible and pragmatic about, and no longer 'dogmatic and doctrinaire'.

The underlying problem here, though, was a continuing inadequacy of policy formation to take into government. 'There was a very wide range of literature on the nationalised industries, much of it by Labour supporters and sympathisers, but this had not led to a clear and agreed policy position,' notes Tomlinson on the situation by 1964. 'There was an instinctive distaste for the extent to which the Conservatives had emphasised their commercial nature, but no agreement on how Labour should change this, or with what it should be replaced.' The experience of two Labour-backing economists, Michael Posner and Richard Pryke, was instructive. Financial targets, they argued in these pre-election years, did not necessarily lead to better management, given that nationalised industries could always raise prices in order to get round such targets. Instead, they contended, a methodology of efficiency audits, together with scrutinising each decision in broader economic terms (essentially through marginal pricing as opposed to overall average pricing), was a better way forward. They ran, however, into consistent opposition from Wilson's long-standing economic adviser, Thomas Balogh, adamant that their approach to defining 'efficiency' would only serve to thwart public enterprise. 'The public sector will make a vital contribution to the national plan,' Labour's election manifesto would unequivocally declare; but precisely how remained far from certain.[5]

What about the private sector? Back in 1950, Wilson had reflected that 'in this problem of the relation between Government and private

industry we have what is almost a vacuum in Socialist thought'; yet
14 years later, neither his Swansea speech nor the election manifesto
specifically focused on this undeniably important area. Even so,
Labour's thinking *had* developed. During much of the 1950s, and
heavily influenced by Anthony Crosland's revisionist analysis, the
prevailing view was that capitalism was becoming less red in tooth and
claw, especially in the context of the increasing divorce between ownership and control, thereby allowing 'managerialism' – often reasonably progressive and enlightened – to flourish. But in the early 1960s,
once declinism had set in, British capitalism started to come under
a significant degree of fire: lacking accountability; failing to respond
adequately to the scientific revolution; and too often (in the words of
Labour's 1961 *Signposts for the Sixties* which in effect provided the
foundation of the party's 1964 offer to the electorate) 'dominated by
a small ruling caste', needing via a 'major shake-up at the top' to give
way to 'the keen young executives, production engineers and scientists
who are at present denied their legitimate prospects for promotion'.

Yet how, apart from that shake-up of personnel, to make the private sector more efficient? Labour's answer was partly to treat education as much as an 'investment', with an increasingly vocational
purpose (often of a 'tech' nature), as an intrinsic good; partly to ensure
more generally the provision of skills (Wilson telling his Welsh audience that 'to make the best of our brilliant scientists is vital, but it is
just as important to train our great army of technicians, craftsmen,
and skilled workers'); and above all, to pursue *scale*, whether via
mergers or otherwise, in order to achieve the necessary modernisation – through greater investment, through greater R&D – of British
industry. Unfortunately, argues Tomlinson, there were four serious
internal contradictions at the heart of Labour's relationship with the
private sector: between the need to raise investment and an abiding
mistrust of the profit motive; between 'big is beautiful' for economic
reasons and a view of big corporations as overly powerful for all
sorts of other reasons; between a broad acceptance-cum-welcoming
of the new managerialism and the socialist need to have out-and-
out capitalists as their enemy; and between regulation (generally
welcomed) and competition (generally less so). The overall effect,
plausibly maintains another historian, Tudor Jones, was to render
Labour 'less capable than its socialist counterparts in central and

northern Europe of adapting with either enthusiasm or conviction to the principles and practices of a market-led mixed economy'.[6] Still, a spell in power would at least give an opportunity to work through those contradictions where it counted.

Labour was perhaps on firmer ground, at least in theory, when it came to the question of a counter-inflationary incomes policy. After all, the Tories had tried and failed, introducing their 'pay pause' in July 1961 only to have to abandon it ignominiously nine months later; whereas Labour could reasonably claim that, with the party's far closer ties to the trade unions, it could better achieve a workable policy. Inevitably, it was not quite so simple. Although at Scarborough in 1963 the shadow chancellor, James Callaghan, did echo Frank Cousins's phrase about 'a planned growth of wages', the T&G's leader was adamant that the unions would continue to determine wages by 'sitting opposite the employers' – in other words, engaging in that exercise of free collective bargaining so deep in the soul of organised labour – 'until such time as the system changes to ensure that we do get a better rate of return for the labour that we put in'. In May 1964, Wilson and Wedgwood Benn attended an informal dinner at the Connaught Hotel with eight *Guardian* journalists (all of them male, including John Cole and Brian Redhead), where Wilson spoke about various aspects of a future Labour government. 'Incomes policy involves close negotiation with the trade union leaders in the first instance, and the hammering out of the programme which they will accept in the new atmosphere of a new Government,' paraphrased Benn in his diary. 'Public support for this wages policy can be expected to last for at least eighteen months.' Thereafter, continued Wilson, 'people will have to get used to the fact that they may be taking their rise in living standards in the form of social dividends rather than in the form of personal income.'

Similarly hopeful, whatever the evidence to the contrary, was Jim Northcott, a youngish Labour Party researcher whose *Why Labour?* appeared as a Penguin Special around the same time. 'Just because one attempt at an incomes policy has failed, it does not follow at all that nothing of value can be done,' he declared, calling on a future Labour administration to 'give the right lead':

If the Government is resolutely set on rapid economic expansion (so that instead of a bleak freeze there is room for some pay increases for all, and for big increases for some); if it brings in unions and employers so that their cooperation is assured from the beginning; if it creates with its tax and social policies a background of increasing social justice; if it applies its policy, fairly and consistently, not only to the public sector, but also to the private, not only to wages and salaries, but also to income from rent, interest, dividends, and capital gains; if its policy is clearly and fully explained and seen to be practical and sensible and fair – then there is no reason why it should not be freely and effectively accepted.

'This is something,' he added, 'which has been done successfully abroad.' Would Cousins, poised by late summer to become a minister within a matter of weeks, now give some ground? Apparently not, as at the annual Trades Union Congress, at Blackpool in early September, he moved the resolution opposing all forms of wage restraint; at which point, the warning words of the Labour frontbencher Michael Stewart suddenly seemed prescient. 'The Labour Party in office has to have a policy for incomes,' he had observed the previous year in an internal paper. 'It may possibly get into office without committing itself on what it would do; but it would then *have* to do something, and ear-stroking of individual trade union leaders when big claims are put forward is not going to help very much.'[7]

Still more potentially discombobulating to a prospective Labour government was the question of sterling. 'All of us know, and the world knows, that a further devaluation would not be like the last one – a readjustment forced on us four years after the war by the consequences of the war and a hungry post-war world,' Wilson – a minister at the time of that 1949 devaluation – told the Commons in 1961. 'A second devaluation would be regarded all over the world as an acknowledgement of defeat, a recognition that we were not on a springboard but on a slide.' Even so, because of the clear deflationary implications of defending an overvalued pound, the issue was being actively discussed, albeit seldom if ever publicly, by Labour during the year and a half before the 1964 election. 'I am the last survivor of a meeting held in the bowels of the Palace of Westminster immediately after Maudling's 1963 Budget speech,' Anthony Murray recalled in 2018. ' "Will we have to have an early devaluation?" asked Jim Callaghan. Nicholas Kaldor, shaking with suppressed laughter, said,

"We shall certainly have to have an early devaluation. What we are considering now is whether we shall need a *late* devaluation as well." ' Kaldor was but one of Labour-sympathising economists pushing the idea that it would be better for a Labour government to grasp immediately the nettle of devaluing the pound, generally reckoned to be beneficial to exporters, *before* it was forced to do so (whether once or even twice); but the three key politicians – Wilson himself, plus Callaghan and Brown – remained unconvinced, with Anthony Crosland among those adding their private voices to the economists but failing to persuade the troika. A concern to play by the rules of the international financial game and thus not alienate the markets and the central bankers; a fear of the long-lasting political damage if Labour became labelled as the party of devaluation, with all its connotations of national humiliation and the 'soft option'; a preference for long-term structural solutions to the ailments of the British economy; and the strong possibility that devaluation would have to be accompanied by serious cutbacks in domestic consumption – such were perhaps the main reasons why Wilson and the others held firm.

Undeniably, for all the understandable concern about scare-mongering in the right-wing press about the probability of capital flight in the event of a Labour victory, it was a policy stance which transcended the purely rational. 'A difficulty in discussing devaluation as a real possibility for an actual currency (as opposed to an exercise in one of those mental gymnasiums of theory equipped with lots of elasticities and very few countries) is that there is so much emotional capital invested in the exchange rate,' reflected a youngish and leftish Australian-cum-Oxford economist, Christopher ('Kit') McMahon, in his 1964 book *Sterling in the Sixties*. That September, not long after its publication, he moved to the Bank of England, whose patrician gov-ernor, Lord Cromer, had forcibly reminded the Treasury two months earlier that the Bank's fundamental priority – to uphold 'the inter-national standing and use of sterling' – would stay unchanged whoever won the election. 'It was rather an emotional place then,' remembered McMahon years later about the hermetic, anti-intellectual Old Lady of the mid-1960s, 'and merely to mention devaluation was like saying a four-letter word in church.'[8] The relationship between previous Labour governments and the City had been largely poor, even hos-tile; and the determination not to devalue in effect signalled a wish for less choppy waters ahead, quite apart from a sentimental attachment to Britain continuing – even eight years after the Suez Crisis – to play a major role, military and diplomatic as well as financial, on the world stage.

Long after the 1960s had played out, there would be few fiercer retrospective critics of the Labour front bench than Edmund Dell, himself a Labour minister in the 1970s. 'They knew nothing about industry,' he insisted in a 1997 symposium about the historical lessons for New Labour. 'They didn't know what an industrial policy should consist of. They didn't know how long it would take an industrial policy to take effect. They imagined that if they had an industrial policy they would be able to get away without devaluation, even though we were in a state of fundamental disequilibrium.' One of those frontbenchers was Richard Marsh, who in his 1978 autobiography not only took a similar line ('very few members of that Government in 1964 had had recent experience of industrial or commercial activity'), but also argued that, in addition, Labour at that time had lacked 'sufficient resources' to enable it to 'seriously question or argue with the massive Civil Service machine', citing the Industrial Training Bill as a typical example. 'The costings of the Labour Party's proposals in 1964 were far more than the country could possibly accommodate. This was not surprising given the way they had been developed. Each set of proposals had been produced by small groups of people in their spare time, frequently in meetings in London hotels on wet Sunday afternoons, with very little research support.' David Edgerton goes further, claiming that the 'notoriously low' levels of education within the Labour Party, in part because of a reliance (except in the field of welfare policy) on 'state experts rather than on its own', meant that 'one looks in vain (until the 1970s) for an elaborated set of arguments from the left for alternative ways of running the economy to that practised by the Conservatives in the 1950s, except for making general arguments about planning and putting the interests of the nation first'. 'What is harder still to find,' he goes on, 'is anyone setting out a general case, and methods, for a new national calculus which would work out what was best for the nation in terms of both equity and efficiency' – a shortfall epitomised by the lack of 'distinctive criteria for nationalised industries, though they were nationalised on the basis that they should indeed be run on principles concerning their national importance'.

Given that Callaghan as shadow chancellor plunged himself into a series of economic seminars at Oxford's Nuffield College, it is tempting to argue that he perhaps exaggerates; though the economist Ian Little, who organised those steep-learning-curve sessions, would recall ruefully that Callaghan 'tended to steer the argument into political channels before all the economic issues had been fully explored'. What about Wilson himself? Dell's verdict – 'a statistician marketing himself as an economist' who was still stuck in the Attlee era and had never 'understood the full implications of the fact that his economic management, did he ever come to power, would take place in a more open economy than he had left in 1951' – was damning, with probably an uncomfortably strong element of truth.[9] Even without the economy under Maudling's stewardship being in a dangerously overheated state, it would not have been all that difficult in the late summer of 1964 to predict that an imminent Labour government was liable to stand or fall by the quality and effectiveness of that economic management.

*

Of course, such concerns were not really at the heart of the New Jerusalem dream, or at least once full peacetime employment had been more or less achieved on a seemingly permanent basis. Rather, that dream was about cradle-to-grave security; about more and better housing; about an active, informed and responsible citizenry; and about greater equality. It was over these and related areas, not the question of what to do about a deteriorating balance-of-payments position, that many left or leftish pulses were – after almost 13 years of Conservative rule – now quickening.

Nothing carried a greater emotional weight than the pursuit of greater equality, whether of outcome or of opportunity. 'If you don't feel strongly about equality,' Hugh Gaitskell had written in 1956 soon after succeeding Clement Attlee as Labour leader, 'then I think it is very hard to be a genuine Socialist, and if we were to abandon this, then I think there would be very little left to distinguish us from the Tories.' Eight years on, Labour's concept of equality was still essentially class-based, with little focus on either racial equality or gender equality. 'Concern with the effect of full employment and affluence

on the working classes after 1945 rarely extended beyond the traditional boundaries of male workers, despite the effect these had on the
female population,' reflect Amy Black and Stephen Brooke in their
survey of this latter vacuum in Labour thinking and policies between
1951 and 1966. 'The new realities of working-class communities,' they
elaborate, 'included profound transformations in gender relations,
whether through changes in the physical geography of such communities through housing programmes, the impact of the welfare state,
affluence, and increasingly liberal mores on the patterns of family
and sexual life, and, not least, the continuing process of "deskilling"
in industry and the increasing number of full- or part-time married
women workers in the economy.' All of these aspects, and many
more, were largely marginalised, as also were Labour's organisations
for women, traditionally separate from the main party structure. 'We
all run our women's conferences,' complained in 1964 one of Labour's
still relatively rare female MPs, Lena Jeger, 'as if only women cared
about children, as if men were not parents, as if consumer protection was entirely the affair of tired, little women with string bags; as
if the soft-faced men who did well out of the war had nothing to do
with costs and prices and profit and values; as if no man ever bought
mutton-labelled lamb or cared about how his wife was looked after at
the maternity hospitals ...' 'Presumably,' she went on in sarcastic vein
to her female audience, 'you neglect Southern Rhodesia, EFTA [the
European Free Trade Association], Algeria and unemployed school
leavers to concentrate on the price of cabbages and the quality of
nappies, and then the men will pat your shoulders and say you are a
"splendid little woman."'[10]

How by this time, then, did the male-dominated, male-oriented
Labour Party envisage achieving, especially for the working class, a
greater measure of equality? Predicated on the hoped-for fruits of a
planned and fast-growing economy, it identified three main possible
ways: through fiscal means; through welfare provision; and through
structural reform in the education system.

'The standard of fairness we ought to adopt,' a delegate told the
Scarborough conference in October 1963, 'should be to shift the
burden of taxation from those who earn their living by work by
hand or by brain, to those who derive their income from speculation or title to wealth.' In fact, the Conservative government had

the previous year, largely to try to get the trade unions on-side and accept pay restraint, brought in a capitals tax (CGT); but in practical operation it was so focused on short-term speculative gains as to be more or less voluntary, thereby leaving the ground clear for Labour to propose something more long term, more thoroughgoing and thus potentially more redistributive. 'The present situation where the largest gains are made, not through hard work but through the untaxed rewards of passive ownership or Stock Exchange speculation, must be ended,' duly declared the eventual election manifesto about the intention to tax capital gains. By contrast, there was at this stage relatively little serious political appetite for a wealth tax on the largest private fortunes, a tax viewed as less relevant than CGT to securing consent for an incomes policy; but there did exist a potentially greater appetite for a bespoke corporation tax. 'Between 1951 and 1962,' noted Jim Northcott in his *Why Labour?* Penguin Special, 'revenue from income tax and surtax on individuals more than doubled, while revenue from income tax and profits tax on companies rose by only a quarter.' Even so, when it came to it, the manifesto entirely omitted to mention the possibility of such a tax.

Indeed, more generally, it does seem that in these years leading up to the 1964 election, Labour's whole approach to the question of taxation was essentially flawed: far too much reliance on an external tax expert in the person of the economist Nicholas Kaldor; relatively little discussion on the subject; and what there was betraying what Tomlinson has characterised as 'a strong but perhaps naïve faith in the redistributive capacity of direct taxation', especially given problems of evasion as well as the steady fall since the mid-1950s in the income tax threshold, thereby making the main means of direct taxation a less than progressive instrument. Altogether, he plausibly contends about Labour and taxation, 'very little attempt was made to look at this issue at all systematically' – including, of course, in relation to the uncomfortable, time-honoured conundrum of whether egalitarian-minded taxation was realistically likely to improve rates of investment and of economic growth in ways which went beyond short-term economic management.[11]

What about the role of welfare? 'Social policy was,' argues one historian, Howard Glennerster, 'even more central to the Labour Party's ideology in the 1960s than it had been in the 1940s'; further, during these intervening years 'the emphasis of Labour policy began to shift to a greater concern with equality in society rather than merely equality of access to state services.' It was inequality in social security – a sense of two nations, notwithstanding the intended universality of the modern welfare state – which in 1964 particularly concerned Northcott, who identified 'sharply contrasting welfare provisions':

> On the one hand are those in private schemes, some of whom are very generously provided for. On the other hand are the rest, who must rely on the increasingly inadequate provisions made by the community. And the gap between these two standards of provision is growing wider all the time. It is both incongruous and tragic that as the nation grows richer it should at the same time be more deeply divided between those who have adequate provision for their social security and those who, usually through no fault of their own, have not.

By this time, confirming the important policy document which Richard Crossman had launched in April 1963, Wilson was publicly committed to two potentially major reforms. 'In the long run,' he told a large audience at Birmingham Town Hall in January 1964 as he set out his 'New Britain' vision, 'our system of graded benefits and graded pensions will ensure half-pay in retirement, in sickness and old age, to the average paid worker, and rather more than half-pay at somewhat reduced contributions to those whose earnings are at the lower end of the scale'; while as for the short term, namely 'the urgent problems of existing pensioners', Wilson promised that 'one of our first acts will be to introduce what we call the "income guarantee", a guaranteed minimum income available to them all'.

The story of how these two ambitious pledges came to be made, and what then happened to them after the election, is told by Stephen Thornton. His account emphasises the difficult circumstances by 1964: not only the startling growth of private sector pension membership (some eight million in 1956, but over twelve million by 1967), but also how what he calls 'the Beveridge strait-jacket', in other words the state pension's deliberately low flat-rate levels, was liable to have the effect of prioritising an improvement in basic benefit rates over more radical reforms. Nor did it help, here as in some other areas, that

Labour in opposition had been so short of detailed policy-planning human resources that by the time of the election its plans for social security were still, as Thornton puts it, 'rather muddled'. 'The basic point remains,' observed in March 1964 a senior official at the Ministry of Pensions and National Insurance after scrutinising the proposals, 'that the Labour Party has not committed itself to any details of how its scheme would work or how benefit calculations would be made.'[12] Seven months later, on election day, that was still essentially the case.

The third main way of pursuing greater equality was – in the year that the PM's nephew, Robin Douglas-Home, published a novel, *Hot for Certainties*, acclaimed by Frederic Raphael as a 'savage' attack on the public school system – an old chestnut. 'Once they are free from dependence and fees,' predicted Northcott hopefully, 'the public schools should be able to make a greater contribution to the nation's education, without being unfair or consolidating social divisions'; and soon afterwards, the manifesto devoted all of one sentence to the matter, asserting that Labour in power would set up 'an educational trust' – whatever precisely that meant – 'to advise on the best way of integrating the public schools into the state system of education'. It was, of course, a difficult and invidious issue, though surely among the most important in the whole post-war story, whether in terms of equality of opportunity or, ultimately, equality of outcome.

'The vice of British education,' declared Richard Crossman (himself a Wykehamist) in January 1964, 'is the educational apartheid which divides our children into two nations from the age of five'; while that spring he was appearing on *Any Questions?* when a member of the audience at Bristol Cathedral School (a direct-grant grammar school) asked, 'Does the panel think that since the majority of our national leaders send their children to fee-paying schools, this is a vote of no-confidence in the state system of education?' In response, he did not deny the truth of the question, before adding that 'the biggest job of the next Government after the next election is to end this appalling separation which creates this appalling problem which parents have to face today'. The public schools themselves were understandably anxious about what lay ahead, and not long before the election a few headmasters invited Crossman and George Brown to a London club in order to elicit their views. Brown, a governor of Repton College (situated in his Belper constituency), was no revolutionary on this question, so the real interest lay in his colleague. 'Crossman turned out to be a devotee of the new comprehensives, in which he felt sure the brilliant, given good teachers, could flourish just as well as in the scholars' "College" at Winchester,' recalled one of those heads present. 'The independent schools would have to become comprehensive, even if it took some time. They did not have to be abolished, but they must change radically. He talked fluently, listened not at all, and left quite early.'

All the time, irrespective of Labour's willingness and readiness – or otherwise – to achieve integration, a larger irony was unfolding. Whatever the rights and wrongs of the 11-plus system, to which Labour was now unequivocally committed to abolishing, the fact was that between 1959 and 1967 the public schools' share of Oxbridge places fell from 55 to 38 per cent; and it was grammar-school products who almost entirely made up the difference. 'My friends and competitors were as likely – possibly more likely – to come from the great Lancashire and Midlands grammar schools as from my old school or Winchester or Harrow,' William Waldegrave would remember about his experience in the mid-1960s of leaving Eton and going up to Corpus Christi, Oxford. 'They were confident, clever and at least as widely cultured as we were ...' In the event, a meritocratic takeover – or, at the least, a serious challenge – was soon to be stopped in its tracks. This is not for a moment to say that there were not other ways available in which the historic engines of privilege could have been made much less egregiously powerful; but for all the inherent flaws of counter-factual history, it was still a resonant retrospective calculation, on the part of one leading public-school headmaster, Eric Anderson, that '60 per cent of the public schools would have gone under if the grammar schools had remained'.[13]

Yet, of course, over and above specific policy issues, more fundamental questions were still in play – not least whether Labour by 1964 was at last in something like sync, which palpably in 1959 it had not been, with what, taken as a whole, was becoming a more affluent, more mobile, more privatised society than Britain had been in the immediate post-war years? Wilson's modernising, 'white heat' agenda certainly helped to give the impression that, as the country had changed, so too had the party. But in truth, it remained to a significant extent a party – indeed, a whole labour movement – stuck in a puritanical

A mother and her five daughters outside their house. Manchester, 1963.

A woman washes some clothes in a deep sink at the Boundary Street Area Laundry, in Bethnal Green. London, 1964.

Crowds gather to watch firemen fight the blaze at a fashion store in Oxford Street, holding up the arrival of an ambulance and several fire engines. London, 2 March 1963.

A dalek prowls the streets. London, 20 August 1964.

Julie Christie and Dirk Bogarde in between takes of John Schlesinger's film, *Darling*, outside Lord's cricket ground in St John's Wood. London, 29 September 1964.

A northern wind. Leeds, February 1965.

At the tills. Cardiff, 16 May 1963.

Pat Swindells and her children on their way home. Salford, November 1964.

Jimmy Greaves running out at Old Trafford, as Tottenham Hotspur are about to play Manchester United. Manchester, 26 September 1964.

Landscapes old and new. Newcastle, 1962.

Christine Keeler and Mandy Rice-Davies in a pub near the Old Bailey during a lunch break in the trial of Stephen Ward. London, 22 July 1963.

Northern shops. 1962–65

Stanley Matthews playing for Stoke City five days after his fiftieth birthday. Stoke-on-Trent, 6 February 1965.

past: instinctively mistrustful of, and often condescending towards, not only consumerism, but also such regrettable phenomena as television (especially the commercial variety), suburbia and popular and youth culture. 'Affluence, whether washing machines, rock 'n' roll or home ownership, did not have innate political meaning,' observes Lawrence Black at the end of his definitive study, *The Political Culture of the Left in Affluent Britain, 1951–64*. 'Rather, the left contrived to alienate itself from affluence by describing it so unfavourably.'

Nor did it help that Labour still possessed, in some seemingly hard-wired way, the top-down, statist assumptions – about the nature of public ownership, about the workings of the welfare state, even about cultural hierarchies – that had so characterised the well-meaning, progressive 'activators' of the 1940s and had prompted Michael Young, author of Labour's 1945 manifesto, to move away from high politics. Democracy, he had argued three years later in his seminal *Small Man, Big World*, would work only if it was practised on a human scale; the needs of the family, in all their diversity, should be at the heart of Labour policy; and it was a central task of public intellectuals, whether himself or others, to understand the lives and aspirations of the people.

In 1964 itself, a kind of flashlight moment came on the second Friday in September. Was, asked a member of the *Any Questions?* audience in the Memorial Hall, West Parley, Dorset, the building of large council estates the right way to house people unable to buy a property, 'or is this another case of setting people apart rather than forming an integral society?' 'We all like the idea of a multi-class society, an integrated society, and in many ways it's almost certainly a better one,' responded the always perceptive critic and novelist Marghanita Laski, before going on:

> But this doesn't seem to be what most people prefer today. You have examples like Stevenage New Town, for instance, which was definitely planned with houses for rent for all economic classes of the community. And after it had been running a very few years, the richer people moved out and preferred to live elsewhere. And it has been said – and considerable interviewing has been done by both sides – by the richer and the poorer, that they would sooner live apart. This doesn't seem the most hopeful or pleasant thing that

we could wish, but there certainly does seem to be a strong tendency today in this direction. When it comes down to it, the people
who are actually concerned don't seem to want – at least in urban
communities – to live in multi-class societies. I believe they're the
poorer for it, but people must, to some extent, do what they want.

A fellow panellist, the up-and-coming, modernising Labour politician Richard Marsh, would have none of it, attacking as 'silly simple
snobbery' the idea that 'there's a difference between the little council
house occupier and the little owner-occupier'. 'People have got to live
somewhere,' he continued, 'let's cut out this silly idea that you can
divide the British people into little watertight compartments – some
nice people live here and some other people not quite so nice live somewhere else. Let's mix them all up together and I think everybody'll
benefit as a result of it.'

Let's mix them all up together ... A noble aspiration, as Laski
agreed; but her scepticism about whether that was what a deeply
class-conscious, status-conscious society really wanted was surely
justified. Ultimately, indeed, can one really be sure that the majority
of people, when it came to it, truly desired greater equality of outcome? Certainly not most of the middle class (the carnivores anyway,
as opposed to the herbivores); certainly not the skilled working class,
resolutely determined to maintain wage differentials; and perhaps not
even the unskilled working class – stubbornly more interested, in the
mordant but quite possibly not inaccurate words of the High Tory
commentator T. E. Utley, 'in the inequality of horses than the equality
of men'.[14] Uncomfortable truths, all of them, but at this stage only
barely acknowledged, if that. The obvious danger, though, is of being
too binary. 'Socialism', after all, meant many different things to many
different people; while various, too, and not necessarily compatible
with each other, were the reasons – and emotions – for sustaining a
close involvement with Britain's main left-of-centre party. At this particular point, with Labour on the cusp of returning from the political
wilderness, a quartet of men represented, in their contrasting ways, a
range of possible 'socialist' futures: Harold Wilson, Frank Cousins,
Anthony Crosland – and, much less high-profile, the late David Logan.

'Socialism, as I understand it, means applying a sense of purpose
to our national life,' Wilson told his Birmingham audience in January

1964. 'Purpose,' he went on, 'means technical skill', and he set out an explicitly meritocratic vision: 'If you fly the Atlantic in a jet, you want to be sure the pilot knows his job, that he's been trained for it. If you're in hospital, you feel more confident if you know that the surgeon has given his lifetime to fitting himself for his work. Pilot or surgeon: it matters not who his father was, or what school he went to, or who his friends are.' But at the same time, Wilson emphasised that this was 'not to equate, as our opponents affect to do, Socialism with technocracy': 'The essential leavening which Socialism brings to the industrial revolution of our age is the leavening of humanity, which was so clearly absent from Britain's first industrial revolution.'

Yet was Wilson, in any meaningful sense, a man of definite and determined political vision? Richard Crossman for one was doubtful, calling him in February 1963, just before he became leader, 'certainly not an intellectual', but instead 'an agile manoeuvrer and something of the demagogue'; while Benn in his diary, between April and June 1964, successively described Wilson as temperamentally unwilling 'to fight a stand-up battle with his colleagues for the things in which he believes', as informing disappointed *Guardian* journalists that 'there were no votes from a Labour point of view in being very tough with the public schools', and as 'so terribly conservative' when it came to any questions of constitutional reform. A perhaps more disinterested perspective was that of the journalist Geoffrey Goodman, who had got to know Wilson reasonably well since the early 1950s. In his retrospective account, he would agree that Labour's leader had been 'never very strong on socialist theories', and was 'no philosopher or political poet in the genre of a Bevan', that indeed there was 'none of the revolutionary romantic in the Wilson bloodstream'. Goodman added, though, a crucial rider: 'What he did eventually develop was a tremendous instinct to understand what the Labour Party was all about: social justice rather than revolution. He saw the Labour Party as the instrument to correct social injustice and in that sense economic inequality.' Such, in short, was 'the essence of Wilsonian socialism'.

Even so, it was not an essence which necessarily always came out strongly – or at least as strongly as some might have wished – in 1964 itself. 'I've been digging for your vision: what is it, Mr Wilson?' a palpably rather frustrated Brian Blake (of the BBC's North Regional Staff) asked him that February at the end of a lengthy interview:

It's [replied Wilson] a vision – this may be a shock to some people – it's a vision, I think, that has got a certain nationalist streak in it. I want to see Britain stand for something. There is an international vision because of the problem of world hunger, world peace, but I am nationalist enough, or I have enough national pride, to feel that Britain has got to play a very big part in all of this. You might call me a Little Englander in consequence, but that is part of my vision. The other is a vision in which every family has got a chance to live its life in the way it wants, without the unemployment and the insecurity that we knew in bygone years, without having to wait ten or fifteen years on the waiting list for a house – because there's no family life until you have a home of your own, with the kids having a real opportunity to develop whatever talents are in them. But beyond that, I think we've got to think not only in terms of our working life and what we are going to earn, and what we are going to produce, but in terms of the fuller use of the leisure that I hope the scientific revolution is going to create. That is my vision for this country.

'Is it enough?' asked Blake. 'I think,' came back the answer, 'it's enough to be going on with.'[15]

Frank Cousins, strongly left-wing leader since 1956 of the giant T&G union, might well have been among the doubters, given how disappointing he had found his 1963 Scarborough conversation ('not talking the same language') with Wilson's shadow chancellor, James Callaghan. The mismatch was unsurprising, albeit Callaghan and he shared similarly ungilded backgrounds. In 1964 an *Observer* profile of Cousins, after explaining how he had 'learned his Socialism the hard way' – 'He was born the eldest of 10 children of a Nottingham miner and himself went down the pit at the age of 14: his trade unionism still has that totally loyal, coal-scarred, aggressive edge about it that people only seem to learn in the mining areas' – stressed how 'uncompromising' his socialist beliefs were. Yet what, from precisely that day in Scarborough, gave a whole extra dimension to those beliefs was 'white heat' itself, with its beguiling promise to harness socialism with science in a mutually beneficial way. 'After nearly a decade in office, a period dominated almost entirely by his struggle to disentangle trade union thinking from past myths and its own defensiveness, Cousins now began to feel that there was at last a remarkable opportunity for further advance,' noted (in 1979) Geoffrey Goodman in arguably the key passage of his exhaustive and almost wholly sympathetic biography of Cousins:

> He somehow felt that industrial modernisation, by its very nature, would compel fundamental changes in the organisation of British society; that the changes already taking place in the struggles of industry, powered as they would be increasingly by scientific innovation and the need for capital resources beyond the means of conventional capitalism, would bring nearer the day of socialism in Britain. He was enough of a Marxist to believe that the growth of technology and the rise in working-class living standards and opportunities would not erode the 'need for socialism', as some claimed, but would, in fact, provide a necessary foundation for it. The vision was there, even if the blueprint was not. For neither Frank Cousins nor anyone else on the Left in the Labour Movement had sat down to work out a precise political and economic framework; nobody had faced up to the contradictions and complexities involved in trying to transform the system into a socialist one. They sensed that a 'new order' was arriving and that this must inevitably expedite progress towards socialism, but no one knew quite how this was to be achieved ...

'The attractions of vague terms such as "technology", "science", "a new order" were,' further reflected Goodman, 'tempting and often overwhelming ... The road to socialism seemed to be paved with computers. By some alchemy of electronic magic – it was even contemplated – capitalism itself, and its social mores, might be undermined not by class war or revolution but by the inevitabilities of science and the demands of industrial modernisation, forcing economic and political change on a hitherto unthinkable scale.'[16] Cousins, as Goodman made clear, was far from the only socialist to be seduced in this way; but even at the time, let alone how things panned out, he was probably the most important.

'White heat' does not seem to have particularly stirred Anthony Crosland, firmly established as Labour's philosopher-king since *The Future of Socialism*, his 1956 tour de force. By the early to mid-1960s he was still – especially as revealed in *The Conservative Enemy* (1962), sub-titled *A Programme of Radical Reform for the 1960s* – broadly on the same revisionist tack: on the one hand, adamant as a live-and-let-live social liberal that continuing denigration by his party of affluence and the affluent fatally showed a 'priggish self-satisfaction, a contempt for the judgement of ordinary people and an indifference to their interests'; on the other, a committed egalitarian highlighting as 'offensive to compassion and humanity, let alone to socialist principles' what he described as 'the contrast between the ample and often luxurious lives of the better-off classes, and the constricting circumstances of the "submerged tenth" still lacerated by poverty or filthy housing'. Nothing, to judge by this book, got more under his skin than the public schools – 'this privileged stratum of education, the exclusive preserve of the wealthier classes, socially and physically segregated from the state educational system, is the greatest single cause of stratification and class-consciousness in Britain' – and he demanded that a future Labour government 'assimilate them into the state sector', 'democratize their entry and so destroy their present socially exclusive character' and 'create a more genuine equality of opportunity by limiting the power of the rich to buy social privilege through buying a privileged education'. Crosland's was, in the round, a bracing vision. Yet it was also, in some fundamental sense, a paternalist and even snobbish one. A devotee of great architecture, he wanted city centres to 'preserve what beauty we still have left, and create a little more', even as he spoke dismissively of northern cities, with their 'unsightly miles of dismal Victorian housing, schools, chapels, mills, factories and industrial debris'; he condemned advertising outright as 'fatuous', 'raucous', 'misleading' and 'totally false'; and he endorsed as 'surely right' the BBC's underlying post-war Reithian mission that its audiences would over time steadily graduate upwards, typically on the radio from the easy listening of the Light Programme to eventually the intellectual uplands of the Third.[17] Whole tracts of northern cities may have been ugly, advertising may not always have been entirely truthful, much of the Light's offerings may have been undemanding pap – but that did not mean that the typical Labour voter did not want or expect them as part of their lives.

The improvement of minds had never been at the top of Davie Logan's agenda. 'Alderman Logan, who lived in Rycroft Road, Fazakerley,

Liverpool, amid the terraced houses and fish and chip shops which make up Scotland Road, the constituency he has represented since T. P. O'Connor resigned thirty-five years ago, began his political life in 1885, from which time he took part in every election in the division,' recorded an obituary of this staunchly Catholic son of a ship's cook, after he had died in February 1964 at the age of ninety-two. By profession a pawnbroker, he had indeed been Liverpool Scotland's MP since 1929; and a third of a century later, a future *Guardian* editor, Peter Preston, got to know him. 'What a tale he might tell – except that he didn't,' recalled Preston a further three decades on about this 'wizened scrap' of a man, memories prompted by watching in 1996 the first episode of *Our Friends in the North*:

> He had his memory. He still had his seat in Parliament. But there wasn't an ounce of romance to a relentlessly matter-of-fact rendition of meetings attended and decisions reached. He had never thought of himself as a player on any kind of political stage. He went here and there, did this and that; and habitually came back to Scotland Road where his constituents queued for interviews. Kindly, shrewd, diligent: without a sliver of vaulting emotion ...

'They built things and knocked things down,' added Preston about Logan and his patient, pragmatic, incremental, non-ideological like – still in 1964, for all the party's increasing middle-classness, the beating heart of Labour. 'Today they'd be knocking down the things they built. They wouldn't begin to understand stakeholder economics; but nor would they give Arthur Scargill the time of day. Get on with it lad. Get bloody weaving. And turn that stupid TV off.'[18]

*

Then, as ever, the Labour Party was far from comprising the entirety of the British left. Even so, its apparent imminence to power did see a significant shift towards the party by at least some independent socialists – including among what remained of the 'First' New Left, which since 1961, five years after the Soviet invasion of Hungary that had led to its creation, had been in perceptible decline. One such, albeit very much on his own terms, was the political scientist Ralph Miliband, father of

David and Ed. A Jewish refugee from Nazism, he had fully set out his
stall in his 1961 book *Parliamentary Socialism*, in effect a sustained,
historically based Marxist attack on how Labour's unbending 'devo-
tion' since 1900 to the parliamentary system had inevitably led to a
whole series of compromises and accommodations ('The Sickness
of Labourism') which had fundamentally undermined its effectiveness as an anti-capitalist political party. But by December 1963, after
attending a semi-private meeting with Wilson, he was starting to think
that there might be possibilities in some kind of 'serious Left parliamentary lobby if and when a Labour Government comes in'. 'The
one thing that may be said for Wilson,' he continued to a friend, 'is
that, being such an opportunist, being in effect the very epitome of
Centrism, real pressure from the Left might find him receptive – but it
will have to be real pressure, well organised and clear-sighted ...' Four
months later, Miliband and the labour historian John Saville (a key
figure in founding the New Left) co-edited the *Socialist Register*, the
first issue of a long-standing annual series; and in their own article they
urged 'the creation and proliferation of Labour Left pressure groups,
made up of constituency and trade union activists, *for limited purposes
and in relation to specific issues*', such as steel nationalisation. Among
those reviewing the symposium as a whole was Albert Hanson, professor of politics at Leeds University. 'The central weakness is that
no one tries to answer the question "What is socialism?",' he wrote
in the *TLS*. 'Throughout, there is an assumption that some kind of
"socialist" answer exists to every problem. Not one of these writers
clearly explains why the particular solution of his choice should be
labelled "socialist", and there is never the hint of the existence of any
problem which cannot be satisfactorily understood by the application
of socialist criteria.' And, fairly or otherwise, he concluded that 'the
reader interested in discovering the precise purposes of a group of
radical writers is at least entitled to a reasonably careful definition of
the nature of their politico-economic ideals'.[19]

In around 1963, the 20-year-old future historian Sheila Rowbotham
was a fascinated observer, in the front room of E. P. Thompson's
Halifax home, of two other key New Left figures:

Lawrence Daly, dark, burly and balding, sat heavy and still in the
armchair, a powerful, purposeful man. Edward [Thompson], in

contrast, spoke and moved quickly, jabbing the air as if he was trying to break through some invisible barrier. They were talking about a break in the New Left, about how they had wanted a very different, much broader movement. Their lives had gone separate ways; Lawrence was preoccupied with the union now. Edward looked down, his head on one side, and said that a chance had been missed. I was too shy to ask what he meant. 'We failed,' he remarked to the floor, and then turned and looked at me as if they were including me in the conversation.

Daly had, ever since the New Left's creation, been its emblematic working-class representative; and his Fife Socialist League, challenging Labour/Communist electoral dominance in West Fife, had been the New Left's major – arguably sole – organisational achievement. But by this time, he was indeed increasingly focused on union matters. In early 1964, after going down the pit for the last time as a working miner, he became (having won the election by a big majority) general secretary for the Scottish area of the National Union of Mineworkers; the Fife Socialist League was dissolved that spring; and in late July, while on holiday in an old cottage up in the hills of Glen Lethnot, he explained at length to a sympathetic friend where he now was politically following the League's dissolution:

> We might have taken a different view if, since 1957, we had seen any real sign of the emergence of a new, Socialist force on a national scale. But our hopes that the New Left might be the basis for such proved vain. The New Left Review is now in the hands of some young academics whose chief attribute, as you obviously recognise, is their ability to make simple statements sound quite unintelligible ...
>
> I just cannot see them organising a MOVEMENT, for they seem to possess no organisational talent and they still have no clearly-defined ideological position. They claim a vague type of Marxism and recently appear to be flirting mildly with Maoism. I am hoping rather desperately that they will not swing suddenly from philosophic anarchy to political dogma.

Accordingly, though noting the emergence of the *Socialist Register* as a welcome contrast to the *New Left Review*, Daly saw no alternative but to apply 'collective action along Socialist lines ... from *inside* the Labour Party': 'Minority groups on the Left, who dared make an electoral challenge in May [a reference to the recent local elections], were severely repulsed and I think the "Be loyal to Labour" call will be more powerful than ever for the first two or three years of a Wilson Government. I don't think the other Left groups are going to do much more than sloganize.' Overall, it was not a prospect about which this charismatic but clear-sighted man felt hugely enthusiastic. 'I am not optimistic about any rapid advance for the Left in Britain in the near future,' he ended, 'but I feel our task must be to strengthen political consciousness in the Trade Unions and local L.P.'s.'[20]

Little optimism, too, from Thompson. Why, by around this 1963/4 time, just as his epic *The Making of the English Working Class* was establishing him almost overnight as the country's leading social historian, did he believe that he and his comrades had 'failed'? Partly no doubt because of the New Left's lack of tangible achievement; partly because of the way in which it had fissured, including over control of the *New Left Review*, leaving him a somewhat isolated presence; partly because his recently acquired membership of the Labour Party felt like an admission of defeat; and partly because, for 'socialists like ourselves', as he told Daly on New Year's Eve 1963, 'everything is rigged against our political intervention for some time ahead'. A further cause of Thompsonian despair (emotions never knowingly undercooked) was, in the course of 1964, the series of articles by Perry Anderson and Tom Nairn in the *New Left Review* – written individually, but soon known collectively as the Anderson–Nairn theses. The most celebrated was Anderson's 'Origins of the Present Crisis', offering a reading of English history in which, over some three centuries, 'a supine bourgeoisie produced a subordinate proletariat', as the latter tamely accepted 'timid and dreary' Fabian gradualism, ultimately leading to twentieth-century 'Labourism', loftily condemned by the wealthy, intellectually gifted Old Etonian as 'most stolid and mundane of political movements'. That appeared in the *NLR*'s January/February issue; and it was followed, almost certainly arousing Thompson's even greater ire, by Nairn's take on 'The English Working Class', in effect accusing him of having failed in *Making* to acknowledge on the one hand the extent to which the working class remained in subjection to the bourgeoisie, on the other hand the extent to which that working class needed what Nairn called 'theory' if it was ever to escape a controlling hegemony. Certainly, neither Anderson nor Nairn invested any real hope in a future Labour government. Did Thompson himself have any such hope? Perhaps just a little, especially through the person and agency of his pet working-class leader. 'IF from your position in the Scottish NUM and Fife (& presumably Labour Party) you were able to put pressure on a Wilson Govt to do any of these things: a) Introduce new industries to Fife under new forms of *municipal* or perhaps co-operative control; b) Introduce new experimental forms of democratic control in selected pits – it seems to me that this would give a point of real leadership to the movement in the country,' he had written to Daly in that New Year's Eve despatch from Halifax. 'We have talked in general terms about these things for long enough,' he went on. 'What we now require is real examples and experiments ...'[21]

It was not quite a vision – and undeniably it had little in common with that of a younger member of the New Left. Likewise a historian (though in his case only just starting out as one), the mercurial Raphael Samuel sent a memorable letter to the sociologist Peter Willmott in spring 1964 shortly after the GLC elections had seen 94,000 Londoners, especially in middle-class suburbs, vote for Communist candidates. 'I must admit that – with everything I think about the CP itself – I find the fact intensely encouraging,' he declared, before going on:

The entire English class system may be on the point of going into reverse. The middle class plainly *wants* to identify with the working class ... And when you think of Hoggart and the Institute [of Community Studies]; and of *Saturday Night and Sunday Morning* and Joan Littlewood; and of *Coronation Street*, isn't it plain that there have been deep cultural preparations for what is, otherwise, so surprising a change? Why should everyone want to go on being more and more middle class? Isn't it possible that people trapped in those giant blocks along London Wall would prefer to install a silk weaver's loom, say, or an engineering lathe? that they would like the computers to give the wrong answers?; and the lifts to dawdle at each floor? ...

The revolution, plainly, is preparing; and it will be a quiet revolution; a very English revolution, circumspect and unobtrusive – understated, one might say. People will simply stay at home, pottering about in the garden every day, instead of going up to town. The telephones will stop ringing; the discrete office commands will go unheeded; gentility will vanish and bluntness will be the order of the day.

Fast as Mr Wilson seeks to abolish the old working class, a new one will arise. Tall factory chimneys will trail smoke over Croydon; there will be pit shafts and furnaces; the spacious gardens of, say, Norwood – or Sutton and Cheam (where a Communist polled 2,500 votes) – will be filled in with back alleys and Roller Skating boys ... The fitted carpets will be taken out of the pubs; the frosted glass restored ...[22]

In 1964 itself, all this was, of course, an idle dream; yet as a romantic left-cum-counter-cultural dream for taking back control from a particular version of modernity, it accurately reflected the impulses of an increasingly radically minded younger generation, largely unmoved by the traditional language and assumptions of British socialism.

14

So Much Better in our Own Caravan

Britain in summer 1964: not exactly a liberal place. At a school in Chester, on a sunny day near the end of term, 11-year-old Martin Newell was day-dreaming in the back row waiting for an English lesson to begin. The usual form teacher was away, so instead it was Mrs Lightfoot in charge. 'She's middle-aged, wears a black cardigan, a tweedy skirt and spectacles. We've heard that she's nice.' Suddenly, though, she apparently spotted something she did not like and started walking in Newell's direction:

> She speeds up through the aisle between the desks, intent on remedying whatever it is she's seen at the back of the classroom. Perhaps one of the paintings behind me is hanging crooked. She's moving faster, getting closer. She'd better slow down soon, or she'll hit the wall. She stops just in front of my little desk. She draws back her hand, and she slaps me full force on my left cheek.
>
> The result is dramatic. My face is burning with embarrassment. There's a high-pitched whine in my left ear, a tear is pushing its way out of my eye and I'm having difficulty catching my breath. The sound of the slap seems to echo round the classroom. By the time I focus, she's back in front of the class, looking at me sternly. She spits, 'no one smiles in my class.' I am completely confused. Has she made a mistake? Was I really smiling? This is Martin Newell, good boy, not usually in trouble for much. What have I done. Numb with shock, I sit there in absolute silence, trying to look like I'm paying attention. But the lesson does not begin.

Instead, still staring at me, she says, 'I think we are waiting for something.' Maybe she's going to pick on someone else. 'I am still waiting.' I'm scared now. I think I'm going to piss myself with fear. I have no idea what this woman wants. She asks my friend Steven, 'Steven, do you know what we are waiting for?'

Steve mumbles, 'Yes, Miss.'

She asks Duncan and David. They both seem to know what we are waiting for. She focuses on me again. 'Martin Newell, are you so stupid that you still don't know what we are waiting for?' In a shaky voice, I tell her that I am sorry but I really do not know. 'Tell him, Steven.'

Steven speaks up a little. 'An apology, Miss?' I am completely confused now. She's belted me full in the face, for no reason that I can think of and she wants me to apologise.

She stares at me again. 'Well?' I open my mouth but no words come, the lump in my throat feels like it will choke me. Tears course down my burning face as I try to say the required words, but nothing comes. She realises I am broken and contents herself with 'I'll be keeping a close eye on you from now on, my lad.'

A few weeks later, at 8 a.m. on 13 August, two young men met the ultimate punishment: Peter Allen at Liverpool's Walton Prison and Gwynne Evans at Manchester's Strangeways. They were a pair of petty criminals whose planned robbery had gone wrong, resulting in the violent death of a middle-aged Cumbrian laundry van driver, John ('Jack') West. 'At the last minute he seemed to make some sort of effort to throw himself, but he didn't get a chance,' recalled in 2014 former prison officer George Donaldson about the hanging of Evans. 'The lever dropped, the door opened and down he went. It was all over.' Later that month, in Southall, bus driver Amar Singh was sent home from work for not wearing the regulation cap. 'I cannot believe that there is so much discrimination and prejudice in such a civilized and cultured society, and that a person cannot have freedom to practise his own faith,' he told the *Middlesex County Times*. 'Is it a crime to be honest and practise one's faith? London Transport say they want their employees to be happy, and to wear my turban would make me so.'[1]

*

During this time, between roughly mid-July and mid-September, there was still plenty of unfinished business left over from the first half of the summer. An intense autumn of party politics awaited, but temporarily anyway the nation's attention lay elsewhere. In South Wales, following criticism in a local paper, an array of teenagers vigorously defended the Rolling Stones's provocative appearance on *Juke Box Jury* ('they could have changed to gain the admiration of the adults,' declared Martyn Powell of Pwllgwaun, Pontypridd, 'but they were courageous enough not to'); in north-west Essex and east Hertfordshire, the likely downside of siting London's third airport at Stansted at last registered ('it is not meet,' preached the Vicar of Broxted, 'to take the children's bread and cast it to the dogs'); in *Emergency – Ward 10*, or, rather, in the hospital garden just outside, the white doctor and the black surgeon at last got to be seen kissing; and, after the *Sunday Mirror* allegations had, quite justifiably, caused him to be linked with the East End gangster Ronnie Kray, the seldom publicity-shy Bob Boothby magnanimously accepted an out-of-court settlement of £40,000. 'If one is incapacitated for life by the negligence of a motorist,' observed Evelyn Waugh, 'one is lucky to get £4,000.' Still, on 27 July, one political moment – coming almost a quarter of a century after his and his country's finest hour – did perhaps cut through. 'During Question Time he seemed anxious to know whether anybody was talking about him,' noted the Conservative MP Sir John Langford-Holt, before sitting with Churchill 'for about an hour in the Smoking Room'. Gerald Scarfe marked the occasion with a wholly unsentimental sketch of a senile and decrepit near-nonagenarian on his last day in the Commons; *The Times*, which had commissioned him, rejected it; and it was left to Peter Cook to put it on the cover of *Private Eye*.[2]

The modern stopped for no one. At 1 p.m. on Thursday the 30th, three days after Churchill's parliamentary farewell, Blackburn's telephone system belatedly switched over to STD (subscriber trunk dialling), enabling subscribers to make trunk calls direct instead of having to go via an operator and ask for a number. 'Bring all of Britain (and in time the Continent too) to your fingertips,' boasted a Post Office pamphlet; while at the formal ceremony opening the new telephone exchange in Jubilee Street, attended by the usual civic dignitaries as well as 'leading personalities in business and professional life', the senior telecommunications superintendent, Mr J. C. Singleton, had an important message: 'The person at the other end must remember not to hang up when he hears the pips – he must realise it is somebody trying to reach him from a coin box.' Some five weeks later, far higher pro-file was the opening by the Queen of the Forth Road Bridge. It linked South Queensferry, near Edinburgh, to North Queensferry, across the River Forth in Fife; it was Europe's longest suspension bridge; seven men had died in its construction; unlike almost all road bridges in England, it involved significant payment by motorists; posters with the nationalist message '2s 6d toll – it's time we voted SNP' were vis-ible along the royal route; and the Queen herself, after being driven over the bridge, made the return journey on the last of the ferries that had been crossing the Forth for nine centuries. Ian Jack, who had spent much of his childhood in North Queensferry (shadowed by the epic Victorian engineering feat, the Forth Railway Bridge), was pre-sent that foggy day. 'A large part of the reasoning for the road bridge,' he later acknowledged, 'was the need to remove Fife's insularity – the county is bounded on three sides by estuaries and sea.' Even so, 'what happened besides was that Fife became a dormitory for Edinburgh', as 'housing estates spread haphazardly across farmland remote from public transport but near new roads'. In short: 'Fife was never the same again.'

Restless times also on the small screen. On *Coronation Street*, Jack Rosenthal coming up with a playful pastiche of *High Noon* (Len Fairclough a reluctant Gary Cooper); Ken Loach directing some of the episodes of *Diary of a Young Man*, a six-part series by Troy Kennedy Martin and John McGrath which used voice-over commen-tary and still pictures as a deliberate attack on TV drama's naturalist conventions; and the arrival on BBC 2 of *Late Night Line-Up*, an almost instant monument to 'sixties' liberal humanism, as open-ended as the hours it kept, in which a regular team (soon including Michael Dean, Joan Bakewell and Tony Bilbow) would, along with much else, lead discussion and interviews about the evening's programmes, on ITV as well as BBC. No newcomer, though, attracted more attention than BBC 1's twice-weekly serial *Swizzlewick*, about a corrupt local council in a fictional Midlands market town, but with Mary Whitehouse as a palpable side-target in the character of the busy-body Mrs Felicity Smallgood, for ever on the lookout for immoral behaviour. Critical reaction was epitomised by *Punch*'s Alan Coren claiming that, 'having trouble with my craw', he could barely write about it; while among the Viewing Panel, the comedy-drama began on 18 August with a poor Reaction Index of 40 ('neither dramatic nor comical') and got worse, down by 8 September to a desperate 25 ('this load of tripe ... this feeble series ... just a lot of silly nonsense'). Still, not everyone watching it, or indeed any programme, reached for the 'off' switch, to judge by the BBC's director of television, Kenneth Adam, who in *The Times* reckoned that a sizeable minority of viewers were 'addicts': not only persistently complaining that each night their fix closed down too early, but during a recent technicians' strike even willing to turn on just to look at the test card.[3]

Elsewhere across the cultural landscape, the *TLS*'s glowing review of Margaret Drabble's *The Garrick Year* ('she has the cogency of an Iris Murdoch without the creamy symbolism') contrasted sharply with its view of Murdoch's own *The Italian Girl* (too much 'mere preposterous contrivance', even 'unintentional comedy of events'); Adrian Mitchell enthused over B. S. Johnson's novel *Albert Angelo* ('his writing sings ... he walks like a fiery elephant'); Penelope Gilliatt was surprisingly tolerant about *Carry On Spying* (eighth in the series, but a career-changing debut in it for Barbara Windsor), noting generally of their broad appeal that 'the comedy is appallingly laborious and planted, but it makes millions of people laugh more than a first-rate free-wheeling wit like the Goons' or a first-rate piece of plot-making like Feydeau's'; on the Home Service, *The Critics* belatedly discussed Joe Orton's *Entertaining Mr Sloane* ('really very funny,' thought John Gross, but 'brutal, unpleasant, and infinitely unfunny' according to Pamela Hansford Johnson); for Alan Brien, the main attractions of the London first night of Alan Ayckbourn's *Mr Whatnot* ('has a taste rather like Vitrac diluted with cherryade') were Ronnie Barker ('milks all he can from the role of the old-fashioned buffer') and 'a very pretty and bright girl called Judy Cornwell whom I have never seen before and would like some time to come across in a play'; while at Drury Lane, the Lerner and Loewe musical *Camelot* received a dusty response from Bamber Gascoigne ('intensely boring ... the tinselly settings, jokes, lyrics and tunes seem more suited to a pantomime and Snow White than to a modern musical and King Arthur').[4] All paled, though, this late summer compared to two major theatrical events.

'Peter Brook's staggering production is masterly in its manipulation of sound and movement and its perfectly co-ordinated teamwork,' wrote Anthony Heap on 20 August after the first night of 'a remarkable theatrical experience' at the Aldwych in which 'Glenda Jackson cuts a poignantly pathetic figure as Charlotte Corday'. The RSC's *The Persecution and Murder of Marat as Performed by the Inmates of the Asylum of Charenton under the Direction of the Marquis de Sade*, immediately controversial and soon known as *The Marat/Sade*, was adapted by Adrian Mitchell from Peter Weiss's original; set indeed in the bath house of an asylum, it marked the *ne plus ultra* of Brook's 'theatre of cruelty'; and among the company, Diana Rigg was so disappointed not to play Corday that not long afterwards she headed towards television. Not every critic loved it, but none denied its visceral impact. 'Mr Brook's collection of deformed lunatics, with their crippled limbs and writhing mouths, and their pints of blood, red, blue and black, acting a revolutionary play written by de Sade, are a terrifying spectacle,' recorded Harold Hobson. 'When they advanced on the audience at the end, homicidal and convulsive, I nearly died of fright.' Altogether, the experience came as close as perhaps anything could to 'total theatre', helped by the brilliance of the stage designer Sally Jacobs, who (in her obituarist's words) 'placed the extraordinary ensemble riot of orgiastic violence, disputation and lunacy on a pattern of small pools sunk in the floor, covered with duckboards, with benches around the periphery, pipes and water jets everywhere, a fully lit stage, no props, no black-out in the audience, and no curtain'.

Just under three weeks later, Heap was at another first night. 'Not so much a play,' he noted after returning home from the Royal Court, 'as a long, wearisome series of monologues, diatribes and one-sided telephone conversations artlessly designed to vent the author's social spleen and air his jaundiced views on life in general.' In short: 'Formless, plotless, pretentious, incoherent, tedious and monotonous, the piece appears to possess neither point nor purpose.' Yet as ever with a John Osborne play, *Inadmissible Evidence* (with a superb Nicol Williamson as the main character, the middle-aged Bill Maitland) had its defenders – not just some of the critics ('a modern *Peer Gynt*,' claimed Bernard Levin), but someone seldom associated with modern drama. 'Apart from the sentiments in the diatribe – which I heartily endorse – it is the most heart-rending and tender study of every man who is not atrophied,' John Betjeman wrote immediately afterwards to Osborne. 'We want to avoid giving pain and we want to be left in peace. Love makes us restless and we resist it. I felt increasingly that the play was about *me* ...' What about the first-night audience as a whole? Taking keen notes, and reckoning that the playwright was 'rather disastrously' ahead of the faithful, was *Punch*'s temporary drama critic:

> The audience was uniquely the Royal Court claque – unpretentiously pretentious, come to worship the cardboard rebel with which they have so often been confronted in the press. This bleak, grim but, more important, compassionate play had them worried. What was he trying to do? Were we meant to take this seriously? Or laugh continuously perhaps? Every reference to the *Daily Express*, or Godfrey Winn, every Osborne epigram was seized on not only with delight but also with relief. Now they knew what their leader wanted them to do.

'The intellectual snobbery – it's not social snobbery – that makes ice-cream sales so low at the Royal Court made the theatre the wrong place for *Inadmissible Evidence*,' concluded David Frost, given that 'what the audience wanted was a lot more good straightforward bitterness about the *Sunday Times*' colour supplement.'[5]

The Beatles continued to occupy a significant chunk of the nation's head space. 'They are not charming, not handsome ... they are not witty,' declared in early August the *Daily Mail*'s TV critic Monica Furlong after watching an interview. 'I would rather have listened to Wilde or Shaw or Chesterton or Sydney Smith talk for ten minutes, than have an hour in the company of these four monumental bores.' Tellingly, the flood of letters over the next few days broke five to one in her favour. Even some teenagers might have nodded their heads. 'The music was terrific but at times I disliked the Beatles themselves as they were so rude, especially John Lennon,' reflected Veronica Lee at about the same time after going to Exeter to see *A Hard Day's Night*. 'Ringo,' she conceded, 'was surprisingly pleasant.' Either way, a critical mass of new London-based groups, and not just the Stones, was now poised for great things. On 28 July, as they all played with their own obscure groups at the Albion in Rainham, 17-year-old Steve

Marriott first encountered two future Small Faces in Ronnie Lane and Kenny Jones; Manfred Mann in mid-August had their first no. 1 with 'Do Wah Diddy Diddy'; and in early-to-mid-September (exact date unknown), Pete Townshend of the High Numbers (not yet the Who) smashed up his guitar for the first time before a handful of Mods at the Railway Tavern outside Harrow and Wealdstone station. Above all, there were the Kinks, in time the most 'British' of groups. Written and sung by Ray Davies, but owing much of its considerable instant impact to his brother Dave's fuzz guitar riff, 'You Really Got Me' was released on 4 August and by the end of the month was storming to the top of the charts. 'I never thought we'd get this far,' Ray told NME as it was clear they had a hit on their hands. 'Course, our parents are pleased at what's happened. They can't quite believe it. They keep going around mumbling, "Strewth, that mob have actually got a job." They can't quite believe it.'[6]

Sport this August featured two resonant, essentially northern moments. 'Test Match relatively exciting as Trueman got his 300 wickets,' recorded Lee on Saturday the 15th about events at The Oval where England were playing Australia. 'Occasions like that are always quite emotive as the commentators make so much of it.' They did indeed, including John Arlott on the radio as he acclaimed 'Fred Trueman's 300th Test wicket – the first man in the history of cricket to achieve this figure'. Trueman himself, a Yorkshire miner's son through and through, celebrated that evening by going to *The Black and White Minstrel Show* at the Victoria Palace. 'Ladies and gentlemen,' announced his friend Leslie Crowther at the end, 'in the wings stands a great man who has just achieved a record in cricket that has never been done before'; and, to a standing ovation, Trueman came on to the stage in tears. A week later, the focus was Anfield, where the defending league champions hosted Arsenal. 'Welcome to *Match of the Day*, the first of a weekly series on BBC2,' declared Kenneth Wolstenholme as he introduced the highlights. 'As you can hear, we are in Beatleville.' With the new channel still unavailable on the great majority of TV sets, only 75,000 watched; but it was the start of a Saturday evening institution, and a turning point in football's hitherto uncertain and suspicious relationship with television, duly commemorated by a 3–2 win for Liverpool against a background of the swaying Kop lustily singing away to Beatles and Gerry and the Pacemakers songs.[7]

For millions, of course, these late-summer weeks were holiday time, which among many other things meant it was carnival time. The annual Salford Carnival saw Miss Jennifer Jones crowned Carnival Queen by the ubiquitous Jimmy Savile; at 'Carnival Saturday' in Bognor Regis, the Fire Brigade Social Club deserved better than second place for their washing-machine-themed float, complete with a topical banner ('BLOOM, BOOM, DOOM') running its entire length; while at the Isle of Sheppey and Sheerness-on-Sea Carnival, the local paper noted 'disturbing gaps in the crowd', not helped by it coinciding with Leysdown's gala day. Another perhaps symptomatic falling off was in the number of agricultural horses – only 19 entries in five classes – at Malton Agricultural Show; though the hunter, pony and cattle classes all had record entries, with a local MP, Robin Turton, winning the Heigholme Cup for champion female beef shorthorn. Elsewhere, Church Stretton's day *en fête* came on August Bank Holiday (still early in the month) with the town's annual Traction Engine Rally. 'It was a glorious day, and Mr Owen the station master was in great form in control of all transport,' Vere Hodgson told friends:

> Stretton was packed with thousands of cars and families from all over the country. The racing was loudly applauded … then they had competitions. A woman was blindfolded and had to find her own engine by the sound of the whistle … Then, of course, the vintage cars from all over the Midlands were much admired and did their procession … I am always so thrilled to see people enjoying such innocent amusement with children running around and getting lost and nothing very efficient, the sun shining and everyone in a good humour. There was something quite Victorian about it … No hooligans around. Thank goodness no Mods or Rockers!

There was also that hardy phenomenon the annual flower show, though sadly seldom with an accompanying cricket match. Entries at Rustington in West Sussex totalled 619, almost double the tally three years earlier. 'The numerous events included the flower and produce, allotments, flower arranging, cookery, wine, handicrafts and children's fancy dress competitions, and a pet show featuring an award-winning litter of kittens,' the local paper duly recorded for posterity. 'The Parry Silver Challenge Bowl was won by Miss P. A.

Tart, a member of Rustington Society of Floral Art who won two of the three floral arrangement classes. Winner of the blue ribbon for the best exhibit in the show was Mr H. Ellis with his collection of vegetables and the junior gardener diploma was carried off by a Miss Lucy Roberts.' Justifiable pride for all of them; but that Saturday night a marquee serving as an extension to Rustington Village Hall slashed in the sides and roof by vandals, causing 'quite expensive' damage.

Trouble, too at the major seaside resorts. At Blackpool's Empress Ballroom, where the Rolling Stones played on 24 July, worse-for-wear Glaswegians caused a serious riot, involving crystal chandeliers smashed, seats torn, a Steinway grand piano destroyed, bottles hurled, some fifty people treated in hospital, and the relatively innocent group (absent Brian Jones's deliberately provocative effete posturing) given an indefinite ban from appearing in the town – a ban not lifted until 2008. Nine days later, on the south coast on Bank Holiday Sunday, the 'Battle of Hastings', largely fought on the beach between Mods and Rockers, saw Scotland Yard's so-called 'Riot Squad' flown down from London and 18 arrests made; while that same day on Brighton beach, memories of the Whitsun violence resulted in 'not a single family of holidaymakers in sight', with the local paper adding that 'teenagers have taken over'.[8]

None of this, though, was the norm. In a favoured destination of working-class south Londoners, it was business as usual, indeed even better than usual. 'As far as our members are concerned, Littlehampton is packed,' the chairman of the town's Hotel Association declared at the end of July. 'The position is good for the rest of the summer. My own hotel is booked solid until September 19.' Still, there were always the grumblers, and Scarborough Corporation considerately kept open during August a suggestions box near the Town Hall. Some shelter at the coach station for coach and taxi queues, requested a Sheffield visitor; a bus service to Scalby Mills, proposed a Halifax man; and more pedestrian crossings, asked visitors from both Carlisle and Rotherham. Increasingly, as traditional seaside destinations were starting – but only just – to come under challenge from continental resorts, it was facilities and attractions which now mattered more than previously. 'The new pool is the latest amenity provided at the caravan camp, which is by far the biggest in Britain with a peak season population of 13,000,' noted the report of the opening in late August of a heated, open-air swimming pool at Porthcawl's Trecco Bay – a memorable opening as a local dignitary cut the tape with a pair of golden scissors and then, 'before a group of bathing beauties' could make their 'first graceful plunge into the water', several hundred impatient children rushed forward together and dived in for a far bigger splash. Always, dotted around the coast, there was Butlin's, including at Filey, where on the first Saturday of September 'a packed audience of holiday-makers and local people' were at the Sun Lounge for the final of that holiday camp's talent competition:

> Fifteen winners of the weekly talent contest took part, and the man who came out on top was Albert Fothergill, a baritone from Blackburn, who won with 'Sergeant Major on Parade' and 'Lucky Old Sun'. Runner-up was Ron Thompson, of Hull, a magician who managed to cut a girl's head off with a guillotine, and have her back in one piece at the end of his act. Third place went to a young singer, Tony London, of Barnsley, who sang 'The Wedding' …

Working class, yes; northern, yes; but not quite the world of the *New Left Review*.

Nor likewise for two mothers, the Beatles-loving first one recalled half a century later by Caroline Dearden:

> We lived in Liverpool and that hot summer, the sash windows were all pushed up to let in a breeze and the music blasted out into the street, where we kids played hopscotch, or skipped, or chased each other on the patch of bare ground opposite (a cleared bombsite).
>
> Dad was away in the Territorial Army, on a short break from his job as a train driver. For the whole fortnight, Mum wrote to him three times a day, unaware of how much ribbing this earned him from the other lads. In between Mum's trips to the post box, she hovered by the front door, keeping a lookout for the postman, playing 'Please Mr Postman' over and over again. If a letter from Dad arrived, I'd run indoors and we would sit together in the parlour where she would read the letter out loud.

The other mother was Barking's Pat Scott, whose diary recorded in late August a ten-day holiday in her family's second home, the caravan on Canvey Island:

Lovely sunny day. I took the children to the beach but my head got very bad. I didn't take my glasses.

Again scorching – it really is perfect weather. We went to Tewkes Creek. It was lovely & quiet there. You can see the small sailing boats coming up the creek.

Still scorching. On the beach all day.

Cold & windy today but we still spent all day on the Beach at Crabbing Pool.

Scorching again. This weather is absolutely perfect. So far its a really good holiday. Its so much better in our own caravan.

Hotter still. Spent day at Leigh Beck & at tea time started to walk to Lobster Smack – 4½ miles away. It took a long time but well worth it. The sun was just setting & the pub is very nice. We had shandy & bread, cheese & onions – lovely. Then got bus back home.

On Tewkes Creek again. Club in evening. 3 new groups all very good. Stephen danced all evening.

Went to Southend by bus. It was hot again. It wasn't such a good idea. Very crowded. We went in to watch the Bowling on the Pier & just stayed long enough to see the Lights come on. We went home by train.

On the beach again. On the island down at Leigh Beck.

We had our dinner & all afternoon cleaned up caravan. Phoned for a taxi at 6 p.m. Took all luggage to Car Park but by 7.30 no taxi. Ted phoned again & they said no cars could pick us up because all traffic held up. Eventually man from No 8 caravan offered us a lift. It took 1¼ hours to get to Benfleet. Awful traffic jam, about 10 miles long. Got home by 9.30.

A fortnight later, she started general office duties in a very small plastics firm in Becontree Avenue: 10 a.m. to 3 p.m., £5 a week, and her first paid job for 18 years. 'Everyone was very nice, even the dog.'⁹

Quite suddenly in these weeks, between 26 August and 13 September, the question of gender seemed everywhere: a reaction per-haps against an apparent recent upsurge in the sexual objectification of women, including not just Bond films, but that summer's brief but much-publicised 'topless' craze.

'Women are among the toughest people I know,' began Kingsley Amis's contribution to *Queen*'s symposium on 'Woman: A Special Kind of Hell'. 'Their ability to come out on top of a situation – getting their own way, putting you in the wrong – exceeds even children's.' The other male contributors were Clancy Sigal ('more and more, I am inclined to the archaic view that women were born to be either priestesses of the light or to serve those men, often deluded, fanatic and starved of life, who see themselves as bearers of the light') and R. D. Laing (an even windier piece), while among the home side was Sheila Kitzinger, author of the recent *The Experience of Childbirth* and now declaring that 'uterus envy can exist as well as penis envy'. The youngest contributor – 17-year-old Polly Toynbee, who had already 'compèred and interviewed on the *Sunday Break* television show and is consultant to radio's *The Teen Scene*' – offered a typology of teenage girls in which they divided into Mods, Rockers, tickets, beats, pseuds and debs. Tickets? 'A type of sub-Mod, imitating the Mods but always three months behind,' she explained. 'The Tickets are in the clubs like the Bedsitter in Notting Hill Gate, but they spend most of their time in coffee bars or, still worse, even Wimpy bars. Some of them have even descended to the Bingo Halls.' And she added that '*Ready, Steady, Go!* is now a ticket show, although it has to call itself Mod to get an audience'. Less than a week later, *Vogue* included an interview by Nell Dunn with the 26-year-old artist and actress Pauline Boty:

Men think of you just as a pretty girl? – No. They just find it embarrassing when you start talking. Lots of women are intellectually more clever than lots of men. But it's difficult for men to accept the idea.

If you start talking about ideas they just think you're putting it on? – Not that you're putting it on. They just find it slightly embarrassing that you're not doing the right thing.

What do they want to talk about? – Well, they want you to listen.

Next up was educational panjandrum John Newsom in the *Observer* on 'The Education Women Need', arguing that the current folly was 'to educate girls into being imitation men', whereas far better was for girls to be educated 'in terms of their main social function – which is to make for themselves, their children and their husbands a secure and suitable home, and to be mothers'. '*All* education is, in a sense, vocational, vocational for living,' he concluded. 'And nobody can escape from the vocation of being male or female. The mistake is to think that they are the same.' Three days later, at the Royal Court on 9 September, John Osborne's Bill Maitland pronounced on another folly, that of men wooing or cajoling: 'Pray God I am never so old, servile or fumbling that I ever have to wriggle through that dingy assault course. Do you like it? Do you want it? – those are the only questions I have ever thought worthwhile going into.' Two days further on, the latest in Granada's *It's a Woman's World* series of TV plays was *Laura* by Margaret Drabble, acclaimed by the *New Statesman's* John Holmstrom for expressing 'vividly and comically the desperation of a young flat-bound mother with her university education painfully festering inside her'. And next day, BBC 2 began a six-part series on *The Second Sex*, with the first one featuring five women, including Elizabeth Jane Howard and Edna O'Brien, talking about 'Men as Lovers'. The male reviewers did not love it: the *Daily Telegraph's* P. J. K. (probably the poet and journalist P. J. Kavanagh) found the experience 'rather like watching a striptease which ends before a couple of veils have fallen with most of the panellists clinging desperately to them and stopping short of full revelation of their feelings and views'; Philip Purser in the *Sunday Telegraph* was dismissive of 'the all-girls-together gossip'; and Maurice Wiggin in the *Sunday Times* pronounced loftily that the rest of the series 'depends on keeping the talking bee from becoming a gabble'. The sequence ended that same Sunday, the 13th,'with four women writing in the *Observer* short pieces 'Against Newsom', among them Katherine Whitehorn. 'I have been supremely happy as a much-educated woman – not just happy and educated but happy because educated, able to do what I am cut out to do,' she insisted. 'I always thank my stars I was born in a century where one got a choice – where all women did not have to be domesticated all the time just because most women want to be domesticated some of the time. It seems I was even luckier than I thought, to catch the brief patch of opportunity between the Victorian age and Sir John Newsom's.'

A question of education, too, for the pregnant Julia Ballam, who in June, at the end of her first year, had been told by her Oxford college, St Hilda's, that she could return in October provided she was married by then. She duly became Julia Gold, but what about her scholarship? 'I am, of course, deeply grateful to the college in allowing me to continue my studies,' she wrote on 12 September to the college's Visitor, Lord Evershed. 'However, the loss of my scholarship – primarily a punishment in an academic direction – seems inappropriate for a social misdemeanour, now rectified. The scholarship was originally awarded on academic merit, and so it is extremely discouraging, after a year's hard work, to be deprived of it.' That hard work had included a distinction in her first-year examinations, and she went on:

> The loss of status is probably harder to bear than that of the emoluments, particularly as I am determined to maintain a high standard of work throughout my career at Oxford. Nevertheless, as you may appreciate, my finances during the next two years will be under a severe strain, and the more so as my mother has been unable to give me any assistance since my father's death, two years ago; the money would therefore be more than useful in covering the high costs of essential text books.

'May I apologise again,' she ended her appeal, 'for taking up so much of your Lordship's valuable time.'[10]

*

That same Saturday, six days after the launch of the *Observer*'s colour supplement, a crowded event in the Josephine Suite of the Café Royal had the IPC's Cecil King and Hugh Cudlipp celebrating and extolling the imminent birth of the *Sun*, successor to the *Daily Herald*. Appropriately, the evening began with a presentation by Mark Abrams, the sociologically minded marketing man who some months earlier had, by request, written a detailed analysis of 'The Newspaper Reading Public of Tomorrow' – an analysis which by August was reported to be on the desks of every member of the new venture's editorial staff. Arguing that Britain had changed radically from the mid-1950s, when it was still 'a society with a style of life basically shaped by the depressions of the 1930s and the wars of the 1940s', Abrams identified a dozen key trends:

1. The expectation of a visibly rising standard of living for everyone even within the short run.
2. Rise of new occupations and industrial techniques so that today manual workers in manufacturing industries form less than 30 per cent of working population.
3. Widespread increase in demand for education at all levels.
4. Emergence of independent, prosperous, self-conscious teenage society with distinctive leisure activities.
5. Very early marriage and child bearing.
6. Proportion of married women at work jumped to 1 in 3.
7. Appreciably younger population.
8. Television in every home and more newspaper pages read.
9. Growth of leisure activities.
10. Movement to suburbs. Workmates and neighbours no longer identical.
11. Wide interest in sociology (knowing about ourselves) and wider interest in the arts.
12. Secular, rather than ideological, approach to politics and parties.

'The general impact of all these changes,' declared Abrams, 'is that age stratification has become at least as important as class stratification in the new Britain.' But, crucially, he added, 'the whole structure of the mass media is organised to cater for class difference'. Or put another way, there now existed a veritable gap in the market.

His masters seem to have been convinced. 'THE GROWTH GENERATIONS OF THE SUN: CHARACTERISTICS OF OUR CHANGING SOCIETY' was the title of a pre-launch booklet, probably written by Abrams himself and aimed squarely at potential advertisers. On paper anyway, the vision presented to them was a compelling one:

The SUN will attract expanding minds. It will therefore link with that aspect of national growth which is demanding many more Oxfords. Not hallowed; not mellowed but WANTED NOW, in brick, to shape managerial cadres for an urgent technological age whose better-paid jobs require higher standards of qualification ...

The Growth Generations mean the new salary earners who have changed the national labour 'mix'. They also mean the many multiple-income working-class families living suburban style. They also mean younger, less class-conscious people spending their affluence on living and leisure patterns which were formerly social preserves ...

We are moving from a pyramid-shaped society (i.e. most incomes in the lower sector) to a diamond-shaped society (i.e. most incomes in the middle sector). We are achieving a wide levelling in personal consumption. Over a wide range of products, working-class spending is much the same as middle-class. You may therefore think that SUN readers will be classless as consumers ...

Who could possibly resist? 'The SUN is not just another newspaper. It is a sociological event thrown up, of necessity, by the new social demands of our times.'[11]

The official logo, though, awaited the Café Royal launch – 'The Only Newspaper Born Of The Age We Live In', accompanied by a huge orange blob against a black background. After Cudlipp had given 'a characteristic display of verbal fireworks to set the occasion alight,' recalled Geoffrey Goodman, 'then came the advertising men to talk about the "new image" of the paper – aimed at "an entirely new readership", whatever that was supposed to mean. Nothing about tradition, history and all that stuff. No mention of any post-war generation or commitment. The melody that bounced round the room was "we are now living in a new world – a world of leisure – shorter working hours – consumer spending – liberation", etc. The clichés were in regiments marching onward ...' Perhaps they believed in all this guff, but did Cudlipp and the others closest to him? Not according to one of the young, newly hired journalists. 'A dummy lead about the Queen' had 'made James Cameron [a *Herald* star] remark that any paper that led on the royal family was unlikely to be exploring new frontiers (although he put it more colourfully),' remembered Michael Leapman four decades later about the *Sun*'s pre-Murdoch history. While at the Café Royal 'troop rallying', Cudlipp let slip that 'the paper was to have all the *Mirror*'s qualities but in a more respectable format, so executives wouldn't be ashamed of carrying it into the office'. In short, notwithstanding that it would be full size rather than tabloid, 'the top executives, all from the *Mirror*, were not going to let sociology deflect their red-top instincts'. But the problem, of course, was the invariable rule that 'papers that pretend to be something else head for trouble'.

The *Herald* bowed out on Monday the 14th – the readership way down on its prime, but still roughly double that of *The Times*, *Financial Times* and *Guardian* combined – and the *Sun* rose on Tuesday the 15th, the first new popular daily for 34 years. A front-page article set out its credo: an 'independent' paper 'designed to serve and inform all those whose lives are changing, improving, expanding in these hurrying years'; a paper welcoming 'the age of automation, electronics, computers' and ready to campaign 'for the rapid modernisation of Britain'; a paper 'with a social conscience'; and 'above all, a gay – as well as informative – paper for those with a zest for living'. Inside pages included columns by Cameron ('I am dead against soldiers and land-owners and people with names like Douglas-Home'), Dee Wells (criticising the police for how long they had taken to recognise that their own Harry Challenor was mentally unbalanced) and Clement Freud (billed as 'the new voice of sport'); a two-page photo feature, ahead of its premiere later in the week, on *Goldfinger* ('the film in which Shirley Eaton is painted gold all over and Honor Blackman shows she is the toughest sex-cat on both the big and little screens'); a full-page 'PROBE', announced as a regular daily feature and focusing today on 'WHAT YOUR DOCTOR THINKS ABOUT THE BIRTH PILL'; and, billed as another regular page, 'Pacesetters', featuring Terence Conran ('brought an English farm-house simplicity to modern furniture when he created tables with the scrubbed pine look') and Cathy McGowan ('personifies the swinging fashions of millions of unknown young people who are unconsciously pacesetters themselves').

What about politics? The very first of the front-page articles of faith may have declared the paper to be 'politically free', but when it came to it no one seriously expected it to support any party other than Labour. Indeed, in proclaiming itself to be a paper for 'the leaders of tomorrow', those leaders were, pointedly enough, identified as 'more likely to emerge from a College of Advanced Technology than from Eton or Harrow'.[12] And, as it happened, the confident expectation was that, this very day, Cameron's favourite Old Etonian would be announcing 15 October – exactly a month away – as the date for the long-awaited general election.

15

It Doesn't Make any Difference

The election had not, of course, been entirely out of sight during the previous two months. In late July there was clear political intent when five out of Birmingham's seven Conservative MPs (Aubrey Jones and Sir Edward Boyle the liberal-minded exceptions) issued a statement pointing to the recent race riots in Harlem, taking a hard line on immigration, and highlighting 'the frictions' when 'different cultures live side by side'; in early August the *Leeds Weekly Citizen*'s columnist 'Albion' declared that 'the trouble with Sir Alec and the whole terrible Tory tribe is that they are stuck with a feudal mentality in a potentially brave new world of social, scientific and technological revolution', with the 32-year-old Bernard Ingham adding that 'all the rag bag lot of them are about to meet their Waterloo'; and later that month the two main parties each had a TV spot. 'The Labour Party political broadcast was on tonight and compared to last week's Conservative broadcast was brilliant,' noted Veronica Lee at home in Devon. 'We were talked to like intelligent, thinking human beings; the Conservatives talked to us as if we were sub-normal six year olds.' 'Daddy,' she went on, 'was so annoying because he is determined to find no good in the Labour Party so he childishly rattled the bag of coke.' That was on the 26th; but next day was a reality check for all concerned, as the latest NOP had the Tories in the lead for the first time in almost three years, destroying at a stroke the conventional wisdom that Labour was on course to a certain victory, albeit Gallup shortly afterwards had them ahead by six points.

Battle, though, was really joined in September: on Friday the 11th, the launch of Labour's manifesto *The New Britain*, promising to ensure that, especially through planning and modernisation, the British again became 'THE GO-AHEAD PEOPLE WITH A SENSE OF NATIONAL PURPOSE, THRIVING IN AN EXPANDING COMMUNITY WHERE SOCIAL JUSTICE IS SEEN TO PREVAIL'; and next day, a razzmatazz Labour rally at Wembley's Empire Pool, including music (the Grimethorpe Colliery Institute Band, Humphrey Lyttelton, African drummers), a comic monologue (Harry H. Corbett in *Steptoe and Son* mode) and readings (Vanessa Redgrave in a maternity smock). Would it be enough?

In Mayfair, one Saturday in August, the fast-driving, property-developing father of the future historian Richard Davenport-Hines had, in his black Alvis with the hood down, made a sudden U-turn, forcing the black taxi behind into an emergency halt:

> As we completed the U-turn and passed the stationary taxi, my father stopped, looked at its driver and gave a harsh, defiant laugh: he was proud of having a chuckle that made people lose their temper or, if they were already angry, re-double their rage. The taxi driver was furious, temporarily powerless, but not, he reminded us, permanently disempowered. As my father drove off chortling, his victim shouted after him the deadly threat: 'Wait until October!'

'"A Labour voter," my father said witheringly.'[1]

'Surprise, surprise, there's going to be a general election,' Gerald Priestland informed BBC 2 viewers on the early evening of Tuesday, 15 September. 'And the date – you'll never guess – is October the 15th.' That evening, both Sir Alec Douglas-Home and Harold Wilson were interviewed on TV, as well as the Liberal leader, Jo Grimond. Sir Alec's interrogation had come with a little local turbulence, though whether it was for real or just play-acting is impossible to say. 'Well, Prime Minister, I think I'd better give you an outline of what I'm going to ask,' his interviewer, George Ffitch, had said beforehand. 'I thought first of all I'd put to you what are the real issues in this election.' To which the PM had replied with a frown: 'Oh, I'm not doing anything like that. I'm not going to talk politics. I agreed to go on to discuss the constitutional significance of October 15th, and that's all.' In the event, all three interviews went ahead as planned, with Wilson by general consent faring worst, handicapped by a lack of crisp, sound-bite answers. Philip Larkin, in his year of fame, remained unmoved. 'No doubt the Labour party will be triumphant,' he predicted to Monica Jones. 'In a way I can't believe it matters an awful lot. All the party manifestos w^d sound like Communism, 100 years ago.'[2]

'BILLERICAY first again?' wondered the *Billericay Times* on the 16th about a bellwether seat, also with the most voters, and remarkably the first in both 1955 and 1959 to declare on election night; Wilson that day came to Stevenage to support Shirley Williams, a rising but so far unblooded Labour star, prospective candidate for Hitchin, and adamant that after the Tory go-slow on the issue since 1951, 'we want generations of New Towns, so that people rotting in the slums of the big cities can move to the New Towns to start a new life'; Larkin next morning in Hull wearily attended a lengthy departmental meeting ('I am wearing my Rolling Stones shirt with college tie, but feel rather unhappy'); that Thursday evening saw the premiere of *Goldfinger*, with Sean Connery still as 007, Honor Blackman as Pussy Galore, and the critics divided ('glossy, entertaining, often funny nonsense,' according to Richard Mallett, but Isabel Quigly finding in its prevailing violence 'the most overtly fascist of this insanitary series'); 'not much taken with The Sun,' noted Anthony Heap on Friday, though conceding that 'a paper proclaiming itself to be "born of the age we live in" and purporting to appeal primarily to the younger generation is hardly likely to appeal to me who takes a dim view of both'; the newly launched Conservative manifesto, *Prosperity with a Purpose*, offered little fresh or exciting; and watching the second of *The Second Sex* series, 'Men as Husbands', the TV critic John Holmstrom reckoned it 'excellently chaired by Joan Bakewell' and 'harder-hitting' than the first, with the 'saturnine' Brigid Brophy claiming that only about 10 per cent of the population, irrespective of gender, had any talent for marriage. Saturday was busy enough – in Skegness the start of the 1965 Caravan Exhibition, in Solihull some 3,000 pop fans ('they screamed; they cheered; they wept') gathering outside a church for the marriage of two of the Applejacks, in Bradford the archaeologist Sidney Jackson giving a lecture at the Mechanics Institute ('what a gloomy Victorian hole'), on TV not only a new series of *Dixon of Dock Green* ('a refreshing simplicity & wholesomeness') to delight Nella Last, but also *Last Night of the Proms* (Sir Malcolm Sargent getting an appreciative response as he talked about 'Mads and Rotters') – before

on Sunday the *Observer*'s female readers largely laid into Sir John
Newsom: 'a throwback to the eighteenth century "salon" style of
existence' (Mrs Stella Haward of Banstead); 'women at present make
up one-third of the country's labour force and the economy cannot
do without them' (Dora Russell, second wife of Bertrand); 'I want to
be capable of doing more than just arranging flowers and preparing
meals for my all-knowing husband' (16-year-old Alison Hall from
Leeds).[3]

Swizzlewick on Monday the 21st prompted a typically low RI of
39 ('nothing about it seems real at all'); next day the London opening
of the Liverpool-set musical *Maggie May* caused the critic Ronald
Bryden to regret Lionel Bart's 'Wagnerian compulsion to mytholo-
gise combined with minuscule musical gifts'; and Violet Bonham
Carter reflected after a phone conversation with the *Sunday Times*'s
William Rees-Mogg that 'his opinion of Home is still abysmal & he
has a "foible" for Wilson which I deplore'. That evening, her main
man, Jo Grimond, was first up on the BBC's *Election Forum*, as the
party leaders responded on successive nights to questions sent in by
viewers. The Liberal leader was by some way the most impressive of
the three, whereas Wilson on Wednesday resorted too often to 'I'll
be absolutely honest about this' and Douglas-Home on Thursday
made a disastrously patrician reference to pensions as 'donations'.
On Friday, the *Daily Telegraph* launched its weekly colour magazine;
Jocelyn Brooke regretfully recognised in Elizabeth Taylor a novelist
sadly out of joint with her time ('she writes an elegant, witty prose,
has a decent respect for the Queen's English, and is not obsessed by
crime, violence, madness or homosexuality'); Sowerby Bridge Ladies'
Circle finished three solid months of jam-making ('I must admit I am
getting a bit tired of the sight and smell of it,' their community service convenor, Mrs Sanderson, told her local paper) by selling it all
for charity from a stall in the local market place; on *Any Questions?*,
from Southsea, Edward du Cann in reply to a question asking what
the team considered 'the political canvasser's most essential item
of equipment' elicited laughter and applause by quipping to the
chairman, 'Freddy [Grisewood], may I say at once, a pair of pretty
legs'; and in Barrow-in-Furness, an increasingly disheartened Last as
usual watched TV (including Bob Monkhouse in a short-lived sitcom,
The Big Noise, about a disc jockey) before taking to her 'blessed bed'.

'One of the nights I dread,' she recorded, 'for I'm firm about my husband stripping & changing his underclothes, though to get him to take a bath is beyond me. Still I do know he is reasonably clean.'

Next day, the 26th, a different person's Saturday evening viewing might have been *Match of the Day* (BBC 2, 7.05–7.55, Manchester United v Tottenham Hotspur, 4–1 home win, RI of 65, some viewers critical of Kenneth Wolstenholme's tendency to 'state the obvious'), followed by *The Billy Cotton Band Show* (back for a new series, BBC 1, 7.55–8.40), followed without switching channels by *Dr Kildare* and then a party political broadcast (PPB) for the Conservatives. 'Sir Alec will never play Hamlet,' commented Anthony Howard, 'but on this occasion he proved himself a passably effective Polonius.' That same evening, listening in Keighley to his radio, Kenneth Preston was unimpressed by the absence of favourites, including book reviews: 'Most things appear to be being swept clean for the benefit of the general election. I think we ought to complain.' While not so far away, at the Odeon in Bradford, by now familiar scenes at a Rolling Stones concert included hundreds of teenage girls rushing the stage, a thin blue line trying to hold them back, a series of objects (autograph books, scarves, sweets, home-made toys) hurled in the direction of the group, mass fainting, a wall panel crushed near the stage. Later that weekend, while the supersonic strike-and-reconnaissance TSR-2 made its maiden flight from Boscombe Down, stand-out political news was the *Sunday Telegraph*'s Gallup poll, showing the Tories half a point ahead – their first Gallup lead for more than three years and attributable, according to the paper's suddenly optimistic Peregrine Worsthorne, to Labour's failure since losing power in 1951 to 'slough off' its 'irrelevant, Socialist, cloth-cap, working-class associations, which preclude it from being a genuine alternative party in an increasingly classless Britain'.[4]

On Monday a big *Daily Mirror* splash on the election ('Whose finger on the tranquiliser?', exposing an apparent Tory plot to 'keep the election quiet') failed to prevent a rise in the FT 30-Share Index; Edward Gardner, Conservative candidate in Billericay, played his trump card by telling a press conference that he intended to respond to 'the amount of feeling in Billericay and Wickford about the New Town [i.e. Basildon]', especially on the part of disgruntled rate payers, by urging the government to give those two largely middle-class places a separate urban district council; *Blue Peter* (still the preserve of Christopher Trace and Valerie Singleton, but with John Noakes soon to join them) was promoted to twice-weekly; and Wilson in Labour's PPB 'put up his usual competent, efficient performance,' judged Howard, 'without ever getting near to scoring the breakthrough that the Labour Party badly needs at the present stage of the campaign'. Next day, some two dozen visiting Russian architects were so impressed by what they had seen the evening before of the Bull Ring that, noted the *Birmingham Evening Mail*, 'they got up early and went to have another look at it before breakfast'; 'Stop the TV sex plays' was the *South Wales Echo*'s headline for a letter from Queenie Evans of Salem, Llandeilo, despairing of how 'promiscuous sex is portrayed as a natural fulfilment of one's life'; and that Tuesday night, the Light Programme launched *Through Till Two* – Jimmy Young presenting the music for the two hours before midnight, Steve Race for the two hours afterwards, listeners invited to phone in with requests (though their voices not actually heard), election forgotten, and the two pivotal days of the campaign only hours away.

On the face of it, Wednesday the 30th began badly for Labour – NOP now putting the Tories ahead by almost three points, share prices duly rising sharply – and then got worse, as a sleep-deprived Wilson in his morning press conference implausibly attributed an unofficial stoppage at the components firm Hardy Spicer (key for the whole motor industry) to political motives. 'I must say,' responded minutes later at the Conservative press conference a palpably amused Reginald Maudling, 'that's a rum one – Tory shop stewards going round sabotaging Mr Wilson's election! Really!' But fortunately for Wilson, a smoking gun now lay at hand, in the form of the newly published trade figures for the second quarter of the year, revealing a sharp deterioration in Britain's balance of payments. Hitherto, against the wishes of his economic adviser Thomas Balogh, he had largely refrained from attacking the government's management of the economy, not wanting to be accused of causing an actual or potential run on sterling; but that evening, in his speech at Norwich, he went for the jugular, accusing Douglas-Home of having engaged in a John Bloom-style act of deception by knowingly propagating the myth that the economy was in sound shape, when in fact the country was borrowing at the rate of 'more than a million pounds a day'. Elsewhere, Henry Brooke told a barrage of youthful hecklers at Orpington that 'the constituency must not make a fool of itself as it did two years ago', a reference to Eric Lubbock's famous by-election victory for the Liberals; Virginia Graham went to see John Osborne's *Inadmissible Evidence* and, she told her friend Joyce Grenfell, was so disgusted by it being 'a monologue with diarrhoea' that she left early amid 'a great many other seats thumping up'; while at Stamford Bridge, 'a lean little chap with an unruly mop of dark hair' starred in Manchester United's 2–0 win. 'He was rarely,' added the *Daily Telegraph*'s Bryon Butler, 'where the book says a left winger should be.' The reaction of the Chelsea crowd (some 60,000) to a dazzlingly virtuoso performance was remarkable. 'At the end,' reported the *Daily Mirror*, 'they stood and acclaimed him. They gave him their hearts … who will forget it?'[5] George Best had come to town.

The diarists began October, with polling day exactly a fortnight away, for the most part as stubbornly apolitical as they had been during September. Daphne Meryon in Emsworth 'hurried through kitchen routine, then spent remainder of morning making cover for second camping mattress and a white cover for one of the spare-room electric blankets'; Henry St John in Acton noted without comment that Soho's Windmill Theatre ('which I visited on several occasions from about 1941') was to close at the end of the month; and Madge Martin in Oxford gloried in the weather ('still beautiful – this September was the sunniest for 53 years, and we are promised 3 more fine weeks'). An exception was Phyllis Willmott. 'The polls seem to be swinging away from Labour,' she reflected this Thursday. 'Sad for the politicians like Wilson. If he is "out" now he could never hope to be in as a "young" P.M.' Another left-of-centre diarist was suddenly more hopeful. 'The trade crisis has given us our opening and a chance to alert a partly apathetic public to the consequences of Tory rule if they are returned,' Anthony Wedgwood Benn observed – even as share prices continued to soar, even as Lord Cromer, the Bank of England's strongly anti-Labour governor, was covertly ensuring that the latest gold and currency figures, due to be issued next day, would show a fall that was politically containable. But if, predictably enough, there was no help for Labour from that quarter, there was from Hardy Spicer's chairman, Herbert Hill, who in his Mayfair offices sounded off to reporters about the strikers: 'They are people who are not of very high

intelligence. If they were, they would understand the issues involved
here economically. I feel very much that they are "poor dears" and
am very sad for them ...' Almost immediately, the patronising phrase
'poor dears' was rivalling Douglas-Home's 'donations' in the Labour
armoury; and, at a stroke, Wilson had escaped from his blunder the
day before. No Thursday was complete, of course, without *Top of the
Pops*. In the TV room at Glasgow's Barlinnie prison, five minutes were
still left in the prisoners' daily ration of an hour's viewing when, with
David Jacobs announcing a performance of the current no. 1, the set
was abruptly switched off, the lights went out and a riot kicked off,
involving chairs thrown, windows smashed and one man hurt. The
act they had missed? Herman's Hermits, with 'I'm Into Something
Good'.[6]

Riots, too, this week in Belfast – after Ian Paisley had demanded
the removal of a tricolour from the Republican headquarters there –
but receiving little coverage in a mainland press increasingly preoccupied with the election. 'Buyers Hopeful Of Tory Election Victory
Send Steels, Insurances, Properties Well Ahead' was the *FT*'s optimistic headline on Friday the 2nd, yet in the event this proved a day
of three significant positives for Labour: NOP reporting a 4½ per
cent swing to the party in Coventry South, an emblematic marginal;
the news that arrangements had been made for increased borrowing
powers from Europe's central banks; and a successful, hard-hitting
PPB by a fired-up but semi-sober George Brown ('he hectored, he
tub-thumped, he did not smile once,' noted an appreciative *New
Statesman*). Saturday had Shirley Williams on the campaign trail, as
she toured seven Hertfordshire villages, though 'on many occasions'
finding, after she had made her stump speech on the village green,
that front doors left slightly ajar were then hastily closed as she
approached them and that 'no amount of persuasion' would induce
those inside to come out again for 'a political discussion'. The big
national political news was on Harvest Sunday, with Gallup giving
Labour a 4½ per cent lead – for Benn as for all his colleagues, 'a wonderful tonic'. That morning, Frederick Ward drove from Bristol to
Torquay: 'Apart from one glimpse of church activity, I saw nothing
in the 100 miles journey which even suggested it was a Sunday. The
roads were full of cars coming and going, but not a sign of children
going to Sunday school, not a church bell.' Later, in Hyde Park during

the hour and a half before sunset, the photographer Robert Freeman took what would be the moody, atmospheric cover (autumn leaves in the background) of *Beatles for Sale*. Less than festive, too, in Barrow for Nella Last's 75th birthday. 'The Palladium Show not starting till just before 9 o'clock meant only having half of it. I've got my husband to watch T.V. till 9.30 odd times but he won't extend it for even The Palladium Show.' Unequivocally too late, at 11.05 on ITV, was the first outing of *The Eamonn Andrews Show*: chat from Sugar Ray Robinson, Willie Rushton, Terry-Thomas and Honor Blackman (mercilessly interrogated about her fear of spiders); the bare-footed Sandie Shaw singing her newly released '(There's) Always Something There to Remind Me'; and the whole thing, in its way an American-style pioneer on British TV, inducing despair from one critic. 'A temple to the god Show-biz,' declared *Punch*'s Angela Milne, 'this sorry programme invites us to worship those Personalities of Stage, Screen, Etc, who trot from the wing, to sit at Mr Andrews's desk and then move on to the sofa for the ensuing badinage.' 'So help me,' she added, 'if I go near it again.'

Monday the 5th saw Daphne Meryon spending 'most of afternoon ironing and listening to radio play in kitchen', Shirley Williams in Labour's PPB executing 'a neat manoeuvre with a shopping basket to make the point about rising prices', and closing day for nominations: 1,757 candidates contesting 630 seats; Conservatives and Labour contesting virtually all those seats, the Liberals somewhat over half (365); minor party candidates almost doubling to 135; only 56 women out of the 1,258 candidates put up by the two main parties; and of the 630 Conservative candidates, 417 privately educated.[7]

As ever in a general election, there were many local flavours and individual stories: in Aberdeen South, for example, Lady Tweedsmuir and Donald Dewar as a notably contrasting pair of candidates; in Birmingham All Saints, Labour's Brian Walden inveighing against the iniquities of 'private landlordism'; in Bodmin, Peter Bessell for the Liberals successfully ensuring that no gossip about his London mistress reached Cornwall; in Brighouse and Spenborough, James Pickles insisting that 'the radical Liberal Party' was 'the true alternative to perpetual Tory rule'; in Brixton, after the Tory candidate's voice had given out, John Major taking on his speaking engagements; in Buckingham, Labour's Robert Maxwell roaring around the local villages in a red Land Rover and seeking to crush hecklers who accused him of being a foreigner with the riposte, 'I chose this country – *did you*?'; in Cardiff South-East, Ted Dexter for the Tories taking on Callaghan and accusing Labour of having a 'look after every man' philosophy ('you don't have to bother whether the man is honest, whether a man is hard-working, what his effort is into the community – you look after him just the same'); in Chester, the Labour agent, John Prescott, despairing of his fruity-voiced, Old Etonian candidate, the publisher Anthony Blond, who on venturing into council estates 'would insist on peering through people's letter-boxes'; in Edinburgh Central, Nicholas Fairbairn going canvassing 'looking every inch a Tory' with his 'square bowler straight out of the nineteenth century, a double-breasted waistcoat of imposing elegance and a great gold watch fob'; in Fife East, Labour's representative a 26-year-old solicitor and future leader, John Smith, two years after winning the *Observer* Mace debating competition; in Fife West, Lawrence Daly being accused in a leaflet by the Communist candidate Bill Lauchlan of having done 'an "OLD PALS" act' with the Labour candidate Willie Hamilton (already a renowned anti-royalist), prompting Daly to counter-attack that 'if Mr Lauchlan ever had power in this country the democratic rights of the people of Britain would disappear'; in Finchley, Margaret Thatcher answering 'a wide variety of questions with a barrage of official statistics'; in Hertford, Anna Harman (mother of Harriet) standing for the Liberals and going hard for the Conservative vote ('Liberals do not believe in a restrictive society … We believe in free enterprise and freer competition'); in Hertfordshire East, Dennis Potter conceding that 'politics sometimes seems to be just a matter of slogans picked out in garish neon' ('happy families beam back at us in ten-foot high photographs, toothfully begging us not to throw away our standard of living'), but adamant that Labour stood for 'a desire for change based on a revulsion against unprincipled chaos, economic drift, unhindered profiteering and moral callousness'; in Kinross and West Perthshire the Communist C. M. Grieve (better known as the poet Hugh MacDiarmid) standing against the PM mainly in order to make the point that it was undemocratic for the party to be excluded from the airwaves; in Liverpool Toxteth, the postmaster-general, Reginald Bevins, vulnerable after the eventual 6.5 per cent settlement with the post workers was widely seen as inflationary; in Orpington, Norris

McWhirter warning voters that democracy was not a 'kind of cricket match', in which sides took turns to have an innings; in Paddington, Jimmy Edwards taking his role as Tory candidate with evident seriousness ('even my trombone is laid up in cocoons'); in Poplar, another Tory candidate, Kenneth Baker, outlining the Conservative case to a quizzical-looking docker and being met with the question, 'Mate, what have I got to conserve?'; in highly marginal Preston North, the French-speaking Julian Amery persuading the Mother Superior of a French Carmelite nunnery to allow the nuns to vote (all but one of the 15, she reassuringly told him, would vote Conservative, with the non-voter due to do penance that day); in Richmond and Barnes, B. S. Johnson doing the hard yards (mainly canvassing) for the Labour candidate, fellow writer Alan Brownjohn; in Rochester and Chatham, also highly marginal, the defending Conservative, Julian Critchley, noting that 'all good candidates run scared', but worried that over the past five years he had, according to one report, 'spent less time in the area than some observers think good for him'; in Roxburgh, Selkirk and Peebles, a son of the manse, David Steel, making his debut; in Saffron Walden, all three candidates coming out against the Stansted proposal; and in Torrington, the Labour candidate David Owen being singularly unimpressed by the Liberals' man, Mark Bonham Carter (grandson of Asquith, son of Lady Violet, exuding 'the cultivated effortless superiority that marks out many of those who pass through Balliol College, Oxford').[8]

The PPB for the Conservatives on the 6th featured Edward Heath – 'with his artificial fruity intonations and his tube-train ticket-machine delivery,' mused one critic about the choice, 'he is precisely the type of bore that one would go to the other end of the room to avoid at a party' – but the real action that Tuesday evening was on the hustings. In Plymouth, responding to a heckler shouting 'What about Profumo?', Quintin Hogg retorted angrily, 'If you can tell me there are no adulterers on the front bench of the Labour party you can talk to me about Profumo'. Any adulterers in particular? The great majority in the audience would have had little if any idea; but the immediate working assumption among those in the political know was that Hogg was referring to Wilson's alleged relationship with Marcia Williams, his 'hugely able and immensely strong-willed' (Roy Hattersley's words) political secretary. Wilson himself was speaking in Birmingham's old covered market in the Bull Ring, where against persistent heckling from Young Conservatives he gave a political masterclass. 'Harold shot each sniper dead – even if not always straight between the eyes,' recalled Hattersley (a local candidate and one of the warm-up acts). 'A florid lady in the front row shouted, "You're a liar." Harold grinned, almost affectionately, in her direction. "Say that again and I'll mention Henry Brooke." Even the ranks of Edgbaston could scarce forbear to cheer.' At one point, amid general laughter, the alarm on his wrist-watch suddenly started to ring. 'Wilson held up both arms in a majestic call for silence before he gripped the edge of the podium and, staring straight ahead, began to give a solemn warning about the state of the economy. Ninety seconds of the rally were being broadcast live on the nine o'clock news.' It was a common enough tactic in later years – but not in 1964. Douglas-Home, meanwhile, that Tuesday was first in Leeds – where unremitting heckling from university students made him lose his temper, remarking that 'the Labour Party must be very hard up if they have to hire these people' – and then in Bradford. There, in a set-piece speech, he turned for the first time in the campaign to the subject of immigration. Strongly defending the 1962 Act, and claiming that without it 'there would now be an additional 300,000 immigrants with their families – an influx of nearly a million people', he accused Labour and the Liberals of having 'opposed it all along the line'. As for present and future policy:

> Any immigrant who enters Britain is treated just like every other British citizen. But the immigrants themselves will realize how much it is in their own interests to avoid the social and economic problems which have created so much trouble elsewhere. Most people will agree that it is necessary to keep the conditions and the number of permits under the strictest review, and to strengthen the safeguards against evasion.

Nine days before polling day, and speaking in one of the main centres of immigration, the PM had, as Paul Foot put it, 'thrown his hat into the ring'.[9]

A particular West Midland constituency (situated between Birmingham and Wolverhampton) would, of course, for ever be associated with the question of immigration and race. 'As we get nearer the election and bigger issues come up,' Smethwick's Labour candidate, the somewhat aloof Patrick Gordon Walker, had hopefully predicted at the start of September, 'the immigrant problem will become less prominent.' He reckoned without the determination of his Conservative opponent, Peter Griffiths, to keep the issue absolutely front and centre, amid growing national attention. 'Integration,' he told a journalist in mid-September, 'is meaningless in Smethwick. The white people don't want it and the immigrants, most of whom are Sikhs, love their culture too fiercely to give it up.' At one of his meetings, on 29 September, responding to a grey-haired woman who said that she wanted immigration stopped at once lest 'in twenty years' time we shall be ruled by them,' he declared in unblushingly populist mode: 'This lady has put over the kind of thing I have heard on hundreds and thousands of doorsteps. Without fear or favour I will put forward what I hear because I believe that is the duty of an MP. If it suits the people of Smethwick I will say it.' Unsurprisingly, his formal election address pulled no punches:

> I shall press for the strictest possible control of immigration. We British must decide who shall or shall not enter our country. So vital a matter cannot be left to other Governments. Overcrowding and dirty conditions must be ended. There must be no entry permits for criminals, the unhealthy or those unwilling to work. Our streets must once again be safe at night.

Soon afterwards, in early October, stickers and leaflets with the overtly racist message 'If you want a n— neighbour vote Liberal or Labour' started to be seen around the constituency, with Gordon Walker handing to the police one such leaflet taken from the notice board of the Sandwell Gospel Hall.

The final week of the campaign at Smethwick – a week which included Air Commodore Sir Frank Whittle's 1,000-word address to the electors, urging them to back Griffiths as one of the few Conservative candidates 'who has the guts to speak out' and describing immigrants as mainly those 'who have failed to make the grade in their own country and are attracted to the benefits of the "Welfare State," with all its hand-outs to all comers' – was dominated by rumours and slurs. 'Patrick Gordon Walker's daughters married black

men', 'Patrick Gordon Walker sold his house at Smethwick to the
blacks', 'Because most of the blacks have leprosy, they are building
two secret leper hospitals in the town' – such, according on the 13th
to *The Times*'s notable Midland correspondent Brian Priestley, were
some of the rumours which Liberal canvassers had picked up in recent
days, while he added that the words 'N— lover' had been daubed over
some of Gordon Walker's posters. 'Vile – It's All in Black and White'
was the title of Priestley's piece, and he had no doubt about who was
responsible for the way in which 'the great issues of the day are all
twisted and perverted by the question of colour'. 'In the creation of
this electoral atmosphere, the Conservative Party at Smethwick has
played a leading role,' he insisted. 'The evidence is there in black and
white in the files of the local newspaper. It is plain and undeniable.
Over a period of years if Smethwick has ever been in danger of for-
getting the immigrant problem, the Conservatives have not scrupled
to remind people of it.'[10]

Yet ultimately – despite Smethwick; despite Birmingham Perry
Barr, where the Conservative campaign was almost as exploitative of
fears; despite Southall, where the British National Party (BNP) candidate targeted Labour voters on an anti-Sikh platform; despite Eton
and Slough, where in one of the biggest wards no Labour election
committee functioned on behalf of Fenner Brockway because its secretary disapproved of his liberal views on race – immigration proved
to be the dog which, taken overall, failed to bark. The much-cited
example was Deptford: on paper, fertile territory for a populist Tory
campaign, but in practice the candidate went to some lengths to dial
down the temperature. Much hinged on the party leaders and those
around them. Douglas-Home, despite what he said at Bradford, seems
to have made a conscious decision – to what extent based on principle,
to what extent on calculation (including nervousness about a backlash)
is impossible to know – to try to keep the issue largely invisible; while
Wilson, conscious of a Gallup poll in August showing that potential Labour voters were even more in favour of a complete ban on
new immigrants than potential Conservative voters were, played the
issue circumspectly, though with a good line when challenged about
how 'there are a lot of people in this country, possibly including some
of this audience, who are alive today because of what has been done
within the National Health Service by coloured doctors and nurses'.

The crucible, then as later, was the West Midlands, where apart from the obvious high-profile exceptions of Smethwick and Perry Barr, a broad consensus just about held between the candidates of the two parties – a consensus favouring on the one hand tight controls on numbers, on the other hand the pursuit of greater integration, or at least non-discrimination. Among the Tory candidates was Enoch Powell in Wolverhampton South-West; and in an article in his local paper he stressed the equal importance of both aspects, declaring that provided a firm lid was kept on already dangerously high numbers, then he and his party would unequivocally want 'to see the coloured immigrants no less integrated into the life and society of what is now their homeland than any other group, such as the Jewish community or the thousands of Poles in Britain today', even if 'generations will pass before this large and sudden influx has been fully assimilated into the society of this country'. What about the electorate itself? A week before polling day, a *Birmingham Evening Mail* reporter was in the city's Locarno ballroom to talk to first-time voters, including two young women living in Hattersley's Sparkbrook constituency, both with 'strong opinions' about immigration:

Pauline [a secretary with a Birmingham stationery firm] said she thought the situation had got out of hand. Immigrants had flooded into Birmingham in their thousands, depriving white couples of a chance to have their own homes. 'I am not in favour of a hate campaign against the coloured people, but I think charity should begin at home,' she said.

Similar sentiments were expressed by her friend [manageress of a showroom for a nationalised industry]. 'It is all very well for the politicians to talk about tolerance and understanding, but they don't have to live in Sparkbrook,' she said.

A few days later, the paper printed a revealing letter. 'Many residents in the Midlands will tell you there is no greater fear than finding that a house in one's street has been sold to a coloured immigrant and that it now houses up to 50 persons,' wrote 'A Sufferer' from Wolverhampton. 'If one has a heavy mortgage outstanding one has to clear this before one can move. In many cases one sells at a loss.'[11]

Back in what was still overwhelmingly monocultural Britain, the campaign was entering its last week or so. On the 7th, the *Mirror*'s splash had the powerful voice of Marjorie Proops directly addressing the PM:

> When I contemplate the three or four million who still, in 1964, have to trudge down backyards, or share squalid outside lavatories with countless other citizens – I am overwhelmed with scorn for you and the rest of the never-had-it-so-good brigade.
>
> *Has your Lady, Sir Alec, ever had to lug hot water to a tub in the kitchen to bath her young? Or herself? Or you come to that? Ever had your back scrubbed in a bath in the kitchen? ...*
>
> The trouble with you, Alec, is you've seen too many Tory ladies in flossy hats beaming at you and clapping their hands at your patronising little jokes.
>
> Of course, these ladies love you. You are good for *them*.

Few more adoring than that morning at Hitchin Corn Exchange, as (reported the local paper) 'a very confident Sir Alec Douglas-Home, looking more youthful than his television image reflects, survived sporadic heckling from Labour Party supporters and was cheered to the echo by Conservatives in the crowd of well over 600', with the accompanying front-page photo indeed showing a row of mainly elderly ladies standing up and applauding him vigorously. Elsewhere this Wednesday, the *Billericay Times* printed the political advice of Basildon's Rev. Keith Wood to his flock ('your Christian responsibility is to vote for the party whose policies correspond most closely to the will of God as you understand it UNLESS one of the candidates is an altogether outstanding man or woman'); an RI of 77 greeted the autumn return of *Animal Magic* ('a programme, many claimed, of never-failing interest to children and adults alike, always absorbing to a degree, and commendably instructive with, thanks to Johnny Morris, a delicious touch of humour'); Britain's first grassroots gay rights organisation, the North West Homosexual Law Reform Committee was launched in Manchester to campaign for decriminalisation; also in Manchester, 16-year-old Roger Darlington saw *Goldfinger* twice at Oxford Road's Odeon ('cost 4/6, but it was absolutely fabulous, just great'); Pussy Galore herself was the star that evening of the Liberals'

PPB, telling viewers that 'it drives me mad' when people talked about a Liberal vote being a wasted vote – so mad that 'I feel like throwing them over my shoulder'; the psephologists David Butler and Anthony King called on Benn and said that Keith Joseph was far from the only Conservative 'completely dejected by the way the Tory campaign was going', even to the extent of thinking 'it might be a Labour landslide'; and John Fowles, touring the West Country in search of somewhere to live, was in sociological mode:

> An old coaching inn at Shaftesbury. The unchangingness of the small provincial town is a shock: the streets without lights, the rural accents, the incestuousness of it all. In even the smallest town, though, we met the strange new young, who might – accents apart – have come from any country in Europe. Boys with Jesus haircuts and black leather coats and loud voices, girls equally without charm; the roar of unsilenced motorbikes and scooters.
>
> It's not much better inside the hotels, where the English middle classes whisper through their meals and then go and gawp at the screen in the TV lounge. Outside the yobboes shout, inside the last of the *ancien regime* cower over their dying way of life and the protocols of an insipid gentlemanliness.

'Nothing in our lifetimes,' he concluded, 'will break this great window between the two Englands – the "gentry" and the "labouring classes".'[12]

Grumbling, too, next day from Larkin at the start of term at Hull ('the students all look very ugly to me – men with greasy shoulder-length hair, women in characterless indeterminate garments'); while in the *Mirror* the list of 'top people' endorsing Labour included Alan Sillitoe ('because I believe in equality'), Iris Murdoch (no reason given), A. J. Ayer ('more likely to bring about social reform – better than voting Conservative because I'm-all-right-Jack') and the jazz singer Annie Ross ('because I hate class distinction'). That evening saw mixed fortunes for the big two. Speaking at Birmingham's Bull Ring, Douglas-Home received the roughest of rides – not just non-stop heckling and gales of derisive laughter, but also right in front of him the unveiling of (recalled Hattersley) a 'cardboard monster' with 'the body of a pre-historic reptile and the face of Sir Alec'. By

contrast, it was cheers almost all the way for Wilson at Southampton's
Methodist Hall as, watched by a reluctantly admiring Henry Fairlie,
he went through his paces with 'an insulting arrogance which carried
his audience':

7.52 He rose, and began with a bitter attack on the 'faceless fraternity' of land speculators.

7.59 He crushed a heckler who had got in with a reference to the
size of the crowd waiting outside. It was an early and confident
assertion of his superiority. As the applause died, he gave a sudden
shake of his head, like a man ready to attack. There was menace in
every movement now.

8.00 'One thing they *can* plan: an election boom.' It was a joke many
of us [journalists] had heard before, but now he spat it out with a
physical thrust which began with his toes.

8.06 Another heckler was immediately answered and crushed: Mr
Wilson was turning every interruption to his advantage.

8.08 He attacked Mr Selwyn Lloyd's pay pause with superb dema-
gogic power.

8.16 He returned to simple stuff, with an attack on the 'blurred
miasma' of Sir Alec's economic hopes. It was a good phrase, and
delivered with something like music.

8.20 The invective was now brilliant, as he dismissed Mr Hogg as
the 'Minister of Science with a broken computer'. It was rollicking
stuff but with suffused power.

8.23 A heckler on his left was picked up and answered with passages
from one of his previous speeches. Mr Wilson simply seized the
moment of the interruption and converted it to his own advantage ...

Next morning, Friday the 9th, the *Daily Express* unhelpfully reported
George Gale's interview with a pessimistic Rab Butler ('things might
start slipping in the last few days ... they won't slip towards us'),
the *Mirror* generously gave space to Edward Heath ('I want to see
the guts torn out of our older industrial cities and new civic centres
and shopping areas built there, the older houses torn down and new
ones in their place'), and the traditionally Conservative-supporting
Economist came out endorsing Labour ('the riskier choice' but 'the

better choice', being less likely to 'stick in the mud'). By this time Joe Coral had Labour at 9–4 on to win, while by the end of trading the stock market had suffered over the past week its worst fall – 5.5 per cent – for many years.[13]

As ever, the voters themselves remained, if not quite noises off, then certainly not centre stage, though in Brighton the evening paper did supply some vox pop from the highly marginal Kemp Town division:

> I think Labour will give us better pensions and we won't have to go to the national assistance. Labour's for the working people. The Prime Minister is all right for people with plenty of money. *(Mrs Emily Keeley, seventy, 'floating voter')*
>
> It doesn't make any difference. I've got my job to do and I'll do it whoever gets in. *(Ian Sweetman, twenty-four, window cleaner, not voting)*
>
> People only vote how their parents voted. What's said now doesn't make any difference to them. All I can see is that you get the party leaders on television and they shout insults at each other. Who wants to vote for people like that? *(Peter West, twenty-four, also not voting)*

BBC 2 that evening had *The Second Sex*'s penultimate episode ('Men as Superiors', with Vanessa Redgrave among those taking part); and at Bradford's Gaumont, the Beatles began their autumn tour. Everything was satisfyingly all Sir Garnet ('fans waving banners and trying to break through the barrier of police at the front, throwing objects ranging from gonks to autograph books on to the stage'), while later on the group arrived unexpectedly at the Cavalier Club in Holmfield, near Halifax, where they enjoyed a few drinks and signed autographs before turning in. 'A bunch of charming lads, very lively and witty' was the verdict of the club's owner, Fred Pearson.

Things got worse next day for the PM: at his press conference a disastrous opening sentence ('I think I can confidently say that morale in our party is as high as it could possibly be expected to be'), followed by an almost equally disastrous whistle-stop tour of London marginals where, as Anthony Howard and Richard West put it in their flavourful, instant-history account of the campaign, 'something in Home's aloof manner seemed to exacerbate hecklers', with Home himself never learning how to deal with them, 'let alone largely hostile crowds'. Typical was a meeting by Clapham Common: provoked by constant shouting of 'Good Old Baillie' (a nod to *Private Eye*'s 'Baillie Vass' nickname for him), a sulky looking Home finally snapped ineffectually: 'One of these days, this boy down here who is continually interrupting will do a few days' work for a fair wage.' Also this Saturday, Larkin gave Monica Jones a political update ('Kingsley saying he is going to vote Labour: postal vote from Majorca I bet'); Julia Gold informed her college's Visitor that she was now dropping her appeal about the loss of her scholarship, saying that she had been 'wrongly advised' to submit it in the first place, apologising again for having taken up so much of Lord Evershed's 'valuable time', and (abjectly enough for someone who as Julia Briggs would become one of the most spirited literary critics of her generation) signing herself 'Your humble servant'; and many people stayed up late to watch the opening ceremony of the Tokyo Olympics, transmitted live by satellite. 'Very clear,' noted Judy Haines. 'Cliff Michelmore sounded as though he had been celebrating. He fumbled for words, and sometimes gave up completely.' Next morning the *Sunday Telegraph* had Gallup giving a commanding 6 per cent lead to Labour; Virginia Graham cheered herself up by writing to Joyce Grenfell about how she had 'caught a glimpse of our future leaders on the telly – people like Mr Callaghan, & Mr Healey, & they all looked *horrid*, all of them enormously fat & flabby with wet mouths & boot button eyes!'; Nella Last reckoned that the outcome was still 'any one's guess – mine is that the Conservatives will win', with a majority of 23 her best estimate; and Haines shared the anxious, apolitical preoccupation of many. 'I think the Queen is very brave to face so cheerfully and composedly the French Canadians, who are hostile to the throne at this time. It will be a great relief to many when she and the Duke are safely home again …'[14]

Three days to go. On Monday morning a tube strike began in London – definitely not good news for Labour – while Hogg at a press conference unforgettably declared that 'if the British public fall for the Labour party's programme, they will be stark staring bonkers', probably cementing Labour's latest odds of 3–1 on. As for the Liberals, he dismissed them as 'insignificant and meaningless', a remark which failed to deter Kenneth Williams for one. 'I see now that the obvious answer is to vote Liberal,' he reflected. 'The other two are obviously the "choix d'embarras" & there is something innocent and honest about the Libs.' Labour's final PPB was that evening. 'A touch of idealism (one imagined him saying beforehand) is what the campaign needs at this stage; and with some skill he succeeded in suggesting it,' observed the *Spectator*'s J. W. M. Thompson about Wilson's key contribution, albeit 'he left it to Lord Attlee, looking very old and shrewd in his armchair, to summon up Labour's past – and he managed to invoke Winston Churchill while doing so.'

On Tuesday morning, the tube strike still on, an outlier poll in the *Daily Express* gave the Conservatives a majority and the stock market some temporary heart, but few of the experts took it all that seriously; 'I long for a Labour victory,' the BBC's director-general, Hugh Carleton Greene, told his future wife, adding that he had 'never felt so intensely about an election'; that evening the return of Harry Worth in *Here's Harry* delighted Madge Martin and her husband ('we love this kindly, bemused comedian') but quite a number of other viewers felt that he had 'overplayed the "bumbling" act' and 'lost some of his sense of unselfconscious "lunacy"'; not quite bumbling for Douglas-Home in the last Conservative PPB, with Thompson noting not unkindly that 'he has no great gift for the business, but he toils on, a sense of earnestness getting through the hesitations and the tension'; speaking for Labour in Battersea was Attlee, his brief, staccato, barely audible speech ending memorably that 'if on Friday I hear that a Labour government has been elected, I shall die happy'; and late that Tuesday evening, the Queen was driven home from London Airport, with a crowd lining the Cromwell Road as she passed by. 'There were some young in open cars in the middle of the road,' Virginia Graham reported to her friend, '& when Q. came, in a lit up car, they honked horns & all we elderly types rushed forward, waving our hankies & shawls and crutches – & then, we all burst into tears and went home.'[15]

Next day, with the tube strike in its final stages, David Bruce, the American ambassador, weighed up the electoral probabilities. Unsure whether Wilson, for all his virtuoso campaigning, had decisively shed a certain reputation for being 'tricky and unreliable', he thought it not impossible that the Liberals would hold the balance of power; while as for the Conservatives, he noted some signs that the female vote was shifting in the direction of the PM. It was not one of the great

Wednesday afternoons in Barrow, where Last, after providing a lunch of 'cooked brisket of beef with vegetables', was unable to coax her husband out to enjoy some autumn sunshine. 'I said "You are going to vote tomorrow, even if I go by myself & ask that some one calls in a car for you. You are getting deeper & deeper into a rut" – I mean it!' Polling was now only hours away, and that evening saw two notable speeches in the city of the moment: in Liverpool's St George's Hall, with up to five thousand squeezed in and at least two thousand outside in the square, Wilson (whose constituency was nearby Huyton) delivered for one final time his central message that the election was not only about the need for modernisation, but also about the contrast between a party 'concerned only to conserve power for an unrepresentative minority' and a party 'engaged on a crusade'; while elsewhere in the city, at West Derby High School, Harold Macmillan was given 'a largely attentive and respectful hearing' as he told a packed hall that this was probably the last speech he would ever make on a platform and reminded them of their solemn duty, 'Don't take a leap in the dark'. The northern meritocrat or the lingering grandee? There seemed little doubt which way the spirit of the age was pointing. And later that evening, as a large and exuberant crowd almost carried Wilson and his wife back to the Adelphi Hotel, the chant rang out, 'We love him, Yeah, Yeah, Yeah'.

Across many of the nation's schools, this had been the week of mock elections, and a small (no doubt skewed) sample suggests that, politically speaking anyway, that apparently prevailing zeitgeist still had some way to go. In five grammars, a clean sweep for the Tories – at Slough, at both the ones in Hitchin, at Harrow County School for Boys, and in Shropshire at Adams' Grammar School in Newport, where Jeremy Corbyn was one of reputedly only two Labour supporters – but at Laurence Marks's comprehensive in north London a victory for the Communist candidate ('he explained Communism to us all and I thought it sounded really good'). As for private schools, the Conservative candidate at St Paul's Girls' School won twice as many votes as her Labour rival; at Lancing, David Hare standing for Labour was comfortably defeated; and so, too, Christopher Hitchens at The Leys, unable to prevent an overall Tory majority. The fee-paying exception was progressive Bedales, where the extrovert and determined Conservative candidate ('We fight on and we fight to win!'), Gyles Brandreth, lost to Labour by 17 votes ('I had only prepared a victory speech – so I gave it anyway!').[16]

That result was declared on Thursday the 15th itself. At the last, the two most trusted opinion polls – NOP and Gallup – both gave Labour a solid if unspectacular lead of 3.1 and 3.5 per cent respectively; Bernard Levin in the very pro-Conservative *Daily Mail* announced he was voting Labour, on the grounds that it was Wilson alone who had 'the requisite will, understanding and capacity' to meet the challenge of the fast-dawning world of 'technology, Russians, computers, diplomacy, Americans, exports, power-blocs, Africans, poverty, wealth and the future'; Anthony Burgess in the *Listener*, after quoting approvingly a correspondent living in Poole who had referred to *Puke Box Jury*, asked, 'How can we march against an enemy whose chief weapon is nausea?'; a BBC spokesman announced that *Swizzlewick* was ending on 11 November ('the initial idea and presentation have not quite "jelled" as we hoped'); and the clerk of the weather produced the wettest day for weeks, especially in the Midlands and south-east during the evening hours that were traditionally the strongest Labour-voting hours. Almost certainly most professional sportsmen voted Conservative, but not two cricketers from contrasting backgrounds as, standing by the Red House pub at the top of Baker Street while waiting to be taken to the airport for MCC's tour of South Africa, they heard coming out of a loudspeaker the booming voice of the Tory candidate for Marylebone, Quintin Hogg. 'As his car went past, I waved a fist and shouted something,' recalled Tom Cartwright, a staunchly Labour man. 'And there was Michael Brearley beside me, and he was doing the same.'

Among the diarists, Daphne Meryon in Emsworth reported early to her local Conservative office and spent the morning 'driving various elderly people to the poll'; poor Nella Last in Barrow, after a sick and feverish night, managed to struggle out to vote, apparently with her husband in tow; Betty Allen in Poulton-le-Fylde fatalistically watched her washing getting soaked in the rain; Madge Martin in Oxford voted Conservative, while noting 'no excitement here'; Kenneth Preston in Skipton High Street enjoyed some brief sunshine and similarly observed 'not a lot of electioneering in evidence'; Kenneth Williams in Hogg's constituency walked to the school at Lisson Grove and in the event voted Tory ('it's the only practical thing to do'); Judy Haines in Chingford barely mentioned the election; Grace Taylor in Ruislip voted in the afternoon, before spending £1 7s 6d as she collected from the menders her husband's black shoes and her own black bootees; and Pat Scott in Barking, after a 'very busy' day at work, voted at around eight despite 'a really bad headache'.

As she did so, the Beatles were playing at Stockton-on-Tees (Paul earlier telling a TV interviewer that the politician's lot was 'a hard day's grind'), the Kinks were at Guildford (with Billy J. Kramer & the Dakotas, Cliff Bennett & the Rebel Rousers, and the Yardbirds also on the bill), and Jacqueline du Pré performed at London's Goldsmiths' Hall; on BBC 1, *Steptoe and Son* was delayed by an hour from its usual eight o'clock slot, following direct pressure from Wilson, worried about absentee voters; and at nine o'clock, as Ron Grainer's familiar 'Old Ned' signature tune struck up and the latest serio-comic drama began in Oil Drum Lane, the polls closed.[17]

*

A stress on Britain's independent nuclear deterrent as opposed to building up conventional forces and strengthening the UN; the lingering, post-*Non* question of the Common Market, as well as relations generally with Europe; the extent of economic planning; completing the denationalisation of the steel industry or renationalising it; attributing restrictive practices more to management or to union failings; sticking largely to existing housing policies or repealing the Rent Act and setting up a Land Commission; the extent of ambitions for the social services and the costing of such ambitions; leaving the educational structure alone or phasing out the 11-plus and seeking to integrate private schools within the state system – on all these matters there existed a legitimate policy choice between the two main parties that may or may not have weighed on the collective minds of the voters as this Thursday they had exercised their democratic will. On the basis of some 1,750 interviews in eighty different constituencies, conducted during the three weeks immediately after the election on behalf of the political scientists David Butler and Donald Stokes, the strong probability is that the overwhelming majority of voters did not deliberately weigh up such issues before making their cross. Typical was the question of Britain's entry into Europe (the Conservatives largely positive, Labour largely negative), on which fully half of interviewees had no opinion either way; when electors did have specific views on specific issues, those views tended to be 'weakly formed' and liable to change; while as for a larger ideological orientation, three out of five voters had no real recognition of the terms 'left' and 'right'. The fact remained, Butler and Stokes reflected in their analysis of the data, that 'the politician, the journalist and the political scientist all tend to encounter people whose interest in politics is grossly unrepresentative of their fellow citizens', as exemplified by the way in which 'those whom an M.P. confronts at a local party meeting, innocent though they are by Westminster standards, will still have much more developed ideas about current policy issues than the average elector'.[18] On what basis, then, *did* the electorate make up its mind?

Their primary explanation came to be known, following the publication of *Political Change in Britain* (1969), which also included the fruits of 1963 and 1966 interviews, as the 'Butler–Stokes model'. Several decades later, the political scientist David Denver helpfully and concisely summarised it:

Three concepts lay at the heart of the model – socialisation; class voting; and party identification (or 'partisan self-image' as they called it). The emphasis was on the importance of long-term factors in determining party choice. At the individual level, voters largely inherited from their parents (especially their fathers) both a class location and a tradition of party support. As the individual came of age, then they developed a party identification and an awareness of the links between classes and parties. When an election came along, this generalised support was translated almost automatically into a vote for the relevant party. Because it was a product of long-term factors, voters were generally stable in their party choice, rarely switching between parties in successive elections. At the level of the electorate, the 'twin pillars' of class voting and party identification sustained a stable two-party system in which electoral change was slow and minimal …

Butler and Stokes did not deny that, at any one election, it did matter – especially when it came to potential last-minute 'switchers' – how the personalities of the respective party leaders, along with the images of their parties, were responded to by the electorate. These, though, were inherently short-term factors – and, in the big Butler/Stokes picture, only relatively marginal in any overall assessment of how voters voted as they did. Social class, above all, still ruled.

Yet there was one other dimension to voter choice – a dimension which, Denver argues, Butler and Stokes did indeed identify, but at the same time perhaps significantly underplay. This was 'valence' issues: the term itself coined by Butler and Stokes, and in essence referring to issues on which the parties were in broad agreement about the ends to be pursued, but where the electorate had to make a judgement about their relative competence in securing those ends. And, for the broad electorate, no issue was more 'valence' in character than the whole area of managing the economy, with its direct impact – for good or ill – on their own economic wellbeing. Or, put bluntly, did voters on 15 October 1964 instinctively reckon, irrespective of their own social background and 'partisan self-image', that Sir Alec Douglas-Home and his party or Harold Wilson and his party represented the better bet when it came to achieving greater job security and a higher standard of living for themselves and their families?

Of course, elections by this time were in some sense increasingly becoming TV elections. Even in 1959, almost three-quarters of homes had had television sets, whether owned or rented; now the box in the corner was near-ubiquitous, residing in 90 per cent of homes, with four-fifths of people saying they received most of their information about politics from television. On the whole, it was no one's finest hour. In 'The Muffling of Television', written just as the campaign got under way, Anthony Howard justifiably complained that television's election coverage had already been 'sewn up by the party machines more tightly than ever before', with the politicians ensuring that 'no candidate may ever run the risk of being confronted by an actual elector'; instead, 'the most that the parties will contemplate is a hand-picked group of journalists who themselves must not apparently be more than three in number'. In short, and lamentably, 'the party machines' were being 'aided and abetted by the timid bureaucracies of the BBC and the ITA'. Nothing significantly changed in the rules of the game as they were played out over the next few weeks, and on 10 October, five days out, the *Liverpool Echo* referred bitterly to how 'thanks to the decision of the All-Party Committee on political broadcasting, politicians are protected at this general election time from being confronted on live television with a public audience'. Even so, all that said, there was still considerable coverage: in addition to 13 PPBs and a plethora of news bulletins, *Election Forum* had the party leaders being questioned on the basis of some 18,000 postcards sent in by voters; BBC 1's constituency-based *Election Gallery* 'produced', in the words of one observer, Martin Harrison, 'lively, if not always authoritative, discussions with peers, non-candidates and experts', albeit handicapped by the absence of actual ministers or candidates; ITV's *This Week* focused on major issues; and both channels included a variety of regional programmes.

Is it possible to reach an overall qualitative assessment? Perhaps not, but undeniably the relationship between politics and television was still very much a work in progress. 'The day still lies ahead,' concluded Harrison, 'when the broadcasters will disclose a major party's evasion of debate as readily as they will report similar conduct by the Communists; when they resolve to defeat attempts to frustrate discussion or coverage; when they consider the public mature enough to laugh at elections [a reference to the liquidation of *TW3*]; and when the system of political broadcasting itself can be freely debated on the air.' Another dissatisfied viewer was the critic Derwent May. 'I think that there is a widespread feeling,' he wrote after it was all over, 'that at the next election the parties have got to let themselves be questioned to the limit – to offer up for full scrutiny their analysis of the situation as it stands, and, without tying their hands to an impossible extent, to give a detailed justification of all they propose to do about it.'[19]

Elections come, elections go. 'Well, an' sooa we're baan to have another General Election,' declared not long before polling day the 'Owd Joss ...' columnist of the *Huddersfield Weekly Examiner*, 'an' Ah will say Ah's be reight glad when it's all ovver, shuse which way it gooas.' It would be wrong, though, to assume automatically a high degree of disengagement on the part of the electorate: TV audiences for PPBs were up on 1959, albeit, at an average all-channel audience of 26 per cent of the population, some 8 per cent less than the average all-channel audience for the entirely non-political programmes being broadcast on the corresponding dates/times in 1963; turnout was a more than respectable 77.1 per cent, down on 1959 but up on 1955; and David Watt, main political commentator for the *Spectator*, boldly claimed that 'public meetings have never been so well attended since

1950 and possibly since 1945'. Even so, the greater weight of evidence points to significant levels of disengagement. Take meetings: in north-east Hampshire, the *Aldershot News* reported that they had been poorly attended compared to 1959; in Glasgow, the biggest crowds flocked not to political gatherings, as had once been the case during elections, but instead this autumn to the Modern Homes Exhibition in the Kelvin Hall; while in Birmingham Sparkbrook, Labour's eve-of-poll rally simply failed to take place because, Hattersley would rue-fully recall, 'nobody except the speakers turned up'. More generally, it was also, though again obviously with exceptions, a quiet election. 'A lot of colour has drained away' was the regretful verdict of the *Preston Herald*'s 'Argus Round the Town' columnist; and in Holborn and St Pancras, Anthony Heap had 'yet to hear a loud speaker van going round the streets' with less than a week to go. Instead, he went on, 'one has to look far and wide to find candidates' posters in windows. As for canvassers, we've had one young girl call on us on behalf of Labour, no one from the Tories.' Such was broadly the tenor of *New Society*'s Paul Barker, who spent the campaign in Halifax. 'The voters,' he found after a serious investigation involving much knocking on doors, 'stayed away from meetings (where they wouldn't have learned much anyway); they would rather watch television than talk to canvassers (and they would prefer that television not to be political); husbands and wives rarely talked politics even with one another.' Ultimately, the prevailing mood – in this as arguably in any election – was one of fatalism; and in Hammersmith, that fatalism came as a disagreeable shock to one ultra-committed, round-the-clock canvasser:

> I fervently wanted Labour to win [remembered Vanessa Redgrave], and was puzzled by the large numbers of housewives and old-age pensioners in the council flats who told me wearily and politely that the election of a Labour government would bring nothing they needed. 'It won't change anything,' they said, 'we'll still be living like this. Labour don't care any more than the Tories.' 'Oh, they *do*, I'm sure they do,' I protested ...[20]

*

Election night itself was, for those who stayed up (which most of the diarists did not), predominantly a televisual experience: on ITV,

Alastair Burnet, political editor of ITN and editor-designate of *The Economist*, as anchorman; on BBC, the inevitable and inimitable Richard Dimbleby – flanked by David Butler and Ian Trethowan, and looking slimmer than usual – 'dominated with his powerful calm and fingernails'. The BBC's 'giant television studio', added 'Pendennis' of the *Observer*, 'looked like a sexy casino devoted to some preposterous gambling. About 200 people sat or stood in the room: on a platform were Robin Day and Cliff Michelmore, waiting for interview-fodder. At the back were rows and rows of pretty girls in pink dresses, sitting at tables, sorting out papers and scattering them round the pundits. At one side was the grey computer, the silent boss of the operation.' The human proceedings were indeed overwhelmingly male: all those pronouncing in the studio; all those reporting from outside the studio; and virtually all the interviewees. 'The count is on,' Dimbleby welcomed viewers at 9.25, but over the next half-hour attention was more or less equally divided between the news of Khrushchev's fall in Russia – news that one day earlier might have significantly helped the Tories – and whether Billericay would be the first seat to declare. As for predictions, the safest came from the ever-articulate Canadian political scientist Robert McKenzie, never far from his trusty swingometer, at around 9.50: 'We're in for a hard day's night.'[21]

And so it duly was, for viewers quite as much as for the political class:

10.00 Cheltenham in fact first. Solid 4½ per cent swing to Labour, somewhat more than what was needed across the country for the party to win an overall majority.

10.12 Salford West. Small swing to Labour (Stanley Orme).

10.19 Salford East. Sizeable swing to Labour (Frank Allaun).

10.24 'Billericay is still panting' (Dimbleby).
Wolverhampton North-East. First West Midland seat. Only 1 per cent swing to Labour (Renée Short).
Guildford. Conservative hold, but Butler noting big increase in Liberal vote.
Wolverhampton South-West. Enoch Powell winning, with swing to Labour of less than 1 per cent.

10.26 Billericay. Brigadier Todhunter, High Sheriff of the county, announcing Conservative hold, with 2.4 swing to Labour not enough in the night's first marginal. Butler also now predicting 'a hard day's night' before outcome sure.

10.40 Butler announcing computer's first prediction: Conservative majority of 20 over Labour.

10.53 Twenty results in. 'It's going to be terribly close' (Trethowan).

10.56 Michael Charlton at Holborn and St Pancras South reporting on Labour's Lena Jeger regaining seat from Geoffrey Johnson Smith.

11.00 Liverpool Exchange. Swing to Labour (Bessie Braddock) of 8 per cent. Latest betting odds: Labour now at 3–1 on.

11.10 Barnstaple. Much-increased majority for Jeremy Thorpe.

11.15 Labour winning in Stockport for first time since 1920s.

11.19 Computer forecast: Labour majority of 31 over Conservatives.

11.21 Liverpool Toxteth. Tory minister Reginald Bevins defeated on 9.9 per cent swing.

11.36 McKenzie: 'I have no doubt whatever in my mind that Labour is headed for a good win.'

11.43 Smethwick. Alderman C. B. Williams, Mayor of Smethwick, standing on balcony with the candidates and attempting to announce result to noisy crowd below. Three warnings in a grumpy Black Country accent: 'Do you mind if I have my say now? ... I do not propose to read this to bedlam ... If you can't be quiet, you'll wait until you are.' Williams eventually able to give the result, producing a large cheer when clear that Peter Griffiths – raising his arms in jubilation – had won. Patrick Gordon Walker smiling gamely. 7.2 per cent swing to the Conservatives, more than double the national swing to Labour. 'Well, this is the most fateful single result of the election' (Trethowan).

11.48 Birmingham All Saints. Labour gain (Brian Walden) with swing to it of only 0.8 per cent. Paddington. Jimmy Edwards defeated.

11.51 Marylebone. Quintin Hogg holding on despite notably large swing to Labour.

11.56 Reporter asking Gordon Walker why his opponent had won. 'A dirty campaign based on immigration ... working up race feelings.'

11.59 Birmingham Perry Barr. The other Conservative gain in the West Midlands after playing the race card.

12.01 Birmingham Sparkbrook. Labour gain (Roy Hattersley), attributed to local prevalence of unemployed car workers.

12.04 Huyton. Hugely increased majority for Harold Wilson (calling results elsewhere 'moderately encouraging').

12.17 Southall. Reduced Labour majority. 'The colour issue does seem to be coming up in these election results' (Butler).

12.21 Hampstead. Huge swing of over 10 per cent, biggest of the night, against the Home Secretary, Henry Brooke, particular *bête noire* of *TW3*.

12.25 Hitchin. Shirley Williams in.

12.31 Day interviewing Keith Joseph. Ashamed of Smethwick? 'The Tory party has disassociated itself from any use of racial, of course it has.' A new leader if the party lost? 'Good lord, no.'

12.34 Rochester and Chatham. Julian Critchley defeated.

12.37 Brierley Hill. Increased Conservative majority. 'The Birmingham area, the Black Country is diverging from the national pattern' (Butler).

12.38 John Morgan interviewing Wilson. 'Do you feel like a Prime Minister? – Quite honestly, I feel like a drink.'

12.45 Orpington. Liberals retaining fairly comfortably.

12.54 McKenzie expecting overall Labour majority of around 20.

12.57 Vox pop in Cardiff. 'If we put Dexter in, we're putting young blood into Parliament' (elderly lady).

1.05 Michelmore interviewing Sir Gerald Nabarro (not standing in the election) and Lord Boothby. Boothby calling the Smethwick result 'the most disgusting thing that's ever happened in British politics'; Nabarro seeing it as part of a pro-conservative trend in the West Midlands because of economic prosperity there; Boothby turning to Nabarro and saying, 'May I ask you just one question, where was the phrase coined, "If you want a n— for neighbour, vote for Labour"?'; Nabarro replying, 'Birmingham, Alabama', and looking very pleased with himself, slapping his thigh.

1.15 Finchley. Margaret Thatcher holding the seat. 'Fairly predictable' (Dimbleby).

1.16 Day interviewing Hogg. 'I see no reason why anyone should be ashamed of Mr Gordon Walker losing his seat.'

1.21 McKenzie: 'We still I think can look to a Labour majority but not a great one.'

1.28 Eton and Slough. Fenner Brockway beaten by 11 votes. 'The racial element again' (Butler).

1.30 McKenzie: 'I want to emphasise the fact that the game isn't wholly over.'

1.33 Wilson returning to Liverpool's Adelphi Hotel.

1.39 Day interviewing Barbara Castle, hoarse after weeks of campaigning. Would she like a post in Wilson's Cabinet? 'Yes, please.' Day remarking that her voice reminded him of Lauren Bacall.

2.03 Cardiff South-East. Comfortable win for James Callaghan over Ted Dexter.

2.09 With a woman hovering behind with a full tray of sandwiches and cups of tea, Butler giving computer's latest prediction: overall Labour majority of 16.

2.20 Dunbartonshire East. Jimmy Reid (Communist) comprehensively losing his deposit.

2.32 Dimbleby announcing that he had heard from 'the outside world' that 'viewers would like to have a quick look at some of the girls who are working around us in the studio and doing such an invaluable job'. Camera focusing on a series of young women in the background.

2.46 Brighton Kemp Town. After five recounts, declaration postponed for the night.

2.47 Michelmore interviewing the *Sunday Telegraph*'s Nigel Lawson. 'The time-for-a-change feeling has proved to be very strong indeed', but 'the British people don't wholly trust the Socialists'.

3.06 Day interviewing downbeat Dexter (the majority against him of almost 8,000 'rather bigger than the scores I'm used to') and avuncular Callaghan.

3.21 Preston North. Julian Amery holding on by 14 votes, the third Tory win by a majority of less than 20. No mention of nuns.

3.43 Trethowan anticipating overall Labour majority of around 11.

4.06 Over two-thirds of results now declared. Final comments of the night. Trethowan: all very tight. Butler: the key marginals to determine next day whether Labour's overall majority would be in the order of 10 to 12 or 'something much more hair's breadth'. McKenzie: 'The whole nation must be on tenterhooks.'

The marathon nocturnal broadcast ended at 4.12; no prizes for guessing the recent hit number that played it out.

'I felt so wretchedly ill when I crawled down to make the fire, not even the news about the Election bothered me.'[22] Nella Last in Barrow had also been too unwell to stay up the night before, and now on Friday morning she missed the BBC's coverage resuming at eight o'clock. Over the next three hours, Labour by seven votes took Brighton Kemp Town, its first-ever Sussex seat, and Mark Bonham Carter lost at Torrington. By 11 a.m., with 199 results still to come, Labour was 67 seats ahead of the Conservatives; but with most of the rest being rural, Conservative-voting constituencies, everyone knew that that lead would narrow considerably. A slow but sure burner awaited for loyal BBC viewers:

11.23 Day interviewing Wilson by phone; Wilson himself in a train just south of Bletchley; Day telling him the latest BBC forecast was an overall majority of eight. 'Well, we just have to wait until the votes are all counted and the results declared, won't we?' A few more questions deadbatted, then Wilson's voice lost as the train going into a tunnel.

11.30 Kenneth Allsop doing vox pop from outside the Stock Exchange. One stockbroker saying the outcome was looking 'problematical', another (top-hatted) talking about Wilson's 'clap-trap'.

12.08 David Dimbleby reporting from Euston station. Top-hatted station master greeting Wilson, accompanied by Mary Wilson clutching an enormous cuddly panda bear. More deadbatting from Wilson – surrounded by an enthusiastic crowd, including building workers otherwise busy transforming the station – before heading off to Transport House in Smith Square.

12.45 Buckingham. Dimbleby senior announcing that one of the dozen or so key marginals left had been won for Labour by 'Captain' Robert Maxwell.

12.46 Maldon. Labour failing to take one of the East Anglian marginals still to declare.

12.48 The Wrekin. Another key marginal held by the Conservatives.

12.50 Eye and Peterborough. Two more Conservatives holds. 'I must say I think things are looking rather worrying for the Labour Party' (Butler). Ealing North. Labour, after a series of recounts, winning by 27 votes.

12.52 Epping. Dimbleby reporting a Labour gain (Stan Newens) in a constituency including a 'rapidly growing' New Town, in fact Harlow.

12.55 Day interviewing Jo Grimond. Understandable emphasis from Liberal viewpoint on the 'gross imbalance' between the votes cast (some three and half million) and the seats won (likely to be six or seven).

12.57 Norfolk South-West. Conservative gain. 'Makes life very difficult indeed for Labour' (Trethowan). 'The position now is extremely dramatic' (McKenzie).

1.02 Cleveland and Dover. Labour winning both, and Butler commenting that it was now almost sure to get an overall majority, however narrow.

1.12 McKenzie smoking a small cigar and anticipating an 'agonising situation' all through the afternoon.

1.18 McKenzie calling a hung Parliament 'a distinct possibility'.

1.19 Day interviewing George Brown (on screen, in Transport House). In truculent mood, Brown first accusing

McKenzie of anti-Labour bias and then refusing to allow him to respond ('I'm not here to have a debate with Robert McKenzie, that's not what you asked me to come for'). As for Grimond's suggestion of possible Labour concessions to the Liberals, including over electoral reform: 'Don't worry yourself quite so much about Mr Grimond, you have an obsession with him.' Things getting friendlier near the end. Day: 'May I call you brother?' Brown: 'If you wish, I would be very flattered and delighted.' Day: 'Goodbye, Mr Brown.' Brown: 'Goodbye Brother Day.' Grins all round, and camera panning to an amused, mildly incredulous Dimbleby. 'Well, three rousing good cheers and a Happy Christmas to all our readers.'

1.29 Dimbleby caught on screen eating a sandwich (probably cheese and salmon).

1.33 King's Lynn. Labour gain by 104 votes – one they were 'desperately' needing to win (Trethowan).

1.36 Butler identifying Meriden and Bedfordshire South as the two crucial seats if Labour to get over the line.

1.41 Hertfordshire East. Dennis Potter defeated.

1.43 Hertford. Anna Harman defeated.

1.46 Bedfordshire South. Conservative hold – 'a blow to Labour' (Butler).

1.51 'We wait for Meriden' (Dimbleby), geographical heart of England.

A tense three-quarters of an hour followed, before at last the two crucial results came through:

2.37 Meriden. Labour gain, by 383 votes.

2.48 Brecon and Radnor. Labour hold, so now up to the magic figure of 315 seats – enough, in effect, for an overall majority.

3.07 McKenzie expecting overall majority of four.

3.12 Dimbleby in sceptical tone reading out statement by Hogg: 'I kept my mouth shut during the campaign, but I thought it would come out like this.'

3.22 Sir Alec finally seen emerging from No. 10. Cheers from almost entirely male crowd. 'I'm going to see the Queen.'

3.49 Day interviewing Lord Attlee, rather more talkative than usual. 'Do you think Mr Wilson is likely to have trouble with the so-called left wing of the Labour Party, or do you think they're likely to keep themselves in check? – I don't think he'll have any trouble, no.' 'What advice do you give to Mr Wilson? – My advice is to go right ahead on your programme.'

3.58 Shots of Wilson, accompanied by his family, coming out of Transport House to go to the Palace and kiss the Queen's hand.

Five minutes later, the Daimler drove through the gates. And from the watching Alan Whicker, only one possible line: 'They're changing the guard at Buckingham Palace.'

It was an undeniably historic moment, with Labour back in power after 13 years in political exile. Two obvious questions now presented themselves. How had they managed to win? And why by such a slim margin (an overall majority of four, as it turned out)?

Wilson was undoubtedly fortunate in his opponents, though for different reasons. 'Alice Douglas-Home lost it for them' was Kenneth Williams's blunt, semi-humorous view of why the Tories had lost; and widespread agreement existed, not least on the part of the commentariat, that a different leader, whether Rab Butler or Reginald Maudling, would almost certainly have been a better bet than the 14th Earl. The PM's failings, though, were not the only reason that whereas Labour's share of the vote (44.1 per cent) remained virtually unchanged compared to 1959, the Conservatives dropped by six full points, down to 43.4 per cent – a drop in significant part attributable to the Liberal share rising from 5.9 per cent to 11.2 per cent. Much was down to Grimond being by some way the best TV performer of the three leaders. 'An engaging person' and the equal of the others in sincerity and intelligence, reckoned the *Spectator*'s J. W. M. Thompson; while according to his biographer, 'if his carefully contrived, errant forelock was already familiar to television audiences by the time the campaign began, by polling day it had secured a place in their hearts'. What about the general zeitgeist? On the face of it, it was all pointing in a pro-Labour direction: an out-of-touch Establishment under challenge from a relatively youthful and decidedly non-Etonian leader combining old-style passion and oratorical skill with new-style meritocratic professionalism; and that compelling image supplemented by the siren calls of modernisation and planning to bring British industry up to date and halt the country's much-talked-about economic decline. Crucially, the whole amounted to a package calculated to appeal to middle-class voters in greater numbers than at any time since 1945. It should, in short, have been a landslide.

But, of course, it was not, perhaps for two main reasons. One was economic: Britain may indeed have been in relative decline, i.e. compared to some other countries, and the warning lights were starting to flash about the immediate outlook; yet what mattered more to most voters in their booths on 15 October was that unemployment was low, the economy was booming and the average standard of living had dramatically improved since the Tories had come to power in 1951. Indeed, when Gallup on the eve of the campaign asked voters which party was better able to maintain prosperity, the Conservatives had the edge by no less than 47 to 34 per cent. Or, to put it another way, why change horses if one was still, to coin a phrase, never having it so good? The other main reason concerned Douglas-Home himself: an overall electoral liability perhaps, but far from solely a liability. Particularly suggestive evidence comes from a Labour canvasser in Oxford. 'What surprised me a great deal was the support enjoyed by Douglas-Home from within the ranks of older working-class voters,' recalled Tariq Ali. 'Time and again one would encounter an expression of genuine affection for the Tory leader from those who were, in any conceivable sense, his polar opposites. The phrase used most often in his favour was that he was a "gent" and had "been at it a long time".'[23] A dignified and patently honest aristocrat in a society that in some fundamental, deep-lying ways was still conservative and hierarchical, with a strong abiding sense of deference: perhaps, after all, Sir Alec was not quite so much a man out of his time.

Even so, he was this Friday afternoon a man out of office. 'No complaints,' he told Derek Hart and Reginald Bosanquet in a joint interview at 4.08, just after Dimbleby had taken a phone call and told viewers not to be startled 'too much' by the news that China had exploded an atomic bomb. 'Everything's happening today, isn't it?' added Dimbleby, while the ex-PM reflected that 'one must take the rough and smooth in public life – win well at times and you must lose well at others'. Soon afterwards, a lengthy filmed portrait of Wilson's life meant (as far as one can tell from YouTube) that BBC viewers actually missed the moment, at around 4.30, when the Yorkshireman achieved his life's ambition and entered No. 10. Minor consolations, not long after five o'clock, were Day interviewing the Labour veteran Manny Shinwell (calling Wilson 'perhaps the most competent Prime Minister we've had in this country I should think for the whole of this century') and Allsop interviewing Fenner Brockway (attributing his defeat to 'an underlying attitude of opposition to the large immigrant population in Slough').

By now the end of the marathon was nigh, with little left bar a quickfire series of vox pops. 'I don't think it'll be any different at all' (man at Euston station). 'I think they will do things, they're very sincere' (veteran railwayman at Lime Street station, Liverpool). 'I think it's important we settle down quickly' (man on street in Cardiff). The BBC's final interviewee was fed by Harold Webb, just outside Lime Street station. Toothier than ever, Ken Dodd played it purely for laughs: Knotty Ash 'a margarine seat'; Harold Wilson not at number 10, but instead Cilla Black; Knotty Ash's black-pudding pickers on strike as the most pressing issue of the day; and the 'Tatty bye' sign-off. One way and another, it was Merseyside's election. And a very last word goes – how could it not? – to the Beatles. 'What will happen if they nationalise you?' an ITN interviewer was reported as jokingly asking them. To which came back (from John?) the instant reply: 'Don't take our money, Mr Wilson.'[24]

PART THREE

16

Can I Help You?

Any Questions? that Friday evening, coming from the Royal Pavilion at Brighton, was inevitably dominated by the election – applause for the almost equally inevitable Bob Boothby when he reiterated that 'the Smethwick election was the most disgusting thing that's happened in the public life of this country' – though the most memorable moment came near the end, with a question about whether the old songs were better than the new ones. Another panellist, the Conservative politician-cum-journalist Bill Deedes, struck a conciliatory note – 'I believe that the Beatles have got harmony and I believe that if you really put your ear to it and try, you can understand and like what they do' – but not Boothby: 'Well, you've got to try damned hard, that's all I can say.' For viewers, the final episode of BBC 2's *The Second Sex* (Joan Bakewell chairing a discussion on 'Men as Equals') was immediately followed at 9.30 by BBC 1's debut outing of *The Kathy Kirby Show*, watched by 21 per cent of the population. 'It was clear' (reported audience research) 'that Kathy Kirby was often considered far too limited to carry a show of this kind – a pleasing appearance and a no more than passable voice, which, in many viewers' estimation, was all this artist had to offer, was just not enough, and her lack of talent in all other directions had been, these viewers indicated, all too apparent in her "coy" introductions and disastrous attempts at humour and dancing.' A 'pleasing appearance' perhaps; but her *Times* obituary almost half a century later would refer to 'her blatant sex appeal' and how during her few heady years at the top 'she was known as "Wet Lips"': ultimately, qualities unlikely to gain her an enduring place in this particular nation's puritanical heart.

A handful of female diarists had their own take on an undeniably historic day:

> David at choir practice – nothing on television, so I just knitted! Bed fairly early – tired. Labour Govt in – majority of 4! *(Betty Allen, Poulton-le-Fylde)*

> Labour is now in power but not with a big majority. Hope they don't ruin the country. *(Gladys Hague, Keighley)*

> A very close fight, which Labour *just* won. Very little excitement anywhere, and I fear I don't care very much, like many others. I don't like the *look* of the new Prime Minister, Mr Harold Wilson, but one never knows. *(Madge Martin, Oxford)*

> We had to queue for a long time and the house was packed. *(Daphne Meryon, Emsworth, on going to see* Goldfinger *in Cosham)*

The fifth diarist was Alison Uttley, weeks away from her eightieth birthday as she pinned her patriotic faith on the goodness in human nature: 'Now the Cons will I hope help, and not heckle too much as Labour tries to clear up the mess.'[1]

At least one Conservative was cheerful enough in this hour of defeat. 'Sorry, old cock' were the immortal words of Reggie Maudling to Jim Callaghan, as the latter replaced him at No. 11 and was about to discover a trade deficit running at £800 million, double what he had expected. Next morning, on Saturday the 17th, after some £25 million of Britain's sterling reserves had flowed out of London the day before, he, Wilson and George Brown (in charge of the newly created Department of Economic Affairs) made the fundamental decision not to devalue sterling – a decision for which they would receive much criticism over the years, mainly on the grounds of its incompatibility with planned growth, yet which was probably unavoidable. The inside story came a quarter of a century later from Wilson's close ally, Edward Short:

> What is not generally known is that the devaluation option was not really available to us because, well ahead of the election, an understanding had been reached on behalf of the Labour Opposition

with Alfred Hayes, President of the New York Federal Reserve Bank, that if we became the Government we would not devalue the pound. In return we received a promise of massive American support for sterling if it should be needed.

This understanding was, I believe, reached without any authority from the Shadow Cabinet but bound the Wilson Cabinet, though I doubt whether most of them knew of its existence.

As for the intrinsic rights and wrongs, an eloquent case for the defence would be made in another ministerial memoir, that of the economically very literate Douglas Jay (who later this Saturday would become President of the Board of Trade), arguing not only that the economic case for devaluation was in itself far less compelling than it had been at the time of the 1949 devaluation, but also that in relation to two key groups – the British electorate and the overseas holders of sterling – there would have been no moral grounds for such an instant, about-turn devaluation, quite apart from a natural reluctance on Wilson's part to allow Labour to be portrayed as the party of devaluation. So, a parity of $2.80 it would continue to be; *contra* Jay, the opportunity was thereby lost for a burst of export-led growth; and, given the difficult budgetary position and outlook, the troika must have known in their bones that hard pounding lay ahead.[2]

Of course, barely anyone at the time knew of the decision that had been taken. Instead, this autumn Saturday, the ailing Nella Last recorded with justifiable satisfaction that she had 'managed to get the fire going & breakfast ready when my husband came down'; Anthony Heap spent the afternoon in Kentish Town buying his son 'another second hand navy blue raincoat for 22/6'; John Thaw had his first TV starring role in the crime drama *Redcap*, albeit initially shown only in the Midlands; while over on BBC *The Billy Cotton Band Show*, with Mrs Mills stepping in for the unwell Russ Conway, had Matt Monro with 61 per cent near the top of the 'enjoyed very much' table, but Rolf Harris and Ted Rogers (35 per cent each) languishing near the bottom. The overall RI was 70, and in the words of one grateful housewife, 'If anyone was feeling down in the dumps or fed up with life (and who doesn't sometimes?) they would have had a tonic tonight.' Including Kenneth Williams? 'One thing is certainly true about me at the present moment: I have no desire for *life*,' he confessed to himself. 'Even as I write this, the awful feeling of guilt about such an admission makes me want to erase it. Why on earth commit such a thing to paper? I suppose all diarists are lonely and uncreative people.'[3]

*

Over the next week, Enoch Powell in the *Sunday Telegraph* took stock of what he saw as declining working-class support for trade unions and predicted that 'in the end the Labour party could cease to represent labour'; Kingsley Amis in Mallorca wrote to friends it was 'a pity that power-crazed, pipe-smoking creep has got into No 10', though adding it was 'a substantially greater relief that that twitching upper-class buffoon is out of it'; Anthony Wedgwood Benn, the new postmaster-general, got his feet under the desk, telling the principal messenger 'that I should be bringing a pint mug, a packet of teabags, a big spoon and a box of saccharine to save him the absurdity of making me trays of tea'; Judy Haines stayed up late to watch the Tokyo Olympics and applaud 'Ann Packer winning the 800 metres in fine style to make Great Britain's 4th gold medal'; Benn, after reluctantly kissing the Queen's hand at Buckingham Palace, 'did the most miniature bow ever seen'; Veronica Lee went to 'the Negro Blues Festival' at Bradford ('I shouldn't think there was anyone in the audience over 25 ... I wonder what happens to people'); Dagenham's Sandie Shaw, recalled by Bob Stanley as the singer who 'did it for all the girls left stood up in the rain', went to no. 1 with '(There's) Always Something There to Remind Me'; BBC 2's much-praised series *The Great War* began its run on BBC 1 ('looks like being the best thing ever done on television,' reckoned Anthony Heap); and, watching at Old Trafford as Manchester United thrashed Aston Villa 7–0, the *Guardian*'s Brian Crowther acclaimed the 18-year-old George Best as 'a slippery player' who 'goes through defences like a knife through butter without employing any such exaggerated movements as the Matthews shimmy'.[4]

On Wednesday the 28th, the *Forres, Elgin & Nairn Gazette* reported without comment that Bailie S. Vass, chairman of the Nairn Burgh Licensing Court, had refused an application by the Scottish Co-operative Wholesale Society for an off-sale licence, but given 'no reason for the decision'; the new Minister of Housing and Local Government, Richard Crossman, told a press conference that the rebuilding of old towns would become 'an increasingly important preoccupation' in his department; and BBC 1's debut 'The Wednesday Play' saw the head of drama, Sydney Newman, playing safe at this stage with an adaptation (*A Crack in the Ice*) of a Nikolai Leskov story (RI an uncontentious 64). Later that week, the announcement that the Queen would be giving up the use of the eight-coach Royal Train was interpreted as a tactful nod to the new Labour government; 'Mrs Wilson's Diary' (initially written by Richard Ingrams and Peter Cook, with illustrations by Willie Rushton) began in *Private Eye*; Slater Walker's Jim Slater revealed the formation of Investment Analysis Limited in order to exploit what he enticingly called 'special situations'; young Kathleen Perry went after work to Earl's Court to inspect the Motor Show ('saw fab Thunderbird'); and the *Sun* finished October, its first full month, with an acceptable but not stellar average daily circulation of 1.47 million. The *News of the World* began November with an almost ritualised attack on the Rolling Stones ('five indolent morons' who 'give the feeling that they really enjoy wallowing in a swill-tub of their own repulsiveness'), before next day an *Evening News* article by Leslie Thomas focused on the newly formed International League for the Preservation of Animal Filament. 'It's really for the protection of pop musicians, and those who wear their hair long,' explained 17-year-old David Jones of Plaistow Grove, Bromley, about his non-existent organisation. 'Anyone who has the courage to wear hair down to his shoulders has to go through hell. It's time we united and stood up for our curls.' 'Dozens of times,' added the already publicity-conscious future David Bowie, 'I've been politely told to clear out of the lounge bar at public houses. Everybody makes jokes about you on a bus, and if you go past navvies digging in the road, it's murder!'[5]

Another evening paper preferred to focus on ATV's new five-days-a-week serial, due to go out for the first time at 6.30. 'It should do well,' predicted the *Birmingham Evening Mail*, explaining that it would be largely set in 'a motel somewhere in the Midlands run by a widowed Meg Richardson (Noele Gordon)'. 'The sets are convincing,' added the paper optimistically; and altogether, on the basis of a sneak preview of early episodes, '*Crossroads* starts acceptably: the test of

durability has yet to come.' To begin with, it seems to have been transmitted on ATV only, with for instance Rediffusion in London preferring a talent show called *Search for a Star* and TWW in Wales and the
West sticking to the American sitcom *Father of the Bride*; while over
on BBC 1, the direct competition was the doomed *Swizzlewick*. The
main driving force behind the new serial was its Australian producer
Reg Watson, who for years had been pestering ATV's Lew Grade
to let him try an American-style soap; the writers were Peter Ling
and Hazel Adair, the combo behind BBC's *Compact*; Tony Hatch
provided a typically seductive theme tune; and Jill Richardson (played
by Jane Rossington) got the ball rolling by answering the telephone
with the words, 'Crossroads Motel, can I help you?'. The first episode
does not survive, but we know the outlines of the plot: a construction
worker causing problems for Meg and her daughter Jill; young Brian
Jarvis feeling miserable on his birthday; his unemployed father, Dick,
hoping to get a job at the local pottery firm; and Dick's wife Kitty,
overseeing the newsagents near the motel, keen to have her husband
out from under her feet and back into work. Next day, the *Evening
Mail*'s headline summed up the verdict of its TV reviewer on a soap
set to be a source of local pride-cum-embarrassment: 'This looks a
winner from the start.'[6]

Monochrome, of course, for the time being; and also for the
time being, no people of colour at the Crossroads Motel – presumably situated not all that many miles from Smethwick, whose
recent election result had continued to reverberate over the past
fortnight. 'It is not colour prejudice or racial intolerance,' Enoch
Powell insisted barely 48 hours after that result, 'to say that only
if substantial further addition to our immigrant population is now
prevented, will it be possible properly to assimilate the immigrants
already here, which in turn is the only way to avoid the evils of
the colour question.' And, he added, 'Conservatives will have only
themselves to blame if they acquiesce in a taboo being placed on
issues which are live and real to millions.' Over the rest of October,
the correspondence pages of the national newspapers had plenty of
letters on the subject; while in the controversy's epicentre, where
ten local ministers had signed a letter condemning Peter Griffiths'
victory, the *Smethwick Telephone* allowed more or less full vent to
prevailing emotions:

The mud-throwing that has gone on against Smethwick people and Mr Peter Griffiths is disgusting. I was under the impression we are free people, able to vote as we please. So why should the clergy and other prominent people of this country tell us how to vote? *(Smethwickian and proud of it)*

May I say in reply to all the outsiders and local clergymen who have expressed their 'concern' and 'disgust' over the result of the election in Smethwick, that I am proud that Smethwick has, in the words of Sir Frank Whittle, had the courage to show the red light on immigration. I think Peter Griffiths fought a clean campaign and he is, in my opinion, the right man for the job. *(J. H. Burford, 43 Stony Lane, Smethwick)*

The great majority of people in Smethwick dislike having coloured immigrants living in the town, although they will obviously not be prepared to say so openly. *(V. B. Penn, 58 Bishopton Road, Smethwick)*

There was the odd exception. 'We had the great privilege and opportunity to rise above the wrong which rejects the brotherhood in our black neighbour,' lamented Constance Harris of 43 Rosefield Road, Smethwick. 'We failed!'

Then on 3 November, the day after *Crossroads* had hit the Midlands' screens, Harold Wilson in the House of Commons raised the political temperature. Breaking off seemingly spontaneously in the middle of his opening address on the Queen's Speech, he referred to Griffiths as 'a Parliamentary leper' so long as he held his seat – immediately provoking uproar and a mass walk out, as some twenty-plus Conservatives followed the example of the Birmingham MP Geoffrey Lloyd. Three days later, the letters in the *Daily Mail* were uniformly hostile to the PM's attack. 'Does Harold Wilson know what it is to walk through a once-pleasant street, to see all the indescribable squalor of a shanty-town displayed in what were once pretty English front gardens?' asked Mrs D. Hardman of Central Hill, Upper Norwood. 'Wilson is deluded if he thinks resentment at Smethwick is isolated. His leper colony at the House of Commons is populated (in spirit) by millions.' Perhaps this was true; for when, about this time, Gallup asked respondents whether they 'would be pleased' to have a 'coloured' person as their neighbour, friend, friend to their children, workmate, employer or in-law, fewer than 5 per cent enthused about the prospect.

Attitudes in Smethwick itself continued to harden, at least to judge by two well-publicised episodes in mid-November. One centred on the Pritam Singhs (father, mother, six children), whose home in Oldbury Road – a general stores, its windows recently smashed in – was due to be demolished in a redevelopment scheme. Now, Smethwick Council was giving them a four-bedroom house in Great Arthur Street – the first time it was moving 'a coloured family' into a council house since the Price Street protest three years earlier. 'I do not mind having them next door so long as they keep themselves to themselves and do not interfere with us,' observed a prospective new neighbour, Sidney Bowser. Another neighbour, an anonymous house-wife, was less tolerant: 'It is not right, is it? They should not be moved in along with us.' The other episode, days later, turned, embarrass-ingly enough, on Smethwick Labour Club, with Pakistani-born Ajore Ali, a member for 26 years, revealing that his 23-year-old, half-white son Oscar had been refused admission there. 'Yes, it's true,' admitted the club's secretary, Leonard Mason. 'Mr Ajore Ali is a member, but he was enrolled a long time ago when there was hardly any coloured people in Smethwick.'[7]

Back on the 3rd, later on the same day as the 'leper' moment, the Commons was treated to an 18-minute maiden speech by Robert Maxwell, loftily ignoring shouts from MPs on all sides to cut it short; on Guy Fawkes night, Philip Larkin in Hull went to see *Goldfinger* ('All right,' he told Monica Jones, 'but back to the dawn of the cinema, sinister orientals, cliff hanging & all'); the *Bideford & North Devon Gazette* reported on the 6th that 'street photographers who use monkeys are not to be banned from Clovelly'; that evening on *Any Questions?*, a question about 'the B.O.A.C. bikini girl', following a protest from a Labour MP about the airline's latest ad, prompted the veteran broadcaster Wynford Vaughan Thomas to reflect, 'I was brought up to believe that a lady ought to have something to get hold of, a luscious armful, she didn't seem to have quite enough about her, but I'd be very happy to find her in Montego Bay'; and on Saturday, the clash at Goodison Park between Everton and Don Revie's recently promoted Leeds United featured an early sending off, brutal tackling, missiles raining on to the pitch, the visitors' black South African winger Albert Johanneson being subjected to Merseyside versions of Zulu chants (as inspired by *Zulu* the film), and the referee being forced to take the players off the pitch for ten minutes, in a vain effort to cool things down.[8] 'I like the relation of the English to their language as they speak it,' Lionel Trilling from his temporary base at Balliol College, Oxford, wrote next day to Allen Ginsberg, 'but it isn't of the kind that is likely to yield poetry. And in general I have the sense that everything here conspires to prevent a lively literature.' The big Oxford story, though, was at Oriel College, where on the 11th it was front-page news that the servants ('scouts') were threatening to go on strike in protest against the declining quality of the undergraduates – 'an absolute shower,' said their head man, Steward Cyril Phillips, adding 'the thing I loathe about modern undergraduates is their whining'. Different concerns for Tony Benn, confirming to the press later that Wednesday that his sons were now going not to fee-paying Westminster but instead to Holland Park Comprehensive ('I hope,' he reflected privately, 'it does something to get comprehensives moving'); and also for David Jones, appearing next evening on *Tonight* to defend what was now more straightforwardly called The Society For The Prevention Of Cruelty To Long-Haired Men. 'Did you get this off the Rolling Stones really?' asked Cliff Michelmore at the end of a sceptical but not unfriendly interview. 'No,' came back the reply, 'that's stupid.'

'EDGWARE GIRL IN NEW TV SERIES' now proudly announced the *Edgware Times*. The girl was Eleanor Bron; and the series was *Not So Much a Programme, More a Way of Life*, successor to *TW3* almost a year after its axing. Scheduled to go out each week late on Friday and Sunday as well as on Saturday, it duly began on Friday the 13th, in theory with three hosts, but David Frost invariably dominating proceedings. Successive RIs that first weekend of 49, 46 and 51 reflected a significant degree of viewer disappointment from those who had been electrified by the generally harder-edged *TW3*, while the response of the critics to the mixture of set-piece sketches and impromptu chat was at best tepid: 'not as good as the old, inspired casualness of *TW3*' (Peter Black); 'a sort of intellectual's *Eamonn Andrews Show*' (John Holmstrom); 'no excuse for the banality, the sponginess, the pointless twitting and twittering' (E. S. Turner). For

many, the main bright spots were John Bird (soon making a speciality of his impersonation of Harold Wilson) and Eleanor Bron herself, especially as the pro-Tory political hostess Lady Pamela Stitty ('I
think people have been jolly unkind about Alec ... he's forceful and
dynamic'). Within days, Bron was receiving an anonymous fan letter
from Brighton:

> Not a very good effort, dear girl – in fact a pretty lousy feeble one.
> You're not a bit like Sir Alec, I'm afraid – too common by far. You
> are more like Nasser, dear girl – same FOREIGN look.
>
> You'll have to do better than this, girlie – what about Patrick
> Gordon Walker [Foreign Secretary despite losing his seat]? Now
> you DO look a bit like him, hook nose and all!
>
> Do leave poor Sir Alec alone – he's very charming you know,
> and strangely, at least half we dull English happen to like him
> immensely. Why not have a go at fat little runt Wilson – see if you
> can be un-biased, like a big girl should be. Try again – or get off!

Did Larkin watch the programme that opening weekend? Perhaps
not, but he was certainly aware of it. 'Satire, Christ,' he exclaimed
to Monica Jones. 'Really, when you come to think of it, wasn't life
during the war *morally purer* than life during peace?'[9]

On Tuesday the 17th, ten days after the Battle of Goodison Park, the
literary critic and football aficionado Karl Miller told a journalist that
he had no problem with dirty play and spectator aggression ('at least
they *care* – violence is a sure guarantee of earnestness'); four months
after Gallup had revealed only one in ten voters wanting complete
freedom of entry for non-white immigrants from the Commonwealth,
the debate in the Commons on the annual renewal of the 1962 Act
conclusively demonstrated relatively little difference between the
positions of the two front benches, both in favour of control; and
BBC TV's flagship arts programme, *Monitor*, passed the editorial-
cum-presentation baton from Huw Wheldon to Jonathan Miller. The
result was its lowest-ever RI (41), with many viewers muttering about
'too clever by half' and finding particularly objectionable the 'long
stint' of 'pseudo-highbrow chatter' with Susan Sontag. *Punch*'s E. S.
Turner, calling Miller 'brightly infuriating', was little kinder, while
even the *Guardian*'s TV critic, Mary Crozier, found the 25-minute

discussion between Miller and Sontag about popular culture largely 'pretentious'. Next evening's Wednesday Play saw it for the first time tackling a contemporary British theme, with Alun Richards's *The Big Breaker* about Welsh provincial life gaining an RI of 68 ('the play seemed very real, viewers often said'); later in the week, the *NME* had Dusty Springfield declaring 'I wish I'd been born coloured', though adding 'I see how some of them are treated and I think, "thank God I'm white"'; and Anthony Heap's Saturday turned on his 8-year-old rented TV set having conked out the day before:

> Call in at Grays Inn Radio on way to Market and buy a 66 guinea 19 inch Ultra set for £60 and our old Murphy [radio] in part exchange – plus a 35/- indoor aerial for the new channel on '625 lines' (BBC 2).
>
> Delivery is promised for 4.0 but at 3.15 we get a message that it won't be coming till 'between 6.0 and 7.0.' Actually it arrives at 9.15, so that by the time it's been installed and tried out on each channel, this week's instalment of The Great War is over and I've scarcely seen any of it. Exasperating!

Still, it was all relative. Sometime this month, on a damp and misty late afternoon, Shirley Baker took one of the great twentieth-century photographs: in the foreground, a pregnant 29-year-old mother, Pat Swindells, on her way home from school, accompanied by two small boys and a baby in the pram; in the background, three newly built tower blocks; and more immediately behind the family, a flattened urban landscape looking for all the world like Dresden the morning after. 'They were pulling down the houses here to build flats – there was a lot of regeneration going on in Salford then,' she would recall half a century later. 'We lived close by, in two rooms behind a shop. We slept in one room – me, my husband and the children – and lived in the other. The boys were being brought up in horrible conditions; we didn't even have a bath. In the front, a man repaired teeth; I cleaned the shop for him every day and he paid for my milk.' As for the drastic slum clearance, hers was an implicit acceptance of its inevitability; and a few years after Baker's photograph, the family moved into 'a nice big council house near the football fields, for the boys to play in', and 'I thought I'd won the pools'. 'It was,' she added on the eve of her eightieth birthday, 'a happy marriage at first. Aren't they all? But I did leave him when the boys were all grown up; I was too scared to leave any earlier.'[10]

*

By the time of Heap's TV frustrations, Britain was moving into a full-scale sterling crisis. During the Labour government's early weeks, the City – viscerally hostile – had just about given it the benefit of the doubt, in the context of an undeniably difficult economic legacy left by Maudling and co. Even so, at the annual Mansion House bankers' dinner on 3 November, it was clear that Callaghan as the new chancellor and Lord Cromer as governor of the Bank of England (not yet independent in its monetary policy) were coming from very different places. After Callaghan had optimistically invited the City's 'co-operation' in a 'joint effort to create a fairer, a more productive and more progressive society', and on a day in which the Queen's Speech had announced the government's intention to abolish prescription charges and increase pensions, the far from politically neutral central banker not only stated gravely that 'the future prosperity of this country at home and its power in the world abroad depends above all on the strength of the pound', but insisted that 'we must reduce expenditure in this country which distracts resources from contributing to the top priority of closing the [balance of] payments gap'.

Eight days later, 11 November, saw Callaghan's emergency Budget. Taken as a whole, it was (in the words of Callaghan's biographer Kenneth O. Morgan) 'mildly deflationary'; but the hostages to fortune, in terms of possible reaction on the part of the City and the broader international financial community, were its increased social expenditure (especially pensions and benefits) on the one hand, its pledge to introduce a corporation tax and amplified capital gains tax on the other. 'Callaghan on TV [in his evening broadcast] made a good show as the good-humoured, sensible, non-class man,' noted one well-disposed and especially perceptive diarist, Phyllis Willmott. 'I must say he did seem "more straight", more lively, more "with" than "above" "the people" than the Tories have ever seemed ... *Our* taxes are up ... I'm glad enough that we should be poorer for the sake of the really poor *and* the New Britain.' 'But,' she asked herself, 'what about everyone else?'

A fair question, not least given the 6d rise in the standard rate of income tax. In the event, while the initial City response was that the first Labour Budget since 1951 could have been a lot worse (the *FT*'s 'Lex' observing that 'none of the feared frightfulness was in evidence'), it was the foreign exchanges which took against it almost from the start – essentially on the grounds that it had been insufficiently tough – and proceeded to give sterling a bad day on Thursday the 12th. Next day, not only did sterling have a torrid time, but the mood in the domestic equity market was (according to the financial journalist Kenneth Fleet) 'something approaching despair' as stockbrokers and institutional investors began to catastrophise about the new taxes (corporation and capital gains) in the absence of specific detail about either their rates or their mechanics once they were introduced the following spring. By the end of the day, Cromer was pushing Callaghan to increase Bank rate from 5 to 6 per cent and thereby restore 'confidence' in 'the future stability of the currency'; while Virginia Potter, an American who was married to a former officer in the Grenadier Guards and had lived for many years in Brixham (where her husband was a champion yachtsman), expressed something of the mood of the solidly Conservative-supporting middle class. 'Of course Wilson is hoping for a snap election in the Spring – and assuming all the pensioners and widows who will now get more money, will vote for him, then God help us,' she wrote that day to her mother. 'One wouldn't mind paying more I/Tax if it would help the country to get on its feet, but it will only cause inflation. I think the most frightening thing is that we have two *Hungarians* [Nicholas Kaldor and Thomas Balogh] as economists behind Wilson and Callaghan – Expect they are Communists!?'[11]

Monday the 16th was the Lord Mayor's annual banquet at Guildhall: Wilson in stipulated white tie expressing his unshakeable determination to keep the pound 'riding high', but both George Brown and Benn rebellious enough to wear black tie. 'As we left dinner,' noted the latter, 'some City bigwig shouted, "Why aren't you properly dressed?" I didn't hear him but he caught Caroline [Benn's wife] by the arm and repeated it to her. She was extremely angry.' The rest of the week unfolded with a certain inevitability: on Tuesday and Wednesday, equities failing to recover, sterling under renewed pressure, foreign exchange reserves continuing to drain away; later on Wednesday, after Wilson had earlier accused Cromer to his face of 'deflationary prejudices', the PM overriding the more compliant Callaghan and refusing to bow to the governor's demand for an immediate 1 per cent rise in Bank rate to 'stop the outflow'; on Thursday, with markets predictably disappointed by the lack of a Bank rate rise, the outspoken Brown lambasting currency speculators as the 'gnomes of Zurich'; on Friday, against the backdrop of a terrible day in the markets requiring a serious rearguard action by the Bank of England in the foreign exchange market, Cromer now pushing for Bank rate to go up to 7 per cent, even as another City panjandrum, Sir George Bolton, was referring in his diary to '£ under immense pressure' and 'Roly [Cromer] trying to educate Wilson & Co about life'; and on Saturday, once it became clear there was going to be no direct American help to shore up sterling (whatever the promises earlier in the year), ministers reluctantly agreeing to raise Bank rate on Monday morning from 5 to Cromer's desired 7 per cent. Altogether it was, reflected Richard Crossman on Sunday, 'the kind of classical financial crisis socialist governments must expect when they achieve power and find the till empty'. Next day, the initial response of markets to the interest-rate hike was cautious; but by this time the damage had been done to whatever confidence – arguably always nugatory – the City and its friends had had in the new government.

The two ensuing, highly charged days, Tuesday the 24th and Wednesday the 25th, paid for all. Tuesday began with the *FT* accusing Labour generally of a fatal 'tendency to underrate the importance of things, like markets and foreigners, which its traditional philosophy does not cover' and continued with some eight or nine hours of heavy selling of sterling and desperate attempts by the Bank, increasingly in danger of exhausting its cash reserves, to prop up the currency. Late that evening, confronted at a memorable summit meeting at No. 10 by Cromer demanding serious deflationary action – including a credit squeeze, a reduction in the level of the recently introduced import surcharges, and the naming of a specific target figure for a reduction in public expenditure – if an international rescue package was going to be arranged, Wilson held firm:

Commenting on the suggestion that there might be difficulty in getting central bank assistance, the Prime Minister said that if central banks and their governors were going to impose a situation in which a democratically elected government was unable to carry out its election programme, then he would have no alternative but to go to the country. He would expect to win overwhelmingly on that xenophobic issue and would then be free to do anything he liked – devaluation included.

Faced by this explicit threat (realistic or otherwise) of a 'bankers ramp' election, Cromer quite sensibly took a step back from the brink. He promised he would indeed do his best over the next 24 hours to persuade central bankers around the world to contribute to such a package – but *without* giving them a binding promise from the UK government that it would adopt the policies that Cromer believed to be necessary. By seven o'clock on Wednesday evening, after another terrible day for sterling and following numerous telephone calls from Threadneedle Street, a $3 billion credit from foreign central banks had been secured. It was undeniably a remarkable achievement on the Bank's part; but as Alec Cairncross, the government's economic adviser, would recall years later, it received 'small thanks' from ministers, despite having put its 'neck on the block'.

For all concerned, it had been a thoroughly bruising episode, ultimately about a competing choice of priorities: politicians with a democratic mandate putting social purposes as their first priority, whereas the very different assumptions shared by the City and the holders of sterling were simply those that suited themselves best (though they may also have believed in them). Was there a way of squaring the circle? In early December, fighting a heavy cold, the PM was interviewed on *This Week* by George Ffitch; and Wilson was adamant that, despite early squalls, he was still wholly committed to modernisation and to expansion:

> The problem is to galvanise British industry, to get exports going, to modernise industry … Already we're hard at work with the new Ministry of Technology, with Mr Brown's Department of Economic Affairs, working out a dynamic plan for expansion … Above all, we are going to get away from the rather slothful attitudes in industry, we are going to have a modern, dynamic, robust and competitive economy …

Fine aspirations, but, of course, the City would remain the City, and Labour would remain Labour, involving for the foreseeable future a high degree of mutual ignorance, prejudice and even demonisation. Previous Labour governments had already suffered grievously from bankers (whether central, merchant or clearing) stubbornly unwilling even to try to see a bigger socio-economic picture, so memories and resentments ran understandably deep; whereas with so much accumulated wealth and privilege at its disposal, the strangely cloistered – and still fiercely tribal – Square Mile should have been capable of a more mature and rounded approach. Eloquent testimony would come the following summer, when (in the context of another Labour/City controversy) *The Economist* looked back at the previous autumn and claimed, presumably with justification, that 'anybody who went to the City at this time was apt to be met with the retailing of venomous personal slanders against every cabinet minister under the sun, and to be disturbed by the spectacle of men in charge of millions of pounds of investable funds who solemnly propounded that the policy of this rather conservative Labour Government was motivated by a deep-laid international communist plot'.[12] Faults on both sides, to be sure; but the greater blame, going well beyond a new administration's tactical errors, surely lay with the men of money, so devoid of imaginative sympathy.

*

'They mistake violence for strength,' reflected Leonard Woolf on 26 November (the day after the rescue) about the new Labour government, 'and though I think their economic measures were generally right they seem to have messed things up by the crude way they put them into operation.' That Thursday, at least one student in increasingly chilly Leeds was struggling with a rising discipline, not always nourishingly taught. 'Hateful Robertson gave us a lecture on our flippant attitude to sociology and the God, [Talcott] Parsons,' noted Veronica Lee. 'I wanted to cry throughout the lecture as I couldn't understand, I know I never shall, and I've got the dread of this essay hanging over me. I just can't get the relevance of functionalism.' Next day was pop day: 'I Feel Fine' released; Virginia Ironside's interview with John Lennon appearing in the *Daily Mail* ('Mums? Yes, well,

it's a good thing, isn't it, that the mums are coming round to us');
and that evening the Beatles appearing on *Ready, Steady, Go!*, but
not Twinkle. 'I think they are being very childish and should face up
to life,' the 16-year-old said from her home in Malden, Surrey, about
RSG's refusal to let her perform 'Terry', her new song about a motor-
cyclist with a death wish. On Saturday, John Fowles went for dinner
to Edna O'Brien's 'Putney human zoo' and met Rita Tushingham ('a
peaked, bright-eyed face; a "nice kid" who happens to answer the
age's need for a lowest common denominator heroine, an epitome of
chirpy lower-class unpretentiousness; a figure they can "feel" with;
identify with, in the jargon'); the BBC on Sunday evening celebrated
Churchill's imminent ninetieth birthday with a variety programme,
scripted by Terence Rattigan and presented by Noël Coward, featuring music-hall songs of his youth ('I believe,' wrote Vere Hodgson,
'the Dear Old Man looked in and loved it all'); *Punch* on 2 December
featured not only Robert Robinson mulling over the popular press's
treatment of recent financial events ('the hallucination that the £ was a
decent little chap who had been adopted by a bunch of warm-hearted
foreigners who were all having the best brought out in them by Roly
was hard to resist'), but two pages of Peter Dickinson's sharply witty
verses ('From Slum to Chic') about the quite rapidly spreading process of gentrification ('One day the shop abandoned Silver Shred/And
offered Oxford marmalade instead'); the novelist C. P. Snow, who was
now Lord Snow with a position at the new Ministry of Technology,
told the Lords that 'we've got to change the climate of society at least
enough to respect those who make the wealth'; and that Wednesday
evening's *Z-Cars* was the last classic episode, in the sense of being
written by the great John Hopkins. 'Made me wish I could live to
the year 2000 to see the fruition of some of the wonderful schemes
for re-building our principal towns,' commented a secretary on BBC
1's *The Rape of Utopia*, a vivid documentary shown on Thursday
about the remodelling of Britain's cityscapes. Unsurprisingly, given
the title, not every viewer was quite so thrilled about what would lie
ahead in the twenty-first century. 'The magnitude of modern architecture looked more terrifying than inviting, it was said several times,'
noted audience research, 'with, in "rectangular masses", a possibility that individuality and character would be sacrificed to material
improvement.'[13]

Straight after this programme came *Gallery*, showing highlights of the evening's debate at a packed Oxford Union. 'Extremism in the defence of liberty is no vice, moderation in the pursuit of justice is no virtue' ran the motion; main speaker against it was the Conservative MP Humphrey Berkeley; and, supported by the Communist poet Hugh MacDiarmid, principal speaker for it was Malcolm X, the best-known member of the Nation of Islam, a black separatist organisation. 'I've never addressed such a well-dressed white audience before,' he whispered to Tariq Ali shortly before speaking – a speech in which he asserted that 'my reason for believing in extremism, intelligently directed extremism, extremism in defence of liberty, extremism in quest of justice, is because I firmly believe in my *heart*, that the day that the black man takes an uncompromising step, and realizes that he's within his rights, when his own freedom is being jeopardized, to use any means necessary to bring about his freedom, or put a halt to that injustice, I don't think he'll be by himself'. The applause at the end lasted for a full 90 seconds; but despite that ovation, those present – members of the Oxford Union and their guests, almost certainly comprising an audience of largely right-wing sympathies – defeated the motion by 228–91. The margin would probably have been wider, but for how Malcolm X in his speech, to quote Tariq Ali, 'broke with black separatism in public, declaring that interracial marriages were fine and that blacks and whites had to get together to fight the system'.

Three days later, on Sunday the 6th, another black visitor was in equally eloquent action. 'Morality cannot be legislated, but behaviour can be regulated,' Martin Luther King declared from the pulpit of St Paul's. 'The law cannot make a man love me, but it can stop him lynching me, and that is quite important.' Among those present was the 21-year-old Darcus Howe, future uncompromising campaigner for racial justice. 'Martin Luther King's attack on the "demolition of self-worth" that was at the heart of racism, was the first time I had heard a black person make a challenge about our position,' he would recall; and accordingly, 'I started, like many blacks, to taste the possibility of remodelling our lives'. After the sermon, Dr King gave a press conference. 'I think it's a fact now, and everybody knows it, that there are growing racial problems in Britain as a result of the large number of coloured persons from the West Indies, from Pakistan and

India who are coming into the country,' he told ITN. 'And it is my feeling that if Britain is not eternally vigilant and if England does not, in a real sense, go all out to deal with this problem now, it can mushroom and become as serious as the problem we face in some other nations.'[14]

Over the next week or so, Kenneth Williams went to the Warner in Leicester Square to see *Carry On Cleo* ('the content was diabolical', notwithstanding his own immortal line 'Infamy! Infamy! They've all got it in for me!'); the Crathorne Committee on the law and Sunday observance recommended some liberalisation ('I think that it is about time that the cinema people were allowed to please themselves and not to be dictated to by antique laws regarding Sunday entertainment,' positively responded C. L. Fowler, president of the Huddersfield and District Cinemas Association, to his local paper, though conceding that 'the feelings of managers and staff are mixed on the subject of opening on Sunday afternoons'); Alison and Peter Smithson's latest act of brutalism, the *Economist* building in St James's, was formally opened, prompting the pro-modernist – but not zealously so – architectural critic Diana Rowntree to observe that 'the plan speaks in spaces rather than in solids, and harks back to the narrow, unexpected courts of the City of London'; Daphne Meryon 'tied up parcel for Oxfam', a name and cause starting to become increasingly prominent; Twinkle managed to get a slot on *Top of the Pops*, albeit 'many viewers objected strongly' to a song 'which they claimed was "so horribly morbid" as to deserve to be banned'; the ire was even greater for presenter Jimmy Savile ('comment by those who freely expressed their feelings was liberally larded with such terms as "this nutcase"; "this obnoxious 'thing'"; and "this revolting spectacle"'); the BBC announced its intention from January to provide more accessible and story-driven Wednesday Plays; Alan Watkins in the *Spectator*, looking ahead to eventual life after Sir Alec, noted that the Conservatives had 'long ceased being the party of the land', were now 'ceasing to be the party of big business', and instead were 'becoming, or trying to become, the party of the consumer'; and 18-year-old Ashok Chudasama arrived in cold Blackburn. 'It was bleak and, living up to its name, it was black: the buildings were all black, the many mill chimneys were all black, my future seemed black,' he remembered about having left Tanzania to try his luck in the Lancashire textile industry. 'I was amazed at the row upon row of terraced housing that seemed to go off in all directions, climbing right up to the grey sky. I stood and shivered and wished I was back in Dar Es Salaam with all the warmth and colour of East Africa around me.' Two years older, a pop critic was already disillusioned by the scene. 'I honestly think that if I hear one more rhythm and blues number sung by some crumby white group with long hair from Barnes, I shall scream,' Virginia Ironside informed a friend. 'The whole Mersey thing is collapsing fast ... the Beatles are still alright, so are the Stones and a few others, but the rest have died – usually after one hit ... Cathy McGowan struggles on ... she won't last long though ... she's already getting dated ...'[15]

'John and I enjoyed our kipper tea in peace and "The Count of Monte Cristo", a Bob Hope, Pauline Goddard Film & Square World,' recorded Judy Haines in Chingford on Sunday the 13th; and she added that 'Pam returned in time for Kipling', referring to a series of dramatisations of his stories which was also a favourite of Vere Hodgson ('Kipling is returning to favour'). All reasonably standard fare, but the BBC was about to show three TV programmes that were each of real resonance. No watershed on Tuesday the 15th, as Peter Watkins' documentary *Culloden* between 8.15 and 9.00 reconstructed in pioneering, almost post-modern style the last pitched battle on British soil, letting his viewers work out for themselves – in the later words of Alex Cox, who watched it on his tenth birthday and instantly resolved to be a pacifist – 'the parallels between what the Americans were doing in Vietnam and what the English had done to the Scots'. 'This, one felt, is what it was really like; this is war,' declared one appreciative critic, Maurice Wiggin. 'It was that most uncommon experience, a television programme which went on working in the mind ...' An hour later, the third edition of the new-look *Monitor* (presenter: J. Miller; producer: M. Bragg) was a double-header: first, the highly articulate Susan Sontag in conversational battle with the highly articulate New York architect Philip Johnson; then, enabling a respectable overall RI of 61, a Patrick Garland film, 'Down Cemetery Road', in which John Betjeman went to Hull to interview Philip Larkin, though doing much of the talking himself. 'A likeable man', writing poetry that was 'never obscure', was viewers' favourite verdict on Larkin, while a watching Anthony Burgess 'experienced one of those rare glimmerings of conviction: here is a poet who is going to be major'. Third up in the sequence, next evening on BBC 2 at 9.55, was the debut episode ('Entente Cordiale') of *The Likely Lads*. 'Apprentices Terry and Bob,' previewed the *Radio Times*, 'discover that a French girl they met while on holiday in Spain is planning to visit them ...' The setting was an electrical workshop; it was the first sitcom to feature working-class Geordies; viewers, awarding it an RI of 69, gave the thumbs-up ('a good working-class story without the kitchen sink ... natural comedy at its simple best ... very good and down to earth – just the way two boys would talk to each other'); and the discerning Wiggin reckoned that 'there's definitely something there'.[16]

During the Christmas run-up – this year, in all self-respecting toy shops, the very zenith of the Dalek craze – Henry St John visited Lyons in South Kensington, only to find service almost at a stand-still ('a man in the queue could hardly contain himself for impatience, and, addressing a man in front of me rather than me, remarked that if it were not for the coloured people we should not get anything to eat'); three male experts discussed in the *Lancet* the side effects of oral contraceptives, i.e. the pill, and noted that on the positive side of the ledger was increased pleasure in sexual intercourse, 'which some people remark upon with gratitude'; Anthony Heap took a Sunday afternoon wander around 'the unfamiliar locality of Shoreditch and Hoxton – a wilderness of decrepit old slums, drab new blocks of council flats, and desolate wasteland even more depressing than I'd imagined it to be'; and nine months after Radio Caroline, another pirate station anchored off the Essex coast, Radio London, began broadcasting (first British music radio station to have American-style hourly news bulletins, irreverent 20-year-old jingle-specialist Kenny Everett an early presenter). 'A white Christmas after all,' recorded Judy Haines on Christmas Day. 'It was predicted and then the forecasters funked it. Well, it was certainly cold enough for it.' The day was notable for the death of Claudia Jones, founder of the Notting Hill Carnival as well as the *West Indian Gazette*; while in the evening, millions tuned in for BBC 1's *Christmas Night with the Stars*, thereby through a seven-minute spot giving national exposure to the exploits of Bob and Terry (with BBC 2 still only being watched by those in London and the Midlands who had the right receivers). On Boxing Day B. S. Johnson was at the City Ground to report for the

Observer on Nottingham Forest v Spurs, an experience that would be his starting point for *The Unfortunates*; V. S. Naipaul's London letter next day for the *Illustrated Weekly of India* lamented the 'blinkered cosiness' among British novelists and playwrights, so that 'people like myself, unwilling or unable to enter these private cultural sports, have no business here'; *Crossroads* from the 28th was available for viewers in London and the Home Counties; Blackburn's 116-year-old clock tower was demolished on the 30th; 'the Beatles are as good as ever,' Kingsley Amis informed Robert Conquest, apparently non-ironically, on New Year's Eve; and the middle-aged artist Keith Vaughan saw in the New Year mingling with a quarter of a million of the young (what he termed 'Generation X') between Piccadilly Circus and Trafalgar Square. 'I did not notice one ugly or uncomely person,' he noted admiringly in his diary. 'Fleet-footed, warm-hearted, tender, perplexed, they were good to look at and good to be with … The fountains were full of wet boys instead of water. The roads were blocked with stationary traffic. But in two hours I saw not one clumsy, brutal or vicious gesture. All was in good sport and good heart.'[17]

During that second half of December, two moments – one of them historic, the other truly awful – would come to seem connected. The first was at 11.14 p.m. on Monday the 21st: two decades after the Labour MP Sydney Silverman had been unable to persuade the Attlee government to repeal the death penalty, and after a sometimes emotional eight-hour debate (Silverman's voice choking as he reached his peroration), the Commons at the crucial second reading endorsed by 355 votes to 170 his bill to abolish capital punishment for all types of murder. Among those joining him was the newly converted Henry Brooke, former Tory home secretary; among those voting on the other side were Quintin Hogg, Margaret Thatcher and William Whitelaw. 'At last the gallows have gone,' recorded Tony Benn, and a younger diarist shared his satisfaction. 'I am pleased that no-one again will be hanged in this country,' reflected Laurence Marks, 'because what if we hang the wrong man … or woman come to that? Was Hanratty guilty? Well if he wasn't it's too late to do anything about it now, isn't it.' Five days later, on Boxing Day at Silcock's Wonder Fair in the Ancoats district of Manchester, Myra Hindley and Ian Brady abducted ten-year-old Lesley Ann Downey. They took her to their home, where (in all probability) Brady raped her before murdering her. 'Nothing in criminal behaviour before or since has penetrated my heart with quite the same paralysing intensity,' remembered John Stalker, then a CID officer, about listening to the recording that Brady made as he tortured his victim. All the evidence suggests that in late 1964 only a minority of the public, perhaps only a quarter, were in favour of the abolition of the death penalty.[18] Even so, most of the abolitionists at Westminster assumed this was effectively the end of the story, certainly once Silverman's bill had become law in November 1965; but perhaps inevitably, and certainly understandably, it was not quite so simple as that.

*

Back at the start of 1965, Harold Wilson's first New Year Honours list was notable for its absence of any hereditary peers – an absence prompting the *Sunday Telegraph's* T. E. Utley to argue that, albeit 'hereditary social privilege and hereditary political duty' rang somewhat hollow in 'contemporary Britain', a strong case remained for the principle of hereditary peers, with their 'sense of obligation' and 'moral incentive', as well as tending to 'have more in common with the average citizen than have that citizen's elected representatives'. Saturday 2 January saw the start of *World of Sport*, ITV's rival to *Grandstand*: fronted by Eamonn Andrews, it focused heavily from the start on horse racing (the Haileybury-educated John Rickman politely doffing his hat to his largely working-class viewers) and professional wrestling (Kent 'Greetings, grapple fans' Walton the already well-established commentator, Jackie 'Mr TV' Pallo almost a weekly fixture, but the masked, Samurai-style Kendo Nagasaki, real name Peter Thornley, deemed for several years too over the top to be allowed to appear); two days later, Anthony Heap grumbled about inflation ('the Odeon cinemas now charge 4/- and 3/6 for stalls and 5/6 for circle seats'); T.S. Eliot died; British Railways was now British Rail, with the soon-to-depart Dr Beeching unveiling that Monday at the Design Centre what would become the classic double-arrow logo; and on Wednesday the 6th, BBC 1 relaunched its so-far rather faltering Wednesday Play. 'WARPED PLAY ABOUT NASTY PEOPLE' was the gratifying headline in next day's *Daily Telegraph*, as L. Marsland Gander laid into *Tap on the Shoulder*, a story (written by James O'Connor, directed by Ken Loach) of crooks being accepted into the Establishment. But for all it being 'depraving' as well as 'warped', Gander did concede 'there was no denying the dramatic quality'; and altogether, it marked 'a provocative start for the BBC's new Wednesday night series, for which many new plays have been found'.

According to taste, these were ominous or enticing words. A recent BBC survey had asked over a thousand members of its Viewing Panel about what *type* of TV plays – women generally much keener on the genre than men – that they had a predisposition to 'like very much'. The findings, given by percentage of respondents reacting positively to mention of a particular type, were revealing enough:

> with detective story plots – 56
> based on real events in the past – 47
> dealing with real present-day problems – 42
> about ordinary nice people – 34
> meant to be amusing (but not farcical) – 32
> with a wartime setting (any war) – 27
> about working-class life – 25
> in costume (historical settings) – 22
> of science fiction – 21
> about modern teenagers (or young people) – 13
> with plenty of violent action – 13
> with strong sex interest – 11
> relying largely on fantasy – 7
> relying on ideas, with little or no story or plot – 2

Soon afterwards, in February 1965, another survey – this time on ITV's behalf – asked viewers about plays on all channels. 'It is often difficult to know what the play is about,' concurred 68 per cent; 60 per cent agreed that 'they don't have enough plays that all the family can watch'; 53 per cent that 'they give too much emphasis to sex'; and the proposition that 'they concentrate too much on the seamy side of life' had 52 per cent nodding their heads.[19]

The day after the gracious royal tap on the shoulder, the *Listener*'s TV critic was in fiery mood ('my New Year resolution,' declared Anthony Burgess, 'is to form a new *Davidsbund* to fight the

Philistines, the disc-jockeys, the intellectual adulators of pop-tripe, the negritudinizers, and the grovellers before the slack-mouthed youth'); 31-year-old twin brothers Ronald and Reginald Kray were remanded on a charge of demanding money by menaces; and on *Top of the Pops* (Twinkle now banned), Alan Freeman, by announcing Sounds Orchestral's 'Cast Your Fate to the Wind' as 'Cast Your Wind to the Fates', won the imperishable nickname 'Fluff'. Entertainment highlight on Saturday the 9th, hours after viewers had reacted poorly ('how silly she looked with all that black on her eyes and those awful false eyelashes') to Dusty Springfield's make-up on *Juke Box Jury*, was the debut, on BBC 2, of *Not Only... But Also*, starring Peter Cook and Dudley Moore, with John Lennon as special guest reading two of his poems. Not everyone loved it. Judy Haines's husband John was 'tired and not in mood for that', while the TV critic Philip Purser found it 'pleasant but surprisingly subdued, almost cosy'. But viewer reaction generally was positive, with a 'very promising' RI of 67 and particular appreciation 'because it did not rely for its humour on politics, crime or crude satire'. Or to quote Harry Thompson, 'thus was born the most successful sketch show of its age, if not of all time' – at the heart of which were 'the Pete and Dud dialogues, semi-improvised conversations between the cloth-capped, working-class Cockney *alter egos* of the two performers', all set against 'the Dagenham milieu' that Moore himself knew intimately.[20]

The day after that debut, George Melly wrote his first pop music column for the *Observer* ('for anyone over 20 who can listen without bias it's a mild stimulant'), but the big story of the next two or three days was the press's quite sudden concentrated focus on the London County Council's intention to close down Risinghill, a co-educational comprehensive in a poor part of Islington where the twin crimes of the school's head, Michael Duane, were his banning of the cane and of expulsions. Later that week, on Friday the 15th, Reyner Banham's stout defence of the Smithsons' *Economist* building ('a characteristic 50 years late, London's flat, dozy skyline is at last beginning to exhibit the physiognomy of a 20th-century metropolis') included a sharp poke at Ian Nairn (his wish to fill up the piazza around the new building 'with stalls, kiosks and the like' dismissed as a 'routine sentimental craving to cram every public space with "life", "spontaneity" and all that medieval Merrie-Merrie'); the *NME*'s Derek Johnson acclaimed 'I Can't Explain', first single by the Who, as 'a pounding shuffle-shaker ... insidious and insistent'; and it was announced that Sir Winston Churchill had had a stroke and, at his home at 28 Hyde Park Gate, was (in Lord Moran's words) 'slipping into deeper sleep'. Five days later, the great man still alive, Cecil Beaton noted in his diary that he had recently photographed the charismatic young actor David Warner ('half ape, half lanky hero ... face covered with spots ... great charm'), while that evening the first series of *The Likely Lads* ended: a sky-high RI of 83, with praise from viewers including 'an excellent tonic for the end of a tiring day!' and 'so realistic of two young men's lives consisting of "birds", "pubs" and "fun"'. Next evening, the 21st, Beaton was at the Warner in Leicester Square for the royal charity première of the film of *My Fair Lady*, for which he had designed the costumes. Sadly he found it 'an anti-climax'; and even worse: 'The people, unknown Jews who could afford the £100 tickets. They looked ugly and dreary ...'[21]

This Thursday was by-elections day. Most of the attention was focused on Leyton, whose Labour MP, Reginald Sorensen, had been elevated to the House of Lords so that Patrick Gordon Walker – controversially defeated at Smethwick in October – could re-enter the Commons and thereby continue as foreign secretary. Right from the start it made headlines. Gordon Walker's first press conference, on 4 January, was marked by Colin Jordan, thuggish leader of the British National Party, bursting in and making 'Keep Britain White' noises; three days later, Jordan's attempt to mount the platform at Gordon Walker's meeting at Leyton Town Hall, amid a flurry of flour bombs being launched by Jordan's henchmen, ended only when the defence secretary, Denis Healey, physically knocked him off stage; and soon afterwards, the BBC postponed until after polling day John Hopkins' Wednesday Play, *Fable*, described as 'a parable in which Britain is shown under coloured rule, with apartheid operating in reverse'.

Sniffing the wind with a week to go, one journalist questioned 15 voters in Northumberland Road, a huddle of terraced houses off one of Leyton's main streets, and found four of them expressing 'opposition to coloured immigration', including three traditional Labour voters 'frank in their opposition to Mr Gordon Walker's reputation for racial tolerance'. The candidate himself, a sincere and well-meaning patrician to his bones, was struggling to connect. 'He is simply not good at making contact with people,' observed Alan Watkins. 'The whole business of apprehending complete strangers and inquiring after their health, work and families is clearly distasteful to him. He would much rather be composing a stern note to Indonesia.' The reporter Lewis Chester agreed about the shortcomings of this 'reluctant hostage of the Smethwick legend': 'He uses expressions like "jolly good" and "like billy-o". He describes the Tories as "the other fellows" and invariably calls his wife "sweetheart". He is not setting Leyton on fire.' Inevitably, added Chester, the contrast with the displaced Sorensen – 'homespun, local man' who had been Leyton's MP for 32 years – was proving a 'discomforting' one; and all the local betting was that Gordon Walker would be 'very lucky to hang on to his handsome inheritance of an 8,000 Labour majority'. On the 21st itself, after a final Nazi-saluting, thunderflash-throwing intervention the previous night by Jordan and co., the voters of Leyton indeed made their displeasure apparent, as by 205 votes they narrowly elected the Tory candidate Ronald Buxton (who had not followed the Griffiths example and played the race card), with the result declared shortly after midnight. 'I did so hope, and indeed half-forecast,' reflected Phyllis Willmott next day, 'that dowdy but respectable little Leyton would sweep him [Gordon Walker] home and give concrete evidence of disgust with the Smethwick affair.'

As the political analysts now went into overdrive, it became reasonably clear that although the sensational outcome was not solely about race, and that both the rising cost of living and the 'carpet-bagging' aspect had also played a significant part, the Labour man would probably not have lost without it. When Mark Abrams's Research Services Ltd interviewed in Leyton on the Friday a representative sample of almost two hundred voters, it found that 'among respondents as a whole the main blame was put upon race feeling', while 'as far as Labour supporters were concerned, this was the explanation offered by one-third of them'. Even so, emphasised Abrams in his summary, 'the bulk of the answers, in one way or another, turned on resentment that the by-election was a crude party operation that rode roughshod over people's feelings – to suit the government's interests they had been deprived of a popular local man and having forced on them in his place a stranger, a "throw-out" from Smethwick'. The *Sunday Times* that Friday also did a survey, with four reporters interviewing

91 electors and finding that although traditional Labour voters 'generally expressed the view that the country had too many immigrants, few expressed immediate concern about coloured immigrants in Leyton' (of which there were about three thousand). Taking the interviews as a whole, moreover, 'virulent remarks about "the blacks" were exceptional' – and indeed, 'the subject does not appear to have changed many votes'. A final word on Gordon Walker himself went to a library attendant who had switched to the Tories: 'I didn't think much of him, not with that Nazi Jordan helping him. He was at all his meetings, wasn't he?'

The other by-election was at Nuneaton, where again the long-standing Labour MP had been persuaded to take a life peerage – this time so that Frank Cousins, the new Minister of Technology, could secure a Commons seat. Here, though likewise there was natural resentment about an outsider being parachuted in, it was a somewhat different story: not only no 'colour' factor, but also a contrast in campaigning skills. 'On his fleeting doorstep expeditions,' noted the *Guardian*'s Peter Preston about Cousins in action, 'he speaks the people's language, talks with a faint, awkward unease which projects the "bully with the block vote" as human, sincere, and concerned'; while in his speeches his humour was 'quick, cutting, and simple'.[22] In the event, the Labour majority was more than halved, but Cousins was still safely home. His transition from trade unionist to Labour politician had, in retrospect anyway, a particular resonance. Over the next 14 years, the relationship between organised labour and the party created to represent it would be closer, more symbiotic, and sometimes more troubled than it had ever been – an ultimately problematic relationship that in unwitting practice did much to pave the way for Thatcherism.

17

A Tremendous Ferment at the Lower Levels

Some chronological snapshots from the first few weeks of 1965: Ray Gunter, down-to-earth and multi-tasking Minister of Labour, appointing a three-man tribunal to sort out the pay dispute in the municipal bus services; Jack Dash, unofficial dockers' leader, continuing to relish ('we're enjoying it') their ability to maintain a ban on weekend working in the Port of London; a one-day walk out over pay at the Luton factory of Vauxhall Motors, with assembly lines there idle for the first time since the General Strike almost forty years earlier; Gunter publicly laying into restrictive practices on both sides of industry ('I suspect that we tend to pat ourselves on the back about them sometimes, and pride ourselves on historical continuity and the richness of our traditional way of life'); a strike at the Caterpillar tractor factory near Glasgow, after the men complaining that supervisors were using stop watches to check them at work; London dockers largely ignoring appeals from the Transport and General Workers' Union (T&G) to return to weekend working; a Darlington taxi proprietor, Monty Sherman, dismissing his 13 drivers after they had gone on strike for better pay and conditions ('I expect my men to work 80 hours a week for £10'); Gunter's praise for the national newspaper industry having set up a high-level joint management-union board to improve efficiency, in turn prompting one labour correspondent to point out that 'the newspaper industry in addition to all its other inefficiencies is just about the most riddled in the country with trade union restrictive practices'; Ian Mikardo, Labour MP for Poplar, insisting that 'you can't blame the dockers for becoming bloody-minded when, after they've done a hard week's work and ten hours' overtime, they hear a thirty-hour-a-week stockbroker demanding that the dockers should work seven days a week'; the National Union of Railwaymen (NUR), unhappy about the admission of private road hauliers to the terminals, continuing to block British Rail's plan to initiate liner trains between Glasgow and London; and at London Airport on Saturday the 23rd, some six hundred engineers walking out of talks with their own union officials – amid claims that those officials had 'got their heads together with the management to ride rough-shod over the men' – and thereby causing BEA (British European Airways) to cancel over a hundred scheduled flights, though an emergency service of one flight an hour to the Continent was maintained.[1]

The larger context to industrial relations this winter was the 'statement of intent' about productivity, prices and incomes that, under George Brown's vigorous auspices, the government, the TUC (Trades Union Congress) and employers' organisations had signed on 16 December. Two months earlier, on election night, Frank Cousins and the TUC's general secretary, George Woodcock, had dead-batted Cliff Michelmore's questions about the probability of an incomes policy under a new Labour government; but now, the TUC was showing itself willing to entertain such a policy, with its chairman, Lord Collison, declaring the statement to be 'rooted in the view that a planned economy is essential if the community is to prosper, and that the growth of incomes should be within the compass of such a plan'. After the recent failure of the Conservative government's incomes policy (Selwyn Lloyd's 'pay pause'), was this a game-changing moment? Brown himself certainly did not undersell it. 'History is being made here today,' he announced at the high-profile signing ceremony at Lancaster House. 'It is a victory for the nation as a whole, a demonstration to the world that the British people are still prepared to respond to the needs of the country in peacetime no less than in wartime.' Inevitably, the individual unions were somewhat less convinced, though in the course of the next month or two they largely fell into line with the TUC's wishes, in effect a signal that they were going to give a new, friendlier government some sort of chance. These included the T&G, whose Harry Nicholas (deputising for Cousins) offered a less than full-throated endorsement. 'We do not regard the joint statement as in any way inferring that there is going to be anything which could be classified as a wage freeze,' he explained in early January. 'The difficulty everyone is going to face is what sort of machinery will be established to make it effective. We accept a planned economy and this is the initial move towards that planning.' Or in trade union parlance, a 'planned growth of incomes' was an admissible target; but 'wage restraint' was very definitely not.

Back in December itself, press reaction to the Lancaster House agreement had been largely – if provisionally – to see it as a rare piece of good news in a very difficult economic situation. 'MR GEORGE BROWN has achieved in sixty days what eluded MR MAUDLING for months,' began *The Times*'s leader, taking satisfaction in how the minister heading the newly created Department of Economic Affairs had 'coaxed unions' and employers' representatives to agree on the outline of an incomes policy'. Then came the inevitable note of scepticism:

> The next step is to hammer out the right machinery to examine incomes and prices with one aim in mind, to pronounce whether increases in either are against the national interest. This is where the difficulties begin. Even when a twin-headed body is established it is far from certain that its terms of reference will make economic sense. Even if they do, they must be made effective on the shop floor and in the board room ... So much has been written about an incomes policy since MR SELWYN LLOYD first began to hint at it over four years ago that far too much is now expected of it. The practice may give the lie to the hopes. More important, the Government may convince themselves that the battle is over. It is only just beginning ...

Predictable scepticism, too, from the *Daily Telegraph*, in an editorial headed 'GOOD INTENTIONS':

> If a wages policy is not to consist merely of uniform restraint, some wages must be allowed to increase while others are deliberately kept constant. What is the criterion to be? If efficiency is the supreme end (and the document contains many hopeful allusions to this goal),

the Government must try, in the advice which it gives to unions and managements, to reproduce in some measure the conditions of a free economy – to offer higher wages where more labour is needed and to penalise redundancy. But at the very outset of the document the Government introduces the much larger and vaguer idea that the benefits of increased productivity are to be distributed 'in a way that satisfies the claims of social need and justice.' Here is a quite different concept, and one which could easily make havoc of the whole notion of a dynamic economy.

Beyond this, of course, is the more earthy question of whether any union engaged in promoting a wage claim which, by *force majeure*, it could bring to success, will be restrained by any consideration of the public interest, however it may be defined. Nothing in recent history suggests that this will be so ...

The *Guardian* for its part, applauding the 'sensible and above all courageous' action of the signatories, emphasised the political aspect, in particular how the fact of Selwyn Lloyd having 'made the first moves towards an incomes policy' meant that potentially it was a policy which could now be pursued along bipartisan lines.[2] And indeed, as long as both main parties continued to believe almost unquestioningly in the current corporatist consensus – economic planning, implemented by men of good faith sitting around a table in a smoke-filled room – this was not necessarily an impossible dream.

*

In 1965 some 9.7 million people were trade union members, amounting to 42.4 per cent of the total British workforce; but *within* that workforce, whereas the proportion of male members of unions was 51.5 per cent, female density was only 25.9 per cent – a discrepancy in part reflecting the fact that most of the increase in female employment since the war had been in part-time work. The number of individual trade unions was gradually coming down (629 in 1965, compared with 781 at the end of the war), but deep-lying historical reasons meant that organised labour in Britain was appreciably more fragmented than in most other countries, including major differences and divisions between craft unions, industrial unions and general unions. Among those 629 unions, the big three by size of membership were the T&G, the Amalgamated Engineering Union (AEU), and the General and Municipal Workers' Union; while old behemoths like the National Union of Mineworkers (NUM) and the National Union of Railwaymen were in fairly rapid numerical decline – NUR membership dropping by more than 20 per cent since 1950 – as their industries contracted. By contrast, white-collar trade unionism was very much on the rise: at least 1.5 million members by this time, with ASSET (Association of Scientific, Technical and Managerial Staffs) more than doubling in a decade and NALGO (National and Local Government Officers' Association) increasing by over 50 per cent. 'White-collar unions are basically antipathetic to political militancy,' one observer, Peter Preston, pointed out this January. 'Civil servants cannot thump the tub of socialism; non-manual unions traditionally draw back from the tougher, wilder tactics of the manual workers – and even when their leaders are Left wing, the membership tends to stay uncommitted.' On the face of it, the omens were not good for conventional assumptions about the trade union vote automatically going to Labour; and even at the recent general election it was estimated that well over a quarter of trade unionists had voted Conservative.[3]

Harold Wilson's more immediate preoccupation during the winter of 1964/5 was to start to make good on his seductive electoral promise that only a Labour government was capable of thoroughly modernising the undeniably creaky British economy. Inescapably, this involved – if the promise was to be anything like fulfilled – doing something about the unions that went beyond the question of an incomes policy. But what exactly? By mid-January it was clear that the government was poised to announce a Royal Commission to examine the whole subject; and, welcoming the prospect, the *Guardian* instanced the sort of questions that such an inquiry should be tackling:

What is the chief aim of the shipbuilding unions? Do they exist, in their own estimation, primarily to protect their members against exploitation or do they exist to help build good ships efficiently so that the shipyards and their members shall prosper? Why do some unions perpetuate restrictive practices and the overmanning of machines? Is it because their members prefer idleness to work or are they afraid of the sack or of learning new techniques? Questions like these have mystified the public for many years ...

At which point, presumably a nod of the head from George Woodcock, the high-minded and bushy-eyebrowed intellectual who had been the TUC's general secretary since 1960. During the intervening years he had been largely unable to persuade the union leaders sitting on the TUC's General Council of the necessity to a) reform the structure of British trade unionism, b) look constructively at the bigger economic picture when it came to wage policy, and c) try to think long and hard about the underlying purpose of unions – though at least the TUC's recent signing up to the statement of intent had revealed a degree of progress in that second task. Crucially, Woodcock saw the role of an objective and comprehensive inquiry as fundamentally educational: for the politicians; for the public; and, not least, for trade unionists themselves, including their leaders. According to the well-informed journalist Peter Jenkins, Woodcock's attitude towards most of the members of the General Council was 'a disdain tempered only by charity'.[4] Yet ultimately, it was those union leaders who held the whip hand, not the man with an Oxford first in PPE.

A gallery of ten trade unionists – actual or emerging leaders by the mid-1960s, and inevitably all-male – suggests a range of qualities less easy to dismiss.

Ted Hill (born 1899). On *Any Questions?* in May 1963, when a question about the current strike in the shipyards provoked the Labour politician Barbara Castle into insisting that 'there's no more patriotic and typical Englishman in Britain today than Ted Hill', the audience responded with (according to the transcript) 'LOUD PROTEST'. In the sometimes grey world of British trade unionism, the president of the Amalgamated Society of Boilermakers, Shipwrights, Blacksmiths, and Structural Workers was the unquestionable exception – in Anthony Sampson's words, describing him in action at the TUC's annual conference, 'an enormous Cockney, shaped like a hippo, with a deep voice growling "nuffink", "where is 'e?" or "get on wiv it"'. Hill's politics over the years were extreme left-wing, though he was never a Communist; he called all bosses a 'thieving bunch of rascals'; he declared before the election that he would not trust the Tories 'further than I can throw them – and I'm an old man'; he denied all charges of unpatriotism ('I am as good a ruddy Englishman as anybody'); and, as a shrewd as well as tough negotiator, he fought ferociously for his members' interests. 'He had,' noted the *Guardian* after his death in 1969, 'a strong feel of what the people he represented would accept, and what they wouldn't. Will such sensitiveness be common when – and if – British trade union leaders are drawn from men who have not lain under the belly of a ship themselves?'[5]

Sir William Carron (born 1902). 'Leader in Bevin mould' had been the same paper's headline, less than a fortnight earlier in 1969, following the death of Bill Carron. Like Hill, his trade unionism had been forged in the harsh realities of British industrial life between the wars; but there the similarities almost ended. 'He is a short, bald man with a jutting chin, large shrewd eyes, small turned-up eyebrows and the impassive expression of a mandarin,' wrote Sampson in 1965 about the AEU's president, knighted two years earlier. 'He is unpompous, fond of photography and television, not attracted by banquets, and completely dedicated … As the right-wing head of a left-wing union, he has had awkward situations, but he is tough, persistent, with superb stamina: he can go on arguing till late at night, unswerving and good-humoured. He is one of the most loved and respected men in the movement.' Carron was indeed the right-wing head (1956–67) of a left-wing union, including (especially among its shop stewards) a strong Communist element. How did he manage it? 'His opposition was never hysterical, but hard, practical, and clear,' noted one obituarist about Carron's awareness that 'common sense and hard bargaining without political aggressiveness could command a powerful, if often inarticulate, following in the union'; while another recorded approvingly how he had 'battled against irresponsible shop stewards in many industrial disputes in shipbuilding and aircraft and motor manufacture'. His culminating achievement was the three-year agreement that he reached with employers in late 1964, covering the wages, hours and holidays of three million engineering workers – a generous settlement hailed by Carron himself as 'the most far-reaching agreement concluded in my time'. But what about trade unionists generally, the great majority of whom lacked the industrial muscle of the AEU, Britain's leading craft union? 'My own industry, without any logical reasons, is entitled to as many rings of protection as any in the

United Kingdom,' Carron imperturbably told the Royal Commission set up by the Labour government in 1965. And, with what the labour observer-cum-historian Robert Taylor would call 'the arrogance of craft power', this devout Roman Catholic went on: 'We are entitled to our views, whether logical or not, and our view is that for our protection we are going to keep the situation which has existed in a fairly satisfactory way ... I am not going to justify this at all.'[6]

Will Paynter (born 1903). 'A forceful leader – short, wiry, and eloquent in a soft Rhondda accent' was how Sampson described the man from South Wales who had gone down the pits at fourteen, been in the Communist Party since the early 1930s, been in the International Brigades during the Spanish Civil War, been president of the South Wales Miners' Federation during the 1950s, and since 1959 had been general secretary of the NUM. 'He has never lost touch with his fellow-miners,' added Sampson. 'He sits in a polished office in London with red leather chairs and white telephones, but is constantly away touring the pit-heads, and though he lives at Edgware two of his seven sons are miners.' Crucially, Paynter's day job trumped his political allegiance – or in his own subsequent words, 'loyalty to the trade union and its decisions came first'. Almost ceaseless pit closures made the 1960s an intensely difficult time for the coal industry, and – whatever the ultimate rights and wrongs of those closures – the unforgiving economic backdrop was the context for a notably constructive relationship between Lord (Alf) Robens, the former Labour minister who was now chairman of the National Coal Board (NCB), and Paynter. Robens's account of his *Ten Year Stint* would be full of praise for the miners' leader: for a June 1964 speech at St Helens (the annual gala of the Lancashire miners) where Paynter urged acceptance of the NCB's offer of an additional 9s 6d a week on the minimum wage as being the most the industry could afford; for his role later that same year in backing a new, unified wages structure for the industry, ultimately leading in 1966 to the National Power Loading Agreement – a role heavily criticised by union militants, but in the event, through uniting the coalfields, laying the foundations for the major strikes of the 1970s; and perhaps above all, for his palpable integrity. Paynter himself was sharply critical of the TUC's General Council (from which he had been voted off in 1961), mocking its 'statesmen' for having lost touch with the rank and file. 'There's a tremendous ferment at the lower levels: it's got to be harnessed somewhere,' he told Sampson. 'And when the recession comes, the young people will be much more rebellious than *we* were. They don't have the restraint and inhibitions that we had. The difference between the workers' share and the employers' is as great as it ever was.'[7]

Richard Briginshaw (born 1908). 'Tall, powerfully built, always seeming to have returned from a sun-bronzed holiday, carefully coifed silver-grey hair over a strong bespectacled face, he looked more like a newspaper baron than a trade-union leader'; 'a froggish face adorned with heavy, horn-rimmed spectacles, "the aging Tarzan", as he was known, meant to make his presence felt'; 'had a way of making provocative statements followed by a firm, half-smiling stare from behind his heavy spectacles' – the obituarists of Dick Briginshaw, in truth more widely known as 'Briggie', would in due course have a bit of a field day. Born into a printer's family in Lambeth, and serving a printing apprenticeship while still a boy, he rose by 1951 to become general secretary of one of the key Fleet Street unions, the National Society of Operative Printers and Assistants (NATSOPA), a position he held until 1975. Few doubted either his self-confidence ('I bring to my job a first-class brain and I bring it panache') or his autocratic tendencies (a veteran trade unionist comparing him, after his death, to the Teamsters' leader, Jimmy Hoffa). Politically, he always identified himself as left wing; and in June 1964, as it became clear that the *Daily Herald* would soon be ceasing publication and that its successor (the *Sun*) would be appreciably less rigidly aligned to either Labour or trade union interests, he was reported as prime instigator to launch a new left daily, possibly under the old *Daily Herald* title. Was the backing realistically there? 'This initiative is being pressed by the owner of the Pergamon Press and Parliamentary Labour candidate, Mr Robert Maxwell, who has informed Mr Briginshaw he is ready to finance all or part of the venture himself.' It never happened; and in 1969 Briggie's dislike of Maxwell would do much to ensure that the ownership of the *Sun* went instead to an Australian rival.[8]

Sidney Greene (born 1910). General secretary of the NUR from 1958 to 1975, Greene was like Paynter in having to face the inescapable reality of a rapidly shrinking industry, and like Carron in being the moderate, right-wing leader of a union whose executive was usually left wing in its instincts. 'He rarely appeared ruffled, even on the brink of a national strike slipping in and out of his union headquarters, opposite Euston station, looking like a bank clerk: a slender figure, always immaculately dressed,' recalled the veteran labour observer

Geoffrey Goodman in his 2004 obituary of 'the senior surviving member of that generation of trade union leaders who, from the 1950s to the end of the 1970s, were hardly ever off the front pages of every national and regional newspaper, seemingly in perpetual combat with whatever government was in power'. Greene's was in its way another classic trajectory: son of a horse-drawn van driver; the father out of work when the son left elementary school at the age of fourteen and found a berth as a messenger boy in the Great Western Railway goods office at Paddington station; promotion there to a porter; and by his late twenties, playing an increasingly active union role. Rail rationalisation was well under way, even before Beeching, by the time he became general secretary; and over the next decade, Greene (in Goodman's words) 'ploughed his own shrewd and moderate furrow', including when necessary a nicely calculated line in brinkmanship. Reputedly his disinclination to go over the brink was fuelled in part by his wife (and perhaps also his three daughters) consistently reminding him of the hardship that strike action would impose on railway women. Whatever the truth of that, his commitment to the social as well as economic benefits of the railways – indeed, the railway culture as a whole way of life – never faltered. It was a commitment which, he insisted to Sampson in 1965, involved serious responsibilities of leadership: 'You've got to make the rank and file feel that they've got a niche in the industry.' And he went on, soberly and judiciously: 'I'm a bit afraid of the extent of our economic strength, I hope we never have to use it: it can so easily turn public opinion against us.'[9]

Jack Jones (born 1913). Ascetic, short of small talk, dogged rather than inspirational in his oratory, Jones possessed what one unsympathetic obituarist called a 'gaunt consistency' which by the 1970s would make him a true power in the land. His life story was wholly authentic: son of a Liverpool docker, he was in his mid-teens when he went to the docks, joined the T&G, and quickly became a shop steward; in his mid-twenties he not only served as a Labour councillor in Liverpool, but fought in the Spanish Civil War and was badly wounded; and from 1939 he had a full-time union base in Coventry, where through the 1940s and 1950s he built up membership and developed a distinctive policy of shop-floor power – an agenda, in Goodman's words, 'based on encouraging shop stewards to in effect assume the role and influence of factory floor managers', thereby 'giving greater authority to the trade unions'. Leader of the T&G for most of those years was the right-wing Arthur Deakin, who in effect all but blacklisted Jones; but once the left-wing Frank Cousins became general secretary in 1956, that all changed, as first he gave Jones greater authority in the Midland region as a whole and then, in 1963, brought him to London to become third in the union hierarchy. Second was the rather colourless Harry Nicholas, who took over as acting general secretary when Cousins became Minister of Technology; but everyone knew that Cousins had Jones firmly designated for the top job sooner rather than later. Yet if his circumstances were changing, nothing else was or indeed would. 'He never,' reflected Goodman in his warm 2009 obituary, 'shifted from his commitment to socialist ideals, immovably determined, sometimes difficult even with his closest friends, rarely disposed to take criticisms lightly, sometimes lacking charitable humour, but always with unflinching integrity. He was not the easiest companion, yet he was the kind of man anyone would respect.'[10]

Hugh Scanlon (born 1913). Jones's future 'terrible twin' was also born in 1913, some seven months later and in his case in Australia. But most of Scanlon's largely fatherless childhood was spent in Manchester, where he attended Stretford Elementary School; every lunchtime and evening he delivered bread for a weekly wage of 3s 6d, while an evening paper round earned him another 2s; on his fourteenth birthday he started work at the giant Metropolitan Vickers plant at Trafford Park; three years later he joined the AEU; and by his early twenties he was a shop steward. Many years followed of relentless if humdrum union activity, with Manchester firmly his growing power base, before in 1963 he alarmed the AEU's national executive (presided over by Bill Carron) by securing election to it, albeit after three recounts and a challenge in court. Virtual ostracism on the executive now followed, leaving the Scanlon of the mid-1960s unhappy but unbowed. The potential affinity with Jones was starting to emerge, an affinity brilliantly captured by Peter Jenkins, for much of the 1960s the *Guardian*'s labour correspondent. 'They were left-wing socialists (indeed, both were former Communists) but they had broken from the tradition of centralism,' he would write in 1970:

> They knew where the industrial power of the workers now resided – on the shop floor – and it was there they expected it to find

its political expression. They were interested in workers' control, a subject for which the TUC had shown a disinterest enlivened only by distaste. Both men were hard trained in the jungle warfare of piecework – the purest example of man-to-man combat in the power struggle between management and men. They were much closer to the anger of the shop floor than were the trade union leaders of the old Establishment; they were more sympathetic towards it and more ready to release it. Socialism, if it came, would result from this struggle, Scanlon and Jones believed, not from cosy chats in London between the trade union movement and what called itself a Labour Government.

And Scanlon the person? 'A slight, unassuming figure, his eyes glinting behind gold-rimmed spectacles,' noted an obituarist of one of the century's most demonised trade unionists, 'Scanlon was, by common agreement, a skilful negotiator for his cause. He was a fluent speaker, and his strengths included his calmness under fire. Away from the negotiating table, he could be sociable and a good raconteur.'[11]

Joe Gormley (born 1917). Born in a large Lancashire mining village (Ashton-in-Makerfield) between Wigan and St Helens, a bullying father who beat the children's mother when drunk, down the pits at fourteen – Gormley, too, was cast from an unromantic working-class mould. Over the next 28 years, he worked as a face-worker in 11 different collieries. 'Underground, Joe couldn't be sent to the wrong job,' recalled James Fairhurst, a friend from the 1930s. 'He could work at any task, quickly and skilfully, and even those who disliked him – he had no real enemies – had to admit that he was one of the best workers ever to go down a pit.' The life-changing epiphany came one day during the war, as he and 38 other miners sat in the canteen, waiting to go down the pit. 'He suddenly thought of his family and of the life without choice which faced most miners. His temper, never slow at rising, boiled over. "Why the hell do we go down?" he shouted. "We ought to tell them to get stuffed." The late shift got up as one man and adjourned to the pub. Gormley had called his first strike.' Over the many years of union activity that followed, and as he climbed the NUM ladder, this staunch Catholic was in fact usually to be counted among the moderates, always among the anti-Communists, but – contrary to what some thought – was never right wing. He was opposed to women going down the pits and believed firmly in the closed shop ('I don't care if a man lapses his union membership – it simply means that he won't get down the mine'). By the mid-1960s he was Lancashire area secretary – having faced down Communist accusations of ballot rigging – and on the national executive. The 'battered cherub', as he increasingly looked with his memorable eyebrows and would soon start to be called, was on his way. Or in Fairhurst's words, 'a native shrewdness, great physical strength and energy, a considerable articulateness and a love of miners and mining ensured that he was a popular choice as a leader'. And he added of the Gormley long before he became a household name: 'My enduring memory is of seeing him moving among the miners in the canteen of Bold Colliery [in St Helens] collecting money for some fellow worker who was off sick.'[12]

Frank Chapple (born 1921). Brought up in out-and-out poverty in Hoxton, leaving school at fourteen to become an electrician, involved in the Normandy landings, gradually after the war becoming disenchanted with his youthful Communism, Frank Chapple would never doubt that the turning point of his life had come in June 1961, shortly before he turned forty. Then, in a historic High Court judgement, Communist leaders in the Electrical Trades Union (ETU) were found to have engaged in ballot-rigging on an industrial scale; and over the rest of the decade, as right-hand man to the union's president, Les Cannon, he not only drove out most remaining vestiges of Communist influence, but did much to modernise the working of the union. By 1965 he was *de facto* general secretary, from 1966 actual general secretary; but this almost defiantly working-class man (breeding racing pigeons his favourite hobby) with a strong line in Cockney invective, thick jet-black hair, and an impish grin across his broad face as he called himself 'an awkward bugger', undeniably had something about him that transcended the easy stereotype. An awkward bugger no doubt; but as Goodman recognised from personal experience, that favourite self-mocking description was also 'a form of protective psychological armour helping to conceal the much more sensitive, shrewdly intelligent, courageous and often complex character that lay behind the controlled jauntiness of the Chapple carapace'. And, paradoxically enough, this tough, unblinking negotiator, a taker of few prisoners, had as his favourite aphorism that coined many years earlier by the Conservative politician Arthur Balfour: 'Nothing in the world matters very much and very little matters at all.'[13]

Clive Jenkins (born 1926). The obituarists in 1999 let themselves go: 'As noisy as the champagne corks popping about him ... the most immodest of men ... names dropped easily from his lips ... the self-opinionated, over-confident little man from Port Talbot ... sharp features, comfortable shape and sardonic Welsh voice ... a residual taste for logic-chopping and excessive legalism ... always appeared to be involved in a permanent love affair with himself and the word "arrogant" could have been invented specially for him.' Yet for all that, Jenkins's achievement was genuine and considerable, being the man who, as the labour correspondent Keith Harper would put it, 'introduced the middle classes to trade unionism'. His childhood in the South Wales of the 1930s had been desperately poor, with the family sharing the same water as once a week they bathed in front of the fire in an old zinc tub; the death of his father meant that instead of going to grammar school, this precocious child had to leave school at fourteen and go to work in the local metal industry; by his early twenties he was a full-time divisional officer for ASSET, at this stage a small white-collar union mainly comprising junior staff in engineering; by 1961 he was general secretary; and over the next seven years it more than tripled in membership, helped partly by middle-class insecurities in a changing labour market, but above all by Jenkins's unabashed flair for promoting both union and self. 'He brings to his union an ingenious energy,' noted Sampson in 1965. 'ASSET has started its own insurance company, advertises for members on television, and has bought small holdings in all the large companies in which it has membership – so that Jenkins can complain at shareholders' meetings.'[14] His political views were left wing; those of the overwhelming majority of his members were decidedly not; but as long as he brought home the bacon in the form of improved pay and conditions, they could regard that unbridled self-confidence, allied to a manifest quick intelligence, as assets to be grateful for if not exactly to cherish.

In all, then, ten trade unionists: for the most part, somewhat short of imagination; for the most part, too (Jenkins the obvious exception), slow to realise important ways in which the world was changing – not just the increased importance of things like education and training, industrial design, strategies for competitiveness, and so on, but also the gradual but remorseless erosion of class loyalties as the shape of the economy began to shift away from manufacturing and towards services. Yet whatever their failings, they and their colleagues were, taken as a whole, far more *interesting* people, with richly authentic backgrounds, than the monolithic condescending-cum-caricature retrospective version of the unions, all too prevalent since the 1980s, has glibly assumed. Or put another way, history written by the victors is not the only history.

*

'Underlying the rising strikes trend were economic factors such as full employment and rising prices and social factors such as rising expectations and a less deferential workforce,' reflects the historian Howard Gospel about the 1960s. 'The trend also reflected institutional factors such as the growing organisation and assertiveness of shop stewards and the weakness and inability of collective bargaining procedures to cope with the changed circumstances.' Undoubtedly it was, by the early to mid-1960s, a rising strike trend. During the 1950s, never more than 800 strikes were recorded annually, excluding mining strikes; but in 1960, the total was well over a thousand, and in 1964 almost 1,500 (again in both cases excluding mining strikes). Even so, it was hardly yet 'the British disease': in a league table covering 1964–6 of 15 developed economies, the UK came sixth for number of stoppages per 100,000 employees (16.8 as annual average, compared to 63.8 for Australia and 32.9 for Italy) and a positively harmonious ninth in terms of number of working days lost per 1,000 employees (annual average of 191, way below the Republic of Ireland's 1,620). Of all strikes in Britain during these three years, government figures found that at least 95 per cent were unofficial, in other words not sanctioned by the executive of the relevant union or unions; but they tended to be on a significantly smaller scale than the official strikes, which despite their relative infrequency accounted for 30 per cent of working days lost. Still, unofficial strikes accounting for some 70 per cent of those lost days: it was a sobering enough figure. And when in 1968 the Royal Commission (chaired by Lord Donovan) on trade unions eventually reported, its most celebrated passage came early and unambiguously: 'Britain has two systems of industrial relations.

The one is the formal system embodied in the official institutions. The other is the informal system created by the actual behaviour of trade unions and employers' associations, of managers, shop stewards and workers.'[15]

So, what in practice was 'actual behaviour' by the mid-1960s? Even if one takes just three industries – coal mines, docks, motor cars – it is inevitably a mixed picture that emerges.

Not least in the coalfields: there in 1963, noted one quantitative survey, 'miners in Scotland were roughly three times as strike-prone than those in Lancashire and the West Midlands, about ten times more strike-prone than those in the East Midlands and Kent, and more than thirty times as strike-prone as miners in the North East'. Published that same year was a Liverpool University study of disputes in four pits in the Lancashire coalfield, from which it clearly emerged that workers whose wages fluctuated from week to week were far likelier to be involved in a dispute than those whose wages were more stable; and that the more disputatious were almost invariably the faceworkers, especially the fillers and packers – for whom, under variable physical conditions and under increasing mechanisation, the main causes of their fluctuating pay packets lay ever more outside their control. Even so, the *overall* trend of mining strikes was by this time on a downward trajectory: in 1958 almost two thousand recorded strikes; in 1960 almost 1,700; and in 1963 less than a thousand. This decline of militancy was not, according to the historians Peter Ackers and Jonathan Payne, solely due to greater job insecurity in a rapidly shrinking industry. Rather, they emphasise how the greater moderation – in most coalfields anyway – reflected not only a raft of positive incremental reforms in the industry since nationalisation in 1947, but also an appreciation (albeit sometimes grudging) of how the NCB had responded from 1957 to the near-existential threat posed by cheap oil in a way that would have been inconceivable in a privately owned industry:

> In line with its stakeholder ethic, the board accepted a moral obligation to minimise the social costs of closures and their impact on the coal communities. Measures such as the 'Pick Your Pit' scheme assisted displaced miners to relocate. Moreover, the NCB accumulated large coal stocks to avoid massive lay-offs. The output

of profitable open-cast mining was reduced by as much as 50 per cent to avoid having to dismiss skilled underground workers, and there were strict controls on recruitment. Above all, the NCB subsidised the continued operation of weak, high-cost coalfields, such as those in parts of Scotland, which were no longer commercially viable.

Morale, though, undoubtedly slumped, as reflected accurately by the increasingly pervasive phenomenon of absenteeism. In 1958 total rates of absence passed 14 per cent for the first time since nationalisation, by 1961 they were over 15 per cent, by 1964/5 they were averaging 16 per cent; and as the knowledgeable labour correspondent Eric Wigham observed in general in his 1961 Penguin Special, *What's Wrong with the Unions?*, 'the time lost through absenteeism is fifty times as much as the time lost through unofficial strikes'.

If there was a canary in the mine, as it were, suggesting some serious discord ahead, it was perhaps the way in which the Colliery Consultative Committees now began to move away from substantive issues (production, absenteeism, safety, welfare) and towards more trivial matters (issues in one Warwickshire pit in 1964 including draughts in the canteen, the weakness of canteen tea and the provision of Brylcreem machines). Liverpool University's Lancashire study had already shown most miners' very limited awareness of the potentialities of the consultative committees as channels for meaningful dialogue with managers; but by now, whatever was happening collaboratively at national level between, say, the NCB's Robens and the NUM's Paynter, that particular inclusive, participatory aspect of the nationalisation vision was starting to fade quite fast in the pits themselves – and in its place a growing fatalism-cum-cynicism on both sides.[16]

A 'scarcely tamed jungle' where 'to qualify for the fall-back payments when no work was available, men were still required to present themselves in the hiring pens of a freezing morning before light was up'; rough work, harsh seasonal ups and downs, the stevedore's life running in families, closed communities; 'working on the hook', as the phrase went, or 'sharpening the claw'; 'the docker right or wrong' as the prevailing ethos; 'incessant unofficial stoppages and unconscionable restrictive practices' ... Such in 1989 were the

unsentimental recollections of Peter Jenkins of his time back in the
1960s reporting on the docks. They were recollections prompted
by Margaret Thatcher bringing 'to a belated end' the 'intolerable
arrangement' of the National Dock Labour Scheme, created in 1947
by the Attlee government as a means of precluding compulsory redundancy of dockers, and which had become during intervening decades
'the sacred cow of the T&G, untouchable by a Labour government'.
Dockland, whether in London or elsewhere, was undeniably a world
of its own. In December 1964, weeks after Ray Gunter had set up an
inquiry into the docks under the Appeal Court judge Lord Devlin
partly to resolve an immediate nationwide dispute over the wages,
and partly to offer long-term solutions about restrictive practices, a
northern reporter from the hardly right-wing *Guardian* brought one
aspect of that world to vivid life:

From behind the long line of lorries waiting to go into Sandon
Dock, Liverpool, to unload, waves of dockers flow across the dock
road and disappear into public houses, betting offices, dockside
cafes, and side streets. It is 1.30 pm – half an hour after lunch – and
the afternoon 'welt' is settling in.

'Welting' – the practice whereby part of a gang takes an unofficial break while the rest continues working – is firmly entrenched
in Liverpool ...

During a recent visit to part of the Sandon and Canada dock area,
soon after the official lunch break had finished, groups of dockers
went out past the dock police. In half an hour about a hundred men
had drifted from the two docks.

These scenes were repeated at other places along the dock road
where ships were being unloaded. Outside Gladstone Dock, at
the Bootle end of Shore Road, the local betting shop, canteen, and
public-house were all filled by 2.30 pm. In the betting shop – clearly
serving the docks as the area is not residential – 50 men waited for
the race results. As some left, others came to take their places. Over
a hundred men sat and smoked in a large canteen down the road,
and the pub was similarly filled.

Meanwhile ships were being manned by gangs under full strength.
On one, four men were in each of the five hatches, instead of the
normal eight for a deep-sea ship; no rail men could be seen (there

should be five); and only three 'hatch' men on the ship, instead of five.

Dockers look upon the 'welt' as a practice they have won over the years, justified in terms of the insecurity of their work and wages. One thought that production and bonus rates were unaffected since the men remaining worked twice as hard. He was not worried about piece rates being lost since they were only a small part of his wages.

He added: 'With good overtime at the weekends I can gross £17 a week, but it is the insecurity that is the trouble. I'm sure that the men would be prepared to give up most of these practices if they could be guaranteed a good wage each week.'

Under the perhaps understandably caustic headline 'Betting, drinking – and sometimes working at the docks', this piece of reportage ended with two telling sentences about where the balance of power apparently lay: 'Recently the employers have seemed reluctant to intervene, perhaps out of fear that open obstruction might lead to something more serious. One employer argued that it was better that a ship was slow in getting away than that it never got away at all.'

Devlin and his colleagues (Hugh Clegg, the academic expert in industrial relations, Jack Scamp, the personnel manager at GEC renowned for his 'trouble-shooting' prowess, and the NUM's Sidney Forde) certainly had plenty to get their teeth into. Lying at the heart of the problem they faced, in functional terms anyway, was the entrenched system of casualised labour, in effect the virtual absence of durable contracts of employment. 'The extent of industrial conflict over the wage-effort bargain was unsurprising,' comments the historian Peter Turnbull, 'given the almost infinite variation inherent in dock work in respect of vessel, cargo, stowage, equipment, gang composition, and ultimately weather.' Nor did the fragmented union situation help: the mighty T&G, whose national docks secretary from 1956 to 1975 was Tim O'Leary, a moderate finding it difficult to exercise more than limited authority; the tiny but obdurate, and persistently militant, National Amalgamated Stevedores and Dockers Union, always known as the 'blue union' because of the colour of its membership card; and, closest of all to the rank and file, the already legendary Jack Dash, leader of the unofficial London Docks Liaison Committee and remembered by Jenkins as 'a diminutive Cockney spell-binder who performed on "the stump" outside the gates of the Royal Docks'. Dash's world view, noted one obituarist, was simple enough:

> The *Daily Mirror*? 'That navvies' comic.' The TUC? 'There are more knights around the table than there were at King Arthur's. If I'd had my way they wouldn't be knighted but neutered.' Class? 'There are only two classes: the owners of industry and those who work in it. The ones who like to call themselves middle-class are just snobbish failures. They've failed to get away from the working classes into the owner classes.'

Was dockland militancy also about something else? Turnbull thinks so, arguing that in the post-war world 'tighter discipline' (whether from management or from centralised collective agreements) 'and the obligations imposed on the dockers for more regular attendance were at odds with their cherished "freedom" of choosing when, for whom, and on what cargoes to work. In other words, while the majority of dock strikes could be "attributed" to working conditions, the anomalies of piecework, and "playing the game" [i.e. docker solidarity], the wider influences of the dockers' occupational culture cannot be ignored and were forcefully articulated in many strikes.'[17] By the mid-1960s this was a very fixed habit of mind; and it was unlikely to be shifted whatever the constructive reforms that Devlin and co. might suggest.

Cultural factors, too, on the shop floors of the almost equally strike-prone British motor industry. 'If the car industry has a public image, it is one of perpetual strikes on seemingly trivial issues,' noted – probably accurately – the journalist Graham Turner in his 1964 Pelican survey *The Car Makers*. 'The 1961 tea-break affair at Ford summed up for many people what they had already instinctively felt – that car workers were fickle, moody, and temperamental and that they had had life rather too good for too long for their own or anybody else's welfare.' Yet if that was the stereotype, what was really going on? Unfortunately, prior to Huw Beynon's *Working for Ford* (1973) we have no intimate contemporary accounts of the industry's shop floors that go beyond the essentially functional and set workplace activism against a background of cultural as well as economic norms and realities.

But, fortunately, what we do now have is Jack Saunders' *Assembling Cultures* (2019), a nuanced and persuasive study of Britain's car factories between 1945 and 1982 which does just that. 'Declinist accounts encourage us to consider industrial conflict as pathological rather than as a way car workers set about remaking their world,' he reflects at the outset. And with a nice even-handedness he adds, surely rightly, that 'the changing forms that workplace activism took should be more than mere fodder for analysing what went wrong with manufacturing or what waylaid the progress of socialism'.

The world that Saunders depicts, as it had taken shape by around the mid-1960s, was one of what he terms 'decentralised direct democracy': shop stewards at the centre of it; the closed shop an unquestioned assumption; workshop assemblies open to all union members in the particular shop, often around forty or so; and every opportunity for those present to make significant contributions to debates. Inevitably, pay was sometimes the focus, and Saunders quotes the retrospective description by Frank Henderson (one of several hundred shop stewards at the British Motor Corporation's giant plant at Longbridge) as being that of a typical negotiation:

> The management tended to say, 'This is as much as we can possibly afford. We cannot afford any more. The vehicle won't be economic if we pay what you are asking for.' The shop steward would say, 'The blokes won't stand for that and we'll walk out.' The steward would report back to the blokes. They would say bugger this, put their coats on and walk off home, usually an hour or so before knocking-off time, then come back in the next morning and the gaffer would say, 'Now look here, let's start talking sensibly about this.'

Bugger this indeed ... But crucially, shop steward-led activism, almost wholly dependent on the backing of the relevant shop or section, was far from being solely about pay. 'In 1967,' notes Saunders, 'wages at Rootes' Stoke Aldermoor plant [in Coventry] made up just 15 per cent of all issues discussed on the JSSC [joint shop stewards' committee], with stewards spending the rest of their time debating hours and job security (26 per cent), casework pertaining to individuals and their rights (4 per cent), union democracy and organisation (28 per cent), issues external to the factory (10 per cent) and working conditions (13 per cent).' And he goes on:

> Sections brought to these meetings issues ranging from complaints over union rights, lay-offs, transfers, line speed, demarcation and overtime to less conventional issues like the provision of a 'rehabilitation department' for workers currently unfit for production. Stewards brought up disputes relating to management neglect of ill workers, accident prevention and factory cleanliness. With its intense focus on the nature of everyday life, sectional activism could widen the type of issues that featured in collective discussion and gave workers new opportunities to develop collective views on a wider range of subjects related to conditions at work.

Ultimately, argues Saunders, what was under way by this time in a largely booming industry was something not wholly short of a revolution in workers' expectations and moral values, above all about the potential greater degree of collective agency on the part of the shop or the section. 'That a group of workers had the right to expect treatment no worse than their peers; that management should fulfil its obligations to its workforce; that change, of whatever sort, should be negotiated, agreed and compensated for; and that skill and merit should be properly recognised' – such, claims Saunders, was the value system which lay behind the flood of small-scale strikes in the motor industry during much of the 1960s. Unsurprisingly, and as he fully accepts, 'this culture of workgroup democracy produced in some shops intense group discipline', a discipline which 'could be unforgiving towards both reluctant trade unionists and rule-breakers'. All in all, it may not have been a particularly liberal, pluralist sort of democracy; nor was it likely to presage anytime soon a lengthy period of industrial peace; but as a form of workplace activism, mainly far removed from the world of the union chiefs, it did involve, in Saunders' words, 'the creation of spaces in which the dominant societal norms around industrial relations and legitimate class hierarchies could be contested or ignored'.[18]

Meanwhile, across trade unionism as a whole, including workplace activism, two groups of traditionally marginalised workers still remained – despite occasional protestations to the contrary – largely marginalised. 'Britain's new black workers encountered a range of responses from trade unionists at all levels, from welcome and support to grudging acceptance and racist discrimination,' three leading labour historians have observed in their joint overview of the 20 years after the war. 'If many were accorded support', and here they cite the example of Bill Morris, future general secretary of the T&G, 'hostility caught the eye and the headlines. At the extremes it was embodied in resolutions of shop stewards' committees, branches and regional bodies, and even in strikes to enforce the "colour bar", against immigrant workers.' They are especially critical of the TUC's General Council, which not only 'took few positive initiatives' to combat racism at the workplace, but was even at times positively opposed to such initiatives, declaring in 1964 that it did not consider any affirmative action to be 'necessary or desirable'.

Typical enough was the motor industry, including at Longbridge, where according to Saunders' research, 'negotiations with management reveal a reluctance to deal with industrial grievances that touched on race relations'. Indeed, on one occasion in 1967, 'the works committee, whilst agreeing off the record that black workers were excluded from better jobs because of a supposed lack of "suitability" for fast-paced production, joined management in denying the existence of a colour bar'. 'Whether or not,' he adds, 'the Longbridge leadership genuinely believed the manifestly racist trope that semi-skilled production work was beyond their members from the Caribbean and South Asia, they were certainly unenthusiastic about having an open debate on the issue.' Elsewhere in the West Midlands, it was much the same at Alfred Herbert's, a kingpin of the Coventry engineering industry. There, notes its historian of the shop-floor politics, 'clear lines of racial segregation' were still firmly in place by the mid-1960s in both the engineering shops and the foundries – segregation, above all between white skilled workers and Asian day labourers, which the shop stewards did little if anything to oppose. A telling episode of not-so-covert racism occurred in the winter of 1965/6, as it emerged that the company intended to recruit more non-white workers in order to deal with a serious labour shortage. 'Imigrent labour – request gone to Coy' read a somewhat cryptic entry in the union records; but some weeks later, the nature of that request was made clear in another entry: 'Re couler imigrent's Coy would not accept our points no more wag'.[19]

The other marginalised group was almost as entirely predictable:

There is not much evidence [wrote Nancy Seear in 1966 in a research paper for the Donovan inquiry] that men trade unionists as a whole, with many outstanding personal exceptions, have been greatly concerned with the position of women workers except in circumstances in which the exploitation of women has been seen as a threat to the position of men ... Even since the Second World War there has been little evidence of active assistance for women in the union movement as a whole. As long ago as 1957, Lord (then Mr) Carron of the AEU pointed out that girls were eligible for engineering apprenticeships. It is difficult to believe that if his union had really wanted to see an improvement in training opportunities for girls, the figures a decade later would be as low as those quoted in Table 3 [showing that apprentices in manufacturing industries were still overwhelmingly male]. If the unions were concerned to improve the status of women, steps would be taken to bring women into positions of influence within the union movement itself ... In the Transport and General Workers' Union, with 195,577 women comprising 13 per cent of total union membership, there are only two women national officers, no women officers at all at regional or district level, one woman on a trade group executive, and one woman member of the TUC General Council ... Neither in relation to employers nor in internal trade union affairs does it appear that the trade union movement as a whole has regarded the position of women as a matter calling for vigorous action.

The historian Chris Wrigley, in his overview of women in the labour market and in the unions by this time, does not dissent, pointing to the prevailing male, sometimes macho, culture in most trade unions, noting the general lack of interest in relation to part-time workers (largely female), and above all emphasising how, if left to themselves, 'British trade union leaders repeatedly backed away from taking decisive action to bring about equal pay or to remedy other female inequalities'.

Specific case studies endorse these damning judgements. At Alfred Herbert's, 'the traditional view of women as a subordinate part of the workforce to be displaced when men's employment was threatened remained strong', as typified by a 1961 minute: 'Re crane drivers it was proposed we ask management to employ only male labour in future. This was carried.' At Longbridge and elsewhere in the motor industry, not only did, wherever possible in mixed sections, 'men tend to be adopted as representatives', but 'for most of the 1960s, women's lower wages went largely unquestioned in sectional bargaining'. While in the Leeds clothing industry, a largely female workforce was firmly excluded from occupying the skilled positions, above all in the cutting room, with the result that female rates of pay rarely rose above two-fifths of the male level. 'The stance of the NUTGW (National Union of Tailors and Garment Workers) on gender divisions in the workplace, consistently determined by securing the best possible deal for the male workers, was reactive and short-sighted,' notes Katrina Honeyman about the industry in general as well as in Leeds. One particular episode which she records spoke volumes. In 1965 the management at the Gateshead branch of Alexandre Ltd, a Leeds-based company, was found to be introducing girls into the cutting room as choppers out. Whereupon, 'because Alexandre's justification for this lamentable course of action was the shortage of male labour, the union scoured the neighbourhood for suitable boys, and "following local enquiries by union officials as to the availability of boys, the firm has now dropped its insistence on employing women"'. As Honeyman rather ruefully reflects, about a still essentially nineteenth-century culture ill-fitted for changing times, 'the image of officials of the union combing the streets of Gateshead for available boys reveals the intensity of their commitment to the traditional gender division of labour'.[20]

*

'Keep your end up,' George Aldridge, a recently retired shop steward at Longbridge, implored his fellow shop stewards in July 1964, 'because I feel the workers will have an uphill fight after the General Election.' And after a reference to 'the Bosseing Class', he ended: 'I reminded a Gentleman the other day; 1. That the Farmer grows for all; 2. The Brewer brews for all; 3. The Baker bakes for all; 4. The Workers pay for all; 5. At the End the Workers have got B—all.'

All the evidence, though, suggests that the vast majority of trade unionists at this time far from fitted the stereotype of the unforgiving class warrior – forever embodied in the popular consciousness by the character of Fred Kite in the satirical film *I'm All Right, Jack* (1959) – and instead had an essentially different focus. Take a trio of submissions to the Donovan inquiry: a research paper (in part by W. E. J. (Bill) McCarthy, an acknowledged authority on industrial relations) found that, whether it was shop stewards or rank-and-file trade unionists, prevailing attitudes were overwhelmingly non-militant; another academic expert, B. C. (Ben) Roberts, emphasised how 'interviews with strikers show that they care little for the effects of their actions on other sections of society', with Roberts adding that 'this lack of social concern almost certainly reflects the values of an affluent society and is related to other forms of egocentric money-dominated behaviour'; while according to the AEU's submission, seeking to explain-cum-justify demands for higher wages, 'the fact that our people can plan to shape their lives without the ever-pressing fear of unemployment and poverty has released in them an acquisitive urge – a trait previously capable of expression by only a section of the community'.[21]

Perhaps unsurprisingly, only a tiny proportion of trade unionists – well under 1 per cent – were also members of the Communist Party, for all the CP's attempts to establish workplace branches. Moreover, the branches themselves tended to be less than vibrant and outward-looking, prompting one veteran activist to reflect sadly in 1964 that 'in spite of all we have said and written from time to time, very few factory branches had been involved in the issues outside their own factories'. 'By 1965,' notes the historian John McIlroy, 'evaluation of forty-three workplace branches found four carrying out "outstanding activity", twelve conducting "regular work of all types", fifteen performing "some organizational work, literature sales, meetings", eleven confining themselves "mainly to trade union work", while a further nine had "no organization whatsoever". There was an absence of CP factory papers.' 'This suggests,' he adds, 'that even allowing for decline in the number of branches there was disarray in many listed as functioning.' Still, who knew what the industrial and political future would hold? CP branch secretary at Longbridge in the 1960s was

Derek Robinson, who even as an apprentice toolmaker in his teens had taken a self-study course in Marxism. 'Everything that happened in that factory the party branch discussed,' remembered the much-demonised 'Red Robbo' of late 1970s legend. 'We then went out into the factory and argued for the line whatever it may be ... I got to know lots and lots and lots of stewards and I was constantly assessing people, opening up discussions ...'[22]

By contrast, the links of the trade union movement to the Labour Party remained close, whether through the political levy (requiring active contracting out), or the block vote of individual unions at the party conference, or the sponsorship of Labour MPs (in 1964 almost two-fifths of the parliamentary party). Did this really mean, though, that a Labour government would be uniquely well placed to land an effective incomes policy? Even without the benefit of hindsight, warning signals were apparent. The TUC may in late 1964 have reluc-tantly signed up to the theoretical principle of such a policy, but Frank Cousins, writing in the T&G's journal in 1963, had already made clear his ultimate allegiance to free collective bargaining ('if we do not fulfil the purposes for which members join unions, to protect and raise their real standard of living, then the unions will wither and finally die'); the growing reach and autonomy of militant shop stewards, especially in the engineering industry, was starting to cast doubt on whether national leaderships could actually deliver on any agreement with government, even a Labour government; there was no evidence that the increasingly touted concept of a 'social wage' – as opposed to hard cash in the pocket – had any real resonance with trade union members; and, perhaps most crucially, the movement as a whole, even at the very top, had little appetite for grappling with the big national picture. Early in 1965 the American central banker Al Hayes noted a phone conversation he had just had with James Callaghan: 'The major problem is the budget. Apparently, the chancellor has not made up his mind on just what should be done. He said he had approached the TUC for their ideas, and they simply turned the question back to him ...'

Power without responsibility? Stanley Baldwin's famous descrip-tion of the press barons already had the potential to become applicable to an emerging fifth estate; and when, back in November 1963 in a TV discussion about the working class, Anthony Crosland had observed that 'there is a very real sense of power among trade unionists – you go and talk to them and they know that in the last resort nothing can be done without their approval', the undertone of foreboding was unmistakable. Even so, he perhaps privately reflected, the unions were still generally seen in a positive light, thereby doing little harm to Labour's image and popularity. Indeed, in September 1964 shortly before the election, when Gallup asked its annual question, 'Generally speaking, and thinking of Britain as a whole, do you think that trade unions are a good thing or a bad thing?', no less than 70 per cent saw them as the former – the highest number, no one knew at the time, for almost the next quarter of a century.[23]

One close observer broadly comfortable in the mid-1960s with the general direction of travel was the industrial sociologist Alan Fox. His inter-war childhood had been a working-class one in Enfield; he had left school at fourteen; during the war he had been awarded the DFM for his hazardous role as a photographer on aerial reconnaissance over Burma; in 1956, as a young, Oxford-based academic, he had coined the term 'meritocracy' subsequently popularised by Michael Young; and now, still Oxford-based, he was increasingly recognised as one of the key experts on industrial relations. His 1966 paper for Donovan exemplified the assumptions of the 'Oxford School', whose fellow members included Hugh Clegg and Allan Flanders. In it, he argued for the desirability of an essentially pluralist approach, one which saw the industrial organisation as (in Jim Phillips' summarising words) 'not a "team" united by common purpose but a coalition of different, sometimes divergent, and occasionally conflicting interests'. Accordingly, 'unions were the organised expression of the workforce's legitimate sectional interest and so could provide a highly positive input, helping realistic employers to manage the conflict that was an unavoidable feature of the industrial enterprise'. A 'pluralistic' perspective, in which employers and trade unions enjoyed an equal social and moral status, was, insisted Fox to Donovan, 'more congruent with modern reality, and would make for more rational decisions'. A notable political-cum-intellectual journey lay ahead; and in later years he would look back on what had ultimately been behind the thinking by this time of the Oxford School:

> Most of us held, explicitly or implicitly, a 'reformist' view of society and the desirable type of change to be sought within it. This was

often little more than an extrapolation of Britain's social development over the past century. While there was no assumption of
automatic social 'progress', it was supposed that the incremental
concession of political rights and social welfare in the past gave rise
to a reasonable assumption of its continuation into the future. Some
of us hoped and believed that this long-term historical process would
eventually produce a less unequal, democratic-socialist society. In
the meantime it made sense to help the reform process along in
any reasonable way one could. As applied to industrial relations,
this meant furthering and enlarging, through teaching, research,
and practical involvement in industry, that long-growing system
by which trade union representatives at all the relevant levels –
industry-wide, regional, workplace or any combination of these –
negotiated settlements of terms and conditions of employment with
management, and participated in a range of economic, social and
political decision-making or advisory bodies covering wide areas of
the national life. The aim was the extension of a rational order regu-
lating industrial relations which was fairly negotiated between independent associations or groups on both sides. It was a continuation
of an influence exerted by reformers – some of them in government
service – from the 1860s. Trade unions themselves were seen, by
most of us, as fully legitimate associations to be encouraged ...

'Since at this time even Conservative governments were more than
ready to take and act on the same view, we were hardly being politically
controversial,' added Fox about what he eventually came to see by the
disenchanted 1970s as almost tantamount to Whiggish assumptions
of automatic progress. 'On the contrary, we were showing ourselves
prepared to work within, and actively promote the health and smooth
working of, a framework of assumptions, attitudes, institutions and
practices which had been developing constitutionally for a century
and which had helped to keep Britain a relatively peaceful society.'

Of course, employers and workers did not, in daily practice in
1960s Britain, enjoy anything like an equal social and moral status.
Perhaps they should have. A detailed study, published in 1967, of
disputes in the motor industry found that two motivations were
dominant: on the one hand, the demand that wages should be 'fair'
in comparison with other workers; on the other hand, the claim that

workers had property rights in a particular job, whether in relation to other workers or, under threat of redundancy, against the employer. 'The remarkable thing about these objectives,' justly reflects the far from left-wing social historian Harold Perkin, 'is how closely they paralleled those of the salaried professions':

> Demarcation disputes between occupations and issues of differential pay between more and less skilled workers mirrored professional demands for the monopoly of the particular service and for payment commensurate with its superior value. The manual workers' opposition to redundancy without adequate notice and compensation for the workers' property in the job was the precise equivalent of the professional's demand for protection of his human capital. Control over the work process was what every self-respecting professional demanded as of right ... The demarcation enforced in the name of the public interest by the barrister and the solicitor, the architect and the builder, the optician and the ophthalmic surgeon, were species of the same genus as those enforced by trade unionists on the shop floor, the building site, or in the shipyard ... The British working class, in other words, was imbued, for good or ill, with precisely the same outlook on the terms and conditions of work as the professional middle class.[24]

This was not, to put it mildly, a conclusion reached all that often in grumbling saloon-bar conversations.

18

A Feeling of Pride

'Churchill lies dying,' wrote Phyllis Willmott on Friday, 22 January 1965, in the same entry as her disappointed reflections on the Leyton by-election result:

> And even though I barely noticed the man at his 'finest hour' – he always seemed to overdo things in the eyes of the full-blooded younger me – there is a sense of history's leaving in his dying. He may go on for days; but even the length of his passing seems to give pause. With him goes, probably, our last 'greatness' as a nation. The old world of Britain supreme goes with him to the grave.

That evening, an enforced Cabinet reshuffle saw Michael Stewart go to the Foreign Office and Anthony Crosland to Education; Saturday was a slow-news day; and on Sunday morning, shortly after eight o'clock, various somewhat disgruntled ministers gathered at Liverpool Street station in order to go to Sandringham to be sworn in as Privy Councillors, with Frank Cousins' expostulation – 'Whose fucking idea was it that we should be here on this job, this morning?' – earning him a frosty look from the nearby Sir Michael Adeane, the Queen's private secretary. A few minutes later came the news that the world had been expecting. As ever among the diarists, Henry St John rose to the occasion, devoting one whole sentence to the matter: 'Sir Winston Spencer Churchill, politician, whom I saw driven in an open car along Whiteladies Road, Bristol, about 20 years ago, died at about 8 a.m. aged 90, after a stroke (cerebral thrombosis) on January 15th.'

Reactions generally seem to have had a distinct generational split. 'I did not really feel any personal loss as he was the hero of another generation,' explicitly noted 16-year-old schoolboy Roger Darlington; 'people heave (secretly of course) a sigh of relief,' Alan Macfarlane, an undergraduate at Worcester College, Oxford, told his parents; while in Veronica Lee's student household in Leeds, 'Val and I felt fairly sad, but Di said he was a war-mongering old bugger'. Less scepticism, however, among the elderly. 'We shall not look upon his like again and we owe to him a debt that can never be repaid,' solemnly recorded Kenneth Preston in Keighley. 'If only,' he added, 'we had such a leader now to get us out of the mess we are in and give us the same sense of purpose and loyalty ...' Inevitably it was a day rich in private reflections as well as public tributes, with perhaps few of the former matching in eloquence as well as emotion Nella Last's in Barrow:

> I was not surprised – or 'grieved'. I'd done my grieving of these last few days, to see his fire abating, to see even he could 'grow old & full of years'. Instead of grief a feeling of pride – and gratitude – filled me, that I'd been privileged to 'serve under him', for at Hospital Supply & Canteen in the War we all looked to him & his inspiring words as a spur & encouragement. It was a kind of spur to quote some of his words. They left me with a feeling I'd have liked to be in a position to hear more. That 'we will fight on the beaches, etc' stirred depths in me I didn't know I had ... It was as if his words probed deep & found granite in me, & I knew I'd never give in ...

A more nuanced response came from Hull. 'I thought I heard on the wireless a "flash" that Churchill had died – anyway I put a black tie on: no doubt I shall hear at 6 p.m.,' Philip Larkin wrote that afternoon to his mother. 'I had respect for him, in a way, but not liking – most people w^d put it the other way round, I suppose. He seemed to me to be second rate in quality, but full of energy & respect for the right things. In a war you want second-rate energy, and he was clearly the best man.'[1]

Next day, Monday the 25th, *The Times* devoted its front page to news (as opposed to advertisements) for the first time since the Great War, the *Daily Telegraph* had black-edged columns, the *Daily*

Mirror's 'Cassandra' mourned that 'the sword sleeps in the scabbard', and the *Daily Worker* declared that 'with the death of Churchill the capitalist system has lost one of its most tenacious and able defenders'; Lord Longford, in his capacity as Lord Privy Seal, read to the House of Lords the Queen's message that she had directed that 'Sir Winston's body shall lie in State in Westminster Hall and that thereafter the funeral service shall be held in the Cathedral Church of St Paul'; Larkin commented to Monica Jones, 'I say, aren't they going it for the funeral! It'll be like the Duke of Wellington, won't it ...'; the aged Gladys Langford confessed herself 'wearied by all this nonsense about Churchill's death'; and on that evening's *Coronation Street*, a gently wretched Minnie Caldwell told Ena Sharples, 'I've been thinking of *him*'. An unforgettable, palpably momentous week lay ahead. 'All England is Churchill, at present, rehearsals, lying-in-state – enormous queues of people for Westminster Hall, miles long, in the bitter cold,' noted Pamela Hansford Johnson in the course of it; and indeed, between Wednesday and early on Saturday morning, through the days and through the nights, more than 300,000 people filed slowly past during the lying-in-state. Among them was 16-year-old Laurence Marks, who on Thursday the 28th bunked off school with three others:

I'm not sure why we want to go but I do know my dad would approve so even if I get caught he probably won't give me too bad a telling off. What we weren't expecting was the length of the queue going right across Westminster Bridge. We join it. It is a freezing cold afternoon and my coat isn't very warm, but I am glad I have brought my gloves with me. There must be hundreds of people, perhaps even thousands, waiting to get into the Westminster Hall, inside the Houses of Parliament. It reminds me of cup final day at Wembley.

When we eventually are let into this grand stone hall (we waited for just over three hours, it's a good thing I brought a book. We must be mad) we are led down some stairs, in rows of five across, and we walk toward a sort of raised stepped stage. Churchill's closed coffin stands high on the stage and it's covered in a Union Jack flag and around the coffin are soldiers or guards and candles. There is a black-blue cushion on top of the coffin and on it is some sort of garter or necklace and a lit candle. There is a big gold cross at one end and I take it all in because I might never see anything like it again.

As we get closer to the coffin a woman and her daughter are crying. The woman is actually sobbing. I ask her if she is all right and she blows her nose, dries her eyes and tells me that it's like losing a member of her own family. I ask her, 'Did you know Winston Churchill?' She says she didn't but she felt like she did. I don't understand her tears because it isn't like she ever met Winston Churchill.

We are in and out of the Westminster Hall in about ten minutes. All the men raise their hats or at least take them off their head, and they sort of give a deep bow. I don't. I don't suppose anyone from Holloway County School will have spotted us … I hope, so now we got to get back to Finsbury Park and I hope my mum and dad don't ask me what I did at school today.

Marks added that Cronin, one of the other three, 'says we have just witnessed history and I say that everything we witness will one day be history'.[2]

Life sort of went on. Kenneth More, starring in an ill-advised singing part in *Our Man Crichton* at the Shaftesbury, would recall playing the Wednesday matinee to a house three-quarters empty, as people generally stayed away from the theatre; having delayed it because of the impending Leyton by-election, the BBC did now for its Wednesday Play show John Hopkins' *Fable*, albeit prefaced with a solemn warning that it was 'in no way a forecast of what may happen in this country'; the *TLS* included a short review of R. M. Lockley's *The Private Life of the Rabbit*, a key source for *Watership Down*, and a longer review of Margaret Forster's *Georgy Girl* ('an original piece of work', if 'increasingly slapdash'); the *New Statesman*'s John Morgan whole-heartedly welcomed Crosland's going to Education ('all of us interested in seeing the public schools made genuinely public are delighted by his appointment … it's good to know that in office he feels as passionately about public schools as he ever did'); and on Friday at Alexandra Palace, the Racing Pigeon Olympiad got under way, a largely working-class event though including an entry from the royal loft.[3] Yet in truth, almost everyone was waiting for the truly major event: Churchill's funeral on Saturday the 30th at St Paul's.

'There have been funeral processions before, there have been state funerals of commoners before, and of those who are not commoners, there has not been I think in the whole history of our land a state funeral or an occasion which has touched the hearts of people quite as much as this one is doing today,' Richard Dimbleby assured BBC viewers just before 9.45, as Big Ben struck for the last time that day – signal for the coffin to emerge from Westminster Hall and be lowered on to a grey gun-carriage. There followed a slow, heavily military procession – Dimbleby speaking of 'its richness, its colour, and its pride, and its intense solemnity and feeling and love' – to St Paul's. There, some 3,000 people, including many of the world's leaders past and present, were gathered for the service. The most unplanned moment of a minutely planned day came just before, as the frail, 82-year-old Attlee stumbled going up the steps, causing the Guardsmen just behind him to break step and almost drop the coffin. The service itself, relatively short, was (in Geoffrey Wheatcroft's words) 'magnificently crafted, from "The Battle Hymn of the Republic" as a reminder of Churchill's maternal descent (and maybe of the "special relationship"), to the Hussar trumpeter sounding Cavalry Last Post and Reveille, symbolising death and resurrection, even if Churchill had never pretended seriously to believe Christian doctrine'. Afterwards, the coffin was taken to Tower Pier, and thence upstream on a launch, as the tall and slender crane masts on the other side of the river slowly dipped in salute: an instantly immortal sight, though half a century later one of the crane drivers would insist that he and most of his colleagues had loathed Churchill and that they had only turned up ('We didn't work Saturdays') and performed as requested because they had been paid to do so. The launch deposited the coffin at Festival Pier, close to where the Queen Elizabeth Hall was in the process of being built, and from there it was taken to Waterloo station. Why Waterloo, given that the body's ultimate destination was Bladon in Oxfordshire, more obviously served by a train from Paddington? The legend that it was Churchill's own decision – being one in the eye for General de Gaulle (present on the day) – seems plausible enough. At Waterloo, the coffin was placed carefully on the train; and Dimbleby's voice broke with emotion as he said, 'We shall not – we shall not see it – again – after it's gone in'.[4]

Large crowds lined the routes all day, but for the vast majority it was a television experience, predominantly on the BBC. Most of the diarists – if not quite all – were gripped:

Never before have I watched TV for so long. Never before have I been so absorbed, so interested, so moved …

It was the fundamental simplicity and gravity of the occasion, the passing of a great man, that had made so many people devote their time to his memory, people who had to put up with great cold and discomfort in England at the worst time of the year. One could see the clouds of cold coming from the Queen's mouth. One could see the spectators jumping up and down, flailing their arms to try to get some circulation going …

The sounds of the procession, the marching boots, the horses' hooves, the distant military orders, the gun salutes, the flapping of a frightened bird's wings were all part of the spell. (Cecil Beaton)

I went to watch the Churchill funeral at HEG's house [Harold Gardiner, English teacher at Bedales]. There were a dozen of us and we sat on the floor in their small sitting room, perched on the arms of the sofa etc. I felt bad for HEG and Mrs Gardiner because people were fidgeting and chattering and the Gardiners wanted to concentrate on the service. HEG became quite snappy: 'Be quiet. This man saved your country. If you don't want to watch, you can leave.' No one left. (Gyles Brandreth)

I settled to four hours' viewing. It was a perfect and fitting State Funeral for such a great man. (Judy Haines)

The whole stately and august ceremony superbly presented, both visually and orally, in all its pomp and grandeur. It was an awesome spectacle, profoundly soul stirring and deeply moving. It was great television. (Anthony Heap)

I rose early & breakfast was over before 8 o'clock. I cleared the table & put on the chicken to cook, & we watched B.B.C. Television nearly all morning. I kept doing odd jobs like hurriedly washing up & making morning tea, but my husband didn't even shave till 10.30, so enthralled was he with the Television. So wonderfully 'produced', it could well have been a stage show. Dimbleby's voice & narrative superb. Such a pageant – I longed for colour in the dull cold – but seemingly fine day – the colours of uniformed men & St Paul's Cathedral must have been a glory …

I got lunch ready after 12.30. I thought of that gallant old lady [Clementine Churchill] – Randolph looked all in tho – & hoped they would find a meal ready on the train, & they could both relax before the ordeal of the interment. *(Nella Last)*

It was most moving & beautiful. The slow march of feet, the six or eight men carrying the great heavy coffin, the sailors drawing the gun carriage, the crowds ... Not a hitch, all so smooth, & yet such a huge spectacle ... the music of the bands & all the time their slow tread of feet. *(Alison Uttley)*

Watched the massive funeral procession & service at St Paul's for Winston Churchill. Thank goodness this dreary saga will soon be finished. *(Kenneth Williams)*

I meant to avoid looking at it, knowing full well that once I started I would be mesmerised. Oddly Petie switched it on – just at the point when the coffin was moving into St Paul's. I then became so involved with the difficulties of the bearers – it looked such a very hard and worrying job getting the coffin down the aisle, on to the stand, off again and back along the aisle and, finally and terrifyingly, down the long flights of steps in front of St Paul's. I watched, as I knew I would, from then on ...

There was, all along, though, the worry in the mind about the *class* thing. He was a 'great' man, the man of the hour. My father [working-class, from Lee in south London] was not, is not, perhaps never could have been. But it's doubtful, to put it extremely – no, mildly – if Winston could have been 'great' if he had started where Dad did. And all the carrying and waiting upon, that in a strange way rankled in my subconscious mind, as I watched the relatives, guests and 'toffs' acting with such graciousness and dignity. In contrast to the fumbling, clumsy strength and proud *serving* of the bearers, say. *(Phyllis Willmott)*

Larkin, no TV set of his own, went to the university's Senior Common Room to watch the proceedings (though skipping the service itself). 'I kept being visited by floods of emotion,' he reported to Monica Jones – not least, he added, during 'the silence of the river trip', when 'of course I thought of Arthur being conveyed to Avalon'. Two radio listeners were more critical. 'Some of it was quite moving – I suppose there is a sense of history about it, but the commentators made me feel pukish at times,' reflected Veronica Lee. 'Such low voices, and super-clichéd descriptions, they talked me out of all emotion.' The other was a tea planter's wife, Iris Macfarlane, listening to it in Assam. 'How much more beautiful, dignified & organised it was than Nehru's, and how much less it moved me,' she wrote to her son in Oxford. 'Perhaps because though I admired Churchill I never really liked him, he so signally lacked the qualities I *do* admire – humility, tolerance and kindliness – to be a great war leader one can't afford to have them I suppose?'[5]

The day as a whole had an almost religious feel to it. **'For Ever and Ever ... AMEN'** was the *Evening News*'s main headline, the last word banner-high. And to the left, this passage of comfort:

> You can take tears today and catch them and call them the river that flows through London's heart.
>
> Because they bore him on the Thames today. Do not say he died. Say he rode triumphant. Chugging, Churchillian.
>
> Past the driftwood in that homely, murky blue. To the last harbour of quiet, Bladon.

How much, though, were the mourners lamenting not only the passing of a great man, but with him the conclusive passing of British greatness? The distinguished foreign reporter Patrick O'Donovan certainly thought so. 'This was the last time that London would be the capital of the world,' he wrote in next day's *Observer*. 'This was an act of mourning for the Imperial past. This marked the final act in Britain's greatness. This was a great gesture of self-pity and after this the coldness of reality and the status of Scandinavia.' Indeed, such a reading of the day's significance soon became something like conventional wisdom. 'One could not help feeling,' noted the writer Goronwy Rees in an *Encounter* piece ('After the Ball was Over') later in the year, 'that so public an extravagance of grief and mourning could not really have been inspired by one man, but it was not Churchill the nation was burying, but a part of their own history, not a statesman but an Empire, not a hero but themselves, as they once were and never would be again.' Yet was that *actually* how most British people felt it at the time? Probably not. For older people especially, but not just older people, there was almost certainly not only an unbreakable nostalgic attachment to 'our finest hour' a quarter of a century earlier, but also a deep instinctive reluctance to assume that Britain's best days were automatically behind her. In his own honourable but rather crabby way, Kenneth Preston, retired teacher from Keighley and out-and-out opponent of almost anything modern, arguably spoke for many unabashed patriots in his diary entry that day. After praising the funeral service – which, naturally, he had listened to, not watched – as 'a most impressive affair', including a 'masterly' choice of hymns, he went on:

> It has been suggested by an American commentator, that the exit of Sir Winston marks also the exit of Britain from any sort of world significance. It is a country, so he says, effete and done for. This funeral is the last time it will ever occupy the attention of the world. It is a sobering thought and there are times when one is tempted to feel it is all true, but we have been pronounced dead before and been buried and there has been a resurrection.

Even so, he felt compelled to add in this age of so much that he disapproved of, 'the moral fibre will have to change before that can happen, it is true'.[6]

That Saturday afternoon saw – unlike after Diana's funeral 32 years later, or indeed after the Queen's death in 2022 – a full football programme, including lowly Peterborough United beating Arsenal. 'My dad is more fed up than I am,' noted Marks. 'He lost his war leader, his teams have been knocked out of the FA Cup, and the two horses he backed didn't come in and he lost his money. It's been that kind of Saturday.' Over the next six days, as the world fully returned to normal, Michael Duane, of Risinghill fame/notoriety, appeared on ITV's *Sunday Break* and, according to one critic, 'defended his progressive methods with intelligence and vigour ... he is plainly on the side of children'; on Monday morning at Roger Darlington's much more traditional school in Manchester, 'everybody was talking about Saturday's F.A. Cup 4th Round'; in Cambridge's Arts Theatre, the first try-out week of Joe Orton's new farce, *Loot*, got the dustiest of receptions from critics ('seldom funny ... repetitive and sometimes nasty sense of humour') and punters ('sets a new low level in the "kitchen sink" era') alike; the millionth Mini came off the production line at Longbridge; Vere Hodgson in Church Stretton confessed herself as disgusted by Brigid Brophy on *Not So Much A Programme, More A Way Of Life* ('the sort of intellectual I dislike very much ... undermining all authority in religion and everything else') as she was delighted by going to the Birmingham Rep to see *Charley's Aunt* ('such glorious wholesome laughter for everyone ... no stupid satire, no sex mania, nothing intellectual in the way of self-pity by this group of young people'); the Opposition leader, Sir Alec Douglas-Home, made a speech in Hampstead calling for further tough action on tightening immigration controls; next day in the Commons, Sir Frank Soskice, as home secretary, not only largely followed his recommendations (Tory MPs cheering repeatedly, Labour MPs mainly silent on the benches behind him), but refused a new inquiry into the case of Timothy Evans ('I am quite convinced that it is not really feasible many, many years after the events to arrive at any reliable view'); Ezra Pound stole the show at T. S. Eliot's memorial service in Westminster Abbey; 'You've Lost that Lovin' Feelin'' by the Righteous Brothers went to the top of the charts; and the Variety Club of Great Britain, a year after conferring its 1963 award on the Beatles, voted Eric Morecambe and Ernie Wise as joint personalities of 1964, while at the same time identifying another northerner, Liverpool's Jimmy Tarbuck, as most promising comedian. 'Until a couple of years ago, people in London did not want to know us,' Eric remarked wryly enough to a journalist. 'Then suddenly we were all the rage.'[7]

'An early start to Stoke in the official car,' recorded the housing minister, Richard Crossman, on Saturday, 6 February:

As I was driving through it I suddenly felt, 'Here is this huge, ghastly conurbation of five towns – what sense is there in talking about urban renewal here? Other towns have a shape, a centre, some place where renewal can start, perhaps a university. But if one spent billions on this ghastly collection of slag heaps, pools of water, old potteries, deserted coal mines, there would be nothing to show for the money.' There is nothing in Stoke except the worst of the industrial revolution and some of the nicest people in the world. Alas, there are no modern sophisticated industries. There is just a vast equalitarian working class living in cheap council houses and with very low wage-rates. I didn't see much of the town but I had a good discussion with half a dozen councillors in the lord mayor's parlour. When it was over I felt even more strongly that it was impossible to revive Britain without letting such places as Stoke-on-Trent decline. Indeed, I began to wonder whether it wasn't really better to let it be evacuated: renewal is an impossibility, or alternatively a fantastic waste of money.

Crossman that afternoon addressed a Labour Party regional conference in Hanley Town Hall; but the main action lay elsewhere – at the Victoria Ground, where Stoke City's venerable forward, the recently knighted Stanley Matthews, played his first competitive match for over a year and thereby became, at the age of fifty, the oldest footballer to play in the First Division. Stoke's visiting opponents, perhaps carefully chosen by Matthews, were Fulham, whose 36-year-old left-back, Jim Langley, was known as 'Gentleman Jim'; the crowd of 28,585 was about 8,000 above the usual; almost thirty photographers, together with a large roar of welcome from the crowd, greeted Matthews as he ran out on to the pitch; 'after 10 minutes,' noted a watching Clement Freud, 'condescending phrases like "pretty good for a man of 50" were silenced ... to be replaced by the plain realisation that Stoke had an elegant, perceptive and dangerous footballer playing on their right wing'; the *Evening Sentinel*'s match reporter gloried in how 'Stan showed he still possesses the master touch when he clipped inside some measured passes and then brought the house down with a great effort which would have produced the lead for Stoke but for a wonderful tip over the bar by Macedo'; happily, the home side came back from an early Rodney Marsh goal to win 3–1; and, responding with typical modesty to post-match congratulations, Matthews said, 'Well, yes, I thought I played reasonable,' adding 'I hope I have some games in the future.' But it was not to be; and at the end of the season, 33 years after first playing for Stoke, he reluctantly hung up his boots.[8]

Churchill and Matthews: the passing of two mid-century icons. The end of the post-war era? Yes, in some sense undeniably. But whether the tug of the past would really lose its power – well, that was another matter entirely.

Abbreviations

Abrams	Mark Abrams Papers (Churchill Archives Centre, Churchill College, Cambridge)
Amis	Zachary Leader (ed.), *The Letters of Kingsley Amis* (2000)
BBC WAC	BBC Written Archives Centre (Caversham)
Benn	Ruth Winstone (ed.), Tony Benn, *Out of the Wilderness: Diaries 1963–67* (1987)
Bonham Carter	Mark Pottle (ed.), *Daring to Hope: The Diaries and Letters of Violet Bonham Carter, 1946–1969* (2000)
Brandreth	Gyles Brandreth, *Something Sensational to Read in the Train* (2009)
Crossman (1)	Janet Morgan (ed.), *The Backbench Diaries of Richard Crossman* (1981)
Crossman (2)	Richard Crossman, *The Diaries of a Cabinet Minister*, vol. 1 (1975)
Daly	Lawrence Daly Papers (Modern Records Centre, University of Warwick)
Darlington	Diary of Roger Darlington (private collection of Roger Darlington)
Dee	Diary of Dennis Dee (East Riding of Yorkshire Archives, Beverley)
DM (1)	*Daily Mail*
DM (2)	*Daily Mirror*
DS	*Daily Sketch*
DT	*Daily Telegraph*
Fowles	Charles Drazin (ed.), John Fowles, *The Journals*, vol. 1 (2003)

Fowles	John Fowles Papers (Special Collections, University of Exeter)
FT	*Financial Times*
G	*Guardian*
GDP	Great Diary Project (Bishopsgate Institute, London)
Hague	Frances and Gladys Hague Papers (Keighley Library)
Haines	Diary of Alice (Judy) Haines (Mass-Observation Archive, University of Sussex, The Keep, Brighton)
Halle	Diary of William Halle (Wandsworth Heritage Service)
Heap	Diary of Anthony Heap (London Metropolitan Archives)
Hill	Diary of Jennie Hill (Hampshire Record Office, Winchester)
Hodgson	Diary of Vere Hodgson (Kensington Central Library)
Ind	*Independent*
Ironside	Diary of Virginia Ironside (private collection of Virginia Ironside)
Jackson	Diary of Sidney Jackson (Bradford Archives, Bradford Central Library)
L	*Listener*
Langford	Diary of Gladys Langford (Islington Local History Centre)
Larkin	Anthony Thwaite (ed.), Philip Larkin, *Letters to Monica* (2010)
Larkin	Unpublished letters of Philip Larkin to Monica Jones (Bodleian Library, Oxford)
Last	Diary of Nella Last (Mass-Observation diarist 5353, Mass-Observation Archive, University of Sussex, The Keep, Brighton)
Lee	Diary of Veronica Lee (later Porter) (private collection of Veronica Porter)
Macmillan (1)	Harold Macmillan, *At the End of the Day* (1973)
Macmillan (2)	Peter Catterall (ed.), *The Macmillan Diaries: Volume II* (2011)
Marks	Diary of Laurence Marks (private collection of Laurence Marks)
Martin	Diary of Madge Martin (Oxfordshire History Centre, Oxford)
MM	*Melody Maker*
MRC	Modern Records Centre (University of Warwick)
NME	*New Musical Express*

New Soc	*New Society*
NS	*New Statesman*
NSPSCA	The National Social Policy and Social Change Archive (Special Collections, Albert Sloman Library, University of Essex)
NVLAA	National Viewers' and Listeners' Association Archive (Special Collections, Albert Sloman Library, University of Essex)
NY	*New Yorker*
Ob	*Observer*
P	*Punch*
Partridge (1)	Frances Partridge, *Hanging On* (1990)
Partridge (2)	Frances Partridge, *Other People* (1993)
Preston	Diary of Kenneth Preston (Bradford Archives, Bradford Central Library)
Raynham	Diary of Marian Raynham (Mass-Observation Archive, University of Sussex, The Keep, Brighton)
RT	*Radio Times*
St John	Diary of Henry St John (Ealing Local History Centre)
Scott	Diary of Patricia Scott (Mass-Observation Archive, University of Sussex, The Keep, Brighton)
Selbourne	David Selbourne (ed.), *A Doctor's Life: The Diaries of Hugh Selbourne M.D., 1960–63* (1989)
Spec	*Spectator*
ST	*Sunday Times*
S Tel	*Sunday Telegraph*
T	*The Times*
TLS	*Times Literary Supplement*
Williams	Russell Davies (ed.), *The Kenneth Williams Diaries* (1993)
Willmott	Diary of Phyllis Willmott (Churchill Archives Centre, Churchill College, Cambridge)

All books are published in London unless otherwise stated.

Notes

I ALL SO WORRYING

1. Martin, P5/2J/37, 6 Oct 1962; diary of Georgiana Tench (MRC), Ms
   255/13, 6 Oct 1962; Hill, vol. 30, 6 Oct 1962; *Ob*, 7 Oct 1962; Larkin,
   Ms.Eng.c.7425, fo 71, 7 Oct 1962; *TLS*, 16 Sep 2022 (Ian Sansom); BBC
   WAC, R9/25/2, week 6–12 Oct 1962, R9/7/60–VR/62/562, 7 Oct 1962;
   Michael Willmott (ed.), Rev. Oliver Willmott, *The Parish Notes of
   Loders, Dottery and Askerswell*, vol. 1 (Shrewsbury, 1996), Nov 1962.
2. https://coronationstreet.fandon.com/wiki/Episode_190; *Ob*, 14 Oct
   1962; Lee, 9 Oct 1962; Haines, SxMOA99/34/8/15, 9 Oct 1962; BBC
   WAC, R9/7/60–VR/62/567, 9 Oct 1962; Larkin, Ms.Eng,c,7425, fo 75,
   11 Oct 1962; Ren Yaldren, *A Profile of Stephen Joseph* (Scarborough,
   n.d.), pp. 30–1; https://coronationstreet.fandom.com/wiki/Episode_
   191; *DT*, 11 Oct 1962; Heap, Acc 2243/36/1, 10 Oct 1962.
3. *G*, 11 Oct 1962; *NS*, 19 Oct 1962; *G*, 11 Oct 1962; *Architectural Design*,
   Nov 1962, p. 503; Martin, P5/2J/37, 11 Oct 1962; Douglas Hill (ed.),
   Tribune 40 (1977), pp. 151–2; *South London Press*, 12 Oct 1962; Heather
   Clark, *Red Comet* (2020), pp. 77–8; *L*, 18 Oct 1962; Martin, P5/2J/37,
   12 Oct 1962; papers of Barbara Pym (Bodleian), Ms. Pym 162/1, 13
   Oct 1962; *G*, 15 Oct 1962; Martin, P5/2J/37, 13 Oct 1962; Haines,
   SxMOA99/34/8/15, 14 Oct 1962; *NS*, 12 Oct 1962 (Kathleen Gibberd);
   Stefan Muthesius, *The Postwar University* (2001), p. 114; *Architects'
   Journal*, 17 Oct 1962; *G*, 18 Oct 1962; Mark Lewisohn, *The Complete
   Beatles Chronicle* (1996 edn), p. 81.
4. *Macmillan* (2), p. 506; Tam Dalyell, 'Viscount Muirshiel', *Ind*, 21 Aug
   1992; H. A. Turner et al., *Labour Relations in the Motor Industry* (1967),
   p. 281; *NS*, 2 Nov 1962; *Macmillan* (2), p. 507; Tim Claydon, 'Tales of
   Disorder', in *Historical Studies in Industrial Relations*, Spring 2000,

pp. 18–20; *Ob*, 21 Oct 1962; BBC WAC, R9/7/60–VR/62/592, 21 Oct 1962; Anthony Hayward, 'Don Taylor', *Ind*, 22 Nov 2003; *G*, 22 Oct 1962; *Glasgow Herald*, 26 Oct 1962; *Ob*, 28 Oct 1962; *G*, 22 Oct 1962.

5. Brian Jackson Collection (NSPSCA), C4, file of 'Marriage Sample' interviews, 22 Oct 1962; D. R. Thorpe, *Supermac* (2010), p. 528; Willmott, WLMT 1/25, 25 Oct 1962.

6. *G*, 24 Oct 1962 ('London Letter'); Dee, DDX 829/2, 23 Oct 1962; *Partridge* (1), pp. 128–9; Scott, SxMOA99/97/1/11, 23 Oct 1962; *Ob*, 28 Oct 1962 (Maurice Richardson); *S Tel*, 28 Oct 1962 (Philip Purser); Christopher Hitchens, *Hitch-22* (2010), p. 65; *ST*, 28 Oct 1962 (Maurice Wiggin); Martin, P5/2J/37, 24 Oct 1962.

7. *DT*, 23–25 Oct 1962. Generally on this episode, see Richard Davenport-Hines, *An English Affair* (2013), pp. 132–7.

8. *DT*, 25 Oct 1962; *Brandreth*, p. 35; Lee, 24 Oct 1962; *Fowles*, pp. 534–5; *Stainbeck County Secondary Girls' School Magazine, 1962* (1962), p. 19 (at Leeds Central Library).

9. *Roundhay High School Magazine*, Dec 1963, p. 24 (at Leeds Central Library); *L*, 25 Oct 1962; BBC WAC, R9/7/60–VR/62/599, 25 Oct 1962; Haines, SxMOA99/34/8/15, 25 Oct 1962; *DT*, 25 Oct 1962; *G*, 26 Oct 1962; *DT*, 26 Oct 1962; Halle, D 121/2, 25 Oct 1962.

10. *Ob*, 28 Oct 1962; *South Wales Evening Post*, 26 Oct 1962; Brendan King, *Beryl Bainbridge* (2016), p. 239; *Partridge* (1), p. 130; Halle, 26 Oct 1962; Lee, 26 Oct 1962; St John, 68/47, 26 Oct 1962.

11. *Finchley Press*, 26 Oct 1962; *Evening News*, 23 Oct 1962; *Lynn News & Advertiser*, 26 Oct 1962, 30 Oct 1962; *G*, 27 Oct 1962; Leo McKinstry, *Sir Alf* (2006), p. 201; *NME*, 26 Oct 1962.

12. Ben Watt, *Romany and Tom* (2014), pp. 338–42; Clark, *Red Comet*, pp. 792–6; Juliet Gardiner, *Joining the Dots* (2017), pp. 102–4; *ST*, 28 Oct 1962; Davenport-Hines, *An English Affair*, p. 258; Chris Salewicz, 'Johnny Edgecombe', *Ind*, 18 Oct 2010.

13. *S Tel*, 28 Oct 1962; Lee, 28 Oct 1962; Scott, SxMOA99/97/1/11, 28 Oct 1962; *DT*, 29 Oct 1962; Mark Lewisohn, *All These Years*, vol. 1 (2013), pp. 783–5; Halle, D 121/2, 28 Oct 1962.

14. Hodgson, 29 Oct 1962; *G*, 11 Jan 2014; David Hare, *The Blue Touch Paper* (2015), p. 63; Virginia Nicholson, *How Was It For You?* (2019), pp. 105–6; *T*, 5 Jun 2021; *Independent on Sunday*, 11 Mar 1990; Simon Winder, *The Man Who Saved Britain* (2006), p. 175.

2 AUDACIOUSLY SATIRICAL

1. *DT*, 1 Nov 1962; *Birmingham Post*, 2 Nov 1962; Lewisohn, *All These Years*, vol. 1, pp. 761–2; *TLS*, 2 Nov 1962; BBC WAC, R9/7/61–VR/62/616, 2 Nov 1962; Peter Doggett, *Growing Up* (2021), p. 72; Dee, DDX 829/2, 3 Nov 1962; Hill, vol. 30, 4 Nov 1962; BBC WAC, R9/7/61–VR/62/619, 4 Nov 1962; Martin, P5/2J/37, 5 Nov 1962; Joanna Moorhead, *New Generations* (Cambridge, 1996), p. 40; *Carlisle Journal*, 2 Nov 1962; *Ob*, 11 Nov 1962; Andrew Barrow, *Gossip* (1980 edn), p. 228; Ben Pimlott, *Harold Wilson* (1992), p. 250; BBC WAC, R9/74/3, Dec 1962, R9/7/61–VR/62/636, 11 Nov 1962; Heap, Acc 2243/36/1, 12 Nov 1962; BBC WAC, R9/7/61–VR/62/637, 12 Nov 1962; Tam Dalyell, 'Sir Frederick Corfield', *Ind*, 31 Aug 2005; *Vauxhall Mirror*, 15 Nov 1962; Hodgson, 26 Nov 1962; *DT*, 19 Nov 1962; BBC WAC, R9/7/61–VR/62/645, 17 Nov 1962; *S Tel*, 18 Nov 1962; *ST*, 18 Nov 1962; *Birmingham Post*, 21 Nov 1962.

2. *Yorkshire Post*, 23 Nov 1962; Last, SxMOA1/4/280, 24 Nov 1962; Ned Sherrin, *A Small Thing – Like an Earthquake* (1983), p. 68; BBC WAC, R9/74/3, Jan 1963, R9/7/61–VR/62/655, 24 Nov 1962; Humphrey Carpenter, *That Was Satire That Was* (2000), p. 223; Humphrey Carpenter, *Dennis Potter* (1998), p. 128; Carpenter, *Satire*, p. 223; *L*, 29 Nov 1962.

3. *L*, 29 Nov 1962; *T*, 27–8 Nov 1962; *DT*, 29 Nov 1962; BBC WAC, R9/74/3, Jan 1963.

4. Charles Williams, *Gentlemen & Players* (2012), pp. 168–9; Stephen Fay and David Kynaston, *Arlott, Swanton and the Soul of English Cricket* (2018), pp. 183–5; https://coronationstreet.fandom.com/wiki/Episode_204; *Western Evening Herald*, 28 Nov 1962; Larkin, Ms.Eng.c.7425, fo 112, 2 Dec 1962; https://coronationstreet.fandom.com/wiki/Episode_205; Peter Mitchell, *Momento Mori* (Otley, 1990), p. 102; Ronald Smith, *The Gorbals* (Glasgow, 1999), pp. 33–4; *Architectural Review*, Dec 1962, p. 383; *ST*, 2 Dec 1962; *NS*, 7 Dec 1962; *DT*, 3 Dec 1962; *T*, 3 Dec 1962; Lewisohn, *The Complete Beatles Chronicle*, pp. 84–5.

5. Haines, SxMOA99/34/8/15, 4 Dec 1962; Heap, Acc 2243/36/1, 4 Dec 1962; *(Newcastle) Journal*, 5 Dec 1962; *Derby Evening Telegraph*, 6 Dec 1962; Adam Benedick, 'David Turner', *Ind*, 15 Dec 1990; Heap, Acc 2243/36/1, 5 Dec 1962; *NS*, 14 Dec 1962; *G*, 14 Apr 1998 (John Ezard); *G*, 7 Dec 1962; John Goldsmith (ed.), Stephen Spender, *Journals 1939–1983* (1985), p. 253; Heap, Acc 2243/36/1, 6 Dec 1962; BBC WAC, R9/7/61–VR/62/680, 6 Dec 1962; Martin Gilbert, *'Never Despair'* (1988), p. 1340; *G*, 9 Mar 2013; *Evening Standard*, 7 Dec 1972.

6. *Bonham Carter*, p. 262; *Macmillan* (2), p. 522; *NS*, 21 Dec 1962; Barrow, p. 229; Conservative Party Records (Bodleian Library), CCO 120/4/5, 23 Oct 1962, 6 Nov 1962. See also: Ferdinand Mount, *Cold Cream* (2008), pp. 250–60.

7. *T*, 6–7 Dec 1962; *Bonham Carter*, p. 262; *Macmillan* (2), pp. 522–3; *T*, 8 Dec 1962; *NY*, 11 Dec 1962; *T*, 12 Dec 1962; *TLS*, 18 Nov 2011 (J. C.); *Macmillan* (1), pp. 348–55; Thorpe, *Supermac*, p. 534.

8. *G*, 10 Feb 2016 (Ian Jack); *Macmillan* (2), p. 527; *Sunday Express*, 23 Dec 1962; Hodgson, 26 Dec 1962.

9. Keith Middlemas, 'Sir Robert Shone', *Ind*, 30 Dec 1992; Barbara M. D. Smith, 'Turner, Eric', in *Dictionary of Business Biography*, vol. 5 (1986), p. 571; *T*, 10 Nov 1962; Bert Hopwood, *Whatever Happened to the British Motorcycle Industry?* (Yeovil, 1981), p. 189; *Ob*, 16 Jun 1963 ('Mammon').

10. *T*, 30 Nov 1962; Peter Gillman, 'Supersonic Bust', in *Atlantic Monthly*, Jan 1977, pp. 72–81; *G*, 29 Nov 1962; *DT*, 26 Nov 1962; *G*, 29 Nov 1962. For the fullest account, see: Lewis Johnman and Frances M. B. Lynch, 'A Treaty Too Far?', in *Twentieth Century British History*, 13/3 (2002), pp. 253–76.

11. *NS*, 29 Nov 2013; *NY*, 11 Dec 1962; *G*, 29–30 Oct 1962, 9 Nov 1962, 13–14 Nov 1962.

12. *Prospect*, Dec 2002, p. 18 (Paul Barker); Raynham, SxMOA99/60/1/41, 8 Dec 1962; *L*, 27 Dec 1962; Carpenter, *Satire*, pp. 233–8; Michael Coveney, 'Ned Sherrin', *G*, 3 Oct 2007; Quentin Crewe, 'Bernard Levin', *G*, 10 Aug 2004; Heap, Acc 2243/36/1, 15 Dec 1962; *G*, 22 May 2010; *FT*, 17 Sep 2011; personal information.

13. Clark, *Red Comet*, p. 828; *Architects' Journal*, 12 Dec 1962; Otto Saumarez Smith, *Boom Cities* (Oxford, 2019), p. 44; *Architects' Journal*, 12 Dec 1962; Heap, Acc 2243/36/1, 12 Dec 1962; *G*, 13 Dec 1962; Martin, P5/2J/37, 13 Dec 1962; Chris Salewicz, 'Johnny Edgecombe', *Ind*, 18 Oct 2010; *G*, 14 Nov 2009 (Mark Olden); Tony Jasper, *The Top Twenty Book* (1994 edn), pp. 81–2; Hazel Holt and Hilary Pym (eds), Barbara Pym, *A Very Private Eye* (1984), p. 292; *The Alfred Herbert News*, Nov–Dec 1962, pp. 178–9 (at Coventry Central Library); BBC WAC, R9/7/61–VR/62/695, 15 Dec 1962; *Selbourne*, p. 209; *Wikipedia*, 'Blue Peter'.

14. *G*, 20 Dec 1962; Lewis Chester et al., *Jeremy Thorpe* (1979), p. 45; Keith Richards, *Life* (2010), p. 113; Paul Foot, *Immigration and Race in British Politics* (Harmondsworth, 1965), p. 25; *RT*, 13 Dec 1962; Haines, SxMOA99/34/8/15, 21 Dec 1962; James Stourton, *Kenneth Clark* (2016), p. 311; Lee, 22 Dec 1962; Rob Young, *Electric Eden* (2011), p. 155.

15. Halle, D 121/2, 23 Dec 1962; John Tilbury, *Cornelius Cardew* (Harlow, 2008), p. 147; Jackson, 43D78/52, 23–4 Dec 1962; Walter Hooper (ed.), C. S. Lewis, *Collected Letters*, vol. III (2006), p. 1396; BBC WAC, R9/7/61–VR/62/714, 24 Dec 1962; *South Wales Evening Post*, 24 Dec 1962.

16. Jackson, 43D78/52, 25 Dec 1962; Heap, Acc 2243/36/1, 25 Dec 1962; Hill, vol. 30, 25 Dec 1962; Joe Moran, *Armchair Nation* (2013), pp. 147–8; Ben Pimlott, *The Queen* (1996), pp. 332–3; BBC WAC, R9/7/61–VR/62/715, 25 Dec 1962; Clark, *Red Comet*, p. 833; *Larkin*, p. 314; Ian Addis, *A Passing Game* (Northampton, 1995), p. 145.

17. Raynham, SxMOA99/60/1/41, 26 Dec 1962; Haines, SxMOA99/34/8/15, 26 Dec 1962; Darlington, 26 Dec 1962; Anton Rippon, *A Derby Boy* (Stroud, 2007), p. 95; Graham Brack, 'Où Sont les Neiges d'Antan', in Nick Hornby (ed.), *My Favourite Year* (1997 edn), p. 224; Duncan Hamilton, *Provided You Don't Kiss Me* (2007), p. 33; *Larkin*, pp. 314–15.

3 I DIDN'T LIKE TO ASK

1. Rodney Lowe, 'The Replanning of the Welfare State, 1957–1964', in Martin Francis and Ina Zweiniger-Balgielowska (eds), *The Conservatives and British Society, 1880–1990* (Cardiff, 1996), p. 270; Rodney Lowe, *The Welfare State in Britain since 1945* (Basingstoke, 1999 edn), p. 18; Nicholas Timmins, *The Five Giants* (2001 edn), p. 249; Simon Heffer, *Like the Roman* (1998), pp. 289–90; *T*, 31 Mar 1997 (Roger Bootle); Timmins, p. 250; Philippe Fontaine, 'Blood, Politics and Social Science', in *Isis*, Sep 2002, p. 406; Timothy Raison, 'Macleod and Howe', in *Twentieth Century British History*, 1997 (8/1), pp. 98–100.

2. John Vaizey, *In Breach of Promise* (1983), p. 57; *L*, 11 Aug 1960; Richard M. Titmuss, *Income Distribution and Social Change* (1962), p. 188; Peter Townsend papers (University of Essex), Box 35, 'A Society for People', undated (late 1950s?) typescript.

3. Duncan Gallie, 'The Labour Force', in A. H. Halsey (ed.), *Twentieth-Century British Social Trends* (Basingstoke, 2000 edn), pp. 314–15; Howard Glennerster, *British Social Policy since 1945* (Oxford, 1995), p. 105. For more on the quartet, see: John Steward, *Richard Titmuss: A Commitment to Welfare* (Bristol, 2020); Tom Clark and Kate Green, 'Peter Townsend', *G*, 9 Jun 2009; Sally Sheard, *The Passionate Economist: How Brian Abel-Smith Shaped Global Health and Social Welfare* (Bristol, 2013); Jonathan Bradshaw, 'Tony Lynes', *G*, 24 Nov 2014. For an incisive

survey of the history of poverty, see: Stewart Lansley, *The Richer The Poorer* (Bristol, 2022).

4. Dorothy Cole Wedderburn, 'Poverty in Britain Today – The Evidence', in *Sociological Review*, Nov 1962, pp. 257–82; *NS*, 20 Apr 1962, 31 Aug 1962, 7 Sep 1962, 14 Sep 1962, 21 Sep 1962; Peter Townsend, 'The Meaning of Poverty', in *British Journal of Sociology*, Sep 1962, pp. 219, 225; Wedderburn, 'Poverty', pp. 258, 260, 265; Peter Townsend and Dorothy Wedderburn, *The Aged in the Welfare State* (1965), pp. 14, 95, 108–10.

5. *New Soc*, 10 Jan 1963 (Phyllis and Peter Willmott); Glennerster, *Social Policy*, p. 89; Ken Coates and Richard Silburn, *Poverty* (Harmondsworth, 1970), pp. 13–20; Hilary Rose, 'Rereading Titmuss', in *Journal of Social Policy*, Oct 1981, p. 490; David C. Marsh, *The Future of the Welfare State* (Harmondsworth, 1964), pp. 100–1; Wedderburn, 'Poverty', p. 263; Alan Deacon and Jonathan Bradshaw, *Reserved for the Poor* (Oxford, 1983), p. 105; Virginia A. Noble, *Inside the Welfare State* (Abingdon, 2009), pp. 11, 69, 84–5; David Vincent, *Poor Citizens* (Harlow, 1991), p. 143.

6. *G*, 2 Apr 1963; Stephen Thornton, 'A Case of Confusion and Incoherence', in *Contemporary British History*, Sep 2006, pp. 443–4; *G*, 5 Apr 1963.

7. *Ind*, 14 Jan 1995; *New Soc*, 31 Jan 1963; Heffer, *Like the Roman*, p. 284; Tony Cutler, 'Economic Liberal or Arch Planner?', in *Contemporary British History*, Dec 2011, p. 477; *T*, 24 Jan 1962; Cutler, p. 469; Glen O'Hara, *From Dreams to Disillusionment* (Basingstoke, 2007), p. 188; Charles Webster, 'Conservatives and consensus', in Ann Oakley and A. Susan Williams, *The Politics of the Welfare State* (1994), p. 59.

8. Michael Ryan, 'Health centre policy in England and Wales', in *British Journal of Sociology*, Mar 1968, pp. 36–7; Robert Shepherd, *Enoch Powell* (1996), pp. 232–3; Harold Evans, *My Paper Chase* (2009), pp. 240–4; The Insight Team of the *Sunday Times* (Phillip Knightley et al.), *Suffer the Children* (1979), p. 142; Shepherd, p. 233; *Suffer*, pp. 142–3; Evans, p. 314; *G*, 2 Aug 2014 (Nick McGrath); Evans, p. 311; *G*, 29 Mar 2004 (Mary Kenny).

9. 'Elizabeth Taylor', *T*, Apr 2011; 'Sir George Godber', *T*, 12 Feb 2009; Penny Warren, 'Desmond Julian', *G*, 16 Mar 2020; John Bynner, 'Professor Neville Butler', *Ind*, 10 Mar 2007; Caroline Richmond, 'Katharina Dalton', *G*, 30 Sep 2004, 'Dr Katharina Dalton', *T*, 2 Nov 2004; Philip Rodin, 'Ambrose King', *Ind*, 26 Oct 2000; Nicolas Rea, 'Hugh Faulkner', *G*, 22 Apr 1994.

10. *Selbourne*, pp. 161, 167, 170; John Berger and Jean Mohr, *A Fortunate Man* (Edinburgh, 2016 edn), pp. 12, 15.

11. Ann Cartwright, *Patients and their Doctors* (1967), pp. 3, 6–9, 110–17, 216–20.

12. *London Review of Books*, 7 May 1987; Lorna Sage, *Bad Blood* (2000), pp. 260–1, 252; David Blunkett, *On a Clear Day* (2002 edn), p. 54; Joanna Moorhead, *New Generations* (Cambridge, 1996), p. 41; Richard Hines, *No Way But Gentlenesse* (2016), p. 52; Gardiner, *Joining the Dots*, p. 115; John Lydon, *Rotten* (1994), pp. 18–19.

13. Mary Lindsay, '"Mummy's gone away and left me behind,"' in Margot Waddell and Sebastian Kraemer (eds), *The Tavistock Century* (Bicester, 2021), pp. 47–60; Rick Rogers, *Crowther to Warnock* (1980), chap. 3; *Ob*, 15 Jan 1961, 22 Jan 1961, 29 Jan 1961, 12 Feb 1961; *T*, 18 Feb 1964; *New Soc*, 26 Mar 1964; *NS*, 5 Jun 1964 (Cynthia Walton); 'June Jolly', *T*, 16 Apr 2016.

14. *The Economist*, 22 Jul 1961; Jim Northcott, *Why Labour?* (Harmondsworth, 1964), p. 170; *ST*, 12 Nov 1961 (Susan Cooper); *New Soc*, 21 Nov 1963; *Punch*, 27 May 1964.

15. Ann Cartwright, *Human Relations and Hospital Care* (1964), chaps 3–4, 6–7, 9, 16. For another informative and even more critical survey, see: Gerda L. Cohen, *What's Wrong With Hospitals?* (Harmondsworth, 1964).

16. Charles Webster, 'Investigating Inequalities in Health before Black', in *Contemporary British History*, Autumn 2002, p. 92; *NS*, 3 Jul 1998 (John Lloyd); Charles Webster, *The National Health Service* (Oxford, 2002 edn), pp. 57–9; Vivienne Walters, *Class Inequality and Health Care* (1980), pp. 145–6; Matthew Murray, 'Class and the Welfare State', in Richard Mabey (ed.), *Class* (1967), p. 89; Moorhead, *New Generations*, p. 42.

17. *TLS*, 14 Oct 2005; *G*, 23 May 2018 (Mark Ivory); Rachel Reeves, *Alice in Westminster* (2017), p. 107; *Critic*, 15 Oct 2022 (Kester Aspden); Caryl Phillips, *Foreigners* (2007), p. 194; Diana Melly, *Take a Girl Like Me* (2005), p. 31; Janet Frame, *The Envoy from Mirror City* (1985), pp. 110–11; Kathleen Jones and Roy Sidebotham, *Mental Hospitals at Work* (1962), pp. 57, 59–60, 67–8, 76, 80, 204.

18. Simon Goodwin, 'Community Care for the Mentally Ill in England and Wales', in *Journal of Social Policy*, Jan 1989, p. 37; Heffer, *Like the Roman*, pp. 282–3; Shepherd, *Enoch Powell*, p. 228; Goodwin, pp. 28–41; Jones and Sidebotham, *Mental Hospitals at Work*, p. 20; *G*, 19 Jun 1961 (Kathleen Jones); Jonathan Bradshaw, 'Kathleen Jones', *G*, 26 Oct 2010.

19. Jane Lewis, 'Choice, needs and enabling', in Oakley and Williams, *Politics*, p. 148; Shepherd, *Enoch Powell*, p. 230; Charles Webster, *The Health Services since the War*, vol. II (1996), pp. 124–6; *New Soc*, 2 Apr 1964; *G*, 7 Jul 1964 (M. E. O'Neill).

20. *G*, 23 May 2018 (Mark Ivory); *Ob*, 5 Apr 1964. See also: Cohen, *Hospitals*, chaps 7–8.

21. *G*, 6 Sep 2008; R. D. Laing and A. Esterson, *Sanity, Madness and the Family* (Harmondsworth, 1970 edn), p. 27; *ST*, 15 Aug 1965 (quoted by Penelope Mortimer).

22. Lowe, *Welfare State*, p. 263; *G*, 18 Apr 1963; Marsh, *Future of the Welfare State*, pp. 77–8; Shepherd, *Enoch Powell*, p. 230; Lowe, *Welfare State*, p. 263; Webster, *Health Services*, p. 126.

23. *New Soc*, 24 Jan 1963 to 28 Feb 1963; Phyllis Willmott, *A Singular Woman* (1992), pp. 125–6; Webster, *Health Services*, pp. 121–2; Northcott, *Why Labour?*, p. 60; *Twentieth Century*, Oct 1959, pp. 253–6, 259; Margot Jefferys, *An Anatomy of Social Welfare Services* (1965), pp. 164–5; Eileen Younghusband, *Social Work in Britain*, vol. 1 (1978), p. 45.

24. Julia Parker and Josephine Webb, 'Social Services', in Halsey, *British Social Trends*, p. 532; Younghusband, *Social Work in Britain*, p. 57; Jimmy Boyle, *A Sense of Freedom* (1977), p. 39; Mary Morse, *The Unattached* (Harmondsworth, 1965), pp. 196, 210; Younghusband, *Social Work in Britain*, pp. 207–11; Andrew Roth, 'Lord Morris of Manchester', *G*, 15 Aug 2012.

25. Younghusband, *Social Work in Britain*, p. 173; *Wikipedia*, 'Jack Tizzard'; 'Judy Fryd', *T*, 23 Oct 2000.

26. Lowe, *Welfare State*, p. 272; Townsend and Wedderburn, *Aged*, pp. 68–70; *Ob*, 5 Jul 1964; *ST*, 24 Feb 1963; Caroline Richmond, 'Dame Cicely Saunders', *Ind*, 15 Jul 2005.

27. *Ob*, 5 Jul 1964; Peter Townsend, *The Last Refuge* (162), pp. 41, 4–5, 146–50; *T*, 16 Nov 1962; *NS*, 28 Dec 1962; Townsend, *Refuge*, p. 436.

28. Andrew Denham and Mark Garnett, *Keith Joseph* (Chesham, 2001), p. 105; O'Hara, *Dreams*, p. 133; Stanley Alderson, *Britain in the Sixties: Housing* (Harmondsworth, 1962), pp. 13–17; *G*, 5 Oct 1962; Lowe, *Welfare State*, p. 254; *G*, 5 Oct 1962; John R. Gold, *The Practice of Modernism* (Abingdon, 2007), p. 168; Lowe, *Welfare State*, p. 254.

29. Patrick Dunleavy, *The Politics of Mass Housing in Britain, 1945–1975* (Oxford, 1981), pp. 37–42; *Sociological Review*, Feb 1983, p. 123 (David Rosenberg); Dunleavy, pp. 112, 170, 145–6; Leeds City Council, *Agenda and Verbatim Reports,1963–64* (1964), 3 Jun 1964.

30. Timmins, *The Five Giants*, p. 188; *G*, 5 Oct 1962; Brian Lund, *Housing Problems and Housing Policy* (Harlow, 1996), pp. 121–2; Alderson, *Britain in the Sixties*, p. 94; Keith Jacobs, 'Institutional Housing Practices and Racism', in *History Workshop*, Autumn 1999, p. 200; James Tucker, *Honourable Estates* (1966), pp. 96–8, 116, 70–2.

31. Charles Johnstone, 'The Tenants' Movement and Housing Struggles in Glasgow, 1945–1990' (University of Glasgow PhD, 1992), pp. 96, 105–6, 112; J. B. Cullingworth, *Housing in Transition* (1963), pp. 183–4; Northcott, *Why Labour?*, p. 32; Alderson, *Britain in the Sixties*, pp. 96–7; Peter Shapely, *The Politics of Housing* (Manchester, 2007), p. 72; Alison Ravetz, *Council Housing and Culture* (2001), p. 173. Generally on post-war housing departments, see: Power, *Property*, chap. 4. Generally on tenant associations and patterns of working-class life on council estates, see: Ravetz, chaps 9–10.

32. Timmins, *The Five Giants*, pp. 191–2; Northcott, *Why Labour?*, pp. 32–5; Michael White, 'John Coward', *G*, 11 Jan 2014. For a telling anecdote about Poplar Council's unwillingness to countenance housing associations, see Kenneth Baker, *The Turbulent Years* (1993), p. 23.

33. Lowe, *Welfare State*, p. 254; Tucker, *Honourable Estates*, pp. 88–92; Cullingworth, *Housing in Transition*, p. 200; Stephen McGann, *Flesh and Blood* (2017), p. 173. Generally on the history of council housing, see the rich and suggestive work of John Boughton: his books *Municipal Dreams: The Rise and Fall of Council Housing* (2019) and *A History of Council Housing in 100 Estates* (2022); and his ongoing blog *Municipal Dreams*.

34. *NS*, 15 Mar 1963; *T*, 22 Apr 1963 (H. W. C. Wilson); *New Soc*, 23 Apr 1964.

35. Glen O'Hara, *Governing Post-War Britain* (Basingstoke, 2012), pp. 159–60; Donald Simpson, 'Progressivism and the development of primary education', in *History of Education Society Bulletin*, Autumn 1996, pp. 58–9; J. W. B. Douglas, *The Home and the School* (1964), p. 118; *British Journal of Sociology*, March 1966, p. 81 (Michael P. Carter's review of *Streaming*). For more on Douglas and Jackson, in addition to the books themselves, see: Brian Simon, *Education and the Social Order, 1940–1990* (1991), pp. 344–50; Helen Pearson, *The Life Project* (2016), chap. 2; Kit Hardwick, *Brian Jackson* (Cambridge, 2003), pp. 92–3.

36. George Smith, 'Schools', in Halsey, *Social Trends*, p. 199; Gordon Marsden and Nicholas Henshall, 'Francis Scott', *Ind*, 12 Aug 2004; Stephen J. Ball, 'Accounting for a Sociological Life', accessed online, 16 Jul 2021; Colin Lacey, 'Freedom and Constraints in British Education', in Ronald Frankenberg (ed.), *Custom and Conflict in British Society* (Manchester, 1982), p. 171; *G*, 13 Nov 2007 (Fiona Millar).

37. Gary McCulloch and Liz Sobell, 'Towards a social history of the secondary modern schools', in *History of Education*, 1994 (23/3), p. 275; David Ayerst, *Understanding Schools* (Harmondsworth, 1967), p. 116;

Gary McCulloch, *Failing the Ordinary Child?* (Buckingham, 1998), p. 89; John Webb, 'The Sociology of a School', in *British Journal of Sociology*, Sep 1962, p. 264; *Sociological Review*, Nov 1967, p. 357 (S. John Eggleston, reviewing D. H. Hargreaves, *Social Relations in a Secondary School*); *P*, 10 Jun 1964 (Barbara Wootton); Rogers, *Crowther to Warnock*, p. 67; A. C. H. Smith, *Paper Voices* (1975), p. 165; *Sociological Review*, Nov 1963, pp. 380–1.

38. Alan C. Kerckhoff et al., *Going Comprehensive in England and Wales* (1996), p. 27; Peter Mandler, *The Crisis of the Meritocracy* (Oxford, 2020), p. 55; David Crook, 'Edward Boyle', in *History of Education*, 1993 (22/1), pp. 52–3; Peter Housden, *The Passing of a Country Grammar School* (Edinburgh, 2015), p. 65; Timmins, *The Five Giants*, p. 240; Brian Simon, 'The politics of comprehensive reorganization', in *History of Education*, 1992 (21/4), p. 360; Mandler, *Crisis of the Meritocracy*, p. 60.

39. Mandler, *Crisis of the Meritocracy*, chap. 3; Abrams, ABMS 2/4/11, folder, 'LP. Study of Public Opinion (Political) August 1962–May 1965', August 1962 report.

40. Douglas, *The Home and the School* pp. 52–3; *G*, 1 Sep 1964; Elizabeth Roberts, *Women and Families* (Oxford, 1995), p. 173; Kevin Jefferys, *Retreat from New Jerusalem* (Basingstoke, 1997), pp. 150–1; Simon, *Education*, pp. 288–9; *Newport & Market Drayton Advertiser*, 5 Jul 1963; Lowe, *Welfare State*, p. 216; Simon, *Education*, p. 215.

41. Bryan Appleyard, *The Pleasures of Peace* (1989), p. 95; BBC WAC, R9/7/60–VR/62/609, 30 Oct 1962; Noel Timms, 'Knowledge, Opinion and the Social Services', in *Sociological Review*, Nov 1962, pp. 362–3; *G*, 3 Mar 1963 (R. H. S. Crossman); *New Soc*, 23 Mar 1964.

42. *T*, 15 Jul 1963; *G*, 30 Jul 1963 (Ralph Harris); Phyllis Willmott, *Consumer's Guide to the British Social Services* (Harmondsworth, 1967), pp. 239–46.

43. Brian Jackson Collection (NSPSCA), C4, file of 'Marriage Sample' interviews, 22 Oct 1962; Social Survey of Merseyside (University of Liverpool), D719/1, 27 Feb 1963; *NS*, 19 Apr 1963.

4 NO WARMTH ANYWHERE

1. Heap, Acc 2243/36/1, 27 Dec 1962; Jackson, 43D78/52, 28–9 Dec 1962; Haines, SxMOA99/34/8/15, 30 Dec 1962; Halle, D 121/2, 30 Dec 1962; Heap, Acc 2243/36/1, 30 Dec 1962; Grace Taylor, GDP/318/1963, 31 Dec 1962; *Selbourne*, p. 214; *Partridge* (1), p. 142; Haines, SxMOA99/34/8/16,

1 Jan 1963; Langford, 2 Jan 1963; Dee, DDX829/2, 2 Jan 1963; Martin, P5/2J/38, 2 Jan 1963; Henry Woodley, GDP/162/1963, 2 Jan 1963; Grace Taylor, GDP/318/1963, 3 Jan 1963; St John, 68/47, 3 Jan 1963; Dennis Barker, 'Barry Bucknell', *G*, 27 Feb 2003; Joe Moran, *Queuing for Beginners* (2007), p. 204; Walter Hooper (ed.), C. S. Lewis, *Collected Letters*, vol. III (2006), p. 1403. For a detailed guide to the Big Freeze, see Juliet Nicolson, *Frostquake* (2021).

2. Richards, *Life*, pp. 99–102; BBC WAC, TVART3 – Rolling Stones, 2 Jan 1963; *NS*, 11 Jan 1963; Last, SxMOA1/4/282, 3 Jan 1963; Avril Sandall (née James), GDP/343/1963, 3 Jan 1963; John Fisher, *Tony Hancock* (2008), p. 380; Jonathan Coe, *Like a Fiery Elephant* (2004), pp. 128–9; Mark Lewisohn, *Radio Times Guide to TV Comedy* (2003 edn), p. 51; Peter Mason, 'Chester Barnes', *G*, 31 Mar 2021; *S Tel*, 6 Jan 1963; Willmott, WLMT 1/25, 6 Jan 1963; Grace Taylor, GDP/318/1963, 7 Jan 1963; Scott, SxMOA99/97/1/12, 7 Jan 1963; Philip Purser, 'Tim Hewat', *G*, 4 Dec 2004; Martin, P5/2J/38, 9 Jan 1963; Clark, *Red Comet*, p. 836; *Bonham Carter*, p. 263; Richards, p. 116; Lee, 10 Jan 1963; Ray Galton and Alan Simpson, *Steptoe and Son* (2002), pp. 62–4; *DT*, 11 Jan 1963; *NME*, 11 Jan 1963.

3. Heap, Acc 2243/37/1, 11 Jan 1963; Martin, P5/2J/38, 11 Jan 1963; Grace Taylor, GPD/318/1963, 11 Jan 1963; Graham Payn and Sheridan Morley (eds), *The Noël Coward Diaries* (1982), p. 525; Raynham, SxMOA99/60/1/41, 12 Jan 1963; Lavinia Greacen (ed.), *J. G. Farrell in his Own Words* (Cork, 2009), p. 59; Larkin, Ms.Eng.c.7426, fo 4, 13 Jan 1963; Dee, DDX829/2, 13 Jan 1963; *G*, 14 Jan 1963.

4. *Official Architecture and Planning*, Jan 1963, pp. 32–3; *Birmingham Post*, 15 Jan 1963; *Architects' Journal*, 9 Jan 1963; *Evening News*, 14 Jan 1963, 7 Jan 1963; *Architectural Review*, Jan 1963, p. 94; *Surrey Comet*, 12 Jan 1963; *Selbourne*, p. 219; Carpenter, *Satire*, pp. 244–5; *DT*, 14 Jan 1963; BBC WAC, R9/7/62–VR/63/32, 12 Jan 1963, R9/10/10–VR/63/47, 7 Feb 1963, R9/74/3, Feb 1963; *Ob*, 20 Jan 1963; *MM*, 12 Jan 1963.

5. *Ob*, 20 Jan 1963 (Mervyn Jones); *ST*, 20 Jan 1963 (Maurice Wiggin); *NS*, 25 Jan 1963 (G. W. Stonier); BBC WAC, R9/7/62–VR/63/33, 13 Jan 1963; *L*, 17 Jan 1963; BBC WAC, R9/7/62–VR/63/33, 13 Jan 1963; *MM*, 19 Jan 1963; Robert Shelton, *No Direction Home* (Sevenoaks, 1986), p. 252. See also: *Ob*, 18 Sep 2005 (Casper Llewellyn Smith); Philip Saville, *They Shoot Directors, Don't They?* (Handsworth Wood, 2019), pp. 83–8.

6. Thorpe, *Supermac*, pp. 536–7; John Campbell, *Edward Heath* (1993), p. 129; *NS*, 18 Jan 1963; Thorpe, p. 537; George H. Gallup, *The Gallup. International Public Opinion Polls: Great Britain, 1937–1975*, vol. I

(New York, 1976), pp. 665–6; *Ob*, 20 Jan 1963; Larkin, Ms.Eng.c.7426, fo 13, 20 Jan 1963.

7. Langford, 15 Jan 1963; Selina Hastings, *Evelyn Waugh* (1994), p. 612; Scott, SxMOA99/97/1/12, 15 Jan 1963; Grace Taylor, GDP/318/1963, 16 Jan 1963; Scott, SxMOA99/97/1/12, 16 Jan 1963; Kate Paul, *Journal*, vol. I, *1958–1963* (Hay-on-Wye, 1997), p. 250; Scott, SxMOA99/97/1/12, 17 Jan 1963; Dee, DDX829/2, 17 Jan 1963; Scott, MOA99/97/1/12, 18 Jan 1963; Last, SxMOA1/4/282, 18 Jan 1963; Haines, SxMOA99/34/8/16, 18 Jan 1963; Grace Taylor, GDP/318/1963, 18 Jan 1963; *Selbourne*, p. 221; Brian Brivati, *Hugh Gaitskell* (1996), p. 427.

8. Raynham, SxMOA99/60/1/41, 18 Jan 1963; Hill (ed.), *Tribune 40*, p. 131; Melly, *Take a Girl Like Me*, p. 14; Last, SxMOA1/4/282, 18 Jan 1963; Heap, Acc 2243/37/1, 18 Jan 1963; Brivati, *Hugh Gaitskell*, pp. 428–9; BBC WAC, R9/7/62–VR/63/50, 19 Jan 1963; Susan Crosland, *Tony Crosland* (1982), p. 113; John Campbell, *Roy Jenkins* (2014), pp. 225–6; Michael Tracey, *In the Culture of the Eye* (1983), p. 125.

9. *FT*, 16 Jan 1988; Roy Jenkins, *A Life at the Centre* (1991), p. 148; Philip M. Williams, *Hugh Gaitskell* (1979), p. 775; Austin Mitchell and David Wienir, *Last Time* (1997), p. 22.

10. Henry Hardy and Mark Pottle (eds), Isaiah Berlin, *Building: Letters 1960–1975* (2013), p. 141; *NY*, 2 Feb 1963; David Marquand, *Britain Since 1918* (2008), p. 198; Denis Healey, *The Time of My Life* (1989), p. 297; *Ob*, 27 Jan 1963; *Macmillan* (2), p. 537. See also: George Brown, *In My Way* (1971); Peter Patterson, *Tired and Emotional* (1993), plus Ben Pimlott's review in *G*, 18 May 1993.

11. *Macmillan* (2), p. 537; *NY*, 2 Feb 1963; *Bonham Carter*, p. 264; Pimlott, *Harold Wilson*, p. 256; *G*, 14 Feb 2013; David Marquand, *The Progressive Dilemma* (1999 edn), p. 164.

12. Mitchell and Wienir, *Last Time*, p. 25. Generally on the leadership battle, see: Anthony Howard and Richard West, *The Making of the Prime Minister* (1965), chap. 1; Pimlott, *Harold Wilson*, pp. 254–9; Patterson, *Tired and Emotional*, pp. 121–8; Kenneth O. Morgan, *Callaghan* (Oxford, 1997), pp. 181–3.

13. Gordon R. Thompson, 'The Beatles and "Please Please Me"', https://blog.oup, 11 Jan 2013; *Mojo*, July 2000, p. 69 (Colin Harper); Larkin, Ms.Eng.c.7426, fo 12, 19 Jan 1963; *East Anglian Daily Times*, 22 Jan 1963; https://coronationststreet.fandom.com/wiki/Johnny_Alexander; 'Thomas Baptiste', *T*, 11 Jan 2019; Clark, *Red Comet*, pp. 848–51; Diana Delahoy (née Rendall), GDP/404/1963, 22 Jan 1963; Dee, DDX 829/2, 22 Jan 1963; *Selbourne*, p. 222; Richards, *Life*, p. 111; City of Bradford,

Official Record of Proceedings of Meetings of City Council, 1962–63, pp. 239–51; *(Bradford) Telegraph & Argus*, 17 Jan 2013.

14. Grace Taylor, GDP/318/1963, 23 Jan 1963; *Surrey Comet*, 12 Jan 1963; *Ob*, 27 Jan 1963; Galton and Simpson, *Steptoe and Son*, pp. 68–70, 237; Haines, SxMOA99/34/8/16, 25 Jan 1963; *MM*, 26 Jan 1963; *Mojo*, Nov 1995, p. 30 (Mark Lewisohn); *Ind*, 2 Dec 1994 (Andy Gill); Haines, SxMOA99/34/8/16, 26 Jan 1963; *Evening News*, 23 Jan 1963; *Evening Standard*, 21 Jan 1963.

15. *NS*, 25 Jan 1963; *Ob*, 27 Jan 1963; Daly, 302/3/19, 27 Jan 1963 and n.d.; *L*, 7 Feb 1963 (Peter Green).

16. *Birmingham Mail*, 28 Jan 1963; *Birmingham Post*, 11 Feb 1963; *(Birmingham) Evening Despatch*, 23 Feb 1963; *Architects' Journal*, 30 Jan 1963; Miles Glendinning and Stefan Muthesius, *Tower Block* (New Haven, 1994), p. 235; *Site and Plant*, 15 Feb 1963; Willmott, WLMT 1/26, 7 Feb 1963.

17. *Manchester Evening News*, 31 Jan 1963; *G*, 1 Feb 1963; *L*, 7 Feb 1963 (Peter Green); *DT*, 1 Feb 1963; Hodgson, 1 Feb 1963; *NME*, 1 Feb 1963; *DM* (1), 1 Feb 1963; *Evening Standard*, 2 Feb 1963; Mojo, *Days of Beatlemania* (2002), p. 38 (Johnny Black).

18. *DM* (1), 31 Jan 1963; *Evening News*, 1 Feb 1963; Carpenter, *Satire*, p. 251; BBC WAC, R9/7/62–VR/63/72, 2 Feb 1963; *G*, 31 Oct 2015 (Tedi Millward); 'Meic Stephens', *DT*, 15 Aug 2018; *ST*, 3 Feb 1963; McGann, *Flesh and Blood*, p. 171; *T*, 10 Dec 2010, 22 May 2012 (Paul Simons).

19. *NY*, 2 Feb 1963; *The Week*, 16 Jan 2010; Rippon, *A Derby Boy*, pp. 105–6; *Partridge* (1), p. 145; Clark, *Red Comet*, pp. 835–8; Holt and Pym (eds), Barbara Pym, *A Very Private Eye*, p. 295.

20. *Macmillan* (1), pp. 393, 436–7; Peter Rawlinson, *A Price Too High* (1989), p. 92; Davenport-Hines, *An English Affair*, pp. 222–41; *DT*, 5 Feb 1963; *Williams*, p. 206. For an insight into the feel of the Vassall Tribunal, see Adam Mars-Jones, *Kid Gloves* (2015), pp. 35–9.

21. Lee, 5 Feb 1963; Dee, DDX 829/2, 5 Feb 1963; Halle, D121/3, 5 Feb 1963; BBC WAC, R9/7/62–VR/63/79, 6 Feb 1963; Haines, SxMOA99/34/8/16, 7 Feb 1963; Jack Common papers (University of Newcastle), Ms 77, 7 Feb 1963; *Crossman* (1), p. 971.

22. *Ob*, 10 Feb 1963; Stuart Laing, *Representations of Working-Class Life, 1957–1964* (Basingstoke, 1986), pp. 137–8; *Ind*, 13 Sep 2004; Harold Evans, *My Paper Chase* (2009), pp. 273–8; *Macmillan* (1), p. 397; Evans, p. 238; *The Economist*, 28 Jul 2012 ('Bagehot'); YouTube, *Waiting for Work* (three parts).

23. Mount, *Cold Cream*, pp. 251–5; 'Social Survey of Merseyside' (University of Liverpool, Special Collections and Archives), D719/2.

24. *T*, 9 Feb 1963; *Bonham Carter*, p. 265; *Daily Express*, 6 Feb 1963; *G*, 11 Feb 1963; *Ob*, 10 Feb 1963; *FT*, 11 Feb 1963; Clark, *Red Comet*, pp. 894, 926.

25. Philip Norman, *John Lennon* (2008), pp. 295–6; Lewisohn, *Beatles Chronicle*, p. 100; Michael Turner, *It Won't Be Long* (Oldham, 1998), pp. 17–27.

26. *Ind*, 18 Jun 1999 (Robert Hanks); *Architects' Journal*, 13 Feb 1963; James Woodall, *The Man in the Mirror of the Book* (1996), p. 295; *Benn*, p. 5; *NME*, 15 Feb 1963; Heap, Acc 2243/37/1, 16 Feb 1963; *Daily Express*, 12 Feb 1963; Michael Leapman, *Treacherous Estate* (1992), pp. 20–2; *Ob*, 17 Feb 1963.

27. *Surrey Comet*, 16 Feb 1963; *Roundhay High School Magazine* (Leeds Central Library), Dec 1963, p. 24; Frederick Ward, GDP/145/1963, 19 Feb 1963; Scott, SxMOA99/97/1/12, 20 Feb 1963; *Architects' Journal*, 20 Feb 1963 (R. C. Coombs); Hague, 21 Feb 1963; Dee, DDX 829/2, 22 Feb 1963; Andrew Roth, 'Sir Charles Fletcher-Cooke', *G*, 1 Mar 2001; Lewisohn, *Beatles Chronicle*, p. 88; diary of Martin Phillips, 23 Feb 1963; Ironside, 26 Feb 1963; *Mojo*, Jun 1988, p. 16 (Mark Paytress); *L*, 7 Mar 1963 (Peter Green); Neville Braybrooke (ed.), *The Letters of J. R. Ackerley* (1975), p. 224.

28. *G*, 7 Dec 2001 (Stuart Jeffries); *DT*, 27 Feb 1963; *East London Advertiser*, 8 Mar 1963; Winston G. Ramsey, *The East End Then and Now* (Harlow, 1997), p. 502; *NS*, 8 Mar 1963; *Ob*, 3 Mar 1963; *L*, 14 Mar 1963; *S Tel*, 3 Mar 1963; *NS*, 8 Mar 1963.

29. Leo McKinstry, *Sir Alf* (2006), pp. 209–10; *RT*, 21 Feb 1963; 'Barry Bucknell', *DT*, 22 Feb 2003; *L*, 7 Mar 1963 (John Pringle); *Crossman* (1), p. 986; *NS*, 1 Mar 1963; Abrams, ABMS 2/4/11, part 2 of 4, Nov 1963.

30. *DT*, 27 Feb 1963; Lewisohn, *Beatles Chronicle*, p. 88; *Partridge* (1), p. 150; Dee, DDX 829/2, 2 Mar 1963; *G*, 2 Mar 1963; Hill, vol. 31, 2 Mar 1963; *S Tel*, 3 Mar 1963; Haines, SxMOA99/34/8/16, 3 Mar 1963; *T*, 23 Oct 2008.

31. Heap, Acc 2243/37/1, 4 Mar 1963; J. A. Baker, *The Peregrine* (2017 edn), pp. 146–7; Jackson, 43D78/53, 5 Mar 1963; Hague, 6 Mar 1963; Frederick Ward, GDP/145/1963, 5 Mar 1963; Martin, P5/2J/38, 6 Mar 1963; *T*, 7 Mar 1963.

5 CLOSING THE STATIONS WITH BEAUTIFUL NAMES

1. *G*, 7–8 Mar 1963; Roy Greenslade, *Press Gang* (2003), pp. 176–7; BBC website, 'Halewood plant is a great survivor', 24 Sep 2009; Huw Beynon, *Working for Ford* (Harmondsworth, 1984 edn), p. 101; *Salford City Reporter*, 8 Mar 1963; Dee, DDX 829/2, 8 Mar 1963; Martin, P5/2J/38, 8 Mar 1963; Hill, vol. 31, 8 Mar 1963; *Ob*, 10 Mar 1963 (Maurice Richardson); *NS*, 15 Mar 1963 (G. W. Stonier); Dilwyn Porter, 'Amateur Football in England, 1948–63', in Adrian Smith and Dilwyn Porter (eds), *Amateurs and Professionals in Post-War British Sport* (2000), p. 23; Howard and West, *The Making of the Prime Minister*, pp. 40–1; Lewisohn, *Beatles Chronicle*, p. 88; Haines, SxMOA99/34/8/16, 9 Mar 1963.

2. *DM* (2), 11 Mar 1963; *DT*, 8 Mar 1963; *T*, 12 Mar 1963; Hill, vol. 31, 12–13 Mar 1963; *T*, 15 Mar 1963; *Vauxhall Mirror*, Mar 1963; Greenslade, *Press Gang*, pp. 180–1; *Macmillan* (2), p. 548; *DT*, 18 Mar 1963; *G*, 31 Jan 2013 (Robert Kitson); Greenslade, p. 181; BBC WAC, R9/7/63A–VR/63/166, 17 Mar 1963; Fowles, Ms 102/1/12, fo 52, 18 Mar 1963; Martin, P5/2J/38, 18 Mar 1963.

3. *L*, 18 Apr 1963 (R. J. E. Silvey); BBC WAC, R9/10/10–VR/63/100, report dated 27 Feb 1963, R9/10/10–VR/63/192, report dated April 1963; *L*, 18 Apr 1963; BBC WAC, R9/74/3, Apr 1963 (no. 278); *DT*, 19 Mar 1963; Jack Adrian, 'Charles Simon', *Ind*, 21 May 2002; BBC WAC, R9/74/3, May 1963 (no. 279).

4. John A. T. Robinson, *Honest to God* (1963), pp. 8, 11–23, 82, 118; Lawrence Black, *Redefining British Politics* (Basingstoke, 2010), p. 124; *G*, 22 Mar 1963; *ST*, 24 Mar 1963; *S Tel*, 24 Mar 1963 (Utley); *ST*, 24 Mar 1963 (Ayer); *Ob*, 24 Mar 1963 (Lewis); *DT*, 25 Mar 1963.

5. Hazel Holt, *A Lot to Ask* (1990), p. 196; *G*, 5 Apr 2008; Holt and Pym (eds), Barbara Pym, *A Very Private Eye*, p. 300.

6. Cy Young, 'Charles Chilton', *Ind*, 5 Jan 2013; *G*, 25 Sep 2002 (Eyre), 17 Feb 2014 (Michael Billington); *ST*, 31 Mar 1963; *S Tel*, 24 Mar 1963; *Ob*, 24 Mar 1963; *Spec*, 5 Apr 1963, 12 Apr 1963; *DT*, 5 Apr 1963; *Ob*, 24 Mar 1963; *G*, 8 Jan 2014 (Philip Hedley).

7. Heap, Acc 2243/37/1, 21 Mar 1963; Julian Critchley, *A Bag of Boiled Sweets* (1994), p. 85; Wayland Young, *The Profumo Affair* (Harmondsworth, 1963), pp. 15–16; Davenport-Hines, *An English Affair*, p. 275; Rawlinson, *A Price Too High*, pp. 95–6; David Profumo, *Bringing the House Down* (2006), p. 182; *DM* (2), 22 Mar 1963; Young, p. 18; Profumo, pp. 184–5; Alistair Horne, *Macmillan: The Official*

Biography, vol. 2, *1957–1986* (1989), p. 476; Wendy Pollard, *Pamela Hansford Johnson* (2014), p. 334; Carpenter, *Dennis Potter*, p. 132.

8. *G*, 23 Mar 1963; Profumo, *Bringing the House Down*, pp. 184–5; Martin, P5/2J/38, 23 Mar 1963: Frederick Ward, GDP/145/1963, 23 Mar 1963; Lee, 23 Mar 1963; Haines, SxMOA99/34/8/16, 23 Mar 1963; David Frost, *An Autobiography* (1993), pp. 77–9; Sherrin, *A Small Thing*, p. 79; Greenslade, *Press Gang*, p. 183; Fowles, Ms 102/1/12, fo 53, 24 Mar 1963; *Liverpool Echo*, 25 Mar 1963; Davenport-Hines, *An English Affair*, p. 278; *Liverpool Daily Post*, 26 Mar 1963; Davenport-Hines, p. 277; *DM* (2), 27 Mar 1963; City of Bradford, *Official Record of Proceedings at Meetings of City Council, 1962–3* (1963), pp. 351–7; Davenport-Hines, pp. 278–81.

9. Roger Wilmut, *Tony Hancock 'Artiste'* (1978), p. 249; Ray Connolly (ed.), *In the Sixties* (1995), p. 49; *DM* (2), 30 Mar 1963; St John, 68/47, 30 Mar 1963; 'Teasy Weasy Raymond', *T*, 20 Apr 1992; *DT*, 1 Apr 1963; https://www.lostglasgow.scot/post, 8 Feb 2019, 'Angry Young Man was a theatrical great'; *Ob*, 31 Mar 1963; *NS*, 29 Mar 1963; Margaret Drabble, *A Summer Bird-Cage* (1963), pp. 11, 14, 28, 34, 74, 77, 81, 105, 168, 170, 181.

10. Larkin, Ms.Eng.c.7426, fo 63, 28 Mar 1963; *Ind*, 29 Dec 1990 (Nicholas Faith); Anthony Sampson, *Anatomy of Britain* (1962), p. 544; Robin Jones, *Beeching* (2011), pp. 42–3; *Country Life*, 4 Apr 1963; *Tonight*, 27 Mar 1963 (BBC Archive); *L*, 4 Apr 1963.

11. *G*, 28 Mar 1963; *East Anglian Daily Times*, 28 Mar 1963; *Cambrian News*, 29 Mar 1963; Kenneth Roy, *The Invisible Spirit* (Prestwick, 2013), pp. 305–6; *DT*, 30 Mar 1963; *T*, 30 Mar 1963; *DT*, 30 Mar 1963; *ST*, 31 Mar 1963; *G*, 10 Jun 1963; Thorpe, *Supermac*, p. 505; *T*, 1 May 1963, 30 Apr 1963.

12. *T*, 28 Mar 1963; *G*, 28 Mar 1963; *DT*, 30 Mar 1963; *T*, 3 Apr 1963 (Empson and Arlott), 1 Apr 1963 (Paten); Hodgson, 21 May 1963; Philip S. Bagwell, *The Railwaymen* (1982), pp. 147–56; *Ian Hislop Goes Off the Rails*, BBC Four, 2 Oct 2008; Roy, *The Invisible Spirit*, p. 306; *NS*, 3 May 1963; *T*, 1 May 1963.

13. *Ind*, 29 Dec 1990; Charles Loft, 'The Beeching Myth', *History Today*, Apr 2003, p. 40; *T*, 15 Mar 2013; Ben Beazley, *Postwar Leicester* (Stroud, 2006), p. 153; David Wiggins and Mayer Hillman, 'Railways, Settlement and Access', in Anthony Barnett and Roger Scruton (eds), *Town and Country* (1998), pp. 245–6; *G*, 7 Oct 2019; Gallup, *The Gallup*, p. 682; *DT*, 30 Mar 1963; Frank Ferneyhough, *Steam Up!* (1983), pp. 172–3; *Wikipedia*, 'Slow Train'; *G*, 23 Feb 2013. For a notably well-balanced

discussion on the Beeching Report and its impact, including the freight aspect, see Simon Bradley, *The Railways* (2015), pp. 412–17.

14. *Spec*, 5 Apr 1963; diary of Martin Phillips, 1–3 Apr 1963; *NS*, 5 Apr 1963; *Macmillan* (1), p. 405; BBC WAC, R9/7/63A–VR/63/202, 3 Apr 1963; John Littlewood, *The Stock Market* (1998), p. 116; Heap, Acc 2243/37/1, 3 Apr 1963; Lewis Baston, *Reggie* (Stroud, 2004), pp. 193–5; Littlewood, p. 116; *S Tel*, 7 Apr 1963; David Kynaston, *Till Time's Last Sand* (2017), pp. 454–5.

15. *Private Eye*, 5 Apr 1963; Nicholson, *How Was It For You?*, p. 117; *NS*, 5 Apr 1963; Frederick Ward, GDP/145/1963, 5 Apr 1963; Sir Gerald Nabarro, *NAB 1* (Oxford, 1969), pp. 261–6; *G*, 8 Apr 1963; *T*, 9 Apr 1963; *NS*, 5 Apr 1963 (John Coleman); *G*, 5 Apr 1963 (Richard Roud); *Ob*, 7 Apr 1963 (James Breen); Haines, SxMOA99/34/8/16, 8 Apr 1963; *ST*, 9 Jun 1963 ('Insight'); Natasha Walter, 'Nicolas Walter', *Ind*, 13 Mar 2000; *T*, 15 Apr 1963; Alan Macfarlane, *Oxford Undergraduate, 1960–3* (n.d.), p. 444; BBC WAC, R9/74/3, Jun 1963 (no 280); Scott, SxMOA99/97/1/12, 15 Apr 1963.

16. Greenslade, *Press Gang*, pp. 183–4; Jack Common papers (at University of Newcastle), packet/box 77, letter to Tommy McCullough, 18 Apr 1963; *Ob*, 21 Apr 1963; Walter Hooper (ed.), C. S. Lewis, *Collected Letters*, vol. III (2006), p. 1422; Davenport-Hines, *An English Affair*, p. 285; Payn and Morley (eds), *The Noël Coward Diaries*, p. 532; Hill, vol. 31, 24 Apr 1963; Martin, P5/2J/38, 24 Apr 1963; Hodgson, 30 Apr 1963; Raynham, SxMOA99/60/1/41, 24 Apr 1963; Haines, SxMOA99/34/8/16, 24 Apr 1963; BBC WAC, R9/74/3, Jun 1963 (no. 280).

17. Davenport-Hines, *An English Affair*, p. 240; *East London Advertiser*, 19 Apr 1963; *G*, 26 Apr 1963 (Geoffrey Moorhouse); GDP/280/1963, 27 Apr 1963; Davenport-Hines, p. 240; *Mojo*, Nov 1995, p. 30 (Mark Lewisohn); *T*, 7 Sep 2009; Mojo, *Days of Beatlemania*, p. 46 (Mark Lewisohn); Michael Turner, *'It Won't Be Long'* (Oldham, 1998), p. 39; Lewisohn, *Beatles Chronicle*, pp. 106–7; *T*, 10 Oct 2009 (Bob Stanley); 'Fiona Adams', *T*, 18 Jul 2020; George Melly, *Revolt into Style* (Harmondsworth, 1970), p. 69; Lewisohn, p. 108; 'Gerry Marsden', *T*, 5 Jan 2021; Christopher Sandford, *Mick Jagger* (1999 edn), pp. 57–8; David Hepworth, *Uncommon People* (2017), p. 77; Bill Wyman, *Stone Alone* (1990), p. 136.

18. GDP/47/1963, 11 Apr 1963; *Architects' Journal*, 17 Apr 1963, 24 Apr 1963; *Evening Standard*, 24 Apr 1963; *Architects' Journal*, 3 Apr 1963; *County Express*, 4 Apr 1963; *Surrey Comet*, 27 Apr 1963.

19. Graham McCann, *Frankie Howerd* (2004), pp. 196–8; *DT*, 15 Apr 1963; Heap, Acc 2243/37/1, 21 Apr 1963; Carpenter, *Satire*, p. 255; Lee, 27

Apr 1963; Frost, *An Autobiography*, p. 85; BBC WAC, R9/74/3, Jul 1963 (no 281).

20. *NY*, 4 May 1963 (Panter-Downes); *Macmillan* (1), pp. 406–7; Heffer, *Like the Roman*, pp. 307–9; Reginald Bevins, *The Greasy Pole* (1965), p. 101; *G*, 12 Apr 1963; Adam Macqueen, *The Prime Minister's Ironing Board* (2013), pp. 278–80; *Macmillan* (1), opposite p. 438; Peter Scott, 'The Worst of Both Worlds: British Regional Policy, 1951–64', in *Business History*, Oct 1996, pp. 54–60; Baston, *Reggie*, p. 195; 'Tim Fry', *T*, 18 Jun 2004; *G*, 3 May 1963; *ST*, 5 May 1963.

21. *Wikipedia*, 'Bristol Bus Boycott, 1963'; *G*, 8 May 1963; *S Tel*, 5 May 1963 (Worrell); *Benn*, p. 14; *(Bristol) Evening Post*, 2 May 1963; *G*, 1 Oct 2020 (Kehinde Andrews); *S Tel*, 12 May 1963 (Cockburn); *(Bristol) Evening Post*, 1 May 1963, 8 May 1963. See also: Kehinde Andrews, 'Roy Hackett', *G*, 20 Aug 2022.

22. Steve Holland, 'Tom Adams', *G*, 2 Apr 2020; *S Tel*, 5 May 1963; *Fowles*, p. 554; *Ob*, 5 May 1963; *ST*, 5 May 1963.

23. John Osborne, *Almost a Gentleman* (1991), p. 243; *DT*, 9 May 1963; *T*, 2 Feb 2019; HSBC Archives, UK 0192–0162, 8 May 1963; *DT*, 10 May 1963; Foot, *Immigration and Race in British Politics*, p. 44; St John, 68/47, 11 May 1963; *Brandreth*, p. 45; *ST*, 12 May 1963; Alan Johnson, *This Boy* (2013), pp. 177–8.

24. *DT*, 14 May 1963; Ivan Ponting, 'Bill Nicholson', *Ind*, 25 Oct 2004; Marks, 16 May 1963; *G*, 18 May 1963; *T*, 7 Sep 2009; *S Tel*, 19 May 1963; Haines, SxMOA99/34/8/16, 21 May 1963; Hague, 21 May 1963; Fay and Kynaston, *Arlott, Swanton and the Soul of English Cricket*, p. 199; Richard King, *Brittle with Relics* (2022), p. 102.

25. Connolly, *Sixties*, pp. 49–50; Frank Cousins papers (Modern Records Centre, University of Warwick), 282/8/3/1, 23 May 1963; *MM*, 25 May 1963; *G*, 9 Jan 2021; https://www.wrestlingheritage.co.uk/jackie-pallo; *T*, 7 Sep 2009; Keith Vaughan, *Journals, 1939–1977* (1989), pp. 138–9; Raynham, SxMOA99/60/1/41, 28 May 1963; *Wikipedia*, 'Relko'.

26. *Architects' Journal*, 29 May 1963, 5 Jun 1963, 12 Jun 1963; *L*, 30 May 1963; *Surrey Comet*, 18 May 1963, 1 Jun 1963.

27. Davenport-Hines, *An English Affair*, pp. 288–9; Profumo, *Bringing the House Down*, p. 187; *Macmillan* (2), p. 569; Gavin Gaughan, 'Ray Martine', *G*, 11 Oct 2002; Profumo, p. 188; Davenport-Hines, p. 290; *ST*, 2 Jun 1963; Christopher Simon Sykes, *Hockney: The Biography*, vol. 1 (2011), p. 126; Connolly, *Sixties*, p. 50; Austin Finn, GDP/151/1963, 3 Jun 1963; *(Manchester) Evening Chronicle*, 7 Jun 1963; *T*, 7 Sep 2009; *Nottingham Evening News*, 4 Jun 1963.

28. Young, *The Profumo Affair*, pp. 24–5; Lewisohn, *Beatles Chronicle*, pp. 110–11; *DT*, 6 Jun 1963; Profumo, *Bringing the House Down*, pp. 189–90; *Doncaster Gazette*, 6 Jun 1963; Last, SxMOA1/4/287, 5 Jun 1963; Marks, 5 Jun 1963; Martin, P5/2J/38, 5 Jun 1963.

6 ONE VAST LEER

1. Greenslade, *Press Gang*, p. 184; *Daily Express*, 6 Jun 1963; *DM* (2), 6 Jun 1963; Mount, *Cold Cream*, pp. 258–9; *L*, 13 Jun 1963; Lee, 6 Jun 1963.

2. Philip Norman, *Mick Jagger* (2012), p. 103; *MM*, 8 Jun 1963; Lee, 7 Jun 1963; Larkin, Ms.Eng.c.7426, fo 95, 7 Jun 1963; *L*, 20 Jun 1963; Davenport-Hines, *An English Affair*, p. 294; *S Tel*, 9 Jun 1963; *Ob*, 10 Feb 2002 (Tamsin Blanchard); *News of the World*, 9 Jun 1963; Travis Elborough (ed.), *Our History of the 20th Century* (2017), p. 289; Mark Amory (ed.), *The Letters of Evelyn Waugh* (1980), p. 610; *Partridge* (1), p. 171; *T*, 11 Jun 1963; *DT*, 12 Jun 1963; *DM* (2), 13 Jun 1963; *T*, 13 Jun 1963; Randolph S. Churchill, *The Fight for the Tory Leadership* (1964), pp. 65–7; Larkin, Ms.Eng.c.7426, fo 99, 13 Jun 1963; Michael Cockerell, *Live from Number 10* (1988), p. 91; *DT*, 14 Jun 1963; Heffer, *Like the Roman*, pp. 313–14; Last, SxMOA1/4/287, 16 Jun 1963; *ST*, 16 Jun 1963.

3. Hill, vol. 31, 17 Jun 1963; *DT*, 17 Jun 1963; *NY*, 29 Jun 1963; Young, *The Profumo Affair*, p. 44; Pimlott, *Harold Wilson*, p. 296; John Biffen, *Semi-Detached* (2013), p. 209; Davenport-Hines, *An English Affair*, p. 304; Young, p. 52; Heffer, *Like the Roman*, pp. 315–17; Biffen, p. 210; Critchley, *A Bag of Boiled Sweets*, p. 82; Simon Courtauld, *To Convey Intelligence* (1999), p. 84; Young, p. 61; Selbourne, p. 254; Preston, 6D87/6, 17 Jun 1963; diary of Bert Weibel (Mass-Observation Archive, University of Sussex, The Keep, Brighton), SxMOA99/98, 17 Jun 1963.

4. *DT*, 18 Jun 1963; diary of Donald and Louise Balfour (National Library of Australia), Ms 1010, 18 Jun 1963; *ST*, 16 Jun 2013 ('Fight to the Top'); 'Sir Henry Cooper', *T*, 2 May 2011; *ST*, 5 Jun 2016 (Hugh McIlvanney); BBC WAC, R9/74/3, Aug 1963 (no. 282); *G*, 18 Jun 2001 (Frank Keating); *T*, 19 Jun 1963; John Samuel, 'Sir Henry Cooper', *G*, 3 May 2011; BBC WAC, R9/7/63B–VR/63/355, 19 Jun 1963; Willmott, WLMT 1/27, 19 Jun 1963; Barrow, *Gossip*, p. 232; BBC WAC, R9/7/63B–VR/63/356, 19 Jun 1963; Adam Benedick, 'Bill Naughton', *Ind*, 10 Jan 1992; *G*, 20 Jun 1963; Baston, *Reggie*, p. 198; Heap, Acc 2243/37/1, 20 Jun 1963; Hodgson, 21 Jun 1963; *G*, 20 May 2005.

5. *S Tel*, 23 Jun 1963; diaries of Richard Crossman (Modern Records Centre, University of Warwick), Ms 154/8/27, fo 31, 22 Jun 1963; *ST*, 23 Jun 1963; Davenport-Hines, *An English Affair*, p. 308; *Macmillan* (1), p. 445; V. S. Naipaul, 'Test', in Michael Meyer (ed.), *Summer Days* (1981), p. 177; Alan Ross, *The West Indies at Lord's* (1963), p. 18; *New Soc*, 4 Jul 1963; *NS*, 20 Sep 1963; Preston, 6D87/6, 25 Jun 1963; Lee, 25 Jun 1963; Haines, SxMOA99/34/8/16, 25 Jun 1963.

6. Martin, P5/2J/38, 26 Jun 1963; Robert J. Wybrow, *Britain Speaks Out, 1937–1987* (Basingstoke, 1989), p. 67; *Selbourne*, p. 256; *NS*, 5 Jul 1963 (Roger Gellert); Lewisohn, *Beatles Chronicle*, p. 114; *MM*, 29 Jun 1963; Lewisohn, pp. 113–14; *G*, 29 Jun 1963; *Ob*, 30 Jun 1963; Haines, SxMOA99/34/8/16, 30 Jun 1963.

7. Davenport-Hines, *An English Affair*, pp. 315–16; Lewisohn, *Beatles Chronicle*, p. 114; Scott, SxMO99/97/1/12, 1 Jul 1963; Larkin, Ms.Eng.c.7426, fo 106, 3 Jul 1963; Joe Moran, *On Roads* (2009), p. 67; *G*, 5 Jul 1963; Ironside, 8 Jul 1963; *Architects' Journal*, 17 Jul 1963; *Brandreth*, p. 46; *Smethwick Telephone*, 5 Jul 1963; Balfour, 5 Jul 1963; *Selbourne*, p. 259.

8. *Ob*, 30 Jun 1963; *ST*, 7 Jul 1963; Michael Leapman, 'Ron Hall', *Ind*, 28 Jan 2014; *ST*, 21 Jul 1963; Greenslade, *Press Gang*, p. 187; *G*, 16 Jul 1963 (Mary Crozier); *East Kent Times*, 17 Jul 1963; Denis Gifford, 'Alex Graham', *Ind*, 5 Dec 1991; *G*, 10 Jul 1963; diary of Frank Lewis (Glamorgan Record Office), D51/1/212, 10 Jul 1963; *DT*, 11 Jul 1963 (Eric Shorter); *NS*, 19 Jul 1963 (Roger Gellert); *ST*, 8 Jul 1973; Paul Willetts, *Members Only* (2010), pp. 177–80; David McKittrick, 'Harry Challenor', *Ind*, 23 Sep 2008; Baston, *Reggie*, p. 198; *T*, 13 Jul 1963; Nicholson, *How Was It For You?*, pp. 134–5.

9. Mark Amory (ed.), *The Letters of Ann Fleming* (1985), p. 326; Christopher Sandford, *Mick Jagger* (1999 edn), p. 61; Wyman, *Stone Alone*, pp. 141–2; Anna von Planta (ed.), Patricia Highsmith, *Her Diaries and Notebooks* (2021), p. 763; Michael Tracey, *A Variety of Lives* (1983), p. 215; Hodgson, 15 Jul 1963; Sheffield Local Studies Library, 720.63 SQ (two vols); *G*, 18 Jul 1963; Christopher Martin and Brian Richards, *London Stations – a user's assessment* (Research Institute for Consumer Affairs, 1963), pp. 10–26; Balfour, 20 Jul 1963; *T*, 7 Sep 2009; Payn and Morley (eds), *The Noël Coward Diaries*, p. 538.

10. John H. Goldthorpe and David Lockwood, 'Affluence in the British Class Structure', in *Sociological Review*, Jul 1963, pp. 134–8; The Affluent Worker Collection (NSPSCA), Box 8, 003, 4 Jul 1963, 008, 17 Jul 1963, Box 1, 011, 7 Dec 1962, Box 8, 057, 6 Aug 1963, 002, 4 Jul 1963, Box 9, 050, 6 Aug 1963; John H. Goldthorpe et al., 'The Affluent Worker and the Thesis of *Embourgeoisement*: Some Preliminary Research Findings',

in *Sociology*, Jan 1967, p. 11; Selina Todd, *The People* (2014), pp. 255–62; Jon Lawrence, *Me Me Me?* (Oxford, 2019), chap. 4.

11. *DM* (1), 31 May 1963; *Western Mercury*, 26 Jul 1963; Donald Balfour, 22 Jul 1963; Andrew Denham and Mark Garnett, *Keith Joseph* (Chesham, 2001), pp. 113–14; Ludovic Kennedy, *Truth to Tell* (1991), p. 279; *S Tel*, 4 Aug 1963.

12. Davenport-Hines, *An English Affair*, p. 318; Nicholson, *How Was It For You?*, p. 119; Kennedy, *Truth to Tell*, p. 287; *G*, 23 Jul 1963; *DT*, 23 Jul 1963; Roy, *The Invisible Spirit*, pp. 326–30; Kenney, pp. 292–3, 296–8, 304–5; Greacen (ed.), *J. G. Farrell in his Own Words*, p. 69.

13. *Liverpool Echo*, 23 Jul 1963; Donald Balfour, 25 Jul 1963; *Smethwick Telephone*, 26 Jul 1963; Mark Phythian, 'CND Cold War', in *Contemporary British History*, Autumn 2001, p. 141; *NS*, 26 Jul 1963; Margaret Busby, 'Barry Reckord', *G*, 17 Jan 2012; *G*, 13 Jul 2020 (Michael Billington); *G*, 24 Jul 1963, 27 Jul 1963; 'Mike Winters', *T*, 27 Aug 2013; *S Tel*, 28 Jul 1963; *G*, 30 Jul 1963.

14. *FT*, 30 Jul 1963; Davenport-Hines, *An English Affair*, pp. 322–4; Kennedy, *Truth to Tell*, p. 314; Davenport-Hines, p. 325; *DM* (1), 25 May 2013 (Mangold); Davenport-Hines, p. 325; *G*, 1 Aug 1963 ('London letter'); Kennedy, pp. 316–18; Tracey, p. 231; *G*, 1 Aug 1963; Barrow, p. 234.

15. Nicholson, *How Was It For You?*, p. 120; Davenport-Hines, *An English Affair*, p. 325; *ST*, 8 Jul 1973; Denham and Garnett, *Keith Joseph*, pp. 107–9; BBC WAC, R9/25/2 – LR/63/2112, 1 Aug 1963; Janie Hampton (ed.), *Joyce & Ginnie* (1997), p. 289; Pollard, *Pamela Hansford Johnson*, p. 340; *MM*, 3 Aug 1963; Dave Lipton, 'When the Beatles Played their Final Cavern Show', www.ultimateclassicrock.com, 3 Aug 2015.

16. Dennis Marsden Collection (NSPSCA), Dennis and Pat Marsden's 'Trinity' survey: 25 Jun 1963; 27 Jun 1963; 19 Aug 1963; 20 Jun 1963; 20 Jan 1964 (joint meeting of the committees); undated (late 1964?) draft of second report for Salford Housing Committee; 'Trinity' diary, 10–11 Aug 1963, 16 Aug 1963, 12–13 Sep 1963, 16 Sep 1963; pilot interview, 17 Oct 1963; Pat Marsden's diary, 30 Oct 1963; 'Trinity' diary, 31 Jan 1964.

17. St John, 68/48, 4 Aug 1963; Davenport-Hines, *An English Affair*, pp. 340–1; Larkin, Ms.Eng.c.7426, fos 111–12, 4 Aug 1963; *Smethwick Telephone*, 9 Aug 1963; *G*, 13 Aug 1963; *DT*, 9–10 Aug 1963; *G*, 10 Aug 1963, 13 Aug 1963.

18. *G*, 9 Aug 1963; *T*, 2 Sep 2020 (Bob Stanley); Marks, 9 Aug 1963; Greenslade, *Press Gang*, p. 189; *Wikipedia*, '1964 British betting scandal'; *Mojo*, Jun 1998, p. 17 (Mark Paytress); *Wikipedia*, 'Henry John Burnett'; *G*, 17 Aug 1963; *NS*, 16 Aug 1963 (Adrian Mitchell); *DT*, 22 Aug 1963

(Bryon Butler); *S Tel*, 25 Aug 1963; Lee, 22 Aug 1963; *NME*, 23 Aug 1963; Marks, 23 Aug 1963.

19. *Wisden Cricketers' Almanack, 1964* (1964), p. 309; Fowles, Ms 102/1/12, fos 92–4, 26 Aug 1963; *Wikipedia*, 'Bristol Bus Boycott, 1963'; Davenport-Hines, *An English Affair*, p. 341; *Macmillan* (2), p. 590; Fay and Kynaston, *Arlott, Swanton and the Soul of English Cricket*, p. 202; *G*, 16 Mar 2016 (Harry Harmer); *ST*, 29 Sep 1963 (Maurice Wiggin); Michael McManus, *Jo Grimond* (Edinburgh, 2001), p. 195; Duncan Hamilton, *Immortal* (2013), p. 76; BBC WAC, R9/7/65–VR/63/526, 14 Sep 1963; Lewisohn, *Beatles Chronicle*, p. 122; *ST*, 15 Sep 1963; *Wikipedia*, 'Bristol Bus Boycott, 1963'; *Smethwick Telephone*, 20 Sep 1963; *G*, 18 Sep 1963; Heap, Acc 2243/37/1, 23 Sep 1963; *G*, 24 Sep 1963; Robert Erskine, 'Jeremy Sandford', *G*, 15 May 2003.

20. Patrick Anderson, *Foxed!* (1972), p. 33; Lee, 13 Aug 1963; Kathleen Johnson (née Perry), GDP/193/1963, 1 Sep 1963; *G*, 22 Aug 1963, 30 Apr 2016; BBC WAC, R9/25/2–LR/63/2382, 10 Sep 1963, R9/25/2–LR/63/2454, 24 Sep 1963; 'Richard Briers', *T*, 19 Feb 2013; *NS*, 27 Sep 1963; BBC WAC, R9/7/64–VR/63/472, 16 Aug 1963; Haines, SxMOA99/34/8/16, 31 Aug 1963; Darlington, 12 Sep 1963; Nicholas Timmins, *The Five Giants* (2001 edn), p. 190; Foot, *Immigration and Race in British Politics*, pp. 210–11; Donald Balfour, 22 Aug 1963, 29 Aug 1963, 17 Aug 1963.

21. Michael Coveney, 'Sir Donald Sinden', *G*, 15 Sep 2014; letter received from David Morris, 31 Jan 2010; *S Tel*, 29 Sep 1963 (John Gross); *DM* (1), 26 Sep 1963; Thorpe, *Supermac*, p. 545; Davenport-Hines, *An English Affair*, p. 329; Cate Haste, *Rules of Desire* (1992), p. 192; Davenport-Hines, pp. 329–31; Howard and West, *The Making of the Prime Minister*, p. 60; Greenslade, *Press Gang*, p. 190; Marks, 3 Oct 1963.

7 UNDER OUR NOSES

1. *Encounter*, Jul 1963, pp. 108, 14; *Western Morning News*, 1 Jun 1963; Hodgson, 28 Sep 1963; Payn and Morley (eds), *The Noël Coward Diaries*, pp. 543–5.

2. Dilwyn Porter, 'Downhill All the Way', in R. Coopey et al. (eds), *The Wilson Governments, 1964–70* (1993), p. 23; Gallup, *The Gallup*, pp. 693, 700; Robert McKenzie and Allan Silver, *Angels in Marble* (1968), pp. 229–39; Davenport-Hines, *An English Affair*, pp. 297–9.

3. Frost, *An Autobiography*, p. 89; Davenport-Hines, pp. 344–5; *Benn*, p. 30; *NY*, 3 Aug 1963; David Kynaston, *The City of London*, vol. 4 (2001), p. 334.

4. Sampson, *Anatomy of Britain*, p. 181; W. L. Guttsman, *The British Political Elite* (1963), p. 374; *Encounter*, Jul 1963, pp. 185–7; Jonathan Bate, *Ted Hughes* (2015), pp. 228–30; *NY*, 28 Sep 1963; Paul O'Grady, *At My Mother's Knee ... And Other Low Joints* (2008), pp. 57, 46–7, 200–2.

5. Zachary Leader, *The Life of Kingsley Amis* (2006), p. 504; Alan Travis, *Bound and Gagged* (2000), pp. 166–83; Andrew Motion, *Philip Larkin* (1993), p. 372; Malcolm Bradbury, *The History Man* (1975), pp. 23–8.

6. Andrew Caine, '"The best teenage romp ever!"', *Journal of Popular British Cinema*, 2001, p. 59; *G*, 18 Sep 2009 (Bob Stanley); Travis Elborough, *The Long-Player Goodbye* (2008), p. 171; Richard Nichols, *Radio Luxembourg* (1983), pp. 113–14; Elborough, p. 171; David Simonelli, *Working Class Heroes* (Lanham, Maryland, 2013), p. 23; Nicholson, *How Was It For You?*, pp. 140–1; *London Review of Books*, 17 Jun 2021 (Ian Penman).

7. *G*, 20 Aug 2013 (Wickham), 13 Feb 2006 (Richard Williams); *T*, 20 Feb 1968 (Glynn), 2 Sep 2020 (Stanley); David Simonelli, '"Meet the new boss/same as the old boss"' (University of Tulane PhD, 2001 p. 150; Simonelli, *Heroes*, pp. 64–5.

8. Diary of May Marlor, 16 Sep 1963; 'Ralph Bennett', *T*, 9 Aug 2002; Scottish Life Archive, Edinburgh, W.Ms.1999. 235–8; *G*, 7 May 2013 (Ali); Eric Shorter, 'Clifford Williams', *G*, 22 Aug 2005; John R. Cook, '"Between Grierson and Barnum"', *Journal of British Cinema and Television*, 2004 (1/2), p. 218; Anthony Hayward, 'Michael Grigsby', *Ind*, 17 May 2013; Nicholson, *How Was It For You?*, pp. 123–4; *Ob*, 5 May 1963; Nicholson, pp. 127–8; Veronica Horwell, 'Toni Mascolo', *G*, 16 Dec 2017; *T*, 1 Feb 2002 (Carol Midgley); Michael De-la-Noy, 'The Rev Chad Varrah', *Ind*, 10 Nov 2007; *Ind*, 10 Aug 1996 (Liz Smith), 28 Jul 1997 (Deborah Ross); Steve Holland, 'Peter O'Donnell', *G*, 6 May 2010; Peter Evans, 'Raymond Hawkey', *G*, 31 Aug 2010; Christopher Booker, *The Neophiliacs* (1969), p. 199; *Ob*, 19 May 1963; 'John Wragg', *T*, 6 Aug 2020; Geoffrey Howson, 'H. Martyn Cundy', *Ind*, 8 Mar 2005; Nicholas Tucker, 'Sybil Marshall', *Ind*, 5 Sep 2005; Robin Pedley, *The Comprehensive School* (Harmondsworth, 1963), pp. 199–200; Brian Simon, 'Professor Robin Pedley', *Ind*, 24 Nov 1988; 'Sheila Tracy', *DT*, 3 Oct 2014; 'Ivan Owen', *T*, 20 Oct 2000; 'Peter Richardson', *T*, 21 Feb 2017; Fay and Kynaston, *Arlott, Swanton and the Soul of English Cricket*, pp. 217–19.

9. *Ob*, 26 May 1963; *Wikipedia*, 'It's All Happening'; David Caute, *Joseph Losey* (1994), p. 20; Sheridan Morley, *Dirk Bogarde* (1996), p. 111; Tom Vallance, 'John Schlesinger', *Ind*, 26 Jul 2003; *S Tel*, 18 Aug 1963; Quentin Falk, *Albert Finney* (2002 edn), p. 72; *NY*, 7 Sep 1963; *Ob*, 30 Jun 1963.

10. Booker, *The Neophiliacs*, p. 195; *Macmillan* (1), p. 408; Patrick Marnham, *The Private Eye Story* (1982), pp. 66–9; Booker, pp. 199–200; Davenport-Hines, *An English Affair*, p. 44, *G*, 7 Sep 1963.

11. *G*, 19 Dec 1962; Martin Childs, 'Brian Sollit', *Ind*, 19 Sep 2013; *TLS*, 10 May 2019 (Shahidha Bari); Frost, *An Autobiography*, p. 111; Brian Brivati, 'The End of Decline', paper at Kingston University, 12 Mar 2003; Robert D. Putnam and Shaylyn Romney Garrett, *The Upswing* (2020).

12. John Western, *A Passage to England* (Minneapolis, 1992), p. 60; Leo Abse, *Private Member* (1973), pp. 159–71; *Old Lady*, Jun 1980 (Pamela Clayton), p. 64; Abrams, ABMS 5/37, part 3 of 4, Derek Wright and Edwin Cox, 'Changes in Moral Belief among Sixth-form Boys and Girls over a Seven-year Period in relation to Religious Belief, Age and Sex Difference'; Doggett, *Growing Up*, p. 74; *G*, 7 May 2013 (Stuart Jeffries); 'Denzil Freeth', *T*, 12 May 2020; Andrew Wilson, *Harold Robbins* (2007), pp. 140–1; *T*, 14 Nov 2005 (Nicola Woolcock); BBC WAC, R9/74/3, Sep 1963 (No. 283); Jack Tinkler, *Coronation St.* (1985), p. 42.

13. *Contemporary British History*, Spring 2000, p. 189 (Lawrence Black); *Smethwick Telephone*, 12 Jul 1963; *Ind*, 4 Aug 2001.

14. 'Peter Hall', *The Economist*, 9 Aug 2014; *Ob*, 6 Apr 2003 (David Walker); *NS*, 23 Aug 1963; Wilfred Burns, *New Towns for Old* (1963), pp. 24, 62, 83, 93–5; *Town Planning Review*, Oct 1984, p. 510 (Gordon E. Cherry); Thomas Faulkner, 'Architecture in Newcastle', in Robert Colls and Bill Lancaster (eds), *Newcastle upon Tyne* (Chichester, 2001), p. 239; John Pendlebury, 'Alas Smith and Burns?', in *Planning Perspectives*, Apr 2001, pp. 127–8.

15. *G*, 15 Aug 1963 (Norman Shrapnel); John Winstone, *Bristol As It Was, 1963–1975* (Bristol, 1990), p. 16; *Burnley Express*, 8 Jun 1963; Maxwell Craven, *Derby* (Derby, 2005), pp. 132–3; *Official Architecture and Planning*, Jul 1963, p. 664; James P. McCafferty, 'The Glasgow Inner Ring Road', in Miles Glendinning (ed.), *Rebuilding Scotland* (East Linton, 1997), p. 78; *New Soc*, 9 Jan 1964 (Paul Thompson); *DT*, 10 Jun 2000 (Giles Worsley); *Architectural Design*, Jul 1963, pp. 326–36; Elain Harwood, *Space, Hope and Brutalism* (2015), p. 82; *Williams*, p. 210; Clare Hartwell, *Manchester* (2001), pp. 189–90; *Architectural Design*, Jul

1963, p. 304; *Official Architecture and Planning*, Oct 1963, p. 972 (Leslie Ginsburg); *Architectural Review*, Sep 1963, p. 168.

16. Saumarez Smith, *Boom Cities*, pp. 123, 45; Gordon E. Cherry, *The Politics of Town Planning* (Harlow, 1982), p. 70; Richard Cobb, *People and Places* (Oxford, 1985), p. 190; G, 9 May 1963; *New Soc*, 9 Jan 1964; Harwood, *Space, Hope and Brutalism*, p. 652; Anthony Thwaite (ed.), *Selected Letters of Philip Larkin* (1992), p. 356.

17. *Liverpool Echo*, 23 Jul 1963; G, 12 Feb 1963 (Diana Rowntree); *Builder*, 12 Jul 1963; Dunleavy, *The Politics of Mass Housing in Britain, 1945–1975*, p. 117; *Architects' Journal*, 10 Jul 1963; *Birmingham Evening Mail*, 16 Sep 1963.

18. Gail Armstrong and Mary Wilson, 'Delinquency and some aspects of housing', in Colin Ward (ed.), *Vandalism* (1973), p. 84; Saumarez Smith, *Boom Cities*, p. 138; *Architectural Review*, Jul 1963, pp. 9–11; Saumarez Smith, p. 135.

8 WITH IT

1. Haines, SxMOA99/34/8/16, 27 Sep 1963; *ST*, 29 Sep 1963; *Wigan Observer*, 4 Oct 1963; Sir Robin Day, *Grand Inquisitor* (1989), p. 224; *Benn*, p. 65; *Selbourne*, p. 282; BBC WAC, R9/7/65–VR/63/583, 12 Oct 1963; *NS*, 4 Oct 1963; *L*, 3 Oct 1963; Kathleen Tynan (ed.), Kenneth Tynan, *Letters* (1984), p. 284; Booker, *The Neophiliacs*, p. 211; O'Grady, *At My Mother's Knee … And Other Low Joints*, p. 199; BBC WAC, R9/74/2 – Oct 1963 (no. 180); Last, SxMOA1/4/290, 29 Sep 1963.

2. *Wikipedia*, 'History of BBC television idents'; Wyman, *Stone Alone*, p. 155; Jackson, 43D78/54, 30 Sep 1963; *S Tel*, 6 Oct 1963; *Fowles*, p. 575; *DT*, 1 Oct 1963; James Booth (ed.), Philip Larkin, *Letters Home, 1936–1977* (2018), p. 371.

3. *NY*, 19 Oct 1963; Pimlott, *Harold Wilson*, p. 304; *Macmillan* (2), pp. 599–600; Frank Cousins papers (Modern Records Centre, University of Warwick), 282/8/3/2, 25 Sep 1963, 1 Oct 1963; Roy Hattersley, *Who Goes Home?* (1995), p. 39; Francis Green and David Kynaston, *Engines of Privilege* (2019), p. 39; *DT*, 2 Oct 1963; G, 2 Oct 1963; *Benn*, p. 69.

4. Larkin, Ms.Eng.c.7427, fo 18, 5 Oct 1963; Haines, SxMOA99/34/8/16, 2 Oct 1963; *Macmillan* (2), p. 599; Leeds City Council, *Agenda and Verbatim Reports, 1963–64* (1964), 2 Oct 1963; C. Farrell, 'The Court Lees Approved School Affair', https://www.corpun.com/courtlees. htm; https://whatenglandmeanstome.co.uk; *T*, 4 Oct 1963; *Fowles*, p. 577; Preston, 6D87/6, 3 Oct 1963; Heap, Acc 2243/37/1, 3 Oct

1963; Nicholson, *How Was It For You?*, p. 138; *RT*, 3 Oct 1963; John Hilton Bureau papers (News International Archive), box 18, 5 Oct 1963; *G*, Oct 1963; Abrams, 2/4/11, part 2 of 4, 11 Oct 1963; *Brandreth*, p. 52; *T*, 7 Oct 1963; *G*, 8 Oct 1963; Thorpe, *Supermac*, p. 55; Haines, SxMOA99/34/8/16, 9 Oct 1963.

5. Thorpe, *Supermac*, p. 565; Baston, *Reggie*, p. 203; Anthony Howard, *RAB* (1987), p. 311; Baston, p. 203; Mount, *Cold Cream*, p. 265; *Benn*, p. 68; Mount, p. 264; *Ob*, 13 Oct 1963; *L*, 17 Oct 1963.

6. Heffer, *Like the Roman*, p. 321; Alethia Hayter (ed.), *A Wise Woman* (Banham, 1996), p. 144; Darlington, 10 Oct 1963; Thorpe, *Supermac*, p. 563; *FT*, 11 Oct 1963; Ron Pollard, *Odds & Sods* (1991), pp. 5–6; Baston, *Reggie*, pp. 205–6; Howard and West, *The Making of the Prime Minister*, pp. 74–5; Randolph S. Churchill, *The Fight for the Tory Leadership* (1964), p. 115; Larkin, Ms.Eng.c.7427, fo 23, 11 Oct 1963; *FT*, 12 Oct 1963; *Oldham Chronicle*, 12 Oct 1963 (Edward Hargreaves); Howard, *RAB*, pp. 313–14; *Ob*, 13 Oct 1963; Frederick Ward, GDP/145/1963, 12 Oct 1963.

7. Churchill, *The Fight for the Tory Leadership*, pp. 122–3; *Brandreth*, p. 53; *T*, 14 Oct 1963; Lewisohn, *Beatles Chronicle*, p. 92; *DM* (1), 14 Oct 1963.

8. John Boorman, *Six Days to Saturday* (YouTube); *G*, 4 Aug 2014 (Peter Walker); Churchill, *The Fight for the Tory Leadership*, p. 129; John Campbell, *Pistols at Dawn* (2009), p. 286; *Benn*, p. 70; *Independent on Sunday*, 1 Jan 1995; BBC WAC, R9/7/65 – VR/63/591, 16 Oct 1963; Churchill, p. 130; Preston, 6D87/6, 16 Oct 1963.

9. *Macmillan* (1), p. 514; Thorpe, *Supermac*, p. 577; Hayter, *Wise Woman*, p. 144; Heffer, *Like the Roman*, p. 328; Campbell, *Pistols at Dawn*, p. 287; Churchill, *The Fight for the Tory Leadership*, p. 132; Heffer, p. 329; *Macmillan* (1), p. 515; Campbell, p. 288; Haines, SxMOA99/34/8/16, 18 Oct 1963; William Kirkman, GDP/30/1963–64, 18 Oct 1963; Preston, 6D87/6, 18 Oct 1963.

10. Howard and West, *The Making of the Prime Minister*, pp. 90–1; Preston, 6D87/6, 19 Oct 1963; *Ob*, 20 Oct 1963 (Richard Baerlein); *Ind*, 26 Oct 2013 (Simon Hart); Churchill, *The Fight for the Tory Leadership*, pp. 146–7; Frost, *An Autobiography*, p. 98–9; Cockerell, *Live from Number 10*, p. 98; W. F. Deedes, *Dear Bill* (1997), p. 184; Andrew Denham and Mark Garnett, *Keith Joseph* (Chesham, 2001), pp. 120–1; Baston, *Reggie*, pp. 208–9; Ian Gilmour, *Whatever Happened to the Tories* (1997), pp. 188, 202; Churchill, p. 135.

11. Churchill, *The Fight for the Tory Leadership*, pp. 147–8; *NY*, 9 Nov 1963; Churchill, p. 148; Eric Shorter, 'Peter O'Toole', *Ind*, 16 Dec 2013;

Heap, Acc 2243/37/1, 22 Oct 1963; Antony Sher, *Year of the King* (1985), pp. 124–6; Dominic Shellard, *British Theatre since the War* (1999), p. 103.

12. Henry Phelps Brown, 'Lionel Charles Robbins', *Proceedings of the British Academy, 1987* (1987), pp. 621–2; Guy Ortolano, 'Two Cultures, One University', *Albion*, Spring 2003, pp. 601–2; Mandler, *The Crisis of the Meritocracy*, p. 85; *NS*, 23 Aug 2019 (Harry Lambert).

13. *G*, 24 Oct 1963; Larkin, Ms.Eng.c.7427, fo 33, 27 Oct 1963; *T*, 24 Oct 1963; Mandler, *The Crisis of the Meritocracy*, p. 81; *DT*, 24 Oct 1963; A. C. H. Smith, *Paper Voices* (1975), p. 165; *T*, 29 Oct 1963.

14. Mandler, *The Crisis of the Meritocracy*, p. 79; Robert G. Burgess, 'Aspects of education in post-war Britain', in James Obelkevich and Peter Catterall (eds), *Understanding Postwar British society* (1984), p. 134; *TLS*, 13 Jul 2001 ('Letter from Falmer'); Carol Dyhouse, 'Education', in Ina Zweiniger-Bargielowska, *Women in Twentieth-Century Britain* (Harlow, 2001), pp. 124, 127; R. G. Jobling, 'Some Sociological Aspects of University Development in England', in *Sociological Review*, March 1969, p. 17; *ST*, 14 Jul 1963; *Country Life*, 28 Oct 1965; Harwood, *Space, Hope and Brutalism*, p. 263; *G*, 12 Sep 1963 (Rowntree), 30 Jul 2015 (Gavin Stamp). See also: Muthesius, *The Postwar University*; Tony Birks, *Building the New Universities* (Newton Abbot, 1972), chap. 1; Jules Lubbock, 'The Counter-Modernist Sublime', in *Twentieth Century Architecture*, 2002, pp. 107–18.

15. Sampson, *Anatomy of Britain*, pp. 206–7; David Lodge, *Quite a Good Time to Be Born* (2015), pp. 316, 323, 426; Veronica Porter (née Lee), unpublished autobiography; University of Manchester Union, *Students in Society* (1963), pp. 2–6.

16. *G*, 3 Jan 1964 (Brian Jackson), 10 May 1962 (Brock), 18 May 1962 (Mackenzie); *Ob*, 27 Oct 1963 ('The Meaning of Robbins'); *G*, 3 Jan 1964; John Vaizey, *Britain in the Sixties: Education Tomorrow* (Harmondsworth, 1962), pp. 76–7.

17. Churchill, *The Fight for the Tory Leadership*, pp. 148–50; Foot, *Immigration and Race in British Politics*, p. 45; Haines, SxMOA99/34/8/16, 25 Oct 1963; BBC WAC, R9/74/2, Nov 1963 (No 181); *G*, 26 Oct 1963; *TLS*, 21 Nov 2003 (Lucy Dallas); BBC WAC, R9/7/65–VR/63/611, 26 Oct 1963.

18. *G*, 28–9 Oct 1963; Roy, *The Invisible Spirit*, p. 304; Tom Bower, *Gordon Brown* (2004), p. 8; *G*, 23 Jun 1989; David Powell, *Counter Revolution* (1989), pp. 109–10; *FT*, 30 Oct 1963.

19. Larkin, Ms.Eng.c.7427, fo 36, 31 Oct 1963; William Smethurst, *The Archers* (1996), pp. 93–4; *Hertfordshire Advertiser*, 1 Nov 1963; *NME*,

1 Nov 1963; *Daily Herald*, 2 Nov 1963; *DT*, 2 Nov 1963; BBC WAC, R9/7/66–VR/63/628, 3 Nov 1963.

20. *T*, 5 Nov 1963; *NME*, 8 Nov 1963; Craig Brown, *One Two Three Four* (2020), p. 129; Dave Laing, 'Ross McManus', *G*, 22 Dec 2011; *DT*, 5 Nov 1963.

21. Brown, *One Two Three Four*, p. 129; *DT*, 6 Nov 1963; Leeds City Council, *Agenda & Verbatim Reports, 1963–64* (1964), 6 Nov 1963; *Bonham Carter*, p. 275; *G*, 7 Nov 1963; *DT*, 8 Nov 1963; Carpenter, *Satire*, pp. 277–9; Churchill, *The Fight for the Tory Leadership*, p. 150; *G*, 9 Nov 1963; *TLS*, 7 Nov 1963; Richard J. Evans, *Eric Hobsbawm* (2019), p. 366.

22. *Ob*, 10 Nov 1963; GDP/47/1963, 9 Nov 1963; Betty Allen, GDP/450/1963–1967, 10 Nov 1963; Maud Coote (née Smith), GDP/433/1963, 10 Nov 1963; *T*, 11 Nov 1963; Brown, *One Two Three Four*, p. 128.

23. BBC WAC, R9/7/66–VR/63/641, 10 Nov 1963; Last, SxMOA1/4/292, 10 Nov 1963; GDP/329/1963, 10 Nov 1963; *Brandreth*, p. 55; Darlington, 10 Nov 1963; Diana Griffith, GDP/7/1960–64, 10 Nov 1963.

9 PUT RIGHT OUT OF GEAR

1. Simonelli, *Heroes*, p. 66; St John, 68/48, 11 Nov 1963; *Evening News*, 12 Nov 1963; Paul Allen, *Alan Ayckbourn* (2001), pp. 96–103; *Evening Sentinel*, 13 Nov 1963; *G*, 23 Apr 2016 (George Arnett); David Hendy, *The BBC* (2022), p. 415; BBC WAC, R9/7/66–VR/63/646, 13 Nov 1963; *P*, 27 Nov 1963; *TLS*, 14 Nov 1963; *Northern Echo*, 15 Nov 1963; Matthew Engel, *The Reign*, Part 1 (2022), p. 211; *Smethwick Telephone*, 15 Nov 1963; BBC WAC, *Any Questions?*, 15 Nov 1963; Mary Whitehouse, *A Most Dangerous Woman?* (1982), p. 9; *T*, 18 Nov 1963; *G*, 16 Nov 1963; Walter Hooper (ed.), C. S. Lewis, *Collected Letters*, vol. III (2006), p. 1480; *Selbourne*, p. 286; BBC WAC, R9/7/66–VR/63/653, 16 Nov 1963; *Ob*, 17 Nov 1963; *ST*, 17 Nov 1963; Haines, SxMOA99/34/8/16, 18 Nov 1963; Brown, *One Two Three Four*, p. 191; *P*, 20 Nov 1963; Frederick Ward, GDP/145/1963, 20 Nov 1963; *G*, 21 Nov 1963; 'Veronica, the Dowager Countess of Lucan', *T*, 28 Sep 2017; *Staines & Egham News*, 29 Nov 1963; *T*, 12 Nov 2019 (Matt Dickinson); *Cambrian News*, 29 Nov 1963; Frederick Ward, GDP/145/1963, 21 Nov 1963; Roy Strong, *Self-Portrait as a Young Man* (Oxford, 2013), pp. 204–7; 'Robert Freeman', *T*, 14 Nov 2019; *Liverpool Daily Post*, 22

Nov 1963; papers of Richard (Dick) Etheridge (MRC), 202/S/J/3/2/48, 22 Nov 1963; *T*, 23 Nov 1963; *Daily Sketch*, 23 Nov 1963; *DT*, 23 Nov 1963; GDP/36/1963, 22 Nov 1963; Martin, P5/2J/38, 22 Nov 1963; Grace Taylor, GDP/318/1963, 22 Nov 1963.

2. (*Wolverhampton*) *Express & Star*, 22 Nov 1963; Philip Purser, 'Mike Scott', *G*, 2 Jun 2008; Marks, 22 Nov 1963; *DT*, 23 Nov 1963; Milton Schulman, *Marilyn, Hitler and Me* (1998), pp. 255–7; *Oxford Mail*, 22 Nov 1963; BBC WAC, *Any Questions?*, 22 Nov 1963; information from Michael Frayn; BBC WAC, *Any Questions?*, 22 Nov 1963.

3. GDP/328/1963, 22 Nov 1963; Jackson, 43D78/54, 22 Nov 1963; Last, SxMOA1/4/292, 22 Nov 1963; Kenneth Johnson, GDP/458/Nov 1963–Jan 1964, 22 Nov 1963; Frederick Ward, GDP/145/1963, 22 Nov 1963; Heap, Acc 2243/37/1, 22 Nov 1963; Marks, 22 Nov 1963.

4. *DT*, 11 Dec 2004 (Sir Cliff Richard); Henry Hardy and Mark Pottle (eds), Isaiah Berlin, *Building: Letters 1960–1975* (2013), p. 172; *NS*, 3 Jul 2020; Lord David Sutch, *Life as Such* (1991), p. 31; Ted Dexter, *85 Not Out* (Shrewsbury, 2020), p. 154; *Big Issue*, 18 Nov 2013; Nicholson, *How Was It For You?*, pp. 144–5; Jimmy Boyle, *A Sense of Freedom* (Edinburgh, 1977), p. 111; Alan Johnson, *This Boy* (2013), p. 206.

5. Information from Claire Tomalin; *Northern Echo*, 23 Nov 1963; *Liverpool Daily Post*, 25 Nov 1963; Philip Norman, *John Lennon* (2008), p. 319; Dannie Abse, *A Poet in the Family* (1974), pp. 186–7; *Surrey Comet*, 27 Nov 1963; *DT*, 11 Dec 2004; Nicholson, *How Was It For You?*, p. 145; Lee, 22 Nov 1963; *Oxford Today*, Trinity 2014 (Andrew Bunbury); Martin, P5/2J/38, 22 Nov 1963.

6. *DT*, 23 Nov 1963; *Bonham Carter*, p. 275; Shulman, *Marilyn, Hitler and Me*, pp. 257–9; *Crossman* (1), p. 1041; Shulman, p. 261; *Benn*, p. 78.

7. Darlington, 23 Nov 1963; *Brandreth*, p. 56; Marks, 23 Nov 1963; GDP/307/1961–1963, 23 Nov 1963; St John, 68/48, 23 Nov 1963; Martin, P5/2J/38, 23 Nov 1963; *Oxford Mail*, 25 Nov 1963; *Bonham Carter*, p. 276; *Daily Express*, 23 Nov 1963; BBC WAC, R9/7/66–VR/63/668, 23 Nov 1963; Carol Ann Lee, *One of Your Own* (Edinburgh, 2010), pp. 130–6.

8. Heap, Acc 2243/37/1, 23 Nov 1963; Carpenter, *Satire*, p. 281; *L*, 5 Dec 1963; Hodgson, 25 Nov 1963. YouTube has an audio version of the programme, plus Ned Sherrin's sleeve notes to the original LP recording of the programme.

9. David Goodway, seminar paper at Institute of Historical Research, 1 Feb 1994; E. P. Thompson, *The Making of the English Working Class* (Harmondsworth, 1968 edn), pp. 9–13; *Ob*, 24 Nov 1963; *L*, 5 Dec 1963; *NS*, 29 Nov 1963.

10. Thompson, *The Making of the English Working Class*, pp. 947–58; Selina Todd, 'People Matter', *History Workshop*, Autumn 2013, p. 261; Raphael Samuel, 'Ralph Miliband 1924–1994', *History Workshop*, Autumn 1994, p. 266; Meredith Veldman, *Fantasy, the Bomb and the Greening of Britain* (Cambridge, 1994), p. 194; *TLS*, 18 Feb 2005; *Ob*, 24 Nov 1963; Abrams, ABMS 5/6, file headed Part 2 of 7.

11. Kate Paul, *Journal*, Vol. 1 (Hay-on Wye, 1997), p. 254; *DS*, 25 Nov 1963; *NS*, 22 Aug 2014; Eric Dunning et al., *The Roots of Football Hooliganism* (1988), p. 144; *Liverpool Daily Post*, 26 Nov 1963; Steve Russell, 'John Bloom – Entrepreneur & Would-be Chairman of QPR F.C.', www.indyrs.co.uk/2020/07/john-bloom-entrenpreneur-would-be-chairman-of-qpr-f-c/; *G*, 23 Apr 2016; Foot, *Immigration and Race in British Politics*, pp. 176–8; *(Stoke) Evening Sentinel*, 27 Nov 1963.

12. Saumarez Smith, *Boom Cities*, p. 17; *G*, 28 Nov 1963; *L*, 5 Dec 1963; *Liverpool Daily Post*, 28 Nov 1963; Saumarez Smith, p. 17; *NS*, 29 Nov 1963.

13. *TLS*, 28 Nov 1963; *Spec*, 29 Nov 1963; Simonelli, *Heroes*, p. 26; Hunter Davies, *The Beatles* (1968), p. 204; *Benn*, p. 79; *T*, 30 Nov 1963; Foot, *Immigration and Race in British Politics*, p. 45; Jessica Boak and Ray Bailey, *Brew Britannia* (2014), pp. 8–9.

14. *S Tel*, 1 Dec 1963; *DT* 2–4 Dec 1963, 7 Dec 1963; *S Tel*, 8 Dec 1963; *DT*, 9–12 Dec 1963, 14 Dec 1963; *Ob*, 15 Dec 1963; Anthony Sampson, *Anatomy of Britain Today* (1965), pp. 456–8; *Encounter*, Dec 1963, pp. 78–82; *TLS*, 5 Dec 1963; Mount, *Cold Cream*, pp. 226–7; *The Letters of John Calmann, 1951–1980* (1986), pp. 175–6; *TLS*, 5 Dec 1963; John Muncie, 'The Beatles and the Spectacle of Youth', in Ian Inglis (ed.), *The Beatles, Popular Music and Society* (Basingstoke, 2000), p. 41.

15. *DT*, 6 Dec 1963; Seymour Platt, 'My battle to clear Christine Keeler's name', in *Spectator Life*, 21 May 2021; *DT*, 7 Dec 1963; Platt, 'My battle'; Tam Dalyell, 'Keith Stainton', *Ind*, 16 Nov 2001; *NS*, 6 Dec 1963; *Hull & Yorkshire Times*, 7 Dec 1963 ('Peter Blackman's Disc Gossip'); email from Richard Williams, 31 Mar 2021; Boak and Bailey, *Brew Britannia*, p. 12; diary of Frank Lewis (Glamorgan Record Office, D51/1/212, 6 Dec 1963; Martin, P5/2J/38, 7 Dec 1963.

16. BBC WAC, R9/7/66–VR/63/697, 7 Dec 1963; Diana Griffith, GDP/7/1960/64, 7 Dec 1963; Lee, 7 Dec 1963; Lewisohn, *Beatles Chronicle*, p. 132; BBC WAC, R9/74/2, Jan 1964 (no. 183), R9/7/66–VR/63/699, 7 Dec 1963; Mojo, *Days of Beatlemania*, pp. 76–7 (Johnny Black); *NS*, 8 Nov 2019 (Kate Mossman); Ian Slater and Ian Chapman, 'The Orchids Story', Spectropop; Orchids, 'Love Hit Me', YouTube

(comments); Nicholas Wollaston, *Winter in England* (1965), pp. 11, 40, 50, 67, 80, 98–110.

17. *DT*, 4 Dec 1963; *G*, 8 Dec 1963; Saumarez Smith, *Boom Cities*, pp. 18, 45; *G*, 11 Dec 1963; Saumarez Smith, p. 46.

18. Cecil Beaton, *The Parting Years* (1978), p. 2; *G*, 29 Nov 1963 (Diana Rowntree); Anthony Hayward, 'John Neville', *Ind*, 26 Nov 2011; Martin, P5/2J/38, 12–13 Dec 1963; Willmott, WLMT 1/28, 16 Dec 1963; Norman, *Mick Jagger*, p. 116; Peter Webb, *Portrait of David Hockney* (1988), p. 59; Martin, P5/2J/38, 16 Dec 1963; *Partridge* (2), p. 31.

19. *G*, 26 Nov 1963, 15–16 Dec 1963; *Ob*, 3 Aug 2014; *G*, 20 Dec 1963.

20. *Crossman* (1), p. 1044; Simonelli, *Heroes*, p. 25; *G*, 20 Dec 1963; Martin, P5/2J/38, 20 Dec 1963; Anthony Hayward, 'Michael Ferguson', *G*, 18 Dec 2021; Langford, 23 Dec 1963; *Beatlemania*, pp. 78–9 (Chris Hunt).

21. Anderson, *Foxed!*, pp. 64–5; *(Wolverhampton) Express & Star*, 27 Dec 1963; *T*, 27 Dec 1963; *Ob*, 29 Dec 1963 (Bob Ferrier); Marks, 28 Dec 1963; *ST* 29 Dec 1963; *Ob*, 29 Dec 1963; Heap, Acc 2243/37/1, 31 Dec 1963; Martin, P5/2J/38, 31 Dec 1963; Wollaston, *Winter in England*, pp. 118–19; Benn, p. 86.

10 I SHOULDN'T LIKE TO BE POOR AGAIN

1. Wollaston, *Winter in England*, pp. 119–22, 131–7, 142–8; Diana Griffith, GDP/7/1960–64, 1 Jan 1964; 'Johnny Stewart', *T*, 5 May 2005; BBC WAC, R9/7/67–VR/64/11, 1 Jan 1964, R9/7/67–VR/64/63, 29 Jan 1964; Pierre Perrone, 'Samantha Juste', *Ind*, 20 Feb 2014; *P*, 19 Feb 1964.

2. *T*, 28 Sep 2012 ('The Who: A Mod History'); Doug Hinman, *The Kinks* (San Francisco, 2004), p. 21; Simonelli, *Heroes*, p. 32; Mojo, *Days of Beatlemania*, p. 93 (John Harris); *T*, 26 Feb 1964; Harris, p. 93; *Daily Express*, 28 Feb 1964; *MM*, 8 Feb 1964, 14 Mar 1964; *Evening Standard*, 21 Mar 1964.

3. *P*, 8 Jan 1964; Langford, 18 Jan 1964; Haines, SxMOA99/34/8/17, 7 Feb 1964; *G*, 8 Feb 1964; *Berrow's Worcester Journal*, 21 Feb 1964; *NS*, 28 Feb 1964; Ironside, 14 Jan 1964.

4. Jeffrey Richards, 'New waves and old myths', in Bart Moore-Gilbert and John Seed (eds), *Cultural Revolution?* (1992), pp. 223–4; *Evening Standard*, 5 Sep 1994 (Michael Swain); *Ob*, 26 Jan 1964; Haines, SxMOA99/34/8/17, 21 Mar 1964, 29 Feb 1964, 22 Mar 1964; Last,

SxMOA1/4/294, 7 Jan 1964, 9 Jan 1964; BBC WAC, R9/7/68–VR/64/139, 7 Mar 1964; *NS*, 31 Jan 1964; Willmott, WLMT 1/28, 8 Feb 1964.

5. *G*, 14 Feb 1964; *Country Life*, 30 Jan 1964; *S Tel*, 12 Jan 1964; *ST*, 22 Mar 1964; *Vogue*, 15 Mar 1964; *TLS*, 26 Mar 1964 (John Willett); Norman, *John Lennon*, p. 360; *NME*, 20 Mar 1964; Hampton (ed.), *Joyce & Ginnie*, p. 307; Holt and Pym (eds), Barbara Pym, *A Very Private Eye*, p. 314; Booth (ed.), Philip Larkin, *Letters Home*, p. 290; *L*, 19 Mar 1964; *Fowles*, p. 588.

6. Frederick Ward, GDP/145/1964, 9 Feb 1964; Hugo Vickers, *Elizabeth: The Queen Mother* (2005), p. 388; Anthony Hayward, 'Tony Selby', *G*, 10 Sep 2021; 'Tony Selby', *T*, 21 Sep 2021; Doggett, *Growing Up*, p. 104; Sheila Hancock, *The Two of Us* (2004), p. 126; Doggett, pp. 107–8; 'Pamela Green', *T*, 15 May 2010; Nicholson, *How Was It For You?*, pp. 147–9.

7. *Wikipedia*, 'Fanny Hill'; *S Tel*, 16 Feb 1964; Richard Stott, *Dogs and Lampposts* (2002), p. 97; *G*, 23 Jan 1964, 21 Feb 1964; St John, 68/48, 8 Jan 1964; Wollaston, *Winter in England*, p. 132; *Birmingham Evening Mail*, 6 Jan 1964; *Ob*, 5 Jan 1964; Coe, *Like a Fiery Elephant*, pp. 52–3; 'Paddy Hopkirk', *T*, 25 Jul 2022; *G*, 17 Mar 2010 (Frank Keating); *S Tel*, 8 Mar 1964; *Daily Worker*, 18 Feb 1964; Barrow, *Gossip*, p. 236; Kevin Cann, *Any Day Now* (2010), p. 35; *ST*, 22 Mar 1964.

8. Ronald Smith, *The Gorbals* (Glasgow, 1999), pp. 29–30; Winstone, *Bristol As It Was*, p. 17; Roy Bullock, *Salford 1940–1965* (Salford, 1996), p. 59; *Berrow's Worcester Journal*, 27 Mar 1964, 6 Mar 1964; *Country Life*, 6 Feb 1964 (Christopher Hussey); *G*, 21 Mar 1964; *NY*, 4 Apr 1964; John Furnival and Ann Knowles, *Archbishop Derek Worlock* (1998), p. 121; Ruth Glass et al., *London: Aspects of Change* (1964), pp. xviii–xix.

9. *Tribune*, 3 Jan 1964, 10 Jan 1964; Joe Street, 'Malcolm X, Smethwick and the Influence of the African American Freedom Struggle on British Race Relations in the 1960s', in *Journal of Black Studies*, Jul 2008, p. 935; Geoffrey Moorhouse, *Britain in the Sixties: The Other England* (Harmondsworth, 1964), pp. 102–3; Foot, *Immigration and Race in British Politics*, p. 46; *G*, 18 Feb 1964; *T*, 9 Mar 1964; Study Group on Commonwealth Immigrants, Feb 1964 to Jun 1964, undated background paper, circa Spring 1964 (Labour Party Archives, People's History Museum, Manchester); *G*, 27 Feb 1964.

10. *Ob*, 22 Mar 1964; Wybrow, *Britain Speaks Out, 1937–87*, p. 70; *DT*, 7 Feb 1964; Dennis Barker, 'Chapman Pincher', *G*, 7 Aug 2014; *G*, 18 Mar 1964 (Mary Crozier); *P*, 4 Mar 1964 (Bernard Hollowood); Housden, *The Passing of a Country Grammar School*, p. 67; Michael Armstrong and Michael Young, 'New Look at Comprehensive Schools', *Fabian*

Society, Jan 1964, p. 18; *DT*, 26 Feb 1964; Barrow, *Gossip*, p. 236; Frank Cousins papers (MRC), MSS.282/3/COR/110/21-2, telegram received 30 Jan 1964 from Hugh Cudlipp; *ST*, 16 Feb 1964.

11. *NY*, 15 Feb 1964; Bank of England Archive, G3/131, 21 Feb 1964; Shepherd, *Enoch Powell*, pp. 269–70; Heffer, *Like the Roman*, pp. 347–8; Cousins papers, MSS.282/8/3/1, Mar/Apr 1964; Abrams, ABMS 2/4/11, part 2 of 2, 'Study of Public Opinion', Mar 1964; *Ob*, 5 Apr 1964.

12. Grace Taylor, GDP/318/1964, 6 Jan 1964; Martin, P5/2J/38, 1 Jan 1964; Haines, SxMOA99/34/8/17, 16 Jan 1964; Kathleen Johnson (née Perry), GDP/193/1964-5, 26 Jan 1964, 29 Jan 1964; Betty Allen, GDP/450/1963–1967, 20 Mar 1964; Lee, 23 Mar 1964; St John, 68/48, 25 Mar 1964; Scott, SxMOA99/97/1/13, 1 Jan 1964–21 Mar 1964; Wollaston, *Winter in England*, chap. 17.

13. *G*, 28 Mar 1964; Glendinning and Muthesius, *Tower Block*, pp. 220, 244; Scott, SxMOA99/97/1/13, 27 Mar 1964; Spencer Leigh, 'Simon Dee', *Ind*, 2 Sep 2009; Anthony Hayward, 'Simon Dee', *G*, 31 Aug 2009; Anthony Hayward, 'Ronan O'Rahilly', *G*, 25 Apr 2020; Wyman, *Stone Alone*, p. 199; Holt and Pym (eds), Barbara Pym, *A Very Private Eye*, p. 314; Andrew Taylor, *20th Century Blackburn* (Barnsley, 2000), pp. 94–5; Langford, 30 Mar 1964; St John, 68/48, 30 Mar 1964.

14. *ST*, 29 Mar 1964; *DM* (2), 30 Mar 1964; *G*, 31 Mar 1964; *Ob*, 5 Apr 1964; Viv Albertine, *Clothes Music Boys* (2014), p. 16.

15. *G*, 2 Apr 1964; Wybrow, *Britain Speaks Out, 1937–87*, p. 71; BBC WAC, *Any Questions?*, 3 Apr 1964; *ST*, 12 Apr 1964; *G*, 28 Apr 1964.

16. *T*, 2 Apr 1964; 'Norman Swallow', *T*, 11 Dec 2000; *DT*, 2 Apr 1964; Keith Vaughan, *Journals 1939–1977* (1989), p. 140; *RT*, 25 Apr 1964; Anthony Hayward, 'Tim Brooke-Taylor', *G*, 14 Apr 2020; Francis Wheen, *Tom Driberg* (1990), p. 349; Kathleen Johnson (née Perry), GDP/193/1964-5, 5 Apr 1964; Simonelli, *Heroes*, p. 35; Daran Little, *The Coronation Street Story* (1995), p. 54; Chris Maume, 'Billie Whitelaw', *Ind*, 23 Dec 2014; *G*, 17 Mar 2004 (Samantha Ellis); *Ob*, 12 Apr 1964 (Maurice Richardson); *Which?*, 8 Apr 1964, pp. 100–9; *G*, 15 Apr 1964 (Wayland Young); Ironside, 10 Apr 1964; Amanda Allsop (ed.), Kenneth Allsop, *Letters to His Daughter* (1974), p. 14; Howard and West, *The Making of the Prime Minister*, p. 125; Bullock, *Salford 1940–1965*, p. 59; *T*, 22 Jan 2021 (Martin Hardy).

17. Baston, *Reggie*, pp. 227–8; *FT*, 15 Apr 1964; Baston, pp. 228–9; Kynaston, *Till Time's Last Sand*, pp. 456–7.

18. *G*, 16 Apr 1964; Hague, 15 Apr 1964; Andrew Ward, *The Manchester City Story* (Derby, 1984), p. 56; Mojo, *The Rolling Stones* (2003), p. 14 (Phil Sutcliffe); *G*, 17 Apr 1964; Michael Coveney, 'Leslie Phillips', *G*,

9 Nov 2022; *DT*, 18 Apr 1964 (L. Marsland Gander); *Ob*, 19 Apr 1964; Lewisohn, *Beatles Chronicle*, p. 131; *Berrow's Worcester Journal*, 24 Apr 1964; Marks, 22 Apr 1964; Frederick Ward, GDP/145/1964, 23 Apr 1964; Spencer Leigh, 'Gordon Waller', *Ind*, 23 Jul 2009.

19. Haines, SxMOA99/34/8/17, 20 Apr 1964; Stuart Jeffries, 'Brian Cant', *G*, 21 Jun 2017; Lewisohn, *Radio Times Guide to TV Comedy*, p. 506; Haines, SxMOA99/34/8/17, 20 Apr 1964; Hampton (ed.), *Joyce & Ginnie*, p. 308; Michael Leapman, 'Michael Peacock', *G*, 4 Jan 2020; *Ob*, 3 May 1964; *P*, 6 May 1964; *L*, 21 May 1964.

20. BBC WAC, R9/7/68–VR/64/238, 26 Apr 1964; *P*, 22 Apr 1964; *Ob*, 26 Apr 1964, 3 May 1964; *Smethwick Telephone*, 24 Apr 1964, 1 May 1964.

21. *Daily Herald*, 1 May 1964; *Illustrated London News*, 6 Mar 1964; Lewis Chester, 'T. Dan Smith', *Ind*, 28 Jul 1993; Edward Milne, *No Shining Armour* (1976), p. 52; *Daily Herald*, 1 May 1964; Michael Gillard and Martin Tomkinson, *Nothing to Declare* (1980), p. 60; David Byrne, 'T. Dan Smith', in *North East Labour History*, 1994 (Bulletin no. 28), p. 22; *Ind*, 4 Aug 1993.

22. NVLAA, Box 77; *Birmingham Evening Mail*, 6 May 1964; Moran, *Armchair Nation*, pp. 152–3; NVALA papers, Box 1; *T*, 6 May 1964.

23. Marcus Williamson, 'Paul Almond', *Ind*, 18 Apr 2015; Michael Apted, *7up* (1999), pp. ix, 2, 24, 39–40, 54, 69, 112, 128, 156; *ST*, 10 May 1964.

24. John Lahr, *Prick Up Your Ears* (2002 edn), p. 156; *Evening Standard*, 7 May 1964; *DM* (1), 7 May 1964; *ST*, 10 May 1964; *DT*, 7 May 1964; *G*, 9 May 1964; Hodgson, Whit Monday, 1964; Haines, SxMOA99/34/8/17, 9 May 1964; Frank Ayliffe, GDP/248/1964, 10 May 1964; *G*, 11 May 1964; *DM* (1), 12 May 1964; Heap, Acc 2243/38/1, 11 May 1964; *DM* (1), 12 May 1964; Nicholas Ind, *Terence Conran* (1995), pp. 146–9.

11 MY HUSBAND WON'T DO WITH CHEAP STUFF

1. *ST*, 10 May 1964; *FT*, 16 May 1964; Gardiner, *Joining the Dots*, pp. 112–13; *FT*, 13 Sep 2008; *Ind*, 13 May 1994; *G*, 16 Jan 1965; Ind, *Terence Conran*, p. 155; *FT*, 5 May 1990.

2. *Ind*, 21 Aug 1999; *G*, 29 May 1964; *DT*, 10 Jun 1964; Oliver Marriott, *The Property Boom* (1967), p. 231; *FT*, 1 Dec 1988.

3. 'Aladdin's cave' derives from Peter Mandler's stimulating 'New towns for old', in Becky Conekin et al. (eds), *Moments of Modernity* (1999), p. 224. In general, for an enjoyable as well as illuminating overview,

see Rachel Bowlby, *Carried Away: The Invention of Modern Shopping* (2000).

4. *Smethwick Telephone* 24 Apr 1964 (Joan Best); Marriott, *The Property Boom*, p. 237; *New Soc*, 1 Nov 1962; Martin Johnes, *Wales since 1939* (Manchester, 2012), p. 77.

5. National Economic Development Office, *The Future Pattern of Shopping* (1971), p. 18; Campbell, *Edward Heath*, pp. 151–3; Shepherd, *Enoch Powell*, pp. 268–9; Charles Moore, *Margaret Thatcher*, vol. I (2013), p. 170; Richard Findley, 'The Conservative Party and Defeat', in *Twentieth Century British History*, 2001 (12/3), p. 347; Jock Bruce-Gardyne and Nigel Lawson, *The Power Game* (1976), p. 103; BBC WAC, *Woman's Hour*, 28 Jan 1964; Bruce-Gardyne and Lawson, p. 103; Findley, pp. 352–3.

6. Black, *Redefining British Politics*, p. 47; Frederick Ward, GDP/145/1964, note at start of diary, plus 21 Apr 1964 entry. See in general: Black, chap. 3, for his survey of 'Co-operative Culture and Affluence'.

7. Christine Shaw, *Simon Marks, 1st Lord Marks of Broughton*, in *Dictionary of Business Biography*, vol. 4 (1985), p. 145; Israel Sieff, *Memoirs* (1970), p. 180; *ST*, 28 Oct 1962; Bullock, *Salford 1940–1965*, p. 62. Generally on Cohen, see: David Powell, *Counter Revolution* (1991), chap. 7; David J. Jeremy, 'Sir John Edward Cohen', in *Dictionary of Business Biography*, vol. 1 (1984), pp. 724–9.

8. *NS*, 12 Mar 1965; Alton and Jo Douglas, *Birmingham in the Sixties*, vol. 1 (Studley, 1998), p. 52; Mark Davison and Ian Currie, *Surrey in the Sixties* (Coulsdon, 1994), p. 66; Mark Davison and Paul Adams, *Tolworth Remembered* (Reigate, n.d.), pp. 52–5; Wollaston, *Winter in England*, p. 50.

9. *T*, 17 Sep 1999 (Fraser Nelson); Anthony Rose, 'Ahmed Pochee', *Ind*, 22 Jan 1999; 'Nick Baile', *T*, 15 Oct 2013; 'Sir Noel Stockdale', *T*, 12 Feb 2004; 'Trevor Storer', *DT*, 15 Aug 2013; 'Noel Lister', *T*, 11 Feb 2015; *G*, 21 Jun 2019 (Chitra Ramaswamy); Barbara Hulanicki, *From A to Biba* (2018 edn), pp. 74–83; *Vogue*, May 1964, pp. 58–9.

10. *East London Advertiser*, 7 Jun 1963, 14 Jun 1963; Douglas, *Birmingham in the Sixties*, pp. 56–9; Brian Aldiss, *The Twinkling of an Eye* (1998), pp. 235–6.

11. Kathryn A. Morrison, *English Shops and Shopping* (New Haven, 2003), p. 323; Saumarez Smith, *Boom Cities*, p. 68; John Grindrod, *Concretopia* (Brecon, 2013), pp. 199–200; Peter Shapely, 'Civic pride and redevelopment in the post-war British city', in *Urban History*, 2012 (39/2), p. 321; Morrison, pp. 258, 263–4; *Evening Standard*, 10 Dec 2010; *East Kent Times*, 3 Jul 1963; Paul Morley, *The North* (2013), pp. 16, 227.

12. *Architects' Journal*, 10 Jul 1963; Harwood, *Space, Hope and Brutalism*, p. 380; Owen Hatherley, *A Guide to the New Ruins of Great Britain* (2010), pp. 82–3; Marriott, *The Property Boom*, p. 222; *Ob*, 19 Feb 1967; 'Owen Luder', *T*, 25 Oct 2021; Elain Harwood, 'Owen Luder', *G*, 22 Oct 2021; Saumarez Smith, *Boom Cities*, p. 67.

13. BBC WAC, *Woman's Hour*, 17 Jan 1964; Yvonne Trethewy, *Butchers' shops – the customers' view* (Research Institute for Consumer Affairs, 1964), p. 8; Rachel Bowlby, *Back to the Shops* (Oxford, 2021), p. 126; *NS*, 14 Jan 1965; Rosalind Watkiss Singleton, 'Old Habits Persist' (University of Wolverhampton PhD, 2011), p. 314.

14. Dennis Barker, 'Richard Tompkins', *G*, 11 Dec 1992; *G*, 23 Jun 1989 (Stephen Debenham); Carlo Morelli, 'Constructing a Balance between Price and Non-Price Competition in British Multiple Food Retailing, 1954–64', in *Business History*, Apr 1998, p. 57; *Leicester Mercury*, 25 Nov 1963.

15. *Burnley Express*, 12 Jan 1963; Avram Taylor, *Working Class Credit and Community since 1918* (Basingstoke, 2002), pp. 73, 75; Watkiss Singleton, pp. 309–12.

16. *New Soc*, 21 Apr 1966, 14 May 1964; *Future Pattern of Shopping*, p. 26; Cyril Sofer, 'Buying and Selling', in *Sociological Review*, Jul 1965, pp. 201–2; Tony Judt, *The Memory Chalet* (2010), pp. 130–1.

17. John Benson, *Affluence and Authority* (2005), p. 52; Dennis Marsden Collection (NSPSCA), Pat Marsden, 'Trinity Diary', 5–6 Sep 1963; Daphne Meryon, GDP/44/1964, 8–9 May 1964, 26 Nov 1964; Haines, SxMOA99/34/8/16, 15 Feb 1963, 19 Feb 1963, 27 Nov 1963, 4 Feb 1964, 6 Mar 1964.

18. Michael Young papers (Churchill Archive Centre, Cambridge), YUNG Acc 1911, box titled 'Offprints and press cuttings, 1960–8', Emer Rodnight, 'Attitudes to Spending Money on Consumer Goods and Services'.

19. Sidney Pollard, *The Development of the British Economy* (1983 edn), p. 326; Johnes, *Wales since 1939*, p. 75; *ST*, 2 Aug 1964 (Stephen Fay); Matthew Hilton, 'The Fable of the Sheep, or, Private Virtues, Public Vices', in *Past & Present*, Aug 2002, pp. 238–9; Naomi Sargent, 'Consumer Power as a Pillar of Democracy', in Geoff Dench et al. (eds), *Young at Eighty* (Manchester, 1995), p. 192; *DT*, 29 May 1963.

20. Maurice Healy, 'Eirlys Roberts', *G*, 22 Mar 2008; Black, *Redefining British Politics*, p. 19; Avner Offer, 'British Manual Workers', in *Contemporary British History*, Dec 2008, p. 559; *T*, 3 Jun 1963; Eirlys Roberts, *Which?25* (1982), p. 98; *New Soc*, 5 Aug 1965 (John Barr).

21. *FT*, 4 May 1964; Sampson, *Anatomy of Britain Today*, p. 628; Frank Whitehead, 'Advertising', in Denys Thompson (ed.), *Discrimination and Popular Culture* (Harmondsworth, 1964), p. 23.

22. Sampson, *Anatomy of Britain Today*, p. 629; *FT*, 4 May 1964; *L*, 12 Mar 1964; *Ind*, 3 Sep 2010; Peter York, 'Wally Olins', *G*, 16 Apr 2014.

23. *Woman*, 14 Mar 1964; Whitehead, in *Discrimination and Popular Culture*, p. 34; *New Soc*, 8 Oct 1964 (G. N. Leech); Mark Robinson, *100 Greatest TV Ads* (2000), pp. 8, 26, 51, 44, 64, 114–15.

24. *FT*, 4 May 1964; 'Will Camp', *T*, 28 Jan 2002; *Woman*, 14 Mar 1964; Nicholas Faith, 'Will Camp', *Ind*, 2 Feb 2002.

25. Sean Nixon, *Hard Sell* (Manchester, 2013), pp. 151–3; Illtyd Harrington, 'Robert Millar', *G*, 30 Jun 1994; Robert Millar, *The Affluent Sheep*. (1963), p. 7; James Obelkevich, 'Consumption', in James Obelkevich and Peter Catterall (eds), *Understanding post-war British Society* (1994), pp. 151–2; Nixon, p. 155.

26. *G*, 2 Oct 1961, 11 Oct 1961; *G*, 8 Sep 2020 (Oliver Wainwright); Anderson, *Foxed!*, p. 54.

12 COMPLETELY AGAINST ANY RADICAL CHANGES

1. *G*, 23 Apr 2005; Stuart Jeffries, 'Jean Alexander', *G*, 14 Oct 2016; *DT*, 14 May 1964; Hodgson, 18 May 1964; *Benn*, p. 114; *NS*, 15 May 1964; Scott, SxMOA99/97/1/13, 16 May 1964; Last, SxMOA1/4/298, 16 May 1964; *DT*, 18 May 1964; *T*, 18 May 1964; Clinton Heylan, *Bob Dylan: A Life in Stolen Moments* (1996), pp. 58–9; *MM*, 23 May 1964; *NS*, 22 May 1964.

2. *Williams*, p. 234; *Brighton & Hove Gazette*, 22 May 1964; *DM* (1), 19 May 1964; *Evening News*, 20 May 1964; Richard Weight, *Mod!* (2013), p. 213; Langford, 18 May 1964; *DM* (2), 19 May 1964; *Daily Herald*, 19 May 1964; *Daily Express*, 19 May 1964; Heap, Acc 2243/38/1, 19 May 1964. In general, for a pioneering study of how the seaside battles between the Mods and Rockers triggered a nationwide moral panic, see Stanley Cohen, *Folk Devils and Moral Panics* (1972).

3. *G*, 15 Apr 1964; Richard S. Grayson, 'Mods, Rockers and Juvenile Delinquency in 1964', in *Contemporary British History*, Spring 1998, pp. 24–5; *Brighton & Hove Gazette*, 22 May 1964; *Ind*, 3 Apr 1999 (Williams); *G*, 27 May 2014 (Jeffries); Grayson, p. 24; Paul 'Smiler' Anderson, *Mods: The New Religion* (2013), chap. 12; Twiggy Lawson, *Twiggy in Black and White* (1997), pp. 28–30.

4. Bill Osgerby, '"Well, It's Saturday Night an' I Just Got Paid"', in *Contemporary Record*, Autumn 1992, p. 292; Steve Humphries and John Taylor, *The Making of Modern London, 1945–1985* (1986), pp. 37–8; F. Musgrove, *Youth and the Social Order* (1964), p. 3; John Barron Mays, *The Young Pretenders* (1968 edn), pp. 160–1, 118, 4; E. M. and M. Epple, *Adolescents and Morality* (1966), pp. ix, 213, 218.

5. Philip Abrams and Alan Little, 'The Young Voter in British Politics', in *British Journal of Sociology*, Jun 1965, p. 106; Abrams, ABMS 6/2/8, draft article, 'Earning and Spending: the Teenage Consumer' (Jul 1964); Peter Willmott, *Adolescent Boys of East London* (Harmondsworth, 1969 edn); Lee, 3 Jun 1964, 21–2 Jun 1964, 29 Jun 1964, 6 Jul 1964.

6. Scott, SxMOA99/97/1/13, 18 May 1964; Toby Hadoke, 'Douglas Wilmer', *G*, 29 Apr 2016; *DT*, 19 May 1964; Larkin, Ms.Eng.c.7428, fo 34, 19 May 1964; *P*, 20 May 1964; NVLAA, Box 1, 23 May 1964; *Benn*, p. 115; Peter Shapely, 'Civic pride and redevelopment in the post-war British city', in *Urban History*, 2012 (39/2), p. 221; *T*, 28 May 1964; Roy, *The Invisible Spirit*, pp. 317–18.

7. *Buckie High School Magazine*, Jun 1964, p. 51; *G*, 22 May 1964, 27 May 1964; *ST*, 31 May 1964; *G*, 6 Jun 1964, 16 Jun 1964; Lesley Diack, 'Myths of a Beleaguered City', in *Oral History*, spring 2001, pp. 62–72; Roy, p. 316.

8. *G*, 30 May 1964; BBC WAC, *Any Questions?*, 29 May 1964, R9/7/69–VR/64/308, 30 May 1964; *DT*, 4 Jun 1964; *G*, 5 Jun 1964; *Vogue*, Jun 1964, p. 14; Ironside, 7 Jun 1964; Cann, *Any Day Now*, p. 37; *S Tel*, 7 Jun 1964; 'Val Doonican', *T*, 3 Jul 2015; *G*, 9 Jun 1964, Marks, 8 Jun 1964.

9. *G*, 29 May 2009; *Ob*, 6 Sep 1964 (Gordon Wilkins); *Wikipedia*, 'Smeed Report'; *DT*, 11 Jun 1964; *T*, 17 Nov 2020 (Philip Booth); *DT*, 11 Jun 1964.

10. *G*, 10 Jun 1964; BBC WAC, R9/7/69–VR/64/332, 10 Jun 1964; Greenslade, *Press Gang*, p. 159; BBC WAC, R9/7/69–VR/64/328, 8–12 Jun 1964; *L*, 11 Jun 1964, 16 Jul 1964; Moran, *On Roads*, pp. 174–5; *Wikipedia*, 'Morden Tower'; Lee, 16 Jun 1964; Marcus Williamson, 'Winnie Johnson', *Ind*, 22 Aug 2012.

11. 'Millie Small', *T*, 6 May 2020; *G*, 28 Mar 2019 (Adrian Chiles); BBC WAC, R9/7/69–VR/64/341, 16 Jun 1964; *ST*, 14 Jun 1964; Foot, *Immigration and Race in British Politics*, p. 46; Clifford Hill, *How Colour Prejudiced is Britain?* (1965), p. 209; papers of Richard (Dick) Etheridge (MRC), 202/S/J/3/2/50, 9 Jun 1964.

12. Archives of St Hilda's College, Oxford [CS/101/7/Ballam], Principal to Visitor, 31 Aug 1964; Morgan, *Callaghan*, pp. 188–9; Martin, P5/2J/39, 20 Jun 1964; *Williams*, p. 236; Michael Kandiah, 'Conservative Leaders, Strategy – and "Consensus"?', in Harriet Jones and Michael Kandiah (eds), *The Myth of Consensus* (Basingstoke, 1996), p. 72; *Benn*, pp. 122–3; *P*, 24 Jun 1964; Marks, 27 Jun 1964; BBC WAC, R9/7/69–VR/64/355, 27 Jun 1964; Avril Horner and Anne Rowe (eds), *Living on Paper: Letters from Iris Murdoch, 1934–1995* (2015), p. 266; Todd, *The People*, p. 242; Stuart Jeffries, 'Jean Alexander', 17 Oct 2016; Heap, Acc 2243/38/1, 29 Jun 1964; Lahr, *Prick Up Your Ears*, p. 170.

13. Kathleen Johnson (née Perry), GDP/193/1964–5, 1 Jul 1964; *G*, 28 Jun 2014 (Andrew Martin); *Vogue*, Jul 1964, p. 81; NVLAA, Box 39, early Jul 1964; Wyman, *Stone Alone*, p. 238; Bullock, *Salford 1940–1965*, p. 60; *TLS*, 8 Feb 2019 (James Campbell); *FT*, 6 Jul 1964; *G*, 7 Jul 1964; *Wikipedia*, 'The Beat Room'; Archives of St Hilda's College, Oxford [CS/101/7/Ballam], Trudi Ballam to Kathleen Major, 6 Jul 1964.

14. Wyman, *Stone Alone*, p. 241; *Ind*, 5 Apr 2014; *TLS*, 2 Dec 2005 (J. Stacey Sullivan); Tony Collins, *Rugby League in Twentieth Century Britain* (Abingdon, 2006), p. 103; *Ob*, 12 Jul 1964; *T*, 7 Jul 1964; *Liverpool Daily Post*, 11 Jul 1964; *Big Issue*, 27 Jan 2014.

15. James Lees-Milne, *A Mingled Measure* (1994), p. 77; Beaton, *The Parting Years*, p. 16; *Evening News*, 7 Jul 1964 (Michael Jeffrie).

16. *G*, 9 Jul 1964; Jeffries, 'Jean Alexander'; Wyman, *Stone Alone*, p. 239; *Wikipedia*, 'Opportunity Knocks'; St John, 68/48, 12 Jul 1964; *Independent on Sunday*, 1 Jan 1995 (Stephen Ward).

17. Hare, *The Blue Touch Paper*, pp. 67–8; *DT*, 18 Jul 1964; https://coronationstreet.fandom.com/wiki/Episode_375; *Benn*, p. 131; *G*, 17 Jul 1964; Edward Leeson, *Dusty Springfield* (2001), p. 51; *Wikipedia*, 'Radio 390'.

18. John Bloom, *It's No Sin to Make a Profit* (1971), pp. 197–8; *G*, 10 Jun 1964, 3 Jul 1964; *ST*, 14 Jun 1964 (Maurice Wiggin); *DT*, 9 Jun 1964; *DT*, 18 Jul 1964; *G*, 18 Jul 1964.

19. *Investors Chronicle*, 24 Jul 1964; T. A. B. Corley, *Domestic Electrical Appliances* (1966), pp. 103–4; *NS*, 24 Jul 1964; *T*, 22–3 Jul 1964; Bernard Levin, *The Pendulum Years* (1970), pp. 154–5; 'John Bloom', *DT*, 6 Mar 2019; 'John Bloom', *T*, 12 Mar 2019.

20. *S Tel*, 5 Jul 1964; Charles Raw, *Slater Walker* (1977), chaps 7–9.

13 ENOUGH TO BE GOING ON WITH

1. Pimlott, *Harold Wilson*, p. 264.

2. Glen O'Hara, '"Dynamic, Exciting, Thrilling Change"', in *Contemporary British History*, Sep 2006, p. 383; *TLS*, 11 May 2018 (Ann Pettifor); Andrew Gamble, *Britain in Decline* (Basingstoke, 1985 edn), p. 13; Labour Party, *The New Britain* (1964), p. 6; Harold Wilson, *The New Britain* (Harmondsworth, 1964), pp. 40–1.

3. Paul Foot, *The Politics of Harold Wilson* (Harmondsworth, 1968), p. 151; David Edgerton, 'The "White Heat" Revisited', in *Twentieth Century British History*, 1996 (7/1), p. 53; Geoffrey Goodman, *The Awkward Warrior* (1979), pp. 376–7, 384–5; *Ind*, 25 May 1995; Foot, pp. 148–9.

4. Ilaria Favretto, '"Wilsonism" Reconsidered', in *Contemporary British History*, Winter 2000, pp. 62–4; Wilson, *The New Britain*, pp. 36–7; Andrew Blick, 'Harold Wilson, Labour and the Machinery of Government', in *Contemporary British History*, Sep 2006, p. 346; Jim Tomlinson, 'Managing the economy, managing the people: Britain c. 1931–70', in *Economic History Review*, Aug 2005, p. 568; Alec Cairncross, 'Lord Roll of Ipsden', *G*, 2 Apr 2005.

5. Jim Tomlinson, *The Labour Governments 1964–70*, vol. 3: *Economic Policy* (Manchester, 2004), p. 12; Favretto, '"Wilsonism"', pp. 59–60; Tomlinson, *Labour Governments*, p. 157; Glen O'Hara, '"What the electorate can be expected to swallow"', in *Business History*, Jul 2009, pp. 509–10; Labour, *New Britain*, p. 9.

6. Jim Tomlinson, 'The Labour Party and the Capitalist Firm, c. 1950–1970', in *Historical Journal*, Sep 2004, p. 685; Favretto, '"Wilsonism"', pp. 71–3; Tomlinson, 'Capitalist Firm', p. 697; Radhika Desai, *Intellectuals and Socialism* (1994), p. 118; Favretto, pp. 68–71; Wilson, *New Britain*, p. 35; Tomlinson, 'Capitalist Firm', pp. 697–8, 707–8; Tudor Jones, 'Labour Revisionism and Public Ownership, 1951–63', in *Contemporary Record*, Winter 1991, p. 445.

7. Ilaria Favretto, *The Long Search for a Third Way* (Basingstoke, 2003), p. 92; Morgan, *Callaghan*, p. 187; David Howell, '"Shut Your Gob!"', in Alan Campbell et al., *British Trade Unions and Industrial Politics: Volume One* (Aldershot, 1999), pp. 136–7; *Benn*, p. 109; Jim Northcott, *Why Labour?* (Harmondsworth, 1964), pp. 125–6; Foot, *The Politics of Harold Wilson*, p. 143; Keith Middlemas, *Power, Competition and the State*, vol. 2 (Basingstoke, 1990), pp. 106–7.

8. Foot, *The Politics of Harold Wilson*, p. 140; *NS*, 19 Oct 2018 (Anthony Murray); Crosland, *Tony Crosland*, pp. 120–1; Tim Bale, 'Dynamics of a Non-Decision', in *Twentieth Century British History*, 1999 (10/2), pp. 197–200; Christopher McMahon, *Sterling in the Sixties* (1964), p. 51; Kynaston, *Till Time's Last Sand*, p. 457.

9. Mitchell and Wienir, *Last Time*, p. 46; Richard Marsh, *Off the Rails* (1978), p. 59; David Edgerton, *The Rise and Fall of the British Nation* (2018), pp. 383–4; Robert Skidelsky, 'Ian Little', *Ind*, 6 Aug 2012; Edmund Dell, *A Strange Eventful History* (1999), pp. 303–4.

10. Lowe, *The Welfare State in Britain Since 1945*, p. 283; Northcott, *Why Labour?*, p. 162; Amy Black and Stephen Brooke, 'The Labour Party, Women, and the Problem of Gender, 1951–1966', in *Journal of British Studies*, Oct 1997, pp. 427, 430.

11. Martin Daunton, *Just Taxes* (Cambridge, 2002), p. 285; Hugh Pemberton, 'Taxation and Labour's Modernisation Programme', in *Contemporary British History*, Sep 2006, p. 428; Labour, *New Britain*, p. 13; Pemberton, p. 427; Northcott, *Why Labour?*, p. 103; Pemberton, pp. 427, 436; Tomlinson, *Labour Governments*, pp. 205–6, 211.

12. Glennerster, *British Social Policy since 1945*, p. 96; Northcott, *Why Labour?*, pp. 42–3; Wilson, *New Britain*, p. 20; Stephen Thornton, 'A Case of Confusion and Incoherence', in *Contemporary British History*, Sep 2006, pp. 446–50.

13. *ST*, 19 Apr 1964; Northcott, *Why Labour?*, p. 74; Labour, *New Britain*, p. 14; *Ob*, 26 Jan 1964; BBC WAC, *Any Questions?*, 29 May 1964; John Thorn, *The Road to Winchester* (1989), pp. 92–3; Adrian Wooldridge, 'Reclaiming meritocracy', in *NS*, 21 May 2021.

14. Lawrence Black, *The Political Culture of the Left in Affluent Britain, 1951–1964* (Basingstoke, 2003), chap. 8; David Kynaston, 'Dual Britannia', in *FT*, 19 May 2007; BBC WAC, *Any Questions?*, 11 Sep 1964; Lowe, *The Welfare State in Britain Since 1945*, p. 295.

15. Wilson, *New Britain*, pp. 14–15; *Crossman* (1), p. 972; *Benn*, pp. 105, 109, 117; Geoffrey Goodman, *From Bevan to Blair* (2003), p. 112; *L*, 29 Oct 1964.

16. Frank Cousins papers (Modern Records Centre, University of Warwick), 282/8/3/2, 1 Oct 1963; *Ob*, 25 Oct 1964; Goodman, *Awkward Warrior*, pp. 380–1.

17. Black, *The Political Culture of the Left in Affluent Britain*, p. 194; Kevin Jefferys, *Anthony Crosland* (1999), pp. 81–2; Green and Kynaston, *Engines of Privilege*, p. 40; Saumarez Smith, *Boom Cities*, p. 123; Vaizey, *In Breach of Promise*, p. 94; Jeremy Nuttall, 'The Labour Party and the Improvement of Minds', in *Historical Journal*, Mar 2003, p. 145.

18. 'Alderman David Logan, MP', *G*, 26 Feb 1964; *Wikipedia*, 'David Logan (British politician)'; *G*, 19 Jan 1996.

19. Ralph Miliband, *Parliamentary Socialism* (1972 edn), especially introduction and chap. 10; Raphael Samuel, 'Ralph Miliband, 1924–94', in *History Workshop*, Autumn 1994, p. 266; Michael Newman, *Ralph Miliband and the Politics of the New Left* (2002), pp. 109–10; *TLS*, 18 Jun 1964.

20. Sheila Rowbotham, *Promise of a Dream* (2000), p. 64; Lin Chun, *The British New Left* (Edinburgh, 1993), pp. 18–19; *G*, 4 Feb 1974 (Terry Coleman); Daly, Ms 302/3/4, 26 Jul 1964.

21. Bryan D. Palmer, *E. P. Thompson* (1994), pp. 81–4; Daly, Ms 302/3/4, 31 Dec 1963; *NS*, 19 Mar 1999 (Edward Skidelsky); Tom Nairn, 'The English Working Class', in Robin Blackburn (ed.), *Ideology in Social Science* (1972), pp. 205–6; Daly, Ms 302/3/4, 31 Dec 1963.

22. Willmott, WLMT 1/28, loose insert.

14 SO MUCH BETTER IN OUR OWN CARAVAN

1. Martin Newell, *This Little Ziggy* (Wivenhoe, 2008 edn), pp. 1–3; *Ind*, 11 Aug 2014 (Adam Lusher); Jonathan Oates, 'Southall's Indian history in the 1960s' (draft), citing *Middlesex County Times*, 29 Aug 1964.

2. *South Wales Echo*, 18 Jul 1964; Olive Cook, *The Stansted Affair* (1967), p. 19; *DT*, 1 Jul 1964; Charlotte Mosley (ed.), *The Letters of Nancy Mitford and Evelyn Waugh* (1996), p. 493; Martin Gilbert, *'Never Despair'* (1988), p. 1354; *Evening Standard*, 20 Sep 2017 (Nick Curtis).

3. *Blackburn Times*, 31 Jul 1964; Roy, *The Invisible Spirit*, p. 322; https://news.bbc.co.uk/on_this_day (4 Sep 1964); *Ob*, 6 Dec 2015 (Kevin McKenna); *G*, 5 Jan 2008; email from Ian Jack, 24 Feb 2010; Philip Purser, 'Jack Rosenthal', *G*, 31 May 2004; Anthony Hayward, *Which Side Are You On?* (2004), pp. 36–8; 'Troy Kennedy Martin', *T*, 16 Sep 2009; Mike Appleton and Joan Bakewell, 'Rowan Ayers', *G*, 23 Jan 2008; Nostalgia Central website, 'Swizzlewick'; Doggett, *Growing Up*, p. 103; *P*, 2 Sep 1964; BBC WAC, R9/7/70–VR/64/451, 18 Aug 1964, R9/7/71–VR/64/487, 8 Sep 1964; Joe Moran, *Queuing for Beginners* (2007), p. 178.

4. *TLS*, 23 Jul 1964 (Sarah Curtis), 10 Sep 1964 (Anthony Cronin); Coe, *Like a Fiery Elephant*, p. 159; *Ob*, 9 Aug 1964; *L*, 6 Aug 1964; *S Tel*, 9 Aug 1964; *Ob*, 23 Aug 1964.

5. Heap, Acc 2243/38/1, 20 Aug 1964; Dominic Shellard, *British Theatre Since the War* (1999), p. 115; Chris Bryant, *Glenda Jackson* (1999), p. 61; *ST*, 23 Aug 1964; Michael Coveney, 'Sally Jacobs', *G*, 17 Aug 2020; Heap, Acc 2243/38/1, 9 Sep 1964; Doggett, *Growing Up*, p. 66; John Osborne, *Almost a Gentleman* (1991), p. 245; *P*, 16 Sep 1964.

6. Simonelli, *Heroes*, p. 29; Lee, 9 Aug 1964; *Wikipedia*, 'Steve Marriott'; *T*, 5 Jun 2021 (Will Hodgkinson); Dave Laing, 'Pete Quaife', *G*, 28 Jun 2010; Hinman, *The Kinks*, p. 32.

7. Chris Waters, *Fred Trueman* (2011), pp. 184–6; Roger Domeneghetti, *From the Back Page to the Front Room* (Huddersfield, 2014), p. 187; Matthew Taylor, *The Association Game* (Harlow, 2008), p. 275; John Williams, *Red Men* (Edinburgh, 2010), p. 325.

8. Bullock, *Salford, 1940–1965*, p. 60; *Littlehampton Post*, 1 Aug 1964; *Sheerness Times-Guardian*, 21 Aug 1964; *(Scarborough) Mercury*, 30 Jul 1964; Hodgson, 17 Sep 1964; *Littlehampton Gazette*, 21 Aug 1964; Wyman, *Stone Alone*, pp. 242–4; *Ind*, 28 Mar 2008 (Mark Hughes); *DM* (2), 3 Aug 1964; *Brighton & Hove Gazette*, 7 Aug 1964.

9. *Littlehampton Gazette*, 31 Jul 1964; *(Scarborough) Mercury*, 10 Sep 1964; *South Wales Echo*, 29 Aug 1964; *(Scarborough) Mercury*, 10 Sep 1964; *G*, 17 Jan 2015; Scott, SxMOA99/97/1/13, 21 Aug 1964 to 30 Aug 1964, plus 14 Sep 1964.

10. Doggett, *Growing Up*, pp. 129–38; *Queen*, 26 Aug 1964; *Vogue*, 1 Sep 1964; *Ob*, 6 Sep 1964; Doggett, p. 65; *NS*, 2 Oct 1964; *DT*, 12 Sep 1964; *S Tel*, 13 Sep 1964; *ST*, 13 Sep 1964; *Ob*, 13 Sep 1964; Archives of St Hilda's College, Oxford [CS/1017/Ballam], 12 Sep 1964.

11. Goodman, *From Bevan to Blair*, p. 104; *G*, 15 Aug 1964; Abrams, ABMS 5/40, undated.

12. Goodman, *From Bevan to Blair*, pp. 104–5; *G*, 9 Sep 2004; Huw Richards, *The Bloody Circus* (1997), pp. 181–2; *Sun*, 15 Sep 1964.

15 IT DOESN'T MAKE ANY DIFFERENCE

1. *Birmingham Evening Mail*, 11 Sep 1964; Robert Harris, *Good and Faithful Servant* (1990), pp. 36–7; Lee, 26 Aug 1964; Howard and West, *The Making of the Prime Minister*, pp. 143–4; Labour Party, *The New Britain* (1964), p. 24; Howard and West, p. 142; Davenport-Hines, *An English Affair*, pp. xii–xiv.

2. Email from David Warren, 10 Feb 2022; Howard and West, *The Making of the Prime Minister*, pp. 153–5; Larkin, Ms.Eng.c.7428, fo 118, 15 Sep 1964.

3. *Billericay Times*, 16 Sep 1964; *Hertfordshire Express*, 18 Sep 1964; Larkin, Ms.Eng.c.7428, fo 121, 17 Sep 1964; *P*, 30 Sep 1964; *Spec*, 18 Sep 1964; Heap, Acc 2243/38/1, 18 Sep 1964; D. E. Butler and Anthony King, *The British General Election of 1964* (1965), pp. 111–12; *NS*, 2 Oct 1964; *Skegness Standard*, 16 Sep 1964; *Solihull News*, 26 Sep 1964; Jackson, 43D78/56, 19 Sep 1964; Last, SxMOA1/4/302, 19 Sep 1964; Charles Reid, *Malcolm Sargent* (1968), p. 444; *Ob*, 20 Sep 1964.

4. BBC WAC, R9/7/71–VR/64/518, 21 Sep 1964; *NS*, 2 Oct 1964; *Bonham Carter*, p. 291; Howard and West, *The Making of the Prime Minister*, pp. 159–61; Nicola Beauman, *The Other Elizabeth Taylor* (2009), p. 339; *Halifax Weekly Courier*, 25 Sep 1964; BBC WAC, *Any Questions?*, 25 Sep 1964; Lewisohn, *Radio Times Guide to TV Comedy*, p. 524; Last, SxMOA1/4/302, 25 Sep 1964; BBC WAC, R9/7/71–VR/64/527, 26 Sep 1964; *NS*, 2 Oct 1964; Preston, 6D87/6, 26 Sep 1964; Wyman, *Stone Alone*, p. 260; *S Tel*, 27 Sep 1964.

5. *DM* (2), 28 Sep 1964; *FT*, 29 Sep 1964; *Billericay Times*, 30 Sep 1964; Anthony Hayward, 'Edward Barnes', *G*, 15 Sep 2021; *NS*, 2 Oct 1964; *Birmingham Evening Mail*, 29 Sep 1964; *South Wales Echo*, 29 Sep 1964; Steve Race, *Musician at Large* (1979), p. 159; Butler and King, *The British General Election of 1964*, p. 115; Howard and West, pp. 175–6; Butler and King, p. 116; *Orpington & Kentish Times*, 2 Oct 1964; Hampton (ed.), *Joyce & Ginnie*, p. 317; *DT*, 1 Oct 1964; Duncan Hamilton, *Immortal* (2013), pp. 83–5.

6. Daphne Meryon, GDP/44/1964, 1 Oct 1964; St John, 68/49, 1 Oct 1964; Martin, P5/2J/39, 1 Oct 1964; Willmott, WLMT 1/30, 1 Oct 1964; *Benn*, p. 148; Kynaston, *Till Time's Last Sand*, pp. 456–7; Howard and West, *The British General Election of 1964*, p. 180; *Edinburgh Evening News*, 2 Oct 1964.

7. Roy Greenslade, *Press Gang* (2003), pp. 236–7; *FT*, 2 Oct 1964; Butler and King, *The British General Election of 1964*, pp. 117–18; *Benn*, p. 148; *NS*, 9 Oct 1964; *Hertfordshire Express*, 9 Oct 1964; Butler and King, p. 118; *Benn*, p. 149; Frederick Ward, GDP/145/1964, 4 Oct 1964; Mojo, *Days of Beatlemania*, p. 132 (Lois Wilson); Last, SxMOA1/4/303, 4 Oct 1964; Eamonn and Gráinne Andrews, *For Ever and Ever, Eamonn* (1989), p. 306; *P*, 21 Oct 1964; Daphne Meryon, GDP/44/1964, 5 Oct

1964; *Spec*, 9 Oct 1964 (J. W. M. Thompson); Butler and King, pp. 118–19, 234, 237.

8. Roy, *The Invisible Spirit*, p. 323; *Birmingham Evening Mail*, 10 Sep 1964; Lewis Chester et al., *Jeremy Thorpe* (1979), pp. 61–2; *Halifax Weekly Courier*, 9 Oct 1964; Anthony Seldon, *Major* (1997), p. 21; John Preston, *Fall* (2021), p. 56; *South Wales Echo*, 13 Oct 1964; John Prescott, *Prezza* (2008), pp. 73–4; *Ob*, 11 Oct 1964 (John Crosby); *Wikipedia*, 'John Smith'; Daly, Ms 302/3/4, press statement, 12 Oct 1964; Butler and King, *The British General Election of 1964*, p. 244 (Bernard Donoughue); *Hertfordshire Express*, 9 Oct 1964; Butler and King, pp. 159–60; Patrick Cosgrave, 'Reginald Bevins', *Ind*, 19 Nov 1996; *Orpington & Kentish Times*, 9 Oct 1964; *T*, 6 Oct 1964; Baker, *The Turbulent Years*, p. 23; *T*, 12 Nov 2019; Coe, *Like a Fiery Elephant*, pp. 173–4; *G*, 18 Sep 1964; Roy, p. 323; Cook, *The Stansted Affair*, p. 27; David Owen, *Time to Declare* (1991), p. 74.

9. *NS*, 9 Oct 1964; Butler and King, *The British General Election of 1964*, p. 120; Roy Hattersley, *Who Goes Home?* (1995), pp. 42–4; Howard and West, *The British General Election of 1964*, pp. 188–9; Foot, *Immigration and Race in British Politics*, p. 148.

10. *Smethwick Telephone*, 4 Sep 1964; *Birmingham Evening Mail*, 16 Sep 1964; *Smethwick Telephone*, 2 Oct 1964; Foot, *Immigration and Race in British Politics*, p. 48; *Birmingham Evening Mail*, 6 Oct 1964, 12 Oct 1964; *T*, 13 Oct 1964.

11. Foot, *Immigration and Race in British Politics*, p. 145; Butler and King, *The British General Election of 1964*, p. 366; Fenner Brockway, *Towards Tomorrow* (1977), p. 234; Dennis Dean, 'The Race Relations Policy of the First Wilson Government', in *Twentieth Century British History*, 2000 (11/3), p. 264; *Spec*, 28 Aug 1964 (David Watt); Foot, *Immigration and Race in British Politics*, pp. 146–7; Howard and West, *The British General Election of 1964*, p. 157; Shepherd, *Enoch Powell*, p. 277; *Birmingham Evening Mail*, 9 Oct 1964, 12 Oct 1964.

12. A. C. H. Smith, *Paper Voices* (1975), p. 191; *Hertfordshire Express*, 9 Oct 1964; *Billericay Times*, 7 Oct 1964; BBC WAC, R9/7/71–VR/64/541, 7 Oct 1964; *G*, 29 Sep 2004; Darlington, 7 Oct 1964; *DT*, 8 Oct 1964; *Benn*, p. 152; *Fowles*, p. 617.

13. Larkin, Ms.Eng.c.7429, fo 2, 8 Oct 1964; Davenport-Hines, *An English Affair*, p. 338; Hattersley, *Who Goes Home?*, pp. 40–1; Pimlott, *Harold Wilson*, pp. 313–14; Butler and King, *The British General Election of 1964*, pp. 122–3; Campbell, *Edward Heath*, p. 162; *The Economist*, 10 Oct 1964; *Liverpool Echo*, 9 Oct 1964; *FT*, 10 Oct 1964.

14. *(Brighton) Evening Argus*, 9 Oct 1964; *RT*, 1 Oct 1964; *NME*, 16 Oct 1964; *Halifax Weekly Courier*, 16 Oct 1964; Howard and West, *The British General Election of 1964*, pp. 199, 202–4; Larkin, Ms.Eng.c.7429, fo 5, 10 Oct 1964; Archives of St Hilda's College, Oxford [CS/101/7/Ballam], 10 Oct 1964; Haines, SxMOA99/34/8/17, 10 Oct 1964; Howard and West, p. 206; Hampton (ed.), *Joyce & Ginnie*, p. 318; Last, SxMOA1/4/303, 11 Oct 1964; Haines, SxMOA99/34/8/17, 11 Oct 1964.

15. *Liverpool Echo*, 12 Oct 1964; *Williams*, p. 241; *Spec*, 16 Oct 1964; Butler and King, *The British General Election of 1964*, pp. 208–9; *FT*, 14 Oct 1964; Jeremy Lewis, *Shades of Greene* (2010), p. 440; Martin, P5/2J/39, 13 Oct 1964; BBC WAC, R9/7/71–VR/64/548, 13 Oct 1964; *Spec*, 16 Oct 1964; Douglas Jay, *Change and Fortune* (1980), pp. 295–6; Hampton (ed.), *Joyce & Ginnie*, p. 319.

16. Philip Ziegler, *Wilson* (1993), p. 160; Last, SxMOA1/4/303, 14 Oct 1964; Goodman, *Awkward Warrior*, p. 393; Pimlott, *Harold Wilson*, p. 317; *Liverpool Echo*, 15 Oct 1964; Pimlott, p. 317; *Slough Observer*, 15 Oct 1964; *Hertfordshire Express*, 16 Oct 1964; https://www.jeffreymaynard.com/Harrow_County/Election1964-RSBuckley.htm; Rosa Prince, *Comrade Corbyn* (2016), p. 28; Marks, 16 Oct 1964; Harriet Harman, *A Woman's Work* (2017), p. 5; Hare, *The Blue Touch Paper*, p. 72; Christopher Hitchens, *Hitch-22* (2010), pp. 78–9; *Brandreth*, pp. 73–4.

17. Butler and King, *The British General Election of 1964*, p. 208; *DM* (1), 15 Oct 1964; *L*, 15 Oct 1964; *Liverpool Echo*, 15 Oct 1964; Butler and King, p. 289; Stephen Chalke, *Tom Cartwright* (Bath, 2007), p. 111; Daphne Meryon, GDP/44/1964, 15 Oct 1964; Last, SxMOA1/4/303, 15 Oct 1964; Betty Allen, GDP/450/1963–1967, 15 Oct 1964; Martin, P5/2J/39, 15 Oct 1964; Preston, 6D/87/6, 15 Oct 1964; *Williams*, p. 242; Haines, SxMOA99/34/8/17, 15 Oct 1964; Grace Taylor, GDP/ 318/1964, 15 Oct 1964; Scott, SxMOA99/97/1/13, 15 Oct 1964; Brown, *One Two Three Four*, pp. 261–3; Hinman, *The Kinks*, p. 38; Elizabeth Wilson, *Jacqueline du Pré* (1998), p. 136; Cockerell, *Live from Number 10*, pp. 107–8.

18. Butler and King, *The British General Election of 1964*, pp. 129–41; David Butler and Donald Stokes, *Political Change in Britain* (1969), pp. 449, 175–8, 207.

19. David Denver, 'The 1964 General Election', in *Contemporary British History*, Sep 2007, pp. 296–300; Butler and Stokes, *Political Change in Britain*, pp. 390–1; Martin Harrison, 'Television and Radio', in Butler and King, *The British General Election of 1964*, p. 156; *FT*, 14 Mar 1992 (David Butler); *NS*, 18 Sep 1964; *Liverpool Echo*, 10 Oct 1964; Harrison, pp. 161–81, 184; *L*, 29 Oct 1964.

20. *Huddersfield Weekly Examiner*, 10 Oct 1964; Harrison, in Butler and King, *The British General Election of* 1964, p. 81; Butler and King, *The British General Election of 1964*, p. 342 (Michael Steed); *Spec*, 16 Oct 1964; *Aldershot News*, 9 Oct 1964; *Roy, The Invisible Spirit*, p. 324; Hattersley, *Who Goes Home?*, p. 45; *Preston Herald*, 9 Oct 1964; Heap, Acc 2243/38/1, 9 Oct 1964; *New Soc*, 15 Nov 1964; Vanessa Redgrave, *An Autobiography* (1991), p. 120.

21. *Ob*, 18 Oct 1964. From here, most of the rest of the chapter is based on YouTube's nine-part, near-complete videos of the BBC TV election coverage on 15/16 Oct 1964.

22. Last, SxMOA14/303, 16 Oct 1964.

23. Jefferys, *Retreat from New Jerusalem*, p. 190; *Spec*, 16 Oct 1964; McManus, *Jo Grimond*, p. 209; Steven Fielding, 'Rethinking Labour's 1964 Campaign', in *Contemporary British History*, Sep 2007, pp. 318–19; Tariq Ali, *Street Fighting Years* (2005 edn), p. 100.

24. *DT*, 17 Oct 1964 (L. Marsland Gander).

16 CAN I HELP YOU?

1. BBC WAC, *Any Questions?*, 16 Oct 1964; *RT*, 8 Oct 1964; BBC WAC, R9/7/71–VR/64/550, 16 Oct 1964; 'Kathy Kirby', *T*, 21 May 2011; Betty Allen, GDP/450/1963–1967, 16 Oct 1964; Hague, 16 Oct 1964; Martin, P5/2J/39, 16 Oct 1964; Daphne Meryon, GDP/44/1964, 16 Oct 1964; Denis Judd (ed.), *The Private Diaries of Alison Uttley* (Barnsley, 2009), 16 Oct 1964.

2. Baston, *Reggie*, p. 237; Edward Short, *Whip to Wilson* (1989), p. 37; Jay, *Change and Fortune*, p. 298. For two detailed historical analyses, both broadly on the Jay side of the argument, see: Tim Bale, 'Dynamics of a Non-Decision', in *Twentieth Century British History*, 1999 (10/2), pp. 192–217; Scott Newton, 'The two sterling crises of 1964 and the decision not to devalue', in *Economic History Review*, Feb 2009, pp. 73–98.

3. Last, SxMOA1/4/303, 17 Oct 1964; Heap, Acc 2234/38/1, 17 Oct 1964; Tom Vallance, 'John Thaw', *Ind*, 23 Feb 2002; BBC WAC, R9/7/71–VR/64/552, 17 Oct 1964; *Williams*, p. 242.

4. Heffer, *Like the Roman*, p. 364; *Amis*, p. 655; *Benn*, p. 163; Haines, SxMOA99/34/8/17, 20 Oct 1964; *Benn*, p. 169; Lee, 21 Oct 1964; Bob Stanley, *Yeah Yeah Yeah* (2013), p. 212; Heap, Acc 2234/38/1, 23 Oct 1964; *G*, 26 Oct 1964.

5. *Forres, Elgin & Nairn Gazette*, 28 Oct 1964; *G*, 29 Oct 1964; BBC WAC, R9/7/71–VR/64/571, 28 Oct 1964; Barrow, *Gossip*, p. 240; Carpenter, *Satire*, pp. 291–2; *DT*, 31 Oct 1964; Kathleen Johnson (née Perry), GDP/193/1964–5, 30 Oct 1964; Abrams, ABMS 5/40, part 1 of 2, 7 Nov 1964 (Hugh Holker); Wyman, *Stone Alone*, p. 274; Elizabeth Thomson and David Gutman (eds), *The Bowie Companion* (1993), p. 12.

6. *Birmingham Evening Mail*, 2 Nov 1964; *DT*, 2 Nov 1964; Anthony Hayward, 'Peter Ling', *Ind*, 27 Sep 2006; *Jane Rossington, The Crossroads Years* (1988), p. 4; www.crossroadsmotel.co.uk/fanclub/1964-nov-dec; *Birmingham Evening Mail*, 3 Nov 1964.

7. Heffer, *Like the Roman*, pp. 364–5; *Smethwick Telephone*, 23 Oct 1964; Foot, *Immigration and Race in British Politics*, pp. 65–6; *DM* (1), 6 Nov 1964; Wybrow, *Britain Speaks Out, 1937–87*, p. 73; *Birmingham Evening Mail*, 10 Nov 1964, 16 Nov 1964.

8. Preston, *Fall*, pp. 53–4; Larkin, Ms.Eng.c.7429, fo 27, 7 Nov 1964; *Bideford & North Devon Gazette*, 6 Nov 1964; BBC WAC, *Any Questions?*, 6 Nov 1964; *DM* (1), 9 Nov 1964; Rob Bagchi and Paul Rogerson, *The Unforgiven* (2002), pp. 85–6; Brian Holland et al., 'Sport and Racism in Yorkshire', in Jeff Hill and Jack Williams (eds), *Sport and Identity in the North of England* (Keele, 1996), p. 171.

9. Adam Kirsch (ed.), *Life in Culture* (New York, 2018), p. 350; *DM* (1), 11 Nov 1964; *Benn*, p. 184; Cann, *Any Day Now*, pp. 43–4; *The Pillow Book of Eleanor Bron* (1985), p. 33; BBC WAC, R9/7/72–VR/64/603, 13 Nov 1964, VR/64/606, 14 Nov 1964, VR/64/608, 15 Nov 1964; *DM* (1), 16 Nov 1964; *NS*, 20 Nov 1964; *P*, 25 Nov 1964; Carpenter, *Satire*, p. 295; *Pillow Book*, p. 33; Larkin, Ms.Eng.c.7429, fo 38, 15 Nov 1964.

10. *DM* (1), 17 Nov 1964; *DT*, 27 Jul 1964; Dennis Dean, 'The Race Relations Policy of the First Wilson Government', in *Twentieth Century British History*, 2000 (11/3), p. 266; BBC WAC, R9/74/2, Dec 1964 (No. 195); *P*, 25 Nov 1964; *G*, 18 Nov 1964; BBC WAC, R9/7/72–VR/64/615, 18 Nov 1964; *NME*, 21 Nov 1964; Heap, Acc 2234/38/1, 21 Nov 1964; *G*, 18 Jul 2015.

11. Kynaston, *City*, vol. 4, pp. 299–300; Morgan, *Callaghan*, p. 215; Willmott, WLMT 1/30, 11 Nov 1964; Kynaston, *City*, pp. 300–1; Angela Potter (ed.), *Shared Histories* (Athens, Georgia, 2006), p. 326.

12. Kynaston, *City*, pp. 301–3; *FT*, 24 Nov 1964; Kynaston, *Till Time's Last Sand*, pp. 459–61; Bank of England Archive, OV44/123, 3 Dec 1964; Kynaston, *City*, pp. 307–8.

13. Frederic Spotts (ed.), *Letters of Leonard Woolf* (1990), p. 452; Lee, 26 Nov 1964; *DM* (1), 27–8 Nov 1964; *Fowles*, pp. 622–3; Hodgson, End of the Year, 1964; *P*, 2 Dec 1964; *G*, 3 Dec 1964; Stuart Laing, 'Banging in

Some Reality', in John Corner (ed.), *Popular Television in Britain* (1991), p. 135; BBC WAC, R9/7/72–VR/64/646, 3 Dec 1964.

14. *G*, 20 Feb 2019 (Tariq Ali); Saladin Ambar, *Malcolm X at Oxford Union* (Oxford, 2014), pp. 177, 180, 144; *G*, 20 Feb 2019 (Ali), 3 Dec 2014 (Hugh Muir); Robin Bunce and Paul Field, *Darcus Howe* (2014), p. 25; *G*, 3 Dec 2014.

15. *Williams*, pp. 244–5; *Huddersfield Weekly Examiner*, 12 Dec 1964; *G*, 11 Dec 1964; Daphne Meryon, GDP/44/1964, 10 Dec 1964; BBC WAC, R9/7/72–VR/64/661, 10 Dec 1964; *Daily Express*, 11 Dec 1964; *Spec*, 11 Dec 1964; Ashok Chudasama, 'Experiences of an Immigrant in Blackburn', in Alan Duckworth (ed.), *Aspects of Blackburn* (Barnsley, 1999), p. 112; Ironside, letter to Robin Grove-White, 14 Dec 1964.

16. Haines, SxMOA99/34/8/17, 13 Dec 1964; Hodgson, 24 Nov 1964; *G*, 9 Jul 2005; *ST*, 20 Dec 1964; BBC WAC, R9/7/72–VR/64/670, 15 Dec 1964; Bevis Hillier, *Betjeman: The Bonus of Laughter* (2004), p. 192; *L*, 7 Jan 1965; *RT*, 10 Dec 1964; BBC WAC, R9/7/72–VR/64/664, 16 Dec 1964; *ST*, 20 Dec 1964.

17. Alwyn W. Turner, *The Man Who Invented The Daleks* (2011), pp. 98–9; St John, 68/49, 17 Dec 1964; *G*, 19 Dec 1964; Heap, Acc 2234/38/1, 20 Dec 1964; David Lister, *In the Best Possible Taste* (1996), pp. 42–7; Haines, SxMOA99/34/8/17, 25 Dec 1964; Lewisohn, *Radio Times Guide to TV Comedy*, p. 470; Coe, *Like a Fiery Elephant*, pp. 22, 230; Patrick French, *The World Is What It Is* (2008), p. 242; *DT*, 28 Dec 1964; *Lancashire Evening Telegraph*, 31 Dec 1964; *Amis*, p. 658; Vaughan, *Journals, 1939–1977*, p. 146.

18. *T*, 22 Dec 1964; Reeves, *Alice in Westminster*, pp. 127–8; *Benn*, p. 198; Marks, 22 Dec 1964; Lee, *One of Your Own*, pp. 166–76; 'John Stalker', *T*, 18 Feb 2019; Liz Homans, 'Swinging Sixties', in *History Today*, Dec 2008, p. 48.

19. *S Tel*, 3 Jan 1965; Richard Griffiths, 'John Rickman', *Ind*, 18 Oct 1997; 'Kent Walton', *DT*, 28 Aug 2003; 'Jackie Pallo', *T*, 16 Feb 2006; *Wikipedia*, 'Kendo Nagasaki'; 'Wrestling's Golden Age', BBC Four, 13 Dec 2012; *G*, 4 Jan 1965; Heap, Acc 2234/39/1, 4 Jan 1965; *G*, 5 Jan 1965; Hayward, *Which Side Are You On?*, pp. 46–7; *DT*, 7 Jan 1965; BBC WAC, R9/10/12–VR/65/31, Jan 1965; ITC Archives, 3995709/3001/20, Feb 1965.

20. *L*, 7 Jan 1965; *G*, 8 Jan 1965; Spencer Leigh, 'Johnny Stewart', *Ind*, 4 May 2005; BBC WAC, R9/7/73–VR/65/14, 9 Jan 1965; Haines, SxMOA99/34/8/18, 9 Jan 1965; *S Tel*, 10 Jan 1965; BBC WAC, R9/7/73–VR/65/15, 9 Jan 1965, R9/74/2, Feb 1965 (No. 197); Harry Thompson, 'Dudley Moore', *Ind*, 29 Mar 2002.

21. *Ob*, 10 Jan 1965; Leila Berg, *Risinghill* (Harmondsworth, 1968), pp. 173–6; *NS*, 15 Jan 1965; *NME*, 15 Jan 1965; Barrow, p. 243; Hugo Vickers (ed.), *Beaton in the Sixties* (2003), p. 13; BBC WAC, R9/7/73–VR/65/95, 20 Jan 1965; *Beaton*, p. 15.

22. *G*, 8 Jan 1965; Healey, *The Time of My Life*, p. 297; *G*, 13–14 Jana 1965; *Spec*, 15 Jan 1965; *ST*, 17 Jan 1965; *G*, 21–2 Jan 1965; Willmott, WLMT 1/30, 22 Jan 1965; Abrams, ABMS 2/4/11, part 3 of 4, handwritten report, 'What Happened at Leyton'; *ST*, 24 Jan 1965; *G*, 16 Jan 1965.

17 A TREMENDOUS FERMENT AT THE LOWER LEVELS

1. *G*, 2 Jan 1965, 4 Jan 1965; Richard Hart, *The Vauxhall Story* (Leighton Buzzard, 2002 edn), p. 119; *DT*, 8 Jan 1965; *G*, 11–12 Jan 1965, 14 Jan 1965; *East London Advertiser*, 15 Jan 1965; *G*, 20 Jan 1965; *ST*, 24 Jan 1965.

2. *DT*, 17 Dec 1964; *T*, 17 Dec 1964; *G*, 7 Jan 1965; *T*, 17 Dec 1964; *DT*, 17 Dec 1964; *G*, 17 Dec 1964.

3. Chris Wrigley, 'Trade union development, 1945–79', in Chris Wrigley (ed.), *A History of British Industrial Relations, 1939–1979* (Cheltenham, 1996), pp. 62–7; H. A. Clegg, *The System of Industrial Relations in Great Britain* (Oxford, 1976 edn), p. 65; *G*, 7 Jan 1965.

4. Peter Jenkins, *The Battle of Downing Street* (1970), p. ix; *G*, 19 Jan 1965; Robert Taylor, *The TUC* (Basingstoke, 2000), pp. 143–50; Jenkins, p. 14.

5. BBC WAC, *Any Questions?*, 24 May 1963; Sampson, *Anatomy of Britain Today*, p. 596; 'Lord Hill of Wivenhoe', *T*, 15 Dec 1969; *G*, 16 Dec 1969.

6. 'Lord Carron', *G*, 5 Dec 1969; Sampson, p. 602; 'Lord Carron', *DT*, 5 Dec 1969; *Ob*, 13 Dec 1964; Robert Taylor, *The Fifth Estate* (1980 edn), pp. 321–2.

7. Sampson, *Anatomy of Britain Today*, p. 604; 'Mr Will Paynter', *T*, 13 Dec 1984; Lord Robens, *Ten Year Stint* (1972), pp. 280–1, 17–18, 281–2; Sampson, p. 604.

8. Geoffrey Goodman, 'Lord Briginshaw', *Ind*, 31 Mar 1992; 'Lord Briginshaw', *DT*, 28 Mar 1992; 'Lord Briginshaw', *T*, 28 Mar 1992; Seumas Milne, 'Lord Briginshaw', *G*, 28 Mar 1992; *Ob*, 14 Jun 1964; Goodman, 'Briginshaw'.

9. Geoffrey Goodman, 'Lord Greene of Harrow Weald', *G*, 28 Jul 2004; Tam Dalyell, 'Lord Greene of Harrow Weald', *Ind*, 28 Jul 2004; Sampson, *Anatomy of Britain Today*, p. 605.

10. 'Jack Jones', *T*, 23 Apr 2009; Geoffrey Goodman, 'Jack Jones', *G*, 23 Apr 2009. See also: Jack Jones, *Union Man* (1986).

11. 'Lord Scanlon', *DT*, 28 Jan 2004; Jenkins, *Battle*, p. 126; 'Lord Scanlon', *T*, 28 Jan 2004.

12. Terry Pattinson, 'Lord Gormley', *Ind*, 28 May 1993; Keith Harper and James Fairhurst, 'Joe Gormley', *G*, 28 May 1993; 'Lord Gormley', *T*, 28 May 1993. See also: Joe Gormley, *Battered Cherub* (1982).

13. 'Lord Chapple', *T*, 21 Oct 2004; *G*, 30 Oct 1971 (John Torode); Geoffrey Goodman, 'Lord Chapple', *G*, 22 Oct 2004.

14. Keith Harper, 'Clive Jenkins', *G*, 23 Sep 1999; 'Clive Jenkins', *T*, 23 Sep 1999; Terry Pattinson, 'Clive Jenkins', *Ind*, 23 Sep 1999; Chris Wrigley, 'From ASSET to ASTMS', in *Historical Studies in Industrial Relations*, spring 1999, pp. 55–74; Sampson, *Anatomy of Britain Today*, p. 606. See also: Clive Jenkins, *All Against the Collar* (1990).

15. Howard F. Gospel, 'The management of labour', in Wrigley, *Industrial Relations*, pp. 89–90; Alan Campbell, Nina Fishman and John McIlroy, 'The Post-War Compromise', in Alan Campbell, Nina Fishman and John McIlroy (eds), *British Trade Unions and Industrial Politics*, vol. 1 (Aldershot, 1999), p. 105; Clegg, *System*, pp. 316–17; Stephen Fay, *Measure for Measure* (1970), p. 79.

16. Peter Ackers and Jonathan Payne, 'Before the Storm', in *Social History*, May 2002, p. 203; Clegg, *System*, p. 325; Campbell, *British Trade Unions*: vol. 1, p. 105; Ackers and Payne, 'Storm', p. 198; William Ashworth, *The History of the British Coal Industry*, vol. 5 (Oxford, 1986), p. 297; Eric Wigham, *What's Wrong with the Unions?* (Harmondsworth, 1961), p. 159; Peter Ackers and Jonathan Payne, '"Through a Glass Darkly"', in *Labour History Review*, Spring 2000, pp. 74–6, 80–1; W. H. Scott et al., *Coal and Conflict* (Liverpool, 1963), p. 173.

17. *Ind*, 11 Apr 1989; *G*, 7 Dec 1964; David F. Wilson, *Dockers* (1972), pp. 172–3; Peter Turnbull, 'Dock strikes and the demise of the dockers' "occupational culture"', in *Sociological Review*, May 1992, p. 301; Jim Phillips, 'Decasualization and disruption', in Wrigley, *Industrial Relations*, p. 182; 'Tim O'Leary', *T*, 25 Feb 1991; *S Tel*, 10 Jan 1965 (Peter Paterson); *Ind*, 11 Apr 1989; Christopher Driver, 'Jack Dash', *G*, 9 Jun 1989; Turnbull, p. 302.

18. Graham Turner, *The Car Makers* (Harmondsworth, 1964), p. 79; Jack Saunders, *Assembling Cultures* (Manchester, 2019), pp. 4–5, chaps 2–3.

19. Campbell et al., 'Post-War Compromise', pp. 93–4; Saunders, *Assembling Cultures*, p. 133; Ken Grainger, 'Management Control and Labour Quiescence', in Michael Terry and P. K. Edwards (eds), *Shopfloor Politics and Job Controls* (Oxford, 1988), pp. 97–8, 106.

20. Nancy Seear, 'The Position of Women in Industry', in Royal Commission on Trade Unions and Employers' Associations, *Research Papers 11* (1968), p. 19; Chris Wrigley, 'Women in the Labour Market and in the Unions', in John McIlroy et al. (eds), *British Trade Unions and Industrial Politics*, vol. 2 (Aldershot, 1999), pp. 43–5; Grainger, p. 99; Saunders, *Assembling Cultures*, p. 123; Katrina Honeyman, *Well Suited* (Oxford, 2000), pp. 172–4, 188–92.

21. Papers of Richard ('Dick') Etheridge (MRC), 202/S /J/3/2/51, circa 14 Jul 1964; Kenneth Roberts, *The Working Class* (1978), p. 140; Richard Whiting, 'Affluence and Industrial Relations in Post-War Britain', in *Contemporary British History*, Dec 2008, p. 522.

22. Eric Hobsbawm, 'Afterword', in Campbell et al., *British Trade Unions*, vol. 1, p. 313; John McIlroy, ' "Every factory our fortress" ', in *Historical Studies in Industrial Relations*, Autumn 2001, pp. 98, 101–2; *The Economist*, 11 Nov 2017 ('All out'); McIlroy, 'Every factory', pp. 83–4.

23. John McIlroy and Alan Campbell, 'The High Tide of Trade Unionism', in McIlroy et al., *British Trade Unions*, vol. 2, p. 103; Robert Taylor, 'The trade union "problem" in the Age of Consensus, 1960–1979', in Ben Pimlott and Chris Cook, *Trade Unions in British Politics* (Harlow, 1991 edn), p. 182; Dell, *A Strange Eventful History*, p. 369; Archives of Federal Reserve Bank of New York, Box 615845, 15 Jan 1965; Abrams, ABMS/6/, part 2 of 7, 'Is There a Working Class?'; Wybrow, *Britain Speaks Out, 1937–87*, p. 160.

24. Tony Topham, 'Alan Fox', *G*, 6 Aug 2002; Jim Phillips, 'Industrial Relations, Historical Contingencies and Political Economy', in *Labour History Review*, Dec 2007, p. 219; Alan Fox, *A Very Late Development* (Warwick, 1990), pp. 228–9; Harold Perkin, *The Rise of Professional Society* (2002 edn), pp. 464–6.

18 A FEELING OF PRIDE

1. Willmott, WLMT 1/30, 22 Jan 1965; Goodman, *Awkward Warrior*, p. 428; St John, 68/49, 24 Jan 1965; Darlington, 24 Jan 1965; Alan Macfarlane, *Oxford Postgraduate, 1963–1966* (n.d.), p. 138; Lee, 24 Jan 1965; Preston, fo 1402, 24 Jan 1965; Last, SxMOA1/4/306, 24 Jan 1965; Booth (ed.), Philip Larkin, *Letters Home*, p. 395.

2. *Spec*, 29 Jan 1965 (Christopher Booker); Paul Boyle (ed.), *Cassandra at His Finest and Funniest* (1967), p. 131; *NS*, 29 Jan 1965 (Francis

Williams); Martin Gilbert, *'Never Despair'* (1988), pp. 1360–1; Larkin, Ms.Eng.c. 7429, fo 90, 25 Jan 1965; Langford, 25 Jan 1965; *NS*, 5 Feb 1965 (John Holmstrom); Pollard, *Pamela Hansford Johnson*, p. 355; Gilbert, p. 1361; Marks, 28 Jan 1965.

3. Kenneth More, *More or Less* (1978), p. 202; *G*, 28 Jan 1965; Meic Stephens, 'R. M. Lockley', *Ind*, 17 Apr 2000; *TLS*, 28 Jan 1965; *NS*, 29 Jan 1965; *East London Advertiser*, 15 Jan 1965.

4. Jonathan Dimbleby, *Richard Dimbleby* (1975), p. 386; Geoffrey Wheatcroft, *Churchill's Shadow* (2021), pp. 416–17, 420; *East London Advertiser*, 5 Feb 1965; *NS*, 30 Jan 2015 (Rachel Cooke); *Ind*, 4 Feb 2005 (Raymond Fischer); Dimbleby, p. 387.

5. Vickers (ed.), *Beaton in the Sixties*, pp. 17–18; *Brandreth*, p. 80; Haines, SxMOA99/34/8/18, 30 Jan 1965; Heap, Acc 2234/39/1, 30 Jan 1965; Last, SxMOA1/4/306, 30 Jan 1965; Judd (ed.), *The Private Diaries of Alison Uttley*, p. 272; *Williams*, p. 250; Willmott, WLMT 1/30, 30 Jan 1965; Larkin, Ms.Eng.c.7429, fo 103, 30 Jan 1965; Lee, 30 Jan 1965; Macfarlane, *Oxford Postgraduate*, p. 143.

6. *Evening News*, 30 Jan 1965; *Ob*, 31 Jan 1965; Wendy Webster, *Englishness and Empire, 1939–1965* (Oxford, 2005), p. 217; Preston, 6D87/6, 30 Jan 1965.

7. Marks, 30 Jan 1965; *Sun*, 1 Feb 1965 (Alan Dick); Darlington, 1 Feb 1965; *Cambridge News*, 2 Feb 1965, 5 Feb 1965; *G*, 3 Feb 1965; Hodgson, 2 Feb 1965; *G*, 4 Feb 1965; Humphrey Carpenter, *A Serious Character* (1988), p. 887; *Sun*, 5 Feb 1965.

8. *Crossman* (2), p. 151; *Sun*, 8 Feb 1965; *(Stoke) Evening Sentinel*, 6 Feb 1965; *Stoke on Trent City Times*, 10 Feb 1965; Ivan Ponting, 'Sir Stanley Matthews', *Ind*, 25 Feb 2000.

Acknowledgements

The following kindly gave permission to reproduce copyright material: Roger Darlington; Pamela Hendicott (Judy Haines); Sue Lowndes (Vere Hodgson); Veronica Porter; Wandsworth Libraries & Heritage Service (William Halle); Alison Light (The Estate of Raphael Samuel); Laurence Marks; Duncan Marlor (May Marlor); Nelofer Pazira (Robert Fisk, author and journalist); Diana Griffith; Ferdinand Mount; Celia Kent; Virginia Ironside; Martin Phillips; Josh Benn (The Estate of Tony Benn); Islington Local History Centre (Gladys Langford); Special Collections, Albert Sloman Library, University of Essex (Brian Jackson Collection; Dennis Marsden Collection; National Viewers' and Listeners' Association Archive; The Affluent Worker Collection); Ruth Walton (Betty Allen); Michael Chaplin (Sid Chaplin); Evelyn Abrams (Mark Abrams); Robin Raynham (Marian Raynham); BBC Written Archives Centre (BBC copyright content reproduced courtesy of the British Broadcasting Corporation; all rights reserved); Michael and Lewis Willmott (Phyllis Willmott); Fred Ward (Frederick Ward); Judy Hebert, Nonie Insall, Clare Jury and Richard Meryon (Daphne Meryon); Avril Sandall; Neil Franklin (Grace Taylor); Penelope Ayliffe (Frank Ayliffe); sister and nieces of Maud Coote; Diana Delahoy; Lesley Duncan, née Finn, and Archie Duncan (Austin Finn); Susi Hall (Kenneth Johnson); the Kirkman family (William Kirkman); the estate of Nick Wollaston; Martin Newell; Nella Last, Marian Raynham, Pat Scott, Bert Weibel and Alice (Judy) Haines, reproduced with permission of Curtis Brown, London on behalf of the Trustees of the Mass Observation Archive © The Trustees of the Mass Observation Archive; the estate of John

Fowles (© John Fowles); *Author, author: Every writer has a "How I became a writer"* by Hilary Mantel (Copyright © Hilary Mantel, 2008) reproduced by permission of A.M. Heath on behalf of the estate of Hilary Mantel; The Society of Authors as the Literary Representative of the Estate of Philip Larkin; Faber & Faber (*Clothes Music Boys* © Viv Albertine); Faber & Faber (*Letters Home* and *High Windows* © Philip Larkin); Copyright © O.W. Toad, 2005, reprinted by permission of CAA on behalf of O.W. Toad. In relation to the diaries that are kept at the Bishopsgate Institute's Great Diary Project (an invaluable resource for any British social historian), best endeavours have been made to contact depositors; but any uncontacted depositors, who might wish for changes to be made in any future edition of this book, are encouraged to contact the GDP. And more generally, I apologise for any inadvertent omissions.

All of us of a certain age can remember where we were when we heard that JFK had been killed; I am very grateful to Claire Tomalin and Michael Frayn for sharing their particular memories.

I would like to thank the following archivists for their often very considerable help: Emma Anthony; Mark Aston; Sophie Bridges; Nigel Cochrane; Sarah Demelo; Stefan Dickers; Helen Ford; Marlin Khondoker; Oliver Mahony; Louise North; Polly North; Jonathan Oates; Andrew Riley; Jessica Scantlebury; Liz Wood; Bef Yigezu.

Various friends very generously read all or part of this book at draft stage, offering encouragement and often helpful suggestions: Rachel Bowlby; Mike Brearley; Mike Burns; Tim Curtis; Dil Porter; Veronica Porter; Harry Ricketts; David Ward; and David Warren. I am also grateful to Robin Briggs and Alison Light for comments on specific passages.

Many thanks also to Amanda Howard (Superscript Editorial Services) for transcribing my audio tapes; to Richard Collins for his copy edit; to David Atkinson for compiling the index; to Catherine Best and Patric Dickinson for reading the proofs; to my agent Georgia Garrett and her assistant Honor Spreckley; and, at Bloomsbury, to my former editor Michael Fishwick, my present editor Jasmine Horsey, and her colleagues Francisco Vilhena and Molly McCarthy.

My greatest debt remains to my wife Lucy.

New Malden
April 2023

Image credits

Index

A Note on the Type

The text of this book is set in Linotype Stempel Garamond, a version of Garamond adapted and first used by the Stempel foundry in 1924. It is one of several versions of Garamond based on the designs of Claude Garamond. It is thought that Garamond based his font on Bembo, cut in 1495 by Francesco Griffo in collaboration with the Italian printer Aldus Manutius. Garamond types were first used in books printed in Paris around 1532. Many of the present-day versions of this type are based on the *Typi Academiae* of Jean Jannon cut in Sedan in 1615.

Claude Garamond was born in Paris in 1480. He learned how to cut type from his father and by the age of fifteen he was able to fashion steel punches the size of a pica with great precision. At the age of sixty he was commissioned by King Francis I to design a Greek alphabet, and for this he was given the honourable title of royal type founder. He died in 1561.